5th Edition

The Production *of* Reality

For Peter Kollock (1959–2009). May your spirit of mindfulness live on in these words.

5th Edition

The Production *of* Reality

Essays and Readings on Social Interaction

Jodi O'Brien

Seattle University

Los Angeles | London | New Delhi
Singapore | Washington DC

For information:

Pine Forge Press
An Imprint of SAGE Publications, Inc.
2455 Teller Road
Thousand Oaks, California 91320
E-mail: order@sagepub.com

SAGE Publications Ltd.
1 Oliver's Yard
55 City Road
London, EC1Y 1SP
United Kingdom

SAGE Publications India Pvt. Ltd.
B 1/I 1 Mohan Cooperative Industrial Area
Mathura Road, New Delhi 110 044
India

SAGE Publications Asia-Pacific Pte. Ltd.
33 Pekin Street #02-01
Far East Square
Singapore 048763

Printed in the United States of America.

Library of Congress Cataloging-in-Publication Data

The production of reality: essays and readings on social interaction / editor, Jodi O'Brien. — 5th ed.
     p. cm.
Includes bibliographical references and index.
ISBN 978-1-4129-7944-3 (pbk: acid-free paper)
    1. Social psychology. I. O'Brien, Jodi.

HM1033.O27 2011
302—dc22   2010032471

This book is printed on acid-free paper.

10 11 12 13 14 10 9 8 7 6 5 4 3 2 1

Acquisitions Editor:	David Repetto
Editorial Assistant:	Maggie Stanley
Production Editor:	Karen Wiley
Copy Editor:	Teresa Herlinger
Typesetter:	C&M Digitals (P) Ltd.
Proofreader:	Penny Sippel
Indexer:	Sheila Bodell
Cover Artist:	Cleofas Ramírez Celestino
Cover Designer:	Candice Harman
Marketing Manager:	Erica DeLuca
Permissions Editor:	Karen Ehrmann

CONTENTS

PART V

PRODUCING SOCIAL ORDER THROUGH INTERACTION 249

PREFACE

In my class syllabus for a course in social psychology, I make this statement:

> The main goal of this course is that you understand how we become social creatures and how, through our everyday interactions with one another, we make and remake ourselves and our social worlds. One important implication of the ideas covered in this course is that if we understand how it is that we participate in the construction of our own realities, then we can take a more active and purposeful approach toward making this the sort of world in which we want to live.

During the production of this book, I was reminded of a scene in the film *Annie Hall*, wherein Woody Allen's character, Alvy Singer (as a young man), reports that he is depressed because he has read that the universe is expanding. As the universe expands, it changes shape. Consequently, what we think we know about it changes as well—whatever we think we know today may change tomorrow. Believing that this will eventually mean "the end of everything," the young Alvy refuses to do his homework: "What's the point?" he sighs.

Indeed, what's the point in learning anything if, in fact, everything that we learn now will be invalid later on?

WHAT'S THE POINT?

The Production of Reality was initially compiled in order to provide students with a social psychology text that was useful and relevant to their everyday lives. One thing that you will probably learn in your sojourn through higher education, if you haven't already, is that there are many voices, many points of view, and many ways of learning and knowing. Diversity and complexity are hallmarks of life in the new millennium. Our social universe is continually expanding, and as it expands, so too does our stockpile of knowledge. Even more profound is the fact that the more we learn about our social universe, the more it changes shape. How do we make sense of this shifting and complexity? This is one of the most significant questions of our times. Several relatively new fields of study (for example, cultural studies) have emerged in the past few decades with the aim of exploring this particular question. Scholars within established disciplines—such as anthropology, law, communications, English, history, philosophy, and even geography—have also taken up this question. The commonality across disciplines of the themes of global expansion, diversity, and complexity is a sign of the importance of this inquiry. It is an exciting time to be a part of this intellectual dialogue.

Sociologists and social psychologists have been exploring for more than a century to map patterns of human social behavior. As sociologists, we know a great deal about patterns—how to look for them, how to read them, and how to interpret the consequences. In particular, sociologists have a lot to contribute regarding "structured relations of power." *Structured* is the operative word in this phrase. Sociologists and social psychologists know a great deal about "structure" and the ways in which it matters in everyday life. Anyone who wants to make sense of her or his own life needs an understanding of the underlying patterns and material conditions that make up the particular cultural milieu in which he or she lives. Racism, for example, is a persistent problem in U.S. society. The tools for understanding and potentially eradicating racism can be forged through an understanding of *why* and *how* people, even self-professed nonracists, are stuck in a social groove that produces patterns of racism. These "grooves" or "ruts" are what sociologists mean when we talk about "social patterns" and "social structures."

New Emphases for the Fifth Edition

The Production of Reality is about human behavior, or "social psychology." The intent in each edition has been to ground social psychology in the experiences of students and to provide an understanding of the forces that shape our feelings, thoughts, and actions. The emphasis in this edition is on how we can be more awake in the world, how we can better see the patterns that we use to organize our own lives. Most human behavior is largely routine and mindless. Studying the whys and hows of the forces that shape us can actually give us more freedom. When we understand the social roots of our feelings, thoughts, and actions, we are better able to adjust to them in ways that bring greater contentment and less suffering. Thus, this edition provides you with a tool kit for understanding yourself and society in ways that are intended to be liberating.

A central theoretical framework for this exploration is symbolic interactionism. *Symbolic interactionism* offers a theory of self and society whereby people create their own stability through interactions with one another. People participate in these stabilizing processes as a way of establishing social anchors—anchors of meaning—in constantly changing seas. The experiences of "authenticity," "meaning," "value," and "self-worth" are embedded in social relations. Who you are—your ideas of what you think you can do and who you think you can be—is shaped by the social relations in which you participate. The "structure" of these social relations, including the meaning that they hold for you, is shaped in turn by your participation. We are all better equipped to grapple with the timely questions of "What is real?" and "What is good?" by studying the social-psychological structure of social relations.

A *multivocal* perspective is another focus in this edition. The book is intended as one contribution to the current dialogue of complexity and diversity. Complexity is a hallmark of a *relevant* social science. I am hopeful that readers of this text will gain an understanding of this complex, expanding terrain so that they can navigate their own life currents more clearly.

THE LOGIC OF THE BOOK

This book is organized as a combination of essays and readings. The *essays* introduce relevant themes and concepts and raise questions intended to awaken you to the mysteries of human social life. These essays constitute the theoretical logic of the book. The *readings* have been selected to illustrate and elaborate various aspects of social interaction that are described in the essays. The readings span several decades and represent many different voices and points of view. Some of the readings are considered sociological classics—articles that every well-educated student should be familiar with. Some of the language and examples used by the authors of some of these older pieces may seem outdated and even offensive. I encourage you to read these selections as a form of social history as well as social theory. In other words, ask yourself what it was that was different about the times in which these authors wrote. Can you be critical and still comprehend why the ideas might have been groundbreaking at the time they were written? The contemporary readings include research studies, narrative essays, and some fiction. It is likely that different readings will resonate for different readers. As you read these diverse selections, consider why it is that certain types of writing and particular themes seem more or less appealing to you. What does your own response as a reader indicate about your social biography?

MANY QUESTIONS, YOUR OWN ANSWERS

The general intent of this book is to immerse you in the puzzles and issues of contemporary social psychology and to provide a framework from which you can begin to construct your own understanding of the social world. Toward this end, many questions are posed, and you are invited to reflect on them in light of the concepts and theories presented in the book. As you will discover in reading this text, there are no absolute or final answers to the most important human questions. This is because we are constantly creating new ways of understanding ourselves and our social worlds. Through our ability to think and communicate, we are expanding our social universe. The material in this text is intended to provide you with a framework for understanding this creative social-psychological process (as well as for avoiding some of the pitfalls that appear when we fail to recognize our own involvement in the process). It can be useful to approach this material as a set of building blocks that you can assemble and reassemble to construct a framework for making sense of your own life.

If you (unlike Woody's character) are willing to do your homework, I am confident that your own universe of knowledge will expand in useful and profound ways.

ACKNOWLEDGMENTS

The creation of any product is always a collective enterprise. There are many who have helped to shape this book. The members of the Pine Forge Press production staff continue to be patient, helpful, and encouraging allies in my efforts to push beyond the boundaries of the traditional textbook. Acquisitions editor David Repetto stepped deftly into the shoes of his predecessor, Jerry Westby, in doing the preliminary work necessary to launch a new edition of this book. Editorial assistant Maggie Stanley went the extra mile on several occasions. I am especially grateful for her tenacity and creativity in locating the artist for the cover art and procuring permissions for some of the less accessible articles. I am also grateful to Ani Durini Romero (Mexico City) for her generous resourcefulness in picking up the painting that was used for the cover art and rendering it into a usable form for reproduction. A huge thanks to Jennifer Hamann for her keen research assistance. Production editor Karen Wiley has had her professional eye on every aspect of the production process. My thanks for making this journey so smooth. Teresa Herlinger has been a copy editor extraordinaire. In addition to her stellar expertise in editing the manuscript, her wit and insight kept me motivated and inspired throughout the final stages of production.

My commitment to bridging the gap between teaching and scholarship has been fostered by role models such as Hubert (Tad) Blalock, Howard Becker, Fred Campbell, Karen Cook, and Judy Howard. Over the course of my career, my commitment has been continuously renewed through interactions with colleagues who struggle valiantly in the quest to provide relevant and useful knowledge for students. I am repeatedly impressed with the dedication of these teacher-scholars. I am also tremendously grateful for the honest and constructive comments from the reviewers of this book. For the current edition, these reviewers included the following: Heather Shay, North Carolina State University; Norman Goodman, Stony Brook University; Scott R. Harris, Saint Louis University; Matthew Immergut, Purchase College, SUNY; Suzanne B. Kurth, University of Tennessee, Knoxville; Lorien Lake-Corral, University of Arizona; Jeanne Mekolichick, Radford University, Virginia; Gretchen Peterson, California State University, Los Angeles; Erica Owens Yeager, West Virginia University; and Steve Swinford, Montana State University.

Much of my thinking as it developed in this book is the result of generous conversations with students. I thank them for sharing their intellectual passion and for trusting me to be open to learning from them. I am fortunate to have several friends and colleagues who are always responsive to my requests for feedback or my need for inspiring company. They include Michele Berger, Karl Bryant, Mark Cohan, Wendy Chapkis, Shari Dworkin, Sarah Fenstermaker, Mako Fitts, Gabriella Gutierrez y Muhs, Pierrette Hondagneu-Sotelo, Kevin

Krycka, Tom Linneman, Kari Lerum, Nancy Naples, Peter Nardi, Gary Perry, Ken Plummer, Rich Serpe, Cecilia Ridgeway, Beth Schneider, Arlene Stein, Eve Shapiro, Pepper Schwartz, Judy Taylor, Verta Taylor, and Christine Williams. Carol Lombardi, who copyedited the third edition, gets credit for the Woody Allen reference. Steve Rutter, the founder of Pine Forge Press and the person responsible for the original version of this book, is a true visionary in the field of textbook production. I am honored to have his friendship. Thanks especially to my good buddy Val Jenness for always reminding me that laughter really is the best medicine. As always, thanks to Ron Obvious just for being there. Y para Gloria, mi compañera hermosa, gracias por todo.

Jodi O'Brien

ABOUT THE COVER ARTIST

Cleofas Ramírez Celestino (1955–) was born in the village of Xlitla, Guerrero, Mexico. She began painting at age 7. Her primary medium is oil on amate. She paints to survive and sells her art on the streets in the marketplaces of Mexico City. Her lively paintings illustrate the everyday life and rituals of the indigenous people of Central Mexico. Ramírez Celestino's paintings have caught the attention of collectors, activists, and educators and have been featured in books that combine art and poetry as an endeavor to keep the Náhuatl language alive. Sadly, as is often the case with poor artists from small villages, Ramírez Celestino rarely receives acknowledgment or compensation for the use of her art. The painting featured here is titled *Bailando Nuestra Realidad* ("Dancing Our Reality"). It was painted specifically for this edition of *The Production of Reality* at the author's request.

PART I

INTRODUCTION

A father said to his double-seeing son, "Son, you see two instead of one."

"How can that be?" the boy replied. "If that were true, I would see four moons up there in place of two."

—Idries Shah (1972), *Caravan of Dreams*

I have come to see that knowledge contains its own morality, that it begins not in neutrality but in a place of passion within the human soul. Depending on the nature of that passion, our knowledge will follow certain courses and head toward certain ends.

—Parker Palmer (1993), *To Know as We Are Known*

1

WHAT IS REAL?

Jodi O'Brien

In rural villages, religious festivals are an important part of the local culture. A documentary film crew was around to record one of these events in another country. The film shows brightly colored decorations, music, dancing, and a variety of delicious and special foods made for the festival. The special treats are clearly a highlight for everyone, especially the children, who crowd around the stands. In the middle of one crowd of children waiting for a treat is a very large stone bowl. A large stone pillar rises out of the center of the bowl. The pillar seems alive. It is completely covered by shiny black beetles crawling around and over each other. The person in charge takes a tortilla, spreads some sauce on the inside, grabs a handful of live beetles, and fills the burrito with them, quickly folding the tortilla so that the beetles cannot escape. Playfully pushing the beetles back into the tortilla between bites, a gleeful child eats the burrito with relish. Would you be willing to try a beetle burrito? Is a strip of burnt cow muscle (also known as a steak) inherently any more or less desirable than a beetle burrito? If you had grown up in that village, would you be eating and enjoying beetle burritos? What does your answer have to say about the social and cultural origins of what seems like an almost biological trait—our tastes in food?

In his book *The Te of Piglet* (1992), Benjamin Hoff recounts the following narratives, based on the writings of Chinese Taoist philosophers:

> A man noticed that his axe was missing. Then he saw the neighbor's son pass by. The boy looked like a thief, walked like a thief, behaved like a thief. Later that day, the man found his axe where he had left it the day before. The next time he saw the neighbor's son, the boy looked, walked, and behaved like an honest, ordinary boy.
>
> A man dug a well by the side of the road. For years afterward, grateful travelers talked of the Wonderful Well. But one night, a man fell into it and drowned. After that, people avoided the Dreadful Well. Later it was discovered that the victim was a drunken thief who had left the road to avoid being captured by the night patrol—only to fall into the Justice-Dispensing Well. (p. 172)

What sort of reality do these Chinese tales illustrate? Does the essence of the neighbor boy or the nature of the well change? Or do people's perceptions change? Consider occasions when your perceptions of someone or something may have been influenced by your own momentary experiences. Is it possible that reality depends on how you look at something? How much does your point of view depend on your own interests?

Consider further: A group of employees from a local business gathers every night after work to share drinks and conversation. They express dissatisfaction with the conditions of their job and the unethical behavior of the boss. Several of them recall occasions of being mistreated or harassed. As the evening progresses, they become emboldened by this sharing of experience and some of them even threaten to confront the boss. The next day, life resumes as usual at work. Each of the employees goes about her or his job with competence. In the presence of the boss, each is quiet and respectful. The status quo prevails. Think about the difference between the late-night and workday activities of these people. What is the source of the disparity between the behaviors in each setting? Are these people being any more or less truthful in either situation? What forces compel people to change their circumstances? What forces constrain resistance in the face of injustice?

These scenarios have in common a focus on the intersection between social forms of expression and individual perceptions, tastes, and behaviors. In each case, a taken-for-granted body of cultural knowledge influences individual action. Children in some villages consume beetles with gusto, whereas others might look on in horror. Yet we all feel that our personal tastes are reasonable.

A person's reactions to the world depend on how he or she defines the situation. The definition of the situation can differ from moment to moment, depending on what the person is inclined to see. Someone's actions may appear perfectly reasonable in one situation and then appear unreasonable in another. Indeed, a great deal of human behavior appears unreasonable and illogical if viewed out of context.

Cultural beliefs and practices include rules about what is "real" and what is "not real." These rules are often taken for granted, and usually we follow them without being aware of them. These rules are not necessarily based on logic or sensory perception. The study of culture and behavior involves figuring out these rules and making them explicit. This book is about how human beings learn and conform to the rules of reality in various situations. These rules enable us to organize and to make sense of our experiences and to share our understanding with others.

When people interact with one another, they do so according to shared cultural rules. The result of this interaction is a set of meaningful patterns that we think of as society. It is important to note that these rules are constructed by human beings and that they are meaningful only within a specific social context. In other words, behavior is contextually meaningful. Taken out of context, many behaviors appear contradictory, silly, or even immoral. For instance, how is it that you know to modulate your voice to a whisper in certain spaces, or the difference between when to hug and when to shake hands in a social situation? Why is "making fun of someone" funny in some settings and cruel in others? Where do we draw the line, or, more importantly, how do we know what the line is? How do people know what to expect and what to do in different contexts, especially in situations that may appear contradictory? How do we learn the rules, lines, and boundaries of reality? The ability to distinguish between contexts and to behave in accordance with social expectations is a defining feature of humanness. It is also the main subject of this book.

What Is Humanness?

Various branches of social and natural sciences have different perspectives on the nature of humanness. There are also a variety of theological perspectives on what it means to be human. Each of these perspectives focuses on different aspects of the human experience, for example, our physiological ability to use tools due to an opposable thumb, or our ability to conceive of and orient ourselves toward the existence of a higher being. Recent developments in the fields of biotechnology and genetic engineering, as well as computer-mediated communications, also contribute to conversations about the nature of humanness. Current debates about stem cell research; genetic social engineering; and the "realness" of online, computer-mediated relationships indicate that our definitions of humanness are always in flux. For instance, what are the implications of artificial limbs and organs or cloning on how we understand humanness in relationship to the body? How do we determine the realness of human relationships conducted entirely through virtual media such as the Internet? The rules for deciding what is human and who is "real" shift and change in response to contemporary social, cultural, and technological developments.

In this book, I invite you to explore the nature of humanness from the perspective of social psychology. Social psychology is the study of the relationship between the individual and the rules and patterns that constitute society. Most sociologists and psychologists agree that human behavior is shaped to some extent by physiological, biological, and neurological processes that are beyond the scope of social psychology. However, social psychologists emphasize that the majority of the activities people engage in on a day-to-day basis constitute *social* behavior—behavior that is both influenced by and expressed through social interaction. According to social psychology, the human is a *socialized* creature who is self-aware and able to make sense of thoughts, feelings, and actions and to communicate this awareness with others. Through communication we are able to learn and share cultural rules, expectations, and values. In this way, the human is both an *individual* with separate thoughts and feelings and a *socialized* being who is able to understand and coordinate her or his activities and ideas in response to others.

Humanness Is Achieved Through Symbolic Interaction

The production of meaningful realities occurs through human interaction. In other words, we "practice" social reality every time we interact with others. Human culture is achieved through interactions among individuals who share highly complex, richly nuanced definitions of themselves and the situations in which they participate. We *learn* to be human, and our learning depends on and is achieved through interactions with other humans. The basis for meaningful human behavior is in our capacity for language—not just definitions and grammar, but metaphor. Consider, for example, a computer that is directed to translate the sentence, "The spirit is willing but the flesh is weak" into Russian. The computer has the necessary vocabulary and grammar to make this translation, but it translates the phrase as "The vodka is good but the meat is rotten." The computer provides a literal translation, but the translation does not convey the intended meaning of the phrase (Scheff, 1990). One of the most remarkable aspects of human behavior is our ability to learn, share, and create nuanced, metaphorical meaning. This nuanced comprehension is what enables us to engage in very complex behavior and to know the difference between various cultural rules and contexts.

The focus in this book is on how we learn these cultural rules and the ways in which we practice them through our everyday interactions. According to many social psychologists, these interactions form the basis of human existence. The aim is to demonstrate how humans learn to participate in culture and ultimately to produce and reproduce themselves and their various cultures. We will explore a number of questions: What cognitive and emotive capacities are necessary for people to be able to engage in meaningful social interactions? How is social behavior affected by a disruption of these processes? How do interactional dynamics shape our behavior and our sense of who we are and what we can do? How do these processes contribute to the production of culture? How is it possible that, through our own behavior, we may be perpetuating cultural systems to which we may think ourselves opposed (e.g., racism)? The general aim is to explore the social foundations of mind, self, and culture. The framework for this exploration is a theoretical perspective known as symbolic interactionism.

Symbolic Interactionism

There are several different forms of social psychology. This book is written according to a subfield of social psychology known as *symbolic interactionism.* Each of the many approaches to the study of human social behavior has strengths and limitations, and I encourage you to become familiar with them. Through many years of teaching and study, I have come to appreciate symbolic interactionism as a perspective that offers one of the most useful frameworks for understanding human behavior in a social context. In other words, this perspective provides excellent tools for understanding the complexity of our own behavior.

For instance, have you ever wondered why you feel so strongly about something in one situation and completely different in another, or why your self-esteem seems to blossom in some circumstances and shrivel in others? Symbolic interaction provides the tools for understanding how we can simultaneously have what seems to be a stable personality and also be constantly shifting in our experiences, values, and points of view. At the social level, symbolic interaction provides a framework for understanding how society can also seem both stable and constantly in flux. Most importantly, this perspective invites us to wake up to the ways in which we ourselves create and perpetuate social routines that may or may not be good for us. In short, symbolic interactionism portrays the human as an active cocreator

6   PART I ❖ INTRODUCTION

in both individual and social experience. To the extent that we become aware of these processes, we are better equipped to participate in our own liberation.

Three points are noteworthy regarding symbolic interactionism in contrast to other social psychological perspectives:

1. Symbolic interactionism gives primacy to the social situation over individual psychology. In other words, behavior is assumed to be organized primarily in response to social factors.

2. The focus of study is on observable behavior, but the cause of this behavior is assumed to be nonobservable processes of individual interpretation. In other words, behavior is based on subjective interpretation of the social environment instead of being a direct response to objective stimuli.

3. Symbolic interactionism uses *interpretive* methodologies. The researcher attempts to take the perspective of the subject and to interpret the context in which the behavior takes place. In other words, the researcher tries to "look over the shoulder" of the subject or group of interest. Some of the methods used to gather information about human relations include fieldwork, interviews, and participant observation. The aim is to understand how humans see and enact their own beliefs and ideals and to trace the implications of these beliefs and actions.

Symbolic interactionism is conducted at the intersection of individuals and society. From this perspective, it is not possible to make sense of one without incorporating the other. The challenge for symbolic interactionism has been to represent society in a way that avoids reification—in other words, to model social patterns and relationships as the products of ongoing individual activity. At the same time, symbolic interactionism must account for the observation that existing social patterns do influence and constrain individual actions. The ultimate aim of symbolic interactionism, as presented in this book, is to place the individual and society on the same level and to analyze the reciprocal relationships between individual action and social patterns and institutions. Social life is conceived as a dynamic web of reciprocal influences among members of a social group. This web is made up of the interactions of individuals. Individuals spin and re-spin the web. At the same time, they are influenced by the existing patterns of previously spun strands.

The organization of this book is intended to provide you with a tool kit for understanding self and society. These tools or topics include language and self-awareness, symbolic communication and socialization, self development, interaction with others, and the production of social life. I use the metaphor of "production" to illustrate that social life is something we create together. The first basic tenet of symbolic interaction is that society is socially constructed. What this means is that through our engagement with others we are constantly generating cultural meaning and rules. Each of the sections of this book will explore aspects of this process.

CONCLUSIONS

The theory determines what we can observe.

—Albert Einstein

What is reality anyway? Nothin' but a collective hunch.

—Trudy the bag lady (from Jane Wagner's [1986]
The Search for Signs of Intelligent Life in the Universe)

So, what is real? According to the symbolic interactionist perspective, "truth" and "reality" are determined by the context in which they are practiced. Does this mean that anything goes? Far from it. Reality may differ across social groups, but within each group, a taken-for-granted system of knowledge establishes boundaries about what is real, true, and right. A central line of inquiry in symbolic interactionism is uncovering what these boundaries consist of and how members of a community produce and reproduce their systems of knowledge through their interactions. For instance, symbolic interactionists have noted that people living in modern, Western cultures act as if their reality is based on a "natural" truth (things are the way they are because nature intended them to be that way). Other cultures might have a faith-based reality (things are the way they are because a transcendent god intends them to be that way). These realities include complex, culturally specific rules for how one can know things. Thus, people in one society may believe in the existence of germs that cause illness. They may invest considerable resources to develop the technology necessary to "see" and "control" these germs. In another culture, people may invest similar resources to perfect ceremonies and rituals to "see" and "communicate with" the spirits that control health and well-being.

Cultural rules about what is real are often contradictory as well. It is fascinating to observe human behavior and culture to see the ways in which seemingly contradictory systems of reality exist side by side. For instance, in the United States, systems of rationality and Christianity often coexist, despite some apparent contradictions. Even so, contradictory belief systems have rules for navigating the contradictions. For example, it is considered normal for the president of the United States to make statements such as "one nation under God" in his speeches. But if he were to say that he was leading the country based on "visions" he received from God, people might question his abilities. Similarly, citing your religious beliefs as a basis for not dating someone is considered reasonable, but these same beliefs are unacceptable as a reason for not paying taxes. Knowing which cultural rules apply in specific contexts is considered "common sense" or "what everybody knows."

In place of the question, "What is real?" try asking, "What are some of the beliefs and practices that make up commonsense realities? What are the implications and consequences of these realities? How do different realities depict the world and the place of humans in it?" These questions remind us to scrutinize our own rules of interaction and their implications for self and society. We must make the "taken for granted" explicit. One of the major strengths of the symbolic interactionist perspective is that it encourages us to see our own roles as authors in the human story and, ideally, to take responsibility for the scripts we produce and the parts we play.

ORGANIZATION OF THE BOOK

One general aim of this book is to establish a foundation for understanding symbolic activity based on human thought processes (social cognition) and then to use this foundation to address questions about social order and change. By way of summary, the basic components of this foundation are symbols, the social self, interaction, and social patterns. The materials in this book are organized to present a picture of society as the product of human interactions based on the use of shared social symbols that are incorporated into human conduct through cognitive-emotive processes. Because humans derive cognitive schemas from cultural patterns, these processes reflect a preexisting social structure. Through our interactions with one another we learn, enact, reproduce, and potentially change this structure.

Part I introduces some of these basic components and explores the general idea of socially constructed realities.

In Part II, the focus is on the ways our thoughts and feelings reflect cultural learning and values as well as distinct, private, personal experiences. For symbolic interactionists, the key to this puzzle is the *symbol,* an abstract representation of something that may or may not exist in a tangible form. For example, *table* is the symbolic representation of a class of objects constructed from hard substances and designed to serve certain purposes. *Guilt* symbolizes a feeling that you are probably familiar with, but it has no actual, physical referent. Complex combinations of symbols used for communication are known as *language.* Through language, humans are able to identify meaningful symbols; understand cultural expectations; and incorporate these expectations into conscious, reflexive behavior. Language is the encyclopedia of human culture. It is also through language that humans generate, conserve, and alter social structure.

The focus of Part III is the social self. The first emphasis is on the way in which we learn, through our capacity for language, to recognize our own actions as aspects of an entity we call "self." The second emphasis is on the interactional or social aspects of self development: Through our interactions with others, we learn to attach meaning to our own behavior, feelings, and thoughts and to assemble this meaning into a coherent pattern that becomes a stable self. This section also explores some of the ways in which self-image is shaped and influenced by social contexts including history and computer-mediated environments.

In Part IV, we explore the process of "socialization," or the way in which humans learn social rules and routines and cultural values. One of the questions that drive the discussion in this section is that of how different people with relatively similar backgrounds and experiences come to have different ideas and expectations and to behave in different ways. The concept of "reference groups" provides a useful and intriguing answer to this question and illustrates the ways in which people organize and evaluate their own behavior in terms of the expectations of specific groups or ideas of groups.

The topic of Part V is social interaction. Social relationships, such as love or power, are given meaning and come to life when they are acted out by members of a social group. These patterns are discernible in the encounters of everyday life, such as conversations. Basic interaction requires people to project an image of what part they wish to play, what part they want others to play, and how they intend to define the situation. For an interaction to proceed smoothly, the actors must agree on a definition of the situation and perform it together. Even arguments, as we will discuss, hold to a particular definition of the situation ("this is a fight") and follow specific rules of interaction. In addition to defining situations, people negotiate how they will define themselves and others.

The social construction of reality is the focus of Part VI. In this section, we begin to put together the ideas and concepts from the previous sections to develop a theory of the production and reproduction of social realities. The key point of this section is that realities are social constructs that exist through shared expectations about how the world is organized. These realities are quite fragile, because they depend on the participation of people who are socialized to comprehend and perform patterns and rituals that follow highly structured (but often unrecognized) rules of interaction. Ironically, these implicit rules can be made explicit by violating them and forcing interaction to a confused halt. We discuss several "violations" as a way of demonstrating how to "see" the rules of interaction. An important question in this section is why certain patterns of reality endure so well, given that they are based on such fragile dynamics.

In Part VII, I invite you to consider how people grapple with multiple perspectives and contradictions. People have the ability to occupy multiple positions and are able to take on a variety of roles and behaviors. However, many of these positions are contradictory and thus present dilemmas for individuals and groups who seek to establish meaningful patterns of existence. I do not attempt to resolve these contradictions. Rather, my intent is to draw your attention to the point that social life is dynamic and complex. Our understanding of who we are and of what is meaningful is forged through the process of wrestling with everyday contradictions.

The Epilogue is an essay on the implications of this material for living a meaningful life. Once we wake up to the mindless patterns of everyday routine, how do we practice staying awake and remain connected to ourselves and others in a meaningful, liberated way?

REFERENCES AND SUGGESTIONS FOR FURTHER READING

Hoff, B. (1992). *The Te of Piglet.* New York: Penguin.

Palmer, P. (1993). *To know as we are known.* San Francisco: Harper.

Scheff, T. (1990). *Microsociology: Discourse, emotion, and social structure.* Chicago: University of Chicago Press.

Shah, I. (1972). *Caravan of dreams.* Baltimore: Penguin.

Wagner, J. (1986). *The search for signs of intelligent life in the universe.* New York: HarperCollins.

REALITY AS A COLLECTIVE HUNCH

Most of us know that different cultures have distinct values and beliefs. Everyday life also consists of patterns of thinking, organizing time, and making sense of things in ways that differ across cultures and between groups of people. The readings in this section illustrate some of the differences in how people perceive everyday reality.

"Islands of Meaning" is written by sociologist Eviatar Zerubavel. In this essay, he gives many examples to illustrate the ways we carve up our lives with respect to divisions such as time and geography. We tend to think of these divisions as natural, but Zerubavel demonstrates that these divisions are actually social creations that are so entrenched that we come to think of them as natural.

"The Search for Signs of Intelligent Life in the Universe" is a selection from a popular Broadway play written by Jane Wagner and performed by Lily Tomlin. In this excerpt, the character Trudy the bag lady ponders the meaning of life and the arbitrariness of cultural rules for what is real.

READING QUESTIONS

1. As you read the articles in this section, think of examples of cultural rules that you take for granted and assume to be fixed in nature.

2. What does it mean to say that cultural rules are "arbitrary"?

3. Consider your relationship to time. Do you think people's rhythms have been altered by the invention of digital clocks that carve time into units of seconds, versus clocks that signal only quarter hours? What about people who organize time in terms of the sun only?

4. Spend a day thinking of yourself as an anthropologist from Mars. What do you see when you look at your world from the perspective of an outsider?

1

Islands of Meaning

Eviatar Zerubavel

(1991)

In the beginning . . . the earth was unformed and void . . . and God divided the light from the darkness. And God called the light Day, and the darkness He called Night.[1]

The very first act of the Creation was one of dividing. It was through being separated from one another that entities began to emerge. The first day was thus spent on dividing the light from the darkness while the next two were dedicated to separating the waters under the heaven from those above it as well as from the dry land.[2] Indeed, according to Genesis, the first three days of the Creation were devoted exclusively to making distinctions.

Like most cosmogonies, the biblical story of the Creation is an allegorical account of the process through which we normally create order out of chaos. These theories of the origin of the universe almost invariably describe the formation of essences (the heavens, the earth, life) out of a boundless, undifferentiated void.[3] Distinctions, they all tell us, are at the basis of any orderliness.

Separating entities from their surroundings is what allows us to perceive them in the first place. In order to discern any "thing," we must distinguish that which we attend from that which we ignore. Such an inevitable link between differentiation and perception is most apparent in color-blindness tests or camouflage, whereby entities that are not clearly differentiated from their surroundings are practically invisible.[4] It is the fact that it is

differentiated from other entities that provides an entity with a distinctive meaning[5] as well as with a distinctive identity that sets it apart from everything else.

The way we cut up the world clearly affects the way we organize our everyday life. The way we divide our surroundings, for example, determines what we notice and what we ignore, what we eat and what we avoid eating. By the same token, the way we classify people determines whom we trust and whom we fear, whom we marry and whom we consider sexually off limits. The way we partition time and space likewise determines when we work and when we rest, where we live and where we never set foot.

Indeed, our entire social order is a product of the ways in which we separate kin from nonkin, moral from immoral, serious from merely playful, and what is ours from what is not. Every class system presupposes a fundamental distinction between personal features that are relevant for placing one in a particular social stratum (for example, occupation, color of skin, amount of formal education) and those that are not (for example, sexual attractiveness, height, intelligence), and any society that wishes to implement a welfare or retirement policy must first distinguish the well-to-do from the needy and those who are fully competent to work from those who are "too old." By the same token, membership in particular social categories qualifies us for, or disqualifies us from, various benefits, exemptions, and jobs.[6] It is the need to distinguish "us" from "them" that likewise generates laws against intermarriage, and the wish to separate mentally the "masculine" from the "feminine" that leads to the genderization of professions and sports.

It is boundaries that help us separate one entity from another: "To classify things is to arrange them in groups . . . separated by clearly determined lines of demarcation. . . . At the bottom of our conception of class there is the idea of a circumscription with fixed and definite outlines."[7] Indeed, the word *define* derives from the Latin word for *boundary,* which is *finis.* To define something is to mark its boundaries,[8] to surround it with a mental fence that separates it from everything else. As evidenced by our failure to notice objects that are not clearly differentiated from their surroundings, it is their boundaries that allow us to perceive "things" at all. These lines play a critical role in the construction of social reality, since only with them do meaningful social entities (families, social classes, nations) emerge out of the flux of human existence. Examining how we draw them is therefore critical to any effort to understand our social order. It also offers us a rare glimpse into the not-so-orderly world that underlies our social world, the proverbial chaos that preceded the Creation.

Boundaries are normally taken for granted[9] and, as such, usually manage to escape our attention. After all, "Nothing evades our attention so persistently as that which is taken for granted. . . . Obvious facts tend to remain invisible."[10] In order to make them more "visible," we must suspend our usual concern with what they separate and focus instead on the process by which we cut up the world and create meaningful entities. In short, we must examine how we actually separate entities from one another, whether it be humans from animals, work from hobby, official from unofficial, or vulgar from refined.

The way we cut up the world in our mind manifests itself in how we construct age, gender, and ethnicity as well as in how we arrange food in supermarkets and books and movies in bookstores and video stores. It is manifested as well in how we divide our homes into separate rooms, and in our sexual taboos. Conventional metaphors such as *closed, detached,* and *clear-cut* similarly reveal how we experience reality as made up of insular entities, while our need to keep such discrete islands of meaning neatly separate from one another is evident from our gut response to ambiguous creatures.

The way we draw lines varies considerably from one society to another as well as across historical periods within the same society. Moreover, their precise location, not to mention their very existence, is often disputed and contested within any given society. Nonetheless, like the child who believes the equator is a real line[11] or the racist who perceives an actual divide separating blacks from whites, we very often experience boundaries as if they were part of nature. . . .

Things assume a distinctive identity only through being differentiated from other things, and their meaning is always a function of the particular mental compartment in which we place them. Examining how we draw lines will therefore reveal how we give meaning to our environment as well as to ourselves. By throwing light on the way in which we distinguish entities from one another and thereby give them an identity, we can explore the very foundations of our social world, which we normally take for granted.

At a time when political and moral distinctions are constantly blurred—when the international order we have regarded for nearly half a century as a given is virtually collapsing and our definitions of work, art, and gender are in flux—the very notion of a social order is being questioned. At such a point it is therefore critical for us to understand the actual process by which we establish boundaries and make distinctions. How we draw these fine lines will certainly determine the kind of social order we shall have.

* * * * *

The first man who, having enclosed a piece of ground, bethought himself of saying "This is mine," and found people simple enough to believe him, was the real founder of civil society.[12]

We transform the natural world into a social one by carving out of it mental chunks we then treat as if they were discrete, totally detached from their surroundings. The way we mark off islands of property is but one example of the general process by which we create meaningful social entities. . . .

CHUNKS OF SPACE

The perception of supposedly insular chunks of space is probably the most fundamental manifestation of how we divide reality into islands of meaning. Examining how we partition space, therefore, is an ideal way to start exploring how we partition our social world.

The way we carve out of ecological continuums such as continents and urban settlements supposedly insular countries and neighborhoods is a classic case in point.[13] Despite the fact that Egypt and Libya or Chinatown and Little Italy are actually contiguous, we nevertheless treat them as if they were discrete. Such discontinuous perception of space is nicely captured by the map shown here, which almost literally lifts Montana out of its actual context. Not only does it represent that state as a discrete three-dimensional chunk jutting out of a flat backdrop, it also portrays both the Missouri River and the Rocky Mountains as if they indeed broke off at its borders.

Spatial partitions clearly divide more than just space. The lines that mark off supposedly insular chunks of space often represent the invisible lines that separate purely mental entities such as nations or ethnic groups from one another, and crossing them serves to articulate passage through such mental partitions. That is why we attribute such great symbolic significance to acts such as trespassing[14] or crossing a picket line and regard the crossing of the Red Sea by the ancient Israelites coming out of Egypt as an act of liberation. That is also why the Berlin Wall could represent the mental separation of democracy from communism and why opening the border between Austria and Hungary in 1989 could serve as a symbolic display of the spirit of glasnost.

Often abstract and highly elusive, mental distinctions need to be concretized. Wearing different sets of clothes, for example, helps substantiate the mental distinction between business and casual or ordinary and festive, just as color coding helps us mentally separate different types of information we put in our notebooks, calendars, or files. Choosing among different variants of a language (such as the one used for speeches and the one used for intimate conversations) likewise helps express the mental contrast between the formal and the informal.[15] In a similar manner, we often use differentiation in space to reinforce mental differentiation. Partitioning our home into separate rooms, for example, helps us compartmentalize our daily activity into separate clusters of functions (eating, resting, playing, cleaning) as well as mentally separate culture (study) from nature (bathroom)[16] or the formal (living room) from the informal (family room). Along similar lines, separate aisles in music stores help reinforce the mental separation of classical and popular music, just as separate floors of department stores help us keep the worlds of men and women separate in our mind. In a similar manner, we express discontinuities among supposedly separate bodies of information by relegating them to separate drawers, newspaper sections, and library floors; and keep different categories of food separate in our mind by assigning them to separate pages of restaurant menus, chapters of cookbooks, aisles of supermarkets, and sections of the refrigerator. Similar forms of zoning help give substance to the mental contrasts between even more abstract entities such as the sacred and the profane,[17] the permitted and the forbidden,[18] the dangerous and the safe, and the good and the evil.[19]

The mental role of spatial partitions is also evident from the way neighborhood boundaries graphically outline rather elusive social class differences.[20] Even more revealing is the way separate bathrooms in the army help articulate status differences between officers and soldiers. The conspicuous absence of doors from rooms we define as public likewise highlights the role of spatial partitions in keeping the private and public spheres separate.[21] "A lock on the door," notes Virginia Woolf in her aptly titled study of privacy and selfhood, *A Room of One's Own*, "means the power to think for oneself."[22] It is the realization that the definition of our selfhood is at stake that makes us so sensitive to the symbolism of having the license to close the door to our room or office.

BLOCKS OF TIME

The way we divide time is evocative of the manner in which we partition space. Just as we cut supposedly discrete chunks like countries and school districts off from ecological continuums, we also carve seemingly insular segments such as "the Renaissance" or "adolescence" out of historical continuums. Such discontinuous experience of time is quite evident from the way we isolate from the flow of occurrences supposedly freestanding events such as meetings, classes, and shows, some of which we further subdivide into smaller though still discrete particles—meals into courses, baseball games into innings.[23] It is also manifested in our ability to create stories with beginnings and ends as well as in the way we break down novels, sonatas, and plays into chapters, movements, and acts.

In a similar manner, we isolate in our mind supposedly discrete blocks of time such as centuries, decades, years, months, weeks, and days, thus perceiving actual breaks between "last week" and "this week"[24] or "the fifties" and "the sixties." That is why many of us may not carry over sick days from one year to the next and why officials try to use up their entire budget before the end of the fiscal year. A similar discontinuity between successive tax years also leads some couples to plan the births of their offspring for December, even to the point of inducing those that would naturally have occurred in January.

Central to such discontinuous perception of time is our experience of beginnings, endings, and "turning points." Most revealing in this regard is the sense of conclusion we experience as a performance, picnic, or season is coming to an end,[25] the radical change we expect at the turn of a century or a millennium or even between two contiguous decades, and the experience of a "fresh" start (or "turning over a new leaf") often associated with the beginning of a "new" year. Even in services that operate around the clock, night staff are often expected to allow the day ("first") shift a fresh start with a "clean desk."[26] A pregnant friend of mine who came back to the same clinic that had handled her previous pregnancy within the same year was asked to provide her entire medical history all over again, as she would now be considered a "new" case.

Temporal differentiation helps substantiate elusive mental distinctions. Like their spatial counterparts, temporal boundaries often represent mental partitions and thus serve to divide more than just time. For example, when we create special "holy days," we clearly use time to concretize the mental contrast between the sacred and the profane.[27] In a similar manner, we use it to give substance to the equally elusive contrast between the private and the public domains, using, for example, the boundary of the workday to represent the mental partition between being "on" and "off" duty.[28] Groups likewise use the way they periodize their own history to highlight certain ideological distinctions, as evident, for example, in the Zionist use of "the Exile"[29] or the American use of "the Great Depression" or "Vietnam" as discrete historical eras. The boundaries of the Sabbath, the workday, and "the Vietnam era" clearly represent major mental discontinuities. Like neighborhoods, drawers, and wings of museums, what they define are clearly more than mere chunks of time.

FRAMES

Temporal differentiation often entails an experience of discontinuity among different sorts of reality as well. Transitions from televised news to commercials or from live coverage to replay, for example, obviously involve more than just breaks in time. Along similar lines, warmup and "real" jumps in long-jump competitions are clearly anchored not only within two distinct blocks of time but also within two separate realms of experience, as are comments made before meetings begin and those included in the official minutes.[30]

Spatial differentiation often entails similar experiential discontinuity. The knight on the chessboard and the glass of water on the table are obviously situated not only within two distinct chunks of space but also within two separate "realities." That is also true of what occurs on and off the stage or inside and outside the picture frame.

Crossing the fine lines separating such experiential realms from one another involves a considerable mental switch from one "style" or mode of experiencing to another, as each realm has a distinctive "accent of reality."[31] At the sound of the bell that signals the end of a boxing match, as brutal punches are instantly transformed into friendly hugs, our entire sense of what is real is dramatically altered. That also happens, of course, when actors enter the stage and are immediately transformed into fictional characters. Picture frames similarly remind viewers that they cannot smell the flowers or eat the apples they see in pictures,[32] as pictorial space is "a structure altogether different from the real space we experience. Within actual space an object can be touched, whereas in a painting it can only be looked at; each portion of real space is experienced as part of an infinite expanse, but the space of a picture is experienced as a self-enclosed world. . . . [The work of art] builds a sovereign realm."[33]

It is precisely that quality that makes frames the ideal prototype of all boundaries delineating the various realms of our experience,[34] those mental lines that separate ordinary reality from the "worlds" of art, dream, play, and symbolism as well as off-the-record from official statements, parenthetical from ordinary remarks,[35] the metaphoric from the literal, satire from sheer slander, commentary from pure coverage, parody from plagiarism, and maneuvers from actual war. Framing is the act of surrounding situations, acts, or objects with mental brackets[36] that basically transform their meaning by defining them as a game, a joke, a symbol, or a fantasy. Play, for example, is actually "a name for contexts in which the constituent acts have a different sort of relevance . . . from that which they would have had in non-play. . . . The essence of play lies in a partial denial of the meanings that the actions would have had in other situations."[37]

A frame is characterized not by its contents but rather by the distinctive way in which it transforms the contents' meaning. The way framing helps de-eroticize what we normally consider sexual is quite suggestive of the remarkable transformational capacity of frames. The party frame, for example, allows even perfect strangers to hold one another while moving together in a pronounced rhythmic fashion (though only while the music is playing).[38] In a similar manner, in the context of art, respectability is granted to otherwise obscene literary passages and poetic metaphors as well as to nude modeling and photography,[39] just as the play frame helps de-eroticize games such as "house" and "doctor." Ordinary sexual meanings are likewise antisepticized by science, which allows genital display in anatomy books, and medicine, which de-eroticizes mouth-to-mouth resuscitation and gynecological examinations.[40]

In cutting chunks of experience off from their surroundings, frames obviously define not only different but also separate realms of experience. In delineating a space which the viewer cannot enter, picture frames, for example, "[cut] the artist's statement off from the room in which it is hung,"[41] thus visually articulating an experiential cleavage between ordinary reality and the artistic realm.[42] Supposedly bounded, experiential realms do not spill over into one another,[43] and the "reality" of any object is therefore always confined to the boundaries of the particular frame within which it is situated. That is why it is so difficult to prolong a dream after waking up or to sustain an erotic experience when someone knocks on the door, as well as why we normally do not hold others responsible for any harm they may have caused us in our fantasies. Along similar lines, terrified as we are by Captain Hook, Darth Vader, or the Wicked Witch of the West when we read about them or watch them on the screen, we nonetheless know that they can never step out of the fictional frames in which they belong and therefore cannot really hurt us.

Picture frames also make us disregard the wall surrounding the picture.[44] Like them, all frames basically define parts of our perceptual environment as irrelevant, thus separating that which we attend in a focused manner from all the out-of-frame experiences[45] that we leave "in the background" and ignore. Thus, for example, when we play checkers, the material of which the pieces are made is considered totally irrelevant to the game and, therefore, out of frame. In fact, when a piece is missing, we often replace it with a coin, totally disregarding the latter's ordinary monetary value. Likewise, within an erotic context, we normally perceive others as attractive or not, ignoring ordinary distinctions based on social class, status, or ethnic origin.[46]

Moreover, frames make us ignore entire acts or objects despite their obvious physical presence in the situation. At concerts, for example, we usually disregard such acts as replacing a mouthpiece or wiping spittle off one's horn, which are clearly not part of the framed performance in which they are visually embedded. We likewise ignore "background" activity such as nail biting or doodling at meetings and routinely skip page numbers and translators' notes when reading books.[47] And just as we exclude from the game frame such accidents as unintentionally knocking a piece off the chessboard (in sharp contrast to removing deliberately a captured piece), we also instruct jurors to ignore "unacceptable" evidence presented to them.

The experiential discontinuity between what is situated "inside" and "outside" frames also applies to human objects, as mere presence at a social situation may not always guarantee inclusion in the frame surrounding it.[48] In social gatherings, full-fledged participants are often surrounded by a mental partition[49] that keeps mere bystanders practically "out of focus." (Such discontinuity becomes apparent when we poke fun at those who laugh at jokes that were not addressed to them or when cardplayers scold kibitzers who offer unsolicited advice: "Who asked you, anyway?")[50] Cabdrivers, waiters, stenographers, and children are often assigned such out-of-frame status. So are technicians installing equipment at rock concerts, attendants who clean after the animals at circuses, food vendors at sports events, and photographers at weddings, all of whom are clearly situated outside the entertainment frame that surrounds everyone else. Despite their obvious physical presence at these situations, they are considered "non-persons"[51] and thus relegated to the out-of-frame "background." That is also why we sometimes fail to notice the very presence of those we assume do not understand the language we speak or the topic we discuss.[52]

CHUNKS OF IDENTITY

The manner in which we isolate supposedly discrete "figures" from their surrounding "ground" is also manifested in the way we come to experience ourselves.[53] It involves a form of mental differentiation that entails a fundamental distinction between us and the rest of the world. It is known as our sense of identity.

The most obvious form of identity is the experience of an insular self that is clearly cut off from one's surrounding environment,[54] a self with "clear and sharp lines of demarcation" that we experience as autonomous and "marked off distinctly from everything else."[55] Such self presupposes the experience of some "ego boundary"[56] that marks the "edge" of our personhood,[57] the point where we end and the rest of the world begins. Such boundary is at the heart of the fundamental experiential separation of what is "inside" the self from what lies "outside" it.[58]

The experience of a self presupposes some "psychological division from the rest of the world."[59] It is a product of a long process that begins when, as infants, we psychologically disengage ("hatch") from our initial "symbiotic" relationship with our most immediate other, usually our mother.[60] As a result of such process of individuation, we withdraw from a somewhat fluid reality into one where the self as well as other individuals with sharp and firm contours seem to emerge as discrete entities that are clearly separate from their environment.[61]

The self is but one particular focus of identity. There are many other answers to the existential question of where we end and the rest of the world begins, and they all involve supposedly bounded clusters of individuals (a family, a profession, a political party, a nation) who experience themselves collectively—and are usually perceived by others—as insular entities[62] clearly separate from everyone else. In short, we experience ourselves not only as "I" but also collectively as "we," that is, as liberals, baseball fans, Muslims, women, humans. It is such perceptions of social clusters as discrete entities that lead us to regard a marriage between a Christian and a Jew or an Armenian and a Pole as "mixed."

The experience of such discrete entities presupposes a perception of some boundaries surrounding them.[63] Even a couple going steady experiences some clear partition separating them from others around them.[64] Such fine mental lines help us perceive a fundamental discontinuity between insiders and outsiders, those included in a social cluster and those who are left outside its confines. Only in relation to those lines do sentiments such as fidelity, loyalty, or patriotism, for example, evolve, and only in relation to them do we learn whom we can trust and of whom we should beware, who is available to us as a sexual partner and whom we must avoid. These are the boundaries that basically define the mental entities we come to experience as "us" and "them." They constitute the basis of our sense of identity and determine much of the scope of our social relations.

Mental Fields

Early in life, space is the only mode available for organizing a self.[65] Indeed, our individuation begins with the development of locomotor functions such as crawling, which allow us to literally withdraw from others.[66] Later we establish some nonspatial sense of selfhood,[67] actualizing our separateness by acts such as saying no[68] and experiences such as ownership of toys, yet the basic way in which we experience the self and its relations with others remains spatial nonetheless. We thus associate selfhood with a psychological "distance" from others[69] and experience privacy (including its nonspatial aspects, such as secrecy) as having some "space" for ourselves or as a "territory" of inaccessibility surrounding us.[70] We experience others as being "close" to or "distant" from us and portray our willingness or unwillingness to make contact with them using topological images such as "opening up" (or "reaching out") and being "closed" (or "removed").[71] We also use the image of "penetration" to depict the essence of the process of becoming intimate.[72]

Similar spatial imagery captures our experience of groups as bounded, "closed"[73] entities that one almost literally "enters" and "exists."[74] We thus "*in*corporate" members into, "expel" them from, and assign them "central" or "marginal" places in groups. We also use images such as "*extra*marital" (or "*out of* wedlock"), "mobility,"[75] and "knows his place"; perceive actual social "distance"[76] between blacks and whites or senior and junior executives; and mentally locate "distant" relatives in terms of the number of "steps" they are "removed" from us.[77] Such mental geography has no physical basis but we experience it as if it did.

We likewise use spatial images to depict supposedly discrete chunks of professional jurisdiction (boundary, turf, territory, arena)[78] as well as knowledge. We thus perceive academic disciplines as surrounded by mental "walls"[79] and works as lying on the "fringes" of sociology or outside our "area" of expertise, and regard those whose interest does not transcend the confines of their "field" as "limited" or "narrow minded." Similar spatial imagery seems to underlie our perception of the *extra*curricular, *extra*judicial, and *eso*teric as well as of insular "domains" such as work, religion, or art.

Somewhat similar is our experience of the fine mental lines that separate acceptable from unacceptable behavior—the assertive from the rude, the funny from the crude. We basically "confine [ourselves] to a particular radius of activity and . . . regard any conduct which drifts outside that radius as somehow inappropriate or immoral. . . . Human behavior can vary over an enormous range, but each community draws a symbolic set of parentheses around a certain segment of that range and limits its own activities within that narrower zone."[80] Our quasi-spatial experience of such "normative outlines" of society[81] is quite evident from our use of verbs such as "*trans*gress" or "*ex*ceed" (which literally mean to step or go beyond), prefixes such as "over-" (as in "*over*ambitious"), "out-" (as in "*out*law"), or "extra-" (as in "*extra*vagant"), and metaphors such as "line of decency"[82] or "limits of authority."

In a somewhat similar manner, we also "enter" conversations, go "out of" business, portray breakthroughs as the crossing of a Rubicon[83] or a forbidden frontier,[84] and can appreciate a cartoon depicting someone reaching a line demarcated by the sign "Boundary of Self Respect."[85] Similar spatial imagery also underlies such concepts as "*extra*ordinary," "*out*standing," or "*ex*otic."

Spatial metaphors pervade much of our thinking.[86] In a wide variety of contexts, we use them to depict purely mental relations among entities. In fact, we basically experience reality as a "space"[87] made up of discrete mental fields delineated by mental "fences"[88] that define[89] and separate them from one another. Given the significance of proximity in perceptual grouping (the closer things are to one another, the more we tend to perceive them as a single entity[90]), we use closeness as a metaphor for conceptual similarity,[91] essentially seeing difference in terms of mental distance.[92] We thus consider similar mental items as belonging "together"[93] and different ones as being "worlds apart," and we may even try to locate an item "exactly halfway" between two others.[94]

A foremost prerequisite for differentiating any entity from its surrounding environment are exceptionally strong intra-entity relations.[95] A mental field is basically a cluster of items that are more similar to one another than to any other item. Generating such fields, therefore, usually involves some lumping. As we group items in our mind (that is, categorize the world), we let their similarity outweigh any differences among them. As a result we perceive mental fields as relatively homogeneous lumps and regard their constituent items as functionally interchangeable variants ("allo-" variants) of a single unit of meaning.[96] Even when we notice differences among them, we dismiss them as totally irrelevant[97]—"making no difference"— and consequently ignore them.

Thus, despite the obvious differences among them, we regard the prefixes of the adjectives "*in*accurate," "*im*proper," "*dis*honest," and "*un*usual" as functionally equivalent variants of a single morpheme.[98] We regard them as basically "the same" because no confusion of meaning is likely to occur if one of them is substituted for another (that is, if we say "disaccurate" or "unproper"). Nor do we normally attribute much significance to the difference between right-eye and left-eye winks, which we perceive as functionally interchangeable variants of a single gesture,[99] or between a kiss and an affectionate look, which we often substitute for each other as tokens of intimacy.[100] Along similar lines, we usually ignore the obvious difference

between 490- and 540-millimicron-long light waves, regarding both as variants of the color "green,"[101] and casually substitute pretzels for potato chips as party snacks. And though clearly aware of the difference between thirty-one- and twenty-eight-day blocks of time, we nonetheless regard both as structurally equivalent variants of the unit "month"[102] and expect identical monthly paychecks for January and February. Along similar lines, we usually perceive conventional historical periods as relatively homogeneous stretches, often lumping together events that occurred centuries apart from one another yet within the same "period" (as in "the Middle Ages").[103]

In a similar manner, we establish social clusters in our mind by regarding all cluster members as similar and ignoring all differences among them, as when we lump together all those whose income falls below a certain "poverty line" as an undifferentiated lot—"the poor." We generally tend to downplay differences within our own group as well as among others,[104] as evident from the extremely broad categories ("Orientals") in which we lump those who came to America[105] or from various catchall categories for outsiders, such as the ancient Greek "barbarian," the Armenian *odar*,[106] the Gypsy *gadjo*, or the Jewish *goy*.

Ignoring intracluster differences and regarding all cluster members as basically "the same" often results in stereotypes, as when racists claim that all blacks are lazy or that all Orientals look alike. Nonetheless, without some lumping, it would be impossible ever to experience any collectivity, or mental entity for that matter. The ability to ignore the uniqueness of items and regard them as typical members of categories is a prerequisite for classifying any group of phenomena. Such ability to "typify"[107] our experience is therefore one of the cornerstones of social reality.

RITUAL TRANSITIONS

Most of the fine lines that separate mental entities from one another are drawn only in our own head and, therefore, totally invisible. And yet, by playing up the act of "crossing" them, we can make mental discontinuities more "tangible." Many rituals, indeed, are designed specifically to substantiate the mental segmentation of reality into discrete chunks. In articulating our "passage" through the mental partitions separating these chunks from one another, such rituals, originally identified by Arnold Van Gennep as "rites of passage,"[108] certainly enhance our experience of discontinuity.

The various rites we perform when we cross the equator, tropic of Cancer, or arctic circle[109] are perfect cases in point. In dramatizing our passage through these imaginary lines that exist only on maps, they certainly make them more "tangible" (somewhat like the road sign Welcome to Massachusetts). In a similar manner, we also dramatize the mental discontinuity between the public and private domains by knocking on the door before entering a room as well as by altering our appearance, as in the following caricature of a stereotypical return home, "from 'a hard day at the office': a banal scene in which the social passage is signified by the man successively removing his hat . . . taking off his jacket, stripping away his tie (exaggerated gesture), opening his shirt collar. . . . A whole set of statements about the contrast between [home] and the 'larger world' is going on."[110] Along similar lines, soldiers coming home even for a few hours often change into civilian clothes just to actualize their "exit" from the military world. Lowering their voices on entering church similarly helps congregants substantiate the mental separation of the sacred from the profane, whereas the ritual apology ("I beg your pardon") we offer on entering each other's

"personal space" likewise promotes our experience of an insular self.

In a similar manner, weddings substantiate the boundaries of the family, whose crossing transforms people into spouses and in-laws. They also signal, of course, the crossing of the mental partition that separates marriage from singlehood, just like puberty rites[111] (or modern equivalents such as obtaining a driver's license or going for the first time to an R-rated film), which dramatize the transition from childhood to adulthood. (The fact that we rarely celebrate divorces and usually articulate second weddings considerably less than first ones suggests that entering marriage entails a much greater break in identity than exiting or reentering it.) In dramatizing the moments of entering and exiting it, birth and death rituals[112] likewise substantiate the experience of life as a discrete block of time (as well as the mental contrast between life and nonlife). The need to substantiate the way we segment time into discrete blocks also accounts for the holidays we create to commemorate critical transition points between historical epochs[113] as well as for the rituals we design to articulate significant changes in our relative access to one another—greetings, first kisses, farewell parties, bedtime stories.[114] Changes of lighting or background music likewise signal transitions among successive segments of theatrical performances, films,[115] rock concerts, and circus shows, whereas ritual switches from sitting to standing help to "punctuate" religious services[116] and demarcate featured solos in jazz.

The ritual of raising the curtain before the beginning of a show[117] and the almost obligatory "once upon a time" or "and they lived happily ever after"[118] that signal crossings of the line separating fairy tales from "real" life similarly serve to substantiate the boundaries of frames.[119] So do the ritual glove touch or kickoff that prefaces sports events, the suspension of meter that signals the dissolution of the poetic frame,[120] and the caption "The End" that used to announce the conclusion of films. (Within films, conventional cues such as soft focus, overexposure, change from color to black and white, and suspension of background music often signal transitions from characters' here and now into their memories, fantasies, or dreams.) Along similar lines, organ preludes are often used to announce a religious frame,[121] "soft" music (and candlelight) a romantic frame, and dance music (and hors d'oeuvres) a party.

By switching from one language to another or even from standard to colloquial speech, we often articulate transitions from formality to informality or from just talking to quoting.[122] In a similar manner, speakers often clear their throats to announce the conclusion of their informal introductory remarks (just as chairpersons use gavels to announce the formal parts of meetings), change their tone to signal diversions from the general thrust of their talk to "parenthetical" remarks, and sit down to announce the beginning of the more informal question-and-answer part.[123] Children likewise use a change of voice to "enter" the make-believe frame[124] and the ritual call "Time" to exit from a game in order to tie a loose shoelace or get a drink.

Along similar lines, by punishing deviants who transgress its moral boundaries, society not only forces us to see that such lines do indeed exist but also demarcates their precise "location." Like weddings, funerals, and bedtime stories, punishment is a ritual that dramatizes the act of crossing some mental partition. In substantiating the mental segmentation of human behavior into acceptable and unacceptable, it serves to "locate and publicize"[125] moral edges:

> The deviant is a person whose activities have moved outside the margins of the group, and when the community calls him to account for that vagrancy it is making a statement about the nature

and placement of its boundaries. . . . Members of a community inform one another about the placement of their boundaries by participating in the confrontations which occur when persons who venture out to the edges of the group are met by policing agents. . . . Whether these confrontations take the form of criminal trials, excommunication hearings, courts-martial, or even psychiatric case conferences, they [demonstrate] where the line is drawn. . . . Morality and immorality meet at the public scaffold, and it is during this meeting that the line between them is drawn. . . . Each time the community moves to censure some act of deviation, then, and convenes a formal ceremony to deal with the responsible offender, it . . . restates where the boundaries of the group are located.[126]

Moral boundaries remain a meaningful point of reference, of course, only as long as society indeed curbs all attempts to transgress them.[127] When society fails to punish deviants who venture beyond the limit of what it defines as acceptable, members will wonder whether such a line really exists.

Only the need to announce crossings of frame boundaries prompts us to indent quotations like the one above on a page of text[128] and only the need to substantiate an insular self compels us to say grace before we ingest parts of the environment into our body through the act of eating. Substantiating the insularity of conventional chunks of space, time, and identity is likewise the only reason for the rites we perform around doorsills,[129] the birthday cards[130] and New Year midnight kisses with which we "punctuate" life as well as history, and the various initiation rites (such as baptism, adoption, and naturalization) by which we dramatize the incorporation of new members into religious communities, families, or nations. Such rituals of "passage" are all products of some basic need to substantiate in our acts the mental discontinuities we perceive in our mind. As such, they play a major role in our ability to think analytically.

NOTES

1. Genesis 1:1–5.
2. Ibid., 6–10.
3. See, for example, Paul Seligman, *The Apeiron of Anaximander* (London: Athlone Press, 1962).
4. Gyorgy Kepes, *Language of Vision* (Chicago: Paul Theobald, 1951 [1944]), p. 45; Wolfgang Köhler, *Gestalt Psychology* (New York: New American Library, 1947), pp. 84, 93.
5. See also Ferdinand de Saussure, *Course in General Linguistics* (New York: Philosophical Library, 1959 [1915]), pp. 116–22; Michel Foucault, *The Order of Things* (New York: Vintage, 1973 [1966]), p. 144.
6. Paul Starr, "Social Categories and Claims in the Liberal State," in Mary Douglas, ed., *How Classification Works* (Edinburgh: Edinburgh University Press, forthcoming).
7. Emile Durkheim and Marcel Mauss, *Primitive Classification* (Chicago: University of Chicago Press, 1963 [1903]), p. 4. See also Karl W. Deutsch, "Autonomy and Boundaries according to Communications Theory," in Roy R. Grinker, ed., *Toward a Unified Theory of Human Behavior* (New York: Basic Books, 1956), pp. 278–79; Anatol Rapoport, "Statistical Boundaries," in *Toward a Unified Theory of Human Behavior*, p. 308. In Hebrew, the words for *classifying* (*sivug*) and *boundary* (*syag*) indeed derive from the same root.
8. Kenneth Burke, *A Grammar of Motives* (Berkeley: University of California Press, 1969 [1945]), p. 24. See also Gottlob Frege, "Logic in Mathematics," in *Post-humous Writings* (Chicago: University of Chicago Press, 1979 [1914]), pp. 155, 179, 195, 229, 241; Joan Weiner, "The Philosopher Behind the Last Logicist," in Crispin Wright, ed., *Frege—Tradition and Influence* (Oxford: Basil Blackwell, 1984), p. 72n.
9. Don Handelman, "The Ritual Clown: Attributes and Affinities," *Anthropos* 76 (1981):340.
10. Gustav Ichheiser, *Appearances and Realities* (San Francisco: Jossey-Bass, 1970), p. 8.
11. See also Henning Henningsen, *Crossing the Equator* (Copenhagen: Munksgaard, 1961), pp. 99–101.
12. Jean Jacques Rousseau, "A Discourse on the Origin of Inequality," in *The Social Contract and Discourses* (New York: E. P. Dutton, 1950 [1754]), p. 234.

13. See also Robert C. Tryon, *Identification of Social Areas by Cluster Analysis* (Berkeley: University of California Press, 1955), p. 71.
14. Barry Schwartz, "The Social Psychology of Privacy," *American Journal of Sociology* 78 (1968):747.
15. Charles A. Ferguson, "Diglossia," *Word* 15 (1959):325–40.
16. Stanley J. Tambiah, "Animals Are Good to Think and Good to Prohibit," *Ethnology* 8 (1969): 423–59; Pierre Bourdieu, "The Berber House," in Mary Douglas, ed., *Rules and Meanings* (Harmondsworth, England: Penguin, 1973 [1971]), pp. 98–110.
17. Robert Hertz, "The Pre-eminence of the Right Hand: A Study in Religious Polarity," in Rodney Needham, ed., *Right and Left* (Chicago: University of Chicago Press, 1973 [1909]); Barry Schwartz, *Vertical Classification* (Chicago: University of Chicago Press, 1981).
18. Kurt Lewin, *Principles of Topological Psychology* (New York: McGraw-Hill, 1936), p. 44.
19. Helms, *Ulysses' Sail*, pp. 22–31.
20. Gerald D. Suttles, *The Social Order of the Slum* (Chicago: University of Chicago Press, 1968), pp. 13–38, 225; Albert Hunter, *Symbolic Communities* (Chicago: University of Chicago Press, 1982 [1974]), pp. 84, 88.
21. See also Schwartz, "The Social Psychology of Privacy," pp. 747–49.
22. Virginia Woolf, *A Room of One's Own* (San Diego: Harcourt Brace Jovanovich, 1957 [1929]), p. 110. See also Woolf, pp. 4, 109; Christopher Alexander et al., *A Pattern Language* (New York: Oxford University Press, 1977), pp. 669–71.
23. On such segmentation of everyday life, see Kenneth L. Pike, *Language in Relation to a Unified Theory of the Structure of Human Behavior* (The Hague: Mouton, 1967 [1954]), pp. 73–82; Roger G. Barker and Herbert F. Wright, *Midwest and Its Children* (Hamden, Conn.: Archon, 1971 [1955]), pp. 225–73; Roger G. Barker, ed., *The Stream of Behavior* (New York: Appleton-Century-Crofts, 1963).
24. Zerubavel, *The Seven-Day Circle*, pp. 121–29. See also Zerubavel, pp. 102–6 and Zerubavel, *Patterns of Time in Hospital Life*, pp. 98–101. That is why nurses can take four-day blocks off only if no more than two of these days are within "the same" week (*Patterns of*

Time in Hospital Life, p. 21; *The Seven-Day Circle*, pp. 128–29).

25. See also Barbara H. Smith, *Poetic Closure* (Chicago: University of Chicago Press, 1968), pp. 2–4.

26. Zerubavel, *Patterns of Time in Hospital Life*, pp. 31–32.

27. Zerubavel, *Hidden Rhythms*, pp. 101–37; Zerubavel, *The Seven-Day Circle*, pp. 118–20.

28. Zerubavel, *Hidden Rhythms*, pp. 138–66.

29. Yael Zerubavel, "The Last Stand: On the Transformation of Symbols in Modern Israeli Culture," (Ph.D. diss., University of Pennsylvania, 1980), pp. 301–21; Yael Zerubavel, "Collective Memory and Historical Metaphors: Masada and the Holocaust as National Israeli Symbols" (paper presented at the meetings of the Association for Jewish Studies, Boston, December 1987).

30. See also Roy Turner, "Some Formal Properties of Therapy Talk," in David Sudnow, ed., *Studies in Social Interaction* (New York: Free Press, 1972), pp. 367–96.

31. Alfred Schutz, "On Multiple Realities," in *Collected Papers* (The Hague: Martinus Nijhoff, 1973 [1945]), vol. 1, pp. 230–31. See also William James, *The Principles of Psychology* (Cambridge: Harvard University Press, 1983 [1890]), pp. 920–23.

32. See also Gregory Bateson, "A Theory of Play and Fantasy," in *Steps to an Ecology of Mind* (New York: Ballantine, 1972 [1955]), pp. 187–88; Marion Milner, *The Suppressed Madness of Sane Men* (London: Tavistock, 1987), pp. 80–81, 225–26.

33. Georg Simmel, "The Handle," in Kurt H. Wolff, ed., *Georg Simmel, 1858–1918* (Columbus: Ohio State University Press, 1959 [1911]), p. 267.

34. Bateson, "A Theory of Play and Fantasy," pp. 184–92; Erving Goffman, *Frame Analysis* (New York: Harper Colophon, 1974).

35. See also Goffman, ibid., pp. 496–559; Erving Goffman, *Forms of Talk* (Philadelphia: University of Pennsylvania Press, 1981), pp. 144–57, 173–86, 226–327.

36. Schutz, "On Multiple Realities," p. 233; Goffman, *Forms of Talk*, pp. 251–69.

37. Gregory Bateson, *Mind and Nature* (New York: E. P. Dutton, 1979), p. 125.

38. See also Georg Simmel, "Sociability: An Example of Pure, or Formal Sociology," in Kurt H. Wolff, ed., *The Sociology of Georg Simmel* (New York: Free Press, 1950 [1917]), pp. 47–53.

39. Goffman, *Frame Analysis*, pp. 77–78; Murray S. Davis, *Smut* (Chicago: University of Chicago Press, 1983), pp. 216–19.

40. Joan P. Emerson, "Behavior in Private Places: Sustaining Definitions of Reality in Gynecological Examinations," in Hans P. Dreitzel, ed., *Recent Sociology No. 2* (London: Macmillan, 1970), pp. 74–97; Davis, *Smut*, pp. 219–24.

41. Goffman, *Frame Analysis*, p. 412.

42. Rudolf Arnheim, *Art and Visual Perception* (Berkeley: University of California Press, 1967 [1954]), p. 231; Edward T. Cone, *Musical Form and Musical Performance* (New York: W. W. Norton, 1968), p. 15; Meyer Schapiro, "On Some Problems in the Semiotics of Visual Art: Field and Vehicle in Image-Signs," *Semiotica* 1 (1969):224; Boris Uspensky, *A Poetics of Composition* (Berkeley: University of California Press, 1973), p. 143; Rudolf Arnheim, *The Power of the Center* (Berkeley: University of California Press, 1982), pp. 50–52, 63.

43. Schutz, "On Multiple Realities," pp. 230–33.

44. Bateson, "A Theory of Play and Fantasy," p. 187.

45. Goffman, *Frame Analysis*, pp. 201–46.

46. Davis, *Smut*, pp. 29–30.

47. Michel Butor, "The Book as Object," in *Inventory* (New York: Simon & Schuster, 1968), pp. 50–51; Goffman, *Frame Analysis*, pp. 227–30. See also Erving Goffman, *Behavior in Public Places* (New York: Free Press, 1963), pp. 43, 50–53; Goffman, *Frame Analysis*, p. 220.

48. Goffman, *Frame Analysis*, pp. 224–25; Goffman, *Forms of Talk*, pp. 131–40.

49. See, for example, Erving Goffman, *Encounters* (Indianapolis: Bobbs-Merrill, 1961), pp. 65–66; Harland G. Bloland, "Opportunities, Traps, and Sanctuaries: A Frame Analysis of Learned Societies," *Urban Life* 11 (1982):87ff.

50. See also Goffman, *Encounters*, pp. 63–64.

51. Erving Goffman, *The Presentation of Self in Everyday Life* (Garden City, N.Y.: Anchor, 1959), pp. 151–53; Goffman, *Behavior in Public Places*, p. 84; Goffman, *Frame Analysis*, p. 207.

52. Our assumption, however, may be false. Traveling in Europe and speaking together in Hebrew, my wife and I were once surprised on a bus by the woman sitting in front of us, who turned and asked us in Hebrew something about the weather. It was a subtle hint designed to remind us that "nonpersons" may interact with us in a far more "focused" way than we realize.

53. Heinz Werner, *Comparative Psychology of Mental Development* (New York: International Universities Press, 1957 [1940]), pp. 452–53; Witkin et al., *Psychological Differentiation*, p. 5; Herman A. Witkin, "Psychological Differentiation and Forms of Pathology," *Journal of Abnormal Psychology* 70 (1965):319.

54. Victor Tausk, "On the Origin of the 'Influencing Machine' in Schizophrenia," in Robert Fliess, ed., *The Psychoanalytic Reader* (New York: International Universities Press, 1948 [1919]), vol. 1, p. 68; Witkin et al., *Psychological Differentiation*, p. 14; Witkin, "Psychological Differentiation and Forms of Pathology," pp. 320–21.

55. Sigmund Freud, *Civilization and Its Discontents* (New York: W. W. Norton, 1962 [1930]), p. 13.

56. Tausk, "On the Origin of the 'Influencing Machine.'"

57. Paul Federn, "The Ego as Subject and Object in Narcissism," in *Ego Psychology and the Psychoses* (London: Imago Publishing Co., 1953 [1928]), p. 285.

58. Paul Federn, "Ego Psychological Aspect of Schizophrenia," in *Ego Psychology and the Psychoses*, p. 225. See also Tausk, "On the Origin of the 'Influencing Machine,'" p. 69; Jean Piaget, *The Construction of Reality in the Child* (New York: Basic Books, 1954), p. 281; Ernst Prelinger, "Extension and Structure of the Self," *Journal of Psychology* 47 (1959):13–23; Witkin et al., *Psychological Differentiation*, p. 134.

59. Nancy Chodorow, *The Reproduction of Mothering* (Berkeley: University of California Press, 1978), p. 68. See also Otto Fenichel, *The Psychoanalytic Theory of Neurosis* (New York: W. W. Norton, 1945), pp. 35–36.

60. Margaret S. Mahler and Kitty La Perriere, "Mother-Child Interaction during Separation-Individuation," in Margaret S. Mahler, *Separation-Individuation* (New York: Jason Aronson, 1979 [1965]), p. 36; Margaret S. Mahler, "On the First Three Subphases of the Separation-Individuation Process," in *Separation-Individuation*, pp. 121–22; Margaret S. Mahler et al., *The Psychological Birth of the Human Infant* (New York: Basic Books, 1975), pp. 52–54, 63.

61. Arthur Koestler, *The Act of Creation* (New York: Macmillan, 1964), p. 292.

62. Donald T. Campbell, "Common Fate, Similarity, and Other Indices of the Status of Aggregates of Persons as Social Entities," *Behavioral Science* 3 (1958):17–18. See also Reuben Hill, *Families Under Stress* (Westport, Conn.: Greenwood, 1971 [1949]), pp. 3–5; Fredrik Barth, *Ethnic Groups and Boundaries* (Boston: Little, Brown, 1969), p. 9.

63. See, for example, Kurt Koffka, *Principles of Gestalt Psychology* (New York: Harbinger, 1935), p. 665; Hill, *Families Under Stress*, pp. 3–5; Kai T. Erikson, *Wayward Puritans* (New York: John Wiley, 1966), pp. 11, 13, 196; Richard Handler, *Nationalism and the Politics of Culture in Quebec* (Madison: University of Wisconsin Press, 1988).

64. Mark Krain, "A Definition of Dyadic Boundaries and an Empirical Study of Boundary Establishment in Courtship," *International Journal of Sociology of the Family* 7 (1977): 120. See also Erving Goffman, *Relations in Public* (New York: Harper Colophon, 1972), pp. 19–23.

65. Sigmund Freud, *The Ego and the Id* (New York: W. W. Norton, 1962 [1923]), p. 16; Stanley R. Palombo and Hilde Bruch, "Falling Apart: The Verbalization of Ego Failure," *Psychiatry* 27 (1964):250, 252, 256.

66. Mahler and La Perriere, "Mother-Child Interaction," p. 36; Margaret S. Mahler, "On Human Symbiosis and the Vicissitudes of Individuation," in *Separation-Individuation*, pp. 85–86; Mahler, "On the First Three Subphases," pp. 124–25; Mahler et al., *The Psychological Birth of the Human Infant*, p. 72; Louise J. Kaplan, *Oneness and Separateness* (New York: Touchstone, 1978), pp. 191–98.

67. See, for example, James, *Principles of Psychology*, pp. 280–83.

68. Kaplan, *Oneness and Separateness*, p. 200.

69. Werner, *Comparative Psychology of Mental Development*, p. 452.

70. Georg Simmel, "The Secret and the Secret Society," in Kurt H. Wolff, ed., *The Sociology of Georg*

Simmel (New York: Free Press, 1950 [1908]), pp. 321–22; Goffman, *Relations in Public*, pp. 38–39; Eviatar Zerubavel, "Personal Information and Social Life," *Symbolic Interaction* 5 (1982):102–5.

71. See also Lewin, *Principles of Topological Psychology*; Maria A. Rickers-Ovsiankina, "Social Accessibility in Three Age Groups," *Psychological Reports* 2 (1956):283–94; Maria A. Rickers-Ovsiankina and Arnold A. Kusmin, "Individual Differences in Social Accessibility," *Psychological Reports* 4 (1958):391–406; Prelinger, "Extension and Structure of the Self."

72. Irwin Altman and Dalmas A. Taylor, *Social Penetration* (New York: Holt, Rinehart and Winston, 1973).

73. Max Weber, *Economy and Society* (Berkeley: University of California Press, 1978 [1925]), pp. 43–46; Campbell, "Common Fate," p. 22.

74. Arnold Van Gennep, *The Rites of Passage* (Chicago: University of Chicago Press, 1960 [1908]), pp. 103, 113.

75. Pitirim A. Sorokin, *Social and Cultural Mobility* (New York: Free Press, 1964 [1927]), p. 133. See also Sorokin, pp. 1–10; Pierre Bourdieu, "The Social Space and the Genesis of Groups," *Theory and Society* 14 (1985):723–44.

76. Georg Simmel, "The Stranger," in Kurt H. Wolff, ed., *The Sociology of Georg Simmel* (New York: Free Press, 1950 [1908]), pp. 402–8; Robert E. Park, "The Concept of Social Distance," *Journal of Applied Sociology* 8 (1924):339–44.

77. See, for example, Ward H. Goodenough, "Yankee Kinship Terminology: A Problem in Componential Analysis," in Stephen A. Tyler, ed., *Cognitive Anthropology* (New York: Holt, Rinehart and Winston, 1969 [1965]), pp. 269–71; David M. Schneider, *American Kinship* (Chicago: University of Chicago Press, 1980), pp. 23, 73.

78. Eliot Freidson, *Doctoring Together* (Chicago: University of Chicago Press, 1980 [1975]), pp. 69–85; Carol L. Kronus, "The Evolution of Occupational Power: An Historical Study of Task Boundaries between Physicians and Pharmacists," *Sociology of Work and Occupations* 3 (1976):3–37; Andrew Abbott, *The System of Professions* (Chicago: University of Chicago Press, 1988).

79. Margaret Mead, "Crossing Boundaries in Social Science Communications," *Social Science Information* 8 (1969):7.

80. Erikson, *Wayward Puritans*, p. 10.

81. Ibid., p. 12.

82. "Next: R-Rated Record Albums?" *Newsweek*, August 26, 1985, p. 69.

83. "Botha Goes Slow," *Newsweek*, August 26, 1985, p. 27.

84. Elihu Katz and Daniel Dayan, "Contests, Conquests, Coronations: On Media Events and Their Heroes," in Carl F. Graumann and Serge Moscovici, eds., *Changing Conceptions of Leadership* (New York: Springer-Verlag, 1986), p. 139.

85. *Newsday*, January 30, 1986, Part 2, p. 19.

86. Mark Johnson, *The Body in the Mind* (Chicago: University of Chicago Press, 1987).

87. Fred Attneave, "Dimensions of Similarity," *American Journal of Psychology* 63 (1950):516–56; Charles E. Osgood et al., *The Measurement of Meaning* (Urbana: University of Illinois Press, 1957), pp. 86, 89–97; Foucault, *The Order of Things*, pp. xviii–xix, xxii; Richard Beals et al., "Foundations of Multidimensional Scaling," *Psychological Review* 75 (1968):132; Samuel Fillenbaum and Amnon Rapoport, *Structures in the Subjective Lexicon* (New York: Academic Press, 1971), p. 4; J. Douglas Carroll and Myron Wish, "Multidimensional Perceptual Models and Measurement Methods," in Edward C. Carterette and Morton P. Friedman, eds., *Handbook of Perception, vol. 2: Psychophysical Judgment and Measurement* (New York: Academic Press, 1974), pp. 425–26; Eugene Hunn, "Toward a Perceptual Model of Folk Biological Classification," *American Ethnologist* 3 (1976):515; Robert Darnton, *The Great Cat Massacre and Other Episodes in French Cultural History* (New York: Vintage, 1985), p. 192; Frederick L. Bates and Walter G. Peacock, "Conceptualizing Social Structure: The Misuse of Classification in Structural Modeling," *American Sociological Review* 54 (1989):569n.

88. Anthony F. Wallace and John Atkins, "The Meaning of Kinship Terms," *American Anthropologist* 62 (1960):67.

89. The Hebrew words for *fence (gader)* and *definition (hagdara)* indeed derive from the same root.

90. Max Wertheimer, "Untersuchungen zur Lehre von der Gestalt," *Psycholo. Forsch.* 4 (1923): 301–50.

91. See also Werner, *Comparative Psychology of Mental Development*, pp. 222–25.

92. See, for example, Attneave, "Dimensions of Similarity"; Osgood et al., *The Measurement of Meaning*, pp. 89–97; Warren S. Torgerson, *Theory and Methods of Scaling* (New York: John Wiley, 1958), pp. 250, 260ff; Werner S. Landecker, "Class Boundaries," *American Sociological Review* 25 (1960):873; Roger N. Shepard, "The Analysis of Proximities: Multidimensional Scaling with an Unknown Distance Function," *Psychometrika* 27 (1962): 126; R. E. Bonner, "On Some Clustering Techniques," *IBM Journal of Research and Development* 8 (1964):22–32; Warren S. Torgerson, "Multidimensional Scaling of Similarity," *Psychometrika* 30 (1965):379–93; Peter M. Blau and Otis D. Duncan, *The American Occupational Structure* (New York: John Wiley, 1967), pp. 67–75, 152–61; Beals et al., "Foundations of Multidimensional Scaling," p. 127; Jack B. Arnold. "A Multidimensional Scaling Study of Semantic Distance," *Journal of Experimental Psychology* 90 (1971):349–72; Fillenbaum and Rapoport, *Structures in the Subjective Lexicon*; Abraham A. Moles, *Théorie des Objets* (Paris: Éditions Universitaires, 1972), pp. 59–61, 74; Stephen K. Reed, "Pattern Recognition and Categorization," *Cognitive Psychology* 3 (1972):382–407; Peter H. A. Sneath and Robert R. Sokal, *Numerical Taxonomy* (San Francisco: W. H. Freeman, 1973), p. 119; Carroll and Wish, "Multidimensional Perceptual Models," p. 393; Robert R. Sokal, "Classification: Purposes, Principles, Progress, Prospects," *Science* 185 (1974):1119; Victor Turner, "Metaphors of Anti-Structure in Religious Culture," in *Dramas, Fields, and Metaphors* (Ithaca: Cornell University Press, 1975 [1974]), p. 294; Alfonso Caramazza et al., "Subjective Structures and Operations in Semantic Memory," *Journal of Verbal Learning and Verbal Behavior* 15 (1976): 103–17; Hunn, "Toward a Perceptual Model," p. 515; Carol L. Krumhansl, "Concerning the Applicability of Geometric Models to Similarity Data: The Interrelationship between Similarity and Spatial Density," *Psychological Review* 85 (1978): 445–63; Edward E. Smith and Douglas L. Medin, *Categories and Concepts* (Cambridge: Harvard University Press, 1981), p. 105.

93. See, for example, Kurt Goldstein and Martin Scheerer, "Abstract and Concrete Behavior: An Experimental Study with Special Tests," *Psychological Monographs* 53 (1941), #2, pp. 59–60, 75–82, 103–7, 128.

94. Foucault, *The Order of Things*, p. 136.

95. Köhler, *Gestalt Psychology*, p. 93; Federn, "Ego Psychological Aspect of Schizophrenia," p. 222; Talcott Parsons, *The Social System* (New York: Free Press, 1964 [1951]), p. 482; Campbell, "Common Fate," pp. 18–20; Bonner, "On Some Clustering Techniques," p. 22; Smith, *Poetic Closure*, pp. 23–24; Robert R. Sokal, "Clustering and Classification: Background and Current Directions," in J. Van Ryzin, ed., *Classification and Clustering* (New York: Academic Press, 1977), p. 7; Smith and Medin, *Categories and Concepts*, pp. 110–11.

96. See also Jerome S. Bruner et al., *A Study of Thinking* (New York: John Wiley, 1956), pp. 2–4; Stephen C. Johnson, "Hierarchical Clustering Systems," *Psychometrika* 32 (1967):242; Yehudi A. Cohen, "Social Boundary Systems," *Current Anthropology* 10 (1969): 109–11.

97. Foucault, *The Order of Things*, p. 140.

98. On "allomorphs," see Pike, *Language in Relation to a Unified Theory*, pp. 164, 176–77, 206; Dwight Bolinger, *Aspects of Language* (New York: Harcourt, Brace & World, 1968), pp. 58–63. On their functional phonological analogues, "allophones," see Roman Jakobson, *Six Lectures on Sound and Meaning* (Cambridge: MIT Press, 1978 [1942]), pp. 28–33; Pike, *Language in Relation to a Unified Theory*, pp. 44–46, 325–28; Mario Pei, *Glossary of Linguistic Terminology* (New York: Columbia University Press, 1966), p. 10; Bolinger, *Aspects of Language*, pp. 43–44.

99. See Ray L. Birdwhistell, *Kinesics and Context* (Philadelphia: University of Pennsylvania Press, 1970), pp. 166, 193–95, 229.

100. Murray S. Davis, *Intimate Relations* (New York: Free Press, 1973), pp. 76–77.

101. Umberto Eco, *A Theory of Semiotics* (Bloomington: Indiana University Press, 1976), p. 77.

102. See also Zerubavel, *Patterns of Time in Hospital Life*, p. 4.

103. See also Y. Zerubavel, "The Last Stand," p. 309.

104. Henri Tajfel, *Human Groups and Social Categories* (Cambridge, England: Cambridge University Press, 1981), pp. 115–16, 121, 133, 243.

105. See also Richard Williams, *Hierarchical Structures and Social Value* (Cambridge, England: Cambridge University Press, 1990).

106. Howard F. Stein, *Developmental Time, Cultural Space*. Norman: Oklahoma Press, 1987), p. 6.

107. Berger and Luckmann, *The Social Construction of Reality*, pp. 30–34, 54–58; Schutz and Luckmann, *The Structures of the Life-World*, pp. 73–79, 238–41.

108. Van Gennep, *The Rites of Passage*.

109. Henningsen, *Crossing the Equator*.

110. Marshall Sahlins, *Culture and Practical Reason* (Chicago: University of Chicago Press, 1976), pp. 181–82n.

111. Van Gennep, *The Rites of Passage*, pp. 65–88.

112. Ibid., pp. 50–64, 146–65; Robert Hertz, "A Contribution to the Study of the Collective Representation of Death," in *Death and the Right Hand* (Aberdeen, Scotland: Cohen and West, 1960 [1907]), pp. 80–86; Michael C. Kearl, *Endings* (New York: Oxford University Press, 1989), p. 95.

113. Y. Zerubavel, "Collective Memory and Historical Metaphors."

114. Goffman, *Relations in Public*, pp. 73–94; Davis, *Intimate Relations*, pp. 56ff; Stuart Albert and William Jones, "The Temporal Transition from Being Together to Being Alone: The Significance and Structure of Children's Bedtime Stories," in Bernard S. Gorman and Alden E. Wessman, eds., *The Personal Experience of Time* (New York: Plenum, 1977), p. 131. See also Emanuel A. Schegloff and Harvey Sacks, "Opening up Closings," *Semiotica* 8 (1973):289–327; Stuart Albert and Suzanne Kessler, "Processes for Ending Social Encounters: The Conceptual Archaeology of a Temporal Place," *Journal for the Theory of Social Behavior* 6 (1976):147–70; Goffman, *Forms of Talk*, p. 130.

115. See also John Carey, "Temporal and Spatial Transitions in American Fiction Films," *Studies in the Anthropology of Visual Communication* 1 (1974):45.

116. Pike, *Language in Relation to a Unified Theory*, p. 76.

117. On ways of invoking or suspending the theatrical frame before the introduction of the curtain, see William Beare, *The Roman Stage* (London: Methuen, 1964), p. 179; Elizabeth Burns, *Theatricality* (New York: Harper Torchbooks, 1973), p. 41.

118. Michel Butor, "On Fairy Tales," in *Inventory* (New York: Simon & Schuster, 1968 [1960]), p. 213.

119. For a general discussion of "metamessages," see Gregory Bateson et al., "Toward a Theory of Schizophrenia," in *Steps to an Ecology of Mind* (New York: Ballantine, 1972 [1956]), p. 222; Bateson, "A Theory of Play and Fantasy."

120. Smith, *Poetic Closure*, pp. 24–25. See also pp. 50–95, 98–150, 158–66, 172–86.

121. Cone, *Musical Form and Musical Performance*, p. 13.

122. Jan-Peter Blom and John J. Gumperz, "Social Meaning in Linguistic Structure: Code-Switching in Norway," in John J. Gumperz and Dell Hymes, eds., *Directions in Sociolinguistics* (New York: Holt, Rinehart and Winston, 1972), pp. 425–26; John J. Gumperz, *Discourse Strategies* (Cambridge, England: Cambridge University Press, 1982), p. 76.

123. Goffman, *Forms of Talk*, p. 176.

124. Holly Giffin, "The Coordination of Meaning in the Creation of a Shared Make-Believe Reality," in Inge Bretherton, ed., *Symbolic Play* (Orlando, Fla.: Academic Press, 1984), p. 86.

125. Erikson, *Wayward Puritans*, p. 11.

126. Ibid., pp. 11–13.

127. Ibid., p. 13.

128. Butor, "The Book as Object," pp. 54–55.

129. H. Clay Trumbull, *The Threshold Covenant* (New York: Charles Scribner's Sons, 1906), pp. 3–12, 25–28, 66–68.

130. Vered Vinitzky-Seroussi, "Classification of Special Days and Specific People" (paper presented at the annual meeting of the Midwest Modern Language Association, Kansas City, November 1990). See also Esther Lavie, "Age as an Indicator for Reference in the Construction of Social Contexts" (Ph.D. diss., Tel-Aviv University, 1987), pp. 242–81.

REALITY AS A COLLECTIVE HUNCH

2

The Search for Signs of Intelligent Life in the Universe

Jane Wagner

(1986)

Here we are, standing on the corner of
"Walk, Don't Walk."
You look away from me, tryin' not to catch
my eye,
　but you didn't turn fast enough, *did* you?

You don't like my *ras*py voice, do you?
I got this *raspy* voice
'cause I have to yell all the time
'cause nobody around here ever
LISTENS to me.

You don't like that I scratch so much: yes, and
excuse me,
　I scratch so much
　'cause my neurons are
　on *fire.*

And I admit my smile is not at its Pepsodent best
'cause I think my
caps must've somehow got
osteo*porosis.*

And if my eyes seem to be twirling around like
fruit flies—
　the better to see you with, my dears!
　Look at me,
　you mammalian-brained LUNKHEADS!

I'm not just talking to myself. I'm talking to
you, too.

And to you
and you
and you
and you and you and you!

I know what you're thinkin'; you're thinkin' I'm
crazy.
　You think I give a hoot? You people
　look at my shopping bags,
　call me crazy 'cause I save this junk. What
should we call the
　ones who
　buy it?

It's my belief we all, at one time or another,
secretly ask ourselves the question,
"Am *I* crazy?"
In my case, the answer came back: A
resounding
　YES!

You're thinkin': How does a person know if
they're crazy
　or not? Well, sometimes you don't know.
Sometimes you
　can go through life suspecting you *are*
　but never really knowing for sure. Sometimes
you know for sure
　'cause you got so many people tellin' you you're
crazy
　that it's your word against everyone else's.

Another sign is when you see life so clear sometimes
  you black out.
This is your typical visionary variety
who has flashes of insight
but can't get anyone to listen to 'em
'cause their insights make 'em sound so *crazy!*

In my case,
the symptoms are subtle
but unmistakable to the trained eye. For instance, here I am,
standing at the corner of "Walk, Don't Walk,"
waiting for these aliens from outer space to show up.
I call that crazy, don't you? If I were sane,
I should be waiting for the light like everybody else.

They're late
as usual.

You'd think,
as much as they know about time travel,
they could be on time *once* in a while.

I could kick myself.
I told 'em I'd meet 'em on the corner of "Walk, Don't Walk"
'round lunchtime.
Do they even know what "lunch" means?
I doubt it.

And " 'round." Why did I say " 'round"? Why wasn't I more
  specific? This is so typical of what I do.

Now they're probably stuck somewhere in time, wondering
  what I meant by
" 'round lunchtime." And when they get here, they'll be

dying to know what "lunchtime" means. And when they
  find out it means going to Howard Johnson's for fried
  clams, I wonder, will they be just a bit let down?
I dread having to explain
tartar sauce.

This problem of time just points out
how far apart we really are.
See, our ideas about time and space are different
from theirs. When we think of time, we tend to think of
  clock radios, coffee breaks, afternoon naps, leisure time,
  halftime activities, parole time, doing time, Minute Rice, instant
  tea, mid-life crises, that time of the month, cocktail hour.
And if I should suddenly
  mention *space*—aha! I bet most of you thought of your
  closets. But when they think of time and space, they really think
  of
Time and Space.

They asked me once my thoughts on infinity and I told 'em
with all I had to think about, infinity was not on my list
  of things to think about. It could be time on an ego trip,
  for all I know. After all, when you're pressed for time,
infinity may as well
not be there.
They said, to them, infinity is
time-released time.
Frankly, infinity doesn't affect
me personally one way or the other.

You think too long about infinity, you could go stark raving mad.

But I don't ever want to sound negative about
going crazy.
I don't want to overromanticize it either, but
frankly,
goin' crazy was the *best* thing ever happened
to me.
I don't say it's for everybody;
some people couldn't cope.

But for me it came at a time when nothing else
seemed to be
working. I got the kind of madness Socrates
talked about,
"A divine release of the soul from the yoke of
custom and convention." I refuse to be
intimidated by
reality anymore.
After all, what is reality anyway? Nothin'
but a
collective hunch. My space chums think reality
was once a
primitive method of
crowd control that got out of hand.
In my view, it's absurdity dressed up
in a three-piece business suit.

I made some studies, and
reality is the leading cause of stress amongst
those in
touch with it. I can take it in small doses, but as
a lifestyle
I found it too confining.
It was just too needful;
it expected me to be there for it *all* the time, and
with all
I have to do—
I had to let something go.

Now, since I put reality on a back burner, my
days are
jam-packed and fun-filled. Like some days, I go
hang out

around Seventh Avenue; I love to do this old
joke:
I wait for some music-loving tourist from one
of the hotels
on Central Park to go up and ask someone.
"How do I get to Carnegie Hall?"
Then I run up and yell,
"Practice!"
The expression on people's faces is priceless.
I never
could've done stuff like that when I was in my
right mind.
I'd be worried people would think I was *crazy*.
When I think of the fun I missed,
I try not to be bitter.

See, the human mind is kind of like . . .
a piñata. When it breaks open,
there's a lot of surprises inside. Once you get the
piñata
perspective, you see that losing your mind
can be a peak experience.

I was not always a bag lady, you know.
I used to be a designer and creative consultant.
For big
companies!
Who do you think thought up the color scheme
for Howard Johnson's?
At the time, nobody was using
orange and aqua
in the same room together.
With fried clams.

Laugh tracks:
I gave TV sitcoms the idea for canned laughter.
I got the idea, one day I heard voices
and no one was there.

Who do you think had the idea to package
panty hose
in a plastic goose egg?

One thing I personally don't like about panty hose:

When you roll 'em down to the ankles the way I like 'em, you

can't walk too good. People seem amused, so what's a little

loss of dignity? You got to admit:

It's a look!

The only idea I'm proud of—

my umbrella hat. Protects against sunstroke, rain and

muggers. For *some* reason, muggers steer clear of people

wearing umbrella hats.

So it should come as no shock . . . I am now creative consultant to

these aliens from outer space. They're a kinda cosmic

fact-finding committee. Amongst other projects, they've been

searching all over for Signs of Intelligent Life.

It's a lot trickier than it sounds.

We're collecting all kinds of data

about life here on Earth. We're determined to figure out,

once and for all, just what the hell it all means.

I write the data on these Post-its and then we study it.

Don't worry, before I took the consulting job, I gave 'em my whole

psychohistory.

I told 'em what drove *me* crazy was my *last* creative consultant

job, with the Ritz Cracker mogul, Mr. Nabisco. It was

my job to come up with snack inspirations to increase sales.

I got this idea to give Cracker Consciousness to the entire

planet.

I said, "Mr. Nabisco, sir! You could be the first to sell the

concept of munching to the Third World. We got an untapped

market here! These countries got millions and millions of

people don't even know where their next *meal* is *coming* from.

So the idea of eatin' *between* meals is somethin' just never

occurred to 'em!"

I heard myself sayin' *this!*

Must've been when I went off the deep end.

I woke up in the nuthouse. They were hookin' me up.

One thing they don't tell you about shock treatments, for

months afterwards you got

flyaway hair. And it used to *be* my best feature.

See, those shock treatments gave me new electrical circuitry

(frankly, I think one of the doctors' hands must've been wet).

I started having these time-space continuum shifts, I guess

you'd call it. Suddenly, it was like my central nervous system

had a patio addition out back.

Not only do I have a linkup to extraterrestrial channels. I also got a hookup with humanity as a whole.

Animals and plants, too. I used to talk to plants all the time;

then, one day, they started talking back. They said, "Trudy,

shut up!"

I got like this . . .

built-in Betamax in my head. Records anything.
It's like somebody's using my brain to dial-switch
through humanity. I pick up signals that seem
to transmit
snatches of people's lives.
My umbrella hat works as a satellite dish. I
hear this
sizzling sound like white noise. Then I know it's
trance time.
That's how I met my space chums. I was in one
of my trances,
watching a scene from someone's life, and I
suddenly sense
others were there
watching with me.

Uh-oh.
I see this skinny
punk kid.
Got hair the color of
Froot Loops and she's wearin' a T-shirt says
"Leave Me Alone."
There's a terrible family squabble going on.
If they're listening to each other,
they're all gonna get their feelings hurt.

I see glitches—
Now I see this dark-haired actress
on a Broadway stage. I know her. I see her all the
time outside
the Plymouth Theater, Forty-fifth Street . . .

Dial-switch me outta this!
I got enough worries of my own.
These trances are entertaining but distracting,
especially since
someone *else* has the remote control, and if the
pause button
should somehow get punched, I could have a
neurotransmitter
mental meltdown. Causes "lapses of the
synapses." I forget

things. Never underestimate the power of the
human mind to
forget. The other day, I forgot where I put my
house keys—
looked everywhere, then I remembered
I don't have a house. I forget more important
things, too.
Like the meaning of life.
I forget that.
It'll come to me, though.
Let's just hope when it does,
I'll be in . . .

My space chums say they're learning so much
about us
since they've begun to time-share my trances.
They said to me, "Trudy, the human mind
is so-o-o strange."
I told 'em, "That's nothin' compared to the
human genitals."
Next to my trances they love goin' through my
shopping bags.
Once they found this old box of Cream of
Wheat. I told 'em, "A
box of cereal." But they saw it as a picture of
infinity. You know
how on the front is a picture of that guy holding
up a box of
Cream of Wheat
and on *that* box is a picture of that guy holding
up a box of
Cream of Wheat
and on *that* box is a picture of that guy holding
up a box of
Cream of Wheat
and on *that* box is a picture of that guy holding
up a box of
Cream of Wheat . . .

We think so different.

They find it hard to grasp some things that
come easy to us,

because they simply don't have our frame of reference.

I show 'em this can of Campbell's tomato soup.
I say,
"This is soup."
Then I show 'em a picture of Andy Warhol's painting
of a can of Campbell's tomato soup.
I say,
"This is art."

"This is soup."

"And this is art."

Then I shuffle the two behind my back.

Now what is this?

No,
this is soup
and *this is art*! . . .

Hey, what's this?

"Dear Trudy, thanks for making our stay here so jam-packed and
fun-filled. Sorry to abort our mission—it is not over,
just temporarily scrapped.

We have orders to go to a higher bio-vibrational plane.

Just wanted you to know, the neurochemical imprints of our
cardiocortical experiences here on earth will remain with us
always, but what we take with us into space that we cherish the
most is the 'goose bump' experience."

Did I tell you what happened at the play? We were at the back
of the theater, standing there in the dark,
all of a sudden I feel one of 'em tug my sleeve,
whispers, "Trudy, look." I said, "Yeah, goose bumps. You
definitely
got goose bumps. You really like the play that much?" They said
it wasn't the play
gave 'em goose bumps,
it was the audience.

I forgot to tell 'em to watch the play; they'd been watching
the *audience*!

Yeah, to see a group of strangers sitting together in the dark,
laughing and crying about the same things . . .
that just knocked
'em out.
They said, "Trudy,
the play was soup . . .
the audience . . .
art."

So they're taking goose bumps
home with 'em.
Goose bumps!
Quite a souvenir.

I like to think of them out there
in the dark, watching us.
Sometimes we'll do something and they'll laugh.
Sometimes we'll do something and they'll cry.
And maybe one day we'll do something so magnificent,
everyone in the universe will get
goose bumps.

RESEARCHING SOCIAL LIFE

Social researchers who work from the perspective of symbolic interactionism face the challenge of trying to understand what people themselves think they are doing. It is not enough simply to observe a behavior. Symbolic interactionists are interested in people's *interpretations* of the situation and their own behavior.

"Truth, Objectivity, and Agreement" is a fun essay written by social methodologist Earl Babbie. Babbie wants his readers to understand that everyone, even scientists, interpret information based on preexisting ideas. This subjectivity is a fact of human experience. Scientists and other systematic researchers deal with their own subjectivity by creating rules for observation and explicit theoretical starting points. One implication is that there is no "objective" truth. Truth is arrived at through "intersubjective" agreement about what is being observed and how to observe it.

"Perspective in Social Science" is an essay by social psychologist Joel Charon. Charon's central theme is that just as individual perception is shaped by perspective, so too is the scientific research process. He describes social science as a distinctive perspective or point of view on human social life and provides a framework of the basic assumptions and ideas that shape contemporary social science research.

READING QUESTIONS

1. Think of some examples of "intersubjective" agreement. Why do we believe the intersubjective truths proposed by some groups and not others?

2. Do you think you have to be similar to members of a culture to understand them (e.g., do you have to be a priest to understand a culture of priests)? Or is it possible to devise methods that would enable you to "put yourself in another's shoes" or "look over their shoulder" to gain insight into their worldviews and experiences?

3. What methods do you currently use in your own life when you're trying to understand someone else?

4. According to Charon, what are some of the basic assumptions of social science? How are these assumptions the same as or different from other contemporary perspectives on human social life, e.g., religious or humanistic perspectives?

RESEARCHING SOCIAL LIFE

3

Truth, Objectivity, and Agreement

Earl Babbie

(1986)

Science is often portrayed as a search for the truth about reality. That sounds good, but what is *truth*? What is *reality*? Look those words up in a good dictionary, such as the *Oxford English Dictionary,* and you'll find definitions like "the quality of being true" and "the quality of being real." Beyond these basic tautologies are some additional definitions (from the *OED*):

Truth:

- Conformity with fact; agreement with reality
- Agreement with a standard or rule; accuracy, correctness
- Genuineness, reality, actual existence
- That which is in accordance with fact
- That which is true, real, or actual; reality

Reality:

- The quality of . . . having an actual existence
- Correspondence to fact; truth
- Real existence

Definitions of the words *true* and *real* are similar:

True:

- Consistent with fact; agreeing with reality; representing the thing as it is
- Agreeing with a standard, pattern, or rule; exact, accurate, precise, correct, right

- Consistent with, exactly agreeing with
- Conformable to reality; natural
- In accordance with reality

Real:

- Having an objective existence; actually existing as a thing
- Actually present or existing as a state or quality of things; having a foundation in fact; actually occurring or happening
- Consisting of actual things

These definitions point to the inherent circularity of language, which is inevitable as long as we use words to define words. In this case, things are true if they're real and real if they're true. The relationship between truth and reality can also be seen in the preponderance of words dealing with agreement: *conformity, accordance, correspondence, consistent with, representing.*

Here's a useful way of seeing the relationship between truth and reality: It is possible to make statements about reality; those that agree with (conform to, are consistent with, represent) reality are true. None of this tells us what truth or reality is, however. It only tells us about their relationship to one another.

Other words in the definitions we've seen may clarify the meanings of truth and reality—words such as *actual, existence,* and *fact.*

Actuality:

- The state of being actual or real; reality, existing objective fact

Actual:

- Existing in act or fact; really acted or acting; carried out; real

Factual:

- Pertaining to or concerned with facts; of the nature of fact, actual, real

Fact:

- Something that has really occurred or is actually the case
- Truth attested by direct observation or authentic testimony; reality

Existence:

- Actuality; reality
- Being; the fact or state of existing

Exist:

- To have place in the domain of reality, have objective being

By now, the incestuous circularity of language is getting a little annoying. Consider this abbreviated search for truth:

Truth is "That which is real; **reality.**"

Reality is "Having an actual **existence.**"

Existence is "**Actuality;** reality."

Actuality is "Existing objective **fact.**"

Fact is "**Truth** attested by direct observation."

In addition to the circularity of these relatively few words defining each other, let's take a cue from the definitions of *exist* and *existence* and add the term *being*.

Being:

- Existence
- That which exists or is conceived as existing

Be:

- To have or take place in the world of fact; to exist, occur, happen
- To have place in the objective universe or realm of fact, to exist
- To come into existence
- To be the case or the fact

For the most part, these new words simply add to the circularity of definitions that is becoming very familiar in this exercise. . . .

From time to time throughout these definitions, and now in the definition of *be,* the quality of objectivity has appeared as part of the background of a definition. In these cases, *real* does not just have existence, it has "objective existence"; *actuality* is not just a matter of fact but of "objective fact." Now, to *be* is to have a place in the "objective universe." Implicit in these uses is the contrast between objectivity and subjectivity.

Subjectivity:

- The quality or condition of viewing things exclusively through the medium of one's own mind or individuality
- The character of existing in the mind only

Subjective:

- Relating to the thinking subject, proceeding from or taking place within the subject; having its source in the mind

In stark contrast, *objective* is defined this way:

Objective:

- That which is external to the mind

The truth about *truth* eventually comes down to the recognition that we know most of the world through our minds. Moreover, we recognize that our individual minds are not altogether reliable. We have colloquial phrases such as "a figment of your imagination," and we realize that people often "see what they want to see." Simply put, the subjective realm refers to the possibly inaccurate perceptions and thoughts we have through the medium of our minds, yours and mine, whereas the objective realm refers to that which lies outside and is independent of our minds. We often term that objective realm *reality,* and term *true* a statement that accurately describes reality.

A couple of snags lie hidden in this construction of objectivity. First, neither you nor I, perceiving reality through our subjective minds, can know whether we perceive it accurately or not. The following scene should make the matter painfully clear.

Imagine that you are sitting in a room that has a small window with a view into another room. A light located in the other room can be turned on or off. Reality in this illustration is simply whether the light is on or off in the other room. Truth is a function of your ability to say accurately whether the light is on or off.

At first impression, nothing could be simpler. I turn the light on in the other room, and you say, "The light is on." I turn it off, and you say, "The light is off." This would be a model of objectivity.

The defect in this model is that your mind and its subjectivity have not been taken into account. But imagine that the small window before you has two shutters. The first shutter has a picture of the other room with the light on, and the second has a picture of the room with the light off. Sometimes the first shutter will close your view of the other room, sometimes the second shutter will, and sometimes there won't be any shutter—but you'll never know.

Now when I ask you whether the light is on in the other room, you will answer based on what you see, but what you see may be the open window or it may be one of the shutters. If you see one of the shutters, the scene you see may correspond with the real condition of the room or it may not.

Relating this illustration to real life, however, you would not be conscious of the possibility that you were looking at a shutter; instead, you would think that what you perceived was reality. You would feel sure that you knew the truth about whether the light was on or off because you saw it with your own eyes. And even if you became aware of the existence of the shutters, you couldn't be sure of reality because you still wouldn't know if what you were seeing was the other room or one of the shutters.

The point of this illustration is that you have no way out. In the normal course of life, you cannot be sure that what you see is really there. But there's a bigger problem than this. Given the subjectivity of your mind, you can't be sure there is *anything* out there at all. In the two-room illustration, maybe there is no window and no other room—only two shutters. Maybe it's all in your mind. How could you ever know?

The answer to both of these dilemmas is the same. If you can't be sure that what your mind tells you is true, you can at least gain some confidence in that regard if you find that my mind has told me the same thing. You say the light is on, and I say the light is on: case closed. Now you may feel doubly sure you know the light is on, not to mention that there's a window, a room, and a light.

Ultimately, our only proof of objectivity is intersubjectivity, and some dictionaries even define *objectivity* that way. When different subjects—with their individual, error-prone subjectivities—report the same thing, we conclude that what they report is objective, existing, actual, factual, real, and true.

Thus, the basis of truth is agreement. Basically, things are true if we agree they are. When Copernicus first said that the earth revolved around the sun, few people agreed; today, most people agree. We say that this view is not only true today but was true when Copernicus first expressed it, and was even true before Copernicus. But we say all that *today* when virtually everyone agrees with the view. Moreover, if all the world's astronomers were to announce a new discovery showing the sun revolved around the earth, we'd soon be saying that Copernicus was wrong and that the sun had always revolved around the earth, even before Copernicus.

When you think about the past history of agreements that were eventually overturned, you won't find much basis for confidence in what you and I now agree to be so. . . . [M]ost of what we "know" today will be thrown out as inaccurate tomorrow.

Where does science figure in all this? What about social science? Don't they offer an exception to this? Aren't they a dependable channel to the truth?

Ultimately, science—social or otherwise—also operates on the basis of agreement: in this case, agreement among fellow scientists. But there are some differences. Scientists recognize that knowledge is continually changing. They know that what they know today may be replaced tomorrow. In fact, the goal of science is to keep changing the truth.

Scientists are aware of the power of subjective biases and are explicitly committed to avoiding them in their research. Social researchers have an advantage in this respect, since bias itself is a subject matter for social science. On the other hand, social researchers have a disadvantage in that their subject matter—religion and politics, for example—is more likely to provoke personal biases than is the subject matter of the natural sciences.

For scientists, observation is a conscious and deliberate activity, whereas it is generally casual and semiconscious for most people in normal life. Thus, you might mistakenly recall that your best friend wore a blue dress yesterday, when it was really green. If you had been recording dress colors as part of a research project, however, you wouldn't have made that mistake.

Moreover, scientists have developed procedures and equipment to aid them in making observations. This also avoids some of the mistakes we make in casual observations. For example, scientists are explicit about the basis for their agreements. Rules of proof are contained within the system of logic prevailing at the time.

More important, perhaps, in the context of this essay, scientists are explicit about the intersubjective nature of truth. Peer review is an established principle: Scientists review each other's work to guard against errors of method or reasoning. Scientific journals perform what is called a gatekeeper function in this regard. Articles submitted for publication are typically circulated among independent reviewers— other scientists knowledgeable in the area covered by the article. Unless the reviewers agree that the article represents a sound and worthwhile contribution to the field, it will not be published.

Scientists are by no means above error, however. Being human, they are susceptible to all the human foibles that afflict nonscientists. Though the scientific enterprise commits them to keeping an open mind with regard to truth, individual scientists can grow attached to particular views. . . .

To understand the nature of science, it is essential to recognize that scientific knowledge at any given time is what scientists agree it is. Because scientific proof is fundamentally based on agreement among scientists, scientific knowledge keeps changing over time. It is probably unavoidable that we see this evolution of scientific knowledge over time as a process through which we get closer and closer to the truth. This view cannot be verified, however. All we can know for sure is that what we know keeps changing.

We can't even bank on views that haven't changed for a long time. Bear in mind, for example, that the idea that the earth was stationary and the sun moved was accepted much longer than our current view has been. Years ago, when I was living in a house on the slopes of a volcano in Hawaii, I took comfort in knowing that the volcano hadn't erupted for 25,000 years and hence probably wouldn't ever erupt again. Then I learned that its previous period of dormancy had been longer than that.

In the case of scientific knowledge, changes are generally occurring faster, not slower, than in the past. . . . [W]hat we learn about social life is often changed by just having the knowledge we've gained. On the whole, then, we'd do better simply to settle for the thrill of discovery than to worry about whether what we've discovered is the ultimate truth or simply a new and currently useful way of viewing things.

RESEARCHING SOCIAL LIFE

4

The Perspective of Social Science

Joel Charon

(2008)

Social science is a perspective. That means it is one way of understanding the human being. Because it is a science, it has much in common with natural sciences. Yet, it is to some extent distinct from natural science, and it is important to recognize that there are several perspectives within social science, each unique to some extent yet sharing some qualities. This chapter is an attempt to introduce social science as a perspective and to lay out in very rough form some of the various perspectives within social science, especially sociology, psychology, and social psychology.

It is probably best to start with an important philosopher who lived at about the time social science was beginning to be developed. His name was Immanuel Kant (1724–1804). Kant was a believer in God, a Christian who was concerned about the assault of reason and science on traditional religious belief as well as about the feeble attempts of religious thinkers to defend their grounds through the tools of rational argument. Kant (1781/1952) wanted to understand the limits of reason and science. He was critical of attempts by religious people to defend the metaphysical world through reason, for he felt it was an impossible task and therefore a waste of time. And, after all, he argued, reason is not everything, and we need to understand certain aspects of the universe through something other than reason and science.

He argued that there are two worlds of reality: a world of phenomena and a world of noumena. The world of *phenomena* is the world we can experience with our senses; it is open to scientific and rational investigation. Science observes the world of phenomena—the natural world—and reason orders those observations. The world of *noumena* is above scientific investigation; it cannot be approached by empirical observation because it is not physical or empirical. Although many people have attempted to approach this world through reason, they have failed.

Kant is saying that, although we can imagine the world of the noumena, reason and science, limited to the world of phenomena, cannot be used to investigate it. In a sense, Kant then is arguing that science is a *perspective* sensitizing the investigator to part of the world—the natural, phenomenal world—but that science is unable to sensitize us to another world, nor should we use it to try.

One of the reasons that Kant is important to us is related to how he applied this philosophy to an understanding of the human being. Physical objects such as plants, livers, wastepaper baskets, dogs, and tape recorders are clearly in the world of phenomena and therefore subject to scientific investigation, and God, heavenly angels, and the Devil are clearly noumena. But in which world does the human being belong? If we are in the world of phenomena, we are physical, we are part of the natural universe, we can be investigated and fully understood through the tools of science. If we are noumena, however, then we are beyond science, not understandable as part of the natural, physical universe. Kant argued that we are both; we are phenomena, subject to the laws of nature, open to science, and "subject to natural necessity"; that is, our behavior is subject to natural cause. On the other hand, we are also noumena, the "human soul," at least in part, containing a will that is *free.* The human being is conceptualized here as both *passive,* in that individuals are caused, shaped, and driven by forces beyond their control, and *active,* in that individuals are also controlling, shaping, acting, free.

Social Science as a Perspective

It is maintained here that social science is a *perspective.* Since its beginning, it has attempted to apply the tools of science to understanding the human being. As a perspective, it has made certain

assumptions, the most important being that the human being is phenomenal, caused, open to scientific measurement, and not an active agent in relation to his or her environment—not self-determining or free. As social scientists, we assume causality in social life, and our goal is (perhaps must be) to uncover that causality.

One is reminded of the cocktail party where the bright new college graduate with one sociology course and one psychology course under his belt is impressing everyone with how much he understands about human behavior. The conversation goes something like this:

"That's silly. You're not free to do anything," he brags.

"Of course I am. I decided what I believe and where I go," the innocent citizen responds.

"Take the girl you're with here tonight. Did you freely choose to bring her?"

"Of course."

"Aha." (I've got you, he says to himself.) "You are attracted to her because she is in the 'right' social class. She reminds you of your mother. She is approximately at your own level of physical attractiveness." Etc., etc., etc., etc.

"Wow!"

Most of us are amazed at the predictability of human behavior and at all the social and psychological causes of behavior that social scientists have been able to amass. But as Peter Berger (1963: 124) has noted, "Freedom as a special kind of cause is *excluded* from this system." The exclusion of freedom is one of science's central assumptions. The purpose of science is to isolate cause, not freedom, so it must, in the end, be considered as excluding some things about the human being. This is not, of course, to criticize science; it is merely to try to isolate its limits as a perspective.

Social scientists seem to be becoming increasingly aware of the fact that social science is a *perspective,* that it makes certain assumptions, that it sensitizes and desensitizes the investigator, that it has a certain conceptual framework (e.g., "empirical," "cause," "independent variable," "dependent variable," "measurement"), and that it can never reveal the whole truth about the human being.

Indeed, social science might even lead us to a misleading or even false picture of the human being. Charles Hampden-Turner (1970) argues this idea in his thoughtful book *Radical Man.* He describes social science as a *perspective* and then concludes that it is clearly a biased one by its very nature: It is consistently a politically *conservative* one, and it must inevitably lead the social scientist to take a conservative view of the human being, systematically ignoring a host of important human qualities. Hampden-Turner (pp. 1–15) takes the position that the social-scientific perspective by its very nature:

1. *Concentrates on the repetitive, predictable, unvariable aspects of the human.* In a sense, social science assures a "compulsive, obsessive, and ritualistic" human subject, rather than recognizing the centrality of creativity and novelty to human life.

2. *Concentrates on "visible externalities,"* that which is "exposed to the general gaze," rather than the subjective world of dreams, philosophies, and the whole mental life of those whose physical movements we observe.

3. *Concentrates on the various parts of the person,* analyzing the parts in order to understand the whole. In a sense, "the human is indivisible" and "we are left with the same problems as all the king's horses and all the king's men."

Hampden-Turner criticizes the scientific perspective on other grounds, too, but the point that he makes for our discussion here is that social science is a perspective, and what emerges from it is a picture of the human being that is far from objective and "value free." That perspective may indeed be as conservative and biased as Hampden-Turner describes it, or it may be less so; on the other hand, it may be even more biased than any of us realize. The treatment of social science as a perspective has only recently been investigated seriously, so it is difficult to know the nature of its bias. But it does indeed appear that in order to be scientific, we have to focus on those aspects of the human that are open to measurement. It is important to recognize that there are qualities left untouched because of our scientific search, even qualities that are measurable but not perfectly open to our contemporary instruments of investigation.

Social science is a perspective; it is an important approach to understanding the human being; it has produced much that has helped us predict, control, improve, and even mess up the condition of the human being. It is not complete, for no perspective can be complete, and it is a bias, but it is a most important perspective for understanding, as witnessed by its results over the past two hundred or more years.

Within social science there are, of course, many perspectives (we might call these *subperspectives*), and each one is thought unique in its approach to the human being. Each one pulls out some aspects of reality, emphasizing those, and in a sense ignores other aspects of reality picked up by other social sciences.

SOCIOLOGY AS A PERSPECTIVE

Sociology is the study of society. It is the study of how society works and how society is an important cause of human action. In fact, it is not just the study of society, but the study of all organized life, from small groups and formal organizations to communities and society. It begins with the assumption that humans have always existed within society, that society is the source of our qualities as a species (for example, conscience, language, mind, self), and that it is the source of our qualities as individuals (interests, values, talents, ideas, and so on).

Sociology is the study of the human being in society as well as of how society gets inside the human being. Society is external to the human being, yet through socialization society is internalized and becomes part of each person. Society is made up of social patterns, developed in the past and important to each of us living in society.

For example, social structure is a social pattern in society. Social structure was formed in the past, and we are all placed in it at birth and as we go through life. We are placed in a class position in social structure, and gender and ethnic group memberships are also positions. We live within a political structure, and in every organization we encounter an authority structure. Even the small groups we exist in develop structures that influence us.

Another social pattern that exists in society is culture. Culture is the consensus developed by people over a long history. It is their shared view of reality, the basic ideas, values, and rules they have come to believe in. That culture is something we are born into and are socialized to accept. Its ideas become our truths; its rules become our morals; its values become what we regard as important in life.

We are also born into a society that has developed a particular set of social institutions. These are the grooves that are there for us to follow and participate in. We live within hundreds of institutions: Some, for example, are political institutions; others might be economic, familial, religious, military, criminal justice, educational, health care, or recreational. So, in U.S. society, the corporation, private health insurance, a volunteer army, and public education exist as social institutions. How the individual acts in society is shaped by such grooves. In *Invitation to Sociology*, Peter Berger (1963) describes the power of society in his conclusion to Chapter 4:

> We are located in society not only in space but in time. Our society is a historical entity that extends temporally beyond any individual biography. Society antedates us and it will survive us. It was there before we were born and it will be there after we are dead. Our lives are but episodes in its majestic march through time. In sum, society is the walls of our imprisonment in history. (p. 92)

To the sociologist, therefore, humans exist within a massive reality—society—developed historically, regarded by us as legitimate, telling us what to do and what to think, and shaping our behavior through a variety of mechanisms.

But society also exists within all of us. In a sense we agree to this imprisonment precisely because the society has penetrated us through socialization; we have, in a real sense, become what society has demanded. This is the role of socialization and it is an important part of what sociology examines. Berger (1963) continues:

> Society not only controls our movements, but shapes our identity, our thought and our emotions. The structures of society become the structures of our own consciousness. Society does not stop at the surface of our skin. Society penetrates us as much as it envelopes us. Our bondage to society is not so much established by conquest as by collusion. . . . The walls of our imprisonment were there before we appeared on the scene, but they are ever rebuilt by ourselves. We are betrayed into captivity with our own cooperation. (p. 121)

Sociology is a perspective that thinks of the human being as an actor. We act out roles. Think of roles as scripts handed out to us in the positions we fill in an organization. A male in society, a student, a sociology major, an employee at a department store, and an unemployed shoe sales-man are all positions in society, and all of them direct what the actor does in the organization. This concept is significant because sociologists tend to see actors as changing all through life, from situa-tion to situation, because we change our roles in society and because society itself changes. How we act in life, then, is tied, once again, to society.

There is, in this perspective, a lot of determin-ism. That is, humans are thought to be linked to society, products of society, controlled by society. The purpose of sociology is to understand this link and to understand how society itself works. Many sociologists will claim that I am exaggerating the determinism of sociology, and perhaps I am, but it is important to see this determinism as central to any social-scientific perspective that seeks to understand *why* humans act the way they do. Sociology describes society as an important cause of human action. Its whole conceptual framework aims at this relation between society and individ-uals, as do its studies. Sociology has a different perspective than other social sciences, such as psy-chology, since its focus is society. Sociology's per-spective is useful because it does help explain a great deal about human behavior. Its perspective, however, can sensitize us to only part of the pic-ture, and it is really up to other social-scientific perspectives to help us understand the other parts.

PSYCHOLOGY AS A PERSPECTIVE

If sociology is most easily defined as the study of society, then psychology is most easily defined as the study of the person. It is an understanding of how the person works and how the characteristics of the person influence what he or she does.

Psychology is similar to sociology in some ways. It has a particular perspective, and it is a social science. As a science, it attempts to apply the tools developed in natural science. More than sociology, it has relied heavily on the controlled laboratory experiment (indeed, some psycholo-gists will define a perspective as scientific only if the controlled laboratory experiment is the norm), and it has usually considered the human being as part of nature, in the world of phenomena, moved by natural laws, created, shaped.

Because there are many schools of psychology (each can be called a perspective), there are differ-ences among psychologists. Psychologists, how-ever, as do sociologists, seem to share certain assumptions, ideas, and concepts, sensitizing the investigator to certain aspects of the human being while neglecting others. Let us emphasize again that a focus is not a fault; it is a limitation of every perspective, and there seems to be no way to escape it: Perspectives are absolutely essential for understanding, but by their very nature they do not capture the whole of reality.

The threads of the psychological perspective are not always clear, and there is always a danger that someone who is not a psychologist will mis-take the perspective. However, it seems that all schools of psychology emphasize the following:

1. The *individual organism,* shaped by various combinations of heredity and environment, social and nonsocial forces.

2. An underlying belief that a person's perfor-mance at any point is tied to previous expe-rience. This can be labeled a *predispositional orientation.* For example, in psychoanalysis this means that very early childhood train-ing causes one to act later on in a certain manner; in learning theory, previous condi-tioning causes behavior; in Gestalt psychol-ogy, it may be the person's conceptual framework or cognitive structure developed in the past that is all-important.

3. An attempt to explain behavior in relation to the *organism.* Change is explained in relation to change *in the organism;* stability of behav-ior is due to the stability *in the organism.*

4. A focus on *personality traits,* qualities of the person developed over time, such as aggressiveness, shyness, lack of self-confidence, and compulsiveness. Some psychologists would call a person's attitude a trait, and some would even call intelligence and habits traits. Whatever these qualities are called, they are similar in that they have been developed earlier in the person's life, become a part of the person, and are brought into a situation, causing behavior. The term *personality* or *person* implies that these traits constitute a system, a network of qualities, an interrelated set of qualities. A stability within the person is assumed—from past to present and from situation to situation. One's actions are thought to be the result of "the way the person is."

5. The idea that behavior is not situational or structural but *personal and trait related,* even though social situations might influence traits over the long run. Roles and social patterns such as structure, culture, and institutions are not the focus of investigation.

6. The idea that cause is located *in the individual's past.* That is where traits come from. What we do know has roots in our past. We act the way we do because of how we developed as a person.

COMMONALITIES AND DIFFERENCES BETWEEN SOCIOLOGY AND PSYCHOLOGY

It should be emphasized here that the psychological perspective differs significantly from the sociological. Although both emphasize studying human behavior, one (psychology) focuses on how the person develops, how the person works, and how the person's qualities influence behavior from situation to situation. The other (sociology) focuses on how society develops, how society works, and how society's qualities influence the individual in different situations. In psychology, change happens to or within the organism, whereas in sociology change occurs in society, in the individual's roles in society, in different organizations one belongs to.

In both cases, the focus is on the human being's behavior, behavior that is caused by forces beyond the individual's own will. The individual is conceptualized as passive in relation to these forces; that is, we are shaped, we are not actively shaping our behavior or our environment as individuals. By taking a scientific perspective, social science has focused on those aspects of the human being molded by the biological, physical, and social worlds. The purpose of social science has been to try to identify those forces.

There are, of course, exceptions to a deterministic and passive view of human beings in both sociology and psychology. Erich Fromm provides one such exceptional view in psychology, as do perhaps such psychologists as Carl Rogers and Abraham Maslow. Indeed, clinical psychology tends to emphasize the active human more than academic psychology does. Cognitive psychology in recent years has taken psychology more in the direction of an active conception of the human being. In sociology, Max Weber is a fine example of someone who takes a more active approach, as do phenomenology and dramaturgical sociology.

It is, in my opinion, the passive, determined, and nonreflective human being who has been portrayed in both psychology and sociology for the past two hundred years. We sometimes will claim that humans really are active beings, but in our academic pursuits, determinism is usually at work. This approach seems perfectly understandable since the goals of social science have always been to examine the human as part of the natural universe, governed by laws that can be discovered through careful research. A liberal education in social science tends to create an image of the human as being caused or shaped by factors in the natural world, as are all other living organisms. Indeed, other social science perspectives (such as anthropology, economics, geography) do seem not to question this image but, on the contrary, to reinforce it.

THE PERSPECTIVE OF SOCIAL PSYCHOLOGY IN PSYCHOLOGY

Of all perspectives in social science, social psychology is the most difficult to describe. Some would argue that it is not a perspective at all but a conglomeration of topics and studies with little unity. Others will argue that it is a discipline in its own right, with roots in both psychology and sociology but with its own distinct history and subject matter.

It is useful to realize that two social psychologies have developed, sometimes influencing each other but often developing as parallel and without overlap. We might call one "psychology social psychology" and the other "sociological social psychology."

Psychological social psychology has its roots, to a large extent, in Gestalt psychology, an important perspective in psychology first developed in the late nineteenth and early twentieth centuries. Gestalt psychology emphasizes the central importance of perception in human behavior: The human being acts according to how the situation is perceived. Gestalt psychologists have attempted to isolate various principles of perception in order to better understand how the individual organizes the stimuli he or she confronts. Gestalt psychology as such is entirely psychological in its orientation, but because of the work of some Gestaltists—especially Solomon Asch and Kurt Lewin—a social dimension was added to the framework, which greatly influenced the direction of social psychology.

The social psychology that developed out of Gestalt psychology focuses on interpersonal influence. "Social psychology," writes Elliot Aronson (1992), is the study of social influence, "the influences that people have upon the beliefs and behavior of others" (p. 6). The basic question to be answered is how other people around us influence our thoughts, feelings, and behaviors. The focus is on the social situation, and the most important idea is that human beings—whatever else they may bring to a situation—are influenced by what goes on in that situation. What I do influences you; what you do influences me. The study of social influence includes how speakers influence our thoughts, how groups form our attitudes, and how people influence us to like them. In this social psychological perspective, human thought and behavior are thought to change according to the influence of others.

By far the most important topic investigated in social psychology has been attitudes and attitude change. An *attitude* is usually conceptualized as a person's set of beliefs and feelings toward an object that predisposes the person to act in a certain manner when confronted by that object (or class of objects). Studies have usually attempted to examine how an individual's attitudes are formed and changed through the influence of other individuals. Attitudes, it has been assumed, are useful traits to study because they lead to behavior. Therefore, the strategy for changing behavior implied in social psychology has been to change one's attitudes. Although the usefulness of studying attitudes as predictors of behavior is increasingly being questioned, studying attitudes is still seen by most social scientists as one of social psychology's most useful concepts. For most people, attitudes are fascinating to study, and they seem to most of us to be basic to our action in real situations. Nothing seems so important to many people as knowing how to change such attitudes as prejudice. The belief that attitudes are important and that attitude change is possible is, in a sense, an optimistic view of the future, implying that we can improve the world simply by changing people's attitudes.

Social psychology is also the study of how *other people influence our behavior.* Conformity, obedience, power, leadership, and attraction are some of the exciting topics covered in the field of social psychology. Interpersonal communication, group decision making, and propaganda are also important. The key to the perspective seems to be, as Aronson states, interpersonal influence, the importance of the social situation in influencing attitudes and behavior. The human being is conceptualized as a "social animal" in the sense that he or she adjusts his or her action to the action of others in the social situation.

There is a great similarity between the perspective described here as psychological social psychology and the sociological and psychological perspectives discussed earlier. That similarity is that there is a continuing focus on cause, the assumption being that something inside or outside the actor influences what he or she does. The purpose of all three perspectives is to uncover that cause. Social psychology looks at other people in the situations we act in. Others influence us through what they say and how they say it, by persuading us and manipulating us, by acting as models or by teaching us directly. Others form our attitudes and influence our behavior *despite* our attitudes. Whatever we bring to the situation (our traits) must be balanced with the social situation itself if we are going to understand human behavior. Whatever social patterns of society play themselves out in what we do, the social situation will still matter. Together, these three perspectives explain a lot of why human beings act as they do. Together, they tell us to look at the social situation, who the person is, and the society within which the person exists. There is overlap among them, but each has a different focus, and whichever one we study or focus on will lead us down a path that emphasizes one of these three aspects rather than the others.

THE PERSPECTIVE OF SOCIAL PSYCHOLOGY IN SOCIOLOGY

Another approach to social psychology exists within the discipline of sociology. Sociologists study social psychology described above; they borrow heavily from it in their work; and they make contributions to it. This social psychology can be thought to be a link of sorts between sociology and psychology. It is psychology in its focus on the person within a social situation where other individuals influence what we do; it is sociology in its focus on the social situation. It is distinct from much of psychology by deemphasizing the person as cause; it is distinct from much of sociology by deemphasizing the power of social patterns and society at large.

There are many perspectives—or schools—of social psychology within sociology, and each has a distinct focus. Some sociologists focus on group dynamics and attempt to uncover the patterns that emerge in small groups. There is an exchange perspective also—very important to the study of family and gender interaction—emphasizing power relationship in face-to-face interaction.

Part of the distinction between the sociological approach to social psychology and the psychological is that the real focus of the sociological is on the concept of *social interaction.* Morris Rosenberg and Ralph Turner (1981) see this distinction as central: Social interaction, they argue, is ongoing action that actors take toward one another back and forth; it is not a one-way, causal influence of other people or groups on the individual that matters as much as what takes place between and among actors as they interact—for example, the negotiation of identity or culture or the development of social structure. Rosenberg and Turner also draw attention to the fact that sociological social psychology places emphasis on *researching real-life events,* such as interactions at a bar or in a kindergarten class. Psychological social psychologists, on the other hand, are far more likely to use surveys or laboratory experiments. Related to this distinction is the fact that sociological social psychology emphasizes *socialization,* the various ways that individuals learn to become members of society—learn the patterns of society in face-to-face interaction. Thus, for example, *identity* becomes a central concept, since the creation of identity is thought to arise through social interaction, and ongoing social interaction is understood as central to the whole socialization process.

The most important way of understanding the distinction between the psychological and sociological approaches to social psychology is to recognize the tremendous importance that a perspective called *symbolic interactionism* has within sociology. No perspective in sociology has influenced our understanding of social interaction, socialization, and the social nature of the human being as much as this perspective. It is quite different from sociology, psychology, and psychological social psychology. It influences mainstream sociology when it comes to "socialization," and it is almost always an integral part of all approaches to social psychology within sociology.

The roots of symbolic interactionism are different from the roots of other social-scientific perspectives, and its insights are also different. It is limited because it is a perspective, and whether it is useful depends on whether it helps us understand the human being. It is part of the social-scientific tradition, yet it also tries to stand apart from the determinism that characterizes most social science perspectives.

1. *The perspective of symbolic interactionism grows out of pragmatism* and is heavily influenced by Charles Darwin's work. It emphasizes the uniqueness of the human being in nature, especially the fact that human beings act back on their environment rather than passively respond to that environment. The phrase *symbolic interactionism* gives away the focus of this perspective: To understand the human being, we need to study interaction, and interaction of human beings relies heavily on the use of symbols.

2. *Human beings are symbol users.* George Herbert Mead saw the use of symbols as our essence. Symbols have a distinct meaning to the symbolic interactionist, and they contribute a great deal to the nature of our reality and the nature of our society. They are the key to our uniqueness.

3. *Human beings possess a self.* We are able to act back on ourselves in situations. We are not only actors in the world, but we are also the object of our own actions. This quality, as is the use of symbols, is part of our essence and makes possible a vast array of actions we are capable of.

4. *Human beings engage in mind action.* We talk to ourselves about our environment. We understand our environment; we solve problems and organize our actions according to goals we determine for ourselves.

5. *Human beings regularly take the role of the other.* As we act in the world, we constantly take account of other people around us, and we direct our actions accordingly. This ability is part of what we do when we engage in mind action, and it changes considerably the nature of how we act in relation to others.

6. *Human beings act along a continuous stream of action,* interacting with others and engaging in mind action, determining goals, and seeing objects in relation to goals. We have to understand action as continuous, directional, and determined by decisions we make along the way.

7. *Human beings interact with one another.* Social interaction is different from simple

social influence, and it is difficult to dissect. It should be seen as the source of what we all are as individuals and as the source of society.

8. *Society is any instance of (a) social interaction in which actors (b) cooperate over time and (c) develop culture.* Two people, a small group, a community, or thousands of people interacting constitute a society. Individuals exist in many societies. Instead of society being an entity created in the past and imprisoning the actor, society is dynamic, continuously being created and recreated, continuously shaped by actors in interaction, and held together not by force but by the voluntary commitment of the actors involved.

9. *Erving Goffman is one of the most important theorists in sociology whose ideas are built on the principles outlined in this perspective.* Goffman's ideas are central to understanding human interaction and human society.

10. *Symbolic interactionism is guided by certain scientific principles* in its search for understanding and is applicable to many issues and situations—everyday and academic.

REFERENCES

Aronson, Elliot. 1992. Th*e Social Animal,* 6th ed. San Francisco: Freeman.

Berger, Peter. 1963. *Invitation to Sociology.* Garden City, N.Y.: Doubleday.

Fromm, Erich. 1973. *The Anatomy of Human Destructiveness.* New York: Holt, Rinehart & Winston.

Hampden-Turner, Charles. 1970. *Radical Man.* Cambridge, Mass.: Schenkman.

Kant, Immanuel. 1952. *The Critique of Pure Reason.* Trans. J. M. D. Meiklejohn. In *The Great Books of the Western World.* Ed. Robert Hutchins. Chicago: Encyclopedia Britannica. (Orig. pub. 1781)

Rosenberg, Morris, and Ralph Turner. 1981. *Social Psychology.* New York: Basic Books.

PART II

HUMANS AS SYMBOL-USING CREATURES

Human beings act toward things on the basis of the meanings that the things have for them.

—Herbert Blumer (1969), *Symbolic Interactionism*

The limits of my language mean the limits of my world.

—Ludwig Wittgenstein (in Lee, 1980)

SHARED MEANING IS THE BASIS OF HUMANNESS

Jodi O'Brien

Imagine that you have just been kicked in the knee. How do you respond? Your immediate physical response is probably an upward jerk of the leg. Perhaps a rush of air and a surprised gasp escape your lips. In a behaviorist's terms, the blow to the knee is considered the stimulus, and your direct, physical response is your jerking leg and cry of pain. This physical response to the stimulus of being kicked is the same for most humans.

In addition to this physiological response, you are likely to have reactions that are not as predictable. How do you respond to the person who kicked you? You may kick the person in return. You may apologize for being in the way. You may flee. Your response to the person who kicked you depends on how you *interpret* the incident. Do you perceive it to be an act of aggression, an accident, a playful joke? Your interpretation of the incident is in turn based on the situation and the cues you pick up from the person who kicked you. If you are in a crowded space and the kicker smiles apologetically, you are likely to interpret the act as an accident and to respond accordingly. If you have been reading quietly in an empty room and the kicker glares at you menacingly, you are more likely to interpret the kick as an act of aggression than as an accident.

Symbolic interactionists are interested in the process of assigning meaning to actions and in the responses that follow. The meaning that you assign to being kicked determines how you will respond to the kicker and, in turn, how the kicker will respond to you. That is, how you *perceive* the incident will determine how you *feel* about it and your subsequent course of action. This perception will also be the basis for how you store the event in your memory and recall it later.

A jerk of the knee and a cry of pain may be predictable, universal, physical responses. However, there is nothing inherent in the interpretation that can be placed on the event. To symbolic interactionists, the most interesting aspects of human behavior are those that take place when we assign meaning to our own actions or interpret the actions of others. Although it is possible to chart direct stimulus–response patterns in human behavior, symbolic interactionists maintain that these patterns are of limited interest in understanding human behavior and institutions. Most noteworthy behavior involves a process of *interpretation* between stimulus and response. Thus, the interesting question for the student of human behavior is not what the objective stimulus is (for example, the blow to the knee) but what *meaning* the receiver of the kick assigns to the stimulus (that is, how the blow is perceived). It is the process of assigning meaning that determines how people feel and act.

Symbolic interactionists claim that symbolic activity mediates between stimulus and response. This essay explores the implications of being symbol-using creatures who interpret the world. We will also discuss human thought as a process of symbolic gestures achieved through the acquisition of language. From this perspective, social behavior is a manifestation of shared patterns of symbolic meaning.

Physical reality seems to recede in proportion as man's symbolic activity advances.

The philosopher Ernst Cassirer makes this assertion in his essay on humans as symbol-using creatures (see Reading 5). For Cassirer, symbol-using creatures do not exist in a direct state of nature. To exist in a state of nature is to be nonconscious, nonreflective, and nonsymbolic. In such a state, the organism is propelled directly by the forces of nature, which include internal physiology and the external environment. In contrast, the symbolic creature is able to comprehend, comment on, and organize behavior in accordance with abstract representations that are removed from the state of nature. This does not necessarily imply that humans are "superior" to animals, nor does it suggest that we do not have an animal form (biologically and physiologically). The point is that most noteworthy human activity is symbolic (abstracted from a direct state of nature). Thus, the symbolic interactionist focuses on human behavior and culture *primarily* as expressions of meaningful symbol systems.

A comparison with elephants illustrates this point. When elephants meet, one places its trunk in the mouth of the other. Body temperature and fluids in the mouth indicate whether each elephant is in a state of arousal or aggression or is passive. This encounter triggers the appropriate response—copulating, fighting, fleeing, or traveling together. The elephants, as far as we can tell, do not think about this encounter; they do not interpret the event and assign meaning to it. They simply engage in a series of stimulus–response behaviors with each other in a direct state of nature.

The difference between humans and elephants is that humans do not respond directly to the physical environment. Rather, humans impose symbolic interpretations on experiences and draw conclusions based on these interpretations. It is true that we are attuned to odors and other physiological manifestations of our fellow humans and that we may experience these directly rather than through a process of interpretation. But most of our responses to others are determined by our *interpretation* of various cues. These cues include physiological features, gestures, and accessories and adornments, such as clothing and other symbolically meaningful items.

Those of you who have driven across a border into another country know that it is the duty of border guards to ascertain whether you are bringing merchandise into (or out of) the country in violation of international or national laws. These guards cannot read your mind, nor can they experience directly whether you are telling the truth when you claim not to be carrying illicit goods. The guards must infer your intentions based on symbolic cues, such as the type of car you are driving, your gender, and the style of your clothes and hair. In other words, the guards guess at your integrity based on their symbolic interpretation of you and the situation. Similarly, the police officer who stops a motorist cannot experience directly whether the accosted driver will be hostile or compliant. The officer must make an inference based on available symbolic cues.

Consider the process of cue interpretation you engage in when you are trying to figure out if the person across the room is flirting with you. In such a situation, you have no direct knowledge of the person's actual mood or intentions. Is this someone who is a potential date? If you approach, will the person be hostile or receptive? Before making a move, the individual trying to assess the situation is likely to consider many cues and will probably discuss the cues with a group of friends before deciding to act. All of this is interpretive behavior.

Social psychologists are interested in the signs people use to make inferences and the reliability of these signs for predicting the intentions of others. This predictability is not a function of directly reading the "natural" world. Rather, it is the product of the symbolic codes through which we assign meaning to objects. Human behavior is not determined directly from our encounters with the physical world. Our bodies are physical entities that exist in the physical world, but our experience of our own bodies, of other people, and of things in our environment is anchored in the internal conversation that constitutes our conscious thought.

SYMBOLIC MEANING: IT'S THE NAME, NOT THE THING

Herbert Blumer is credited with first use of the term *symbolic interactionism* to define the approach to the study of human behavior and society that we have been discussing (Fine, 1990). Blumer (1969), who was a sociologist at the University of California, Berkeley, suggested three basic premises:

1. Humans act toward a thing on the basis of the meaning they assign to the thing.

2. Meanings are socially derived, which is to say that meaning is not inherent in a state of nature. There is no absolute meaning. Meaning is negotiated through interaction with others.

3. The perception and interpretation of social symbols are modified by the individual's own thought processes. (p. 2)

Naming (Assigning Meaning)

When we make sense of a person, space, or occasion, we attach meaning to it. This process is known as *naming*. Naming has three elements: a label, a cognitive-emotive evaluation, and a recommended course of action. The conceptual names we have for persons, spaces, and things include each of these three components. Consider a round, hollow tube made of glass with a single closed end. We can label it a glass. But *glass* is a fairly abstract term, and we might each be imagining a different type of glass. Let's say that we further narrow the meaning of the label by imposing additional classifications—for example, the glass has a stem attached. This description suggests a wineglass, which we may evaluate subjectively as, perhaps, an elegant sort of glass or a decadent sort of glass. Regardless of the specific glass that each of us has in mind, we are in agreement as to its general purpose. That is, we know the recommended course of action toward the object that we have labeled a glass: It is a container from which we can drink.

Philosophers, linguists, and cognitive social psychologists agree that to name something is to know it. This process of object identification is central to human perception and appraisal. Humans name things and then respond according to the implications carried by the name. They do not respond to the essence of the thing itself. Thus, we say that human behavior involves not just a response to a stimulus but a process—naming—that mediates between stimulus and response.

Try the following exercise. Work up some saliva in your mouth. How does it feel? Now spit it into a glass. How does it look? Now drink it up. Most of you will probably respond to this last request with some hesitation. Yet we have simply asked you to reabsorb a substance that, in fact, you swallow continually all through the day. Why did you hesitate? Probably because you have an aversion to spit. This aversion is not a direct response to the natural essence of the substance. It is an aversion to the *name,* not the thing. Your reaction is based on a symbolic process whereby you have conceptualized bodily fluids that have left the body as repulsive. The name *spit* implies an evaluative response ("Yuck!") and a course of action (avoidance). You do not respond to the nature of the fluid. Instead, you assign meaning to the fluid and respond to that meaning. Cassirer reminds us of the words of the Greek philosopher Epictetus: "What disturbs [people] are not things, but their opinions and fancies about things."

Symbols and Signifying

Emotional and behavioral responses to environmental stimuli are shaped by this naming process. Thus, behavior differs not in response to a particular stimulus but in response to the meaning human actors assign to the stimulus. Recall Jane Wagner's "The Search for Signs of Intelligent Life in the Universe" (Reading 2) in Part I. In this story, Trudy the "bag lady" is giving lessons about earth life to some "space chums." She attempts to explain the difference between a can of Campbell's soup and Andy Warhol's painting of a can of Campbell's soup. One is soup, the other is art. Warhol's rendering of the can of soup is not merely a stand-in image for the soup itself; rather, as "art" it constitutes a class of meaning unto itself. In contemplating the painting, a person doesn't consider whether the actual soup tastes good; instead, the person evaluates the "worth" of the painting based on what he or she knows about art. "Soup" and "art" are both abstract ideas, although each term conjures a different meaning. These different meanings imply different lines of action or responses toward the object. Similarly, the "conversation" we are now having, in which we are removed from one another's immediate presence, would not be possible if we did not share the abstract ideas of "book," "reading," and a similar symbolic system called "written English."

What are these symbols that we use to assign meaning to our experiences? Symbols are abstract representations. Brand names are a form of symbolic representation that even young children are familiar with. Many parents are familiar with the exasperation of trying to locate, not to mention pay for, a pair of shoes that a teenager insists he or she *must* have. It's often the case that the materials and construction of the desired brand differ little from those of other brands, but the brand itself stands for something—in this case, being hip or cool—and in a social world, this makes all the difference.

Consider another example: A rectangular piece of cloth with red and white horizontal stripes and a blue square in the upper left-hand corner filled with white stars has significance beyond this physical description—it is a symbol, an abstract representation, of the United States of America.

A flag is a symbol not only of the nation "for which it stands," but also of the social convention of dividing the world into mutually exclusive geopolitical units known as "nations." The U.S. flag not only stands for what is considered uniquely American, but also symbolizes a *distinction* from other nations. To be American is also to *not be* Russian, for example. Thus, a symbol defines both what something is and what it is not. The essence of the item you hold in your hands at this moment is tree pulp (assuming you are reading this as an actual book and not electronically) flattened and pressed into connected sheets with splotches of ink all over them. Most likely you do not think of the item this way, but rather as a book with abstract symbols in the form of written language for you to absorb. It is also likely that you do not consider the book as a source of toilet paper, although its natural essence has properties similar to those of the materials in toilet paper.

The study of semiotics and sociolinguistics is the study of the cultural systems of meaning that are conveyed through various symbolic representation. Roland Barthes (1964/1967), for example, has studied food symbolism. All societies have cultural systems that *signify* what foods can be eaten and what foods should be excluded, how certain foods are supposed to be grouped (for example, breakfast, lunch, dinner, or appetizers, main courses, desserts), and the various rituals of use ("table manners," "picnics," "feasts"). Trudy's space chums have difficulty comprehending the distinction between "soup" and "art" because they do not share the symbolic understanding whereby an apparently similar material image is *assigned* to entirely different domains of meaning (food/art). In both examples, the symbolic system *signifies* how things are supposed to be grouped (classified) and how we are supposed to feel about them. Thus,

Naming = assigning symbolic meaning to things/persons/events

Symbolic meaning = a sign system that conveys messages regarding how to feel about and respond to the thing/person/event

Harlem Renaissance artist and writer Langston Hughes wrote a story called "That Powerful Drop" to illustrate the significance of symbolic meaning within specific cultural contexts. In the story, Hughes's characters ponder the significance of "Negro blood." Physiologically, there is no difference between white and black blood. However, in the context of this story—the 1950s Southern states—identifying certain people as having "Negro blood" conveys the symbolic message that black blood is less desirable and more problematic than white blood. Technically speaking, the characters in the story cannot see one another's blood, nor can most of us most of the time. It's not the blood per se, but the idea of what the blood stands for—in this case, skin hues and phenotypical characteristics such as nose and other facial features that are presumed to signify one's standing as a human being in relation to other human beings. This racial marker is mutually understood by people who share a cultural system of meaning premised on racial differentiation and prejudice. In a culture in which differentiation is based more on class position than on race, the phenotypical characteristics associated with "blood" might be overlooked, but people's accents—do they sound educated or not?—might be highly notable and symbolic.

Symbols, Experience, and Culture

Because symbols are abstractions, we can use them to transcend the concrete environment and to have experiences that are not rooted in time and space. Abstraction also allows us to remember, fantasize, plan, and have vicarious experiences. When we imagine something, we formulate an image, a symbolic representation, of something that is not present in the immediate state of nature. Remembering is a similar activity. When we fantasize and make plans, we are manipulating symbolic images. Vicarious experience allows us to learn by observing the actions of others; we need not experience everything ourselves to comprehend what someone else is experiencing. This is a key element in individual survival and in the transmission of culture.

Symbolic interactionists claim that without symbol systems, human experience and culture would not be possible. To comprehend the significance of the human ability to engage in symbolic abstraction, consider how much time you spend in the presence of your intimate friends versus how much time you spend thinking, remembering, fantasizing, and planning about them. Ask yourself if it would be possible for you to experience "love" for someone if you could not imagine (represent conceptually) the person when he or she was not actually physically present.

A great deal of human symbolic activity involves learning to sort and group people into social roles (for example, stranger, teacher, judge, soldier, priest, and so on). Culturally specific expectations are associated with different social roles. For example, we think, feel, and behave very differently with "friends" than we do with "grandparents."

In a case study titled "Yes, Father-Sister" (see Reading 6), neurologist Oliver Sacks describes a woman who has lost the ability to recognize and name people according to recognized social groups. She has a neurological dissolution associated with language processing that has left her without "any 'center' to the mind." She is no longer able to comprehend or express symbolic *meaning*. All social roles are the same for her and can be interchanged at will. Thus, someone in her presence can be "Father," "Sister," or "Doctor" at any given moment. Imagine how disconcerting it would be if one of your parents called you indiscriminately "child," "parent," "lover," "salesclerk." People who are unable to engage in appropriate symbolic activity are islands, isolated from meaningful relationships. They are unable to access and express the cultural "script" that others share and find significant.

THE SOURCE OF SYMBOLIC SYSTEMS OF MEANING: LANGUAGE

The primary way by which humans exchange symbolic meaning is through language. Language is a system of symbols that allows humans to communicate and share abstract meaning. Language gives humans the capacity to become social creatures—which is to say, the capacity to comprehend and to participate in culture.

The basic unit of language is the word. Words are symbols that denote the meaning of something. Words can be conveyed through writing, speech, and sign. The power of words to represent the range of human activity can be seen in the following exercise: Try listing words for as many emotions as you can think of. Then read your list to someone else. Chances are that the person will comprehend the states of being that each word suggests. Now, select an emotion word that is well understood among those who share your language and attempt to communicate this emotion to someone through direct physical contact without the use of words. General emotions such as anger, lust, and fright may possibly be communicated by touch. However, it is likely that the list of emotion words that you generated conveys a much wider range of emotion and greater emotional subtlety than you can communicate effectively without resorting to words. Does this exercise show that there are more emotions than there are ways of expressing them? No. It implies that there are as many emotions as there are words for describing them.

Words give meaning to our experiences. In many instances, a physiological state of arousal is meaningless and may even go unnoticed until the experience has been named. Consider, for example, a young man who, while traveling by plane, experiences a queasy stomach and sweaty palms. He is unable to ascertain whether he is experiencing airsickness or attraction to the woman sitting next to him. Both experiences entail the same physiological responses, but different courses of action are deemed appropriate, depending on whether one labels the experience "nausea" or "love."

Meaning consists not only of isolated words or names, but also of the additional ideas and experiences associated with particular words. An instructive exercise is to note words that have parallel definitions but carry very different connotations. *Bachelor* and *spinster* are one example. They are defined, respectively, as the male and female state of being unmarried. But *spinster* raises much less attractive images in the minds of most people than does the term *bachelor.* Language comprehension involves much more than just knowing words. Meaningful communication is based on shared understanding of a *cluster of meanings* associated with particular words. Recall the discussion of "naming"—words are the basis of naming and provide not only identification of objects, but also instructions for how to feel and respond to objects and situations that we encounter.

Language and Social Behavior

Language, thought, and social behavior are closely related. We interact with each other by observing ourselves and steering our behavior according to our interpretations of the expectations of others. This process is internal; we *talk* with ourselves about how to name situations, how to name our role in the situation, and how to assign meaning to others in the situation. We determine recipes for action based on the meaning we assign to the situation and experience feelings about the situation depending on how we have defined it. Without language, we would be unable to assign meaning to our own actions or to bring our actions into line with the expectations of our culture. We would be unsocialized.

Language and Socialization

Much research has been done on the relationship between language acquisition and human development. Researchers are particularly interested in the few documented cases of "feral children"—children raised in isolation from adult human interaction. In the 1940s, sociologist Kingsley Davis described the case of a young girl who was subjected to extreme isolation during crucial developmental years (see Reading 7). In presenting her case, Davis pursued the hypothesis that social intercourse is necessary for the development of language and intellectual activity. Without exposure to language, children do not achieve the ability to engage in normal human activities.

Further information about the relationship between language and social behavior comes from studies of people who have experienced damage to the language centers of the brain. The neurological disorders that result from such damage are referred to as *aphasia*. These disorders usually impair a person's ability to engage in normal social interactions. Recall the woman described by Oliver Sacks who could no longer recognize social roles and therefore responded to everyone as if they were anything that popped into her mind.

Other researchers have documented similar consequences of aphasia (see, for example, Lindesmith, Strauss, & Denzin, 1991). In one tragic case, a well-known symphony conductor contracts a virus that impairs his neurological language center. As a result of this impairment, his conceptual memories are wiped out to the extent that he no longer recognizes his own wife. When she hugs him, his sense of smell and touch serve as triggers that remind him, briefly, who she is. Thus reminded, he sobs and clings to her and asks where she has been for so long. Minutes later, when she returns to his room from taking a break, the entire scene is played over again. Without the capacity for language, specifically the ability to formulate a concept of "wife" and retain all his memories of her as wife in his mind, the man simply doesn't know who she is.

Together, these curious and often tragic cases suggest to neurologists, linguists, and social psychologists that the relationships among the brain, language, and social behavior is highly complex and also crucial for what we consider "normal" human behavior.

Language and Thought

As powerful as a single word may be in assigning meaning, the full power of language is in the relationships among words, or the *structure* of language. Words are juxtaposed in such a way as to convey one meaning rather than another. For example, the words *cat, dog,* and *chases* each suggest a particular meaning. The first two are nouns that denote certain types of four-legged mammals, and the third is a verb that names a particular action. Presumably we have a shared understanding of the general class of meaning to which these words refer. Now, consider the alignment of the words "dog chases cat" and "cat chases dog." Do both combinations suggest the same event? Try writing other possible combinations of these three words. How many of these combinations make sense to you?

The structure of language, called *syntax,* comprises the rules of grammar. Syntax allows humans to combine words to create strings or clusters of meaning more complex than the meaning suggested by isolated words. The syntax of a language also permits us to convey entirely different meanings by recombining symbols, as in the example of *cat, dog,* and *chases.* Another interesting feature of syntax is that humans appear to learn and use the rules of language without necessarily being aware of what these rules are. For example, although most people can give an example of a "yes or no" question (for instance, "Is your car red?"), very few could state the formal rules for constructing such a sentence. Nevertheless, people recognize when the rules have been violated. (We will return to this simple but profound point in Part IV in discussing the similarities between language syntax and "social grammar." As with rules of grammar, people are implicitly aware of the rules of interaction and recognize when these rules have been violated, but they cannot state explicitly what these rules are.) Thus, the power of language derives from the human ability to employ rules to convey meaning without necessarily being aware of the rules. Humans are continually able to represent new meanings, and these novel combinations will be understood by others, provided that the combinations follow accepted syntactical structure.

Linguists refer to the ability to formulate novel but mutually understood statements as the *generative* property of language. Humans generate their own ideas and codes of meaning; in other words, language and meaning are not predetermined by nature. The extent of this generative ability is profound—it allows small children to formulate novel sentences (rather than just repeating preprogrammed speech) and nuclear physicists to develop abstract and complex theories.

Nonetheless, not all combinations of words are equally meaningful or likely to be generated. What is intriguing is that people can ascertain the difference between "gibberish" and mutually comprehensible strings of words.

The meaning of what is generated is determined by the underlying structure of the language, or the particular "patterns of discourse." Different languages entail distinct patterns of meaning. These language patterns profoundly influence culture. In short, different languages provide different ways to make sense of ourselves, others, and our circumstances.

During the past few decades, social scientists have debated whether language shapes thought or thought comes before language. George Herbert Mead (see Reading 11) theorized that, in the process of learning language, the mind develops and becomes structured in a manner that reflects the individual's culture. Anthropologists, too, have pursued the claim that distinct languages cause people of different cultures to view and think about the world differently. For instance, many anthropologists demonstrate ways in which different cultures divide up "time" and "space" as expressed in their various languages. Some cultures express time in a nonlinear way as compared with Western linear conceptions, for example. Think about what your relationship to time might be if you could refer only to the concepts of "now" and "not now" and had no notion of "past" or "future."

Language: Innate or Socially Produced?

Scholars agree that language is a bedrock of human behavior and social life. There is disagreement, however, about whether the capacity for language is socially learned (nurture) or physiologically innate (nature). Linguists such as Noam Chomsky consider language an innate human ability. Chomsky (1972) has made a convincing case that the "deep structure" of language is more complex than anyone could "learn" through social contact alone. He argues instead that one feature of the human brain is an inborn "computational modality." That is, humans are "hardwired" to comprehend and generate abstract representations and to piece together complex strings of words that require them to compute various possible lines of meaning and association. This activity is so complex and so unavailable to general consciousness that, according to Chomsky and his supporters, it would be impossible for children to perform the incredible mental gymnastics required to communicate if the brain were not hardwired for language.

One of Chomsky's students, Steven Pinker, author of the popular book *The Language Instinct* (1994), offers a simple but noteworthy illustration of the computational modality using these three statements:

Ralph is an elephant.

Elephants live in Africa.

Elephants have tusks.

Pinker continues thus:

> Our inference-making device [innate computational processor] . . . would deduce "Ralph lives in Africa" and "Ralph has tusks." This sounds fine but isn't. Intelligent you, the reader, knows that the Africa Ralph lives in is the same Africa that all the other elephants live in, but that Ralph's tusks are his own. (Pinker, 1994, p. 79)

Pinker's point is that people make this distinction on the basis of common sense, but there is nothing in the words themselves that conveys this common sense; thus, the meaning is not logically explicit. The fact that people can make the distinction without hesitation is, for Pinker, a demonstration that people "know" things independently of the words used to express them. Thus, the way people think about and structure understanding precedes the language they use to express this understanding. Language itself contains so many ambiguities and oversimplifications that humans must have a larger picture in mind before speaking; otherwise, we would be unable to fill in the blanks and sort through the ambiguities with such unconscious ease.

Rather than debate the nature/nurture aspects of language, there is a more useful and accurate (albeit more complex) way to think about human behavior. Chomsky is probably correct, in part—the aptitude for abstraction and linguistic computation is innate; it is a fundamental property of humanness. But what is the *source* of the conceptual abstractions that the mental processors are acting on? This puzzle is the untold story in contemporary linguistics.

Let's return to Ralph the elephant. If humans were preprogrammed with information, infants would be born knowing all there is to know about elephants, Africa, and tusks. Clearly, this is a silly speculation. Let's assume, then, that we comprehend the distinction between the sharing of one Africa by many elephants and the possession of tusks by single elephants because we have learned a distinction between being physically located in a space and possessing physical traits. Our ability to generalize these experiential observations and to incorporate them in language is the computational element that Chomsky refers to.

Language, Thought, and Social Interaction

Our capacity for the abstraction and computation necessary to process language may be innate, but the actual content is *learned* through social contact. What Chomsky and colleagues can't tell us, as observers trying to make sense of human behavior, is the *significance* of Ralph in particular and of elephants, tusks, and Africa in general. This significance—people's attitudes, feelings, and behavior toward such strings of words—is determined by the context in which the words appear and the attributes people have learned to associate with these contexts. This is a social process. That is, the human capacity for the abstraction and computation necessary to process language may be innate, but the actual content is learned through social contact. Adults use language to teach children not necessarily how to think about, say, elephants, tusks, or Africa, but what to think about these things—and subsequently, how to respond. People don't need to be taught how to respond physiologically—for example, *what* to do physically when kicked in the knee. But the range of possible *social* responses to being kicked that occur to a person, and her or his understanding of their appropriateness and consequences, are the result of having been taught, through language, what he or she should think about the incident. The name that we each ascribe to an experience acts as a sort of shorthand that shapes our subsequent thoughts about how to respond to the situation. In this way, language, experience, and thought continually interact—they are mutually determining.

A helpful analogy is the relationship between computer hardware and software: Here, the human brain is the hardware and language the software. Humans are born with brain hardware that enables us to engage in complex, computational, abstract, representational thought, but the content—*what* we process—is input by others who provide us with meaningful ideas through the activity of language. In the same way that a computer cannot operate in a fully functional manner without being switched on and fed some software, there is considerable evidence that children who are not exposed to language fail to develop normal conceptual abilities.

Oliver Sacks (1989) explores this issue in his book about the congenitally deaf, *Seeing Voices*. On the basis of several case studies, Sacks asserts that those born without hearing are endowed with the same intellectual capacity as those who can hear. But in an oral-based culture, the congenitally deaf, in the absence of aural stimulation, fail to develop conceptual thought. The cognitive hardware of the congenitally deaf child may be in perfect working order, but the hearing impairment (deficient perceptual hardware) gets in the way of the necessary start-up. The child's language ability never really gets turned on. For this reason, many deaf children are mistakenly assumed to be developmentally disabled. However, when a congenitally deaf infant is exposed to sign language, the child not only proceeds along a normal course of cognitive development, but actually begins to communicate in sign earlier than hearing infants learn to talk. Some specialists suggest that the ability for communication is switched on before the infant's vocal cords are physically ready for speech. Signing infants don't have to wait for their vocal cords to develop.

Studies of "feral children"—children raised in isolation, who are often assumed to be developmentally disabled—suggest similar conclusions. The capacity for abstract thought may be innate, but in order to develop this capacity, the child must be exposed to language-based social interaction. When the child lacks such access, he or she is effectively denied access to the "switch" (language-based interaction) and the "software" (a specific language) through which conceptual thought develops. The implication is that humans require social stimulation and exposure to abstract symbol systems—language—in order to embark upon the conceptual thought processes that characterize our species.

Thus, human experience is given meaning and is organized through language, and the ability to form complex strings of words and to communicate verbally is innate. But the source of the meaning assigned to the words is social.

Experience and Conceptualization

In the late 1600s, the philosophers Gottfried Leibnitz and John Locke are said to have exchanged letters in which they debated the following question: Imagine a man who is born blind. How will he learn the difference between the concepts "triangle," "square," and "circle"? Like all children, he can be given blocks to play with. The "platonic solids" consist of blocks that are triangular, cubed, and round. The blind man could learn to tell the difference through his sense of touch. He could *feel* each one and be told the name, and then, whenever someone mentioned the name (for example, "triangle"), he would have an *idea* of what the triangle was. Now here is the question: What would happen if the man were suddenly able to see, and the three different blocks were set in front of him? Would he be able to *see* the difference and name them accordingly, or would he still have to *feel* each one? According to Locke, the man would not necessarily be able to *see* the different shapes. His *conceptual* understanding of the shapes would be based in his *experience* of touch. Leibnitz disagreed. He believed that the man would be able to conjecture what each was, based on the concept that he held in his mind (a concept that was rooted in the experience of touch, not sight).

One of the questions that interests sociolinguists is the relationships among experience, perception, and conceptualization. In the title case from his well-known book, *The Man Who Mistook His Wife for a Hat,* Oliver Sacks (1987) describes a man who has retained his ability for abstraction but has lost the "commonsensical" meaning tracks used in ordinary, day-to-day conversation. While trying to figure out what is wrong with the man, Sacks holds up a glove and asks him what he sees. The man studies it for a bit and then declares that it appears to be "some sort of container with five out-pouchings." Technically, this is an accurate description of the item. But is it meaningful? Sacks notes that "seeing" is a matter of conceptualization, not just sensory perception. We use our conceptual knowledge to make sense of what our senses are seeing. *Meaningful* concepts resonate with experience. A "glove" is really not the same thing as "a continuous surface unfolded on itself with five out-pouchings." The implication is that we learn conceptual meaning *in context*. Socially meaningful concepts reflect specific experiences—experiences that are visceral and imbued with feeling. Thus, when studying how children learn to assign meaning to concrete things in their environment, we have to take into account both the social content and the context of experience.

The Russian linguist and social psychologist Lev Vygotsky wrote extensively on the relationship between language and thought during the 1920s, but his writings have been available in English only since 1960 (for example, Vygotsky, 1961). Writing independently of the North American debate regarding linguistic determinism, Vygotsky, like his fellow Eastern European social scientists, was inclined to see a mutual relationship between individual neurological-cognitive processes and social learning.

According to Vygotsky (1961), children make sense of their environment by grouping things (persons and objects) that seem, through their own experiences, to be connected. The result is "complex thinking," or grouping seemingly related things into "complexes." Concepts generated from the complexes stand in as abstract representations of meaningful relationships between concrete things and experiences. For instance, a child's experiential complex for the family dog might consist of "Ruffy, big, furry, tail, bite." Conceptual thinking replaces the complex when the child learns the general name for the complex—"dog." Initially, the child may attempt to interchange the specific name, "Ruffy," with the general name, "dog." She may also experience fear whenever she hears of a "dog," because her complex or cluster includes the experience "bite."

Comprehending a parent's explanation that "the dog will bite you only if you pull its tail" is an illustration of the child's ability to generalize based on abstract thinking. It is also an illustration of the child's ability to learn vicariously through language. The child needn't experiment with pulling the tail of every dog that she encounters to gain an understanding of the conceptual relationship between tail pulling and biting. Rather, she uses the words to formulate a more general idea and to encode both the specific experience and her general interpretation of it in her memory. Thus, she begins to develop a lexicon of experientially based but socially influenced "names" complete with evaluative and action codes ("Dogs can bite, so beware").

Vygotsky (1961) bridges individual and social-cognitive linguistics through his idea of "pseudo-concepts," generalizations that are like concepts but that are actually complexes:

> In the experimental setting, the child produces a pseudo-concept every time he surrounds a sample with objects that could just as well have been assembled on the basis of an abstract concept. For instance, when the sample is a yellow triangle and the child picks out all the triangles in the experimental material, he could have been guided by the general idea or concept of a triangle. Experimental analysis shows, however, that in reality the child is guided by concrete, visible likeness and has formed only an associative complex limited to a certain kind of perceptual bond. Although the results are identical, the process by which they are reached is not at all the same as in conceptual thinking.
>
> Pseudo-concepts predominate over all other complexes in the child's thinking for the simple reason that in real life complexes corresponding to word meanings are not spontaneously developed by the child: The lines along which a complex develops are predetermined by the meaning a given word already has in the language of adults. . . . This language, with its stable, permanent meanings, points the way that a child's generalizations will take. The adult cannot pass on to the child his mode of thinking. He merely supplies the ready-made meaning of a word, around which the child forms a complex. . . . The pseudo-concept serves as the connecting link between thinking in complexes and thinking in concepts. Verbal intercourse with adults becomes a powerful factor in the intellectual development of the child. (pp. 67–69)

The point that we derive from Vygotsky is that, in normal cognitive development, children operate at the nexus of practical experience and preestablished concepts. Even as they are forming experience-based groupings of things in their environment, children are learning to use ready-made words that are based on conceptualizations that are already socially established. Thus, both the child's own experiences and social influence, through preexisting language, play a role in the development of language and cognition. The resulting conceptual knowledge is a combination of experience and social learning. Concrete experiences enable the child to *comprehend* in an embodied, fully feeling way, but without preexisting language, the child would not be able to transcend the immediate experience and "make sense" of it in a more general way.

LANGUAGE, THOUGHT, AND CULTURE

We can discuss language and cognitive structure from one additional angle. Chomsky and others, in their zeal to make the point that humans have an innate capacity for representational computation, have rejected the notion that the particular language of a culture determines the way in which members of the culture classify persons, objects, and events. Many social scientists disagree and argue instead that language categories do in fact structure the way in which individuals perceive, organize, evaluate, feel about, and respond to their experiences and environments.

Language, as we have already noted, has evaluative and emotive components that make up concepts. Concepts, as Vygotsky details, do not necessarily emerge through direct experience but, rather, are handed down to us through social intercourse with other members of our culture. These concepts shape the way we focus on, categorize, evaluate, respond to, and remember people, objects, and events; in other words, language *does* structure how we think.

Consider the following string of words: *Race is not biologically significant; it is only skin deep.* When considered from a chromosomal perspective, this statement may indeed be correct. But is it representative of social reality as you know it? The chromosomes of humans with brown skin and those with white skin may be identical, but the words *black* and *white* carry an entire history of meaning here in the United States and shape, to a large extent, the way in which Americans are inclined to see, evaluate, and remember others. In short, "race" in the United States is socially significant.

In learning the customs and belief systems of their culture, people learn to classify humans in a variety of ways. They learn that humans can be big, small, short, tall, fat, thin, brown, white, and so forth, and each of these "names" includes emotive-evaluative components and behavioral cues.

Let us stress the point one more time—left to themselves, free of preexisting cultural influence, children would develop "complexes" that reflect their particular experience with their environment. The meaning that they would attach to words (that is, the abstract concepts and names that emerge from complexes) would thus accurately portray the world as they experienced it. Note that this path of learning leads to a process of stereotyping—if the child is bitten by a big fluffy animal that she later comes to name "dog," she may, through experience, later presume that all such creatures are scary. In other words, her conceptual notion would stand in for "real" experience and would shape her response to such creatures. However, as generations of social scientists have demonstrated, children do not learn in a vacuum. More likely, they begin forming complex associations between named objects, people, and spaces by asking, "What's that?" The concepts given to them by others contain preconceived associations that reflect shared cultural evaluations. For example, a child who has no direct experience with lions can still learn to identify a picture of one—and, most important, the child will absorb whatever emotive-evaluative-behavioral cues are expressed by the adults explaining what a lion is. Thus, a child can become "scared" by the *thought* of a lion without ever encountering one, because he or she has been taught that lions are "scary."

This process of "naming" has serious implications for the structure of society. For instance, without ever having encountered a Mexican American before, an Anglo-American middle-class employer can find herself wondering whether a young "Mexican-looking" job candidate from Texas is likely to be "illegal." The sources of such a stereotype are subtle and varied. The employer may not even be aware that she is evaluating the candidate on the basis of a pre-conceived stereotypical framework. Her response is based on a cultural representation and may have no connection to her direct experience or the abilities of the prospective employee.

By studying the way in which names are associated with other emotive-evaluative words, we can learn a great deal about the way in which culture, through language, shapes the thoughts of individuals. The power of language is not simply in words but in the manner in which words can be combined to create clusters of meaning. These associations, which we often take as "common sense," reflect social divisions, not natural ones.

Categorization

The process of naming is an act of categorization. To categorize is to impose conceptual categories of meaning on things. Categories group things in a way that makes them related and gives them order. Cognitively, this is a very efficient operation, similar to a mental filing system (consider the "system" you use to organize your notes and materials for different classes so that you don't have to file through one big heap every time you need something). But categorization also presents problems. In her book *Mindfulness,* Harvard psychologist Ellen Langer (1990; Reading 8) describes these cognitive processes of categorization and some of the pros and cons of this amazing human ability. For instance, when we meet some-one new, we classify the person according to cues such as type of clothing, posture, age, and so on. Based on these cues, we make an immediate assessment based on categorical associa-tions (e.g., well-dressed, older, gray hair = gentleman = safe). We do this in the blink of an eye and largely without thinking about it. This ability for categorical associative thinking enables us to move quickly and efficiently through our daily encounters.

We navigate our way through life by making categorical assessments and responding to the information contained in the category as we have previously learned it. For the most part, this serves us well. We can be efficient in our thinking, and we don't have to experience everything directly in order to know what the situation requires of us. When you enter a "classroom," for example, the category "classroom" implies a particular set of behaviors and expectations. You fall into a behavioral response that is routine, or "mindless." However, if you entered what you *thought* was a "classroom" and heard music and saw people drinking and dancing, your mind would be triggered into a more aware or "mindful" state, and you would begin searching for additional cues in order to make sense of the situation. The way in which we learn to recognize and define social situations is discussed in more detail in Part V. Here, the point is that our abil-ity to make categorical assessments is a product of learning language—when we learn a word or an idea, we learn it as part of a categorical cluster of meanings.

The downside of this process is that we tend to get stuck or trapped in previously learned categories. This can lead to what Langer calls "mindlessness," or behavior that is based on unconscious or semiconscious routine. Mindlessness occurs when we rely on a few symbolic cues to fill in all the blanks. In Reading 8, Langer offers many interesting examples of mind-lessness. The dangers of mindlessness include the omission of other relevant features of the event, object, or person in question and the perpetuation of stereotypes. For example, elderly people or persons with physical disabilities are often assumed to be mentally deficient as well because, stereotypically, it is common to categorically associate physical slowness or inability with mental slowness.

Stereotypes and Default Assumptions

All languages suggest categorical relationships based on notable symbols. In the absence of specific information, people use these general word-based categories to impose meaning on other people, things, and events and to form judgments that they then rely on to guide their behavior. A border guard, in the absence of any other information, may see a male motorist with a shaved head and five earrings in one ear and infer, based on categorical associations among clusters of symbols, that the person is a punker who is trying to smuggle drugs into the country. We all have a tendency to make these types of inferences. What is your general image of the border guard? Where did you get this information? Your ability to envision a border guard, even if you have personally never encountered one, is a process of stereotyping. You conjure up the image based on a classification scheme. Chances are that the border guard you imagine is based on a stereotype. This stereotype is most likely male, wearing some type of uniform, and carrying a gun.

Douglas Hofstadter (1986) is another scholar who writes about stereotypical thinking. He discusses what he calls "default assumptions." Default assumptions are preconceived notions about the likely state of affairs—what we assume to be true in the absence of specific information. Given no other information, when I mention my "secretary," you are likely to assume the secretary is female, because female and secretary are associated stereotypically. In the absence of specific details, people rely on the stereotype as a default assumption for filling in the blanks. Default assumptions have a tendency, in Hofstadter's words, to "permeate our mental representations and channel our thoughts" (p. 137). For instance, given the words *cat, dog,* and *chases,* you are likely to think first of a dog chasing a cat.

This line of thought reflects a default assumption that, all else being equal, the dog is more likely to chase the cat than the other way around. Default assumptions are based on prior experience and knowledge of circumstances. They are useful in that people cannot always afford the time it would take to consider every theoretical possibility that confronts them.

Nonetheless, it is possible that default assumptions are wrong. An interesting question is how might we know if we are wrong. Another is whether we change our default assumptions if the facts of the situation prove us wrong. If, for example, the shaved motorist does not have drugs in the car, will the border guard revise her categorical expectations regarding the association between a male with a shaved head and earrings, and drug use? Or will she reaffirm these general expectations with an account to herself of why this particular incident was not as expected? She may decide that the person does, in fact, have drugs in the car; she was simply unable to find them. Thus, the general category shaved head = punker = drugs is confirmed. Furthermore, the category may now be associated with deviousness as well.

Default assumptions are only one type of language-based categorization. Hofstadter is particularly interested in race-based and sex-based categorization and default assumptions. For instance, if you hear that your school basketball team is playing tonight, do you assume it's the men's team? Most people would assume so unless a "qualifier" were added to provide specific information. In this case, the qualifier would be "the *women's* basketball team is playing tonight." Hofstadter means to show us that language is a powerful reflection of cultural associations and stereotypes. These associations are revealed in the way we use language. The phrase "my black doctor" reflects the cultural assumption that, all else being equal, the speaker knows that his audience does not expect the physician to be black. He adds a qualifier, *black,* to offset the expected default assumption. Similarly, consider the practice of hyphenation in racial and ethnic labeling. Anglo-Americans rarely refer to themselves as such. Rather, the default assumption, in the absence of a qualifier such as Japanese American, is that an American is Anglo and white. The qualifier is considered unnecessary, because it is assumed to be the default. One of the problems with default assumptions such as these is that, in addition to being taken for granted, the categorical associations tend to include notions such as "normal" and sometimes even "culturally desirable."

Hofstadter (1986) offers another exercise for finding culture embedded in language. He refers to these as "language asymmetries" (p. 103). Consider the following terms: *Mr., Mrs.,* and *Miss.* Presumably each is the polite form of address for someone you don't know well. Why are there two terms for women and only one for men? "Well," you might respond, "it's because the Miss/Mrs. lets you know if a woman is married or not." Correct. But why is there no corresponding distinction for men? The asymmetry suggests that a woman's marital status is significant information, whereas a man's marital status is not. Indeed, it is probably the case that in modern Western culture, marital status is one of *the* most important bits of information about a woman. This is reflected in the prominence of language that provides this information. In recent years, the term "Ms." has come into use as an attempt to balance this asymmetry and deemphasize a woman's marital status. However, many professional organizations still instruct their employees to use "Mrs." as the more "appropriate" or "polite" form of address when talking with a woman of marriageable age. Clearly this particular language pattern is deeply engrained in our cultural mind.

Conclusions

By way of conclusion, consider the following statements. These are real headlines that linguist Steven Pinker (1994, p. 79) collected from various newspapers:

Child's Stool Great for Use in Garden

Stud Tires Out

Stiff Opposition Expected to Casketless Funeral Plan

Drunk Gets Nine Months in Violin Case

Iraqi Head Seeks Arms

Queen Mary Having Bottom Scraped

Columnist Gets Urologist in Trouble With His Peers

It's both mundane and amazing that we understand the double meanings and the underlying humor. The computational ability required to recognize these double entendres is innate and universal, but the content of each—or rather, its double content—and, more significantly, the fact that people find the phrases funny, is a consequence of social learning.

The complicated mental process that enables "generative grammar" is a universal human feature. But the lexicon of meanings available to individuals—the concepts through which they make sense of their experiences, encode these in memory, and feel about and act on them—derives from cultural learning. That is, we are interested in what is said, not said, and how it is said—what names do and don't exist and the evaluative-emotive components of those names. Different languages represent reality differently; particular languages highlight certain features of life and leave others in the haze of "preconceived" thought. Names/words/concepts reveal certain lines of action and possibilities to individual humans. In this way, although it may be theoretically possible for all humans to generate infinite and similar grammars and lexicons of meanings, it is not probable that members of a given culture will do so. And that which is unnamed is unknown. This idea has been summarized by the mathematician and philosopher Bertrand Russell: "Language serves not only to express thought but to make possible thoughts which could not exist without it."

The assertion that humans process all experience through socially constructed symbol systems has been a source of both caution and enthusiasm. This tension is expressed n the following quotation from a brooding poet in *Hyperion,* a science fiction novel (Simmons, 1990):

> Words are the supreme objects. They are minded things. As pure and transcendent as any idea that ever cast a shadow into Plato's dark cave of our perceptions. But they are also pitfalls of deceit and misperception. Words bend our thinking to infinite paths of self-delusion, and the fact that we spend most of our mental lives in brain mansions built of words means that we lack the objectivity necessary to see the terrible distortion of reality which language brings.... [Yet] here is the essence of [humankind's] creative genius: not the edifices of civilization nor the bang-flash weapons which can end it, but the *words* which fertilize new concepts.... You see, in the beginning was the Word. And the Word was made flesh in the weave of the human universe. Words are the only bullets in truth's bandolier. (pp. 190–191)

It is important to emphasize that the process of associating meaning with objects, persons, and events is an ongoing negotiation. In making sense of your world, you negotiate abstract meanings with others (interpersonal negotiation), and you negotiate with yourself to maintain a "fit" between your existing conceptual frameworks and concrete experience (intrapersonal negotiation). This negotiation is done through language: Even as you experience "unnamed" thoughts, emotions, and acts, you make sense of them by "fitting" them into the language categories available to you. For instance, if your culture has a category for "lover" that includes the default assumption that the pairing consists of one each of the two sexes, and you are paired with someone of the same sex, then you may find yourself without a "name" for this person when conversing with others who want to know about your attachments. Your experience may lead you to search for "alternative names" that stretch the category of "husband/wife" to include those who have same-sex partners. In this way, you are generating new concepts reflective of individual experience, but the fact that you have to search for a name for what you do is structured by the existing cultural classifications.

"Meaning" is not simply "out there"; it is something that is created and recreated through everyday interactions. The process reflects the complex interplay between individual experience and social structure. Individuals are constantly working to "fit" their individual thoughts and experiences into a form that can be expressed and shared with others. As you read the articles in this section, ask yourself the following: How do significant categories of language carve up my world? How do various concepts shape who I think I can be and what I think I can do? What are some of my default assumptions as a result of having absorbed the concepts of my culture? Am I aware that my language reflects a cultural value system?

References and Suggestions for Further Reading

Barthes, R. (1967). *Elements of semiology.* New York: Hill & Wang. (Original work published 1964)

Blumer, H. (1969). *Symbolic interactionism.* Englewood Cliffs, NJ: Prentice Hall.

Brown, R. (1986). *Social psychology* (2nd ed.). New York: Free Press.

Charon, J. (1989). *Symbolic interactionism* (3rd ed.). Englewood Cliffs, NJ: Prentice Hall.

Chomsky, N. (1972). *Language and the mind.* New York: Harcourt Brace Jovanovich.

Fine, G. (1990). Symbolic interactionism in the post-Blumerian age. In G. Ritzer (Ed.), *Frontiers of social theory* (pp. 117–157). New York: Columbia University Press.

Hofstadter, D. (1986). Changes in default words and images. In *Metamagical themas: Questing for the essence of mind and pattern* (pp. 136–158). New York: Bantam Books.

Langer, E. (1990). *Mindfulness.* Cambridge, MA: Da Capo Press.

Lee, D. (Ed.). (1980). *Wittgenstein's lectures, Cambridge 1930–1932.* Chicago: University of Chicago Press.

Lindesmith, A. R., Strauss, A. L., & Denzin, N. K. (Eds.). (1991). *Social psychology* (7th ed.). Englewood Cliffs, NJ: Prentice Hall.

Mead, G. H. (1934). *Mind, self, and society.* Chicago: University of Chicago Press.

Pinker, S. (1994). *The language instinct: How the mind creates language.* New York: HarperPerennial.

Sacks, O. (1987). *The man who mistook his wife for a hat.* New York: Harper & Row.

Sacks, O. (1989). *Seeing voices.* Berkeley: University of California Press.

Sapir, E. (1921). *Language.* New York: Harcourt, Brace and World.

Simmons, D. (1990). *Hyperion.* New York: Bantam.

Vygotsky, L. S. (1961). *Thought and language* (E. Hanfmann & G. Vahar, Trans.). Cambridge: MIT Press.

SYMBOL USE, LANGUAGE, AND DEVELOPMENT

The readings in this section are illustrations of a basic component of symbolic interactionism.

People respond to things, people, and situations in terms of the *meaning* they assign to the object, person, or event. We do not just respond to stimuli in our environment. We *interpret* the stimuli. Interpretation is an act of assigning meaning. The act of assigning a meaning or definition is known as *naming*. Language is the means for the process of making meaning and making sense of our environment. Language is an organized symbol system that enables us to think, imagine, learn vicariously, plan, direct our own behavior, and communicate with others. It is the basis of social life. Without language, individuals would not be able to learn or understand cultural expectations and would not be able to participate in social life. The study of the relationships among the brain, the mind, language, and culture is a fascinating area of research. The readings in this section illustrate some of the basic ideas that researchers agree on regarding language and social development.

In the classic essay "A Clue to the Nature of Man," philosopher Ernst Cassier describes humans as living in a symbolic world, a world of culturally created ideas, and not in a state of nature. He reminds us that it is our opinions and fancies of things that disturb (or delight) us, not the nature of the thing itself.

"Yes, Father-Sister" is a reading taken from the case files of the well-known neurologist Oliver Sacks. In this case, Sacks presents a woman who has lost the ability to "name" the people she encounters. She no longer recognizes the symbolic cues that enable her to place people into meaningful social categories.

"Final Note on a Case of Extreme Isolation" is a research note written by sociologist Kingsley Davis in 1947. Davis and his contemporaries were interested in the cases of children who had been raised in isolation from normal human interaction. When found, such children are considered more animal than human. They lack many of the basic signs of socialization that even severely developmentally delayed children raised in normal environments possess. Davis reviews the case of Anna and raises the question of whether it is possible for a child who is not exposed to human culture, especially language, by a certain age to ever become fully socialized.

READING QUESTIONS

1. Explain to someone the difference between responding to symbolic cues and responding directly to stimuli.

2. Practice slowing down your thinking in situations and see if you can catch yourself "interpreting" the situation.

(Continued)

(Continued)

3. When you encounter a stranger, what do you notice first in deciding what to think about the person?

4. Think of something that disturbs or frightens you. See if you can trace your feelings to your original experiences of "naming." Is your fear or disgust based on direct experience, or is it based on an idea that you learned from someone else?

5. Consider how often you imagine or think about someone you love. If you had no language or ability for abstract thought, could you remember that person when he or she was not in your presence?

6. Think of an example of something that you've learned vicariously. How much of what you know is based on others telling you things?

7. The forms we use for expressing language influence us as much as the content of the language. Consider how your life might be different if you lived in a culture that had no written language. How would such a culture pass on learning and knowledge? Do you think people in such a culture would have stronger or weaker abilities to memorize?

5

A Clue to the Nature of Man: The Symbol

Ernst Cassirer

(1944)

In the human world we find a new characteristic which appears to be the distinctive mark of human life. The functional circle of man is not only quantitatively enlarged; it has also undergone a qualitative change. Man has, as it were, discovered a new method of adapting himself to his environment. Between the receptor system and the effector system, which are to be found in all animal species, we find in man a third link which we may describe as the *symbolic system*. This new acquisition transforms the whole of human life. As compared with the other animals man lives not merely in a broader reality; he lives, so to speak, in a new *dimension* of reality. There is an unmistakable difference between organic reactions and human responses. In the first case a direct and immediate answer is given to an outward stimulus; in the second case the answer is delayed. It is interrupted and retarded by a slow and complicated process of thought. At first sight such a delay may appear to be a very questionable gain. Many philosophers have warned man against this pretended progress. "L'homme qui médite," says Rousseau, "est un animal dépravé": It is not an improvement but a deterioration of human nature to exceed the boundaries of organic life.

Yet there is no remedy against this reversal of the natural order. Man cannot escape from his own achievement. He cannot but adopt the conditions of his own life. No longer in a merely physical universe, man lives in a symbolic universe. Language, myth, art, and religion are parts of this universe. They are the varied threads which weave the symbolic net, the tangled web of human experience. All human progress in thought and experience refines upon and strengthens this net. No longer can man confront reality immediately; he cannot see it, as it were, face to face. Physical reality seems to recede in proportion as man's symbolic activity advances. Instead of dealing with the things themselves man is in a sense constantly conversing with himself. He has so enveloped himself in linguistic forms, in artistic images, in mythical symbols or religious rites that he cannot see or know anything except by the interposition of this artificial medium. His situation is the same in the theoretical as in the practical sphere. Even here man does not live in a world of hard facts, or according to his immediate needs and desires. He lives rather in the midst of imaginary emotions, in hopes and fears, in illusions and disillusions, in his fantasies and dreams. "What disturbs and alarms man," said Epictetus, "are not the things, but his opinions and fancies about the things."

From the point of view at which we have just arrived we may correct and enlarge the classical definition of man. In spite of all the efforts of modern irrationalism this definition of man as an *animal rationale* has not lost its force. Rationality is indeed an inherent feature of all human activities. Mythology itself is not simply a crude mass of superstitions or gross delusions. It is not merely chaotic, for it possesses a systematic or conceptual form.[1] But, on the other hand, it would be impossible to characterize the structure of myth as rational. Language has often been identified with reason, or with the very source of reason. But it is easy to see that this definition fails to cover the whole field. It is a *pars pro toto;* it offers us a part for the whole. For side by side with conceptual language there is an emotional language; side by side with logical or scientific language there is a language of poetic imagination. Primarily language does not express thoughts or ideas, but feelings and affections. And even a religion "within the limits of pure reason" as conceived and worked out by Kant is no more than a mere abstraction. It conveys only the ideal shape, only the shadow, of what

a genuine and concrete religious life is. The great thinkers who have defined man as an *animal rationale* were not empiricists, nor did they ever intend to give an empirical account of human nature. By this definition they were expressing rather a fundamental moral imperative. Reason is a very inadequate term with which to comprehend the forms of man's cultural life in all their richness and variety. But all these forms are symbolic forms. Hence, instead of defining man as an *animal rationale,* we should define him as an *animal symbolicum.* By so doing we can designate his specific difference, and we can understand the new way open to man—the way to civilization.

NOTE

---

1. See E. Cassirer (1922), *Die Begriffsform im mythischen Denken.* Leipzig: B. G. Teubner.

SYMBOL USE, LANGUAGE, AND DEVELOPMENT

6

Yes, Father-Sister

Oliver Sacks

(1970)

Mrs. B., a former research chemist, had presented with a rapid personality change, becoming "funny" (facetious, given to wisecracks and puns), impulsive—and "superficial." ("You feel she doesn't care about you," one of her friends said. "She no longer seems to care about anything at all.") At first it was thought that she might be hypomanic, but she turned out to have a cerebral tumor. At

craniotomy there was found, not a meningioma as had been hoped, but a huge carcinoma involving the orbitofrontal aspects of both frontal lobes.

When I saw her, she seemed high-spirited, volatile—"a riot" (the nurses called her)—full of quips and cracks, often clever and funny.

"Yes, Father," she said to me on one occasion.

"Yes, Sister," on another.

"Yes, Doctor," on a third.

She seemed to use the terms interchangeably.

"What *am* I?" I asked, stung, after a while.

"I see your face, your beard," she said. "I think of an Archimandrite Priest. I see your white uniform—I think of the Sisters. I see your stethoscope—I think of a doctor."

"You don't look at *all* of me?"

"No, I don't look at all of you."

"You realize the difference between a father, a sister, a doctor?"

"I *know* the difference, but it means nothing to me. Father, sister, doctor—what's the big deal?"

Thereafter, teasingly, she would say: "Yes, father-sister. Yes, sister-doctor," and other combinations.

Testing left-right discrimination was oddly difficult, because she said left or right indifferently (though there was not, in reaction, any confusion of the two, as when there is a lateralizing defect of perception or attention). When I drew her attention to this, she said: "Left/right. Right/left. Why the fuss? What's the difference?"

"*Is* there a difference?" I asked.

"Of course," she said, with a chemist's precision. "You could call them *enantio-morphs* of each other. But they mean nothing to *me*. They're no different for *me*. Hands . . . Doctors . . . Sisters . . . ," she added, seeing my puzzlement. "Don't you understand? They mean nothing—nothing to me. *Nothing means anything* . . . at least to me."

"And . . . this meaning nothing . . . ," I hesitated, afraid to go on, "This meaninglessness . . . does *this* bother you? Does *this* mean anything to you?"

"Nothing at all," she said promptly, with a bright smile, in the tone of one who makes a joke, wins an argument, wins at poker.

Was this denial? Was this a brave show? Was this the "cover" of some unbearable emotion? Her face bore no deeper expression whatever. Her world had been voided of feeling and meaning. Nothing any longer felt "real" (or "unreal"). Everything was now "equivalent" or "equal"—the whole world reduced to a facetious insignificance.

I found this somewhat shocking—her friends and family did too—but she herself, though not without insight, was uncaring, indifferent, even with a sort of funny-dreadful nonchalance or levity.

Mrs. B., though acute and intelligent, was somehow not present—"de-souled"—as a person. I was reminded of William Thompson (and also of Dr. P.). This is the effect of the "equalization" described by Luria. . . .

POSTSCRIPT

The sort of facetious indifference and "equalization" shown by this patient is not uncommon—German neurologists call it *Witzelsucht* ("joking disease"), and it was recognized as a fundamental form of nervous "dissolution" by Hughlings Jackson a century ago. It is not uncommon, whereas insight is—and the latter, perhaps mercifully, is lost as the "dissolution" progresses. I see many cases a year with similar phenomenology but the most varied etiologies. Occasionally I am not sure, at first, if the patient is just "being funny," clowning around, or schizophrenic. Thus, almost at random, I find the following in my notes on a patient with cerebral multiple sclerosis, whom I saw (but whose case I could not follow up) in 1981:

> She speaks very quickly, impulsively, and (it seems) indifferently . . . so that the important and the trivial, the true and the false, the serious and the joking, are poured out in a rapid, unselective, half-confabulatory stream. . . . She may contradict herself completely within a few seconds . . . will say she loves music, she doesn't, she has a broken hip, she hasn't. . . .

I concluded my observation on a note of uncertainty:

> How much is cryptannesia-confabulation, how much frontal-lobe indifference-equalization, how much some strange schizophrenic disintegration and shattering-flattening?

Of all forms of "schizophrenia" the "silly-happy," the so-called "hebephrenic," most resembles the organic amnestic and frontal lobe syndromes. They are the most malignant, and the least imaginable— and no one returns from such states to tell us what they were like.

In all these states—"funny" and often ingenious as they appear—the world is taken apart, undermined, reduced to anarchy and chaos. There ceases to be any "center" to the mind, though its formal intellectual powers may be perfectly preserved. The end point of such states is an unfathomable "silliness," an abyss of superficiality, in which all is ungrounded and afloat and comes apart. Luria once spoke of the mind as reduced, in such states, to "mere Brownian movement." I share the sort of horror he clearly felt about them (though this incites, rather than impedes, their accurate description). They make me think, first, of Borges' "Funes," and his remark, "My memory, Sir, is like a garbage-heap," and finally, of the *Dunciad,* the vision of a world reduced to Pure Silliness—Silliness as being the End of the World:

Thy hand, great Anarch, lets the curtain fall;
And Universal Darkness buries All.

SYMBOL USE, LANGUAGE, AND DEVELOPMENT

7

Final Note on a Case of Extreme Isolation

Kingsley Davis

(1947)

Early in 1940 there appeared . . . an account of a girl called Anna.[1] She had been deprived of normal contact and had received a minimum of human care for almost the whole of her first six years of life. At this time observations were not complete and the report had a tentative character. Now, however, the girl is dead, and with more information available,[2] it is possible to give a fuller and more definitive description of the case from a sociological point of view.

Anna's death, caused by hemorrhagic jaundice, occurred on August 6, 1942. Having been born on March 1 or 6,[3] 1932, she was approximately ten and a half years of age when she died. The previous report covered her development up to the age of almost eight years; the present one recapitulates the earlier period on the basis of new evidence and then covers the last two and a half years of her life.

EARLY HISTORY

The first few days and weeks of Anna's life were complicated by frequent changes of domicile. It will be recalled that she was an illegitimate child, the second such child born to her mother, and that her grandfather, a widowed farmer in whose house her mother lived, strongly disapproved of this new evidence of the mother's indiscretion. This fact led to the baby's being shifted about.

Two weeks after being born in a nurse's private home, Anna was brought to the family farm, but the grandfather's antagonism was so great that she was shortly taken to the house of one of her mother's friends. At this time a local minister became interested in her and took her to his house with an idea of possible adoption. He decided against adoption, however, when he discovered that she had vaginitis. The infant was then taken to a children's home in the nearest large city. This agency found that at the age of only three weeks she was already in a miserable condition, being "terribly galled and otherwise in very bad shape." It did not regard her as a likely subject for adoption but took her in for a while anyway, hoping to benefit her. After Anna had spent nearly eight weeks in this place, the agency notified her mother to come to get her. The mother responded by sending a man and his wife to the children's home with a view to their adopting Anna, but they made such a poor impression on the agency that permission was refused. Later the mother came herself and took the child out of the home and then gave her to this couple. It was in the home of this pair that a social worker found the girl a short time thereafter. The social worker went to the mother's home and pleaded with Anna's grandfather to allow the mother to bring the child home. In spite of threats, he refused. The child, by then more than four months old, was next taken to another children's home in a near-by town. A medical examination at this time revealed that she had impetigo, vaginitis, umbilical hernia, and a skin rash.

Anna remained in this second children's home for nearly three weeks, at the end of which time she was transferred to a private foster-home. Since, however, the grandfather would not, and the mother could not, pay for the child's care, she was finally taken back as a last resort to the grandfather's house (at the age of five and a half months). There she remained, kept on the second floor in an attic-like room because her mother hesitated to incur the grandfather's wrath by bringing her downstairs.

The mother, a sturdy woman weighing about 180 pounds, did a man's work on the farm. She engaged in heavy work such as milking cows and tending hogs and had little time for her children. Sometimes she went out at night, in which case Anna was left entirely without attention. Ordinarily, it seems, Anna received only enough care to keep her barely alive. She appears to have been seldom moved from one position to another. Her clothing and bedding were filthy. She apparently had no instruction, no friendly attention.

It is little wonder that, when finally found and removed from the room in the grandfather's house at the age of nearly six years, the child could not talk, walk, or do anything that showed intelligence. She was in an extremely emaciated and undernourished condition, with skeletonlike legs and a bloated abdomen. She had been fed on virtually nothing except cow's milk during the years under her mother's care.

Anna's condition when found, and her subsequent improvement, have been described in the previous report. It now remains to say what happened to her after that.

LATER HISTORY

In 1939, nearly two years after being discovered, Anna had progressed, as previously reported, to the point where she could walk, understand simple commands, feed herself, achieve some neatness, remember people, etc. But she still did not speak, and, though she was much more like a normal infant of something over one year of age in mentality, she was far from normal for her age.

On August 30, 1939, she was taken to a private home for retarded children, leaving the county home where she had been for more than a year and a half. In her new setting she made some further progress, but not a great deal. In a report of an examination made November 6 of the same year, the head of the institution pictured the child as follows:

> Anna walks about aimlessly, makes periodic rhythmic motions of her hands, and, at intervals, makes guttural and sucking noises. She regards her hands as if she had seen them for the first time. It was impossible to hold her attention for more than a few seconds at a time—not because of distraction due to external stimuli but because of her inability to concentrate. She ignored the task in hand to gaze vacantly about the room. Speech is entirely lacking. Numerous unsuccessful attempts have been made with her in the hope of developing initial sounds. I do not believe that this failure is due to negativism or deafness but that she is not sufficiently developed to accept speech at this time. . . . The prognosis is not favorable. . . .

More than five months later, on April 25, 1940, a clinical psychologist, the late Professor Francis N. Maxfield, examined Anna and reported the following: large for her age; hearing "entirely normal"; vision apparently normal; able to climb stairs; speech in the "babbling stage" and "promise for developing intelligible speech later seems to be good." He said further that "on the Merrill-Palmer scale she made a mental score of 19 months. On the Vineland social maturity scale she made a score of 23 months."[4]

Professor Maxfield very sensibly pointed out that prognosis is difficult in such cases of isolation. "It is very difficult to take scores on tests standardized under average conditions of environment and experience," he wrote, "and interpret them in a case where environment and experience have been so unusual." With this warning he gave it as his opinion at that time that Anna would eventually "attain an adult mental level of six or seven years."[5]

The school for retarded children, on July 1, 1941, reported that Anna had reached 46 inches in height and weighed 60 pounds. She could bounce and catch a ball and was said to conform to group socialization, though as a follower rather than a leader. Toilet habits were firmly established. Food habits were normal, except that she still used a spoon as her sole implement. She could dress herself except for fastening her clothes. Most remarkable of all, she had finally begun to develop speech. She was characterized as being at about the two-year level in this regard. She could call attendants by name and bring in one when she was asked to. She had a few complete sentences to express her wants. The report concluded that there was nothing peculiar about her, except that she was feeble-minded— "probably congenital in type."[6]

A final report from the school made on June 22, 1942, and evidently the last report before the girl's death, pictured only a slight advance over that given above. It said that Anna could follow directions, string beads, identify a few colors, build with blocks, and differentiate between attractive and unattractive pictures. She had a good sense of rhythm and loved a doll. She talked mainly in phrases but would repeat words and try to carry on a conversation. She was clean about clothing. She habitually washed her hands and brushed her teeth. She would try to help other children. She walked well and could run fairly well, though clumsily. Although easily excited, she had a pleasant disposition.

INTERPRETATION

Such was Anna's condition just before her death. It may seem as if she had not made much progress, but one must remember the condition in which she had been found. One must recall that she had no glimmering of speech, absolutely no ability to walk, no sense of gesture, not the least capacity to feed herself even when the food was put in front of her, and no comprehension of cleanliness. She was so apathetic that it was hard to tell whether or not she could hear. And all this at the age of nearly six years. Compared with this condition, her capacities at the time of her death seem striking indeed, though they do not amount to much more than a two-and-a-half-year mental level. One conclusion therefore seems safe, namely, that her isolation prevented a considerable amount of mental development that was undoubtedly part of her capacity. Just what her original capacity was, of course, is hard to say; but her development after her period of confinement (including the ability to walk and run, to play, dress, fit into a social situation, and, above all, to speak) shows that she had at least this capacity—capacity that never could have been realized in her original condition of isolation.

A further question is this: What would she have been like if she had received a normal upbringing from the moment of birth? A definitive answer would have been impossible in any case, but even an approximate answer is made difficult by her early death. If one assumes, as was tentatively surmised in the previous report, that it is "almost impossible for any child to learn to speak, think, and act like a normal person after a long period of early isolation," it seems likely that Anna might have had a normal or near-normal capacity, genetically speaking. On the other hand, it was pointed out that Anna represented "a marginal case, [because] she was discovered before she had reached six years of age," an age "young enough to allow for some plasticity."[7] While admitting, then, that Anna's isolation may have been the major cause (and was certainly a minor cause) of her lack of rapid mental progress during the four and a half years following her rescue from neglect, it is necessary to entertain the hypothesis that she was congenitally deficient.

In connection with this hypothesis, one suggestive though by no means conclusive circumstance needs consideration, namely, the mentality of Anna's forebears. Information on this subject is easier to obtain, as one might guess, on the mother's than on the father's side. Anna's maternal grandmother, for example, is said to have been college educated and wished to have her children receive a good education; but her husband, Anna's stern grandfather, apparently a shrewd, hard-driving, calculating farmowner, was so penurious that her ambitions in this direction were thwarted. Under the circumstances her daughter (Anna's mother) managed, despite having to do hard work on the farm, to complete the eighth grade in a country school. Even so, however, the daughter was evidently not very smart. "A schoolmate of [Anna's mother] stated that she was retarded in school work; was very gullible at this age; and that her morals even at this time were discussed by other students." Two tests administered to her on March 4, 1938, when she was thirty-two years of age, showed that she was mentally deficient. On the Stanford Revision of the Binet-Simon Scale her performance was equivalent to that of a child of eight years, giving her an I.Q. of 50 and indicating mental deficiency of "middle-grade moron type."[8]

As to the identity of Anna's father, the most persistent theory holds that he was an old man about seventy-four years of age at the time of the girl's birth. If he was the one, there is no indication of mental or other biological deficiency, whatever one may think of his morals. However, someone else may actually have been the father.

To sum up: Anna's heredity is the kind that *might* have given rise to innate mental deficiency, though not necessarily.

COMPARISON WITH ANOTHER CASE

Perhaps more to the point than speculations about Anna's ancestry would be a case for comparison. If a child could be discovered who had been isolated about the same length of time as Anna but had achieved a much quicker recovery and a greater mental development, it would be a stronger indication that Anna was deficient to start with.

Such a case does exist. It is the case of a girl found at about the same time as Anna and under strikingly similar circumstances. A full description of the details of this case has not been published, but in addition to newspaper reports, an excellent preliminary account by a speech specialist, Dr. Marie K. Mason, who played an important role in the handling of the child, has appeared.[9] Also the late Dr. Francis N. Maxfield, clinical psychologist at Ohio State University, as was Dr. Mason, has written an as yet unpublished but penetrating analysis of the case.[10] Some of his observations have been included in Professor Zingg's book on feral man.[11] The following discussion is drawn mainly from these enlightening materials. The writer, through the kindness of Professors Mason and Maxfield, did have a chance to observe the girl in April, 1940, and to discuss the features of her case with them.

> Born apparently one month later than Anna, the girl in question, who has been given the pseudonym Isabelle, was discovered in November, 1938, nine months after the discovery of Anna. At the time she was found she was approximately six and a half years of age. Like Anna, she was an illegitimate child and had been kept in seclusion for that reason. Her mother was a deaf-mute, having become so at the age of two, and it appears that she and Isabelle had spent most of their time together in a dark room shut off from the rest of the mother's family. As a result Isabelle had no chance to develop speech; when she communicated with her mother, it was by means of gestures. Lack of sunshine and inadequacy of diet had caused Isabelle to become rachitic. Her legs in particular were affected; they were so bowed that as she stood erect the soles of her shoes came nearly flat together, and she got about with a skittering gait.[12]

Her behavior toward strangers, especially men, was almost that of a wild animal, manifesting much fear and hostility. In lieu of speech she made only a strange croaking sound. In many ways she acted like an infant. "She was apparently utterly unaware of relationships of any kind. When presented with a ball for the first time, she held it in the palm of her hand, then reached out and stroked my face with it. Such behavior is comparable to that of a child of six months."[13] At first it was even hard to tell whether or not she could hear, so unused were her senses. Many of her actions resembled those of deaf children.

It is small wonder that, once it was established that she could hear, specialists working with her believed her to be feeble-minded. Even on nonverbal tests her performance was so low as to promise little for the future. Her first score on the Stanford-Binet was 19 months, practically at the zero point of the scale. On the Vineland social maturity scale her first score was 39, representing an age level of two and a half years.[14] "The general impression was that she was wholly uneducable and that any attempt to teach her to speak, after so long a period of silence, would meet with failure."[15]

In spite of this interpretation, the individuals in charge of Isabelle launched a systematic and skillful program of training. It seemed hopeless at first. The approach had to be through pantomime and dramatization, suitable to an infant. It required one week of intensive effort before she even made her first attempt at vocalization. Gradually, she began to respond, however, and, after the first hurdles had at last been overcome, a curious thing happened. She went through the usual stages of learning characteristic of the years from one to six not only in proper succession but far more rapidly than normal. In a little over two months after her first vocalization she was putting sentences together. Nine months after that she could identify words and sentences on the printed page, could write well, could add to ten, and could retell a story after hearing it. Seven months beyond this point she had a vocabulary of 1,500–2,000 words and was asking complicated questions. Starting from an educational level of between one and three years (depending on what aspect one considers), she had reached a normal level by the time she was eight and a half years old. In short, she covered in two years the stages of learning that ordinarily require six.[16] Or, to put it another way, her I.Q. trebled in a year and a half.[17]

The speed with which she reached the normal level of mental development seems analogous to the recovery of body weight in a growing child after an illness, the recovery being achieved by an extra fast rate of growth for a period after the illness until normal weight for the given age is again attained.

When the writer saw Isabelle a year and a half after her discovery, she gave him the impression of being a very bright, cheerful, energetic little girl. She spoke well, walked and ran without trouble, and sang with gusto and accuracy. Today she is over fourteen years old and has passed the sixth grade in a public school. Her teachers say that she participates in all school activities as normally as other children. Though older than her classmates, she has fortunately not physically matured too far beyond their level.[18]

Clearly the history of Isabelle's development is different from that of Anna's. In both cases there was an exceedingly low, or rather blank, intellectual level to begin with. In both cases it seemed that the girl might be congenitally feeble-minded. In both a considerably higher level was reached later on. But the Ohio girl achieved a normal mentality within two years, whereas Anna was still marked inadequate at the end of four and a half years. This difference in achievement may suggest that Anna had less initial capacity. But an alternative hypothesis is possible.

One should remember that Anna never received the prolonged and expert attention that Isabelle received. The result of such attention, in the case of the Ohio girl, was to give her speech at an early stage, and her subsequent rapid development seems to have been a consequence of that. "Until Isabelle's speech and language development, she had all the characteristics of a feeble-minded child." Had Anna, who, from the standpoint of psychometric tests and early history, closely resembled this girl at the start, been given a mastery of speech at an earlier point by intensive training, her subsequent development might have been much more rapid.[19]

The hypothesis that Anna began with a sharply inferior mental capacity is therefore not established. Even if she were deficient to start with, we have no way of knowing how much so. Under ordinary conditions she might have been a dull normal or, like her mother, a moron. Even after the blight of her isolation, if she had lived to maturity, she might have finally reached virtually the full level of her capacity, whatever it may have been. That her isolation did have a profound effect upon her mentality, there can be no doubt. This is proved by the substantial degree of change during the four and a half years following her rescue.

Consideration of Isabelle's case serves to show, as Anna's case does not clearly show, that isolation up to the age of six, with failure to acquire any form of speech and hence failure to grasp nearly the whole world of cultural meaning, does not preclude the subsequent acquisition of these. Indeed, there seems to be a process of accelerated recovery in which the child goes through the mental stages at a more rapid rate than would be the case in normal development. Just what would be the maximum age at which a person could remain isolated and still retain the capacity for full cultural acquisition is hard to say. Almost certainly it would not be as high as age fifteen; it might possibly be as low as age ten. Undoubtedly various individuals would differ considerably as to the exact age.

Anna's is not an ideal case for showing the effects of extreme isolation, partly because she was possibly deficient to begin with, partly because she did not receive the best training available, and partly because she did not live long enough. Nevertheless, her case is instructive when placed in the record with numerous other cases of extreme isolation. This and the previous article about her are meant to place her in the record. It is to be hoped that other cases will be described in the scientific literature as they are discovered (as unfortunately they will be), for only in these rare cases of extreme isolation is it possible "to observe *concretely separated* two factors in the development of human personality which are always otherwise only analytically separated, the biogenic and the sociogenic factors."[20]

NOTES

1. K. Davis (1940, January), "Extreme social isolation of a child," *American Journal of Sociology,* 45, 554–565.

2. Sincere appreciation is due to the officials in the Department of Welfare, Commonwealth of Pennsylvania, for their kind co-operation in making available the records concerning Anna and discussing the case frankly with the writer. Helen C. Hubbell, Florentine Hackbusch, and Eleanor Mecklenburg were particularly helpful, as was Fanny L. Matchette. Without their aid neither of the reports on Anna could have been written.

3. The records are not clear as to which day.

4. Letter to one of the state officials in charge of the case.

5. Ibid.

6. Progress report of the school.

7. Davis (1940), p. 564.

8. The facts set forth here as to Anna's ancestry are taken chiefly from a report of mental tests administered to Anna's mother by psychologists at a state hospital where she was taken for this purpose after the discovery of Anna's seclusion. This excellent report was not available to the writer when the previous paper on Anna was published.

9. M. K. Mason (1942), "Learning to speak after six and one-half years of silence," *Journal of Speech Disorders, 7,* 295–304.

10. F. N. Maxfield (no date), "What happens when the social environment of a child approaches zero." Unpublished manuscript. The writer is greatly indebted to Mrs. Maxfield and to Professor Horace B. English, a colleague of Professor Maxfield, for the privilege of seeing this manuscript and other materials collected on isolated and feral individuals.

11. J. A. L. Singh & R. M. Zingg (1941), *Wolf-children and feral man.* New York: Harper & Bros., pp. 248–251.

12. Maxfield (no date).

13. Mason (1942), p. 299.

14. Maxfield (no date).

15. Mason (1942), p. 299.

16. Mason (1942), pp. 300–304.

17. Maxfield (no date).

18. Based on a personal letter from Dr. Mason to the writer, May 13, 1946.

19. This point is suggested in a personal letter from Dr. Mason to the writer, October 22, 1946.

20. Singh & Zingg (1941), pp. xxi–xxii, in a foreword by the writer.

CATEGORIZATION, LANGUAGE, AND CULTURE

When we learn language, we also acquire a kind of social encyclopedia that provides us with an entire system of cultural knowledge. The way we talk about things shapes our experiences. Language directs our focus—what we pay attention to and what we ignore. Language also shapes our values and our perceptions. Language can be dissected and examined to reveal underlying cultural beliefs and value systems.

Ellen Langer is a psychologist who studies the ways in which we organize our understanding and experience through language-based categories. "Mindfulness and Mindlessness" is an excerpt from her book on the subject. In this selection, she describes the usefulness of categorical thinking and its relationship to cognitive efficiency (we don't have to think every thought anew all the time). She also illustrates some of the pitfalls of categorical thinking. The reading includes some memorable examples of the problems that can occur when we switch to "automatic pilot" or become "mindless."

"Metaphors We Live By" is written by two psycholinguists, George Lakoff and Mark Johnson. They provide several illustrations of the ways in which metaphors shape our thinking and behavior. For example, the metaphor of "time is money" leads us to organize our behavior in terms of "not wasting time," "saving time," and so forth. We even "spend" time with others.

"Racism in the English Language" is a dissection of language asymmetries and metaphors that convey a cultural value system. Readers are usually surprised at the many examples Robert Moore writes about. Many of these illustrations are aspects of language people rarely think about. Taken together, however, the cultural message indicates deeply entrenched meanings and values.

READING QUESTIONS

1. According to Langer, what are some of the pros and cons of categorical thinking? Consider some examples of "mindlessness" in your own daily routines.

2. Make a list of some of the metaphors discussed by Lakoff and Johnson. Try inserting new words that convey a different meaning. For example, consider the expression, "I'd like to *share* some time with you" rather than "*spend* some time with you."

3. Make a list of "language asymmetries" (see Part II, p. 66, and Reading 10 for definitions) and consider what underlying cultural values these asymmetries indicate.

4. Consider the use of the masculine *he* or *man* to refer to all people. Some people say that this "generic use" is perfectly acceptable because the terms "imply" women as well as men. Others argue that the term not only leaves out half the population, but also perpetuates an image of women as "auxiliary" and men as "central." Discuss this.

5. Discuss the cultural practice of women taking men's names when they marry. What cultural values does this practice convey?

CATEGORIZATION, LANGUAGE, AND CULTURE

8

Mindfulness and Mindlessness

Ellen Langer

(1990)

INTRODUCTION

I don't like the idea of a unitary subject; I prefer the play of a kaleidoscope: you give it a tap and the little bits of colored glass form a new pattern.

—Roland Barthes,
The Grain of the Voice

One day, at a nursing home in Connecticut, elderly residents were each given a choice of houseplants to care for and were asked to make a number of small decisions about their daily routines. A year and a half later, not only were these people more cheerful, active, and alert than a similar group in the same institution who were not given these choices and responsibilities, but many more of them were still alive. In fact, less than half as many of the decision-making, plant-minding residents had died as had those in the other group. This experiment, with its startling results, began over ten years of research into the powerful effects of what my colleagues and I came to call *mindfulness,* and of its counterpart, the equally powerful but destructive state of *mindlessness.*[1] . . .

Social psychologists usually look for the ways in which behavior depends on context. When mindless, however, people treat information as though it were *context-free*—true regardless of circumstances. For example, take the statement: Heroin is

dangerous. How true is this for a dying individual in intolerable pain?

Once alerted to the dangers of mindlessness and to the possibility of bringing about a more mindful attitude by such deceptively simple measures as those used in the nursing home experiment, I began to see this double-edged phenomenon at work in many different settings. For instance, consider the events that led to the 1985 crash of an Air Florida plane that killed seventy-four passengers. It was a routine flight from Washington, D.C., to Florida with an experienced flight crew. Pilot and copilot were in excellent physical health. Neither was tired, stressed, or under the influence. What went wrong? An extensive examination pointed to the crew's pre-takeoff control checks. As the copilot calls out each control on his list, the pilot makes sure the switches are where he wants them to be. One of these controls is an anti-icer. On this day, the pilot and copilot went over each of the controls as they had always done. They went through their routine and checked "off" when the anti-icer was mentioned. This time, however, the flight was different from their experience. This time they were not flying in the usual warm southern weather. It was icy outside.

As he went through the control checks, one by one as he always did, the pilot appeared to be thinking when he was not.[2] The pre-takeoff routines of pilot and copilot have a lot in common with the tiresome safety demonstrations of flight attendants to experienced, glassy-eyed passengers. When we blindly follow routines or unwittingly carry out senseless orders, we are acting like automatons, with potentially grave consequences for ourselves and others.

When the Light's On and Nobody's Home

Out of time we cut "days" and "nights," "summers" and "winters." We say what each part of the sensible continuum is, and all these abstract whats are concepts.

The intellectual life of man consists almost wholly in his substitution of a conceptual order for the perceptual order in which his experience originally comes.

—William James,
"The World We Live In"

Imagine that it's two o'clock in the morning. Your doorbell rings; you get up, startled, and make your way downstairs. You open the door and see a man standing before you. He wears two diamond rings and a fur coat, and there's a Rolls Royce behind him. He's sorry to wake you at this ridiculous hour, he tells you, but he's in the middle of a scavenger hunt. His ex-wife is in the same contest, which makes it very important to him that he win. He needs a piece of wood about three feet by seven feet. Can you help him? In order to make it worthwhile he'll give you $10,000. You believe him. He's obviously rich. And so you say to yourself, how in the world can I get this piece of wood for him? You think of the lumber yard; you don't know who owns the lumber yard; in fact you're not even sure where the lumber yard is. It would be closed at two o'clock in the morning anyway. You struggle but you can't come up with anything. Reluctantly, you tell him, "Gee, I'm sorry."

The next day, when passing a construction site near a friend's house, you see a piece of wood that's just about the right size, three feet by seven feet—a door. You could have just taken a door off its hinges and given it to him, for $10,000.

Why on earth, you say to yourself, didn't it occur to you to do that? It didn't occur to you because yesterday your door was not a piece of wood. The seven-by-three-foot piece of wood was hidden from you, stuck in the category called "door."

This kind of mindlessness, which usually takes more humdrum forms—"Why didn't I think of Susan? She can unclog sinks"—could be called "entrapment by category." It is one of three definitions that can help us understand the nature of mindlessness. The other two, which we will also explain, are automatic behavior and acting from a single perspective.

Trapped by Categories

We experience the world by creating categories and making distinctions among them. "This is a Chinese, not a Japanese, vase." "No, he's only a freshman." "The white orchids are endangered." "She's his boss now." In this way, we make a picture of the world, and of ourselves. Without categories the world might seem to escape us. Tibetan Buddhists call this habit of mind "The Lord of Speech":

We adopt sets of categories which serve as ways of managing phenomena. The most fully developed products of this tendency are ideologies, the systems of ideas that rationalize, justify, and sanctify our lives. Nationalism, communism, existentialism, Christianity, Buddhism—all provide us with identities, rules of action, and interpretations of how and why things happen as they do.[3]

The creation of new categories, as we will see throughout this book, is a mindful activity. Mindlessness sets in when we rely too rigidly on categories and distinctions created in the past (masculine/feminine, old/young, success/failure). Once distinctions are created, they take on a life of their own. Consider: (1) First there was earth.

(2) Then there was land, sea, and sky. (3) Then there were countries. (4) Then there was Germany. (5) Now there is East Germany versus West Germany. The categories we make gather momentum and are very hard to overthrow. We build our own and our shared realities and then we become victims of them—blind to the fact that they are constructs, ideas.

If we look back at the categories of an earlier age, once firmly established, it is easier to see why new ones might become necessary. The Argentinean writer Jorge Luis Borges quotes from an ancient Chinese encyclopedia in which the animals are classified as "(a) belonging to the Emperor, (b) embalmed, (c) tame, (d) suckling pigs, (e) sirens, (f) stray dogs, (g) included in the present classification, (h) frenzied, (i) innumerable, (j) drawn with a very fine camel brush, (k) et cetera, (l) having just broken the water pitcher, (m) that from a long way off look like flies."[4] To be mindless is to be trapped in a rigid world in which certain creatures always belong to the Emperor, Christianity is always good, certain people are forever untouchable, and doors are only doors.

AUTOMATIC BEHAVIOR

Have you ever said "excuse me" to a store mannequin or written a check in January with the previous year's date? When in this mode, we take in and use limited signals from the world around us (the female form, the familiar face of the check) without letting other signals (the motionless pose, a calendar) penetrate as well.

Once, in a small department store, I gave a cashier a new credit card. Noticing that I hadn't signed it, she handed it back to me to sign. Then she took my card, passed it through her machine, handed me the resulting form, and asked me to sign it. I did as I was told. The cashier then held the form next to the newly signed card to see if the signatures matched.

Modern psychology has not paid much attention to how much complicated action may be performed automatically, yet as early as 1896 Leon Solomons and Gertrude Stein looked into this question. (This was *the* Gertrude Stein who, from 1893 to 1898, was a graduate student in experimental psychology at Harvard University, working under William James.) They studied what was then called "double personalities" and which later came to be known as "split personalities," and proposed that the mindless performance of the second personality was essentially similar to that of ordinary people. Ordinary people also engage in a great deal of complex behavior without consciously paying attention to it. Solomons and Stein conducted several experiments in which they were their own subjects, demonstrating that both writing and reading could be done automatically. They succeeded in writing English words while they were otherwise caught up in reading an absorbing story. With much practice, they were even able to take dictation automatically while reading. Afterward, they were completely unable to recall the words they had written but were nevertheless quite certain they had written something. To show that reading could take place automatically, the subject read aloud from a book while a captivating story was read to him or her. Again they found that, after a lot of practice, they could read aloud unhampered while giving full attention to the story being read to them.

Solomons and Stein concluded that a vast number of actions that we think of as intelligent, such as reading and writing, can be done quite automatically: "We have shown a general tendency on the part of normal people, to *act,* without any express desire or conscious volition, in a manner in general accord with the *previous habits* of the person."[5]

An experiment I conducted in 1978 with fellow psychologists Benzion Chanowitz and Arthur Blank explored this kind of mindlessness.[6] Our setting was the Graduate Center at the City University of New York. We approached people using a copying machine and asked whether they would let us copy something then and there. We gave reasons that were either sound or senseless. An identical response to both sound and senseless requests would show that our subjects were not thinking about what was being said. We made one of three requests: "Excuse me, may I use the Xerox machine?"; "Excuse me, may I use the Xerox machine because I want to make copies?"; "Excuse me, may I use the Xerox machine because I'm in a rush?"

The first and second requests are the same in *content*—What else would one do with a copying machine except make copies? Therefore if people were considering what was actually being said, the first two requests should be equally effective. Structurally, however, they are different. The redundant request ("Excuse me, may I use the Xerox machine because I want to make copies?") is more similar to the last one ("Excuse me, may I use the Xerox machine because I'm in a rush?") in that both state the request and give a reason. If people comply with the last two requests in equal numbers, this implies attention to structure rather than conscious attention to content. That, in fact, was just what we found. There was more compliance when a reason was given—whether the reason sounded legitimate or silly. People responded mindlessly to the familiar framework rather than mindfully attending to the content.

Of course, there are limits to this. If someone asked for a very large favor or if the excuse were unusually absurd ("because an elephant is after me"), the individual would be likely to think about what was said. It is not that people don't hear the request the rest of the time; they simply don't think about it actively.

In a similar experiment, we sent an interdepartmental memo around some university offices. The message either requested or demanded the return of the memo to a designated room—and that was all it said.[7] ("Please return this immediately to Room 247," or "This memo is to be returned to Room 247.") Anyone who read such a memo mindfully would ask, "If whoever sent the memo wanted it, why did he or she send it?" and therefore would not return the memo. Half of the memos were designed to look exactly like those usually sent between departments. The other half were made to look in some way different. When the memo looked like those they were used to, 90 percent of the recipients actually returned it. When the memo looked different, 60 percent returned it.

When I was discussing these studies at a university colloquium, a member of the audience told me about a little con game that operated along the same lines. Someone placed an ad in a Los Angeles newspaper that read, "It's not too late to send $1 to _____," and gave the person's own name and address. The reader was promised nothing in return. Many people replied, enclosing a dollar. The person who wrote the ad apparently earned a good sum.

The automatic behavior in evidence in these examples has much in common with habit.[8] Habit, or the tendency to keep on with behavior that has been repeated over time, naturally implies mindlessness. However, as we will see . . . mindless behavior can arise without a long history of repetition, almost instantaneously, in fact.

ACTING FROM A SINGLE PERSPECTIVE

So often in our lives, we act as though there were only one set of rules. For instance, in cooking we tend to follow recipes with dutiful precision. We add ingredients as though by official decree. If the recipe calls for a pinch of salt and four pinches fall in, panic strikes, as though the bowl might now explode. Thinking of a recipe only as a rule, we often do not consider how people's tastes vary, or what fun it might be to make up a new dish.

The first experiment I conducted in graduate school explored this problem of the single perspective. It was a pilot study to examine the effectiveness of different requests for help. A fellow investigator stood on a busy sidewalk and told people passing by that she had sprained her knee and needed help. If someone stopped she asked him or her to get an Ace bandage from the nearby drugstore. I stood inside the store and listened while the helpful person gave the request to the pharmacist, who had agreed earlier to say that he was out of Ace bandages. After being told this, not one subject, out of the twenty-five we studied, thought to ask if the pharmacist could recommend something else. People left the drugstore and returned empty-handed to the "victim" and told her the news. We speculated that had she asked for less specific help, she might have received it. But, acting on the single thought that a sprained knee needs an Ace bandage, no one tried to find other kinds of help.

As a little test of how a narrow perspective can dominate our thinking, read the following sentence:

FINAL FOLIOS SEEM TO RESULT FROM YEARS OF DUTIFUL STUDY OF TEXTS ALONG WITH YEARS OF SCIENTIFIC EXPERIENCE.

Now count how many Fs there are, reading only once more through the sentence.

If you find fewer than there actually are (the answer is given in the notes),[9] your counting was probably influenced by the fact that the first two words in the sentence begin with F. In counting, your mind would tend to cling to this clue, or single perspective, and miss some of the Fs hidden within and at the end of words.

Highly specific instructions such as these or the request for an Ace bandage encourage mindlessness. Once we let them in, our minds snap shut like a clam on ice and do not let in new signals.

NOTES

1. E. Langer & J. Rodin (1976), "The effects of enhanced personal responsibility for the aged: A field experiment in an institutional setting," *Journal of Personality and Social Psychology, 34,* 191–198; J. Rodin & E. Langer (1977), "Long-term effects of a control-relevant intervention among the institutionalized aged," *Journal of Personality and Social Psychology, 35,* 897–902.

2. C. Gersick & J. R. Hackman (1990), "Habitual routines in task-performing groups," *Organizational Behavior and Human Decision Processes, 47,* 65–97.

3. C. Trungpa (1973), *Cutting through spiritual materialism,* Boulder & London: Shambhala.

4. T'ai P'ing (978), Kuang chi [Extensive records made in the period of peace and prosperity]; cited in J. L. Borges (1967), *Libro de los seres imaginarios,* Buenos Aires: Editorial Kiersa S. A., Fauna China, p. 88.

5. L. Solomons & G. Stein (1896), "Normal motor automation," *Psychological Review, 36,* 492–572.

6. E. Langer, A. Blank, & B. Chanowitz (1978), "The mindlessness of ostensibly thoughtful action: The role of placebic information in interpersonal interaction," *Journal of Personality and Social Psychology, 36,* 635–642.

7. Langer et al. (1978).

8. To understand the more complex relationship between automatic information processing and mindlessness, compare E. Langer (1989), "Minding matters," in L. Berkowitz (Ed.), *Advances in experimental social psychology* (pp. 137–173), New York: Academic Press; and W. Schneider & R. M. Schiffrin (1977), "Controlled and automatic human information processing: I. Detection, search, and attention," *Psychological Review, 84,* 1–66.

9. The correct answer is 8. A similar quiz was printed on the business card of the Copy Service of Miami, Inc.

9

Metaphors We Live By

George Lakoff and Mark Johnson

(1980)

The concepts that govern our thought are not just matters of the intellect. They also govern our everyday functioning, down to the most mundane details. Our concepts structure what we perceive, how we get around in the world, and how we relate to other people. Our conceptual system thus plays a central role in defining our everyday realities. If we are right in suggesting that our conceptual system is largely metaphorical, then the way we think, what we experience, and what we do everyday is very much a matter of metaphor.

But our conceptual system is not something we are normally aware of. In most of the little things we do everyday, we simply think and act more or less automatically along certain lines. Just what these lines are is by no means obvious. One way to find out is by looking at language. Since communication is based on the same conceptual system that we use in thinking and acting, language is an important source of evidence for what that system is like.

Primarily on the basis of linguistic evidence, we have found that most of our ordinary conceptual system is metaphorical in nature. And we have found a way to begin to identify in detail just what the metaphors are that structure how we perceive, how we think, and what we do.

To give some idea of what it could mean for a concept to be metaphorical and for such a concept to structure an everyday activity, let us start with the concept ARGUMENT and the conceptual metaphor ARGUMENT IS WAR. This metaphor is reflected in our everyday language by a wide variety of expressions:

ARGUMENT IS WAR

Your claims are *indefensible.*

He *attacked every weak point* in my argument.

His criticisms were *right on target.*

I *demolished* his argument.

I've never *won* an argument with him.

You disagree? Okay, *shoot!*

If you use that *strategy*, he'll *wipe you out.*

He *shot down* all of my arguments.

It is important to see that we don't just *talk* about arguments in terms of war. We can actually win or lose arguments. We see the person we are arguing with as an opponent. We attack his positions and we defend our own. We gain and lose ground. We plan and use strategies. If we find a position indefensible, we can abandon it and take a new line of attack. Many of the things we *do* in arguing are partially structured by the concept of war. Though there is no physical battle, there is a verbal battle, and the structure of an argument—attack, defense, counterattack, etc.—reflects this. It is in this sense that the ARGUMENT IS WAR metaphor is one that we live by in this culture; it structures the actions we perform in arguing.

Try to imagine a culture where arguments are not viewed in terms of war, where no one wins or loses, where there is no sense of attacking or defending, gaining or losing ground. Imagine a culture where an argument is viewed as a dance, the participants are seen as performers, and the goal is to perform in a balanced and aesthetically pleasing way. In such a culture, people would view arguments differently, experience them differently, carry them out differently, and talk about them differently. But *we* would probably not view them as arguing at all: They would simply be doing something different. It would seem strange even to call what they were doing "arguing." Perhaps the most neutral way of describing this difference between their culture and ours would be to say that we have a discourse form structured in terms of battle and they have one structured in terms of dance.

This is an example of what it means for a metaphorical concept, namely, ARGUMENT IS WAR, to structure (at least in part) what we do and how we understand what we are doing when we argue. *The essence of metaphor is understanding and experiencing one kind of thing in terms of another.* It is not that arguments are a subspecies of war. Arguments and wars are different kinds of things—verbal discourse and armed conflict—and the actions performed are different kinds of actions. But ARGUMENT is partially structured, understood, performed, and talked about in terms of WAR. The concept is metaphorically structured, the activity is metaphorically structured, and, consequently, the language is metaphorically structured.

Moreover, this is the *ordinary* way of having an argument and talking about one. The normal way for us to talk about attacking a position is to use the words "attack a position." Our conventional ways of talking about arguments presuppose a metaphor we are hardly ever conscious of. The

metaphor is not merely in the words we use—it is in our very concept of an argument. The language of argument is not poetic, fanciful, or rhetorical; it is literal. We talk about arguments that way because we conceive of them that way—and we act according to the way we conceive of things. . . .

In each of the examples that follow we give a metaphor and a list of ordinary expressions that are special cases of the metaphor. The English expressions are of two sorts: simple literal expressions and idioms that fit the metaphor and are part of the normal everyday way of talking about the subject.

THEORIES (AND ARGUMENTS) ARE BUILDINGS

Is that the *foundation* for your theory? The theory needs more *support.* The argument is *shaky.* We need some more facts or the argument will *fall apart.* We need to *construct* a *strong* argument for that. I haven't figured out yet what the *form* of the argument will be. Here are some more facts to *shore up* the theory. We need to *buttress* the theory with *solid* arguments. The theory will *stand* or *fall* on the *strength* of that argument. The argument *collapsed.* They *exploded* his latest theory. We will show that theory to be without *foundation.* So far we have put together only the *framework* of the theory.

IDEAS ARE FOOD

What he said *left a bad taste in my mouth.* All this paper has in it are *raw facts, half-baked ideas, and warmed-over theories.* There are too many facts here for me to *digest* them all. I just can't *swallow* that claim. That argument *smells fishy.* Let me *stew* over that for a while. Now there's a theory you can really *sink your teeth into.* We need to let that idea *percolate* for a while. That's *food for thought.* He's a *voracious* reader. We don't need to *spoon-feed* our students. He *devoured* the book. Let's let that idea *simmer on the back burner* for a while. This is the *meaty* part of the paper. Let that idea *jell* for a while. That idea has been *fermenting* for years.

With respect to life and death IDEAS ARE ORGANISMS, either PEOPLE or PLANTS.

IDEAS ARE PEOPLE

The theory of relativity *gave birth to* an enormous number of ideas in physics. He is the *father* of modern biology. Whose *brainchild* was that? Look at what his ideas have *spawned.* Those ideas *died off* in the Middle Ages. His ideas will *live on* forever. Cognitive psychology is still in its *infancy.* That's an idea that ought to be *resurrected.* Where'd you *dig up* that idea? He *breathed new life into* that idea.

IDEAS ARE PLANTS

His ideas have finally come to *fruition.* That idea *died on the vine.* That's a *budding* theory. It will take years for that idea to *come to full flower.* He views chemistry as a mere *offshoot* of physics. Mathematics has many *branches.* The *seeds* of his great ideas were *planted* in his youth. She has a *fertile* imagination. Here's an idea that I'd like to *plant* in your mind. He has a *barren* mind.

IDEAS ARE PRODUCTS

We're really *turning (churning, cranking, grinding) out* new ideas. We've *generated* a lot of ideas this week. He *produces* new ideas at an astounding rate. His *intellectual productivity* has decreased in recent years. We need to *take the rough edges off* that idea, *hone it down, smooth it out.* It's a rough idea; it needs to be *refined.*

IDEAS ARE COMMODITIES

It's important how you *package* your ideas. He won't *buy* that. That idea just won't *sell.* There is always a *market* for good ideas. That's a *worthless* idea. He's been a source of *valuable* ideas. I wouldn't *give a plugged nickel for* that idea. Your ideas don't have a chance in the *intellectual marketplace.*

IDEAS ARE RESOURCES

He *ran out of* ideas. Don't *waste* your thoughts on small projects. Let's *pool* our ideas. He's a *resourceful* man. We've *used up* all our ideas. That's a *useless* idea. That idea will *go a long way.*

IDEAS ARE MONEY

Let me put in my *two cents' worth.* He's *rich* in ideas. That book is a *treasure trove* of ideas. He has a *wealth* of ideas.

IDEAS ARE CUTTING INSTRUMENTS

That's an *incisive* idea. That *cuts right to the heart of* the matter. That was a *cutting* remark. He's *sharp.* He has a *razor* wit. He has a *keen* mind. She *cut* his argument *to ribbons.*

IDEAS ARE FASHIONS

That idea went *out of style* years ago. I hear sociobiology *is in* these days. Marxism is currently *fashionable* in western Europe. That idea is *old hat*! That's an *outdated* idea. What are the new *trends* in English criticism? *Old-fashioned* notions have no place in today's society. He keeps *up-to-date* by reading the New York Review of Books. Berkeley is a center of *avant-garde* thought. Semiotics has become quite *chic.* The idea of revolution is no longer *in vogue* in the United States. The transformational grammar *craze* hit the United States in the mid-sixties and has just made it to Europe.

UNDERSTANDING IS SEEING; IDEAS ARE LIGHT-SOURCES; DISCOURSE IS A LIGHT-MEDIUM

I *see* what you're saying. It *looks* different from my *point of view.* What is your *outlook* on that? I *view* it differently. Now I've got the *whole picture.* Let me *point something out* to you. That's an *insightful* idea. That was a *brilliant* remark. The argument is *clear.* It was a *murky* discussion. Could you *elucidate* your remarks? It's a *transparent* argument. The discussion was *opaque.*

LOVE IS A PHYSICAL FORCE
(ELECTROMAGNETIC, GRAVITATIONAL, ETC.)

I could feel the *electricity* between us. There were *sparks*. I was *magnetically drawn* to her. They are uncontrollably *attracted* to each other. They *gravitated* to each other immediately. His whole life *revolves* around her. The *atmosphere* around them is always *charged*. There is incredible *energy* in their relationship. They lost their *momentum*.

LOVE IS A PATIENT

This is a *sick* relationship. They have a *strong, healthy* marriage. The marriage is *dead*—it can't be *revived*. Their marriage is *on the mend*. We're getting *back on our feet*. Their relationship is *in really good shape*. They've got a *listless* marriage. Their marriage is *on its last legs*. It's a *tired* affair.

LOVE IS MADNESS

I'm *crazy* about her. She *drives me out of my mind*. He constantly *raves* about her. He's gone *mad* over her. I'm just *wild* about Harry. I'm *insane* about her.

LOVE IS MAGIC

She *cast her spell* over me. The *magic* is gone. I was *spellbound*. She had me *hypnotized*. He has me *in a trance*. I was *entranced* by him. I'm *charmed* by her. She is *bewitching*.

LOVE IS WAR

He is known for his many rapid *conquests*. She *fought for* him, but his mistress *won out*. He *fled from* her *advances*. She *pursued* him *relentlessly*. He is slowly *gaining ground* with her. He *won* her hand in marriage. He *overpowered* her. She is *besieged* by suitors. He has to *fend* them *off*. He *enlisted the aid* of her friends. He *made an ally* of her mother. Theirs is a *misalliance* if I've ever seen one.

WEALTH IS A HIDDEN OBJECT

He's *seeking* his fortune. He's flaunting his *new-found* wealth. He's a *fortune-hunter*. She's a *gold-digger*. He *lost* his fortune. He's *searching for* wealth.

SIGNIFICANT IS BIG

He's a *big* man in the garment industry. He's a *giant* among writers. That's the *biggest* idea to hit advertising in years. He's *head and shoulders above* everyone in the industry. It was only a *small* crime. That was only a *little* white lie. I was astounded at the *enormity* of the crime. That was one of the *greatest* moments in World Series history. His accomplishments *tower over* those of *lesser* men.

SEEING IS TOUCHING; EYES ARE LIMBS

I can't *take* my eyes *off* her. He sits with his eyes *glued to* the TV. Her eyes *picked out* every detail of the pattern. Their eyes *met*. She never *moves* her eyes *from* his face. She *ran* her eyes *over* everything in the room. He wants everything *within reach of* his eyes.

THE EYES ARE CONTAINERS FOR THE EMOTIONS

I could see the fear *in* his eyes. His eyes were *filled* with anger. There was passion *in* her eyes. His eyes *displayed* his compassion. She couldn't *get* the fear *out* of her eyes. Love *showed in* his eyes. Her eyes *welled* with emotion.

EMOTIONAL EFFECT IS PHYSICAL CONTACT

His mother's death *hit* him *hard*. That idea *bowled me over*. She's a *knockout*. I was *struck* by his sincerity. That really *made an impression* on me. He *made his mark* on the world. I was *touched* by his remark. That *blew me away*.

PHYSICAL AND EMOTIONAL STATES ARE ENTITIES WITHIN A PERSON

He has a pain *in* his shoulder. Don't *give* me the flu. My cold has *gone from my head to my chest*. His pains *went away*. His depression *returned.* Hot tea and honey will *get rid of* your cough. He could barely *contain* his joy. The smile *left* his face. *Wipe that sneer off* your face, private! His fears *keep coming back.* I've got to *shake off* this depression—it keeps *hanging on.* If you've got a cold, drinking lots of tea will *flush it out* of your system. There isn't a *trace* of cowardice *in* him. He hasn't got *an honest bone in his body.*

VITALITY IS A SUBSTANCE

She's *brimming* with vim and vigor. She's *overflowing* with vitality. He's *devoid* of energy. I don't *have* any energy *left* at the end of the day. I'm *drained.* That *took a lot out of* me.

LIFE IS A CONTAINER

I've had a *full* life. Life is *empty* for him. There's *not much left* for him *in* life. Her life is *crammed* with activities. *Get the most out of* life. His life *contained* a great deal of sorrow. Live your life *to the fullest.*

LIFE IS A GAMBLING GAME

I'll *take my chances*. The *odds are against me.* I've got an *ace up my sleeve.* He's *holding all the aces.* It's a *toss-up.* If you play your cards right, you can do it. He *won big.* He's a real *loser.* Where is he when the *chips are down*? That's my *ace in the hole.* He's *bluffing.* The president is *playing it close to his vest.* Let's *up the ante.* Maybe we need to *sweeten the pot.* I think we should *stand pat.* That's *the luck of the draw.* Those are *high stakes.*

In this last group of examples we have a collection of what are called "speech formulas," or "fixed-form expressions," or "phrasal lexical items." These function in many ways like single words, and the language has thousands of them. In the examples given, a set of such phrasal lexical items is coherently structured by a single metaphorical concept. Although each of them is an instance of the LIFE IS A GAMBLING GAME metaphor, they are typically used to speak of life, not of gambling situations. They are normal ways of talking about life situations, just as using the word "construct" is a normal way of talking about theories. It is in this sense that we include them in what we have called literal expressions structured by metaphorical concepts. If you say "The odds are against us" or "We'll have to take our chances," you would not be viewed as speaking metaphorically but as using the normal everyday language appropriate to the situation. Nevertheless, your way of talking about, conceiving, and even experiencing your situation would be metaphorically structured. . . .

The most fundamental values in a culture will be coherent with the metaphorical structure of the most fundamental concepts in the culture. As an example, let us consider some cultural values in our society that are coherent with our UP-DOWN spatialization metaphors and whose opposites would not be.

"More is better" is coherent with MORE IS UP and GOOD IS UP.

"Less is better" is not coherent with them.

"Bigger is better" is coherent with MORE IS UP and GOOD IS UP.

"Smaller is better" is not coherent with them.

"The future will be better" is coherent with THE FUTURE IS UP and GOOD IS UP. "The future will be worse" is not.

"There will be more in the future" is coherent with MORE IS UP and THE FUTURE IS UP.

"Your status should be higher in the future" is coherent with HIGH STATUS IS UP and THE FUTURE IS UP.

These are values deeply embedded in our culture. "The future will be better" is a statement of the concept of progress. "There will be more in the future" has as special cases the accumulation of goods and wage inflation. "Your status should be higher in the future" is a statement of careerism. These are coherent with our present spatialization metaphors; their opposites would not be. So it seems that our values are not independent but must form a coherent system with the metaphorical concepts we live by. . . .

New Meaning

The metaphors we have discussed so far are *conventional* metaphors, that is, metaphors that structure the ordinary conceptual system of our culture, which is reflected in our everyday language. We would now like to turn to metaphors that are outside our conventional conceptual system, metaphors that are imaginative and creative. Such metaphors are capable of giving us a new understanding of our experience. Thus, they can give new meaning to our pasts, to our daily activity, and to what we know and believe.

To see how this is possible, let us consider the new metaphor LOVE IS A COLLABORATIVE WORK OF ART. This is a metaphor that we personally find particularly forceful, insightful, and appropriate, given our experiences as members of our generation and our culture. The reason is that it makes our experiences of love coherent—it makes sense of them. We would like to suggest that new metaphors make sense of our experience in the same way conventional metaphors do: They provide coherent structure, highlighting some things and hiding others.

Like conventional metaphors, new metaphors have entailments, which may include other metaphors and literal statements as well. For example, the entailments of LOVE IS A COLLABORATIVE WORK OF ART arise from our beliefs about, and experiences of, what it means for something to be a collaborative work of art. Our personal views of work and art give rise to at least the following entailments for this metaphor:

Love is work.

Love is active.

Love requires cooperation.

Love requires dedication.

Love requires compromise.

Love requires a discipline.

Love involves shared responsibility.

Love requires patience.

Love requires shared values and goals.

Love demands sacrifice.

Love regularly brings frustration.

Love requires instinctive communication.

Love is an aesthetic experience.

Love is primarily valued for its own sake.

Love involves creativity.

Love requires a shared aesthetic.

Love cannot be achieved by formula.

Love is unique in each instance.

Love is an expression of who you are.

Love creates a reality.

Love reflects how you see the world.

Love requires the greatest honesty.

Love may be transient or permanent.

Love needs funding.

Love yields a shared aesthetic satisfaction from your joint efforts.

Some of these entailments are metaphorical (e.g., "Love is an aesthetic experience"); others are not (e.g., "Love involves shared responsibility"). Each of these entailments may itself have further entailments. The result is a large and coherent network of entailments, which may, on the whole, either fit or not fit our experiences of love. When the network does fit, the experiences form a coherent whole as instances of the metaphor. What we experience with such a metaphor is a kind of reverberation down through the network of entailments that awakens and connects our memories of our past love experiences and serves as a possible guide for future ones.

Let's be more specific about what we mean by "reverberations" in the metaphor LOVE IS A COLLABORATIVE WORK OF ART.

First, the metaphor highlights certain features while suppressing others. For example, the active side of love is brought into the foreground through the notion of WORK both in COLLABORATIVE WORK and in WORK OF ART. This requires the masking of certain aspects of love that are viewed passively. In fact, the emotional aspects of love are almost never viewed as being under the lovers' active control in our conventional conceptual system. Even in the LOVE IS A JOURNEY metaphor, the relationship is viewed as a vehicle that is not in the couple's active control, since it can be *off the tracks,* or *on the rocks,* or *not going anywhere.* In the LOVE IS MADNESS metaphor ("I'm crazy about her," "She's driving me wild"), there is the ultimate lack of control. In the LOVE IS HEALTH metaphor, where the relationship is a patient ("It's a healthy relationship," "It's a sick relationship," "Their relationship is reviving"), the passivity of health in this culture is transferred to love. Thus, in focusing on various aspects of activity (e.g., WORK, CREATION, PURSUING GOALS, BUILDING, HELPING, etc.), the metaphor provides an organization of important love experiences that our conventional conceptual system does not make available.

Second, the metaphor does not merely entail other concepts, like WORK or PURSUING SHARED GOALS, but it entails very specific *aspects* of these concepts. It is not just any work, like working on an automobile assembly line, for instance. It is work that requires that special balance of control and letting-go that is appropriate to artistic creation, since the goal that is pursued is not just any kind of goal but a joint aesthetic goal. And though the metaphor may suppress the out-of-control aspects of the LOVE IS MADNESS metaphor, it highlights another aspect, namely, the sense of almost demonic possession that lies behind our culture's connection between artistic genius and madness.

Third, because the metaphor highlights important love experiences and makes them coherent while it masks other love experiences, the metaphor gives love a new meaning. If those things entailed by the metaphor are for us the most important aspects of our love experiences, then the metaphor can acquire the status of a truth; for many people, love *is* a collaborative work of art. And because it is, the metaphor can have a feedback effect, guiding our future actions in accordance with the metaphor.

Fourth, metaphors can thus be appropriate because they sanction actions, justify inferences, and help us set goals. For example, certain actions, inferences, and goals are dictated by the LOVE IS A COLLABORATIVE WORK OF ART metaphor but not by the LOVE IS MADNESS metaphor. If love is madness, I do not concentrate on what I have to do to maintain it. But if it is work, then it requires activity, and if it is a work of art, it requires a very special *kind* of activity, and if it is collaborative, then it is even further restricted and specified.

Fifth, the meaning a metaphor will have for me will be partly culturally determined and partly tied to my past experiences. The cultural differences can be enormous because each of the concepts in the metaphor under discussion—ART, WORK, COLLABORATION, and LOVE—can vary widely from culture to culture. Thus, LOVE IS A COLLABORATIVE WORK OF ART would mean very different things to a nineteenth-century European Romantic and an Eskimo living in Greenland at the same time. There will also be differences within a culture based on how individuals differ in their views of work and art. LOVE IS A COLLABORATIVE WORK OF ART will mean something very different to two fourteen-year-olds on their first date than to a mature artist couple.

As an example of how the meaning of a metaphor may vary radically within a culture, let us consider some entailments of the metaphor for someone with a view of art very different from our own. Someone who values a work of art not for itself but only as an object for display and someone who thinks that art creates only an illusion, not reality, could see the following as entailments of the metaphor:

Love is an object to be placed on display.

Love exists to be judged and admired by others.

Love creates an illusion.

Love requires hiding the truth.

Because such a person's view of art is different, the metaphor will have a different meaning for him. If his experience of love is pretty much like ours, then the metaphor simply will not fit. In fact, it will be grossly inappropriate. Hence, the same metaphor that gives new meaning to our experiences will not give new meaning to his.

Another example of how a metaphor can create new meaning for us came about by accident. An Iranian student, shortly after his arrival in Berkeley, took a seminar on metaphor from one of us. Among the wondrous things that he found in Berkeley was an expression that he heard over and over and understood as a beautifully sane metaphor. The expression was "the solution of my problems"—which he took to be a large volume of liquid, bubbling and smoking, containing all of your problems, either dissolved or in the form of precipitates, with catalysts constantly dissolving some problems (for the time being) and precipitating out others. He was terribly disillusioned to find that the residents of Berkeley had no such chemical metaphor in mind. And well he might be, for the chemical metaphor is both beautiful and insightful. It gives us a view of problems as things that never disappear utterly and that cannot be solved once and for all. All of your problems are always present, only they may be dissolved and in solution, or they may be in solid form. The best you can hope for is to find a catalyst that will make one problem dissolve without making another one precipitate out. And since you do not have complete control over what goes into the solution, you are constantly finding old and new problems precipitating out and present problems dissolving, partly because of your efforts and partly despite anything you do.

The CHEMICAL metaphor gives us a new view of human problems. It is appropriate to the experience of finding that problems which we once thought were "solved" turn up again and again. The CHEMICAL metaphor says that problems are not the kind of things that can be made to disappear forever. To treat them as things that can be "solved" once and for all is pointless. To live by the CHEMICAL metaphor would be to accept it as a fact that no problem ever disappears forever. Rather than direct your energies toward solving your problems once and for all, you would direct your energies toward finding out what catalysts will dissolve your most pressing problems for the longest time without precipitating out worse ones. The reappearance of a problem is viewed as a natural occurrence rather than a failure on your part to find "the right way to solve it."

To live by the CHEMICAL metaphor would mean that your problems have a different kind of reality for you. A temporary solution would be an accomplishment rather than a failure. Problems would be part of the natural order of things rather than disorders to be "cured." The way you would understand your everyday life and the way you would act in it would be different if you lived by the CHEMICAL metaphor.

We see this as a clear case of the power of metaphor to create a reality rather than simply to give us a way of conceptualizing a preexisting reality. This should not be surprising. As we saw in the case of the ARGUMENT IS WAR metaphor, there are natural kinds of *activity* (e.g., arguing) that are metaphorical in nature. What the CHEMICAL metaphor reveals is that our current way of dealing with problems is another kind of metaphorical activity. At present most of us deal with problems according to what we might call the PUZZLE metaphor, in which problems are PUZZLES for which, typically, there is a correct solution—and, once solved, they are solved forever. The PROBLEMS ARE PUZZLES metaphor characterizes our present reality. A shift to the CHEMICAL metaphor would characterize a new reality.

But it is by no means an easy matter to change the metaphors we live by. It is one thing to be aware of the possibilities inherent in the CHEMICAL metaphor, but it is a very different and far more difficult thing to live by it. Each of us has, consciously or unconsciously, identified hundreds of problems, and we are constantly at work on solutions for many of them—via the PUZZLE metaphor. So much of our unconscious everyday activity is structured in terms of the PUZZLE metaphor that we could not possibly make a quick or easy change to the CHEMICAL metaphor on the basis of a conscious decision.

Many of our activities (arguing, solving problems, budgeting time, etc.) are metaphorical in nature. The metaphorical concepts that characterize those activities structure our present reality. New metaphors have the power to create a new reality. This can begin to happen when we start to comprehend our experience in terms of a metaphor, and it becomes a deeper reality when we begin to act in terms of it. If a new metaphor enters the conceptual system that we base our actions on, it will alter that conceptual system and the perceptions and actions that the system gives rise to. Much of cultural change arises from the introduction of new metaphorical concepts and the loss of old ones. For example, the Westernization of cultures throughout the world is partly a matter of introducing the TIME IS MONEY metaphor into those cultures.

The idea that metaphors can create realities goes against most traditional views of metaphor. The reason is that metaphor has traditionally been viewed as a matter of mere language rather than primarily as a means of structuring our conceptual system and the kinds of everyday activities we perform. It is reasonable enough to assume that words alone don't change reality. But changes in our conceptual system do change what is real for us and affect how we perceive the world and act upon those perceptions.

The idea that metaphor is just a matter of language and can at best only describe reality stems from the view that what is real is wholly external to, and independent of, how human beings conceptualize the world—as if the study of reality were just the study of the physical world. Such a view of reality—so-called objective reality—leaves out human aspects of reality, in particular the real perceptions, conceptualizations, motivations, and actions that constitute most of what we experience. But the human aspects of reality are most of what matters to us, and these vary from culture to culture, since different cultures have different conceptual systems. Cultures also exist within physical environments, some of them radically different—jungles, deserts, islands, tundra, mountains, cities, etc. In each case there is a physical environment that we interact with, more or less successfully. The conceptual systems of various cultures partly depend on the physical environments they have developed in.

Each culture must provide a more or less successful way of dealing with its environment, both adapting to it and changing it. Moreover, each culture must define a social reality within which people have roles that make sense to them and in terms of which they can function socially. Not surprisingly, the social reality defined by a culture affects its conception of physical reality. What is real for an individual as a member of a culture is a product both of his social reality and of the way in which that shapes his experience of the physical world. Since much of our social reality is understood in metaphorical terms, and since our conception of the physical world is partly metaphorical, metaphor plays a very significant role in determining what is real for us. . . .

METAPHOR, TRUTH, AND ACTION

In the preceding section we suggested the following:

Metaphors have entailments through which they highlight and make coherent certain aspects of our experience.

A given metaphor may be the only way to high-light and coherently organize exactly those aspects of our experience.

Metaphors may create realities for us, especially social realities. A metaphor may thus be a guide for future action. Such actions will, of course, fit the metaphor. This will, in turn, reinforce the power of the metaphor to make experience coherent. In this sense metaphors can be self-fulfilling prophecies.

For example, faced with the energy crisis, President Carter declared "the moral equivalent of war." The WAR metaphor generated a network of entailments. There was an "enemy," a "threat to national security," which required "setting targets," "reorganizing priorities," "establishing a new chain of command," "plotting new strategy," "gathering intelligence," "marshaling forces," "imposing sanctions," "calling for sacrifices," and on and on. The WAR metaphor highlighted certain realities and hid others. The metaphor was not merely a way of viewing reality; it constituted a license for policy change and political and economic action. The very acceptance of the metaphor provided grounds for certain inferences: there was an external, foreign, hostile enemy (pictured by cartoonists in Arab headdress); energy needed to be given top priorities; the populace would have to make sacrifices; if we didn't meet the threat, we would not survive. It is important to realize that this was not the only metaphor available.

Carter's WAR metaphor took for granted our current concept of what ENERGY is, and focused on how to get enough of it. On the other hand, Amory Lovins (1977) observed that there are two fundamentally different ways, or PATHS, to supply our energy needs. He characterized these metaphorically as HARD and SOFT. The HARD ENERGY PATH uses energy supplies that are inflexible, nonrenewable, needing military defense and geopolitical control, irreversibly destructive of the environment, and requiring high capital investment, high technology,

and highly skilled workers. They include fossil fuels (gas and oil), nuclear power plants, and coal gasification. The SOFT ENERGY PATH uses energy supplies that are flexible, renewable, not needing military defense or geopolitical control, not destructive of the environment, and requiring only low capital investment, low technology, and unskilled labor. They include solar, wind, and hydroelectric power, biomass alcohol, fluidized beds for burning coal or other combustible materials, and a great many other possibilities currently available. Lovins' SOFT ENERGY PATH metaphor highlights the technical, economic, and sociopolitical *structure* of the energy system, which leads him to the conclusion that the "hard" energy paths—coal, oil, and nuclear power—lead to political conflict, economic hardship, and harm to the environment. But Jimmy Carter is more powerful than Amory Lovins. As Charlotte Linde (in conversation) has observed, whether in national politics or in everyday interaction, people in power get to impose their metaphors.

New metaphors, like conventional metaphors, can have the power to define reality. They do this through a coherent network of entailments that highlight some features of reality and hide others. The acceptance of the metaphor, which forces us to focus *only* on those aspects of our experience that it highlights, leads us to view the entailments of the metaphor as being *true*. Such "truths" may be true, of course, only relative to the reality defined by the metaphor. Suppose Carter announces that his administration has won a major energy battle. Is this claim true or false? Even to address oneself to the question requires accepting at least the central parts of the metaphor. If you do not accept the existence of an external enemy, if you think there is no external threat, if you recognize no field of battle, no targets, no clearly defined competing forces, then the issue of objective truth or falsity cannot arise. But if you see reality as defined by the metaphor, that is, if you do see the energy crisis as a war, then you can answer the question relative to whether the metaphorical entailments fit real-ity. If Carter, by means of strategically employed political and economic sanctions, forced the OPEC nations to cut the price of oil in half, then you would say that he would indeed have won a major battle. If, on the other hand, his strategies had produced only a temporary price freeze, you couldn't be so sure and might be skeptical.

Though questions of truth do arise for new metaphors, the more important questions are those of appropriate action. In most cases, what is at issue is not the truth or falsity of a metaphor but the perceptions and inferences that follow from it and the actions that are sanctioned by it. In all aspects of life, not just in politics or in love, we define our reality in terms of metaphors and then proceed to act on the basis of the metaphors. We draw inferences, set goals, make commitments, and execute plans, all on the basis of how we in part structure our experience, consciously and unconsciously, by means of metaphor. . . .

Metaphors, as we have seen, are conceptual in nature. They are among our principal vehicles for understanding. And they play a central role in the construction of social and political reality. Yet they are typically viewed within philosophy as matters of "mere language," and philosophical discussions of metaphor have not centered on their conceptual nature, their contribution to understanding, or their function in cultural reality. Instead, philosophers have tended to look at metaphors as out-of-the-ordinary imaginative or poetic linguistic expressions, and their discussions have centered on whether these linguistic expressions can be *true*. . . .

We do not believe that there is such a thing as *objective* (absolute and unconditional) *truth,* though it has been a long-standing theme in Western culture that there is. We do believe that there are *truths* but think that the idea of truth need not be tied to the objectivist view. We believe that the idea that there is absolute objective truth is not only mistaken but socially and politically

dangerous. As we have seen, truth is always relative to a conceptual system that is defined in large part by metaphor. Most of our metaphors have evolved in our culture over a long period, but many are imposed upon us by people in power—political leaders, religious leaders, business leaders, advertisers, the media, etc. In a culture where the myth of objectivism is very much alive and truth is always absolute truth, the people who get to impose their metaphors on the culture get to define what we consider to be true—absolutely and objectively true. . . .

AN EXPERIENTIALIST SYNTHESIS

What we are offering in the experientialist account of understanding and truth is an alternative which denies that subjectivity and objectivity are our only choices. . . . The reason we have focused so much on metaphor is that it unites reason and imagination. Reason, at the very least, involves categorization, entailment, and inference. Imagination, in one of its many aspects, involves seeing one kind of thing in terms of another kind of thing—what we have called metaphorical thought. Metaphor is thus *imaginative rationality.* Since the categories of our everyday thought are largely metaphorical and our everyday reasoning involves metaphorical entailments and inferences, ordinary rationality is therefore imaginative by its very nature. Given our understanding of poetic metaphor in terms of metaphorical entailments and inferences, we can see that the products of the poetic imagination are, for the same reason, partially rational in nature.

Metaphor is one of our most important tools for trying to comprehend partially what cannot be comprehended totally: our feelings, aesthetic experiences, moral practices, and spiritual awareness. These endeavors of the imagination are not devoid of rationality; since they use metaphor, they employ an imaginative rationality.

An experientialist approach also allows us to bridge the gap between the objectivist and subjectivist myths about impartiality and the possibility of being fair and objective. . . . [T]ruth is relative to understanding, which means that there is no absolute standpoint from which to obtain absolute objective truths about the world. This does not mean that there are no truths; it means only that truth is relative to our conceptual system, which is grounded in, and constantly tested by, our experiences and those of other members of our culture in our daily interactions with other people and with our physical and cultural environments. . . .

REFERENCE

Lovins, A. (1977). *Soft energy paths.* Cambridge: Ballinger.

CATEGORIZATION, LANGUAGE, AND CULTURE

10

Racism in the English Language

Robert B. Moore

(1976)

LANGUAGE AND CULTURE

An integral part of any culture is its language. Language not only develops in conjunction with a society's historical, economic and political evolution; it also reflects that society's attitudes and thinking. Language not only *expresses* ideas and concepts but actually *shapes* thought.[1] If one accepts that our dominant white culture is racist, then one would expect our language— an indispensable transmitter of culture—to be racist as well. Whites, as the dominant group, are not subjected to the same abusive characterization by our language that people of color receive. Aspects of racism in the English language that will be discussed in this essay include terminology, symbolism, politics, ethnocentrism, and context.

Before beginning our analysis of racism in language we would like to quote part of a TV film review which shows the connection between language and culture.[2]

Depending on one's culture, one interacts with time in a very distinct fashion. One example which gives some cross-cultural insights into the concept of time is language. In Spanish, a watch is said to "walk." In English, the watch "runs." In German, the watch "functions." And in French, the watch "marches." In the Indian culture of the Southwest, people do not refer to time in this way. The value of the watch is displaced with the value of "what time it's getting to be." Viewing these five cultural perspectives of time, one can see some definite emphasis and values that each culture places on time. For example, a cultural perspective may provide a clue to why the negative stereotype of the slow and lazy Mexican who lives in the "Land of Mañana" exists in the Anglo value system, where time "flies," the watch "runs" and "time is money."

A Short Play on "Black" and "White" Words

Some may blackly (angrily) accuse me of trying to blacken (defame) the English language, to give it a black eye (a mark of shame) by writing such black words (hostile). They may denigrate (to cast aspersions; to darken) me by accusing me of being blackhearted (malevolent), of having a black outlook (pessimistic, dismal) on life, of being a blackguard (scoundrel)—which would certainly be a black mark (detrimental fact) against me. Some may black-brow (scowl at) me and hope that a black cat crosses in front of me because of this black deed. I may become a black sheep (one who causes shame or embarrassment because of deviation from the accepted standards), who will be blackballed (ostracized) by being placed on a blacklist (list of undesirables) in an attempt to blackmail (to force or coerce into a particular action) me to retract my words. But attempts to blackjack (to compel by threat) me will have a Chinaman's chance of success, for I am not a yellow-bellied Indian-giver of words, who will whitewash (cover up or gloss over vices or crimes) a black lie (harmful, inexcusable). I challenge the purity and innocence (white) of the English language. I don't see things in black and white (entirely bad or entirely good) terms, for I am a white man (marked by upright firmness) if there ever was one. However, it would be a black day when I would not "call a spade a spade," even though some will suggest a white man calling the English language racist is like the pot calling the kettle black. While many may be niggardly (grudging, scanty) in their support, others will be honest and decent—and to them I say, that's very white of you (honest, decent).

The preceding is of course a white lie (not intended to cause harm), meant only to illustrate some examples of racist terminology in the English language.

Obvious Bigotry

Perhaps the most obvious aspect of racism in language would be terms like "nigger," "spook," "chink," "spic," etc. While these may be facing increasing social disdain, they certainly are not dead. Large numbers of white Americans continue to utilize these terms. "Chink," "gook," and "slant-eyes" were in common usage among U.S. troops in Vietnam. An NBC nightly news broadcast, in February 1972, reported that the basketball team in Pekin, Illinois, was called the "Pekin Chinks" and noted that even though this had been protested by Chinese Americans, the term continued to be used because it was easy, and meant no harm. Spiro Agnew's widely reported "fat Jap" remark and the "little Jap" comment of lawyer John Wilson during the Watergate hearings, are surface indicators of a deep-rooted Archie Bunkerism.

Many white people continue to refer to Black people as "colored," as for instance in a July 30, 1975 *Boston Globe* article on a racist attack by whites on a group of Black people using a public beach in Boston. One white person was quoted as follows:

> We've always welcomed good colored people in South Boston but we will not tolerate radical blacks or Communists. . . . Good colored people are welcome in South Boston, black militants are not.

Many white people may still be unaware of the disdain many African Americans have for the term "colored," but it often appears that whether used intentionally or unintentionally, "colored" people are "good" and "know their place," while "Black" people are perceived as "uppity" and "threatening" to many whites. Similarly, the term "boy" to refer to African American men is now acknowledged to be a demeaning term, though still in common use. Other terms such as "the pot calling the kettle black" and "calling a spade a spade" have negative racial connotations but are still frequently used, as for example when President Ford was quoted in February 1976 saying that even though Daniel Moynihan had left the U.N., the U.S. would continue "calling a spade a spade."

COLOR SYMBOLISM

The symbolism of white as positive and black as negative is pervasive in our culture, with the black/white words used in the beginning of this essay only one of many aspects. "Good guys" wear white hats and ride white horses, "bad guys" wear black hats and ride black horses. Angels are white, and devils are black. The definition of *black* includes "without any moral light or goodness, evil, wicked, indicating disgrace, sinful," while that of *white* includes "morally pure, spotless, innocent, free from evil intent."

A children's TV cartoon program, *Captain Scarlet,* is about an organization called Spectrum, whose purpose is to save the world from an evil extraterrestrial force called the Mysterons. Everyone in Spectrum has a color name—Captain Scarlet, Captain Blue, etc. The one Spectrum agent who has been mysteriously taken over by the Mysterons and works to advance their evil aims is Captain Black. The person who heads Spectrum, the good organization out to defend the world, is Colonel White.

Three of the dictionary definitions of white are "fairness of complexion, purity, innocence." These definitions affect the standards of beauty in our culture, in which whiteness represents the norm. "Blondes have more fun" and "Wouldn't you really rather be a blonde" are sexist in their attitudes toward women generally, but are racist white standards when applied to third world women. A 1971 *Mademoiselle* advertisement pictured a curly-headed, ivory-skinned woman over the caption, "When you go blonde go all the way," and asked: "Isn't this how, in the back of your mind, you always wanted to look? All wide-eyed and silky blonde down to there, and innocent?" Whatever the advertising people meant by this particular woman's innocence, one must remember that "innocent" is one of the definitions of the word white. This standard of beauty when preached to all women is racist. The statement "Isn't this how, in the back of your mind, you always wanted to look?" either ignores third world women or assumes they long to be white.

Time magazine in its coverage of the Wimbledon tennis competition between the black Australian Evonne Goolagong and the white American Chris Evert described Ms. Goolagong as "the dusky daughter of an Australian sheepshearer," while Ms. Evert was "a fair young girl from the middle-class groves of Florida." *Dusky* is a synonym of "black" and is defined as "having dark skin; of a dark color; gloomy; dark; swarthy." Its antonyms are "fair" and "blonde." *Fair* is defined in part as "free from blemish, imperfection, or anything that impairs the appearance, quality, or character; pleasing in appearance, attractive; clean; pretty; comely." By defining Evonne Goolagong as "dusky," *Time* technically defined her as the opposite of "pleasing in appearance; attractive; clean; pretty; comely."

The studies of Kenneth B. Clark, Mary Ellen Goodman, Judith Porter and others indicate that this persuasive "rightness of whiteness" in U.S. culture affects children before the age of four, providing white youngsters with a false sense of superiority and encouraging self-hatred among third world youngsters.

ETHNOCENTRISM OR FROM A WHITE PERSPECTIVE

Some words and phrases that are commonly used represent particular perspectives and frames of reference, and these often distort the understanding of the reader or listener. David R. Burgest[3] has written about the effect of using the terms "slave" or "master." He argues that the psychological impact of the statement referring to "the master raped his slave" is different from the impact of the same statement substituting the words: "the white captor raped an African woman held in captivity."

> Implicit in the English usage of the "master-slave" concept is ownership of the "slave" by the "master," therefore, the "master" is merely abusing his property (slave). In reality, the captives (slave) were African individuals with human worth, right and dignity and the term "slave" denounces that human quality thereby making the mass rape of African women by white captors more acceptable in the minds of people and setting a mental frame of reference for legitimizing the atrocities perpetuated against African people.

The term "slave" connotes a less than human quality and turns the captive person into a thing. For example, two McGraw-Hill Far Eastern Publishers textbooks (1970) stated, "At first it was the slaves who worked the cane and they got only food for it. Now men work cane and get money." Next time you write about slavery or read about it, try transposing all "slaves" into "African people held in captivity," "Black people forced to work for no pay" or "African people stolen from their families and societies." While it is more cumbersome, such phrasing conveys a different meaning. . . .

POLITICS AND TERMINOLOGY

"Culturally deprived," "economically disadvantaged" and "underdeveloped" are other terms which mislead and distort our awareness of reality. The application of the term "culturally deprived" and third world children in this society reflects a value judgment. It assumes that the dominant whites are cultured and all others without culture. In fact, third world children generally are bicultural, and many are bilingual, having grown up in their own culture as well as absorbing the dominant culture. In many ways, they are equipped with skills and experiences which white youth have been deprived of, since most white youth develop in a monocultural, monolingual environment. Burgest[5] suggests that the term "culturally deprived" be replaced by "culturally dispossessed," and that the term "economically disadvantaged" be replaced by "economically exploited." Both these terms present a perspective and implication that provide an entirely different frame of reference as to the reality of the third world experience in U.S. society.

Similarly, many nations of the third world are described as "underdeveloped." These less wealthy nations are generally those that suffered under colonialism and neo-colonialism. The "developed" nations are those that exploited their resources and wealth. Therefore, rather than referring to these countries as "underdeveloped," a more appropriate and meaningful designation might be "over exploited." Again, transpose this term next time you read about "underdeveloped nations" and note the different meaning that results.

Terms such as "culturally deprived," "economically disadvantaged" and "underdeveloped" place the responsibility for their own conditions on those being so described. This is known as "Blaming the Victim."[6] It places responsibility for poverty on the victims of poverty. It removes the blame from those in power who benefit from, and continue to permit, poverty.

Still another example involves the use of "non-white," "minority" or "third world." While people of color are a minority in the U.S., they are part of the vast majority of the world's population, in which white people are a distinct minority. Thus, by utilizing the term minority to describe people of color in the U.S., we can lose sight of the global majority/minority reality—a fact of some importance in the increasing and interconnected struggles of people of color inside and outside the U.S.

To describe people of color as "non-white" is to use whiteness as the standard and norm against which to measure all others. Use of the term "third world" to describe all people of color overcomes the inherent bias of "minority" and "non-white." Moreover, it connects the struggles of third world people in the U.S. with the freedom struggles around the globe.

The term "third world" gained increasing usage after the 1955 Bandung Conference of "non-aligned" nations, which represented a third force outside of the two world superpowers. The "first world" represents the United States, Western Europe and their sphere of influence. The "second world" represents the Soviet Union and its sphere. The "third world" represents, for the most part, nations that were, or are, controlled by the "first world" or West. For the most part, these are nations of Africa, Asia and Latin America.

"LOADED" WORDS AND NATIVE AMERICANS

Many words lead to a demeaning characterization of groups of people. For instance, Columbus, it is said, "discovered" America. The word *discover* is defined as "to gain sight or knowledge of something previously unseen or unknown; to discover may be to find some existent thing that was previously unknown." Thus, a continent inhabited by millions of human beings cannot be "discovered." For history books to continue this usage represents a Eurocentric (white European) perspective on world history and ignores the existence of, and the perspective of, Native Americans. "Discovery," as used in the Euro-American context, implies the right to take what one finds, ignoring the rights of those who already inhabit or own the "discovered" thing.

Eurocentrism is also apparent in the usage of "victory" and "massacre" to describe the battles between Native Americans and whites. *Victory* is defined in the dictionary as "a success or triumph over an enemy in battle or war; the decisive defeat of an opponent." *Conquest* denotes the "taking over of control by the victor, and the obedience of the conquered." *Massacre* is defined as "the unnecessary, indiscriminate killing of a number of human beings, as in barbarous warfare or persecution, or for revenge or plunder." *Defend* is described as "to ward off attack from; guard against assault or injury; to strive to keep safe by resisting attack."

Eurocentrism turns these definitions around to serve the purpose of distorting history and justifying Euro-American conquest of the Native American homelands. Euro-Americans are not described in history books as invading Native American lands, but rather as defending *their* homes against "Indian" attacks. Since European communities were constantly encroaching on land already occupied, then a more honest interpretation would state that it was the Native Americans who were "warding off," "guarding" and "defending" their homelands.

Native American victories are invariably defined as "massacres," while the indiscriminate killing, extermination and plunder of Native American nations by Euro-Americans is defined as "victory." Distortion of history by the choice of "loaded" words used to describe historical events is a common racist practice. Rather than portraying Native Americans as human beings in highly defined and complex societies, cultures and civilizations, history books use such adjectives as "savages," "beasts," "primitive," and "backward." Native people are referred to as "squaw," "brave," or "papoose" instead of "woman," "man," or "baby."

Another term that has questionable connotations is *tribe*. The *Oxford English Dictionary* defines this noun as "a race of people; now applied especially to a primary aggregate of people in a primitive or barbarous condition, under a headman or chief." Morton Fried,[7] discussing "The Myth of Tribe," states that the word "did not become a general term of reference to American Indian society until the nineteenth century. Previously, the words commonly used for Indian populations were 'nation' and 'people.'" Since "tribe" has assumed a connotation of primitiveness or backwardness, it is suggested that the use of "nation" or "people" replace the term whenever possible in referring to Native American peoples.

The term *tribe* invokes even more negative implications when used in reference to American peoples. As Evelyn Jones Rich[8] has noted, the term is "almost always used to refer to third world people and it implies a stage of development which is, in short, a put-down."

"Loaded" Words and Africans

Conflicts among diverse peoples within African nations are often referred to as "tribal warfare," while conflicts among the diverse peoples within European countries are never described in such terms. If the rivalries between the Ibo and the Hausa and Yoruba in Nigeria are described as "tribal," why not the rivalries between Serbs and Slavs in Yugoslavia, or Scots and English in Great Britain, Protestants and Catholics in Ireland, or the Basques and the Southern Spaniards in Spain? Conflicts among African peoples in a particular nation have religious, cultural, economic and/or political roots. If we can analyze the roots of conflicts among European peoples in terms other than "tribal warfare," certainly we can do the same with African peoples, including correct reference to the ethnic groups or nations involved. For example, the terms "Kaffirs," "Hottentot" or "Bushmen" are names imposed by white Europeans. The correct names are always those by which a people refer to themselves. (In these instances Xhosa, Khoi-Khoin and San are correct.[9])

The generalized application of "tribal" in reference to Africans—as well as the failure to acknowledge the religious, cultural and social diversity of African peoples—is a decidedly racist dynamic. It is part of the process whereby Euro-Americans justify, or avoid confronting, their oppression of third world peoples. Africa has been particularly insulted by this dynamic, as witness the pervasive "darkest Africa" image. This image, widespread in Western culture, evokes an Africa covered by jungles and inhabited by "uncivilized," "cannibalistic," "pagan," "savage" peoples. This "darkest Africa" image avoids the geographical reality. Less than 20 percent of the African continent is wooded savanna, for example. The image also ignores the history of African cultures and civilizations. Ample evidence suggests this distortion of reality was developed as a convenient rationale for the European and American slave trade. The Western powers, rather than exploiting, were civilizing and christianizing "uncivilized" and "pagan savages" (so the rationalization went). This dynamic also served to justify Western colonialism. From Tarzan movies to racist children's books like *Doctor Dolittle* and *Charlie and the Chocolate Factory,* the image of "savage" Africa and the myth of "the white man's burden" has been perpetuated in Western culture.

A 1972 *Time* magazine editorial lamenting the demise of *Life* magazine, stated that the "lavishness" of *Life*'s enterprises included "organizing safaris into darkest Africa." The same year, the *New York Times'* C. L. Sulzberger wrote that "Africa has a history as dark as the skins of many of its people." Terms such as "darkest Africa," "primitive," "tribe" ("tribal") or "jungle," in reference to Africa, perpetuate myths and are especially inexcusable in such large circulation publications.

Ethnocentrism is similarly reflected in the term "pagan" to describe traditional religions. A February 1973 *Time* magazine article on Uganda stated, "Moslems account for only 500,000 of Uganda's 10 million people. Of the remainder, 5,000,000 are Christians and the rest pagan." *Pagan* is defined as "Heathen, a follower of a polytheistic religion; one that has little or no religion and that is marked by a frank delight in and uninhibited seeking after sensual pleasures and material goods." *Heathen* is defined as "Unenlightened; an unconverted member of a people or nation that does not acknowledge the God of the Bible. A person whose culture or enlightenment is of an inferior grade, especially an irreligious person." Now, the people of Uganda, like almost all Africans, have serious religious beliefs and practices. As used by Westerners, "pagan" connotes something wild, primitive and inferior—another term to watch out for.

The variety of traditional structures that African people live in are their "houses," not "huts." A *hut* is "an often small and temporary dwelling of simple construction." And to describe Africans as "natives" (noun) is derogatory terminology— as in, "the natives are restless." The dictionary definition of *native* includes: "one of a people inhabiting a territorial area at the time of its discovery or becoming familiar to a foreigner; one belonging to a people having a less complex civilization." Therefore, use of "native," like use of "pagan" often implies a value judgement of white superiority.

QUALIFYING ADJECTIVES

Words that would normally have positive connotations can have entirely different meanings when used in a racial context. For example, C. L. Sulzberger, the columnist of the *New York Times,* wrote in January 1975, about conversations he had with two people in Namibia. One was the white South African administrator of the country and the other a member of SWAPO, the Namibian liberation movement. The first is described as "Dirk Mudge, who as senior elected member of the administration is a kind of acting Prime Minister. . . ." But the second person is introduced as "Daniel Tijongarero, an intelligent Herero tribesman who is a member of SWAPO. . . ." What need was there for Sulzberger to state that Daniel Tijongarero is "intelligent"?

Why not also state that Dirk Mudge was "intelligent"—or do we assume he wasn't?

A similar example from a 1968 *New York Times* article reporting on an address by Lyndon Johnson stated, "The President spoke to the well-dressed Negro officials and their wives." In what similar circumstances can one imagine a reporter finding it necessary to note that an audience of white government officials was "well-dressed"?

Still another word often used in a racist context is "qualified." In the 1960s white Americans often questioned whether Black people were "qualified" to hold public office, a question that was never raised (until too late) about white officials like Wallace, Maddox, Nixon, Agnew, Mitchell, et al. The question of qualifications has been raised even more frequently in recent years as white people question whether Black people are "qualified" to be hired for positions in industry and educational institutions. "We're looking for a qualified Black" has been heard again and again as institutions are confronted with affirmative action goals. Why stipulate that Blacks must be "qualified," when for others it is taken for granted that applicants must be "qualified"?

SPEAKING ENGLISH

Finally, the depiction in movies and children's books of third world people speaking English is often itself racist. Children's books about Puerto Ricans or Chicanos often connect poverty with a failure to speak English or to speak it well, thus blaming the victim and ignoring the racism which affects third world people regardless of their proficiency in English. Asian characters speak a stilted English ("Honorable so and so" or "Confucius say") or have a speech impediment ("rots or ruck," "very solly," "flied lice"). Native American characters speak another variation of stilted English ("Boy not hide. Indian take boy."), repeat certain Hollywood-Indian phrases ("Heap big" and "Many moons") or simply grunt out "Ugh" or "How." The repeated use of these language characterizations functions to make third world people seem less intelligent and less capable than the English-speaking white characters.

WRAP-UP

A *Saturday Review* editorial[10] on "The Environment of Language" stated that language

> . . . has as much to do with the philosophical and political conditioning of a society as geography or climate. . . . people in Western cultures do not realize the extent to which their racial attitudes have been conditioned since early childhood by the power of words to ennoble or condemn, augment or detract, glorify or demean. Negative language infects the subconscious of most Western people from the time they first learn to speak. Prejudice is not merely imparted or superimposed. It is metabolized in the bloodstream of society. What is needed is not so much a change in language as an awareness of the power of words to condition attitudes. If we can at least recognize the underpinnings of prejudice, we may be in a position to deal with the effects.

To recognize the racism in language is an important first step. Consciousness of the influence of language on our perceptions can help to negate much of that influence. But it is not enough to simply become aware of the affects of racism in conditioning attitudes. While we may not be able to change the language, we can definitely change our usage of the language. We can avoid using words that degrade people. We can make a conscious effort to use terminology that reflects a progressive perspective, as opposed to a distorting perspective. It is important for

educators to provide students with opportunities to explore racism in language and to increase their awareness of it, as well as learning terminology that is positive and does not perpetuate negative human values.

NOTES

1. Simon Podair, "How Bigotry Builds Through Language," *Negro Digest,* March 1967.

2. Jose Armas, "Antonio and the Mayor: A Cultural Review of the Film," *The Journal of Ethnic Studies,* Fall, 1975.

3. David R. Burgest, "The Racist Use of the English Language," *Black Scholar,* Sept. 1973.

4. Thomas Greenfield, "Race and Passive Voice at Monticello," *Crisis,* April 1975.

5. David R. Burgest, "Racism in Everyday Speech and Social Work Jargon," *Social Work,* July 1973.

6. William Ryan, *Blaming the Victim,* Pantheon Books, 1971.

7. Morton Fried, "The Myth of Tribe," *National History,* April 1975.

8. Evelyn Jones Rich, "Mind Your Language," *Africa Report,* Sept./Oct. 1974.

9. Steve Wolf, "Catalogers in Revolt Against LC's Racist, Sexist Headings," *Bulletin of Interracial Books for Children,* Vol. 6, Nos. 3&4, 1975.

10. "The Environment of Language," *Saturday Review,* April 8, 1967.

Further Readings

Roger Bastide, "Color, Racism and Christianity," *Daedalus,* Spring 1967.

Kenneth J. Gergen, "The Significance of Skin Color in Human Relations," *Daedalus,* Spring 1967.

UNESCO, "Recommendations Concerning Terminology in Education on Race Questions," June 1968.

Lloyd Yabura, "Towards a Language of Humanism," *Rhythm,* Summer 1971.

PART III

PRODUCING SOCIAL SELVES

We come into this world as individuals, achieve character, and become persons.

—Robert Park (1952),
Human Communities

We talk, therefore I am.

—Anna Quindlen (1989),
Living Out Loud

Tell me who you love and I'll tell you who you are.

—Creole Proverb

WHO AM I?
DEVELOPING CHARACTER

Jodi O'Brien

Who am I? This is one of the most common and persistent questions that we ask our-selves. Consider for a moment what this question implies: We really don't know who or what we are. We are constantly searching for answers to this question. Furthermore, our answers change over the course of a lifetime. Despite this fluctuation in self-understanding, we tend to think of our "self" as something that is knowable and stable. Self-understanding is a central topic in social psychology. Social psychologists consider the self to be an aspect of social interaction. The self—an organized, stable sense of who you are—develops through social interaction with other people. Accordingly, the emphasis in this essay and in the read-ing material that follows is on the *social self.*

There are certainly aspects of who you are that cannot be explained entirely by the theories that follow. For instance, your physiology and aspects of your spirituality can be usefully understood in terms of biology and theology, respectively. However, after reading this material it's likely you will see that theories of the social self are extraordinarily useful in helping you to understand why you think about yourself in certain ways and how these perceptions shape your sense of who you can be, what you can do, and how you feel. This section of the book, Part III, introduces the basic social psychological the-ories of self development. Part VII deals with additional complexities of self-understanding.

Try this exercise: Write down 20 personal responses to the question, "Who am I?" Take a look at your list and see if you notice anything about it. In 1954, social psychologists Kuhn and McPartland published what they called the "Twenty Statements Test." They asked people to give 20 responses to the question, "Who am I?" Most people can do this quickly, without too much thought. What Kuhn and McPartland noted was that people's answers fall into two categories: social roles (e.g., mother, son, sister, boyfriend, student, dentist, conservative, activist, etc.) or personality expressions (e.g., funny, happy, generous, friendly, shy, helpful, trustworthy, etc.). What's interesting about this is that people see themselves in reference to others, either as a role (e.g., when you think of yourself as a father, you are thinking of yourself in reference to your child), or as a characteristic (e.g., I am "hardworking" in the eyes of my employer). This observation led Kuhn and McPartland to conclude that self-image is shaped largely in reference to social roles and other people's impressions of us. This conclusion is consistent with social psychological theories of the self: Our sense of self is formed in terms of social roles or positions and our ideas about what other people think of us.

SELF AS OBJECT

Recall the discussion in Part II about language and the process of "naming" or categorization. In the same way that children learn to group and make sense of their environment by attaching names and creating categories for things, people, and situations, they also learn to make sense of themselves. In other words, self development begins when the child becomes *aware* of its existence as an object in the world. Consider the term *self concept.* In addition to learning concepts such as "dog," "milk," "toys," and so forth, children develop the ability to recognize themselves as an object in the world and to conceptualize that object as "myself." This ability requires the child to develop an inner eye or witness that is capable of observing the child's own behavior and recognizing that this behavior is associated with "self" and not something apart from "self." Pause for a moment and observe your own inner eye or witness. Where is it located? How does it function? Without this ability to see your own behavior, and subsequently to name or categorize it, you wouldn't be able to exercise self-control.

One early thinker who made significant contributions to social psychological theories of the self is George Herbert Mead (see Reading 11). Mead was a social philosopher writing and lecturing in Chicago in the early 1900s. Like his contemporary, Sigmund Freud, Mead was particularly interested in the connections between the development of mind and self and the functioning of society. According to Mead, the human mind and self-awareness develop simultaneously in the process of learning language.

When a child learns language and begins to develop the ability to conceptualize (see Part II) she also learns to conceptualize her "self." When very young children first become aware that they are agents in the world, they are fascinated with their ability to control things in their environment. For example, a toddler will spend many contented hours opening and shutting a door or flipping a switch to an electronic device. This repetitive and seemingly boring action is actually quite exciting for the infant who is suddenly aware that he can make things happen. This becomes even more exciting when a child learns that he can "control" others in her environment. When the child repeatedly throws a toy and an adult picks it up and returns it, the child learns that he can engage in actions that bring about expected responses from others. This initial awareness is the beginning of what Mead refers to as the child's ability to comprehend the self as an object—like other objects in the environment, the child realizes that he is an object himself and that he has agency.

In the same way that children learn the meaning of things, they begin to collect a set of self-object meanings by observing how others label or categorize them. Thus, the child not only learns the concept "ball," but she learns the concept "bad girl" when she throws the ball in the house and someone scolds her. Very young children tend to refer to themselves in the third person: "Ramon is a good boy," "Alex is sleepy," and so forth. They have learned to see themselves as objects and to attach meaning states such as "good" and "sleepy" to their objective being, but they haven't yet internalized the full concept of self.

Many parents might suggest that this internal sense of self becomes most pronounced as the child learns the concept of "mine!" Indeed, as the self concept develops, the child begins to take on a more internal and organized sense of ownership with her own feelings and actions. In this process, the child internalizes the names and categories that others have used to describe her object-self and begins to self-identify with them. Accordingly, a child moves from expressions such as "Ming is a nice boy" to "I am a nice boy." At this point in self development, Ming understands (1) the meaning of "nice," (2) that this characteristic is being attributed to him as a unique being in the world, and (3) that he can cause people to make this attribution by acting or behaving in a certain way. This is an amazing and complex learning process. Child development experts say that we learn more in the first 5 years of life than over the rest of our entire lifetime. During this time, children not only develop the idea or concept of a self, but they also begin to acquire information that forms the basis of their particular sense of what their self concept is—in other words, the general script for their answer to the question, "Who am I?"

I/Me and the Self as a Conversation

Mead uses the terms *I* and *me* to distinguish between the actions or behavior of the person ("I") and the internal awareness, guidance, and evaluation of this behavior ("me"). In other words, the "me" watches or observes the "I" and is able to guide and direct its impulses. This self-direction is usually done in accordance with previously learned ideals about "how" to behave according to significant others. Children still learning this will sometimes engage in a willful behavior, such as pulling the cat's tail and then, after a moment or two, exclaim, "Bad boy!" In this instance, the toddler is learning to link an impulse action ("I") with his ability to observe the action ("me") and evaluate it based on ideas learned from a significant other such as a parent.

Consider a child who is learning to play with an object called a "ball." She learns that a certain activity associated with the ball, such as hurling it across space, meets with particular responses from those around her. She also learns that these responses are either positive or negative and come in the form of reactions toward herself. Thus, she learns that she is the source of the activity that generates the response. She also learns that in certain situations— for example, in an enclosed space—people react more negatively when she hurls the ball than they do when she is on the green stuff called "grass."

The child also learns to distinguish between the responses of differently named persons in her environment. "Mom" may praise her "athletic ability" when she hurls the ball. "Dad" may attempt to "settle her down." By observing the reactions of significant others, the child learns to form complex associations among persons, things, and situations. Most importantly, the child learns what stance to adopt in a given setting in relationship to specific categories of people and objects. This process of learning names and the associated rewards and punishments is the foundation of human socialization.

Socialization will be discussed in detail in Part IV, but for now, the lesson is that we learn to see ourselves and develop an idea of who we are from interacting with significant others.

In doing so, we take on the attitudes, ideas, and values of these significant others. Thus, when children are learning who they are, they are also learning to associate certain actions, social roles, and qualities with specific judgments or evaluations. Through this learning process, they are internalizing social meaning and values, and learning to guide and direct their behavior in accordance with these values.

An example I sometimes share with students, to their amusement, is my own behavior in the presence of a colleague who is completely bald. This colleague is much older than me, and holds a high-ranking administrative position. For reasons I don't entirely understand, I often find myself wanting to rub his head when we sit together in meetings. In my mind, I can see myself reaching out to do this. At the same time, I can see how mortified everyone would be if I followed through on this action. Seeing all this in my mind enables me to resist the temptation to rub his head. Mead would describe the impulse to head-rub as the potential action of the "I." The "me" is the overseer who observes the behavior and intentions of the "I" and brings them into line with cultural expectations: "You can't rub his head! That would be so embarrassing!"

The images and ideals you hold in your mind about proper behavior represent the attitudes and values of your culture. These expectations function as the *generalized other* (internalized social expectations) to give people an "ideal script" for acting the proper role in a situation. In understanding your "self," it is useful to think in terms of a conversation. When you guide, direct, and evaluate your own behavior, you are engaging in an internal conversation. This conversation might be with "generalized" expectations ("Nice people don't pee on the sidewalk."), with your idea of the expectations of a particular group you associate yourself with ("I need a different haircut if I'm going to look as hip as the rest of the gang."), or with some specific person in your life ("My girlfriend is going to be so pissed if she catches me flirting this way."). According to Mead, these internal conversations are the basis of what we think of as our core self. Think for a moment about some of the audiences in your own head. Who are some of the significant people that you find yourself organizing your behavior in response to? What are some of the groups you reference in trying to make decisions about what to do and who to be?

THE SELF AS A PRODUCT OF INTERACTION

The process of identifying or naming behaviors that we come to see as an aspect of "self" involves an internal conversation with the generalized other and people or groups that are important to us. Accordingly, the self is a *social construction* that takes shape through interaction—interaction outwardly with others and, especially, internally through the conversations we have with ourselves about those interactions.

The Looking-Glass Self

In much the same way that we each learn to define the meaning of things in our environment, we learn about who we are through observing the responses of others to us as objects.

Mead was interested in the relationship between mind and self, and the relationship of both to language acquisition and subsequent social engagement. His contemporary, Charles Horton Cooley (see Reading 12), was interested in *how* people acquire the information that they use to form a self-image. Cooley proposed that this process is like a mirror or "looking glass." When we encounter others, we look to see how they are responding to us, similar to looking into a mirror to see how we look. If we perceive the other person to be responding positively, then we feel good about ourselves ("pride," in Cooley's terms). If we perceive a negative reaction, then we feel "mortification." According to Cooley, we get information about who we are and how to feel about ourselves based on what we think others think of us. Cooley called this the "looking-glass self." Both Mead and Cooley emphasize social interaction as a central element in self development. When we interact with others, we are alert to their responses and engage in self-evaluation in accordance to these responses.

The looking-glass self consists of an internal image we generate about our self when we are trying to figure out what others think of us. We gain information about ourselves by casting ourselves in the role of an observer, *imagining* how our actions appear to that person, and then attaching some reaction (such as pride or mortification) to that perception. In short, we imagine what we think someone else thinks of us, and then we judge ourselves accordingly. Cooley refers to these self-assessments based on perceived reactions from others as "reflected appraisals."

According to Mead, Cooley, and most contemporary social psychologists, other people have a great deal of potential to shape our possible selves because we use perceived assessments of others to shape our own self-assessment. In other words, we name our own behavior (including how we feel about it) based on what *we think* others think about us. For example, a teacher whom you admire a great deal may appear to think very highly of your writing. This reflected appraisal may lead you to focus more intently on your writing; in time, your writing may become quite good, and you may begin to see yourself as a "writer." If you have a difficult decision to make regarding whether to take a high-paying job or attend a graduate writing program, you are likely to ask yourself what this teacher would think of your decision. In this process, you literally conjure up an image of yourself and hold it in front of your ideal of your teacher and develop a self-assessment accordingly. You may find yourself thinking, "This teacher will be so disappointed in me if I don't pursue my writing."

Combining the theories of Mead and Cooley yields a theory of self development that suggests that our sense of who we are and our self-evaluations are formed in interaction with others—that is, the self is a *social* process. We develop self-awareness in the process of learning language. During this same process, we derive self-meaning in the form of names and characteristics directed at us from significant others in our environment. These names or characteristics coalesce into an organized self concept and, eventually, become a basis from which we learn to see ourselves (from the inside out) and determine the meaning and value of our actions.

"Significant Others"

According to the theories of Mead and Cooley, we are constantly engaged in internal self-evaluation based on our ideas about what we think others expect of us. However, Cooley made an important distinction in this process: We are not equally sensitive or persuaded by the views of everyone we encounter. We are much more likely to pay attention to and be influenced by the reactions of someone who is significant to us. Long before the term became a popular way of referring to an intimate partner, Cooley (1902/1983) used the term *significant others* to refer to those people whose opinions and influence are particularly important in an individual's self-assessment. Cooley used the concept of "significant other" to explain this process. We pay more attention to the gestures and responses of those who are important to us. As we observe the reactions of those we are close to, we continuously evaluate and reevaluate our own behavior. For instance, consider a young man who identifies strongly with his grandfather as someone who is courageous and honest. While hanging out with a group of friends who decide to rob a store, this particular young man may find himself thinking about how his grandfather would react if he were to observe his grandson engaged in a robbery. Consequently, he might decide not to join his friends; he would rather appear noble in the imagined eye of his grandfather.

Young children form their initial self-image in the presence of adults who feed, shelter, and nurture them. These adults (usually parents) are therefore likely to be the child's first "significant others" and, as such, will have a strong influence on the child's early self-image. As the child matures and comes into contact with others, he or she will develop other relationships that will exert a significant influence on self-image. The beliefs, tastes, and habits of significant others are also an important source of cultural input that we use in trying on and discarding various social identities. Consider some of your own preferences for types of food, clothing, and music. Is there a type of food or music that you thought you didn't like, but you reconsidered because someone you were attracted to liked it? In such instances, you are putting yourself into the position of the other and willing yourself to simulate the other person's experiences. You are motivated to do so because you like the person, and in trying on new ideas and behaviors, you are stretching the boundaries of your own self.

FROM SOCIAL ROLES/IDENTITIES TO SELVES: THE PROCESS OF "BECOMING"

Students of social psychology often point out that we play different social roles in different situations, but we are not equally invested in each of these roles. For example, you may work part-time as a clerk at the local convenience store. Although you spend several hours a week in this "role," it's probably not on your "Who am I?" list. The question is, why do some of our social identities and behaviors take on the significance of an aspect of "self" while others do not? For instance, some people like to play golf but do not necessarily think of themselves as "golfers," while others include this as an important part of who they are. Not everyone who regularly attends church considers "religious" to be part of their self concept. Why is this the case for some and not others? Or what is the difference between someone who says funny things (a behavior) and someone who thinks of "funny" as an aspect of her or his self concept?

Under the right circumstances, we begin to think of everyday behaviors as "identities" and then, perhaps, to incorporate these identities into an organized sense of self. This is likely to occur when people whose opinions we value continually reinforce a specific behavior or identity ("I think you have a great sense of fashion"; "I think you are a remarkable person"; and so forth). The identity becomes solidified into an aspect of "self" as we incorporate it into our internal dialogue (internalization) and hold it up as a reflection of a personal, ideal sense of being. Consider the implications of this process as you reread your "Who am I?" list. Can you describe the social relations or social processes that occurred over time to give you a sense that you are these roles and possess these characteristics?

My own list includes the identity "teacher." How did I come to see myself this way? When I entered graduate school, like most graduate students, I was required to be a teaching assistant as part of my training. Most of us had been undergraduate students ourselves only a few years earlier, and we were quite nervous about playing the role of teacher. One exercise we engaged in was to try to remember a favorite teacher and consider the traits that made her or him a great teacher. With these images in mind, we would then perform the role of teacher in our own classes. All of us had to teach, but only a few of us began to eventually think of "teaching" as a central aspect of who we are. What made the difference? In my case, I received "role support" from several sources. My family thought that my teaching was a neat thing (other than the teaching, they had little concept of graduate school and why I was there). When I talked with them about my studies, we talked mostly about my teaching. This they could understand. I was also invited by the chair of the department to participate in a pilot seminar that was part of a national project aimed at making scholars into better teachers. (Most graduate students receive little or no training to teach.) This seminar functioned as a primary group for me. It became one of my main reference points, and the instructors and fellow participants were significant people to me. Through this seminar, which included a lot of videotaping of our teaching, I began to think constantly about teaching: how to do it, what made it special, and so forth. My new seminar buddies and I talked together about these things as well. Within a few years, I was giving seminars to other graduate students on how to teach. I even wrote articles about teaching. I woke up one day and realized that over the course of several years and through engagement with a specific primary group, I was not just a scholar who also taught classes; I was a *teacher.*

Role support from those who are significant is a central factor in the development of aspects of self that we consider to be core components of who we are. However, significant others can sometimes be a source of conflicting information. In addition to the teaching support I received in graduate school, I also had faculty mentors who considered my teaching activities a waste of time. These professors wanted me to focus on scholarly writing and get a job at a top research school. They worried that I had become "too identified" with faculty at teaching schools and that I would "throw away" a good research career. These conflicts can be painful and difficult to reconcile. I will discuss this idea at length in the section of Part VII titled "Contradictions and Conflict in Self Production." For now, it can be said that the conflicts are also a form of internal conversation that reveal our deepest values and commitments. I valued *both* primary groups— researchers and teachers—and I had significant relationships with mentors in both areas. The depth of my own conflict reflected these social relationships and commitments.

Ultimately, I was able to reconcile my conflict by engaging in an alternative conversation with myself: I didn't have to be one or the other—I could be both. I became aware of this *possible self* (see below) in a conversation with a retired faculty member who was very famous for his scholarly work on social research methods. This famous scholar would visit me in my graduate student cubicle and ask how my teaching was going. He was the one who told me I could do both. He introduced a new possibility into my existing definition of the situation—he reframed it. In so doing, he probably changed the course of my life.

To the extent that I have a current vocation for teaching, I can trace it to the interactional effects of groups who provided me with a vocabulary for thinking about and performing the teaching role, and significant others who provided role support in the form of encouragement. Even those who were discouraging had an impact in making my commitment to teaching even stronger.

"Ossification" of Cultural Roles

Philip Blumstein was one of my mentors in the field of social psychology. He developed a theory to explain how specific social roles and behaviors can evolve into coherent, consistent aspects of self concept through the process of interaction with significant others. Blumstein (1991) was particularly interested in the ways in which evolving selves reflect preestablished cultural ideals—ideals that we may, in theory, not agree with, but which have a tendency to become incorporated into our sense of self when reinforced by significant others. Thus, we are often surprised to wake up and discover that we have "become" something or someone that we could never have imagined.

Blumstein's thesis is that significant others, particularly intimate partners, are important contributors to our sense of self because we value their reflected appraisals so highly. For example, in the process of coordinating activities, a couple may name particular behaviors as identities, such as "provider" or "homemaker." The partners may become attached to, or grow into, these identities through routinization and the reflected appraisals of each other. This is especially likely to be the case when we perform contextual social roles or identities that correspond with highly idealized cultural expectations. For instance, a heterosexual couple who insist, early in their marriage, that they will not conform to gendered expectations about marital roles may find themselves surprised at the extent to which they have fallen into these roles anyway. If they trace it back, they may recognize many small, but cumulatively significant moments when parents, friends, and others have focused on these behaviors and, in order to maintain the interaction, the married individuals may have played the expected social identity. Friends and relatives who constantly comment on a man's "earning power" are singling out this behavior as an important characteristic of a "successful" married man. Each of these interactions reinforces a social expectation that "the man should be the breadwinner." In time, even though he may not think he believes in this expectation, the newly married man may find himself shifting his behavior more and more to fit the expectations of "the married man." Blumstein refers to this process as "ossification," meaning that identities have the potential to harden, like bone, into selves.

I ask my students to engage in the following exercise as a way to illuminate the specific interactional steps that occur in the process of moving from a series of identities or behaviors to internalized self-ideals, especially roles and ideals we may think we are opposed or immune to. Begin a paper with the phrase, "I never thought I would become _____." Then fill in the blank with something that you could never imagine yourself doing (joining a religious cult, becoming a particular type of politician, etc.). Now consider the ways in which persons who are significant in your life could actually change your ideals, beliefs, and sense of who you are.

It can be very useful in your understanding of your self to take some time to ponder your internal conversations; ask yourself who or what you're in conversation with, especially when you experience strong motivation to do something of unease or conflict. This internal "witnessing" can help you become more awake to the processes whereby you incorporate the reflected appraisals of others into your concept of self and then judge and evaluate your behavior accordingly. Recall the lesson on "mindlessness" from Part II: To what extent do "mindless" categories of behavioral expectations shape your internal conversation about who you think you *should* be and what you think you *should* do?

Possible Selves

Hazel Markus and Paula Nurius (1986) are known for their studies on how people develop ideas about who and what they think they can be. So far, this text has emphasized the idea that we learn cultural expectations from others. These expectations include categories and scripts that provide details about appropriate behavior (identities) for various situations. Markus and Nurius are interested in the specific sources of information that individuals have for what roles they think they can play. They are also interested in how this information varies for different people in different walks of life. For instance, your economic background, your racial or ethnic background, and your gender are some of the significant differences that shape ideas about who you think you can be.

Markus and Nurius are particularly keen on studying the details of how we imagine ourselves in possible roles. According to their work, individuals who can "see" themselves in a particular social position are more likely to eventually achieve this position. However, it's not enough to have a general idea of the social role you would like to occupy; rather, you need to be able to imagine the actual *process* of getting into that role. They propose that people who have access to the information, or stories, that provide specific details of how to become a certain self will be more likely to be able to *imagine* themselves going through these steps and, in turn, will be better able to organize their lives so that they achieve their desired positions.

One example of their work focuses on the different expectations of fourth graders who are from either wealthy or low-income families. When asked what they want to be when they grow up, the children from higher-income families usually name a profession such as lawyer, doctor, software designer, and so on. What is noteworthy for Markus and Nurius is the children's ability to describe, in very specific detail, the paths to achieving these professional roles. The children have a well-mapped route, which includes an understanding that they will have to go to college (a good one), graduate school, and so forth. They also understand the detailed steps of how to get there—for example they know they need to score well on college entrance exams such as the SAT.

In contrast, children from low-income families often have highly unrealistic desires—they most frequently want to be music stars or star athletes. When asked how this might come about for them, they have very little idea about what they might have to do to realize these desired selves. According to Markus and Nurius (1986), the difference is in the type of information children receive about the actual processes of becoming specific social roles. If the information is specific and well charted, the children develop a highly articulated sense of a "possible self." They can hold this image in their minds and "rehearse" what it will be like to go through each stage of development toward the imagined end. Children who have no information about the path also have ideals, but they have no real sense of how to perform in each of the phases that leads to these ideals.

Related research on athletic performance demonstrates that athletes who *imagine* themselves going through specific maneuvers actually perform better. These athletes take themselves through a mental workout that enables them to create a mental path through anticipated performance routines. This mental or imaginative process was the basis of an extremely popular book, *The Inner Game of Tennis,* published originally in 1974. The book was subtitled *The Classic Guide to the Mental Side of Peak Performance.* Several related books such as *Inner Skiing* (1977), *The Inner Game of Golf* (1981) and even *The Inner Game of Music* (1986) followed soon after. In these books, author Timothy Gallwey instructed his readers in the usefulness of tuning into the mental or inner dialogue and imagery in order to better manage physical performance. A later book by Gallwey, *The Inner Game of Work* (2001), extends this concept to activities such as the job interview, illustrating that people can mentally prepare for this experience by rehearsing their peak performance. This imaginative process includes engaging in inner dialogues about potential nervousness, feelings of inadequacy, and so forth, and learning to "beat" these "mental opponents."

Markus and Nurius, along with many other educational researchers, observe that children in low-income schools receive very different information from those in high-income schools. Higher-income children are not only "tracked" for professional-level jobs, but they are also exposed to considerable information about the specific steps required to progress toward these professions. For example, teachers and administrators in these schools routinely talk with parents and students about services that provide instruction and sample testing for college entrance exams. These conversations point students toward valuable services, and they also enable the students to imagine themselves in potential roles and to conceive the specific routes for getting there.

Conclusions

One implication of these theories on the *social* self is that the company you keep and the ideas that you cultivate *do* matter. Before parents the world over start jumping for joy and saying, "See, I told you so, that person/group *will* be a bad influence," we should remember that these effects are (1) a process and (2) the result of complex conversations we have with ourselves in which we reference multiple perspectives and consider many different significant others. We are not social robots; the attitudes of others are not simply poured into our heads, causing us to behave unthinkingly, nor are we "Stepford" people who can be easily programmed to fulfill an ideal social role (such as husband or wife). As Mead has stated, the self is an *ongoing conversation*. Significant others are a part of our internal conversations, but just as we do not allow people to act as dictators over our external lives, so we do not allow the imagined "voices" of significant others to dictate our internal lives. We also adopt different reference group perspectives when we evaluate our behavior and make decisions. We conjure up these different perspectives as a way to enable us to see our possibilities from different points of view. Thus, the company you keep will certainly have an impact on your internal conversations and deliberations, but the form this influence takes will be (1) to allow new voices into your conversation—in the form of significant others, and (2) to cultivate new and alternative perspectives from which to make sense of and guide your own behavior.

Far from being robotic influences, a richly cultivated set of reference perspectives can actually make us freer. The processes described in this essay can be used as a guide to becoming more observant or "mindful" of the kind of conversation we are having with ourselves about who and what we can be. Other people and their ideas usually do not have a direct effect on our behavior, but they have an influence to the extent that the *expectations* of significant others make us feel more or less free to make certain choices and to behave in certain ways. One thing to keep in mind is that a broad range of possible selves and a carefully considered set of diverse reference groups will result in self-conversations that provide many different perspectives on how to see and direct your own behavior. This expansion of imagined possibilities provides you with a basis for bringing more individuality to various social roles. For instance, there are many different ways to be a minister or a teacher or a student or a spouse. The specific ways in which you grow into social identities, and eventually make them your own as part of your organized self concept, will depend on the "models" you have for how you can play these roles. The broader your range of possibilities, the more variations you will be able to imagine, and the more individuality you will cultivate.

A final thing to keep in mind as we leave this topic is that significant others and reference groups can operate "oppositionally" as well as directionally. Most of us can recall occasions, at some time or another, when we have been focused primarily on *not* being something or on formulating a point of view that is in *opposition* to a significant other or reference group that feels problematic in our lives. Oppositional self-conversations can be very powerful in leading us to behave in emotionally charged ways. Thus, parents who are inclined to protect their children from "undesirable" external influences might consider whether their ways of doing so are teaching their children healthy ways of trying on various identities and reference perspectives so that they can judge for themselves, or rather, whether their methods are hindering their children from gathering the variety of perspectives that enable healthy self-engagement and development. In the case of the latter, one of the first strong oppositional perspectives the child might develop will be against the parent. In so doing, the child might be less selective about various identities he or she tries on and less inclined to assess the fit of these identities in terms of a thoughtful self process. Instead, in the eagerness to take on perspectives that challenge or oppose the parent, the child may actually eclipse or ignore other significant internal voices that are telling her or him that this identity is not a good fit.

In short, trying on various identities under conditions of support and wisdom leads to the cultivation of a rich and healthy internal conversation whereby we learn the skill of mindful self-assessment and feel able to develop a variety of responses that we can feel good about in difficult situations. Conversely, external attempts to limit the opportunities for "identity play" may lead to less mindful rebellion aimed in opposition to single perspectives. The study of the self as a social process opens up the avenues to greater self-awareness and, consequently, to more nuanced ideas about who we think we can be and what we think we can do.

References and Suggestions for Further Reading

Blumstein, P. (1991). The production of selves in personal relationships. In J. Howard & P. Callero (Eds.), *The self–society dynamic* (pp. 305–322). Cambridge, UK: University of Cambridge Press.

Cooley, C. H. (1983). Looking-glass self. In *Human nature and the social order* (pp. 182–185). New York: Transaction Publishers. (Original work published 1902)

Denzin, N. (1966). The significant others of a college population. *The Sociological Quarterly, 7*(3), 298.

Gallwey, T. (1974). *The inner game of tennis: The classic guide to the mental side of peak performance.* New York: Random House.

Gallwey, T. (1977). *Inner skiing.* New York: Random House.

Gallwey, T. (1981). *The inner game of golf.* New York: Random House.

Gallwey, T. (1986). *The inner game of music.* New York: Random House.

Gallwey, T. (2001). *The inner game of work.* New York: Random House.

Kuhn, M. H., & McPartland, T. S. (1954). An empirical investigation of self-attitudes. *American Sociological Review, 19,* 68–76.

Markus, H., & Nurius, P. (1986). Possible selves. *American Psychologist, 41,* 954–969.

Mead, G. H. (1962). *Mind, self, and society: From the standpoint of a social behaviorist.* Chicago: University of Chicago Press.

Park, R. E. (1952). *Human communities.* Glencoe, IL: Free Press.

Quindlen, A. (1989). *Living out loud.* New York: Random House.

Sandstrom, K. L., Martin, D. D., & Fine, G. A. (2003). *Symbols, selves, and social reality.* Los Angeles: Roxbury. (See especially Chapters 3–5)

Snyder, M. (1987). *Public appearances/private realities: The psychology of self-monitoring.* New York: W. H. Freeman.

THE SELF AS A PROCESS OF INTERACTION

Who am I really? This is a question we often ask ourselves. The psychologist William James once remarked that our selves are as numerous as the number of people with whom we interact. Most people believe that the self is a fixed and immutable set of "core personality traits"—something that we are born with. This section introduces the concept of the self as a social process. Sociologists George Herbert Mead and Charles Horton Cooley were contemporaries of James, writing in the United States in the 1930s. They introduced the idea that people develop a sense of themselves in the same way that they develop an understanding of other social objects and events: We learn to "name" ourselves and our actions. This naming process occurs through interaction, especially with those who are significant to us. We learn how to think and feel about ourselves based on the impressions and "names" others have for us. The readings in this section provide the theoretical basis for understanding the social self.

"The Self, the I, and the Me" is excerpted from the classic writings of George Herbert Mead. Mead discusses the process by which we come to see ourselves as objects and to learn to describe our own actions. As this process develops, so does our ability to conceptualize our own actions as a separate, coherent self.

"Looking-Glass Self" is excerpted from another classic article, this one by Charles Horton Cooley. Cooley proposed that we learn what to think and feel about ourselves by watching how others react to us. Much like looking into a mirror, if we perceive someone as viewing our actions with admiration, then we feel pride. If we perceive them as viewing us with disdain, we feel mortification. Through these "reflected appraisals," we gain information from others about ourselves and our actions.

READING QUESTIONS

1. Make a list of 20 responses to the question, "Who am I?" How many of the characteristics on your list are "social roles"—that is, aspects of yourself that exist only in reference to others (for example, daughter)?

2. If you listed behavioral characteristics (for example, "friendly," "funny," etc.), try to recall how you came to think of yourself this way. Do you have significant others who notice, expect, and reinforce these self-images? How do you feel when you don't behave in ways that are consistent with these expected characteristics?

3. According to Cooley, we rely on the impressions of others in forming our own self-assessments. If we are watching others' perceptions of us, how do we know whether our read of their reaction to us is accurate or not? Does it matter?

4. For a day, practice paying attention to how you are imagining others are thinking of you. What evidence are you using to confirm your impressions of their judgments of you?

11

The Self, the I, and the Me

George Herbert Mead

(1934)

We can distinguish very definitely between the self and the body. The body can be there and can operate in a very intelligent fashion without there being a self involved in the experience. The self has the characteristic that it is an object to itself, and that characteristic distinguishes it from other objects and from the body. It is perfectly true that the eye can see the foot, but it does not see the body as a whole. We cannot see our backs; we can feel certain portions of them, if we are agile, but we cannot get an experience of our whole body. There are, of course, experiences which are somewhat vague and difficult of location, but the bodily experiences are for us organized about a self. The foot and hand belong to the self. We can see our feet, especially if we look at them from the wrong end of an opera glass, as strange things which we have difficulty in recognizing as our own. The parts of the body are quite distinguishable from the self. We can lose parts of the body without any serious invasion of the self. The mere ability to experience different parts of the body is not different from the experience of a table. The table presents a different feel from what the hand does when one hand feels another, but it is an experience of something with which we come definitely into contact. The body does not experience itself as a whole, in the sense in which the self in some way enters into the experience of the self.

It is the characteristic of the self as an object to itself that I want to bring out. This characteristic is represented in the word "self," which is a reflexive, and indicates that which can be both subject and object. This type of object is essentially different from other objects, and in the past it has been distinguished as conscious, a term which indicates an experience with, an experience of, one's self. It was assumed that consciousness in some way carried this capacity of being an object to itself. In giving a behavioristic statement of consciousness we have to look for some sort of experience in which the physical organism can become an object to itself.

When one is running to get away from someone who is chasing him, he is entirely occupied in this action, and his experience may be swallowed up in the objects about him, so that he has, at the time being, no consciousness of self at all. We must be, of course, very completely occupied to have that take place, but we can, I think, recognize that sort of a possible experience in which the self does not enter. We can, perhaps, get some light on that situation through those experiences in which in very intense action there appears in the experience of the individual, back of this intense action, memories, and anticipations. Tolstoi as an officer in the war gives an account of having pictures of his past experience in the midst of his most intense action. There are also the pictures that flash into a person's mind when he is drowning. In such instances there is a contrast between an experience that is absolutely wound up in outside activity in which the self as an object does not enter, and an activity of memory and imagination in which the self is the principal object. The self is then entirely distinguishable from an organism that is surrounded by things and acts with reference to things, including parts of its own body. These latter may be objects like other objects, but they are just objects out there in the field, and they do not involve a self that is an object to the organism. This is, I think, frequently overlooked. It is that fact which makes our anthropomorphic reconstructions of animal life so fallacious. How can an individual get outside himself (experientially) in such a way as to become an object to himself? This is the essential psychological problem of selfhood or of self-consciousness; and its solution is to be found by referring to the process of social conduct or activity in which the given person or individual is implicated. The apparatus of reason would not be complete unless it swept itself into its own analysis of the field of experience; or unless the individual brought himself into the same experiential field as that of the other individual selves in relation to whom he acts in any given social situation. Reason cannot become impersonal unless it takes an objective, non-affective attitude toward itself; otherwise we have just consciousness, not *self*-consciousness. And it is necessary to rational conduct that the individual should thus take an objective, impersonal attitude toward himself, that he should become an object to himself. For the individual organism is obviously an essential and important fact or constituent element of the empirical situation in which it acts; and without taking objective account of itself as such, it cannot act intelligently, or rationally.

The individual experiences himself as such, not directly, but only indirectly, from the particular standpoints of other individual members of the same social group, or from the generalized standpoint of the social group as a whole to which he belongs. For he enters his own experience as a self or individual, not directly or immediately, not by becoming a subject to himself, but only insofar as he first becomes an object to himself just as other individuals are objects to him or in his experience; and he becomes an object to himself only by taking the attitudes of other individuals toward himself within a social environment or context of experience and behavior in which both he and they are involved.

The importance of what we term "communication" lies in the fact that it provides a form of behavior in which the organism or the individual may become an object to himself. It is that sort of communication which we have been discussing—not communication in the sense of the cluck of the hen to the chickens, or the bark of a wolf to the pack, or the lowing of a cow, but communication in the sense of significant symbols, communication which is directed not only to others but also to the individual himself. So far as that type of communication is a part of behavior it at least introduces a self. Of course, one may hear without listening; one may see things that he does not realize; do things that he is not really aware of. But it is where one does respond to that which he addresses to another and where that response of his own becomes a part of his conduct, where he not only hears himself but responds to himself, talks and replies to himself as truly as the other person replies to him, that we have behavior in which the individuals become objects to themselves.

Such a self is not, I would say, primarily the physiological organism. The physiological organism is essential to it, but we are at least able to think of a self without it. Persons who believe in immortality, or believe in ghosts, or in the possibility of the self leaving the body, assume a self which is quite distinguishable from the body. How successfully they can hold these conceptions is an open question, but we do, as a fact, separate the self and the organism. It is fair to say that the beginning of the self as an object, so far as we can see, is to be found in the experiences of people that lead to the conception of a "double." Primitive people assume that there is a double, located presumably in the diaphragm, that leaves the body temporarily in sleep and completely in death. It can be enticed out of the body of one's enemy and perhaps killed. It is represented in infancy by the imaginary playmates which children set up, and through which they come to control their experiences in their play.

The self, as that which can be an object to itself, is essentially a social structure, and it arises in social experience. After a self has arisen, it in a certain sense provides for itself its social experiences, and so we can conceive of an absolutely solitary self. But it is impossible to conceive of a self arising outside of social experience. When it has arisen we can think of a person in solitary confinement for the rest of his life, but who still has himself as a companion, and is able to think and to converse with himself as he had communicated with others. That process to which I have just referred, of responding to one's self as another responds to it, taking part in one's own conversation with others, being aware of what one is saying and using that awareness of what one is saying to determine what one is going to say thereafter—that is a process with which we are all familiar. We are continually following up our own address to other persons by an understanding of what we are saying, and using that understanding in the direction of our continued speech. We are finding out what we are going to say, what we are going to do, by saying and doing, and in the process we are continually controlling the process itself. In the conversation of gestures what we say calls out a certain response in another and that in turn changes our own action, so that we shift from what we started to do because of the reply the other makes. The conversation of gestures is the beginning of communication. The

individual comes to carry on a conversation of gestures with himself. He says something, and that calls out a certain reply in himself which makes him change what he was going to say. One starts to say something, we will presume an unpleasant something, but when he starts to say it he realizes it is cruel. The effect on himself of what he is saying checks him; there is here a conversation of gestures between the individual and himself. We mean by significant speech that the action is one that affects the individual himself, and that the effect upon the individual himself is part of the intelligent carrying-out of the conversation with others. Now we, so to speak, amputate that social phase and dispense with it for the time being, so that one is talking to one's self as one would talk to another person.

This process of abstraction cannot be carried on indefinitely. One inevitably seeks an audience, has to pour himself out to somebody. In reflective intelligence one thinks to act, and to act solely so that this action remains a part of a social process. Thinking becomes preparatory to social action. The very process of thinking is, of course, simply an inner conversation that goes on, but it is a conversation of gestures which in its completion implies the expression of that which one thinks to an audience. One separates the significance of what he is saying to others from the actual speech and gets it ready before saying it. He thinks it out, and perhaps writes it in the form of a book; but it is still a part of social intercourse in which one is addressing other persons and at the same time addressing one's self, and in which one controls the address to other persons by the response made to one's own gesture. That the person should be responding to himself is necessary to the self, and it is this sort of social conduct which provides behavior within which that self appears. I know of no other form of behavior than the linguistic in which the individual is an object to himself, and, so far as I can see, the individual is not a self in the reflexive sense unless he is an object to himself. It is this fact that gives a critical importance to communication, since this is a type of behavior in which the individual does so respond to himself.

We realize in everyday conduct and experience that an individual does not mean a great deal of what he is doing and saying. We frequently say that such an individual is not himself. We come away from an interview with a realization that we have left out important things, that there are parts of the self that did not get into what was said. What determines the amount of the self that gets into communication is the social experience itself. Of course, a good deal of the self does not need to get expression. We carry on a whole series of different relationships to different people. We are one thing to one man and another thing to another. There are parts of the self which exist only for the self in relationship to itself. We divide ourselves up in all sorts of different selves with reference to our acquaintances. We discuss politics with one and religion with another. There are all sorts of different selves answering to all sorts of different social reactions. It is the social process itself that is responsible for the appearance of the self; it is not there as a self apart from this type of experience.

A multiple personality is in a certain sense normal, as I have just pointed out. There is usually an organization of the whole self with reference to the community to which we belong, and the situation in which we find ourselves. What the society is, whether we are living with people of the present, people of our own imaginations, people of the past, varies, of course, with different individuals. Normally, within the sort of community as a whole to which we belong, there is a unified self, but that may be broken up. To a person who is somewhat unstable nervously and in whom there is a line of cleavage, certain activities become impossible, and that set of activities may separate and evolve another self. Two separate "me's" and "I's," two different selves, result, and

that is the condition under which there is a tendency to break up the personality. There is an account of a professor of education who disappeared, was lost to the community, and later turned up in a logging camp in the West. He freed himself of his occupation and turned to the woods where he felt, if you like, more at home. The pathological side of it was the forgetting, the leaving out of the rest of the self. This result involved getting rid of certain bodily memories which would identify the individual to himself. We often recognize the lines of cleavage that run through us. We would be glad to forget certain things, get rid of things the self is bound up with in past experiences. What we have here is a situation in which there can be different selves, and it is dependent upon the set of social reactions that is involved as to which self we are going to be. If we can forget everything involved in one set of activities, obviously we relinquish that part of the self. Take a person who is unstable, get him occupied by speech, and at the same time get his eye on something you are writing so that he is carrying on two separate lines of communication, and if you go about it in the right way you can get those two currents going so that they do not run into each other. You can get two entirely different sets of activities going on. You can bring about in that way the dissociation of a person's self. It is a process of setting up two sorts of communication which separate the behavior of the individual. For one individual it is this thing said and heard, and for the other individual there exists only that which he sees written. You must, of course, keep one experience out of the field of the other. Dissociations are apt to take place when an event leads to emotional upheavals. That which is separated goes on in its own way.

The unity and structure of the complete self reflects the unity and structure of the social process as a whole; and each of the elementary selves of which it is composed reflects the unity and structure of one of the various aspects of that process in which the individual is implicated. In other words, the various elementary selves which constitute, or are organized into, a complete self are the various aspects of the structure of that complete self answering to the various aspects of the structure of the social process as a whole; the structure of the complete self is thus a reflection of the complete social process. The organization and unification of a social group is identical with the organization and unification of any one of the selves arising within the social process in which that group is engaged, or which it is carrying on.

The phenomenon of dissociation of personality is caused by a breaking up of the complete, unitary self into the component selves of which it is composed, and which respectively correspond to different aspects of the social process in which the person is involved, and within which his complete or unitary self has arisen; these aspects being the different social groups to which he belongs within that process. . . .

Rational society, of course, is not limited to any specific set of individuals. Any person who is rational can become a part of it. The attitude of the community toward our own response is imported into ourselves in terms of the meaning of what we are doing. This occurs in its widest extent in universal discourse, in the reply which the rational world makes to our remark. The meaning is as universal as the community; it is necessarily involved in the rational character of that community; it is the response that the world made up out of rational beings inevitably makes to our own statement. We both get the object and ourselves into experience in terms of such a process; the other appears in our own experience insofar as we do take such an organized and generalized attitude.

If one meets a person on the street whom he fails to recognize, one's reaction toward him is that toward any other who is a member of the same community. He is the other, the organized, generalized other, if you like. One takes his attitude over against one's self. If he turns in one direction, one is to go in another direction. One has his response as an attitude within himself. It is having that attitude within himself that makes it possible for one to be a self. That involves something beyond the mere turning to the right, as we say, instinctively, without self-consciousness. To have self-consciousness one must have the attitude of the other in one's own organism as controlling the thing that he is going to do. What appears in the immediate experience of one's self in taking that attitude is what we term the "me." It is that self which is able to maintain itself in the community, that is recognized in the community insofar as it recognizes the others. Such is the phase of the self which I have referred to as that of the "me."

Over against the "me" is the "I." The individual not only has rights, but he has duties; he is not only a citizen, a member of the community, but he is one who reacts to this community and in his reaction to it, as we have seen in the conversation of gestures, changes it. The "I" is the response of the individual to the attitude of the community as this appears in his own experience. His response to that organized attitude in turn changes it. As we have pointed out, this is a change which is not present in his own experience until after it takes place. The "I" appears in our experience in memory. It is only after we have acted that we know what we have done; it is only after we have spoken that we know what we have said. The adjustment to that organized world which is present in our own nature is one that represents the "me" and is constantly there. But if the response to it is a response which is of the nature of the conversation of gestures, if it creates a situation which is in some sense novel, if one puts up his side of the case, asserts himself over against others and insists that they take a different attitude toward himself, then there is something important occurring that is not previously present in experience.

12

Looking-Glass Self

Charles Horton Cooley

(1983)

The social origin of [self] comes by the pathway of intercourse with other persons. There is no sense of "I" . . . without its correlative sense of you, or he, or they. . . . In a very large and interesting class of cases the social reference takes the form of a somewhat definite imagination of how one's self—that is any idea he appropriates—appears in a particular mind, and the kind of self-feeling one has is determined by the attitude . . . attributed to that other mind. A social self of this sort might be called the reflected or looking-glass self:

> Each to each a looking-glass
>
> Reflects the other that doth pass.

As we see our face, figure, and dress in the glass, and are interested in them because they are ours, and pleased or otherwise with them according as they do or do not answer to what we should like them to be; so in imagination we perceive in another's mind some thought of our appearance, manners, aims, deeds, character, friends, and so on, and are variously affected by it.

A self-idea of this sort seems to have three principal elements: the imagination of our appearance to the other person; the imagination of his judgment of that appearance, and some sort of self-feeling, such as pride or mortification.

The comparison with a looking-glass hardly suggests the second element, the imagined judgment, which is quite essential. The thing that moves us to pride or shame is not the mere mechanical reflection of ourselves, but an imputed sentiment, the imagined effect of this reflection upon another's mind. This is evident from the fact that the character and weight of that other, in whose mind we see ourselves, makes all the difference with our feeling. We are ashamed to seem evasive in the presence of a straightforward man, cowardly in the presence of a brave one, gross in the eyes of a refined one, and so on. We always imagine, and in imagining share, the judgments of the other mind. A man will boast to one person of an action—say some sharp transaction in trade—which he would be ashamed to own to another.

The process by which self-feeling of the looking-glass sort develops in children may be followed without much difficulty. Studying the movements of others as closely as they do, they soon see a connection between their own acts and changes in those movements; that is, they perceive their own influence or power over persons. The child appropriates the visible actions of his parent or nurse, over which he finds he has some control, in quite the same way as he appropriates one of his own members or a plaything, and he will try to do things with this new possession, just as he will with his hand or his rattle. A girl six months old will attempt in the most evident and deliberate manner to attract attention to herself, to set going by her actions some of those movements of other persons that she has appropriated. She has tasted the joy of being a cause, of exerting social power, and wishes more of it. She will tug at her mother's skirts, wriggle, gurgle, stretch out her arms, etc., all the time watching for the hoped-for effect. These performances often give the child, even at this age, an appearance of what is called affectation, that is, she seems to be unduly preoccupied with what other people think of her. Affectation, at any age, exists when the passion to influence others seems to overbalance the established character and give it an obvious twist or pose. It is instructive to find that even Darwin was, in his childhood, capable of departing from truth for the sake of making an impression. "For instance," he says in his autobiography, "I once gathered much valuable fruit from my father's trees and hid it in the shrubbery and then ran in breathless haste to spread the news that I had discovered a hoard of stolen fruit."[1]

The young performer soon learns to be different things to different people, showing that he begins to apprehend personality and to foresee its operation. If the mother or nurse is more tender than just, she will almost certainly be "worked" by systematic weeping. It is a matter of common observation that children often behave worse with their mother than with other and less sympathetic people. Of the new persons that a child sees, it is evident that some make a strong impression and awaken a desire to interest and please them, while others are indifferent or repugnant. Sometimes the reason can be perceived or guessed, sometimes not; but the fact of selective interest, admiration, prestige, is obvious before the end of the second year. By that time a child already cares much for the reflection of himself upon one personality and little for that upon another. Moreover he soon claims intimate and tractable persons as *mine*,

classes them among his other possessions, and maintains his ownership against all comers. M., at three years of age, vigorously resented R.'s claim upon their mother. The latter was "*my* mamma," whenever the point was raised.

Strong joy and grief depend upon the treatment this rudimentary social self receives. In the case of M. I noticed as early as the fourth month a "hurt" way of crying which seemed to indicate a sense of personal slight. It was quite different from the cry of pain or that of anger, but seemed about the same as the cry of fright. The slightest tone of reproof would produce it. On the other hand, if people took notice and laughed and encouraged, she was hilarious. At about fifteen months old she had become "a perfect little actress," seeming to live largely in imaginations of her effect upon other people. She constantly and obviously laid traps for attention, and looked abashed or wept at any signs of disapproval or indifference. At times it would seem as if she could not get over these repulses, but would cry long in a grieved way, refusing to be comforted. If she hit upon any little trick that made people laugh she would be sure to repeat it, laughing loudly and affectedly in imitation. She had quite a repertory of these small performances, which she would display to a sympathetic audience, or even try upon strangers. I have seen her at sixteen months, when R. refused to give her the scissors, sit down and make-believe cry, putting up her under lip and snuffling, meanwhile looking up now and then to see what effect she was producing.

In such phenomena we have plainly enough, it seems to me, the germ of personal ambition of every sort. Imagination cooperating with instinctive self-feeling has already created a social "I," and this has become a principal object of interest and endeavor.

Progress from this point is chiefly in the way of a greater definiteness, fullness, and inwardness in the imagination of the other's state of mind. A little child thinks of and tries to elicit certain visible or audible phenomena, and does not go back of them; but what a grown-up person desires to produce in others is an internal, invisible condition which his own richer experience enables him to imagine, and of which expression is only the sign. Even adults, however, make no separation between what other people think and the visible expression of that thought. They imagine the whole thing at once, and their idea differs from that of a child chiefly in the comparative richness and complexity of the elements that accompany and interpret the visible or audible sign. There is also a progress from the naive to the subtle in socially self-assertive

action. A child obviously and simply, at first, does things for effect. Later there is an endeavor to suppress the appearance of doing so; affection, indifference, contempt, etc., are simulated to hide the real wish to affect the self-image. It is perceived that an obvious seeking after good opinion is weak and disagreeable.

NOTE

1. Darwin, F. (1959). *Life and letters of Charles Darwin*. New York: Basic Books, p. 27.

SIGNIFICANT OTHERS AND SELF DEVELOPMENT

The readings in this section expand on the theoretical ideas presented in the previous section and provide illustrations of Cooley's concept of "significant others." According to the theories of Mead and Cooley, we learn how to recognize ourselves and form impressions of behavior based on how we imagine others think of us. For example, two young students with similar academic ability may learn to think very differently about their student "selves" if one has a teacher who treats the student as if her performance is "inspired" and the other has a teacher who considers his questions to be annoying and stupid. The first student, feeling encouraged and praised, may begin to see herself as having tremendous potential and therefore be inclined to study even harder. She may even begin to think of herself as "intellectual." The second student is likely to see himself as nonintellectual and be disinclined to study any more than he has to. Significant others, especially in the early stages of development, have considerable effect on our ideas about who we think we are and what we think we can do.

In his article "A Theory of Genius," sociologist Thomas Scheff uses these theories as a framework for explaining the development of genius. Scheff proposes that significant others exert a powerful influence on self development through the process of "shaming." According to his theory, "genius" is more likely to occur among those who are able to escape the interactional shaming processes that lead us to conform to the status quo.

"Sissy Boy, Progressive Parents" by Daniel Farr is a personal memoir about growing up as a boy who preferred many of the games and activities commonly associated with girls. In a twist on the usual boy-is-bullied-for-being-a-sissy theme, Farr discusses the ways in which the acceptance he felt from his parents enabled him to deal more effectively with the taunts of his peers. Acceptance from significant others such as parents can provide us with a strong and enduring self-esteem, even when confronted with the punishing of peers.

READING QUESTIONS

1. For a few days, keep track of the "audience in your head" when you are making decisions or judging yourself. In these moments, stop and ask yourself who or what is in your mind as you go through the process of self-assessment and self-direction. This exercise can help you identify your significant others.

2. Discuss the idea of "shame" as a process that preserves the status quo. How does this process work interactionally? How does it work internally?

3. Consider experiences in which you have felt shame. Do you avoid certain behaviors or situations because you *imagine* you might experience shame? When you imagine this shame, who or what is the audience in your head?

4. Recall an occasion in which someone's comments to you have lifted your spirits when you were down and made you feel better about yourself and the situation. How is it possible that another person's comments can have such a tremendous impact? Explain the process based on the theories in this section.

SIGNIFICANT OTHERS AND SELF DEVELOPMENT

13

A Theory of Genius

Thomas Scheff

(1990)

The explanation of genius that is most common is that it is a product of inherited genes. Galton (1869) sought to demonstrate this point by studying the family lines of artists, scientists, and statesmen. Cox (1926) conducted a similar but more extensive study. Both show a strong relationship between genius in a certain field, for example, music, and a family background of talent in that field. Bach and Puccini, for example, were both descended from five generations of musicians. Although these two examples are extreme, the relationship is general; most of the great musicians came from families in which there was already musical talent.

This article is aimed not at dismissing the genetic argument but offers an alternative model of explanation which could either complement or replace it, depending on the findings of future research. As has been pointed out many times, family inheritance has both a biological and a social character. In the study of genius it is difficult to disentangle the two since we deal with a small number of cases. Since I propose only a necessary cause, not a sufficient one, there is no need to evaluate the validity of the genetic argument.

The theory proposed concerns two processes of development—one of *talent,* the other of *self-esteem.* I argue that both processes are necessary. The development of talent will be discussed first.

Modern linguistics has (unintentionally) contributed to the issue by the discovery that all humans have genius in language. Since this contention is not obvious, I first review the contribution that linguists have made: the competent use of language is an achievement of such staggering complexity that it seems a miracle.

There is a large literature on the complexity of even the simplest utterances. The attempt to program computers for automatic translation is one of the bases of the new appreciation of the immense intelligence required to use language. There is no way to program a computer to solve a relatively simple problem of competent language use: choosing from among fixed, multiple meanings of a word. This can be demonstrated by . . . the simple statement . . . , "The box is in the pen." Is pen to be construed as a writing instrument or an enclosure? To answer this question, the program would have to have access to an encyclopedia, not merely a dictionary, and would have to have the resources to know how to comb the encyclopedic reference for its relevance to the context in the sentence.

Compared with creating a metaphoric expression or even merely understanding one, words with two or more meanings are very simple problems indeed. There is the story of the computer program which translated the expression "The spirit is willing, but the flesh is weak" into Russian as "The whiskey is good, but the meat is bad," and "Out of sight, out of mind" as "First blind, then insane." These illustrations are apocryphal, but they make the point: using language correctly is a creative process beyond the power of even the most sophisticated computer program, or of living creatures other than humans, for that matter.

It will be helpful here to define what I mean by creative intelligence, the basis of genius. For my purposes, it is the ability to find a new solution to a new problem. In the living world outside humans, creatures that have even a modicum of this ability are very rare. The psychologist Köhler showed that a few of the most intelligent in the most intelligent of the primates, the chimpanzees, had a limited amount of creative intelligence. A representative problem was to reach fruit on a shed that was too high to climb. The ingredients of the solution, jointed sticks and packing crates, were scattered around the yard. Only a few chimpanzees solved the problem: stacking the crates near the shed, carrying the jointed sticks to the top, joining them, using the pole created to get the fruit. This simple problem would confound almost all the non-human living world.

At the other end of the scale of complexity was the problem facing physicists at the turn of the century . . . when it was becoming apparent that classical physics was inadequate for dealing with the accumulating evidence on the nature of the physical universe. Hilbert (cited in Feuer 1982) raised the question of why it was that Einstein solved the problem rather than any one of a group of men, all of whom seemed to be so much better prepared than he: Lorentz, Hilbert himself, Poincaré, Mach, and Minkowski. His question can be used to illustrate my conception of creative intelligence. The others were all more erudite than Einstein, but their very erudition led them to keep applying the old solutions that were no longer appropriate. Only Einstein saw that it was the very successes of classical physics that were standing in the way of a solution. What was needed was not merely modifying the old solutions but discarding them entirely and starting over with new ones.

The physicist Boltzmann (1899) described the problem in general terms. He noted that when a new method yields "beautiful results," many become unconsciously wedded to it; they come "to believe that the development of science to the end of all time would consist in the systematic and unremitting application of it." . . .

Even among humans, many kinds of creative activity are rare: only a few solve an artistic or scientific problem in their lifetimes; that is, they do not create a new solution to a new problem. However, as already suggested, in one field, language, virtually every human by the age of five is a creative genius. Most five-year-olds can understand and even create a correct sentence that they have never heard before. Not infrequently, at a somewhat later age, a child can create a correct sentence that no one has ever heard before. In one field, language, almost everyone is creative, spontaneously creating new solutions to new problems as they arise in everyday life.

How do linguists account for the immense human creativity they have discovered? Chomsky (1957, 1965, 1969) offers what turns out to be a conventional genetic explanation. He suggests that linguistic competence is based on "deep structures," genetically programmed sequences, which would have been called instincts if that term had not been discredited. In his view, all humans are linguistically creative because that creativity has been genetically inherited.

I wish to broaden the linguists' question so that the issue includes all creative genius, not just language use. The question becomes: *Why is it that almost everyone is a genius at language, but only a few rare individuals are geniuses in all other spheres of activity?* As already suggested, Chomsky's answer to this question is genetic; he would assume that language creativity is genetically inherited by everyone and that genius in other areas belongs to only a few individuals with the right genetic inheritance, as Galton and Cox both tried to show.

My alternative explanation does not exclude genetics but opens several new areas of investigation. First, assume that the capacity for creative genius in all spheres of activity, not just in language, is genetically inherited by all human beings. Apparently the human brain is more complex and powerful than the largest and most sophisticated computer. Von Neumann estimated that it is capable of processing 140 million bits of information per second. The philosopher Emerson (whose conception of human nature will figure prominently in this essay) did not know this, of course, but he seemed to sense it: "We lie in the lap of immense intelligence" (1837).

If humans have the capacity for genius in all areas, not just in language, why does genius appear in everyone in language but almost never in other areas? Suppose we assume that the disparity is caused by differences not in genetics but in systems of instruction. That is, it is possible that the system of instruction which leads children to learn language is enormously effective, while the systems of instruction which lead children to learn other activities, such as musical composition or mathematics, are relatively ineffective. These two suppositions raise what seems to me to be a new question. *How is the system of instruction of children in language different from other systems of instruction?*

A careful answer to this question might require considerable investigation. In this paper I will attempt only a provisional answer in order to formulate a rudimentary theory of the origins of genius. I will describe only some of the most obvious characteristics which differentiate language instruction from all other types of instruction.[1]

1. Exposure to language begins at the moment of birth and goes on almost constantly throughout infancy and childhood, and indeed for the whole of the individual's life. In terms of sheer quantity, for most individuals, exposure to language is probably vastly greater than any other type of instruction.

2. Language instruction is supremely interactive. Only very early in infancy is the child merely passively exposed to language. Long before any speech is acquired, parents and others speak directly to the infant, usually seeking a response, any response, to their utterances. The immediate rewarding of the infant's responses, often with boundless enthusiasm, is the beginning of a process of interaction between the infant and competent speakers which instructs the child in correct usage.

3. Virtually all of an infant's prelanguage and language tutoring is with tutors who are, as has already been pointed out above, extraordinarily competent in the subject they are imparting. This characteristic of language instruction surely differentiates it from instruction in other subjects. With subjects other than language, the instructors are often only routinely competent, if that. As will be illustrated below for the case of musical creativity, most of the children who go on to become creative geniuses had been instructed by a teacher, usually a parent or other close relative, of much more than routine competence.

4. Language instruction is built upon the infant's own spontaneous gestures and utterances. Virtually all other systems of instruction require the learner to conform to the conventions of the subject to be learned. With a baby, however, one instructs by responding to its cooing, crying, or babbling with language, thereby gradually but relentlessly shaping native impulses. This characteristic may profoundly influence the results of instruction. It also serves to tie together the two parts of the present argument. Since language instruction appears to be so integral with the infant's spontaneous impulses and gestures, it would probably serve to affirm the infant's sense of self, resulting in small but cumulating additions to the level of self-esteem. By contrast, most other systems of instruction, which require the learner to adapt to an alien system of conventions, may cause small but cumulating deficits of self-esteem.

It is conceivable that a system of instruction for music or mathematics or other subjects could be constructed, as language is, out of the learner's spontaneous activities. In music, for example, the instructor could begin by responding to the infant's pitch and rhythms as if they were musical notes and shaping them as one does with language. Similarly a system of mathematical instruction could be built upon the learner's spontaneous counting activities.

The intention to build upon the learner's spontaneous actions appears to lie at the core of the Montessori method of teaching. Children are allowed to play with instructional toys which usually give rise to spontaneous mathematical, musical, and other types of activity. The teacher is trained to base his or her teaching on these spontaneous activities. Although this is an excellent idea, it is not able to capture many of the characteristics of language instruction in the family setting. It takes place only at certain hours of the day and only when the child has reached school age. The instructor may be at least routinely competent in the Montessori method but only routinely competent, if that, in the special area of music, mathematics, and so on. Finally, the teacher is a stranger, at least at the beginning of instruction, rather than being someone, like a parent or other relative, to whom the learner is already strongly attached.

The ideal teacher for a budding genius would be a close relative who is gifted in the area of instruction, always available because of living in the same abode, who uses the learner's spontaneous acts as the basis for instruction. Also ideal would be the presence in the home of one or more back-up teachers, so that at least one teacher would be always available.

If we look at the families of the greatest composers, these conditions were usually met. Of course there is no way of knowing in detail their methods of instruction. Most of the greatest composers had at least one close relative who was a gifted musician: Bach, Beethoven, Bizet, Brahms, Chopin, Dvorak, Gounod, Grieg, Ives, Liszt, Mendelssohn, Mozart, Puccini, Rossini, Scarlatti, Schubert, Stravinsky, and Vivaldi. It would appear from their biographies that these composers had access to instruction from at least one gifted musician during infancy and early childhood. However, there are three composers who appear to be exceptions: Tchaikovsky, Verdi, and Wagner. I could find no obvious indication that there was a gifted musician available to them from the time of their births. Judging from these three exceptions, it would appear that although access to a gifted teacher from birth is strongly correlated with the appearance of genius, it is not a necessary condition. I will return to this issue after the discussion of self-esteem, below.

One last comment on musical instruction must be made with respect to Mozart, one of the most prodigiously gifted of the great composers. Like most of them, in his earliest years he had access to more than one competent musician. His father, Leopold, was a performer, composer, and teacher of music; and his older sister, Nannerl, a gifted performer. Of great interest for my argument, there is evidence that his father may have been extraordinarily gifted as a teacher of music. His manual of instruction for the violin, now almost two-hundred-years old, is still the standard text for that instrument. The vitality of his written teaching at least suggests that he may have also been a supremely competent teacher for his son.

The fifth characteristic which may differentiate instruction in language from instruction in other fields is the nature of the response to the learner's progress or lack of progress. In language acquisition in infancy, at least, the instructors seem to concentrate on rewarding correct speech rather than punishing error. Many parents seem to regard each new word as a miracle, often completely disregarding errors. One does not expect infants to know how to speak. We feel no contempt for their errors. (This is in contrast to our native reaction to the difficulties foreign adults have with our language.)

At least in the earliest years of instruction, the young learner is not ridiculed for making errors. Perhaps this is one of the reasons for the remarkable effectiveness of learning in language and the ineffectiveness of most other kinds of instruction: early language use may be almost completely free of shame.

In this section I have suggested that the methods that lead to language acquisition are vastly richer than other kinds of instruction. They begin at birth and are virtually continuous during the child's waking hours. They are carried on by a close relative who is extraordinarily gifted in the use of language. One or more back-up teachers are also usually available to ensure continuous training even in the absence of the primary teacher. Language instruction in infancy and early childhood is also intensely interactive, with the learner's getting virtually instant feedback on her or his fluency. I have also suggested that language instruction in the family is built upon the shaping of the learner's native impulses rather than the acquiring of new ones. This method may lead to high levels of self-esteem. A fifth characteristic may also build self-esteem: the overwhelming prevalence of positive, rather than negative, feedback in the early years of language acquisition. There seems to be a moratorium on criticism in the initial response of adults to children's early efforts at language.

The Real and the False Self

I introduce the topic of self-esteem and its relation to genius by referring again to Emerson's thought. He believed that self-reliance was the basic virtue because, he argued, at the core of every human is a self of unbelievable brilliance (1837, 18):

> What is the aboriginal Self, on which a universal reliance may be grounded? What is the nature and power of that science-baffling star, without parallax, without calculable elements, which shoots a ray of

beauty even into trivial and impure actions, if the least mark of independence appear? The inquiry leads us to that source, at once the essence of genius, of virtue, and of life, which we call Spontaneity or Instinct. We denote this primary wisdom as Intuition, whilst all later teachings are tuitions. This aboriginal self is the origin of intuition, and therefore of inspiration, of effortless genius.

Emerson points out that one aspect of genius, the completely accurate perception of reality, is totally involuntary:

> Every man discriminates between the voluntary acts of his mind and his involuntary perceptions, and knows that to his involuntary perceptions a perfect faith is due. He may err in the expression of them, but he knows that these things are so, like day and night, not to be disputed. My willful actions and acquisitions are but roving; the idlest reverie, the faintest native emotion, command my curiosity and respect. Thoughtless people contradict as readily the statement of perceptions as of opinions, or rather much more readily; for they do not distinguish between perception and notion. They fancy that I choose to see this or that thing. But perception is not whimsical, but fatal. If I see a trait, my children will see it after me, and in the course of time all mankind—although it may chance that no one has seen it before me. For my perception of it is as much a fact as the sun.

If all humans have access to boundless intuition and perception, according to Emerson, why is not everyone a genius? The answer he gives is that with few exceptions, everyone is terrified by the specter of being deviants from the collective vision of reality that is held in the community. We conform out of shame.

> A man must consider what a blindman's bluff is this game of conformity. . . . most men have bound their eyes with one or another handkerchief, and attached themselves to some one of these communities of opinion. This conformity makes them not false in a few particulars, authors of a few lies, but false in all particulars. Their every truth is not quite true. Their

two is not the real two, their four not the real four; so that every word they say chagrins us and we know not where to begin to set them right.

Conformity to the popularly held version of what is real and what is possible blinds most individuals to their own inner visions. *Only that person whose self-esteem is so high that he can withstand social rejection will be able to propose new solutions to new problems.* Emerson's formulation of this issue is so lengthy that I have separated and enumerated the main components (emphasis added).

[1] To believe your own thought, to believe that what is true for you in your private heart is true for all men—that is genius. Speak your latent conviction, and it shall be the universal sense; for the inmost in due time becomes the outmost, and our *first thought* is rendered back to us by the trumpets of the Last Judgment.

[2] A man should learn to *detect and watch that gleam of light which flashes across his mind from within,* more than the lustre of the firmament of bards and sages.

[3] Yet he dismisses without notice his thought, because it is his. In every work of genius we recognize our own *rejected thoughts;* they come back to us with a certain alienated majesty.

[4] Great works of art have no more affecting lesson for us than this. They teach us to abide by our spontaneous impression with good-humored inflexibility than most when the whole cry of voices is on the other side. Else tomorrow a stranger will say with masterly good sense precisely what we have thought and felt all the time, and we shall be forced to take with *shame* our own opinion from another.

There are several important ideas in this passage, but they are not developed by Emerson, only mentioned casually in passing. Perhaps the most fundamental basis of his thought is found in (2): "A man should learn to detect and watch that gleam of light which flashes across his mind from within, more than the lustre of the firmament of bards and sages." The key word is "flashes." In the context of the sentence, he seems to be suggesting that the flashes are extremely fast, so fast, perhaps, that unless one trains one's self, it is almost impossible even to become aware of them, much less try them out.

This sentence may serve to clarify what is otherwise a confusing issue in the advice that Emerson gives us. He tells us to trust ourselves but, aside from this sentence, does not give us any further guidance about what self it is that we are to trust. In the passage quoted earlier he calls it the "aboriginal self" and identifies it with intuition and spontaneity. But we have many different types of spontaneous impulses and thoughts, some of which are notoriously unreliable. We need a more specific description of the type of spontaneous intuitive thought.

In the sentence about the gleam of light, Emerson may have provided an important clue to what he meant. He seems to have anticipated Freud's discovery of the unconscious, the "aboriginal self" as Emerson calls it. In order to teach his patients "to learn to detect and watch" the gleam of light, Freud developed the method of free association. He devised a practical workaday technique for giving his patients access to their "aboriginal" selves. Once the patient discovered this access, therapy usually advanced more rapidly.

In systematically applying the method of free association, Freud made a discovery that went beyond Emerson. He found that most of his patients actively resisted acquaintance with their aboriginal selves (the repressed parts of their experiences). . . .

The patient's resistance, Freud later found, was due to unresolved painful emotion that was often also a part of the aboriginal self. I will return to the issue of unresolved emotion below, in the section on shame and guilt. . . .

Emerson's idea and Freud's later work teach that intuitive thought is unsolicited and nonverbal, an "involuntary perception," to use Emerson's term; second, it appears and disappears so rapidly as to seem instantaneous; and finally, it is always the *first* thought, rather than the second, third, or later thought, that is unedited and uncensored and therefore uncompromised by bias. The unsolicited first thought appears always, "invariably" to use Freud's word, to be the most inclusive, complex, and original of our thoughts. (But this is not necessarily true; Emerson was careful to state that intuitive ideas always need to be tested in reality.)

Einstein, when he sought to explain the origins of his creative ideas, often hinted at these characteristics. He usually explained that ideas did not come to him in words but in "images." The greatest of the chess masters also explain their deliberation in a similar way, not in words or moves but in fluid images that come to them involuntarily. Like Einstein, they struggle in their descriptions because they are attempting to describe a nonverbal process in words. . . .

If we return to Emerson's passage, a second idea is suggested in (1), "To believe your own thought, to believe that what is true for you in your private heart is true for all men—that is genius." This statement makes a connection between self-esteem and genius. It evokes the idea, in the strongest possible terms, that what differentiates the genius most strongly from other, ordinary persons is not talent—no mention is made of that—but self-esteem. Emerson seems to suggest that for the genius, his or her unique vision does not lead to a feeling of alienation from others, of being "different," that is, a freak, as is

usually the case, but of feeling connected with others in that what is true for you is also true of all others. In the discussion of the relationship between self-esteem and shame below, I suggest how such an extraordinary high level of self-esteem might come about.

One last thought in the original passage, (4), is in need of elaboration. I refer to the last part of this sentence, about the "whole cry of voices" being on the other side. The implication is that the person who expresses his or her unique vision will be persecuted for it. This sentence again implies a connection between genius and self-esteem. In this case it is implied that one will need a high level of self-esteem in order to withstand the cry of voices. The case of Galileo affords a familiar example. The tragic lives of the mathematician Georg Cantor and the physicist Boltzmann are less familiar. Relentless criticism of their work, which was far advanced over that of their contemporaries, drove Boltzmann to suicide and Cantor to the insane asylum. Emerson's paragraph appears to comprehend, in a single glance, the whole situation of the genius—his inner turmoil and his place in society. . . .

Self-Esteem: Coping With Shame and Guilt

One last reference to Emerson evokes another aspect of genius—single-minded dedication to one's work: "I shun father and mother and wife and brother, when my genius calls me." Once again the image which Emerson evokes refers to a high level of self-esteem, in this case, the absence of guilt. I suggest that self-esteem rests upon a very specific process, the management of shame and guilt, and that this process, in conjunction with the development of talent, gives rise to genius.

I have been using the term "self-esteem" as if its meaning were self-explanatory. Actually, there is no agreed-upon definition of this idea. The nearest thing to be found in the literature is the idea that level of self-esteem concerns the degree to which one has positive feelings about oneself. Although this idea is a good place to start, since it concerns feelings rather than thoughts or images, it is much too vague. It does not tell what kind of positive feeling: joy, love, pride, interest, thrill, and so on. In order to proceed further with the theory of genius, I discuss one particular feeling: shame. I define self-esteem as freedom from chronic shame.

Even a child who has no wish to express a unique vision, who wishes merely to be conventional in every possible way, must run a gauntlet of potentially shaming situations. The problem that the child faces is of almost inexpressible magnitude: in order to become an acceptable member of a community, she must learn a myriad of conventions and execute them in virtually perfect manner, as if each were second nature. There is a further characteristic of the job at hand. The child must learn to suppress her understanding that most of these conventions are completely arbitrary. The question "Why do we kiss on the lips rather than rub noses?" or a similar question is tolerated from a three-year-old, but in an older child it already is taken as intimating frivolousness or worse. These conventions "go without saying"; that is, they are sacred. Even to notice the arbitrariness of conventions, much less make an issue of them, invites ridicule and ostracism.

Rapid learning of a large mass of conventions makes errors inevitable. Mispronouncing a word is as much a part of learning as pronouncing it correctly, yet each error invites scorn or ridicule. (In a family I know, one of the members is still being teased about the time she thought that a friend of the parents named Dennis was a dentist.)

A repeating error, such as lisping, stammering, or stuttering, creates a nightmare of ridicule. Language errors are particularly rife. There are millions of details of pronunciation, inflection, grammar, syntax, and nonverbal gesture that must be performed, letter perfect.

There is a further twist to language that must seem almost diabolical to the learner. On the one hand, the correct use of language requires creativity. As already indicated, one often needs to invent new linguistic solutions for new situations. A vexing problem faced by children, however, is that some of their inventions are accepted but others are ridiculed. . . .

THE SHAME CONSTRUCT

. . . A useful place to start is to compare shame with a much less complex and much more prestigious affect: guilt. In most cases, the feeling of guilt is evoked by a specific and quite delimited act or failure to act, for example, to forget one's spouse's birthday or to scream at one's helpless infant. The thread which seems to be common to the actions or inactions which produce guilt is that they all involve the possibility of injuring another. Whether one person steals another's purse or curses or berates him in public, the victim has been injured.

When a child misunderstands a word like "Dennis," however, or invents a motive for soccer players, no injury has occurred. Harmless errors of these kinds do not produce guilt in the perpetrator but a different emotion: shame. The possibility that one could injure another assumes a potent, powerful, *capable* self. Making a gross error raises a question about the *adequacy* of the self, its basic worth: If you could make an error like that, are you really a person like me, or are you some kind of freak that need not be taken into consideration?

When one feels guilt, one's self feels *intact*. In feeling shame, one experiences what must be the most vertiginous of all feelings, the *disintegration of the self,* or its potential for disintegration. It is for this reason that guilt is infinitely more prestigious than shame. Guilty persons may even feel pride (the reverse of shame) that they are feeling guilt: it shows that they are basically moral persons; that is, they have intact, capable selves.

A vast ocean of errors is built into the child's existence. These errors, for the most part, are unavoidable, as is the normal shame that is the result of making errors. What may be avoidable, however, is to have innumerable experiences lead to *chronic* shame.

Shame is probably the most intensely painful of all feelings. Each person has spent what feels like an eternity of time and effort in constructing a competent, valuable self. The threat of losing that self may be more painful than the threat of losing one's life. In all cultures and historical eras, personal disgrace usually leads to extreme measures, even suicide.

There are two further premises about shame which need to be discussed before I return to self-esteem and genius. Many readers might agree that shame is a profoundly painful emotion but will assume that it seldom occurs and, when it does, one is fully aware of it. I am assuming, on the contrary, that shame is ubiquitous, not only in the lives of children but also in adult life, and virtually invisible. How can one be consumed with shame and still not be aware of it? To understand this issue, I will again review the concept of "unacknowledged shame" and the two forms this type of shame takes: "*bypassed* shame" and "*overt,* undifferentiated shame" (Lewis 1971).

According to Lewis, there are two opposite paths that one can take in order to avoid noticing the feeling of shame: one can bypass the feeling, swallow it, so to speak, so that one does not feel the pain at all (except for one extremely brief instant, when the shame is initially evoked). Although by following this path, one manages to decrease substantially the *intensity* of pain, at the same time the *duration* is increased. The shame is experienced as obsessive ideation or speech. During episodes of compulsive thinking or speaking, one experiences little feeling. On the contrary, one may be aware of an absence of feeling, of blankness or emptiness. Bypassed shame takes the form of too much ideation and too little feeling.

The other form, unacknowledged shame, the overt, undifferentiated type, leads to the opposite experience, too much feeling and too little ideation. One is so flustered by the threat of incompetence (paralysis, disintegration) that one is unable to observe and analyze what is happening. "I feel like a perfect idiot" is one rendering. "Embarrassment," "humiliation," and "mortification" are examples of words used to describe overt shame; "bashfulness," "shyness," "modesty," and "discomfiture" are less-intense but longer-lasting variants.

Many of the commonly used references to undifferentiated painful feelings appear to be shame experiences, or mixtures of shame with another emotion, such as anger: awkward, uncomfortable, foolish, silly, strange, and "in a stew" are examples. In adolescent terminology, one is "bummed," "freaked," or "weirded out." These words appear to be substitutes or euphemisms for shame, just as there are many euphemisms for sexual and "toilet" terms. Shame, like these other functions, appears to be subject to taboo (Scheff 1984).

The discussion so far has focused on shame as a *response,* a stereotyped biopsychological response which is virtually omnipresent in human communities. To describe shame further, it is necessary to shift to the *stimulus* that is common to all situations in which shame arises. This stimulus seems to be social in character: shame appears to be the stereotyped emotional response to a threat of loss of connection to another person or persons. This element is fairly obvious in most cases of overt, undifferentiated shame. One becomes painfully embarrassed and flustered when one "loses face" in public: caught in a lie, a gross error, or caught unawares by an obvious trick (we feel humiliated that we "swallowed it hook, line, and sinker" without a trace of redeeming suspicion).

In bypassed shame, the social source is less obvious since this experience often arises when one is alone. Here is a characteristic moment described by a male college student:

> I am on campus, walking to class. On the way, I am remembering an earlier conversation with a great deal of pleasure. I believe I made a good impression on this woman that I am interested in. But then I remember a remark I made about her ex-boyfriend. At the time I felt witty saying it, but suddenly I saw it from her point of view. I felt like a turd. I kept re-playing that scene, even when I was sitting in class, thinking what I might have said instead.

The obsessive replaying of the scene suggests that this experience involved bypassed shame. It occurred when the student shifted from his point of view to that of the woman. This shift exposes the social nature of the stimulus to bypassed shame. It occurred not in social interaction in the real world, as overt, undifferentiated shame usually does, but in imagined social interaction in the "internal theater," the interior dialogue that goes on in our minds.

The stricken feeling of shame indicated by the phrase "I just felt like an idiot" may occur in actual social interaction. Just as likely, it can occur in solitude, when one is reenacting a transaction from memory or inventing a meeting with another which has never taken place, and may never take place—imagining a conversation with "the man on the street" or with Shakespeare.

In interior dialogue, we are very often engaged with some other person, whose image we create for an inner enactment or reenactment: one's spouse, son, or daughter, boss or subordinate, or even one's self in some other guise, older or younger, in one or another of one's many hats or disguises. This internal theater often results in emotional responses. When we imagine the other as approving or accepting ourselves, we bask in the glow of self-generated pride. When we imagine the other as critical, contemptuous, or scornful, we roast in the hell of self-generated shame or guilt.

EMOTION AND CREATIVITY

The last step in describing the relationship of genius and self-esteem concerns feeling traps (Lewis 1971). Normal emotions—fear, anger, grief, and shame—are usually quite short-lived, a few seconds perhaps. They ordinarily are crisis responses. Referring to anxiety, Freud suggested that it has a "signal function"; it is an interior warning that something is wrong. If normal emotions are short-lived, how is it possible that one may be constantly angry, frightened, and, especially for our purposes here, ashamed? Chronic shame states are significant because they are probably the basis of what is called low self-esteem: one is usually not proud of one's self but ashamed.

The concept of the feeling trap may explain what otherwise might seem to be a paradox: emotional states which are virtually life long. Feeling traps occur when one has an emotional reaction to one's emotional reaction, and another reaction to that reaction, and another and another, and so on, ad infinitum. Panic seems to be one outcome of a fear spiral: of being frightened that one is so afraid. In fear panics, people may stampede like animals, inadvertently killing each other, or, as in the case of voodoo death, die of anoxia. Being ashamed of being ashamed is another spiral that has runaway possibilities: "What an idiot I am (how shameful it is) that I should get so upset (ashamed) over something so trivial." One outcome of this spiral, stage fright, can reach such proportions that the victim is paralyzed in mind and body.

In interpersonal relations, the lethal feeling trap seems to be the shame-rage spiral, of being ashamed that you are angry ("How could I be so angry at someone who loves me? What a monster I am.") and angry at self or at the other that you are shamed: "You asshole. Don't stand around moping over your ego. Get your ass in gear." The anger may be directed at the other rather than one's self: "It's all your fault. You made me feel bad." This particular spiral may be experienced as humiliated fury (e.g., the "wronged woman")—anger bound by shame. This state may not be represented in consciousness, however. Frequently it is not experienced at all since it has been going on so long as a virtually automatic response. Another possibility is that it is experienced as the absence of any feeling at all, as blankness or emptiness.

Another of the isotopic representations of shame-rage is intermittent but lengthy bouts of resentment, jealousy, or guilt. These are all molecules of the same two atoms, but with the anger pointing in different directions. . . . In chronic jealousy, the anger may be pointed at the putative rival or at the love object or at both. In guilt, the anger seems to be pointed back at the self. One is enraged at the self for injuring another and, at the same time, ashamed both of one's actions and of being so enraged ("out of control").

Is there any possibility of escaping from a feeling trap, once caught up? The most common gambit used in daily life seems to be the attempt to talk one's self out of it, which seldom works. Telling one's self "You should be ashamed of being so upset at something so trivial" only sinks one deeper in the trap. In psychotherapy, a frequently used technique is to try to get the victim to express or discharge his anger. This seldom works either because it ignores the shame component of the trap. A common reaction is to become embarrassed (shamed) by the "artificiality" of showing anger when you are "not really mad," which is another variant of feeling that one's anger is not adequately justified, or feeling guilty about being loud or "selfish."

One method which almost always dispels shame is laughter, good-humored or affectionate laughter. This idea is very much in accord with popular belief that laughter relieves embarrassment. Lewis (1983) has shown that it is also supported by Freud's analysis of wit and laughter, although he does not make the idea explicit. Retzinger (1985, 1987) has shown that it is also implied by McDougall's analysis of laughter, although, like Freud, he does not make the sequence explicit.

If one laughs good-naturedly when shame is evoked, it will be quickly dispelled. If one does not laugh, one is often faced with unpleasant after effects. Usually the shamed person will blush or attempt to hide (cover face with hand, look away, try to leave the scene, or at least imagine he has left) or begin to talk or think obsessively. This is the setting for entry into a feeling trap. A common sequence is to become angry or hostile toward the other who is perceived as shaming one, then to feel guilty that one is angry, then to feel ashamed that one is so upset, and so on.

Good-natured laughter, if it occurs immediately when shame is evoked, avoids entry into the spiral. If it occurs when the spiral is in operation, it ends the cycle. Apparently when one laughs during a shame-rage spiral, the dispelling of the shame, which was binding the anger, allows the anger to discharge also. In her video studies of resentment, Retzinger (1985, 1987) has investigated the effects of laughter on anger. In the episodes where laughter occurred during the recalling of a resentment-laden memory, facial flushing and body heat, which are the markers of anger discharge (Scheff 1984), occurred simultaneously with the laughter. Retzinger showed that the frequency, intensity, and duration of verbal and facial anger expressions decreased dramatically after laughter.

The Laughing Genius

Having reviewed the concepts of unacknowledged shame and the shame-rage feeling trap. I return to genius and its relationship to self-esteem. I have argued that for genius to appear, the bearer must have extraordinarily high self-esteem, be able to catch his or her first thoughts in flight, and have the confidence to develop and express these thoughts. There are probably two paths which lead to this level of self-esteem. The first path concerns humane treatment: the budding genius may have undergone less humiliation than others and therefore spent less time in shame-rage spirals than the less gifted. . . .

It seems likely, however, that the development of ways of managing shame would be far more important in the development of self-esteem than the extent to which one was treated with respect or contempt. Shame seems to be an unavoidable aspect of the human condition, even for those who are fortunate enough to have been treated well in most of their relationships. The gamut of errors through which children must pass in learning their culture, and the shame which results, has already been mentioned. A second universal source of shame is that love is always ambivalent. Intimate relationships are invariably a source of

frustration, and therefore of anger, as well as fulfillment, and a source of shame as well as pride. That is, intimacy inevitably leads to a situation in which one is rejected or feels rejected, a basic source of shame.

If, as has been argued here, shame is unavoidable, then self-esteem must rest on effective ways of dispelling shame. The most effective way of dispelling shame, I have suggested, is through laughter. If this is the case, the great geniuses should have been laughers. . . .

Although it is difficult to test the laughing-genius hypothesis with written biographies, it might be possible in interviews with living artists and scientists. I think that the laughing hypothesis probably is much more relevant to a certain type of creator, which I have termed the "easy" creator. These creators work very rapidly and with little revision. Goethe wrote *Werther* in 24 days; Nietzsche . . . wrote *Zarathustra* in 30 days. I suspect that creativity is extraordinarily rapid with this type because there is freedom from self-censure and therefore access to the aboriginal self. Schubert and Mozart were certainly composers of this type, and also the mathematician John von Neumann (the person most responsible for the invention of the computer). By investigating the nature of the emotional lives of these creators, and particularly the amount and quality of their laughter, it might be possible to clarify some of the issues that have been discussed here.

Conclusion

This paper has outlined a rudimentary theory of genius. Creative intelligence may arise out of two interrelated processes, the development of extraordinary talent and the growth of extremely high levels of self-esteem. Extraordinary talent, whether or not it also involves genetic inheritance of talent, also requires a system of highly effective instruction. The model for this system of instruction may be the kind of language instruction children receive for the first five or six years. The formulation of this model raises what may be an important question for investigation: In what ways is early language instruction different from all other types of instruction, and do these differences account for the creativity that occurs in the correct use of natural language?

The second process in the growth of creative intelligence may be the development of high levels of self-esteem. I argue that self-esteem is essentially freedom from chronic shame. This type of shame is usually unacknowledged. It is virtually invisible because it appears in multiform guises. The basic mechanism of chronic shame, it is argued, is the feeling trap, which may convert emotions, normally brief, into lifelong states. Finally it is suggested that chronic shame is most effectively dispelled by good-humored laughter. If this is the case, we should expect to find the genius, especially the easily creative genius, to be a laugher.

One final question: Is there any reason to believe that one or the other of these two processes, the one involving talent, the other, self-esteem, is in any way more important than the other in the appearance of genius? No doubt they are equally important in the lives of most geniuses. However, it seems possible, for theoretical reasons, that the development of self-esteem may be more important. It is possible that the early growth of high levels of self-esteem may allow the potential genius to find the effective instruction needed to develop extraordinary talent. This is one way of interpreting the three deviant cases—Tchaikovsky, Verdi, and Wagner—who do not appear to have had early access to a musically talented teacher. This possibility, like the others suggested here, awaits future research for clarification. . . .

NOTE

1. Howard Becker called to my attention a comparison of schooling and language acquisition which parallels mine, in Paul Goodman, "Education of the Young" (1969).

REFERENCES

Boltzmann, Ludwig. 1899. "The Recent Development of Method in Theoretical Physics." *Monist* 11:229–30.

Chomsky, Noam. 1957. *Systematic Structures.* The Hague: Mouton.

_____. 1965. *Aspects of a Theory of Syntax.* Cambridge, Mass.: MIT Press.

_____. 1969. *The Acquisition of Syntax in Children from 5 to 10.* Cambridge, Mass.: MIT Press.

Cox, Catherine M. 1926, *The Early Mental Traits of 300 Geniuses.* Stanford, Calif.: Stanford University Press.

Emmerson, R. W. 1837/1983. *Essays and Lectures.* New York: Library of America.

Feuer, Lewis S. 1982. *Einstein and the Generations of Science.* New Brunswick, N.J.: Transaction.

Galton, Francis. 1869. *Heredity Genius.* Cleveland: Meridian.

Goodman, Paul. 1969. *New Reformation.* New York: Vintage.

Lewis, H. B. 1971. *Shame and Guilt in Neurosis.* New York: International Universities Press.

_____. 1976. *Psychic War in Men and Women.* New York: New York University Press.

_____. 1983. *Freud and Modern Psychology.* 2 vols. New York: Plenum.

Retzinger, Suzanne. 1985. "The Resentment Process: Videotape Studies." *Psychoanalytic Psychology* 2: 129–51

_____. 1987. "Marital Conflict: Case Study of an Escalating Quarrel." Typescript.

_____. 1987a. "Resentment and Laughter: Video Studies of the Shame-Rage Spiral." In Helen B. Lewis, ed., *The Role of Shame in Symptom Formation.* Hillsdale, N.J.: Erlbaum.

Scheff, T. J. 1966. *Being Mentally Ill.* Chicago: Aldine (2d ed., 1984).

_____. 1984. "The Taboo on Coarse Emotions." *Review of Personality and Social Psychology* 5: 156–169.

SIGNIFICANT OTHERS AND SELF DEVELOPMENT

14

Sissy Boy, Progressive Parents

Daniel Farr

(2006)

Gender is part of our lives from the very beginning. From early on, children begin to conceptualize and integrate an understanding of gender into their identities and actions. Families, the media, and other children continually recreate, develop, and perpetuate regulating behaviors both within and between individuals that work to legitimize and maintain the dichotomous nature of gender. One is either a boy or a girl, a man or a woman. When gender is not evident in this conventional way, there can be disapproval, concern, and even loathing. These responses may torment both girls (tomboys) and boys (sissy boys) who do not conform to dichotomous gender characteristics.

LOOKING BACK AT CHILDHOOD

Applying an autoethnographic analysis of my experience growing up as a gender nonconforming boy—yes, a "sissy boy"—offers insight into the social construction of gender and the manner in which gender is incorporated into the various social organizations and structures that guide our lives. As a sissy boy, I seldom interacted with tomboys so I cannot offer insight into their experience, but I will explore facets of my own early experience as an effeminate male to describe the way gender dichotomy affects those who don't readily fit into one gender category or the other.

Critically evaluating and looking back at one's experience offers a rich tapestry of information about the social world. Informed in part by Arlie Hochschild's concept of the "magnified moment" (1994: 4), I explore several of the key moments and events of my life that have reverberated through my memories. These are happenings which, at the time they occur, seem to tell it all, so to speak. In the process, I point to the many threads of gender socialization and related power dynamics at play in our society, which, oddly enough, work themselves out in the smallest ways, such as through toy selection and favored books.

Growing up I was what many might call a precocious child. I was intelligent, creative, imaginative, and "too" sensitive to fit into the social conception of boyhood. I was the boy who was constantly picked on by my peers for being unmanly, for being a sissy, and later for supposedly being a faggot. I don't know that I can pinpoint when I first realized I was unique and different, but I certainly recognized I was not just unlike other boys, but other children in general, at an early age (at least by first or second grade). The path of my unique childhood is not the same as all other effeminate boys or even other outsider boys in general, but the various experiences

I will examine are ones to which we can all relate in one way or another.

Boy Versus Girl Toys

As children of the late 20th century, many of us have a collection of toys and other recreational and educational objects. Coming from a middle-class background, I was fortunate to have a respectable assortment of toys and tools at my disposal, to help ward off childhood boredom. Looking back to my childhood, I don't think my parents took too strongly to the idea that there were specific toys for boys and specific toys for girls. I know my sister got dolls and I got teddy bears, but at the time I only saw this as their giving us what we each liked.

Is this a matter of what we instinctively prefer or is it what we are taught to prefer? Had I been more like other "normal" boys of my age group, maybe I would have received more action figures and appropriately masculine toys. For example, *Transformers* were all the rage at the time. I don't recall ever expressing desire for, or interest in, them. My one friend had a large collection of these types of toys, but I never found them especially interesting. The time I spent playing with this friend and his toys was more the result of neighborhood proximity than strong feelings of camaraderie. Fortunately, my parents were able to step away from some, though of course not all, of the categorization of toys by gender. Despite the frequent gender stereotyping of toys by parents (see Campenni 1999), my own parents were more open about the types of toys my siblings and I could play with. I was thus able to enjoy "masculine" toys, such as Legos™ and Construx™, as well as "feminine" toys like looms and cooking kits. My parents were exceptional in this way. As far as I knew, they never stereotyped my interests. They never discouraged what my peers viewed with disdain as sissy boy inclinations. To my progressive parents, I was simply their son—the one who was good at so many things and who loved his family— not the boy child in their lives.

One of the favorite toys I received as a child was a Fisher-Price™ loom. It's used to weave yarn into fabric, to make scarves, for example. I didn't view it as a girly type of gift; I saw it as a cool new crafty toy. I still recall the circumstances of receiving the loom; it was an unexpected gift, unassociated with a holiday or birthday. It was new and exciting. As I look back, I can still vaguely see the box. It seems that there was a boy on the box cover. I have unsuccessfully searched online trying to locate a picture of this box. I believe it was a boy on the cover, but it may have been a girl with a "masculine" haircut. This led me to assume that this was a gender-appropriate gift: If there was a boy on the cover, it must have been okay for me to also play with the loom.

The freedom of toy selection I experienced at home was not something I would experience in school. One winter, in second grade, my class had a holiday party and a gift exchange. On the day of the big party, we each drew numbers for the gifts that were sorted as being either a masculine toy or a feminine toy. I was lucky in that I drew the number for the biggest box! After all the boxes were distributed, the tension grew as we all opened our gifts at the same time. My initial excitement of receiving the biggest box was squelched when I opened it to find a Nerf™ football. I was disappointed; I had no clue about what to do with it. I had grown up in a household where sports were rarely, if ever, watched on TV. I promptly made a trade for a cool dinosaur kit where you could put the bones together to build a T-rex. I loved building that T-rex and kept it for many years, but the boys of my class branded me a "wuss" because I didn't want the football. One would think that bones and dinosaurs would be adequately masculine, but a football superseded this in the toy-related hierarchy of masculinity in the classroom.

Hobbies and Books

Through much of my childhood I had an interest in artistic endeavors. Despite my parents' lack of concern for gender-appropriate toys and interests I soon became aware of the gendered division of hobbies and how to regulate and manage the public (school) and private (home) side of this. I had grown up with parents who both enjoyed arts and crafts. From as far back as I can remember, my mother had sewn, quilted, crocheted, and cross-stitched. My father also had interest in crafts, particularly working with wood and stained glass. Given the dangers innate to a wood shop, I was primarily exposed to the fiber arts my mother was working with. From an early age, I found her hobbies intriguing and was eager to learn. I was six or seven when my mother showed me how to cross-stitch. I can still remember the first piece I stitched of a little brown bear.

Looking back, I now know that my interest in cross-stitch must have been challenging for my parents. Sewing is culturally regarded in our society as a craft for women. I feel it was quite progressive of my parents to not have told me "cross-stitch is for girls" and push me toward stereotypical masculine pastimes. I even recall my father's positive support for my first little project. My parents never instilled shame or embarrassment in me because of my "feminine" hobbies.

A growing interest in arts and crafts, combined with my love of books, led me to borrow various arts books [from the library]. Initially, I was vaguely familiar with the craft of crocheting, having seen my mother working with the funny hooked needle. I was curious, so this was the topic of the first of these books I borrowed. I took the book home and taught myself how to crochet, making a white washcloth.

I was proud of that little project, so I took it to school for show-and-tell. This led to another magnified moment, in which I learned one of the harshest lessons of my gender socialization. My classmates picked on me endlessly. I was beginning to see that there were certain hobbies and activities that I might be interested in and had talent in doing, but which could never be shared with

the kids at school. The teacher was supportive and said what a nice job I had done, but the kids were cruel. I was confused. After all, we all took the same art classes. How was this different? I had no idea that this wasn't stuff I was supposed to be doing. I had two options: give up this hobby entirely or continue it at home and keep it secret from my peers. I chose the latter.

Moving Along in School

By the fourth grade, I was selected to join my school district's Academically Gifted Program (AGP). This became another nail in the coffin of my popularity. It's strange how as children we tease and insult both the over-achievers and the under-achievers. I yearned through those years to merely be "average." Alas, I was not, as I was in a special program where I was permitted to leave my regular school one whole day a week and ride a bus to another school to interact with other "gifted" students in a special class. We had access to various academic and activity-experience opportunities. It was a good experience while I was at AGP, at least initially. This was the first time that I had a chance to mingle with peers who seemed to be at my own intellectual level. I also was no longer the main target of harassment in my class. I was grouped with those who I can only assume were also targets in their own schools. In a funny kind of way, it was rewarding to be grouped up with the other nerds, geeks, sissies, and weirdos, one of the first times I didn't feel alone.

Children can be incredibly cruel and I was an easy target, being in a gifted program, being a bit pudgy, being too effeminate, and wearing glasses. It was in fourth grade when I first tried to go on a diet in hopes of fitting in better with my classmates. I knew to hide this from my peers, because, as with so many other things in my world, being on a diet was something girls did, not boys. So even in my aim to fit in better, I was trying to get there by way of non-masculine approved routes (though as adults we know that both men and women go on diets).

During those years of fourth through sixth grade, I found myself becoming increasingly isolated and distant. I was a sad child in many ways. I spent a lot of time reading and doing artistic projects by myself. I struggled with the emotional limitations of schooling, with my inability to fit in with my peers. I spent many nights hiding under my quilt in bed crying about it. I simply could not understand why my peers held such a negative view of me. I tried to reason the circumstances away as being the result of superior intellect, but this didn't work. I'm sure it was not an easy thing for my parents to see me so sad, so I also tried to keep it hidden from them. (Isn't that what boys are supposed to do?) I sought to reconcile some of the emotional strain of the situation by withdrawing and convincing myself that I was fine alone.

Having relocated to a new town towards the end of sixth grade, I merged into the life of junior high school much like my peers. We were all new to the school, with an equally low status in the grade hierarchy, all seeking to establish our standing in the local scheme of things. I was placed in all the advanced classes that were offered. While this was great in that I was with a group of intellectual peers, I also was separated from the majority of my classmates, who I only met in gym, chorus, and maybe in the cafeteria.

During the seventh grade, all students were required to take a home economics class. For the first time, I was able to flaunt my domestic abilities with a needle and thread as well as in the kitchen. From a young age, I had learned to cook, in part because of personal interest, but also in part because I was a Cub Scout. I no longer had to hide the fact that I could cook and sew from my peers, but I did have to be careful in showing how much I knew and how much I enjoyed these activities. I ended up being at the head of my class for home economics and even started helping other students with some of the sewing and embroidery assignments. It was the first

time that the feedback I was receiving from peers was not reinforcing the negative associations of my gender identity in connection with stereotypically feminine activities.

Because the course was required and I was part of a class of high-achieving students, I wasn't seen as a boy participating in feminine activities. Instead, I was just a student who was doing well in class. But as soon as the semester in home economics ended and I entered the wood shop class, I had to send my domestic abilities and interests into the gender closet. This produced another magnified moment, this time highlighting how quickly valued abilities in one context can become a source of embarrassment and taunting in another.

Heading into wood shop, many of my peers expected that I would be uncomfortable and fall flat on my face. I surprised them when they learned that I actually knew as much or more about the tools and equipment as they did. All the time I had spent with my father in the garage had paid off. I was a competent woodworker and did just fine in making the semester's big lamp project. One might think that the ability to fulfill both the roles and tasks traditionally classified as feminine and those classified as masculine would have been regarded positively by my peers. Unfortunately, this was not the case, because the dichotomous nature of gender reared its head once again. While both my feminine and masculine skills required similar abilities—precise measurement, the operation of machines (be it a sewing machine and mixer, or a table saw and drill press), envisioning how differing parts or different ingredients work together to create a final product—the incongruity of being a boy who was successful in the feminine tasks was unacceptable. We seem more likely to recognize difference while remaining blind to the similarity that is demonstrated by differently gendered youth (Messner 1992). This is especially true for boys who demonstrate "feminine" skills.

Third grade brought my first regular visits to the playground. Of course, we had gone outside to play in the past, but it had been intermittent, as the big kids in higher grades were "too wild" and might hurt us. While it is common for children to create single-sex play groups (Martin and Fabes 2001), I found I was more comfortable playing with the girls. They were less violent and didn't always talk about the stereotypically masculine toys about which I had little knowledge or interest. I didn't fit in well and was picked on and posited to the lowest boy status. However, with the group of girls, I was able to be one of the leaders and had a lot of social support from them. I learned how to play cat's cradle at lunch, got to just relax and sit and talk in the sun at play time, and compete on the swings for who could go highest and jump off.

The dread of gym class persisted throughout my junior and high school years. My gym class loathing was reinforced one year when I was placed with students two years my senior because of my academic and choral schedule. That was a very rough year of gym class for me. As one might suspect, my classmates (who seemingly comprised the majority of the football team) were not pleased to have to count me among them. Making matters worse, the gym teacher "inadvertently" mentioned that I was in a class of seniors "because of chorus." Involvement of any male in choir was regarded with disgust by most of the boys in my school.

I had learned to deal with the psychological harm accompanying this masculine departure, but that year I understood that gender violations could also result in physical pain. That fall, one of the games of flag football, which was supposed to be non-contact, resulted in my first cast. This was the first concrete example of my life in which the disapproval of my gender portrayal by my peers, together with the bolstering disapproval of adults (my gym teacher), caused me real harm. I had always wanted to believe that each of my classmates felt different and out-of-place to at least some degree, but from that point on I became increasingly critical and distant from my peers and even wary of the adults of my school. I was disappointed that adults would not present a better example for students, but I now recognize that deeply imbedded categories of masculinity are not only part of youth culture but of adult culture as well.

Athletic interest and involvement have long been held a bastion of masculinity. Being a successful athlete enables men/boys to affirm and define who and what they are, especially in opposition to femininity (Connell 1995; Messner 1992). Having had little athletic interest or skill as a child (and I still don't today), my experience of masculinity was problematized in this regard by my peers as well as the adults of my world. I had become a large-bodied, strongly built youth, with the quintessential football figure. The idea that I was disinterested in the football and wrestling teams seemed utterly foreign to my athletics teachers.

Cub Scouts and Masculinity

While I didn't participate in organized sports in my youth, I did become involved in an organization that is commonly regarded as a cornerstone of masculine childhood socialization, the Cub Scouts. I do not recall if I joined of my own volition or if I had been encouraged to do so by my parents. Looking back, I can see how I might initially have perceived Cub Scouts as the "in thing" to do, but I can also see how my parents, like many other parents, may have been encouraged to involve their sons in activities such as this. My scout troop was small because of the area where I lived. It was just me, Gus (a boy who was even more of an outsider than myself), and Brian (whose dad was our pack leader). Such a small pack was limited in the activities it could undertake. I remember the occasional craft projects and the emergence of my competitive nature as I sought various beads and patches that marked one's ranking and skill as a scout. As the years passed, I obtained quite a few badges, but I did not find the overall experience fulfilling.

While "character development" is the first purpose of scouting, I do not know if I experienced much of this within the Scouts or if, instead, I was encouraged to regard certain behaviors, activities, and characteristics as masculine and thus appropriate, or feminine and thus inappropriate. There were many conflicting messages in this regard. While we primarily participated in "masculine" activities such as woodworking, nature and environmental appreciation, and various competitions such as the building and racing of small wooden cars, we also had an annual cake-baking contest. Fathers and sons were to bake cakes without the help of a mother to raise funds for the troop. At the time, I did not understand why my mother wasn't allowed to help with the cake. I felt that since my mother did most of the cooking and baking at home, she would be the appropriate parent for the task. In other scouting tasks, such as seeking patches, my mother was able to help, so why couldn't she here? The annual cake-baking contest was in many respects a magnified moment, an affirmation for me that men and women were in opposition in our society. To be a real man meant to be separate and independent of girls. Any task a woman could do, a man could do better—if he wanted to.

Cooking and Clothing

While there were conflicting messages conveyed in the cake baking of Cub Scouts, it didn't reduce my interest in cooking. I found I loved mixing and making things in the kitchen. It amazed me that you could put various ingredients together, add heat, and presto! I first learned the miracles of kitchen chemistry through the use of *Bisquick*. I would get up early on the weekend, not only for the cartoons, but to make pancakes for the family. I became quite skilled at it, even though it took many bad pancakes to master the timing. My parents were always encouraging and around the age

of 7 or 8, I received my first cookbook. I loved that book and have kept it. The first real thing I ever made from it was potato salad, which was a hit with the family. Despite all the comfort and praise I received from my family for my cooking and despite my cookbook having pictures of both boys and girls, I somehow knew that this was not something I should mention at school. I was already labeled an outsider; no need to add fodder to my peers' ammunition.

It is odd how, as children, we receive such mixed messages about what establishes various tasks as masculine and feminine. We often see our parents completing similar tasks. If raised in the home of a single parent, with all the adult tasks needing to be accomplished by that one parent, how is it that certain tasks and skills are then demarcated masculine and feminine? I recall most cooking and kitchen tasks being done by my mother, but I can also vividly recall occasions when my father cooked and worked in the kitchen. We probably all experience childhood in this way, but at the same time we create a cultural understanding of gender through the subtle messages surrounding us, such as that while both men and women cook, kitchen and cooking are gendered feminine.

During my early adolescence, like most of my peers, I became fashion conscious. I aspired to dress in style and to fit in. I was never quite able to pull it off. When I was in junior high, I had a pair of jeans that caused me problems and sparked a new wave of taunting. When I sat, the jeans would bunch up in front, causing the zippered area to visibly bulge. At the time, we were having our first big sex education sections in health class. All the sex talk combined with my bulging jeans led one of my male classmates to ask me loudly whether I was gay because I was allegedly looking in his direction while sexually aroused. I was completely embarrassed and angered, prompting another magnified moment.

Regardless of my response, I was branded. No longer was I just a nerd, geek, and sissy boy, but I was to become the gay boy of the class. The months that followed were horrendous. Despite assertions to the contrary, no one listened. Being regarded as gay was the worst thing anyone could be branded.

Dating, Sex, and College

In time, I became increasingly aware of dating and sex. However, unlike many of my peers, I did not date. There were some girls who I had crushes on, but given my outsider and stigmatized status, it did not seem likely that I could get a date. The combination of rumors that I was gay; my participation in music, art, and theater; and my academic achievements put me in a tough spot. Socially, I did spend some time with a small group of my classmates, much of it during lunch. It was reassuring to have some bonds with a group of other nerds, sissies, and outsiders of both sexes. Few members of this group dated or were sexually active as far as I knew, and we were all disparaged to varying degrees by the "populars."

College offered me a clean slate on which I hoped to write a new story. After years of being labeled and taunted for not being masculine enough, I found college to be a liberating experience. I had visions of being a new person, a man who would be masculine and free of taunts and labels, someone who would leave behind gender-bending attributes. But I found I could not be anyone other than who I was—a man who enjoyed sewing and quilting, a man who loved to cook, a man who enjoyed art and music, and a man who became immersed in the soap operas the girls would watch at lunchtime. College was a world away from the one I had known. Not only was I no longer picked on, teased, or taunted, but I was finally accepted by my floormates, classmates, instructors, and co-workers. With this new freedom, I became more confident and outgoing. Those unique "non-masculine" activities and interests that had confined me as a youth now

worked to my benefit, making me special. I reveled in newfound popularity with my peers and found the obstacles that had impeded dating in the past were now all but gone.

THEN AND NOW

As the years have passed, I have often reflected on my past and contrasted my own experience with that of other men with whom I've spoken. I have realized my parents were far more progressive than I had imagined, providing me with a regular refuge at home to be myself. In our culture, the acceptable expressions of masculinity are quite restrictive, but my parents somehow managed to establish an environment that offered flexibility. My parents are not psychiatrists; they had not even acquired college degrees when I was growing up. But they supported my own, as well as my sibling's, choices to live our lives as we chose, to be the individuals we preferred. I believe it is their acceptance and support that made my childhood successful despite the odds.

Today, I am proud to admit that I still partake in many feminine stereotyped activities. I no longer feel shame for the ways that I challenge the stereotypes of gender. Yes, I am clearly a man. I dress in appropriately masculine clothes. I wear my hair in a masculine style. I am "masculine" in many ways. Yet, I suspect my sexual orientation is often in question. Many may wonder—am I gay or am I straight? Were all those taunts and teases of my youth correct? I actually find this to be humorous, something reflecting the need for clear dichotomies. Perhaps some readers did not question my sexuality as they read this chapter, but I suspect that most did, given the "demasculinizing" title of the chapter and the various masculinity-challenging behaviors exhibited throughout my life. I know that I challenge the conceptions of masculinity in numerous ways, but nearly every man challenges our stereotypical beliefs of masculinity in some manner. In practice, gender for many is an endless range of grays.

Yes, many gay men do express recollections of a childhood in which they experienced masculinity in problematic and stigmatizing manners (Savin-Williams 1998). There also are many gay men who experienced a fairly nonproblematic masculine gender identity as they grew up. We see little problem in questioning the experiences of gay men, presuming that somehow their gender inclinations are clear, but we rarely question the gender of heterosexual men whose gender depictions challenge our conceptions of masculinity.

Summing Up

Based on my own social history, I have examined the experience of growing up as a boy/man who embraces stereotypically feminine activities. Through this autoethnography, some of the complexities of socialization have been examined for those who are different. Looking at the education system, one of the primary socialization environments for youth, we can readily recognize the mechanisms of peer policing and gender regulation, which are further linked with society at large. Individuals who do not adhere to dichotomous definitions of masculinity or femininity are often stigmatized, considered polluted, and suspect. Negative responses often conflate sexuality and gender, whose magnified moments showcase difference.

References

Campenni, C. Estelle. 1999. "Gender Stereotyping of Children's Toys: A Comparison of Parents and Nonparents." *Sex Roles* 40: 121–138.

Connell, Robert W. 1995. *Masculinities.* Berkeley: University of California Press.

Hochschild, Arlie Russell. 1994. "The Commercial Spirit of Intimate Life and the Abduction of Feminism: Signs From Women's Advice Books." *Theory, Culture & Society* 11: 1–24.

Martin, Carol Lynn. 1995. "Stereotypes About Children With Traditional and Nontraditional Gender Roles." *Sex Roles* 33(11–12): 727–751.

Martin, Carol Lynn, and Richard A. Fabes. 2001. Research cited in Marianne Szegedy-Maszak, "The Power of Gender." *U.S. News & World Report* 130(22): 52.

Messner, Michael. 1992. *Power at Play: Sports and the Problem of Masculinity.* Boston: Beacon.

Savin-Williams, R. C. (1998). ". . . *And Then I Became Gay": Young Men's Stories.* New York: Routledge.

SELF AND SOCIAL CONTEXT

Sociologist C. Wright Mills described the "sociological imagination" as the ability to see the intersection of "biography and history." The readings in the previous section illustrate the influence of "significant others" in shaping our self concept. The readings in this section provide examples of social context and self development. Our sense of who we are and what we expect our life circumstances to be are directly related to the cultural and historical circumstances in which we find ourselves. As Mills points out, sociology is about understanding how these various contexts influence individual lives. In terms of the theories we have been discussing, social context can be seen as a site in which we gather ideas and information (our "scripts") for making sense of our experiences. Social context also puts us into contact with others who share perspectives that are specific to that context. Accordingly, as we interact with them, we begin to adopt perspectives that reflect the particular contexts in which we live our everyday life. Social context can be as specific as the neighborhood in which you live, the schools you attend, and your particular group of friends. It can also be as general as the civil rights movement, the events of 9/11, the recent financial crisis, and so forth. People are sometimes surprised to learn how much these general conditions and events affect individual lives. Consider, for example, the effects of one very large-scale social pattern, birth rates. We rarely think of ourselves in terms of our "birth cohort," and yet these demographics have a profound effect on the resources, education, jobs, and so on that will be available during our lifetime. Similarly, technological developments have a profound impact on how we live our everyday lives, which in turn shapes our sense of self.

In "The Digital Self," Shanyang Zhao uses Cooley's concept of the "looking-glass self" to explore some of the implications of online communication on self presentation and development. At the time Cooley was writing, the interactional context was largely face-to-face. Zhao asks what happens when our interactions become increasingly mediated through technology. How does this contemporary context shape our sense of self and others? What happens when words on a screen become our "looking glass"?

"Identity Careers of Older Gay Men and Lesbians" invites us to take a step back a few years and look at the historical context of people who identify as gay and lesbian. Sociologist Dana Rosenfeld uses a life-course interview method to learn about the distinct historical conditions that influenced the experiences and self-understanding of older gay men and lesbians. In this article, the interviewees share their recollections of some of the significant events of the days when they were coming of age. Through their stories, Rosenfeld demonstrates the profound effects of social context on the direction and development of a "deviant" identity.

READING QUESTIONS

1. Make a list of some of the memorable social, political, and economic events that occurred early in your life. Trace the effects these events have had on the social context in which you grew up.

(Continued)

(Continued)

2. In considering Zhao's article, one thing to keep in mind is the rapidly changing context for technological communication. Methods that were common just a few years ago (instant messaging, chat rooms, etc.) have now been replaced with text messaging, Facebook, and other new interactional media. How does the social context of "needing to keep up" shape your everyday experiences and sense of self?

3. Researchers have demonstrated that people are much more likely to say insensitive or rude things online than they are in person. Do you think people's desire to treat one another respectfully is different in face-to-face versus online interaction? How might this affect the way we view others as "looking glasses" and the "reflected appraisals" we get from them?

4. Do you think a social context of online interaction sharpens or reduces the line between the "private" self and the "public" self?

5. Interview some of the elders in your life and ask them to describe the events and experiences that had the greatest impact on their beliefs, ideals, and commitments. Do their stories reflect a social context that might be shared by others who had similar experiences?

15

The Digital Self: Through the Looking Glass of Telecopresent Others

Shanyang Zhao

(2005)

[Editor's Note: Computer-mediated communication has changed so extensively in the past decade that it has been difficult for scholars to keep up. Some of the online communication patterns described in this article may seem out of date to contemporary readers. However, despite the changes in forms of electronic communication, the author's main points about the desire for self presentation and recognition among others are still valid. As you read this article, consider how you might apply the concepts to current changes in online communication. For instance, why has Facebook gained such quick popularity and what are the implications of its widespread use for self understanding and presentation?]

People we interact with influence the way we think of ourselves. According to symbolic interactionism, others serve as a looking glass in which we see ourselves (Cooley [1902] 1964). Our view of who we are emerges from our interactions with others. We present ourselves to others as we interact with them, and we come to know ourselves as others react to us. Just as we find out how we look from the reflections we see in the mirror, we learn who we are by interpreting how others respond to us. Others communicate their attitudes toward us not merely in the expressions they give, but more important, in the expressions they "give off" (Goffman 1959). Through both verbal and nonverbal behaviors, others convey to us, either purposefully or unwittingly, their appraisals of our self-presentations, which in turn shape how we view ourselves.

ADOLESCENTS ONLINE

According to the "looking glass" theory, the self is not something we are born with or something that is innate in us; instead, it is something we acquire through interaction with others. In the sense that our perceived appraisals of those we interact with serve as the basis upon which we establish our self-view, we say that we come to see ourselves through the lens of others. Mead's work (1934) postulated that in the context of social interaction, the self evolves gradually through childhood in two main stages. At the first stage, the self is constituted by the organization of the attitudes of the significant others in particular social contexts. At the second stage, the self is constituted by the organization of the attitudes of the generalized other that represent the views of the larger society. As significant others in particular social contexts can bring in different influences, a child may develop multiple selves; but a child learns later to integrate these selves by taking the attitudes of the "generalized other," namely, the view of the larger community to which the child belongs.

Prior to the advent of the Internet, the significant others a child interacted with on a daily basis resided primarily in the world of corporeal copresence. The social world of a teenager in Western society typically consisted of three domains: family, school, and neighborhood. People in these social domains exert different impacts on the formation of self, depending on the stage of development of the child. Research has shown that parents have a dominant influence on their children's sense of self prior to adolescence. As a child grows older, however, the influence of peers increases (Rosenberg 1986). Another finding worth noting here is that a significant number of teenagers have "special adults" outside the family who play an important part in shaping their conception of self (Galbo and Mayer Demetrulias 1996). In most instances, these influential adults are situated in one of the other two domains (i.e., school and neighborhood) of a teenager's life-world. The emergence of the Internet, however, adds a fourth domain—the online life—to the social world of teenagers, hence altering the dynamic of self-acquisition in adolescence.

Since the spread of the Internet in the 1990s, teenagers' involvement in the online world has been increasing at a phenomenal rate. Many teenagers are heavy users of the Internet, as about 42 percent of all the online teens go online every day. Once logged on, they are more likely to engage in multi-tasking, such as browsing Web pages, downloading music, and visiting chat rooms all at the same time. Compared to adults, teenagers are more likely to use the Internet for interpersonal communication. According to the Pew Internet survey conducted in 2000 (Lenhart, Rainie, and Lewis 2001) the three most popular online activities for teenagers are e-mailing, instant messaging,

and chat room discussion. While teenagers and adults are equally likely to use e-mail (92 percent for teens and 93 percent for adults), teenagers are considerably more likely than adults to engage in instant messaging (74 percent for teens and 44 percent for adults) and visiting a chat room (55 percent for teens and 26 percent for adults). These findings suggest that teenagers are more inclined to treat cyberspace as a social place for meeting people and interacting with others.

Most of the people with whom teenagers interact in cyberspace are those they also know offline. The bulk of a teen's online "buddy list," for example, includes school classmates, summer campmates, and friends from other places. Keeping in touch with these people in "telecopresence" [the electronic experience of being copresent with others who are not physically present] helps maintain and strengthen relationships established offline. Another major reason teenagers go online, however, is to meet complete strangers. The Pew Internet and American Life Project in 2000 (cited in Lenhart et al. 2001) reported that 50 percent of those teens who use e-mail, instant messaging, and chat rooms have corresponded via instant messaging or e-mail with people they have never met face-to-face. Twenty-nine percent of older teens and 37 percent of younger teens say that the Internet helps them make new friends whom they would otherwise never meet.

Why do teenagers go online to meet with strangers? There are three possible explanations. First, teenagers are at a stage of life when they begin to explore their place in the world. In making the transition from childhood to adulthood, teenagers are faced with what Erikson's study (1959) called an "identity crisis." As Steinberg's study (1996:307) explains, the maturational and social forces "converge at adolescence," forcing teenagers to "reflect on their place in society, on the ways that others view them, and on their options for the future." To find out who they are and where they belong, teenagers are eager to "leave home" to explore the unknown and mysterious world. But, restrained by limited mobility and adult supervision, most teenagers are able to interact with only the same people in the three familiar domains of their offline world day in and day out. The Internet has changed this situation by opening up virtually the entire world to teenagers, enabling them to visit different places and meet with different people all over the world without actually leaving home. It has been found that:

> Interest in Net-based communications usually starts around age 11 for girls and 13 for boys—basically during adolescence. At these ages, children seek autonomy and the creation of an identity. The Net seems to provide a vehicle to explore the self and for children to establish themselves as independent, self-governing individuals. (Tapscott 1998:56)

Second, teenagers perceive the online world as a safer place to interact with others. Teenagers are socially adventurous and inexperienced at the same time. While they want to go out to meet strangers and make new friends, teenagers are more likely to be oversensitive and easily embarrassed when interacting face-to-face with unfamiliar people, especially people of the opposite sex. Among other things, they worry about the way they look, how others will judge them, and the possibility of being rejected or humiliated by others. In the online world, however, teenagers feel much more comfortable interacting with other people, including complete strangers. As a 16-year-old boy explains:

> Why? Well, online, we have [the] mask of the computer screen. We don't have to worry about what we look like or what other people think of us. Imagine, for instance, meeting a teenager online named Pat. All Pat knows is what you tell Pat. Pat knows what you are feeling and who you REALLY are, based on what you talk to Pat about. Pat doesn't worry about what you look like or what people say about you. (Lenhart et al. 2001:17)

Third, teenagers go online to look for a "soul mate" or someone they can really relate to. The online environment proves to be an ideal place for "heart-to-heart" talks. Protected by disembodiment and anonymity, people in telecopresence are more willing to bare their souls to others, and, as a result, are more likely to find "confidants" who really know them well. It is not uncommon, for example, to hear teenagers describe someone they have met online as "a better friend than anyone else in my life" (Lenhart et al. 2001:17). Despite the fact that others in the anonymous online world are essentially strangers who show up merely as disembodied text messages on the screen, they may be taken very seriously. As one MUD player puts it:

> I don't care how much people say they are, muds (sic) are not games, they are "real"!!! My mud friends are my best friends. . . . They are my family, they are not just some dumb game. (Reid 1995:175)

The Internet, therefore, provides teenagers with a whole new world where they can go and explore the mystery of social life, meet with complete strangers, search for soul mates, and engage in many other social activities without stepping outside of their homes. This means that, for the first time in human history, anonymous and disembodied strangers become important agents of socialization, interacting with youngsters in their homes on a daily basis, and thereby affecting the formation of their self.

THE DIGITAL SELF

In the online world, the disembodied and anonymous others teenagers interact with constitute what Altheide in his research (2002:42) calls the "E Audience," which, like those in the offline world, "invites meaningful participation and displays of self." To differentiate it from the self that emerges from face-to-face interactions with others, I name the self conceived online under the influence of the "E Audience" the "digital self." The digital self is constructed solely through online interaction without the intervention of nonverbal feedback and the influence of traditional environmental factors. As such, the study of the digital self will contribute to our understanding of the processes through which linguistic communications affect the formation of personal identities.

However, it must be noted at the outset that in practice it would be impossible to separate the digital self from other aspects of a person's self-repository. The self is an integrated structure that constantly evolves. To say that there is a "digital self" is not to suggest that a person's self is actually split into physical and digital parts, but to acknowledge the salience of the impact of the "E Audience" on the formation of self in the Internet medium. For the purpose of the analysis being conducted here, the digital self is treated as if it were a separate entity so that the unique influence of others in telecopresence on self-formation can be better highlighted.

The digital self that teenagers come to acquire through interactions with disembodied others in the anonymous online world can be described as (1) inwardly oriented, (2) narrative in nature, (3) retractable, and (4) multiplied. These four characteristics of the digital self are explained in turn below.

Inwardly Oriented

The self is a complex structure that consists of many components and dimensions. Rosenberg's research (1986) has differentiated between "social exterior" and "psychological interior" in self-conceptions. The social exterior of the self pertains to the externally visible aspects of an individual, which include such attributes as height, weight, ethnicity, clothes, and behaviors; the psychological interior of the self, on the other hand, pertains to the less palpable internal world of thoughts, emotions, attitudes, and wishes. Rosenberg found that

in the early years of childhood, an individual tends to focus on the social exterior of the self; upon reaching adolescence, an individual starts to turn inward, paying more attention to the psychological interior of the self.

> More specifically, adolescents tend to say that those who know them best know "what I'm really like," "the real me," "how I feel deep down inside when I'm hurt," "what I really mean." Particularly prominent are references to emotional states. The knowledgeable other understands our deeper feelings: "they know if I'm happy or not," "my feelings," "that I worry a lot," "can tell when I'm sad or when something is wrong," "know my feelings can be hurt easily." (Rosenberg 1986:197)

However, "knowledgeable others" are relatively few in the offline world, for it is hard and often embarrassing for a person to confide his/her innermost thoughts and feelings to others in a face-to-face situation. One may lose control over one's emotions, or freeze up when others lose theirs. Furthermore, revealing too much of one's inner world makes one vulnerable and thereby runs the risk of being taken advantage of. In comparison, "knowledgeable others" are more easily found in the online world, as people appear to be more willing to bare their souls to others in telecopresence. There are several reasons for this. First, people believe that the disembodied text mode in which they communicate with each other in the online world ensures anonymity. Second, because they are able to conceal their offline identities in telecopresence, individuals feel that they can share with others their private thoughts without losing privacy. The possibility of revealing oneself while remaining unseen encourages teenagers to open up their inner world to others through what is known as "self-disclosure":

> Fairly intimate self-disclosure occurs frequently during the first private channel interaction with an individual, and for the most part, the participants

ask and respond easily to questions that, if put to them on such short notice in "real life," could be taken as offensive . . . channel members might confide personal problems or issues with which they are dealing. Within the culture of internet relay chat (IRC), these types of interactions can only be considered natural. (Surratt 1998:114)

The digital self is therefore more oriented toward one's inner world, focusing on thoughts, feelings, and personalities, than one's outer world, focusing on height, weight, and looks. Needless to say, this does not mean that individuals in cyberspace are no longer interested in overt personal characteristics. As a matter of fact, it has been found that when interacting with others in telecopresence, people always conjure an image of what others look like based on the bits and pieces of information gleaned from the disembodied text messages (Stone 1992). These mental projections, often idealized, can help maintain a relationship that might not be able to survive in corporeal copresence.

Narrative in Nature

In the world of corporeal copresence, we rarely need to describe to others how we look as they can see for themselves, nor do we need to tell others what we are because they will come to know us over time. As such, we tend to take our self for granted in face-to-face interaction. This is not the case in the online world, however. When interacting with telecopresent others, especially those we have never met face-to-face, we are obliged to provide some type of self-description. The reason is simple: in text-based online communications we are nothing until we type at the keyboard and others do not know us unless we tell them something. In the process of narrating to others who we are and what we do, the digital self begins to take shape.

In this sense, the digital self is what Thompson (1995:210) calls a "symbolic project" that an individual actively constructs in working out a coherent "narrative of self-identity":

To recount to ourselves or others who we are is to retell the narratives—which are continuously modified in the process of retelling—of how we got to where we are and of where we are going from here. We are all the unofficial biographers of ourselves, for it is only by constructing a story, however loosely strung together, that we are able to form a sense of who we are and of what our future may be.

Telling telecopresent others who we are therefore requires a level of introspection and reflectivity that is not normally exercised in the realm of face-to-face interaction. It is a process in which we take a careful look at ourselves and seek to articulate solely in words what we see about ourselves that we would like others to know (including what we would like others to believe about ourselves even if it is not there). This reflexive process can become challenging and even frightening at times. Below is a perceptive observation by [one of my students] who was attempting to create, for the first time, a weblog for herself:

At first I found it difficult to fill in information on my profile regarding areas of expertise, or even hobbies. I suppose I am not often confronted with situations where I need to describe myself to total strangers. I found the process to be intimidating, leaving me to feel somewhat exposed and vulnerable.

Self-description or introduction takes different forms in the online world. In online chat and instant messaging, for example, self-description begins with the selection of a "screen name" for oneself. A screen name serves as an indicator of what a person claims to be. In the same way that an individual dresses him- or herself in the offline world, a screen name generates a "first impression" of a person on others. As Waskul has written (2003:41), "Without physical presence, screen names become the only initial means by which chat participants can communicate qualities of selfhood that are normally observed, discerned by social cues, or acquired through knowledge of the person." In the online world, it is quite common for people to use more than one screen name. According to the findings of the Pew Internet and American Life Project in 2000 (Lenhart et al. 2001), 56 percent of online teens have more than one e-mail address or screen name, and almost a quarter of boys and one in five girls have more than four online identities. It seems apparent that teenagers are using multiple screen names to compartmentalize their presence in the online world so that they can try out or experiment with different versions of their self. Self-description also comes in the form of self-posted "personal profiles" on listservs, homepages, and weblogs. These autobiographical narratives allow individuals to craft a self in a more careful, elaborate, and coherent manner. By choosing distinctive screen names for themselves and telling interesting personal stories to others, teenagers in cyberspace come to acquire a stable and meaningful self.

Retractable

In corporeal copresence, the self is constrained by the body that contains it. One's body is not one's self, but one's self cannot exist in separation from one's body. As such, once it is formed, our self follows us around like a shadow. Even after we as a person have changed, it takes time for others to change their attitudes toward us. In many situations, the only effective way to shake off an established self is to relocate to a new place where we rebuild our self by interacting with a totally different group of others.

In the online world, however, a given version of one's self can be erased relatively easily. The digital self constructed online is detached from the corporeal body which, in Goffman's research (1959), serves as the "peg" on which the self is hung in face-to-face interaction. The separation of the self

from the body in telecopresence allows individuals to remain unidentified, thus making it possible for them to retract an undesirable self and build a new one without resorting to physical relocation and social uprooting. This proves to be a desirable attribute, for it enables teenagers to "cycle through" multiple versions of their self in the online world while avoiding potential punitive repercussions. As Tapscott points out in his research (1998:92),

> Self-esteem also seems to be enhanced in chat groups because kids can always have another chance—they can adopt another self. In the real world, children can be labeled or isolated early in life and take years to shake it off. You may remember someone in your class who was characterized as a nerd, nose-picker, fatty, or creep—or you may have been that person. A nasty nickname can take years to shake. In cyberspace, if the child doesn't like how he has been characterized, he can adopt a new identity. The other children forget about the old creep and you've got a new self.

Of course, retracting a self, either online or offline, comes with a price. Attached to a self is not only the time and energy one has invested in building it, but also a set of relationships that sustain one's social existence. To retract a self is to abandon all the resources that are associated with it. It is true that the loss is relatively insignificant, to those teenagers who treat their online construction of self merely as a playful "identity game," but the impact may not be so negligible to those who take their online identities seriously.

Multiplied

Multiplicity in self is a reflection of multiplicity in society. In the traditional society, homogeneous communities exhibit a unified collective attitude that fosters a more unitary self in children. Modern societies expose people at an early age to the influence of different ideas, beliefs, and practices, which result in the conception of multiple selves in an individual. The advent of the Internet removes the barriers of physical distance, bringing the dazzling diversity of the entire world to anyone who has access to the World Wide Web. The incursion of cyberspace into the life-world of young people in the Internet era creates a type of self that has been described as "decentered, dispersed, and multiplied in continuous instability" (Poster 1990:6). As Lipton's study (1996:343) describes,

> When the construction of the self happens online in cyberspace, as is occurring at an increasingly rapid rate, taking the attitude of the other becomes awfully complex. It is not just me and my mom anymore. But it is also not just me and my family, or me and my community. Without fixed and distinct communities, the range of potential interactions becomes infinite. These are, after all, so many "others," so many unique identities to choose from. . . . Consequently, there will be no fixed self, but multiple selves, and identity will be further fragmented with each interaction in cyberspace.

However, this appears to be just part of the picture. It is probably true that the Internet has made "the entire world" available at our fingertips, but what is also happening is that most of us go online only to look for what we want to find and filter out what we are not interested in. We are doing this partly because there is simply too much to be seen and partly because we are more free to choose what we like in the online world. The overflow of information combined with the greater freedom of personal choice works to create a self-selected online environment conducive to the formation of a digital self that is more insulated than its offline counterpart.

Self-selection is a prevailing phenomenon in the online world. In instant messaging, for example, teenagers use the "buddy list" to include people they would like to hang out with, and use the "block" function to exclude people they do not want to talk to. In online chat, channel names are instrumental in helping people decide which channels to enter and which channels to stay away from. Once in a chat room, people use the "public channel" to screen for those they can relate to and switch to the "private channel" to hold intimate discussions with them. It is not uncommon to find the public domain of a crowded chat channel virtually empty, with most of the conversations being conducted in "private rooms" among people who like, and perhaps also are like, one another. In addition to being able to seek out like-minded individuals for one-to-one contact, people can form cyber-groups or online communities that consist of only individuals of the same kind. For example, people can establish listservs that only allow authorized individuals to sign up, and they can create web pages that only designated members can subscribe to. Even personal weblogs can be connected to form "blog rings" according to shared interests. Thus, in contrast to face-to-face interactions in the offline world which are often constrained by spatial and institutional arrangements that are not of one's own choice,

> [w]hat computer-mediated communication adds is a greater capacity to avoid public interaction of the kind that would pull one beyond one's immediate personal choices of taste and culture. Discussion groups may transcend the spatial community, but they do so precisely by linking people with similar interests, not by forging links among people sharply different from one another. (Calhoun 1998:385)

Such a capacity to look for and bring together the like-minded on the Internet has contributed to the homogenization of the others one interacts with in the different domains of the online world. Putnam's work (2000:178), for example, has noted that, compared to the offline world, "the virtual world may be more homogeneous, not in demographic terms, but in terms of interest and outlook." Lack of diversity in the appraisals of those with whom one interacts invariably results in the formation of a self that is less "de-centered." The freedom to go where we want to go and be with whom we want to be with may therefore counterbalance the impact of anonymity on self-construction in the online world. Even though anonymity and disembodiment encourage teenagers to experiment with multiple versions of their self, the homogeneity of the attitudes of the like-minded people teenagers choose to interact with in telecopresence may in the end make the resulting digital self more insulated than those formed in corporeal copresence.

CONCLUSION

What happens to the formation of self in the online world? Can people we do not know in person affect how we think of ourselves? Does lacking nonverbal cues from others in telecopresence change the looking glass in which we see ourselves? The present study has provided some preliminary answers to these questions. Analyses of the online experience of teenagers have shown that telecopresent others in the online world do constitute a unique looking glass which generates a digital self that is different from the self constructed offline. The digital self has been found to be oriented inward, narrative in nature, retractable, and multiplied. The digital self is oriented inward toward the world of thoughts and feelings because others cannot see our overt attributes; it is narrative in nature because others come to know us primarily on the basis of what we tell them; it is retractable because others are unable to link our online self-claims to our offline identities; and, finally, it is multiplied because others interact with us in different domains of the online world. As is true in corporeal copresence, those we interact with in telecopresence affect how we perceive ourselves; furthermore, the ways in which we interact with others also play a part in determining the outcome of our self-conception.

It must be mentioned that, although the principle of the looking-glass self is applicable to people of all ages, telecopresent others may affect teenagers more than adults, as teenagers are yet to form a stable view of themselves and thus are more susceptible to the influence of others. As such, it may be true that adults participate in online role-play games mostly for the purpose of self-presentation, and teenagers mostly for the purpose of self-experimentation. Yet, in the sense that the self is a symbolic project to be worked on throughout one's life, others, acting as our "looking glass," always have an impact on our self-perception regardless of whether we are teenagers or adults.

The results of this study regarding the effect of telecopresent others on the conception of self in teenagers have practical implications for parents, teachers, and other agents of socialization. As has been shown, the Internet is not just a new source of information and a new form of entertainment; it is also a new domain of social interaction. The addition of this emergent social domain to the life-world of teenagers has altered the ways in which young people make the transition from adolescence into adulthood, and the long-term societal effect of such alteration remains to be known. The study of the formation of the digital self in teenagers in telecopresence is only a beginning step toward a better understanding of the changing dynamics of socialization in the Internet era.

REFERENCES

Altheide, David L. 2002. "Toward a Mapping of the Mass Media and the 'E Audience.'" Pp. 41–62 in *Postmodern Existential Sociology*, edited by J. A. Kotarba and J. M. Johnson. Walnut Creek, CA: AltaMira.

Calhoun, Craig. 1998. "Community Without Propinquity Revisited: Communications Technology and the Transformation of the Urban Public Sphere." *Sociological Inquiry* 68:373–97.

Cooley, Charles. [1902] 1964. *Human Nature and the Social Order.* New York: Scribner's.

Erikson, Erik H. 1959. "Identity and the Life Cycle." *Psychological Issues* 1:18–164.

Galbo, Joseph J. and Diana Mayer Demetrulias. 1996. "Recollections of Nonparental Significant Adults During Childhood and Adolescence." *Youth & Society* 27:403–20.

Goffman, Erving. 1959. *The Presentation of Self in Everyday Life.* New York: Doubleday.

Lenhart, Amanda, Lee Rainie, and Oliver Lewis. 2001. "Teenage Life Online: The Rise of the Instant-Message Generation and the Internet's Impact on Friendships and Family Relationships." Available online at: http://www.pewinternet.org/Reports/2001/Teenage-Life-Online.aspx.

Lipton, Mark. 1996. "Forgetting the Body: Cybersex and Identity." Pp. 335–49 in *Communication and Cyberspace: Social Interaction in an Electronic Environment,* edited by L. Strate, R. Jacobson, and S. B. Gibson. Cresskill, NJ: Hampton.

Mead, George H. 1934. *Mind, Self, and Society.* Chicago: University of Chicago Press.

Poster, Mark. 1990. *The Mode of Information: Poststructuralism and Social Context.* Cambridge, UK: Polity Press.

Putnam, Robert D. 2000. *Bowling Alone: The Collapse and Revival of American Community.* New York: Simon & Schuster.

Reid, Elizabeth. 1995. "Virtual Worlds: Culture and Imagination." Pp. 164–93 in *Cybersociety,* edited by S. G. Jones. Thousand Oaks, CA: Sage.

Rosenberg, Morris. 1986. *Conceiving the Self.* Malabar, FL: Robert E. Krieger.

Steinberg, Laurence. 1996. *Adolescence.* Boston: McGraw-Hill.

Stone, Allucquere R. 1992. "Will the Real Body Please Stand Up? Boundary Stories About Virtual Cultures." Pp. 81–118 in *Cyberspace: First Steps,* edited by M. Benedikt. Cambridge: MIT Press.

Surratt, Carla. G. 1998. *Netlife: Internet Citizens and Their Communities.* New York: Nova Science.

Tapscott, Don. 1998. *Growing Up Digital: The Rise of the Net Generation.* New York: McGraw-Hill.

Thompson, John B. 1995. *The Media and Modernity: A Social Theory of the Media.* Palo Alto, CA: Stanford University Press.

Waskul, Dennis D. 2003. *Self-Games and Body-Play: Personhood in Online Chat and Cybersex.* New York: Peter Lang.

SELF AND SOCIAL CONTEXT

16

Identity Careers of Older Gay Men and Lesbians

Dana Rosenfeld

(2003)

C. Wright Mills (1959) once argued that biographical narratives are not just accounts of lifelong experience, but are significantly shaped both in form and in content by the ideas and values of the historical period in which they are embedded. How people experience their later years, for example, is strongly influenced by the historical context in which they came of age. This bears especially on their sense later in life of who and what they were and have become—their *identity careers.*

The ways in which identities are shaped by their historical context were strikingly impressed upon me during a recent study I conducted to explore the lives and experiences of older gay men and women (see Rosenfeld 1999). In 1995, I conducted open-ended, in-depth interviews with 50 self-identified gay men and lesbians of various class and ethnic backgrounds, who were aged 64 to 89 years. I identified subjects in the greater Los Angeles area by means of "snowball" sampling and conducted interviews in subjects' homes. I tape-recorded these interviews, collecting demographic information and life histories, which included accounts of current and future concerns, friendship and family networks, religious beliefs and practices, and feelings about the organized lesbian and gay communities.

As I started analyzing the transcripts from these interviews, I immediately noted how the emergence of gay liberation in the late 1960s and 1970s—which divided subjects' lives into an era in which homosexuality was exclusively constructed as a shameful stigma and a new period in which being gay was increasingly viewed as a positive identity—affected their recollections of sexual experiences and the identity issues that flowed from them. A central theme resonated throughout the interviews: These subjects were members of a cohort who formed sexual identities at a time of tremendous change, and they were now constructing narratives of life experiences that reflected just how much their identity careers were still being shaped by these events, even later in life.

Gay Life and Historical Change

Consider the climate for homosexuals who were coming of age or first considering their sexual identities in the early to mid-twentieth century. Throughout my subjects' youth and middle age, homosexuality was defined and treated as a medical, legal, and moral aberration. The medical establishment considered homosexuality to be a disease until 1973, when the nascent gay movement's

lobbying efforts resulted in the American Psychiatric Association's vote to rescind this definition. Homosexuality was widely viewed as an unnatural existence devoid of healthy social, familial, or emotive ties. Indeed, throughout the 1950s and 1960s, medical and psychiatric constructions of homosexuality increasingly informed the popular depiction of gay men and women as isolated, immature, ashamed, and incapable of achieving either personal satisfaction or social integration. These images dominated the limited press coverage of homosexual life, and censorship of gay-positive texts and films kept homosexuals dependent upon a medical and popular literature that stigmatized them (Faderman 1991). These depictions were invoked and elaborated by the federal government during the McCarthy era (Nardi and Sanders 1994: 11), when homosexuals were constructed as security risks by the State Department and other federal agencies (D'Emilio 1983: 43–44). Federal policy toward homosexuality found a natural ally in state and local police, who had a long history of harassing gays and lesbians.

The construction of homosexuality as a pathological condition provided gay men and women with both an identity category in which to place their often-secretive feelings and a language with which to discuss and describe themselves and their position in society. This language, of course, was negative and stigmatizing. As a result, while some homosexuals embraced the stigmatized roles made available by the gay underground (Chauncey 1994), others saw their sexual desires as a condition to be suppressed, remaining single and celibate or adopting heterosexual marriage patterns. Yet others engaged in sexual, social, and emotional relations with other gay men or lesbians, understanding their homosexuality to be an aberrant condition which, while capable of being satisfied, nonetheless required them to pass as heterosexual. While the severe stigmatization of homosexuality was seen by these individuals as merited, they saw their persecution as avoidable through their own attempts at normalization. They condemned both the underground homosexual life that exploded in the post-war years and those immersed in it as unnecessarily legitimating stereotypes of gay men and women, which they figured invited the persecution of all homosexuals.

The civil rights and the New Left movements of the 1960s informed an emergent oppositional stance within the homosexual subculture, which began to formulate homosexuality as a valid identity to be openly embraced and enacted, rather than a stigmatizing condition to be hidden. Both the gay liberation and the lesbian feminist movements (Weitz 1984; Faderman 1991) of the early 1970s called for all homosexuals to condemn both the stigmatized understanding of homosexuality as well as those who continued to embrace this view, and to come "out of the closets and into the streets" (Young 1972) to live openly as gay men and lesbians. This position is the dominant ideology of lesbian and gay communities today.

(Homo)Sexual Identity Careers

My subjects were born between 1906 and 1931 and were aged 39 to 64 when gay liberation began to systematically challenge both the dominant stigmatization of homosexuality and homosexuals' adaptation to it. While most had identified as homosexual according to the stigmatized formulation of homosexuality, living relatively secret lives by passing as heterosexual in public, some had not then identified as homosexual at all, although many had had same-sex desires and relationships. The latter group encountered gay liberation and lesbian feminism at a time in their lives when they were aware of their attraction to members of their own sex, but did not yet view themselves as gay or lesbian. The emerging formulation of homosexuality provided them with a new way of understanding and enacting these feelings, and they

adopted the new homosexual identity that was now available.

When recounting their identity careers, these subjects often described "always knowing" that they were different. They spoke of being attracted to members of their own sex during their early years, often in childhood. When speaking of these early desires, many echoed 77-year-old respondent Manny's (pseudonyms are used throughout) statement that "I knew something was wrong with me all my life." Recognizing and evaluating inchoate desires were, for these subjects, coterminous aspects of the same project: to understand the nature of their desires and their implications for self. They described feeling bewildered about both the meaning of these desires (and, often, their own fulfillment of them) and their implications for identity and value. Brian, aged 74, for example, "kept thinking, 'Well, that's quite different. Is it something you outgrow?' I remember having that in my mind."

Some did not act on this awareness for years, as there was little in the air at the time that encouraged them to develop related identities. Susan, aged 75, reported that when she "was in high school, I was aware of certain girls. And I found myself attracted or interested. But I didn't do anything about it. I just, I was conscious of it. It was one of those things. I lived with it." Similarly, 72-year-old Tex's belief that a man could be attracted to him was "a phase [he] was going through" prevailed well into his marriage. As he explains, he

was attracted to men, the more I fought it, the more I dreamed about it. I thought it was a phase that I would get over, but I didn't. I never tried to put a name for it. I thought I was different. I didn't think anybody else felt like that except me.

Most, however, pursued these desires, still failing to understand their meaning for self. Many experienced their associations and relations as relatively unproblematic. While they "knew" that these were best enacted in certain contexts and not in others, pursuing same-sex relations while unaware of their severely stigmatizing "nature" allowed them to experience these connections as "natural." Jan, aged 68, noted, for example, that she

> didn't label it because I didn't know there was such a thing as a lesbian, it was just the most natural thing in the world. I don't suppose I knew what a homosexual was. If someone had asked me: "I don't have a clue." As I told you I started dating a neighbor kid, even before I got involved with this woman. And I always assumed that I would marry and you know do all this stuff because that was what people did where I grew up.

Most subjects spoke of searching for accounts of these differences in textual and cultural representations and in others' remarks. For example, Rodney, aged 81, wrote to the editor and publisher of a homoerotic "muscle" magazine for advice to "determine where I stood in life." Jeannine, aged 66, and her female lover searched the dictionary for female versions of the word "faggot." Others described pondering their interactions and characterizations to uncover the nature and consequences of their desires. Without exception, the accounts formulated same-sex desires as a pathological yet curable condition. This discourse "explained" subjects' experiences to them in stigmatizing terms, and thus supplied a much-needed identity category. The interpenetration of these messages and responses can be seen in 66-year-old Sharon's account of

> reading medical journals on how to deal with the brain because I thought I was crazy because of being gay. I thought I was insane because it was not normal. Probably by the age of ten or twelve I was getting books at the library on Havelock Ellis and Kraft-Ebbing because I would look up the term homosexual—don't ask me how I found that word—but I would look up the term homosexual and would refer to notes. And it told about all the horrible things that the insane people did, so I thought that's what gay people did.

The stigmatizing discourse of the times provoked the challenge of making the self intelligible and, at the same time, preserving its value in the face of a devalued identity. Subjects described feeling caught between a need to understand and pursue their desires on the one hand and to avoid the negative implications of a stigmatized identity on the other. Recognizing and fulfilling sexual desires served to discredit them, making them subject to ridicule and rejection.

Distancing

Many found the implications of a stigmatized identity so severe that they worked to avoid interpreting their desires in its terms, managing the tension between their desires and the consequences of enacting them by distancing themselves from one, the other, or both. "Distancing" refers to the variety of ways in which subjects modified, weakened, or resisted the applicability of the term "homosexual" to themselves; these consisted of "putting it on the back burner," pursuing heterosexual relations, and cultivating a heterosexual identity.

Those who "put it on the back burner" made same-sex desire a background concern of significantly less importance to them than other interests, needs, and obligations, which, according to them, provided greater rewards. Ryan, aged 81, "would see men that I thought I liked, you know at a distance, and I would like to get better acquainted with them, but I didn't dare go any further than that, and I just let it go at that." Similarly, Marge, aged 81, recalled "staying away from it."

> There was a female that everybody called "old dyke" because she was out and she had a girlfriend. She was almost like an outcast. [Also] conversation would come up with the kids that I would associate with and other people and they would speak of people like this, not only women but men, too, that were feminine. I knew I was connected with it, but

I wanted to stay away from it because I did not want to be ridiculed. I didn't do anything about it. I went out with guys, you know.

For many, distancing included pursuing heterosexual relations. For example, Patricia, aged 77, "had boyfriends," Kate, aged 76, "occasionally would accept a date, usually fixed up by anxious family or anxious friends," and 81-year-old Ryan saw heterosexual relations as "the lesser of two evils." According to Ryan, in his teen years, he was

semi-interested in girls. It was the lesser of two evils, let's put it that way. We would be going to parties or to dances and things like that, I enjoyed dancing in those days, and we enjoyed dinners and bake-outs.

Subjects said they had expected that the frustration of unmet needs and desires would be precluded or offset by replacing those needs with others which were more easily met and which presented no negative implications for self. After her psychoanalysis failed to "cure" her lesbianism, Kate sought to fulfill herself through her job. "I was also deeply involved in my school and my teaching, which was very satisfactory, very all-consuming. And the other stuff I put on the back burner."

For many, however, distancing techniques caused them to see themselves as without value or definition. Dan, aged 70, spoke of defining himself as "active neuter. No sex, nothing" while engaged in distancing. Deborah, aged 74, explained that "I wasn't defining myself at all," and Kate considered herself "a mess, sexually, practically without identity." This distress led some to actively pursue a heterosexual identity, which they saw as providing a fulfilling family life on the one hand and protection from the harassment and ridicule homosexuals faced on the other.

They did this in one of two ways. Some entered conventional heterosexual marriages, less as a means of "hiding" their homosexuality than as a way to achieve a heterosexual identity that provided positive rewards. A few had married, only to

have their homosexual desires emerge and coalesce during their marriages. Luke, aged 69, for example, accounts for his heterosexual marriage by stating that when he "met her I was trying to get away from gay life. I was trying to get out of being gay. I was trying to get out and raise a family and everything. I don't know. I just wanted a family." Mark, aged 71, married when he realized that the man he was in love with

was more interested in what I had to give. Then along came June, my ex-wife. I decided that I was going to give up being gay. I figured that [there] just wasn't any future in it for me. We went to a dance, came home, I took her underneath the porch, I had sex with her. And then four months later, she says, "I'm pregnant." So I says, "Well, better get married." We got married and I gave up Joe. I was 28, 29.

Others constructed a kind of liminal heterosexuality by embracing the medicalized formulation of homosexuality as curable through therapy, which provided a positive and rewarded role and promised a future heterosexual identity. Rather than see themselves as permanently diseased, these subjects embraced the medicalized discourse's most positive version of "pervert"—s/he who is committed to a cure. Although immanently homosexual and thus stigmatized, this constructed them at the same time as adequately oriented to the medical establishment's norms and goals and committed them to achieving a normal life. Seventy-two-year-old Leonard, for example, sought therapy after being fired from the State Department for being homosexual.

So I went to New York at that time, mainly because they had suggested that, you know, therapy in New York was the place. I was gonna get cured. I was in pretty bad shape. I went to therapy with this general idea in mind.

Embracing a New Identity

Several subjects who had had same-sex desires but who did not know how to interpret them described their first sexual or erotic contacts as clarifying these desires, learning how to fulfill them on the one hand and providing insight into "what they were" on the other. Dan, aged 70, for example, reported that he "still wasn't aware of anything" when, in his mid-twenties, he

> wanted to get rid of my glasses, so I went for eye exercises, and the guy giving [them] was gay. So, he started massaging my eyes and things and I was very attracted to him, and then finally he kissed me. And then I was in heaven, you know. And that's when I became aware, when he kissed me in New York.

Meeting and associating with other homosexuals either alone or in groups was key to subjects' interpreting their desires in a new light. At the very least, it showed them that they were not "the only ones in the world" and that there were venues for associating with others like themselves. Many searched for and patronized lesbian and gay bars to determine if they had anything in common with the other patrons. They spoke of feeling as though they belonged "there" ("there" being a subcultural homosexual world). Abby, aged 70, described this happening

> the first time that I went to a bar . . . I was 25. I think it was Bleecker Street, and it was the Swing Rendezvous was the name of the place. It was primarily women. As soon as I walked in there, I don't think it took me very long to realize that this is exactly where I belong. And that was my first introduction.

Subjects also explained how changing relational contexts inspired a reformulation of homosexuality and its relation to self. Many spoke of the emergence of emotional needs that could only be fulfilled through erotic or romantic relationships with same-sex partners. While they had initially limited their same-sex connections to sexual ones that did not, for them, implicate a homosexual identity, these new desires caused them to reexamine their sexual selves. While 75-year-old George, for example, "did homosexual things before," he didn't "realize" he was gay until

> that night that I told Jack. We were sitting in my car, holding hands. This is when I had this wave of emotion, and I turned and looked out the window and I said, "I want to tell you something." And he said, "Don't worry about it, so am I." He was also at the same point where I was. In coming out we were discovering ourselves. I knew that I wanted him; he knew that he wanted me.

The breakup of Mark's marriage provided a new context through which to reassess his sexuality and his future. Having given up "being gay" (see above), he "found out that the straight life wasn't what it's kicked up to be" when he found his wife in bed with his brother. He then "went back to Joe, said 'let's get the hell out of Syracuse.' And Joe and I moved to California. We were lovers for three years after that."

For 66-year-old Mary, her husband's request for an "open marriage" provided the opportunity for experimenting sexually, allowing her to look "at women differently." Her first lesbian affair, "other problems in the marriage," and pressure from her female lover created a need "to make a decision."

> I started going around with a girlfriend of mine who had always played around. And all the men that we ran into, everybody was telling me how good-looking I was and what they could do for me, and I thought, "Oh no." So I don't know, somewhere along the line. . . . And I had always had gay and lesbian friends, and all at once I realized I was looking at women differently than I had before. So, I got myself involved in an affair, and told my husband about it. There were some other problems in the marriage. I finally decided that I needed to make a decision. I didn't like living that way. And of course by this time the other lady had decided that I wasn't ever gonna leave my husband, and so I asked my husband to move.

As a result, she added, "I made a conscious choice to my way of thinking to become a lesbian when I was about forty-three."

For these individuals, who were still engaged in distancing practices when gay and lesbian liberation emerged, the movement provided both a very broad social context through which to form new relationships with gay men and lesbians and a new symbolic framework through which to assess their desires and actions. This granted the opportunity to reformulate oneself not from a non-homosexual to a stigmatized homosexual, but from a non-homosexual self to a liberated gay or lesbian person. Marilyn, aged 66, who encountered lesbian-feminism and the possibilities for a new identity at a meeting of the National Organization for Women in the early 1970s, referred directly to the link between changing times and changing selves.

> It was a gradual process. What really kicked it off for me was reading an article by a woman in the National Organization for Women, and I said, "Hey, that's me." It was just a revelation. I went to the National Organization for Women. I met other women who identified themselves as lesbian. It was the first time that I had lesbians around me, identifiable lesbians. I became involved, we had a march in West Los Angeles and had speakers for hours. It was a *fantastic* time for feminism and gays and lesbians and a lot of energy; it was a great time.

Coming Out to Family Members

For those who identified as homosexual before gay liberation, close relations with family hinged on avoiding discussion of their homosexuality. Those who came out by way of gay liberation, in contrast, were committed to broaching the issue with family members at various times and places.

Members of the first group saw their homosexuality as a private matter that should not be raised as a topic by any members of the family, including themselves. They explained that doing so was unnecessary and could create tensions and even distress for their loved ones. For example, Brian, aged 74, "kept that separate from the family." Even his nephew, to whom he is extremely close, has

> no idea. We're so separated geographically that there's never been any reason to tell [the family], you know, or for them to think anything of it. All they know is, "Oh, he was married once and he's divorced." So it doesn't enter their mind, you see. I haven't felt that there's any reason to talk to them about it; it'd just shock them.

These subjects felt this way even though several felt that their families "already knew." As 77-year-old Manny put it, "I don't tell anybody that I'm gay, but everybody knows. But nobody says anything. It's taken for granted." Declining to discuss their sexuality was not necessarily a matter of passing as heterosexual, but was rather understood as respecting the family's perceived feelings of discomfort and shame were the topic to be raised. Patricia, aged 77, stated that she

> never mentioned it. They all know that I am. My sisters know I am but we've never talked about it. I'm sure my dad and mother [knew but] we never discussed it. They knew when I went to live with Deborah, especially my mother, but never discussed it. It was just something that [they] didn't want to have to go through [or] live with. My sisters are very good friends and I talk to them but we don't discuss anything like this. We discuss everyday life. Things that are going on.

Similarly, Jan, aged 68, describes herself as "still very, very *guarded* in terms of being open with most of the people that I know," explaining that "I guess I came up in the wrong era," expressly tying her biography to history. She feels that

> there are no illusions, everybody who knows me I'm sure knows that I'm a lesbian, I'm sure they do, but it's never discussed. It's not something I would particularly bring up, but I wouldn't *avoid*.

Indeed, these same subjects were upset and insulted when other members of their families disclosed their homosexuality to them. Seventy-seven-year-old Manny described a nephew's including him in the process of coming out to his family as an unwelcome intrusion into the appropriate distance he had established with his relatives. In his view, this was ultimately irrelevant to him and his position in the family.

> I have a nephew that's gay, in Montreal. He's a college kid. And he came out to his mother and father when he was in college. And of course, I went home, and this is part of the family that I don't like. So the mother said, "Manny, call Josh. Manny, call Josh." I said, "Okay, I'll call Josh." So I'm leaving Montreal and I didn't call Josh. So Josh calls me, "Uncle Manny? You're leaving—I'm gay." So I said, "What do you want *me* to do?" You know?

Given the commitment of this set of subjects to keeping their homosexuality private, it is not surprising that the rare instances when they were expected to disclose their homosexuality to others were met with outrage. Sixty-nine-year-old Lillian, for one, felt that her cousin's anger at her failure to come out to him was unwarranted, and his expectation that she come out to him unreasonable. As she explained, his desire that she disclose her lesbianism to him displaced his responsibility for raising the topic onto her shoulders. Since he was the one who saw her sexuality as relevant to their relationship, it was his obligation to ask her about it. To expect her to raise the issue was to expect her to "make an announcement," to gratuitously make her sexuality evident and obtrusive.

> My cousin Louie did something I didn't like and he got very mad at me because I never told him I was gay. I said I never heard of something like that. First of all, I'm not one to wear a sign on my back, and like I told him if he were that curious to know what my lifestyle was, why didn't you ask? If you would have asked me I would have told you, but I'm not about to

come to you and say, "Hey, Louie, I'm gay," you know. I just don't want to deal with that, you know what I'm saying? I mean he's 72 years old. I said, "You're a grown man, if you were that curious, why didn't you ask me? I would have told you. But I'm not about to make an announcement."

Subjects who identified as gay or lesbian by way of gay liberation, however, viewed the discussion of their homosexuality as essential to close relations with family members. Marilyn, aged 66, made this explicit when discussing her relationship to a niece, equating being close with being out (clearly, she was not close to the niece she discusses below).

> If you're asking me close, I'm not out to her. I don't tell her my personal problems. I tell her about, you know, problems with the apartment and other things. But she's not somebody I would go to with relationship problems.

This equation is even clearer when we consider Marilyn's relationship to her cousin, who is "almost like a sister to me" and to whom she did, in fact, come out.

Kate, aged 76, spoke in similar terms of her

> cousin in Chicago to whom I'm out. In an odd sort of way, I'm fond of her. She came the closest to being a sister, simply because for a while, in Texas, we lived near each other and our mothers were not only sisters but very, very fond of each other, and we had a lot of contact as children.

In stark contrast to Manny's account above, these subjects welcomed younger gay people into their lives, offering support and guidance, even help in handling their homosexuality in the context of the family. Seventy-year-old Abby, for example, suspects that

> one of my great-nieces is going to turn around some day and say something to me, and if she does, then I will tell her flat out, and I will tell her where to go

and what to [do], and steer her away from any of the pitfalls that I possibly can. And if I have to run interference for the rest of her family and mine, I will.

Similarly, Susan, aged 75, described how she looked forward to a visit from her granddaughter and her gay friend:

> My whole family's fully aware of who I am and that's what's important to me. . . . My granddaughter's supposedly coming to visit here. She's bringing a couple of friends with her and it so happens, she tells me, one of her friends is gay, a young girl. She said, "I told her about you, Grandma. She'd love to talk to you." I said, "Sure, fine." So they think I'm gonna be an advisor to this young kid. Anyway, it'll be interesting to talk to her. But I think it's kind of cute, that she's gonna take her friend to visit her grandmother who's gay.

While Manny fumed when his nephew told him of his own homosexuality, 66-year-old Sharon was incensed that her brother has not come out to her, interpreting his reticence as an affront to the closeness they'd felt while growing up.

> My brother is not married. He has never said anything to me about being gay. *Ever.* Can you believe it? And he and I were just *this close.* We grew up like twins, there was a year difference. We were very close, he and I were raised very close. Yet he will not tell me he's gay.

BEING OLD AND GAY

Clearly, there are many ways to experience being old and gay. In discussing the impact that homosexuality had on their lives and on growing older, gay men and lesbians often related to family issues in contradictory terms. Many expressed regret that they lacked the "support system" that the traditional family offers. For example, Ryan, aged 81, noted that, for homosexuals, growing older was "much more difficult. I don't think I have the support system, I don't have the family support system that I would otherwise have. I guess that's the main thing." Sixty-six-year-old Ricardo felt that "because we grow old normally separated from families" and heterosexuals "grow old *within* the families," gay aging

> is by definition a little different. You just can't define [yourself] isolated without any relationship to family or society. So in this case you have to project yourself to your family. I don't have any family, possibly because I wouldn't feel comfortable in the heterosexual world. So growing older, it makes a little difference.

At the same time, many also claimed that the absence of traditional family ties made for a better life in old age. For example, Jeannine, aged 66, while recognizing the importance of children as caregivers to older people, saw the family as a potential obstacle to happiness in old age, as the following interview exchange suggests.

Jeannine: They don't have the family support that straights would. They don't have a daughter that's dutifully going to— usually—take care of Mom. Or a son who's going to be an advocate. So, in that sense, they're a little more isolated, they don't have the broad family thing. But it may be a blessing, too. 'Cause I've seen the vultures circle too, with straights.

DR: You mean waiting for Grandma to die so that they can have the Porsche?

Jeannine: Yeah. Or jostling to be nice to her before she dies so that they can have the Porsche.

Several subjects felt that the absence of conventional family relations freed them from constraints and concerns that took their toll on individuals' freedom, appearance, and health. These respondents linked the absence of a conventional family to what they perceived as the relative vitality and youthfulness of the gay and lesbian elderly. For 68-year-old Jan, childlessness is said to free older homosexuals from children's constant reminder of their relatively advanced age, resulting in subjective feelings of youthfulness.

I don't think of myself as old, elderly, or even aging. And I think if I were in the regular mode—a husband and kids, grandchildren—I'd have grandchildren at this point, and a constant *reminder* from all these years that have crept up and having all these generations younger than myself I would tend to feel much older I think than perhaps I do now. [Heterosexuals] usually do age faster.

Others explained that the relative vitality of older homosexuals was due to their freedom from the worries over family, from which heterosexuals suffered. Brian, aged 74, compared his gay friends to his heterosexual friends from his days in the Navy, claiming that the latter's marital and parental roles bring with them "worries" that cause "feebleness":

Maybe gays aren't quite as feeble as straights now. Because I think that these friends I see just don't seem as old as the straight friends that are the same age. They haven't had kids and all this and that. I'm sure that [straight] people have kids, and they're with spouses. It's just maybe a little more worries or something.

Still others, such as Luke, aged 69, described the traditional family as threatening the autonomy and freedom of the elderly. According to Luke, older homosexuals are free from these impositions and hence relatively carefree in their youthfulness. He saw older heterosexuals, in contrast, as vulnerable to institutionalization by their children, which makes them "lonelier."

Their sons and their daughters take them and make them lonelier by putting them in convalescent homes and getting rid of them. When you're gay, no one can do that to you, you have to do it to yourself. So you go on by yourself until you don't have any more strength to go on. And that's why I'm 68 and I still feel like I'm 55.

Some saw their homosexuality as irrelevant to their old age, resisting the narrative linkage of sexual nonconformity, social stigmatization, and their impact on the later years typical of many others. As William, aged 76, put it, "Some people, both gay and heterosexual, age gracefully and some don't. And I don't know that being gay has anything specifically to do with it." Mary, aged 66, felt that "getting old is just getting old, as far as I can tell." To 75-year-old Susan, "You're a person first, aren't you? Gay people get ill, gay people have the same problems that straight people do." For Kate, aged 76, the circumstances under which people age center on social support, which she felt is independent of sexuality. As she explained, the isolation of older persons depends upon

whether they were ever married or had children, what kind of families they have. A straight woman who never married, if she has a loving niece, you know, great. If she doesn't, too damned bad. I think it's a matter of old age *per se* and the kind of friends and the kind of family you have. It's a question of you're single, you damned well better have a support system and/or some sort of family. You know most people that are my age and single do have nieces and nephews, you see. Having been a single child I don't have that. I think that cuts across the whole society in terms of old age. That has nothing to do with the gay/lesbian part. We join the mainstream in old age.

FUTURE COHORTS

In considering future ways of aging among gays and lesbians, we need to avoid a full reliance on the heterosexual/homosexual divide. History has shown that this divide is now not as clear as it was for the older subjects under consideration. Just as the historical era in which my subjects identified as homosexual affected their identity careers, so will the historical era in which future cohorts of lesbians and gays age affect their identities and their views of the later years. Future cohorts of homosexual elderly will have moved through life in the context of concerns and opportunities related to sexuality almost unimaginable a generation ago.

The shape of lesbian and gay families (see Weston 1991), if not legally binding, is nonetheless now part of the discourse and practice of lesbian and gay life. The emergence of same-sex partner benefits, while by no means universal, allows gay men and women to cement their relationships financially and legally, and to move to and from jobs as families, with massive implications for security in old age. This also allows gay men and women to be "out" at work, an almost mind-boggling change from the 1950s, when homosexuality was grounds for immediate dismissal from a job. Indeed, the homosexual "baby boom" of the 1980s and 1990s will undoubtedly have immense consequences for the quality of gay life in old age later in the century. The emergence of gay voting blocs and of gay lobbying will provide a new arena for the political engagement with, and enactment of, diverse homosexual identities and policies in the public sphere. These rapidly developing historical changes will undoubtedly provide new biographical opportunities for future generations of homosexual elders.

Accompanying this is the explosion of venues for the discussion and contesting of homosexual identity in the mass media, which suggests that future cohorts of older gay men and lesbians will have devoted a shorter period of their lives to identity issues surrounding their sexuality. It is doubtful that today's teenagers experiencing same-sex desires will spend as much time plowing through a discourse of difference to interpret their desires. Indeed, the now classic coming out story may become less dramatic and less painful than it has

been, one which seems to have been a narrative watershed for the older subjects of the generation under consideration.

Gay liberation, lesbian-feminism, and queer politics have complicated a field of sexual discussion that had, in my subjects' earlier years, been dominated by an identity landscape almost wholly reliant upon the condemnation of homosexuality. Imagining the future impact of these changes on the identity careers of homosexuals further highlights the importance of the link between biography and history as it relates to ways of aging.

REFERENCES

Chauncey, George. 1994. *Gay New York: Gender, Urban Culture, and the Making of the Gay Male World, 1890–1940.* New York: Basic Books.

D'Emilio, John. 1983. *Sexual Politics, Sexual Communities: The Making of a Homosexual Minority in the United States.* Chicago: University of Chicago Press.

Faderman, Lillian, 1991. *Odd Girls and Twilight Lovers: A History of Lesbian Life in Twentieth-Century America.* Middlesex, UK: Plume.

Mills, C. Wright. 1959. *The Sociological Imagination.* New York: Oxford University Press.

Nardi, Peter M. and Sanders, David. 1994. *Growing Up Before Stonewall: Life Stories of Some Gay Men.* London: Routledge.

Rosenfeld, Dana. 1999. "Identity Work Among Lesbian and Gay Elderly." *Journal of Aging Studies,* 13(2):121–44.

Weitz, R. 1984. "From Accommodation to Rebellion: The Politicization of Lesbianism." In T. Darry and S. Potter (eds.), *Women-Identified Women.* Palo Alto, CA: Mayfield, pp. 233–48.

Weston, Kath. 1991. *Families We Choose: Lesbians, Gays, Kinship.* New York: Columbia University Press.

Young, A. 1972. "Out of the Closets, Into the Streets." In Karla Jay and Allen Young (eds.), *Out of the Closets: Voices of Gay Liberation.* New York: Pyramid Books, pp. 6–30.

PART IV

PRODUCING SOCIAL IDENTITIES AND SOCIAL SCRIPTS

Social structure is an essential element of the reality of everyday life.

—Peter Berger and Thomas Luckmann (1966),
The Social Construction of Reality

To be aware of the idea of social structure and to use it with sensibility ... is to possess a sociological imagination.

—C. Wright Mills (1959), *The Sociological Imagination*

LEARNING THE SCRIPT: SOCIALIZATION

Jodi O'Brien

As we have discussed in the previous sections of this book, humans become social creatures through their ability to formulate language-based systems of meaning. We live in a symbolic universe rather than a direct state of nature. Humans organize their existence into a meaningful reality through symbols, and language is the primary form of symbol. One implication of this thesis is that *social order* exists in the human mind, in the form of meaningful conceptual associations that organize each person's experiences and perceptions. This essay explores how this internal, cognitive system is learned, manifest, and reproduced among groups of people. The central theme of this essay, and the readings that follow, is that people *learn* cultural rules and social expectations. These rules and expectations take the form of *social routines*. As we learn these routines, they become part of our internal system of meaning, and we are able to respond to situations and experiences in ways that are consistent and comprehensible to others who share our culture.

WHAT IS SOCIALIZATION?

As a thought exercise, I ask the students in my classes to consider the difference between someone who is considered "eccentric" and someone who seems socially "off." By "off" we mean those people who don't seem to behave in a manner consistent with our expectations. Students struggle to explain the actual meaning of "off," but most everyone agrees that we know when we encounter someone who is "off." After some discussion, the students usually come to the conclusion that someone who is eccentric *knows* the rules, but *chooses* not to go along with them, whereas the person who is "off" doesn't seem to know or be able to act in accordance with the rules. What is the difference, and what does it mean to "know" social rules and to be able to "choose" to follow the rules or not?

Consider this related phenomenon: Can you give me an example of a "yes" or "no" question? (The preceding sentence is actually one such example.) Your answer is most likely "yes," and you could easily do so. Now, can you give me the grammatical rules for constructing a "yes" or "no" question? Unless you are an expert in English grammar, your answer is most likely to be "no."

As we discussed in the previous sections (Parts II and III), the grammatical complexity of language makes it seem miraculous that most all children are able to learn it with such ease. We all "know" our language—we can speak it, understand it, even have this conversation about what it is—but most of us don't actually know the rules for how it is constructed. When someone speaks "word salad" to you—i.e., forms a sentence that doesn't make sense—you "know" that the sentence is wrong, but you don't necessarily know the grammatical rules for *why* it is wrong. You know correct or incorrect language when you hear it, but you don't know why it is correct or incorrect. Think about that for a minute. The same logic applies to our understanding of social behavior. People who are similarly socialized share certain cultural expectations, and they "know" when these cultural expectations have been violated (i.e., when someone is "off"), but they can't necessarily explain the underlying rules. In this regard, social rules or expectations can be thought of as a form of "social grammar." Language acquisition means that we not only know "words," but we also know the underlying structure for putting words together to form comprehensible meanings. This is grammar. Our capacity to use grammar (even if we don't know the underlying rules) enables us to form sentences and entire complexes of meaning that make sense to others, but seem spontaneous and original. Our capacity for "social grammar" has a similar effect: When we become socialized, we absorb not only random rules or beliefs, but also an entire *structure* of social meaning and routine. It's our capacity for this social grammar that enables us to be spontaneously engaged in social interaction (i.e., we are not robots) while also behaving in ways that are meaningful and consistent for others.

Socialization is the process through which we learn not only cultural beliefs and social rules, but also the underlying *structure* or grammar that enables us to behave individually, organically, and seemingly spontaneously, while at the same time doing so in ways that make sense to ourselves and to others. An important point to keep in mind as you read the following material is that this is a *dynamic* process. We are always learning new ideas, new rules, and new routines, but we incorporate these into an existing structure of socialization so that they take on the qualities of order and consistency rather than chaos and instability.

SOCIAL LEARNING AS A PROCESS OF INTERACTION

Social learning, or "socialization," takes place through interaction with others. By now, the theme of "interaction" should seem like a mantra to you. In Part III, we explored the process of developing a self-concept through interaction with others. Significant people in our environment assign meaning to our actions. They name us and label our behavior in specific ways. As we develop consciousness (become self-aware), we begin to internalize these names, and they form a cluster of self-meaning that we use referentially to make sense of our own feelings and actions. Over time, we become focused on this early established set of self categories or ideas about who we are. We pay attention to experiences and activities that confirm our self-concept. In this way, our behavior becomes routinized, or predictable, and we take on characteristics of a consistent "personality."

Simultaneously with the development of the social self, we are also learning social rules and cultural ideals. Recall the point from Part III: Child development scholars estimate that a child learns more in the first 5 years than in the entire remainder of her or his life. It's no wonder that this is the case when you consider the extent of what the child has to learn in order to participate in human social life: language, a sense of self, cultural beliefs, attitudes and ideals, behavioral expectations, and so on. As I hope you will realize in reading the following material and the remainder of this book, the human capacity for learning and engaging in social action is an amazing thing.

Internalizing Society

Peter Berger and Thomas Luckmann are well-known social theorists, and their book, *The Social Construction of Reality* (1966), has had considerable impact on sociology. In the early sections of their book, Berger and Luckmann focus on the question of how society gets into the individual (see Reading 17). As they note, our everyday lives are shared with others, and it appears that our ability to get along, to comprehend one another, to share similar ideals and expectations, and to coordinate our activities is based on our ability to take on, or *internalize,* the feelings and attitudes of others. As they illustrate, when we see a toddler crying, we do not actually feel the toddler's pain, but we "know" from her crying that she is in distress. Our ability to read the signs of crying as a symbolic indication of distress and, further, to engage in a response of attempting to "comfort" the toddler indicates that we are capable of forming an "objective reality" out of shared, mutually understood signs and symbols.

Consider an older child who observes his crying sibling and asks, "Why is the baby crying?" The father explains that the baby is tired or hungry or is experiencing some related distress. Then the father "comforts" the baby. Observing this, the older child is likely to engage in similar actions of comforting when he next encounters the baby crying (We've all seen very young children attempting to soothe an infant with utterances of "there, there" and similar cooing.). Through this process of observing, asking, and practicing, the child learns the meaning of pain and comforting and the relationship between the two. As he engages in comforting the infant, he is not just acting out a behavior, but he is also taking in the attitudes of a significant other (father) and experiencing these subjectively for himself. When his father praises him later for being a "good brother," he further internalizes these attitudes as associated with an aspect of who he is, and he forms a web of understanding between certain events (baby crying=pain), appropriate attitude (concern), and expected response (comforting). As Berger and Luckmann emphasize, this entire process is very emotionally charged, and the subsequent praise ("good brother") by a significant other (father) has a strong impact on the way in which the child organizes and files this experience and, eventually, makes it a part of himself.

Similar to the process of language acquisition, *primary socialization* is ceaseless and profoundly significant during the first years of human development. During this time, children internalize an entire encyclopedia of cultural attitudes and expectations and, through their simultaneous development of self-awareness, learn to witness and to guide their own impulses in concert with these newly learned cultural expectations or "norms." As we discussed in Part III, Mead referred to this internalized witness as the "generalized other"—the internalization of social expectations and attitudes—and it is this generalized other that we engage in internal dialogue with when we evaluate our own feelings, intentions, and actions. When we find ourselves saying, "Well, that's just the way it's done," or "People will be upset if I do that," we're responding to the generalized other—our own internalization of social attitudes and expectations. We don't actually know who the "they" is that we're referencing; we just know that "they" have certain expectations, and we judge our own behavior in accordance with our perception of this generalized other, or "they."

Consider someone who says, "I feel so badly, I haven't cried at all about my mother's death." This seemingly simple statement reflects a very complicated process in which the person has internalized the social expectations for grief—especially grief regarding a parent—but upon observing herself not crying (a symbolic indication of grief), she "feels badly." In her internal dialogue, she notes her lack of tears and feels this as a judgment from the generalized other that her behavior is an inappropriate response to grief.

Imagine now that the woman shares her "guilt" with someone who has the status of a moral authority—for instance, a pastor or therapist. The therapist tells the woman not to worry, "Many people are unable to cry when someone very close to them dies. It's a perfectly normal response." Upon hearing this, the woman is immediately relieved. Why? Because she has replaced the very general attitude of the generalized other with the more nuanced attitude of a specific moral authority. The potential impact is not only in the therapist's words, but in the social position the therapist holds as a moral authority. This presumed moral status is also an internalized social attitude. We learn to associate certain characteristics, including authority, morality, and so on, with specific social roles, such that we automatically or categorically associate authority with a police officer, morality with a priest, and so forth.

Learning Social Roles and Identities

Much of our primary socialization includes learning the behavioral expectations for specific roles and identities. Mead called this stage of development the "play stage." In the play stage, the child takes on the perceived attitudes of a social role or identity and acts it out. When children don costumes and engage in fantasy play, they are actually socializing one another in the expectations for cultural identities. In this way, they are learning what might be called the "scripts" that are associated with successful social engagement. Various events or situations have a script, and the script includes certain roles or identities as well as the attitudes and behavior associated with those identities. Accordingly, children play house and take on corresponding roles of parents; they play school and enact the roles of teacher/student; and so forth. Observe young children playing at these games, and you will note considerable negotiation about how a specific role is supposed to be played—what is the appropriate attitude, clothing, and so on. Children can be quite tyrannical in these games. This is because they are actually working very hard to learn and practice the meaning of various social roles and the attitudes, identities, situations, and expectations associated with theses roles.

Socialization is a process of learning the gestures, cues, and expectations that enable us to engage in successful social performance of roles and identities (see Part V for a more extended discussion). When we become socialized into a role, we learn how to perform in ways that are consistent with the situation or event associated with that role. For instance, whenever you begin a new job, you learn basic skills of the trade, but you also learn how to convey the attitude associated with the job. New teachers, for example, may be masters of their area of knowledge, but they have to *practice* giving the impression that they are in charge of the class and in control of the situation. Just as young children overplay or insist on certain hyper-stylized behaviors in their fantasy games, a novice teacher may overdo the attempt to be seen as "in charge" and come across as "too authoritative." Likewise, a junior employee who is invited to drinks with the boss for the first time may worry later that she appeared "overeager" in her attempts to convey an impression of interest and respect. Like all new skills, the ability to play the identity in a way that seems appropriate to our socialized understanding of the situation develops with practice. The more practiced we become, the less likely we are to judge our "performance" in accordance with attitudes of the generalized other, and the more likely we are to incorporate the evaluations and opinions of those who are significant to the situation. For instance, as I gained more teaching experience, I became less and less concerned with following some sort of internalized notion of *the* perfect teacher and more concerned with listening to the actual students in my classes for an evaluation of my teaching role.

Sources of Socialization

This raises another interesting question regarding socialization. Where do the attitudes and expectations that we internalize come from? Primary socialization takes place largely under the influence of "significant others." From these individuals we learn the basic knowledge of our society, and we internalize this knowledge as a coherent set of expectations, feelings, and attitudes. This means that our initial learning is shaped almost entirely by those sources with the most proximity to us. This usually includes our parents and other close relatives. Once the child is initially socialized, additional sources become influential. These sources can be in the form of other people or, increasingly, through roles and identities as represented in media.

Initial socialization acts as a filter for these secondary sources, however. By the time they reach school, most children already have intricately socialized matrices of meaning and attitudes in the form of a generalized other that has been strongly etched by the attitudes of their primary significant others. They also have a well-developed self-awareness. Accordingly, all subsequent sources of socialization will be *filtered* through both the existing self-concept and the child's particular version of the generalized other. In other words, the child is not a robot simply taking in sources of social influence unaware; rather, he or she engages dynamically with these sources. As the child's self-awareness expands, so too does the capacity for processing multiple sources of social input. As self-concept stretches to accommodate new experiences and influences, the internal conversation becomes more nuanced and sophisticated and reflects an increasingly diverse set of socialization sources. It's important to keep in mind, however, that we do not simply allow in these sources and file them away to later exert influence over our behavior; we are in fact constantly engaging with new ideas and potential social learning through our internal conversations.

Parenthetically, and at the risk of editorializing, one implication of this is that in assessing the impact of various external sources of social influence (school curricula, television and related media), the pertinent issue is *not* the content itself, but the *quality of the internal conversation* the young person is engaged in *regarding* the content. Children actually have a tremendous capacity for complex thinking (contrary to popular belief). When they are allowed to grapple with complex moral issues, they demonstrate a refreshing ability to think about the situation in novel and intelligent ways. But this ability is also a function of socialization—a social learning process in which complex thinking is modeled for them, just as any other behavior or attitude is.

Accordingly, the most important question is not necessarily what is the content of social influence, but rather, how are we filtering it and talking about it to ourselves? I find it useful to pose this in terms of the question, who or what are the audiences in your head? In addition to significant others, social psychologists use the concept of "reference group" to address the process of internal conversation. Reference groups are groups, real or fictional, that serve both as a source of social learning, similar to significant others, and internal assessment and evaluation. The following discussion looks at the ways in which reference groups are a source of information about attitudes and expectations, and also serve as an important internal witness and voice.

SOCIAL LEARNING THROUGH MULTIPLE SIGNIFICANT OTHERS AND REFERENCE GROUPS

In 1966, sociologist Norman Denzin conducted a study on the "significant others of a college population." Denzin tracked the shifts that students went through during their college careers. He found that most traditionally aged freshmen remained strongly connected to their families and friends "back home." They talked with parents frequently, returned home for holidays and vacations, and were likely to discuss the material they were learning in terms of the beliefs and experiences of their parents and family. However, Denzin noted a distinct shift in students who were midway through their college careers. Sophomores and juniors talked more about their friends at school and were more involved in school-related activities and less interested in what was going on back home.

Denzin was particularly interested in the observation that students in this latter group expressed much more conflict, frustration, and disenchantment with their parents than those in the freshman class. The more advanced students seemed to be experiencing a conflict between the ideals and expectations of new role models (especially faculty, who were sometimes more liberal than the parents) and those of their family. By the senior year, Denzin observed that most students were strongly identified with their college peers, the faculty, and peer groups in the local region. These students expressed beliefs and commitments very similar to those of the faculty and were somewhat disdainful of the ideas they had held just a few years earlier.

According to Denzin, as the students became more identified with their college environment, their attachment to home shifted and, eventually, waned. This process of shifting identification was not always easy; students often experienced tremendous guilt, conflict, and ambivalence. Denzin's interpretation is that these feelings reflect the shift away from significant others whose values and behaviors we have grown accustomed to sharing. Exposure to new groups, new peers, and new environments leads to shifts in alliances and commitments, which in turn lead to shifts in our sense of self. As Denzin notes, the process, while inevitable, is not without some pain, conflict, and grief.

Although Denzin refers to them as "the significant others" of a college population, the shifting perspectives and attitudes that (traditionally aged) students are exposed to throughout their college years can be usefully understood in terms of reference groups. Sociologist Tamotsu Shibutani describes reference groups as *perspectives* that we adopt in accordance with our attachment to particular groups and the ideals they represent (see Reading 18). When observing our own behavior and imagining how it might appear to others, the "others" we have in mind are not the generalized other or specific significant others, but particular groups. Close association with specific groups (or our ideals of what those groups stand for) may lead us to adopt perspectives that are consistent with the behaviors, values, and beliefs of that group. Consequently, when we are making sense of a particular situation, or formulating assessments and making decisions, we use the perspective represented by this group as our reference point. When people use phrases such as "speaking as a [Christian, Democrat, sociologist, etc.]," they are imagining themselves as members or representatives of a particular group and adopting the attitudes that they perceive to be consistent with this group.

Reference groups can be specific groups that we associate with regularly; they can be dispersed groups whose values we have adopted; or they can be imaginary groups whose ideals we have derived from television, film, literature, and other cultural sources. Evaluating self-actions from the perspective of the "honorable hero" would be an example of using an imagined reference group. Our associations with reference groups have a powerful influence on our self-assessments and the decisions we make. A strong identification with particular reference groups is a central factor in the organization of our goals, values, and behaviors. For instance, first-time, newly married people have little or no experience actually being "husbands" or "wives," but the importance of their new social position leads them to identify strongly with these roles and, consequently, to make decisions in terms of what they think the *ideal* wife or husband might do. Major shifts in someone's behavior can usually be traced to the person's use of a particular reference group as a perspective for self-understanding and direction.

In Reading 19, sociologist Pamela Perry explores the development of distinctive perspectives regarding racial awareness and ethnic self-identification among students in two different high schools. Perry's ethnographic study revealed that white students in a predominantly white high school had little or no sense of ethnic self-identification. In contrast, white students in a multiracial high school had a strong ethnic awareness and well-articulated perspectives on race. Perry attributes these different perspectives to differences in reference groups between the two schools. In the multiracial school, race is more prevalent as a frame of reference and, accordingly, students have a more strongly developed understanding of different ethnicities; race serves as a more significant reference group perspective than in the white school, where ethnicity is seen as undifferentiated and therefore insignificant as a self-referential category.

Reference group perspectives also help to explain why people who engage in very similar behaviors may adopt different self-images and, consequently, lead very different lives. For instance, sexologists are interested in the gap between sexual behavior and sexual identification. Studies show repeatedly that a majority of people engage in sexual activity with someone of the same sex at some point in their lives. For example, many high school and college students report that they have experimented with same-sex behavior. Yet not all of these individuals go on to identify as gay or lesbian. Thus, the social psychologist might ask how it is that bisexual *behavior* results in different sexual *identities*. One immediate answer might be that those who don't like the behavior don't continue it. However, this is countered by evidence that indicates that many people who have had same-sex experiences continue to seek them (or would if they had the opportunity); they just don't *identify* as gay or lesbian (or even as bisexual).

In a book called *Lesbian and Bisexual Identities,* sociologist Kristen Esterberg (1997) explores how women who have sex with other women *learn* to identify as either straight or lesbian. Esterberg uses case studies to map the path that women who are behaviorally bisexual take toward a particular sexual identity. The primary influences along this route are significant others and reference groups. Esterberg's case studies suggest that bisexual women who are strongly identified with a boyfriend and with extended family and friends who are actively supportive of this relationship tend to settle into an identity as "straight." Similarly, women who become involved with other women who identify not only as lesbian, but with a gay and lesbian "community," tend to settle into lesbian identities. Repeated interaction with different groups, and the perspectives they represent, lead the women, eventually, to become more strongly identified with one or the other.

This explanation suggests that sexual identities are fluid and shift over time depending on significant attachments and reference groups. Research in this area demonstrates that many people shift back and forth between sexual identities over the course of a lifetime. Reference group theories provide one framework for explaining these shifts, and they also provide a basis for understanding the potential conflict and stress related to certain behaviors: To the extent that we view certain behaviors from the perspective of conflicting reference groups (for example, "I'm a good Christian. How can I be gay?"), we are likely to be caught up in considerable personal turmoil. This kind of self-contradiction is explored more fully in Part VII.

NAMING EXPERIENCE AS A PROCESS OF SOCIAL LEARNING

In the early 1950s, during what has come to be known as the "beatnik era," Howard Becker, a young graduate student, spent his evenings playing jazz piano in Chicago-area nightclubs. Becker noticed that many patrons tried the drug marijuana, but only a few continued to use it. As a budding sociologist, Becker wondered why some people merely "experimented," and others became routine users. He was familiar with the "personality" and "physical" theories of his day, which suggested that those who continued to smoke marijuana were likely to have the sort of personality or physical makeup that inclined them to use drugs. But Becker wasn't satisfied with these theories. They didn't mesh with his observations.

Becker noted that those who continued to use marijuana described it as a "pleasurable" experience; they could rattle off lists of positive effects that they associated with marijuana, and when they introduced the drug to their friends, they tended to pass on this information. He concluded that those who continued smoking marijuana had "learned" to define the experience and the effects as enjoyable. He wrote a paper titled "Becoming a Marihuana User," in which he suggested that people learn to "name" experiences and physical responses (see Reading 20). This naming process shapes a person's reactions to the event—in this case, the smoking of a drug and the corresponding physical reaction. He emphasized that people learn these "names," or responses, through interaction with others. Regardless of how people might feel privately, they get cues from others about how they are expected to feel and behave publicly. They adjust their perceptions and behavior in response to these expectations. This profoundly "social" explanation for individual behavior—even in response to something as physically based as drug ingestion—helped alter the course of sociology and gained young Becker a reputation as a formidable social scientist.

Naming Physical Experience as a Social Act

In thinking about Becker's question—What does it take to become a marijuana user?—consider the possible range of responses from someone who ingests marijuana but doesn't know what it is. As a child, I once accidentally inhaled Clorox bleach. The physical sensation was similar to the one marijuana might produce when it is first inhaled: choking, followed by a burning sensation. When I inhaled the bleach, I thought I was going to die. I was so convinced of my imminent demise that I wrote a note for my parents to find when they came across my body and didn't know how to explain my death. Clearly I did not seek to repeat the experience.

Becker asks a pertinent question when considering the relationship between physical stimuli and human response: Why would someone voluntarily seek out and continue to do something that, if evaluated simply as an undefined physical experience, is not likely to be considered immediately pleasant? Technically, when you first smoke marijuana, you are just as likely to feel as if you had inhaled bleach as you are to feel like you have inhaled something that might be a source of pleasure.

Becker illustrates the process of interaction and learning that helps us to identify an experience with a particular meaning. One of the key points of his article is that getting high is something that must be *learned in interaction* with other, more experienced users. Becker points out, for example, that it is very common for novices not to feel high the first time they smoke marijuana and for an experienced user to smoke a placebo that smells like marijuana and report feeling high. In other words, smoking marijuana is not a simple physiological response to a psychoactive drug but a socially constructed experience that must be identified or named before people are able to recognize the intended effect. The fact that

Becker's article is more than 50 years old is also important for the contemporary reader. It allows us to study a culture in its infancy, before the general public knew much about marijuana and its effects.

Becker's article demonstrates that people do not respond directly to stimuli within a state of nature; rather, through interactions with others, we learn to assign meaning to a particular experience. Even in the case of physiological experiences, we have to learn to identify the effects and determine what is going on in a meaningful way before we know how to respond. Consider another example: How do you know when you are sick? In the course of your daily activities, you may notice aspects of your body or behavior that feel "off." As you become aware of these uncomfortable feelings, you attempt to make sense of them. In doing so, you likely rely not only on your observations of the specific symptoms—scratchy throat, upset stomach, aches and pains—but also on input from others.

One sociologist, Bernice Pescosolido (1992), researched the process of deliberation people use to determine whether they should go to the doctor when something feels "off." Her research suggests that people rely on networks of friends and acquaintances to help them name the experience. People confer with an average of at least seven others before they decide to visit the doctor's office. Other people help us interpret the experience by drawing our attention to specific symptoms ("Do you have a fever? If you don't have a fever, you don't have the flu."), or reminding us of associations we may not have considered ("You've been partying every night for the past 2 weeks, so of course you feel run down."). Pescosolido's study reminds us that we must recognize and name even basic physiological experiences before we can act on them, and this process is usually interactional.

There is some very interesting research done by endocrinologists that shows that men experience regular hormonal fluctuations. Similar to the experiences of menstruating women, these fluctuations may be associated with mood change and related physiological effects such as a decrease or increase in appetite, sexual desire, and so forth. Although the fluctuations may have a pattern and be a source of mood shifts among men, it is unlikely that most men *recognize* the effects of these shifts. Culturally, men simply don't have a "script" for talking about, let alone recognizing, hormonal fluctuations in their bodies. In fact, the prevailing cultural belief is that most men have stable hormones and only women experience hormonal cycles. One conclusion that can be drawn from this research is that a significant physical process may be occurring in men's bodies, but without a name for it, it's not likely to be recognized or understood. Conversely, most women have considerable experience talking with others about bodily symptoms that they learn to associate with a menstrual cycle. Whether or not these symptoms are actually caused by the hormonal shifts that are presumed to be their source, most women talk with one another *as if* this were the case.

These examples illustrate that the ways we make sense of our experiences, even things as basic as bodily functions, are based on interactions with others. In these interactions, we learn how to define our experiences, we learn whether something is supposed to be pleasurable or painful, and we learn the attitudes and postures that are associated with the experience.

Naming Emotional Experience as a Social Act

Even if you don't know what your body is doing, you know your heart, right? One of the most commonly expected and widespread cultural ideals in U.S. society is that of romantic love. Finding "true love" is one of the top-rated goals most people list when asked to rank their life priorities. But where does "love" come from? How do you know when you are experiencing it? What are some of the symptoms of "love"? Ask some of your friends to generate a list of symptoms associated with "falling in love." It's likely this list will include terms such as "distracted," "nervous," "anxious," "giddy," and similar words that convey a sense of being "out of control." Does this sound like fun to you? In the absence of a culturally learned context, an anthropologist from Mars might conclude that the human experience of attraction is similar to the experience of taking a dreaded exam.

Some excellent sociological research has been conducted that studies the ways in which young people learn about love and romance through their interactions with others. Similar to the process of learning to become a marijuana user, or related examples, we *learn* how to be "in love." In "The Development of Feeling Norms Underlying Romantic Love Among Adolescent Females," Robin Simon and colleagues describe the process whereby middle-school girls teach one another the socially expected feelings and attitudes regarding romantic love (see Reading 21). Based on ethnographic research, Simon provides detailed conversational accounts of young people explaining the rules of romance to one another. These rules include well-known adages such as "you should only be in love with one person at a time," and "you shouldn't take someone else's boyfriend." Also included is the admonition that "you must *always* be in love."

The experiences shared by the girls who were interviewed for Simon's research indicate that they use these "rules" as a source of self-evaluation. If they like someone else's boyfriend, they feel guilty. If someone tries to date more than one person, others feel justified in their indignation toward her. Girls who are *not* attracted to anyone worry that there is something wrong with them.

This article illustrates the significance of social learning, especially in the vulnerable formative years. Young people learn powerful lessons from one another about who they think they should be and how they are supposed to feel. The combination of the age vulnerability and the intensity of this socialization results in a deeply entrenched set of cultural attitudes and ideals that can be very difficult to alter. As these young women mature and encounter new ideas and experiences about love and romance, they may still find themselves evaluating their experiences through the socialization they acquired in their early teens.

Conclusions

The foregoing examples demonstrate the significance of social learning as a process through which we not only learn culture attitudes, beliefs, and expectations, but we also internalize them and incorporate them into a core understanding of who we are. In short, through the process of socialization, social norms become integrated into the individual as a perspective, or set of perspectives. These perspectives form the basis of self and social evaluation—we make sense of and judge our own feelings and behavior, as well as that of others, in accordance with these socially learned perspectives.

Socialization is essential to the coordination of social life. It is the basis of social order. One of the most fascinating aspects of social order is that, for the most part, we manage to pull off amazing feats of social coordination without really thinking about it. This production of social order through interaction routines is the subject of Part V. For now, the point to emphasize is that when we internalize social attitudes and expectations—when we gain the perspective of the generalized other—we are learning the social grammar that enables us to engage with others in routine and meaningful interactions.

Many people resist the idea of the "socialized" individual on the premise that socialization turns us into social robots or cultural conformists. This tension is revealed in the common notion of the "individual versus society." However, consider for a moment what you've learned up to this point. We gain consciousness in the form of self-awareness through the acquisition of language. Language not only gives us the means to think and communicate with others, but it also gives us the ability to *recognize* that we are thinking. As soon as we begin thinking and become aware of ourselves, we begin to take the social world into us in the form of organized attitudes, expectations, and perspectives of others. If we did not have this self-awareness, we wouldn't be conscious actors; we would simply be passive respondents. Furthermore, the inner witness that guides our behavior in accordance with the expectations of the generalized other is the basis for our social freedom. The key point here is the *ability* to observe and direct our own behavior. If we were not socialized, we would not have this awareness and we would therefore have no ability for self-engagement or self-control. Consider again the illustration from the beginning of this essay on the difference between the eccentric and the person who is "off." The former is in control of her behavior and therefore "free," whereas the latter can't even participate fully—he has no choice in the matter.

Through socialization, or the acquisition of social grammar, we become capable social "players." We learn the social roles and scripts that enable us to coordinate our activities with others and to communicate meaningfully and successfully. Think for a moment about driving a car. If you wanted to spend all your time driving in any direction and at any speed you desired in a large empty field, you could certainly do so, but chances are you want to drive in places where other people are also driving. Accordingly, you agree to follow the rules of the road. These rules are so mindless or automatic that you rarely think of them. With a few exceptions (e.g., the speed limit on certain occasions), you probably don't feel "oppressed" by the rules of the road. Rather, you recognize that by learning and participating in these shared rules, many people can coordinate a tremendously complex activity and share the road.

An understanding of the influential forces of socialization is key to self-understanding. When correctly understood, the processes of socialization reveal that we have the potential to be *both* overly conforming *and* liberated. The distinction is in our ability for *awareness* of the socialization process. An understanding of the social psychology of self development gives us the ability to scrutinize the sources of influence that form the basis of our core beliefs, expectations, and ideals. In other words, we can use this information to become more mindful of the social routines that we engage in. Recognizing that you are shaped by cultural forces does not take away from your individuality. In fact, students of social psychology often find that they have a better sense of themselves once they learn to identify the cultural influences that are shaping how they think and feel.

Social order exists, in part, because we are committed to our routines and we find meaning in the attitudes and beliefs we have learned through significant others and reference groups. This is simply a fact of socialization. The question we can usefully ask ourselves, if we want to be less "conforming," is to what extent we are *aware* of meaning and values underlying expected social scripts and norms. Are we engaging in them thoughtfully because they are effective (e.g., traffic rules) or meaningful (e.g., celebrating a special event), or are we participating out of habit or internalized guilt and other social pressures that take the form of a coercive inner conversation? Social order based on socialization is not the problem; it's actually an amazing human ability. The issue is not whether we are socialized (we are), but the extent to which we are awake to the socialization process.

REFERENCES

Berger, P., & Luckmann, T. (1966). *The social construction of reality.* New York: Doubleday.

Denzin, N. (1966). The significant others of a college population. *Sociological Quarterly, 7*(3), 298.

Esterberg, K. (1997). *Lesbian and bisexual identities: Constructing communities, constructing selves.* Philadelphia: Temple University Press.

Mills, C. W. (1959/2000). *The sociological imagination* (40th anniv. ed.). New York: Oxford University Press.

Pescosolido, B. (1992). Beyond rational choice: The social dynamics of how people seek help. *American Journal of Sociology, 97,* 1096–1138.

SOCIALIZATION AND REFERENCE GROUPS

The readings in this section provide examples of socialization. Socialization is the process of internalizing the general ideas and expectations of our culture. As children become socialized, they are able to take the "perspective" of society or to imagine what it is that others think, feel, and expect. In this way, they are able to observe and direct their own behavior in harmony with others. Socialization is not a robotic operation whereby "society" is simply poured into the individual; rather, it is a dynamic process through which the developing individual learns to adopt the attitudes and behavior of significant others. This initial mimicking soon becomes a more complex set of willful behaviors and attitudes directed by a maturing internal conversation. This internal conversation reflects the perspectives and ideals of "reference groups." Reference groups are the groups (real or fictional) that we refer to in our internal conversations when we are trying to make sense of things, to decide what actions to take and how to evaluate our feelings and behavior. For example, if you think of yourself as a "leader," you probably have an idea of a general group of leaders whom you admire. When making decisions and judging your own actions, you reference this group in your mind. Or, if you are a devoted Christian, you may find yourself asking, "What would Jesus do?" and using this reference as a perspective for making decisions. Reference groups can be close and tangible, they can be abstract and distant, or they can even be fictitious. Regardless of the form they take, reference groups are a basic source of socialization and exert a strong influence on how we see the world and the choices that we make.

"The Internalization of Society" is a selection from a well-known book, *The Social Construction of Reality*, written by sociologists Peter Berger and Thomas Luckmann. In this short excerpt, Berger and Luckmann discuss the process by which society "gets into" the individual through interaction with significant others. The result is the individual's ability to take the perspective of others. They emphasize that this process includes a necessary emotional component: Our attachment to significant others motivates us to take their perspective and makes socialization a willing rather than a forced process.

"Reference Groups as Perspectives" is written by sociologist Tamotsu Shibutani. Shibutani expands on the theories of Mead and Cooley by introducing the idea that we are particularly concerned about the "reflected appraisals" of groups that are significant to us. According to Shibutani, we use our images of these groups as a reference point, or measuring rod, for defining and evaluating our own actions, beliefs, and values. When we internalize the beliefs and attitudes of specific groups, we have adopted the group's perspective and made it the basis of our own.

School environments provide significant sites for establishing peer reference groups. "Shades of White" is a selection from a book based on a study of two racially distinct high schools. Sociologist Pamela Perry was interested in the racial viewpoints that high school students develop based on the influence of their peers. In this article, Perry demonstrates that white students in predominantly white schools have very different racial perspectives from white students in a racially diverse school.

(Continued)

(Continued)

READING QUESTIONS

1. Make a list of your most cherished beliefs and values and also some of the expectations and goals you have for yourself. Identify the groups reflected in this list of ideals. Now trace the origins of your identification with these groups.

2. Consider an experience where you had to learn a new routine, a new job, new school, or new culture. Who helped you and how? Do you recall a difference between feeling like an "outsider" and gradually becoming more at ease as an "insider"? Explain that difference in terms of socialization.

3. Consider the magazines that you read and the television shows that you watch frequently. For a few days, pay close attention to the types of images you see. What information do you get about who is attractive and popular? About who is successful? About who is a social problem? How are your personal age, gender, race, class, and sexuality most commonly portrayed?

4. Study the photos in your local newspaper for one week. Specifically, count the number of photos of men and of women. Do you notice anything about where pictures of women are likely to be posted in comparison with pictures of men? Count the number of pictures of members of minority groups that appear, and make a note of the context in which they are portrayed. Do you think these images send particular messages about what kind of person is most likely to be a political leader? Fashion expert? Criminal?

17

Socialization: The Internalization of Society

Peter L. Berger and Thomas Luckmann

(1996)

Since society exists as both objective and subjective reality, any adequate theoretical understanding of it must [include] both these aspects.... [T]hese aspects receive their proper recognition if society is understood in terms of an ongoing dialectal process composed of the three moments of externalization, objectivation, and internalization. As far as the societal phenomenon is concerned, these moments ought *not* to be thought of as occurring in a temporal sequence. Rather society and each part of it are simultaneously characterized by these three moments, so that any analysis in terms of only one or two of them falls short. The same is true of the individual member of society, who simultaneously externalizes his own being into the social world and internalizes it as an objective reality. In other words, to be in society is to participate in its dialectic.

The individual, however, is not born a member of society. He is born with a predisposition toward sociality, and he becomes a member of society. In the life of every individual therefore, there *is* a temporal sequence, in the course of which he is inducted into participation in the societal dialectic. The beginning point of this process is internalization. . . .

Only when he has achieved this degree of internalization is an individual a member of society. The ontogenetic process by which this is brought about is socialization, which may thus be defined as the comprehensive and consistent induction of an individual into the objective world of a society or a sector of it. Primary socialization is the first socialization an individual undergoes in childhood through which he becomes a member of society. Secondary socialization is any subsequent process that inducts an already socialized individual into new sectors of the objective world of his society. . . .

It is at once evident that primary socialization is usually the most important one for an individual, and that the basic structure of all secondary socialization has to resemble that of primary socialization. Every individual is born into an objective social structure within which he encounters the significant others who are in charge of his socialization.[1] These significant others are imposed on him. Their definitions of his situation are posited for him as objective reality. He is thus born into not only an objective social structure but also an objective social world. The significant others who mediate this world to him modify it in the course of mediating it. They select aspects of it in accordance with their own location in the social structure, and also by virtue of their individual, biographically rooted idiosyncrasies. The social world is "filtered" to the individual through this double selectivity. Thus the lower-class child not only absorbs a lower-class perspective on the social world, he absorbs it in the idiosyncratic coloration given it by his parents (or whatever other individuals are in charge of his primary socialization). The same lower-class perspective may induce a mood of contentment, resignation, bitter resentment, or seething rebelliousness. Consequently, the lower-class child will not only come to inhabit a world greatly different from that of an upper-class child, but may do so in a manner quite different from the lower-class child next door.[2]

It should hardly be necessary to add that primary socialization involves more than purely cognitive learning. It takes place under circumstances that are highly charged emotionally. Indeed, there is good reason to believe that without such emotional attachment to significant others, the learning process would be difficult if not impossible.[3] The child identifies with the significant others in a variety of emotional ways. Whatever they may be, internalization occurs only as identification occurs. The child takes on the significant others' roles and attitudes, that is, internalizes them and makes them his own. And by this identification with significant others, the child becomes capable of identifying himself, of acquiring a subjectively coherent and plausible identity. In other words, the self is a reflected entity, reflecting the attitudes first taken by significant others toward it;[4] the individual becomes what he is addressed as by his significant others. This is not a one-sided, mechanistic process. It entails a dialectic between identification by others and self-identification, between objectively assigned and subjectively appropriated identity. . . .

What is most important for our considerations here is the fact that the individual not only takes on the roles and attitudes of others, but in the same process takes on their world. Indeed, identity is objectively defined as location in a certain world and can be subjectively appropriated only along with that world. Put differently, all identifications take place within horizons that imply a specific social world. The child learns that he is what he is called. Every name implies a nomenclature, which in turn implies a designated social location.[5] To be given an identity involves being assigned a specific place in the world. Because this identity is subjectively appropriated by the child ("I *am* John Smith"), so is the world to which this identity points. Subjective appropriation of identity and subjective appropriation of the social world are merely different aspects

of the same process of internalization, mediated by the same significant others.

Primary socialization creates in the child's consciousness a progressive abstraction from the roles and attitudes of specific others to roles and attitudes in general. For example, in the internalization of norms, there is a progression from "Mummy is angry with me now" to "Mummy is angry with me whenever I spill the soup." As additional significant others (father, grandmother, older sister, and so on) support the mother's negative attitude toward soup-spilling, the generality of the norm is subjectively extended. The decisive step comes when the child recognizes that everybody is against soup-spilling, and the norm is generalized to "one does not spill soup"— "one" being himself as part of a generality that includes, in principle, all of society insofar as it is significant to the child. This abstraction from the roles and attitudes of concrete significant others is called the generalized other.[6] Its formation within consciousness means that the individual now identifies not only with concrete others but with a generality of others, that is, with a society. Only by virtue of this generalized identification does his own self-identification attain stability and continuity. He now has not only an identity vis-à-vis this or that significant other, but an identity in general, which is subjectively apprehended as remaining the same no matter what others, significant or not, are encountered. This newly coherent identity incorporates within itself all the various internalized roles and attitudes—including, among many other things, the self-identification as a non-spiller of soups.

The formation within consciousness of the generalized other marks a decisive phase in socialization. It implies the internalization of society as such and of the objective reality established therein, and, at the same time, the subjective establishment of a coherent and continuous identity. Society, identity, and reality are subjectively crystallized in the same process of internalization. This crystallization is concurrent with the internalization of language. Indeed, for reasons evident from the foregoing observations on language,

language constitutes both the most important content and the most important instrument of socialization.

When the generalized other has been crystallized in consciousness, a symmetrical relationship is established between objective and subjective reality. What is real "outside" corresponds to what is real "within." Objective reality can readily be "translated" into subjective reality, and vice versa. Language, of course, is the principal vehicle of this ongoing translating process in both directions. It should, however, be stressed that the symmetry between objective and subjective reality cannot be complete. The two realities correspond to each other, but they are not coextensive. There is always more objective reality "available" than is actually internalized in any individual consciousness, simply because the contents of socialization are determined by the social distribution of knowledge. No individual internalizes the totality of what is objectivated as reality in his society, not even if the society and its world are relatively simple ones. On the other hand, there are always elements of subjective reality that have not originated in socialization, such as the awareness of one's own body prior to and apart from any socially learned apprehension of it. Subjective biography is not fully social. The individual apprehends himself as being both inside and outside society.[7] This implies that the symmetry between objective and subjective reality is never a static, once-for-all state of affairs. It must always be produced and reproduced in actuality. In other words, the relationship between the individual and the objective social world is like an ongoing balancing act. . . .

In primary socialization, there is no *problem* of identification. There is no choice of significant others. Society presents the candidate for socialization with a predefined set of significant others, whom he must accept as such with no possibility of opting for another arrangement. *Hic Rhodus, hic salta.* One must make do with the parents that fate has regaled one with. This unfair disadvantage inherent in the situation of being a child has the obvious consequence that, although the child is not simply passive

in the process of his socialization, it is the adults who set the rules of the game. The child can play the game with enthusiasm or with sullen resistance. But, alas, there is no other game around. This has an important corollary. Because the child has no choice in the selection of his significant others, his identification with them is quasi-automatic. For the same reason, his internalization of their particular reality is quasi-inevitable. The child does not internalize the world of his significant others as one of many possible worlds. He internalizes it as *the* world, the only existent and only conceivable world, the world *tout court.* It is for this reason that the world internalized in primary socialization is so much more firmly entrenched in consciousness than worlds internalized in secondary socializations. However much the original sense of inevitability may be weakened in subsequent disenchantments, the recollection of a never-to-be-repeated certainty—the certainty of the first dawn of reality—still adheres to the first world of childhood. Primary socialization thus accomplishes what (in hindsight, of course) may be seen as the most important confidence trick that society plays on the individual—to make appear as necessity what is in fact a bundle of contingencies, and thus to make meaningful the accident of his birth.

The specific contents that are internalized in primary socialization vary, of course, from society to society. Some are found everywhere. It is language that must be internalized above all. With language, and by means of it, various motivational and interpretative schemes are internalized as institutionally defined—wanting to act like a brave little boy, for instance, and assuming that little boys are naturally divided into the brave and the cowardly. These schemes provide the child with institutionalized programs for everyday life, some immediately applicable to him, others anticipating conduct socially defined for later biographical stages—the bravery that will allow him to get through a day beset with tests of will from one's peers and from all sorts of others, and also the bravery that will be required of one later—when one is initiated as a warrior, say, or when one might be called by the god. These programs, both the immediately applicable and the anticipatory, differentiate one's identity from that of others—such as girls, slave boys, or boys from another clan. Finally, there is internalization of at least the rudiments of the legitimating apparatus; the child learns "why" the programs are what they are. One must be brave because one wants to become a real man; one must perform the rituals because otherwise the gods will be angry; one must be loyal to the chief because only if one does will the gods support one in times of danger; and so on.

In primary socialization, then, the individual's first world is constructed. Its peculiar quality of firmness is to be accounted for, at least in part, by the inevitability of the individual's relationship to his very first significant others. . . .

Primary socialization ends when the concept of the generalized other (and all that goes with it) has been established in the consciousness of the individual. At this point, he is an effective member of society and in subjective possession of a self and a world. But this internalization of society, identity, and reality is not a matter of once and for all. Socialization is never total and never finished.

NOTES

1. Our description here, of course, leans heavily on the Meadian theory of socialization.

2. The concept of "mediation" is derived from Sartre, who lacks, however, an adequate theory of socialization.

3. The affective dimension of early learning has been especially emphasized by Freudian child psychology, although there are various findings or behavioristic learning theories that would tend to confirm this. We do not imply acceptance of the theoretical presuppositions of either psychological school in our argument here.

4. Our conception of the reflected character of the self is derived from both Cooley and Mead. Its roots may be found in the analysis of the social self by William James (*The Principles of Psychology*, 1890).

5. On nomenclature, Claude Levi-Strauss, *La Pensée Sauvage* [1962], pp. 253 ff.

6. The concept of the "generalized other" is used here in a fully Meadian sense.

7. Compare Georg Simmel on the self-apprehension of man as both inside and outside society. Plessner's concept of "eccentricity" is again relevant here (*Die Stufen des Organischen und der Mensch*, 1928 and 1965).

SOCIALIZATION AND REFERENCE GROUPS

18

Reference Groups as Perspectives

Tamotsu Shibutani

(1961)

Each person acts on the basis of his definition of the situation. He categorizes the transaction in which he is involved, locates himself within it, and thereby decides upon his obligations. The consistency with which he defines a succession of situations arises from the fact that he generally uses the same perspective, one that he shares with his associates. Once he has adopted a particular point of view it becomes his working conception of the world, and he brings this frame of reference to bear upon each situation he encounters, whether or not anyone else from the group is actually on the scene. Since people with diverse orientations are selectively responsive to different aspects of their natural environment, identical events may be seen in divergent ways. A prostitute and a social worker walking down the same street in a slum area often have remarkably contrasting experiences. The leering men they pass, the drunk sleeping on a doorstep, the drug addict purchasing a "fix"—all are seen differently. But their respective outlooks differ no more than those of a traffic officer and of a motorist stopped for excessive speeding. The offender is irked by the delay; much like a naughty child who has been caught misbehaving, he sulks. If the officer speaks curtly, the motorist is resentful of what he regards to be an unnecessary display of authority. It does not occur to him that only a half hour ago the same officer may have helped load the body of a dead child upon an ambulance, the victim of an accident involving two speeding automobiles. The diversity of interpretations often arises from the fact that key objects, though designated by the same symbols, assume different meanings for different people. It is not surprising, therefore, that immigrants and tourists almost invariably misinterpret much of what they see.

There have been a number of experimental studies demonstrating the manner in which the definition of identical situations varies with perspectives. Among them is one concerning the spectators of a crucial football game between Princeton and Dartmouth on November 23, 1951. It was a fiercely contested match in which a large number of penalties were called. In the second quarter a Princeton star who had been prominently mentioned for All-America honors had to leave the game with a broken nose and a concussion, and in the following period a Dartmouth player was carried off the field with a broken leg. Immediately after the contest there were charges in the press of "dirty" football. A week later undergraduate students in both universities were given a questionnaire concerning the game. All Princeton students described the game as "rough and dirty"; of the Dartmouth students a tenth thought it was "clean and fair," a third judged it as "rough and fair," and the remainder acknowledged that it was "rough and dirty." Of the Princeton spectators nine-tenths insisted that the Dartmouth players had started the foul tactics; but of the Dartmouth observers only a third held their own team guilty, and the rest blamed both sides. When the students were shown a motion picture of the game and asked to note and to evaluate infractions of the rules, the Princeton students detected twice as many violations and rated them as being more flagrant.[1] All of these students were either in the same stadium or were exposed to the same motion picture, but what they saw differed to a remarkable extent.

Divergent meanings can sometimes be reconciled by comparing assumptions, but misunderstandings become less amenable to clarification when differences exist over such fundamental categories as *time*. At first glance nothing appears as simple as the concept of time; it just passes on inexorably in increments like hours or days. But the passage of time is of different significance in different cultures. Precision in keeping time, for example, is relatively unimportant for a peasant, for he begins work soon after dawn and continues until sundown. He harvests his crops when they are ready and rests when weather conditions are such that he cannot work. In a peasant community that is becoming industrialized, however, keeping time takes on a new meaning, for men work by the clock. In some areas the owning of a wrist watch has become a status symbol among those desiring to be in line with the latest trends. At the other extreme are those who work for the railroads, among whom almost everything is measured in terms of accuracy in timing.[2] Such contrasts in the unstated premises about the passage of time sometimes lead people to conclude that others are indolent or unnecessarily aggressive.

Differences in the meaning of categories such as success can lead to serious misunderstandings, for the manner in which men organize their careers depends upon such conceptions. In the United States a high value is generally placed upon success. It is taken for granted that each individual will strive to improve his station in life, and those who do not succeed are often regarded as indigent. But there are many different conceptions of the kinds of goals that are regarded as worth pursuing. In some social worlds men in competitive situations are expected to exert themselves to the utmost to win; victory is all important, and considerations of decency and fair play are viewed as luxuries for "idealists." In intercollegiate athletics, for example, it has been reported that some athletes have been injected with amphetamine and similar stimulants by their coaches to make possible performances far beyond their normal capacity. Those who are familiar with the unreasonable pressures placed upon coaches and athletes view this practice with regret but with understanding. But many others are horrified, wondering what there could be about winning a contest that would justify risking the health of young men. Similarly, in some universities men doing research sacrifice themselves and their families, devoting themselves to their work 365 days a year; some of their colleagues wonder, however, whether anything such men may accomplish could really be worth the unbalanced lives they lead.[3] In some business circles the deception and exploitation of competitors and customers is regarded as perfectly natural; others wonder whether success built upon the misfortunes of other people can really be satisfying, and they condemn those who struggle so feverishly as being "power mad." Assumptions such as these provide the basis for deciding what goals are really worth seeking in life and the manner in which one is to go about pursuing his aspirations.

Many serious misunderstandings arise from differences in certain crucial values, especially in criteria of modesty, cleanliness, and sexual conduct. There are vast differences in standards of modesty. In some social worlds the exposure of the nude body, belching, and flatulence are simply accepted as a natural part of human life; in others such behavior is regarded as unforgivable and is concealed at all cost. The emphasis upon personal cleanliness ranges from high standards of sanitation to the retention of an outward appearance of neatness to a vague awareness of the problem. One person may be amused at those who are constantly washing themselves, while the latter wonder how their associate can possibly stand his own stench. There are norms in all groups concerning what constitutes proper sex conduct; this is true even in groups that are thought by outsiders to be without standards.[4] But there is remarkable variability in these norms, ranging from the open acceptance of sexual excitement as a part of human nature to the puritanical denial of sexuality. Practices that are condemned as sinful perversions in one circle are accepted as the normal part of life in another. Since each group takes it for granted that its own ways are right and natural, people are easily convinced that outsiders are either lewd or unduly inhibited. . . . Because understandings about sex are so deeply ingrained, people generally feel that there is something filthy or unnatural about the practices condemned in their group.

People with diverse cultural backgrounds often have different conceptions of human nature. In each universe of discourse explanations of the things men do are circumscribed by the available vocabulary of motives. There are a limited set of recognized intentions, approved and disapproved, which are thought to depict the natural inclinations of man. There are a limited number of words that are used to label these dispositions, and a motive that cannot be designated obviously cannot be imputed or avowed. Furthermore, in each social world there are shared assumptions as to the kinds of intentions that develop in each standardized context. In our society it does little good for a murderer to insist that his hand had been guided by the spirit of an ancestor for whom he had been named; he is more likely to receive a sympathetic hearing by claiming that he was the victim of a mysterious "inner urge" that he could not understand.

As one compares the perspectives that are shared in diverse social worlds, it becomes apparent that what differs are the premises underlying action. Identical situations are perceived differently because those starting out with unlike assumptions project contrasting hypotheses and are selectively responsive to different sensory cues. What makes the clarification of these divergences so difficult is that the differences are about matters that are taken for granted, matters on which alternatives are not considered. Beliefs concerning the importance of punctuality, cleanliness, or success, convictions about the proper contact between the sexes, as well as assumptions about the nature of love—all these meanings are intertwined with thousands of others into an organized scheme. A successful challenge to any basic assumption can lead to searching questions about all the others. To challenge such fundamental beliefs is to challenge a man's orientation toward life. If he takes it seriously, he may be left dazed and bewildered, not knowing what is true and what is false. . . .

The contention that men think, feel, and see things from the standpoint peculiar to the group in which they participate is an old one which has been repeatedly emphasized by anthropologists and students of the sociology of knowledge. But what makes this hypothesis so important for the study of modern mass societies is the fact that people may assume the perspectives of groups in which they are *not* recognized members, sometimes of groups in which they have never participated directly, and sometimes of groups that do not exist at all. For example, those seeking to raise their status are more responsive to the opinions of people in the social set to which they aspire than to the views shared in

the circle to which they belong. Members of ethnic minorities who are becoming assimilated examine themselves from the standpoint of the dominant group; they often develop strong feelings of inferiority and condemn others in the minority for failing to live up to these outside norms. Servants and slaves sometimes accept the standards of their masters, and adolescent boys in slum areas sometimes adopt the code of the underworld, as they learn of it from motion pictures. There are many people, then, who try to live up to the standards of social worlds of which they learn from vicarious participation—through observation or through the various media of mass communication.

Furthermore, in societies characterized by cultural pluralism each person may acquire several perspectives, for he can participate simultaneously in a number of social worlds. Because cultures are products of communication, a person develops a somewhat different perspective from each communication channel to which he is regularly exposed. Because of the ease with which one can gain access to a variety of channels, he leads a somewhat segmented life, engaging in turn in a succession of quite unrelated activities. Furthermore, the particular aggregate of social worlds of which one partakes differs from individual to individual; this is what led Simmel to declare that each person stands at that point at which the unique combination of social circles of which he is a part intersects.[5] This geometric analogy is a happy one, for it enables us to conceive of the almost endless permutations as well as the varying degrees of involvement in each circle. To understand any particular person, then, one must get a picture of his unique outlook. Since this is the product of his past experiences, real and vicarious, no two people are likely to have an identical outlook.

Since a given situation may be defined from so many different points of view, to understand what a man does, an observer must get at the assumptions with which he begins. One of the most important things to know about a person is what he takes for granted. To take his role and to anticipate what he is likely to do, it is necessary to identify the perspective he is using, the social world in which he is participating in a given act. The concept of *reference group* may be used to designate *that group, real or imaginary, whose standpoint is being used as the frame of reference by the actor.* This provides some notion of the meanings he is projecting upon the scene. Not only can different persons approach the same situation from diverse standpoints, but the same person in different transactions may utilize different perspectives. On a hockey field he has one orientation, and in a classroom he is participating in an entirely different social world. Each man acts, then, for some kind of *audience,* and it is important to know what this audience is and what kinds of expectations are imputed to it.

The reference group supports the values in terms of which a person estimates his own conduct; therefore, his line of activity depends upon the real or anticipated reactions of the other people for whom he is performing. There is a selective sensitivity to others; men are not equally responsive to the opinions of everyone present. Hardened criminals are well aware of the disapproval of most people but are not especially upset. Furthermore, the audience that counts need not consist of people whom one knows personally; frequently reference groups are quite large, and one can have direct contacts only with a few representatives. For example, those in ethnic minorities are usually highly responsive to the demands of others with whom they identify on the basis of common ancestry, but in most cases each knows on a personal basis only a small percentage of those who make up the category. In studying the behavior of human beings it is necessary to get "inside" the actor, to see the situation from his point of view, and the concept of the reference group is useful for this purpose.

There are as many reference groups for each person as there are communication channels in which he participates, and individuals differ considerably in their range of participation. Each lives in an environment of which he is the center, and the dimensions of his effective surroundings are defined by the direction and distance from which news comes to him. Each time a man enters a new communication channel—subscribes to a new periodical, joins a new circle of friends, purchases a television set, or begins to listen regularly to some radio program—he is introduced into a new social world. People who communicate develop an appreciation of one another's tastes, interests, and outlook upon life; and as one acquires new standards of conduct, he adds more people to his audience. Each man's outlook is both shaped and limited by the communication networks in which he becomes involved.

A reference group, then, is any identifiable group whose supposed perspective is used by the actor as a frame of reference in the organization of his perceptual field. Men are usually most responsive to the views imputed to those with whom they are in direct and constant association, but reference groups may also be imaginary, as in the case of artists who are "born ahead of their time," scientists who work for "humanity," or philanthropists who give for "posterity." Such persons estimate their endeavors from a postulated standpoint imputed to people who have not yet been born. They sometimes undergo incredible sacrifices in anticipation of being appreciated by some future audience that presumably would be more sensible than the people who are now living. They are not concerned with immediate rewards and work slavishly for people who may actually never come into existence. There are others who live for a distant past, idealizing some period in history, longing for the "good old days" and constantly criticizing current events from a standpoint imputed to people long since dead—as in the case of the Southerner pining for the days of the Confederacy. There are some people who create a paradise in the next world—Valhalla, Heaven, or the "happy hunting grounds"—and forego pleasures in their present life on the assumption that they will be rewarded after death. An interesting problem is that of ascertaining how perspectives imputed to such imaginary audiences are constructed. One can learn about the typical ways in which people in the "Greek world" presumably lived, acted, and thought by reading history and studying archaeology, but what of the audiences that will not be born for another thousand years? The fact that there is no material basis for such reference groups does not make them any less important.

There are some categories of people with which men occasionally identify which are so amorphous that they may almost be regarded as imaginary groups. Two examples of vaguely defined audiences that play an important part in our society are public opinion and social class. Politicians, administrators, labor leaders, advertising men, and even dictators are constantly concerned with what they call "public opinion." Sometimes even the man of the street may refrain from doing something on the ground that "people won't like it." But who are these "people"? How does one go about ascertaining what it is that the "people" want? Although surveys and polls give some indications, there is no way of knowing for certain until after mass reactions are aroused. Public opinion is the source of so much concern precisely because a miscalculation of what people will tolerate can lead to disastrous consequences—embarrassing demonstrations, the loss of an election, demands for changes that threaten those in privileged positions, or a spectacular drop in the sales of some product. But most of the time those who are concerned with public opinion can only guess, and their conjectures are usually based upon very limited contacts. The same is true of social class. In a study of social stratification in England, where class lines are more clearly drawn than they are in the United States, Bott found that people are class-conscious and do act in terms of their understanding of their class position. But their conception of class structure is often vague and develops from the ways in which the various individuals personally experience

prestige and power in their daily lives. Most people are conscious of class differences, but their conception of the system varies with their experiences. Bott concluded that a social class is a constructed reference group—an audience to which people project their own respective expectations and of which they do not in fact possess accurate knowledge.[6]

Actually, men become acutely aware of the existence of divergent standpoints primarily when they are caught in situations in which conflicting demands are made upon them. While they avoid making difficult decisions whenever possible, these contradictions sometimes force one to choose between two social worlds. Such inner conflicts are essentially struggles between alternative ways of defining a given situation, the options arising from each of two or more perspectives that might be brought to bear upon it. Examples of such dilemmas were provided by William James: "As a man I pity you, but as an official I must show you no mercy; as a politician I regard him as an ally, but as a moralist I loathe him." In playing roles in different social worlds, contrasting expectations are imputed to competing audiences, and sometimes these differences cannot be compromised. The problem is that of selecting the standpoint from which the situation is to be defined. It is in contexts in which alternative definitions are demanded that problems of loyalty arise.

There are individual differences in the flexibility with which one shifts from one reference group to another. There are some people who have a dominant perspective and insist upon defining virtually all situations from this standpoint. Such persons are sometimes reluctant even to acknowledge the existence of other viewpoints and insist that everyone who disagrees with them is wrong. Most people have a limited number of perspectives and are aware of the existence of others, and though they may feel uncomfortable in the company of people whose views are too different, they can tolerate some diversity. Still others change with the wind so that even their close associates are not certain of where they stand. Some can compartmentalize their experiences into units; others apparently find it difficult to do so. . . .

NOTES

1. Albert H. Hastorf and Hadley Cantril, "They Saw a Game: A Case Study," *Journal of Abnormal and Social Psychology,* XLIX (1954), 129–34.

2. Cf. W. Fred Cottrell, *The Railroader* (Stanford: Stanford University Press, 1940); and Hallowell, op. cit., pp. 216–35.

3. Cf. Alvin W. Gouldner, "Cosmopolitans and Locals: Toward an Analysis of Latent Social Roles," *Administrative Science Quarterly,* II (1957–58), 281–306, 444–80.

4. William F. Whyte, "Slum Sex Code," *American Journal of Sociology,* XLIX (1943), 24–31.

5. Georg Simmel, *Conflict and the Web of Group-Affiliations,* trans. Kurt H. Wolff and Reinhard Bendix (Glencoe: The Free Press, 1955), pp. 127–95.

6. Elizabeth Bott, "The Concept of Class as a Reference Group," *Human Relations,* VII (1954), 259–85. Cf. Kurt Riezler, "What is Public Opinion?" *Social Research,* XI (1944), 397–427.

SOCIALIZATION AND REFERENCE GROUPS

19

Shades of White

Pamela Perry

(2001)

"How would you describe white American culture?" I ask Laurie, a white, middle-class senior at Valley Groves High,* a predominantly white, suburban public school near the Pacific Coast of northern California. She pauses, her face looking visibly perplexed as if she did not understand the question or her mind was drawing a blank. Wondering if she heard me over the roar of the cappuccino machine in the background, I awkwardly reiterate, "Like, you know, what would you say white American culture is like?"

"I wouldn't be able to tell you. I don't know." She pauses again and laughs nervously. "When you think about it, it's like—[a longer pause]—*I don't know!*"

About twenty miles away from Valley Groves is the postindustrial city of Clavey. Clavey High School is composed of a brilliant mosaic of students from different ethnic and racial groups, about 12 percent of whom are white. In an interview with Murray, a white, Jewish, middle-class senior, he and I talked a great deal about the consequences of race in the United States and what privileges come with being a white person here. When I probed into his identification with being white or Jewish, he said,

[Cultural pride] doesn't make sense to me. To me it doesn't. I mean, what difference does it make what my great, great grandfather was or his whole

*All names of cities, schools, and individuals in this article are pseudonyms.

generation. That's not affecting my life. . . . I'm still here now. I've got to make what's best for me in the future. I can't harp on what the past has brought.

Laurie and Murray express what the racial category "white" means to each of them. Although their responses differ markedly, they share something fundamental; they perceive white raciality as cultureless. For Laurie, whiteness is not culturally defined. She lives within it but cannot name it. It is taken for granted. For Murray, to be cultural means having emotional attachment to tradition and history. He eschews culture, in this regard, and lives in the present, looking forward.

I chose these two excerpts from qualitative research I carried out in 1994–97 at Valley Groves, a predominantly white, suburban high school, and Clavey, a multiracial, urban high school. The focus of this research was on what differences, if any, the two demographically distinct contexts made on the ways white youth reflected on and constructed white identities. I found that it made a large difference: white students at Valley Groves did not reflect on or define white identity as a culture and social location to the extent that the white youth at Clavey did. Moreover, white identities at Clavey tended to be altogether more variable and contradictory than at Valley Groves. Elsewhere, I argue that these differences in white identities were conditioned by different experiences and structures of interracial association (Perry 1998).

I make a similar argument in this article but with a focus on the only similarity between the ways whites at both schools defined white identity. They defined white as cultureless. By that, I mean that white identity was understood to have no ties or allegiances to European ancestry and culture, no "traditions." To the white youth, only "ethnic" people had such ties to the past. The students would agree with George DeVos (1975) that a "feeling of continuity with the past" distinguishes an "ethnic" group from peoples with more "present-oriented" or "future-oriented" identities (p. 17)—such as whites.

However, although white students at Valley Groves and Clavey shared this perception of white identity, they did not arrive at it by the same processes. In what follows, I present and interpret ethnographic and interview data to argue that at Valley Groves, the tendency for youth to explicitly define themselves and other whites as people without culture came about through processes of *naturalization*—the embedding of historically constituted cultural practices in that which is taken for granted and seems "normal" and natural. At Clavey, culturelessness was achieved through processes of *rationalization*—the embedding of whiteness within a Western rational epistemology and value paradigm that marginalizes or subordinates all things "cultural."

Although there is some scholarly debate over whether there is such a thing as "white culture" (Ignatiev and Garvey 1996; Roediger 1994), my argument here is not so much about whether there is or is not a white culture but about the power whites exercise when *claiming* they have no culture. Culturelessness can serve, even if unintentionally, as a measure of white racial superiority. It suggests that one is either "normal" and "simply human" (therefore, the standard to which others should strive) or beyond culture or "postcultural" (therefore, developmentally advanced).

This work seeks to advance on theories and research in critical white studies, the sociology of education, and racial-ethnic identity formation by vividly illustrating the social construction of white identities and culture in schooling and the ways that different social-structural contexts differently influence constructions of whiteness, including the construction of white as cultureless or the norm. . . .

METHOD AND REFLECTIONS

The vast wealth of excellent scholarship on the social construction of identities in schooling fundamentally shaped my research focus and methodology (Bourdieu and Passeron 1977; Davidson 1996; Eckert 1989; Fordham 1996; Fordham and Ogbu 1986; Kinney 1993; MacLeod 1987; Thorne 1993; Valenzuela 1999). The main focus of my work was what role, if any, close interracial association in school had on the racial consciousness and identities of white youth. Therefore, in choosing my research sites, I looked for two schools: one predominantly white and located in a predominantly white town or city; the other multiracial, minority white and located in a minority white town or city. It also concerned me that the schools be in the same geographical region, of similar size and academic standing, and with student bodies of similar socioeconomic backgrounds to keep those factors as "constant" as possible. I studied census data and school statistics for different towns and cities across the United States before I decided on Valley Groves, which was 83 percent white, and Clavey, which was 12 percent white. Although Clavey was located in a city and Valley Groves a suburb, Clavey was very similar to Valley Groves in all respects besides racial composition, largely due to the fact that Clavey's catchment area encircled a largely middle- to upper-middle-class population. Particularly important for my research was that white students at Clavey were primarily middle class, which allowed me to focus on middle-class whites in both schools.

I spent two and a half years in the schools doing participant observation and in-depth interviewing. Daily practices included sitting in on classrooms with students, hanging out with them during breaks and lunch, attending school club meetings, and participating in student-administrator advisory committees, especially those concerned with race and cultural awareness on campus. I also observed or helped out with after-school programs and events, such as school plays, major rallies, games, and the junior and senior balls of each school. To familiarize myself with the music and leisure activities the students were involved in, after hours I listened to the local rap, R & B, punk, alternative, and classic rock radio stations; bought CD's of the most popular musical artists; went to live underground punk and alternative concerts; read fanzines and other youth magazines; watched MTV; studied music that students dubbed for me; and attended a large rave produced by some Clavey students.

Although I looked somewhat younger than my age (thirty-eight when the research began), I made concerted efforts to minimize the effects of age difference on how students related to me. I did not associate with other adults on campus. I dressed casually in attire that I was comfortable in, which happened to be similar to the attire students were comfortable in: blue jeans, sandals or athletic shoes, T-shirt or sweat-shirt, no jewelry except four tiny hoop earrings—one in one ear, three in the other. I had students call me by my first name, and I did not talk down to them, judge them, or otherwise present myself as an authority figure. To the contrary, I saw the students as the authorities, and they seemed to appreciate that regard. Those efforts, on top of having developed some popular-cultural frames of reference with the students; contributed to my developing some very close relationships with several of the students and fairly wide access to different peer groups and cliques on campus. Having stood in the middle of secret hideouts, food fights, fist fights, tongue lashings, and over-the-top fits of goofiness, I can say that in most cases, I seemed to have little impact on students' behaviors.

My other most apparent traits—race, gender, and middle-class/intellectual appearance—had both positive and negative effects. I connected most readily and easily with girls. The results were that I have more narrative data and in-depth material from girls than boys. At Clavey, however, I did make a few close relationships with boys that I believe helped balance my findings at that school. Similarly, my class background made crossing class differences awkward at times for me and for some participants, particularly working-class males. However, since I was focusing on middle-class white students, my own middle-class whiteness seemed to work mostly on my behalf. With respect to students of color, of which I interviewed quite a few, my race limited my ability to hang out with them in groups at school. Because my focus was on white students, I do not feel this limitation seriously compromises my argument, but deeper perspectives from students of color would certainly have improved it.

I formally interviewed more than sixty students at Valley Groves and Clavey. They included, at Valley Groves, fourteen white youth, one Filipino female, and a group of ten African American students. At Clavey, I interviewed twenty-two white youth, ten African American youth, two Chinese American, one Filipino, and two Latino youth. A little more than half of my interviewees were female and the rest male. Most were middle class, but six were working class.

I did not randomly sample interview participants because I had very specific desires regarding to whom I wanted to speak: liberals and conservatives; whites, blacks, Asians, and Latinos; punks, hippies, homies, alternatives, rappers, and such; high achievers and low achievers; girls and boys; middle class and working class. So I sought out interviewees through multiple methods. Mostly, I directly approached students I observed in classrooms or in their cliques, but I also went to club meetings and asked for volunteers and, for the hard-to-find students, sought recommendations or introductions from youth.

Interviews took place on campus, in coffee shops, and in students' homes and generally lasted two hours. Students and their parents signed consent forms that explained that I was examining racial identities and race relations in the two demographically distinct contexts. In the interviews, I explored youth's experiences at school, their experiences of racial difference, how they thought of themselves racially, how they thought of racial-ethnic others, their cultural

interests and other significant identities, and what types of meanings they gave to their interests and identities. Interviews and informal discussions were also a time for me to discuss with youth my interpretations of school practices, youth cultures, and other events around campus. Students spoke candidly and openly; they seemed eager to talk to an adult who would listen to and treat them respectfully.

The interviews were tape-recorded and transcribed. They and my field notes were manually coded and analyzed along the way to illuminate processes, practices, terms, and conceptions calling for deeper investigation or changes in focus. Along the way, also, I read widely, looking for existing studies and theories that might shed analytical light on my observations. My final coding and analysis were carried out without the aid of software—only colored markers, a Xerox machine, and lots of post-its.

IDENTITY NATURALIZATION AT VALLEY GROVES HIGH: PASSIVE CONSTRUCTION OF WHITE AS CULTURELESS

Valley Groves is a suburban city of roughly 115,000 people. Its residents are solidly white and middle to upper-middle class. In 1990, 83 percent of the population of Valley Groves was white, and the median household income was $42,095. Inside Valley Groves High School's catchment area is Mapleton, a small suburb of about 7,500 people. Ninety percent of Mapleton residents are white, and their median household income in 1989 was $70,000.

The racial and class demographics of Valley Groves and Mapleton cities were reflected in the composition of the Valley Groves High student body and staff. In the 1995–96 school year, white youth made up 83 percent of the school population, followed by Hispanics (7 percent), Asians (5 percent), Filipinos (2 percent), and African Americans

(2 percent). The fifty-three teachers, five administrators, five administrators, three campus supervisors, and fifty-odd service and administrative staff were 85 percent non-Hispanic white. There was only one African American among them.

Raymond Williams (1976) wrote,

> Hegemony supposes the existence of something that is truly total . . . which is lived at such a depth, which saturates the society to such an extent, and which, as Gramsci put it, even constitutes the limit of commonsense for most people under its sway. (pp. 204–5)

At Valley Groves, whiteness "saturated" youths' lived experience. White youth and adults overwhelmed the demographic landscape. When I asked white students at Valley Groves how they would rate their experiences of people of color, most said "very little" or "none at all." In the school yard during lunch or break, students sauntered into the "quad," a large patio area in the center of the campus, to meet with friends and grab a bite to eat. At these times, the most open and public spaces were a sea of blonde- and brown-haired white girls and boys in blue jeans and T-shirts sporting logos of their favorite rock band or skateboard company. The popular and nondescript kids (usually called "normal") occupied the main quad, and the counterculture white students—druggies, skaters, hicks—claimed territory in outside areas adjoining the quad.

Some African American, Asian, or Latino students joined with white friends, and, when they did, they assumed the styles and demeanors of the crowd they were in, be it "popular," "skater," or merely "normal." Then, there were the students of color who clustered in groups of like-kind, racial ethnically. They wore their own styles; spoke in Tagalog, Spanish, or black English; and usually hung out in the cafeteria, classrooms, or distant corners of the campus, locations that kept them virtually invisible to the majority of students in and around the quad.

Similar spatial demographics, in which racial-ethnic difference was placed where it did not challenge the white norm, existed in the classroom structure (Fine 1989). The mainstream students—the popular kids, athletes, and college-bound youth—were in the honors and other high-tracked classes. The "regular" classes were made up of a hodge-podge of different types of youth—middle-class mainstream, working class, countercultural. With the exception of some of the high-tracked math classes, in which Asian American students were overrepresented, high- and regular-tracked courses were disproportionately white, with small numbers of minority youth distributed equally among them. Just where the students of color were I am sorry to say I never learned the answer to, except that one day I saw a large (disproportionate) number of them in a remedial class.

Whiteness saturated Valley Groves' school life not only demographically but culturally as well. The dominant culture at Valley Groves—that which oriented the social organization of students, common styles and practices, and expected behaviors—was homologous with the dominant culture outside of the campus, namely, a white European American culture. By "white European American culture," I refer to two features of American culture, broadly. First, although the dominant culture in the United States is syncretic, that is, composed of the different cultures of the peoples that populate the United States, several of its core characteristics are of European origin. These include, as I have already suggested, the values and practices derived from the European Enlightenment, Anglican Protestantism, and Western colonialism, such as rationalism, individualism, personal responsibility, a strong work ethnic, self-effacement, and mastery over nature. I include, also, carryover or "melted" material cultures of Western, Eastern, and Southern European peoples, such as hamburgers, spaghetti, cupcakes, parades, and line dancing. Second, by virtue of being numerically and politically dominant, whites tend to share certain dispositions, worldviews, and identities constituted by that, especially in predominantly white communities. Currently, a race-neutral or "color-blind" worldview and sense of oneself as normal are examples of that.

At Valley Groves, student cliques and social categories revolved around a norm-other dichotomy in which normal meant that one conformed to the dominant culture and expectations placed on them, and other meant one did not. For example, when I asked Billy how he would describe his group of friends he said,

> "Normal. We don't smoke or drink or anything and [we] wear clothes we would call normal."
>
> "And what is that?" I asked.
>
> "Not oversized, baggy clothes like the skaters wear, or, obviously, we don't wear cowboy hats or boots."

The normal clothes Billy referred to were the styles one might find at mainstream department stores like The Gap: loose, not overly baggy blue jeans; cotton T-shirts and blouses; sundresses; khaki shorts. The kids who did not dress or act normal served to define the boundaries of what was and was not normal. For instance, skaters wore excessively baggy pants and overall filthy clothes; "hicks" wore ten-gallon cowboy hats, tooled-leather boots, and tight jeans with big brassy pants buckles; and druggies flagrantly carried and consumed illicit drugs. (*Flagrant* is the key word here since, as a popular girl told me, "Popular kids do drugs. They just don't want anyone to know it.") Carli, a white girl who considered herself "hippie," referred to the nonmainstream kids as "rebels." She said, "I call them rebels 'cause they know the system sucks."

This norm-other dichotomy was race neutral. Maria, a popular senior of Mexican American descent on her mother's side, told me that the "first cut of students starts with who is popular" and who fits in with the other cliques on campus.

Anyone, regardless of racial-ethnic ascription, could be popular, a skater, a druggie—even a "homie," which, as groups went at Valley Groves, was the most nonwhite. Price of admission was conformity to the styles and demeanor of the group. Hence, black kids who were skaters were not "black skaters," nor were white kids who were homies "white homies"; they were simply "skaters" and "homies," respectively. A white skater I spoke to pointed to an African American boy in his crowd and said, "That doesn't matter. We all love to skate together, hang out together." And when I asked black students if the white kids who were homies were considered "wanna-be black," they looked flatly at me and said, "No." Ron, who was a homie himself, said, "One of the guys who hangs out with us is white. He's not a racist and we've known each other for years."

Students' measuring sticks for gauging normal styles, behaviors, and expectations were the common, everyday practices and the system of rewards at school. On any given day at Valley Groves High, students attended classes and romped into the Quad at break and lunch to purchase anything from fresh cinnamon rolls, cupcakes, rice crispy bars, and fudge for snacks to pizza, hamburgers, meat loaf, and spaghetti for something more substantial. On occasion, leadership students played rock music over the loudspeakers while students talked among themselves in their friendship groups. Circulating through the youth were members of the administrative staff, who would greet students by their first names and engage them in casual conversation, and the team of grounds supervisors, all of whom were greying, middle-aged women. One was affectionately referred to as "Grandma."

"These are all good kids," is what administrators, teachers, and ground supervisors would say to me nearly every time I spoke with them. As Bourdieu (1977) argues, the embodiment of practices and ideas into that which feels normal, natural, and "common sense" requires collective reinforcement and approval. Adult approval rating of the students was high, and they let students know that with their smiles and friendly banter. It was demonstrated also, I believe, through the grounds supervisors, who, by virtue of their title (as opposed to "security") and appearance, demonstrated an implicit trust the adults had that students would, for the most part, comply with expected behaviors. (At least, adults trusted that the white students would comply. Students of color, especially black boys who wore hip-hop styles, told me that they experienced considerable racial profiling by school administrators and the grounds supervisors. This explicitly racial treatment of students of color was either not witnessed by whites or rubbed out of their minds, which I believe played a role in maintaining the pretense of race neutrality on campus.)

At schoolwide rallies and events, collective consensus, reinforcement, and approval of white American norms came from an even wider span of individuals: school adults, other students, and the outside community. Such events seemed to secure a broad consensus of what is true, right, and white but always through nondiscursive practice, never by saying and, thus, never sayable. For example, homecoming—a high school tradition that celebrates the school football team—was a time to raise school spirit and, thus, excite the interest and imagination of the most students possible. It was, for me, an excellent time to observe shared assumptions and normative expectations of students and observe the rewards and sanctions applied to different types of behaviors.

One day during homecoming week, students held rallies in the gym for the entire student body. To the thunder of heavy-metal music, rivers of white students flowed into the gym and took seats in different quadrants of the auditorium reserved for different grade levels. Just before the official ceremony began, two big, husky white males (appearing to be seniors) dragged into the center of the auditorium a small boy (appearing to be a freshman) whose feet and legs were bound with silver duct tape. The crowd laughed and applauded. The two husky guys pumped their fists in the air to encourage the crowd then dragged the boy off center stage. After a brief greeting, members of the student leadership committee introduced the junior varsity and varsity football players. The players came out in succession and formed a line across the middle of the gym floor. The boys were all white except for three black players on the junior varsity team and, on the varsity team, two boys with Hispanic surnames. As his name was called, each player stepped forward to acknowledge the applause. Most did so with an air of shyness or humility, their heads bowed, cheeks blushing, shoulders pulled up to their ears. Two boldly strutted out, trying to play up the roar of the crowd, but their efforts fell flat.

Then, the varsity cheerleaders bolted to center stage, leaping energetically before getting into formation for their choreographed performance. The girls were all thin, some overly so, and wore uniforms with close-fitted bodices that made them look all the smaller. But their body size betrayed their strength. Their routine, driven by the firm beat of a heavy-metal tune, was rigorously gymnastic, with lots of cartwheels, flips, and pyramid constructions that were punctuated by the top girls falling trustingly into the arms of their comrades. Long, silky blonde hair parachuted out with each acrobatic stunt. Through the performance, the audience remained silent and attentive, with an occasional collective gasp at the girls' athleticism, until the show was over. At that time, the cheerleaders received roaring, vocal applause.

On the day after the rally was the homecoming parade. The parade took off from the basketball field and wound its way onto a residential side street. Four adult males, two of whom appeared to be Mexican American, led the parade mounted on prancing horses and wearing Mexican serapes and sombreros. The front two carried large replicas of the California and American flags.

Following the horsemen were two convertibles, one of which was a white Corvette carrying the (white) city mayor, who waved ceremoniously to the onlookers on the sidewalks.

The music of the marching band, which followed closely behind the mayor, announced the arrival of the parade along its path. A group of eight white and one African American female dancers led the band, tossing and spinning colored flags in sync with the beat of the band's percussion section. The fifty musicians in the band, most of whom appeared white with five or six exceptions, marched militarily in tight formation and played their instruments with competence and finesse. Following the band was a procession of American-built pickup trucks carrying, first, the varsity and junior varsity football players, then the "royalty"—the senior "king" and "queen" and underclass "princes" and "princesses"—and finally, an open-bed truck loaded with seniors, hooting and cheering as if their graduation day had already arrived.

The parade made its way through several blocks of residences before returning to the main street and slowly making its way back to the school. Proud parents were perched on the sidewalks with their thirty-five-millimeter and video cameras in hand. Community residents stepped onto their front landings to wave and cheer as the parade passed their homes. Others peered out through large pane windows with cats in arms and dogs at heel.

The homecoming rally and parade were, in my view, packed with assumptions, values, behaviors, and origin stories that privileged white European American perspectives as well as gender, sexuality, and class-based norms (all of which tend to coproduce one another). At the rally, for example, the display of the hog-tied freshman reinforced that white (male) dominance is sustained not only through the subordination of nonwhite others but of "other" whites as well (Hartigan 1997, 1999; Thandeka 1999; Wray and Newitz

1997). Second, the virtues of personal mastery and self-effacement were exemplified by the humble postures of the football players and reinforced by the slights the audience gave to those who presented themselves with more bravado. And, finally, the cheerleaders' thin, bounded physiques and gravity-defying athletic feats demonstrated that the girls had successfully learned to subjugate their bodies and overcome nature.

The homecoming parade, with its display of the national and state flags, American cars, marching band, and school royalty, was a stunning way to observe the coproduction of whiteness, Americanness, citizenship, and gendered codes of conduct. Included was even an origin story of white American colonial victory over Mexico. And, by virtue of who was there and who was not, the knitting together of the themes of mastery, domination, nationhood, and industry with whiteness was seamless. Other cultures in the school and community were not represented in the parade. There were no Filipino dancers, Asian martial artists, or African American rappers. The event was performed by whites and for whites and, thus, little contradicted the cultural and political assumptions at play.

In sum, at Valley Groves High, white people and white European American culture saturated school life. White youth had little to no association with people or cultures that would place whiteness in relief in such a way that students might reflect on it and consciously define it.

No Ties

Given this sociocultural milieu, white youth could say nothing when I asked them to describe white culture; they had no words to describe that which comes naturally. Laurie, whom I quoted at the beginning of this article, struggled to describe white culture and finally succumbed to "I don't know!" Billy, a popular white senior, had a similar response. I asked him what he thought was culturally specific about white American culture. After a long pause in which he said only, "hmmm," he asked, "Like, what's American culture?"

"Uh-huh," I replied.
"Hmmm. [Another long pause]—I don't really know, 'cause it's like [pause]—just [pause]—I'm not sure! I don't know!"

However, Valley Groves' white students were not always speechless about white identity. When my questions probed into the youths' social experiences and identities as whites and not their cultures, they could find something to say. Not too surprisingly, most told me that being white meant you had no cultural ties. Students I spoke to would explain that they had mixed European roots that held no significance to them; therefore they were "just white." For example, I asked Mara, a Valley Groves senior, what she would say if a census taker asked her, straight out without any prompting, "What are you?"

Mara: Like a race?

PGP: Could be a racial category.

Mara: I'd have to answer "Very white." I am, yeah. I am 100 percent white.

PGP: I noticed on your [consent form] you said you had a mix of European backgrounds, and you wrote, "Pretty much WHITE." Is that what "white" means to you, a European mix?

Mara: I just think that there's not much—I don't really think of myself as European. I think of myself as a white American girl. . . . I don't really go back to my roots, though I know I have family and where they come from but they're all white races.

PGP: You don't have any heartfelt devotion to your European past?

Mara: Not really. My family has lived here for generations, so I don't really draw on that.

Laurie had a similar response:

We're a bunch of everything. My great, great Grandmother is Cherokee. Whenever I fill out [questionnaires] about what's my ethnic background I write "white" because everything is so random. We have German, some family from Wales—but that means nothing to me. . . . I don't have ties to anything. I haven't heard about anything my parents have been through except for my grandparents in wars. It's all been about people, not culture.

Answers like Mara's and Laurie's, of which there were many, reflect that, although white youth at Valley Groves may not have thought about whiteness as a culture, they did think about it as a social category (Phoenix 1997), as a "group position" (Blumer 1958) with respect to other racial-ethnic groups. To Valley Groves' students, whites were a group because they did not have culture, and "minorities" did. Through mixed-European and other cultural amalgamation, whites were a new breed, a hybrid, removed from a past that was meaningless to them and for the loss of which they held no remorse.

Valley Groves' whites were speaking from the "postcultural" perspective that Rosaldo (1989) asserts is the perspective of all who are members of the dominant group of Western-style nation states. Naturalized whiteness complements and helps constitute this kind of postcultural identity because of the stability garnered from the fit between societal norms and the constructed identity of whites (powell 1997). The us-them construction revolves around "majority" (those who all look and act normal to one another) and the "minority" (those who do not look or act like the majority). Naturalized whiteness is securely grounded in and validated by the normal way of things in the present and therefore does not seek meaning in a cultural or past orientation.

CLAVEY HIGH SCHOOL: WHEN WHITE IS NOT THE NORM

Once a port of entry for African American, Mexican, and Asian immigration into northern California, Clavey City today has one of the most racially/ethnically diverse populations for its size in the United States. Of its 372,000 residents, 33 percent are white, 44 percent are black, 19 percent are of Hispanic origin, and 15 percent are of Asian origin. Median household income in 1989 was $27,095. More than 16 percent of families in Clavey City live below poverty.

Clavey High School stands like a fortress overlooking a dense urban landscape. The school's magnet academies draw in youth from all over the city, bringing in a mosaic of students from different racial and ethnic groups. At the time of my research, whites comprised 12 percent of the two thousand students at Clavey. African Americans were the majority, making up 54 percent of the school. They were followed in numbers by Asian Americans (23 percent), then Hispanics (8 percent), Filipinos (2 percent), and a few Pacific Islanders and Native Americans. At any given moment during lunch break, one could tour the campus and hear students speaking in standard English, black English ("ebonics"), Eritrean, Cantonese, Mandarin, Korean, Spanish, Spanglish, Tagalog, Samoan, Russian, and Vietnamese, among others.

The racial composition of the administrative and teaching staff at Clavey was also quite diverse. The principal of Clavey was a white male, but the other top administrators, two assistant principals and the dean, were African American. Of all the administrators and their staff, 50 percent were African American, 25 percent were Asian,

and 25 percent were white. Clavey teachers were 53 percent white, 30 percent African American, 8 percent Asian American, 6 percent Hispanic, and 3 percent Pacific Islander.

Life at Clavey High was very different from that at Valley Groves. White youth at Clavey were in daily, up-close association with marked racial and cultural difference to whiteness, and race was the primary means of sorting out who was who and where one belonged in the social organization of the school. Clavey's tracking structure, which I say more about later, was racially segregated, with whites and Asians disproportionately represented in the high-tracked classes and African Americans and Latinos overrepresented in the low-tracked classes. As well, certain areas on the campus were "where the white kids hang out"; others were "where the black (or Asian American or Latino) kids hang out." And student cliques and subcultures were racially marked such that "straights" (who were like "normal" kids at Valley Groves), alternatives, hippies, and punks were all "white people's groups"; rappers, athletes, gangsters, and "fashion hounds" were "black people's groups"; housers, natives, newly arrived, and martial artists were "Asian people's groups"; and so forth. This meant that the styles, slangs, vernaculars, and demeanors that marked identification with a certain clique or subculture simultaneously inferred racial identification. In a word, peer group activities *racialized* youth.

Speaking to this fact and the sanctions that came with crossing racialized boundaries in styles or leisure activities, Gloria, an immigrant from El Salvador, said to me,

> For my race, if you start wearing a lot of gold, you're trying to be black. If you're trying to braid your hair, you'll be accused of trying to be black. I'm scared to do things 'cause they might say, "that's black!" Or if you're Latino and you listen to that, you know, Green Day—that [alternative rock] kinda thing. If you listen to that, then you wanna be white. . . . "Oh my

god, why you listening to that music?" they'd say, . . . Aren't you proud of who you are?

Also different from Valley Groves was the dominant school culture. Overall at Clavey, African American youth claimed the majority of open, public spaces, and black popular cultural forms and practices shaped the normative culture of the school. By "black popular culture," I refer to the music, styles, and other meaningful practices that have risen out of black communities; are linked, if remotely, to diasporic traditions; and, most significantly, mark black identity and peoplehood (Gilroy 1991, 1993; Rose 1994; Wallace 1992). Hall (1992) defines three things that are distinctive of black diasporic culture: (1) *style* as the "subject of what is going on," (2) *music* as the "deep structure of [black] cultural life," and (3) the *body* as "canvases of representation" (p. 27). Gilroy (1991) adds that the body in black culture carries "potent meanings" (p. 226) because it rests at the core of historical efforts of blacks to assert their humanity.

Unlike at Valley Groves, where the dress code did not diverge much from white adult mainstream style, at Clavey, basic elements of black hip-hop style were generalized into the normative styles for all youth. One informant called it the "leveler" style because it made all who wore it "the same." This basic style included clean, oversized, and sagging denim pants or sweatpants; large and long untucked T-shirts or hooded sweatshirts; large, bulky parkas; and sparkling-clean athletic shoes. The look was particularly common for boys, but girls' styles were also influenced by it. Only if and when students wanted to mark a distinctive style and/or racial identification did they embellish on this basic, baggy theme. Duncan, a middle-class, white male skater and "raver" (someone who frequents rave parties) told me,

We all wear baggy pants, right? So parents think! But you find that ravers have cut-off bottoms to their [sagging] jeans, they wear bigger t-shirts they have

hanging out of their pants, they carry packs that's full of crap that they take everywhere.

What Duncan specified as "raver" style, other students specified as "white," particularly the cut-off bottoms to large pants. Other markers of white kids' styles were Van shoes, instead of Nike or Fila brands (which marked black style), and macramé or silver-chain neck chokers.

Informal and formal activities on campus were also shaped by black popular culture. During breaks or at lunchtime, the ambient din of casual conversation was composed of the sounds, words, and inflections of black English and the most recent innovation in "street" slang. Lunchtime events, school rallies, and dances were enlivened with rap and R & B music, predominantly, with an occasional reggae tune or specially requested techno or alternative song. Often, students performed raps on the steps in front of the cafeteria or graced an audience with a spontaneous hip-hop dance performance.

Homecoming week at Clavey, like at Valley Groves, was a time to unite the school and raise the collective spirit. So, leadership students made attempts to appeal to the breadth of diverse interests and cultures of the school with "fashion shows" of traditional or native garments and a variety of games designed to mix students up. At lunch, they played a range of music, from R & B to techno and alternative rock, but songs by African American and Afro-Carribean artists were predominant. The main events—the rally and game—were attended by and played predominantly to a majority-black audience.

The rally took place during lunch on the day of the "big game." Students, of which all but a few were black, crammed into the auditorium to the heartbeat pulse of a rap song. The rally opened with a greeting from the student body president and a soulful a cappella song performed by three African American students. Then the cheerleaders, composed of one white and ten black girls, sprung out onto the gym floor. Their choreographed routine was fluid, rhythmic, and dancelike, with movements drawn from traditional and contemporary African and African American dance forms. To the infectious beat of an upbeat R & B song, the girls playfully flirted with their appreciative audience with beckoning hand and eye gestures. Several boys succumbed to the urge to dance in dialogue with the girls and leapt down to the floor to join them, but they were met by the arresting hands of campus security. Others, boys and girls alike, stood up and swayed or danced in place until the performance was over. Then, the varsity football players were called to line up in the center of the auditorium. The players were African American with the exception of two white boys and one Latino. When each name was announced, the football player leapt forward a few steps and embraced the cheers from the crowd. Each took his moment in the limelight proudly, with his fist in the air or maybe a little dance to augment the roar of his audience.

At Clavey, there was no homecoming parade that extended into the community, like at Valley Groves. At the game, a small procession of vehicles featuring the elected school "emperor" and "empress" circled the football field during half time. There was no marching band, either, but the award-winning school gospel choir sang several lively songs at halftime.

In short, school life at Clavey was heavily infused with styles, music, and activities that marked the identities and cultures of the majority black students. This had a few important implications for the experiences and identities of the white students. First, white was not the norm, either numerically or culturally. Barry, a middle-class, "straight" white male, told me, "School is like a foreign country to me. I come here to this foreign place, then go home where things are normal again." When I asked white students why they did not attend the rallies and dances, they said things like, "I don't enjoy the people," "They don't play my kind of music," and "I can't dance to that music." All in all, the message was that they could not relate to the dominant school culture.

Furthermore, whiteness was not entirely taken for granted. The racial organization of Clavey's social life, curricular structure, and schoolwide activities meant that white students were forced to grapple with their identities as whites and participate in active contestation over the meanings of white identity and culture. No white student I spoke to at Clavey was completely unable to describe something about white culture. All had reflected on it to some extent, even if only to ruminate on how difficult it was to define. And some youth could say a lot about white culture. One white, middle-class senior girl, Jessie, elaborated extensively on differences in attitudes toward food consumption that she noticed between her white, Filipino, and Chinese American friends, and she commented on how much more visible white culture is to her in places outside of California. She said, "Minnesota, Denver and . . . places like that. It seems like . . . you know, you've got the whole thing going on—beer bread, polka, parades, apple pie and things like that."

Most stunning to me about the white students at Clavey was not what they said explicitly about white culture but what they said implicitly. In our discussions about the types of music they liked and why, white students would tell me that they liked rock or punk or alternative music and not rap or R & B because "their" music spoke more to their "interests" or experiences as whites. For example, Kirsten and Cindi were good friends. They both were from middle-class homes, were juniors at the time, and liked alternative rock. Kirsten was white, European American, and Cindi was part white and part Chinese, although she admittedly "looked white" and hung out solely with other white youth. I asked them why they thought students tended to self-segregate on campus:

Cindi: I think there is . . . the factor that some people feel like they may not have very much in common with someone from a different race, which in some ways is true. Because you have, like, different music tastes, different styles of clothes. Also, like what your friends think.

Kirsten: Or like different things you do on weekends.

Cindi: Yeah, so I think that's something that separates the races.

Kirsten: It's kind of interesting because my musical interests have changed. . . . It seems like [in junior high school] everyone, regardless of if they were black or white or Asian, . . . listened to the [local rap and R & B station]. But then I think when you are little you don't really . . . have too much of an identity of yourself. As you get older and mature more you, like, discover what your "true being" is. So then people's musical tastes change. [Later in the conversation] I think punk is more of a "I don't get along with my parents" kind of music and rap is more of "let's go kill someone" music.

Cindi: Punk . . . expresses a simpler anger. It's just kind of like "Oh, I broke up with my girlfriend" . . . something like that. Usually rap has more to do with killing and gangs—stuff that doesn't really relate to me.

In this discussion, Kirsten and Cindi defined white identity and culture in terms of interests and tastes in leisure culture. This "discourse of taste" (Dolby 2000) was the language of choice among all groups of students for articulating racial-ethnic differences. Behind it was the belief that different life experiences accounted for different tastes. Sometimes, white youth named fairly explicit experiences they believed were most common to or defining of whites. Class experience, expressed

by Kirsten and Cindi in terms of the type of neighborhood one lived in, was often evoked by youth. Other times, white youth spoke in terms of intangible but presumably race-based, emotional, aesthetic, and ethical sensibilities they felt when they listened to, say, punk or alternative music but not when they listened to rap.

ACTIVE CONSTRUCTION OF WHITE AS POSTCULTURAL

Ironically, even as Clavey whites demarcated white culture and identity boundaries through their popular-cultural tastes and leisure activities, they also imagined whiteness as cultureless, as postcultural. This was not as explicit as it was at Valley Groves. It would show its face when white students referred to people of color as people with "race" or "ethnicity," as though whites had neither. Tina, a working-class junior who had always been a racial minority in school and had many close black and Latino friends, told me that she "had a lot of ethnicity in [her] family . . . Hispanic, Korean. We all get along." By this she meant that white relatives had married "out" of whiteness and into culture, ethnicity.

Common also was the explicit and implicit definition of white as empty, meaningless, bland, and without tradition. This comment by Eric touches on all of those:

I think it's more difficult [to define white culture] for Americans because the culture of America is more just consumption. In America, we buy stuff, and that's the basis of our culture. If you talk to people who want to come to America?—They want things. TV is a very American thing. We don't have lengthy traditions. . . . A lot has been lost because of the good ol' melting pot. I heard a cool one about a salad bowl—that's what America is, and along comes the dressing and turns everything into dressing flavor. Vegetables all got that white American spin on it.

Note, too, that Eric equates "white" with "American" until his last line, when he specifies "white American." That is a faux pas that whites often fall into because of the dominant construction of white as the "unhyphenated" American standard.

Finally, several Clavey white students told me that they did not like to think about themselves as "white" but as "human." These students also expressed a more explicitly rationalist construction of whiteness that denied the significance of a past orientation and exalted a more individualistic and present- or future-oriented construction of the self. White, middle-class boys expressed this most boldly, which might be expected given that they are triply constructed as the most rational by race, class, and gender.

Murray, whom I quoted at the beginning of this article, best exemplifies this latter perspective. In Murray's comments, we can read several tenets of Western rational thought and a postcultural identity: the irrationality of past-oriented values, the future orientation of the self, and individual responsibility. Daniel was a white, middle-class, "straight" male with some Portuguese ancestry. He made comments similar to Murray's:

> People have suggested I am a person of color or mixed. Then I decided, no, I'm European American. Ancestry doesn't matter. . . . People look back in the past and judge you for it, and I don't think that's right. Sure, people enslaved people. At one time every race had slaves. I think you need to move on and see what's going on now. History is important but you have to work on getting together now and don't use that as a divide.

A few scholars have observed a propensity among whites to deny the significance of the past, slavery particularly, in affecting the life chances of African Americans today. Some argue that this denial is a kind of defensive mechanism whites adopt to exonerate themselves from taking responsibility for the legacies of slavery and past discrimination against African Americans and other minorities (Gallagher 1995). I take a slightly different position and suggest that white identity and culture is constructed in such a way that the values of individuality, personal responsibility, and a future-oriented self create a cognitive inability to see things any other way (see also Alba 1990; Blauner 1989). A past orientation simply does not make sense to many whites from their cultural perspective.

In sum, at Clavey, white culture was not entirely naturalized and taken for granted; it was reflected on and even defined somewhat, particularly through the language of tastes and popular culture. To an extent, however, white students also considered themselves unmarked American, nonethnic, unmarked human, and/or present oriented. In a word, they saw themselves as cultureless. I might add that several students of color I spoke to also were quick to define white culture in terms of styles and tastes but not in terms of tradition. Johnetta, an African American senior, said, "It's hard to generalize [about white culture] because there's no ready answer to what is white culture."

Whereas I have proposed that the naturalization of whiteness greatly facilitated the passive construction of postcultural whiteness at Valley Groves, I suggest that at Clavey, different and more active social processes were in play. Namely, Western rational ways of knowing and making sense of social relations permeated Clavey school and social practices. As I have argued, Western rationalism exiles tradition and culture from the realms of truth and relevance and replaces them with reason. That which is reasonable or rational is separated from and raised above that which is not, like the elevation of mind over body, intellectual over emotional, and order above chaos. Whiteness benefits from those hierarchical dualities by being linked with the higher value of each—with orderliness, self-control, individualism, and rationality, which, not coincidentally, are recognized as standard or normal behaviors.

Otherness is defined in terms of that which is passionate, chaotic, violent, lazy, irrational, and—since marginal to the norm—cultural.

Two school practices in particular stood out for me in terms of the ways they seemed to structure the meanings all youth gave to their experience through a Western rational value paradigm. The first and most obvious of those was the tracking structure. Scholars have long argued that racial segregation in tracking reproduces racial inequalities in the wider society, largely by preparing high-tracked students, who tend to be middle-class white and Asian, better than low-tracked students, who tend to be black, Latino, and poor white and Asian (Gamoran et al. 1995; Oakes 1985, 1994; Oakes and Guiton 1995). Tracking also reproduces racial inequalities by reinforcing, if not constituting, racial stereotypes. Jeannie Oakes (1994) has argued that "all but the most extraordinary schools have their stereotypes and prejudices reinforced by racially-identifiable high- and low-tracked classes" (pp. 86–87). She asserts that tracking "institutionalizes racist conceptions of intellectual capacity" (ibid.). I would add to her argument that tracking also institutionalizes the values of mind over body and self-control over lack of restraint and racializes those who are superior and inferior in those respects.

At Clavey, the high-tracked classes, those designed to prepare students for high-ranking colleges and universities, were 80 percent white and Asian, according to a school survey. Conversely, "preparatory" classes, which filled graduation requirements, were overwhelmingly black and Latino. Remedial classes were 100 percent black and Latino. Although, officially, youth were tracked according to their intellectual or achievement levels, the discourses that surrounded tracking at Clavey suggested that *behavior* (including expected behavior) was just as relevant.

Students in the high-tracked classes were generally understood to be "well-behaved," "good" students. In those classrooms, students acted in the utmost orderly fashion: always listening attentively and taking notes, speaking only when called on. They considered themselves hard working and sophisticated in their abilities to defer gratification, such as to study during lunch instead of hang out and have fun with their friends. They justified their privilege to be in the accelerated classes on these grounds and blamed underachievement on the behaviors of the underachieved. Linda, a white Jewish girl in accelerated classes, represented this viewpoint in the following comment:

> It's so sad because these kids could be pushed so far beyond what they are [doing]. Like, it's unbelievable. When I see a twelfth grader holding a geometry book, I cringe inside me. Because, *you can learn,* you can do it! People are so lazy, they don't care. They have no goals, no ambitions. It's frustrating! I don't get it!

The "lazy" and unambitious kids Linda referred to were black and Latino students in the preparatory classes. Other commonly used terms to describe those classes and the students in them were "bonehead," "rowdy," and "out of control." And, indeed, some of those classes had students who were inattentive or disruptive and who could, on occasion, set the whole class off into a blaze of rowdiness. But those students were aware that they had been assigned to the least valued and negatively stereotyped classes in the school. If they did not hear it through common discourse, they deduced it from the classes themselves. They were overcrowded and short of chairs, books, and other course materials. Sometimes, they did not even have full-time teachers. It is not a stretch to suggest that preparatory students behaved in "bonehead" ways that they thought were expected of them (Baron, Tom, and Cooper 1985; Eder 1981; Ferguson 1998; Lightfoot 1978; Steele and Aronson 1998).

In sum, tracking at Clavey asserted more than, simply, intellectual superiority but also the values of mind over body and self-control over lack of restraint. Furthermore, it marked standard, acceptable forms of behavior—standards within which middle-class whites and Asians were squarely located practically and symbolically.

"Multicultural" programs and discourses were other school practices that positioned whites as the school's most rational and postcultural. At Clavey, there were two main, formal multicultural events: the "cultural assemblies" and "multicultural week." Once every other month or so, an ethnic club—the African American Student Union, the Asian Student Union, Latino Student Union, or the Inter-Tribal Student Union—would put on a schoolwide assembly. A common assembly featured traditional ceremonial dances and rituals, music and song, poetry readings, historically informative slide shows, and clothing displays, all arranged and performed by the students.

Lunchtime activities during multicultural week were another opportunity for students to publicly display elements of their cultural heritage. Each day of the week was designed to feature a particular aspect of a culture—the music, dance, clothing, written texts, or narratives. For example, on a day featuring traditional or national clothing styles, youth held a fashion show in which African American youth in dashikis, Chinese American girls in brocade gowns, and Mexican American youth in ceremonial dance costumes paraded before youth gathered outside the cafeteria.

These events had their merits. They gave voice and visibility to the cultures and perspectives of people historically silenced by white colonialism. African American and Asian youth told me that they enjoyed having the opportunity to present their culture as well as learn about others. I propose, however, that multicultural events at Clavey coterminously reproduced white supremacist, rationalist tenets of white colonialism by making whiteness culturally invisible.

Rosaldo (1989) argues that, "as the Other becomes more culturally visible, the self becomes correspondingly less so" (p. 202). I believe this was true for many Clavey whites. When white students spoke about the assemblies, they usually expressed enthusiastic appreciation for "the chance to learn about so many cultures." But learning about other cultures merely gave them more references by which to define what they were not. As well, when they spoke in this way, it was as if "cultures" were like books—objective things that existed outside of the self but could be consumed to pleasure the self (Farley 1997). In a conversation with four middle-class white girls at Clavey, I asked them how they thought their experience at Clavey would influence their adulthood.

Ann: I think it's going to be a very positive thing. [Melissa interjects: Yeah.] Because it teaches us how to deal with different kinds of people.

Sera: Yeah, you learn more about others. . . . It's a positive experience.

Melissa: Yeah, you gain street smarts. You gain stuff.

Greater knowledge of other cultures was something Ann, Sera, and Melissa appreciated because it gave them tools to enhance their sociability, but it did not make them reflect on their sociocultural location as whites. When other white students at Clavey spoke to me about the value of the multicultural events, they made very similar kinds of statements and inferences. Overall, multicultural events, as "add-on" school practices in which white students could pleasurably gaze on racial-ethnic others without putting themselves on the line, reinforced a sense of whiteness as center and standard (cultureless) and racial-ethnic others (by virtue of having culture to display) as different and marginal to that.

Furthermore, no white students I spoke to questioned why there was not a white-American cultural assembly. Granted, to most this was untenable, largely because it might be taken as a white-supremacist act. I talked to students about school clubs for whites only and they categorically dismissed the idea. One said, "There'd be a riot!" Another said, "It wouldn't be right. It would be taken all wrong." But it was also untenable because, as another student put it, "White is all around. It doesn't need special attention." The idea that white culture does not need special attention (read: white is the norm and standard) seemed to be another message multicultural events gave to white students. As if for the eyes of whites only, multiculturalism at Clavey gave white students new references to add to their mental cache of exotic others while further obscuring the invisible power of white culture.

Conclusion

For a while now, scholars of race and whiteness have understood that the construction of white culture as the invisible norm is one of the most, if not *the* most, pernicious constructions of whiteness in the post–civil rights era. However, very few have examined the everyday social processes by which white people come to think of themselves as normal and culturally empty (Frankenberg 1993; Kenny 2000a, 2000b; Twine 1997), and among those, no one has done a comparative study illuminating the ways that different social-structural institutional contexts influence different constructions of white identity as cultureless. My research suggests that, at Valley Groves, a predominantly white high school, white identity seemed cultureless because white cultural practices were taken for granted, naturalized, and, thus, not reflected on and defined. At Clavey, a multiracial school, white culture was not taken for granted— white youth thought about and defined it to an extent, particularly through their interests and tastes in popular culture. However, in part, whites also reflected on their sociocultural location

through the lens of European American rational authority, which school structures and practices helped construct and reinforce. That lens refracted whiteness into all that was good, controlled, rational, and cultureless and otherness into all that was bad, out of control, irrational, and cultural. It may be that when naturalization processes are not possible because of close interracial association, then rationalization processes must come into play to preserve white hegemony.

This argument has theoretical and practical implications for critical white studies, the sociology of education, and general theories and research in racial-ethnic identity formation. Within critical white studies, there are two prevalent sets of assumptions about white culture that this research advances. The first is that white people experience themselves as culturally empty because whiteness is hegemonic and, therefore, undefined. To disrupt the insidious power of white culture, then, we must expose and define it. My study suggests that this is true but not everywhere the truth. The multiracial experiences of white youth at Clavey suggest that making white culture visible is not sufficient for challenging the construction of white as norm. What is also necessary are efforts to expose, challenge, and transform the rule of reason that frames white culture as rational and, therefore, *beyond* culture, postcultural or even anticultural.

Another assumption among some scholars of critical white studies, particularly "New Abolitionists," is that white culture is experienced as empty because, simply, there is no white culture. I am less concerned with the question of whether there really is a white culture than with what is reproduced through *denying* there is a white culture. The argument I have presented here proposes that the concept of culture denotes more than, simply, a way of life organized around sets of symbolic practices. It connotes a relationship of power between those who "have" culture (and are, thus, irrational and inferior) and those who claim not to (and are, thus, rational and superior). More research and thought needs to go into examining the ways postcultural whiteness is inculcated in daily practice and into the profits whites gain by denying that they have a culture.

This research also contributes to the growing scholarship on social and cultural reproduction in education. Although considerable research has examined the reproduction and subversion of societal norms in schools, including racial norms (for example, Carter 1999; Conchas 2000; Davidson 1996; Fine et al. 1997; Fordham 1996; Kenny 2000a; McCarthy and Critchlow 1993; Valenzuela 1999), more is still needed that closely examines the symbolic impact of certain school practices on how white students make sense of their own identities and the identities of people of color. This research only touched the surface of that and came on some disturbing and unexpected findings, namely, the active construction of postcultural whiteness. Research and evaluations of multicultural and other programs designed to redress racial inequalities have focused primarily on students of color. Important insights might be gained from more attention to white students and the meanings they assign to their experiences of those same programs.

Finally, this research embellishes on theories of racial-ethnic identity formation by vividly illuminating the socially constructed and contingent nature of race. Racial identities are made, not born, and they are made through the interaction of the specific social, structural, political, and cultural composition of a given context (Blumer 1958; Pinderhughes 1997). This means that racial identities are not fixed or uniform but variable and multiple. They may even be contradictory. These observances are often lost among scholars of whiteness and white racism who tend to represent whites and white identities as everywhere and always the same and contradictions as a form of "contemporary race prejudice" (Williams et al. 1999). My research affirms that the hegemonic

construction of white as cultureless is stubbornly persistent but that even *it* is not the same across all contexts. To more effectively dismantle white domination, we need to be aware of and ready to work with its different manifestations and internal contradictions. Future research and antiracist scholarship may benefit from deeper exploration of the variability of white racial identities and the processes by which white racial domination is reproduced and subverted in distinct contexts.

REFERENCES

Alba, Richard. 1990. *Ethnic identity: The transformation of white America.* New Haven, CT: Yale University Press.

Allen, Theodore. 1994. *The invention of the white race, vol. 1: Racial oppression and social control.* London: Verso.

Almaguer, Tomas. 1994. *Racial fault lines: The historical origins of white supremacy in California.* Berkeley: University of California Press.

Apple, Michael W. 1995. *Education and power.* New York: Routledge.

Baron, Reuben, David Y. H. Tom, and Harris M. Cooper. 1985. Social class, race and teacher expectations. In *Teacher expectancies,* edited by Jerome B. Dusek. Hillsdale, NJ: Lawrence Erlbaum.

Blauner, Bob. 1989. *Black lives, white lives: Three decades of race relations in America.* Berkeley: University of California Press.

Blumer, Herbert. 1958. Race prejudice as a sense of group position. *Pacific Sociological Review* 1 (1): 3–7.

Bourdieu, Pierre. 1977. *Outline of a theory of practice.* Cambridge, UK: Cambridge University Press.

Bourdieu, Pierre, and J. C. Passeron. 1977. *Reproduction in education, society and culture.* Beverly Hills, CA: Sage.

Carter, Prudence L. 1999. Balancing acts: Issues of identity and cultural resistance in the social and educational behaviors of minority youth. Ph.D. diss., Columbia University, New York.

Conchas, Gilberto Q. 2000. Structuring failure and success: Understanding the variability in Latino school engagement. Working paper, Harvard Graduate School of Education.

Davidson, Ann Locke. 1996. *Making and molding identity in schools: Student narratives on race, gender, and academic engagement.* Albany: State University of New York Press.

De Vos, George. 1975. Ethnic pluralism: Conflict and accommodation. In *Ethnic identity: Cultural continuities and change,* edited by George De Vos and Lola Romanucci-Ross. Chicago: University of Chicago Press.

Dolby, Nadine. 2000. The shifting ground of race: The role of taste in youth's production of identities. *Race, Ethnicity, and Education 3* (1):7–23.

Dyer, Richard. 1997. *White.* New York: Routledge.

Eckert, Penelope. 1989. *Jocks and burnouts: Social categories and identity in high school.* New York: Teachers College Press.

Eder, Donna. 1981. Ability grouping as a self-fulfilling prophecy: A micro-analysis of teacher-student interaction. *Sociology of Education 54* (3): 151–62.

Essed, Philomena. 1996. *Diversity: Gender, color and culture.* Amherst: University of Massachusetts Press.

Farley, Anthony Paul. 1997. The black body as fetish object. *Oregon Law Review 76* (3): 457–535.

Ferguson, Robert A. 1997. *The American Enlightenment, 1750–1820.* Cambridge, MA: Harvard University Press.

Ferguson, Ronald F. 1998. Teachers' perceptions and expectations and the black-white test score gap. In *The black-white test score gap,* edited by Christopher Jencks and Meredith Phillips, 318–74. Washington, DC: Brookings Institution.

Fine, Michelle. 1989. Silencing and nurturing voice in an improbable context: Urban adolescents in public school. In *Critical pedagogy, the state, and cultural struggle,* edited by Henry Giroux and Peter McLaren, 152–73. Albany: State University of New York Press.

Fine, Michelle, Lois Weis, Linda C. Powell, and L. Mun Wong, eds. 1997. *Off white: Readings on race, power and society.* New York: Routledge.

Fordham, Signithia. 1996. *Blacked out: Dilemmas of race, identity, and success at Capital High.* Chicago: University of Chicago Press.

Fordham, Signithia, and John Ogbu. 1986. Black students' school success: Coping with the "burden of 'acting white.'" *Urban Review 18* (3): 176–206.

Frankenberg, Ruth. 1993. *White women, race matters: The social construction of whiteness.* Minneapolis: University of Minnesota Press.

_____. 1997. *Displacing whiteness: Essays in social and cultural criticism.* Durham, NC: Duke University Press.

Gallagher, Charles A. 1995. White reconstruction in the university. *Socialist Review 24* (1&2): 165–87.

_____. 1997. White racial formation: Into the twenty-first century. In *Critical white studies: Looking behind the mirror,* edited by Richard Delgado and Jean Stefancic, 6–11. Philadelphia: Temple University Press.

Gamoran, Adam, Martin Nystrand, Mark Berends, and Paul C. LePore. 1995. An organizational analysis of the effects of ability grouping. *American Educational Research Journal 32* (4): 687–715.

Gilroy, Paul. 1991. *"There ain't no black in the Union Jack": The cultural politics of race and nation.* Chicago: University of Chicago Press.

_____. 1993. *The black Atlantic: Modernity and double consciousness.* Cambridge, MA: Harvard University Press.

Giroux, Henry. 1996. *Fugitive cultures: Race, violence, and youth.* New York: Routledge.

_____. 1997. Rewriting the discourse of racial identity: Towards a pedagogy and politics of whiteness. *Harvard Educational Review 67* (2): 285–320.

Goldberg, David Theo. 1993. *Racist culture: Philosophy and the politics of meaning.* Cambridge, UK: Blackwell.

Hall, Stuart. 1992. What is the "black" in black popular culture? In *Black popular culture,* edited by Gina Dent, 21–33. Seattle, WA: Bay.

_____. 1996. Introduction: Who needs identity? In *Questions of cultural identity,* edited by Stuart Hall and Paul du Gay, 1–17. London: Sage.

Haney Lopez, Ian F. 1996. *White by law: The legal construction of race.* New York: New York University Press.

Harris, Cheryl. 1993. Whiteness as property. *Harvard Law Review* 106:1707–91.

Hartigan, John, Jr. 1997. Locating white Detroit. In *Displacing whiteness: Essays in social and cultural criticism,* edited by Ruth Frankenberg, 180–213. Durham, NC: Duke University Press.

_____. 1999. *Racial situations: Class predicaments of whiteness in Detroit.* Princeton, NJ: Princeton University Press.

Hill, Mike, ed. 1997. *Whiteness: A critical reader.* New York: New York University Press.

hooks, bell. 1992. *Black looks: Race and representation.* Boston: South End.

Ignatiev, Noel. 1995. *How the Irish became white.* New York: Routledge.

Ignatiev, Noel, and John Garvey, eds. 1996. *Race traitor.* New York: Routledge.

Jacobson, Matthew Frye. 1998. *Whiteness of a different color: European immigrants and the alchemy of race.* Cambridge, MA: Harvard University Press.

Kenny, Lorraine Delia. 2000a. Doing my homework: The autoethnography of a white teenage girl. In *Racing research, researching race: Methodological dilemmas in critical race studies,* edited by France Winddance Twine and Jonathan Warren. New York: New York University Press.

_____. 2000b. *Daughters of suburbia: Growing up white, middle class, and female.* New Brunswick, NJ: Rutgers University Press.

Kinney, David A. 1993. From nerds to normals: The recovery of identity among adolescents from middle school to high school. *Sociology of Education 66* (1):21–40.

Lightfoot, Sara Lawrence. 1978. *Worlds apart: Relationships between families and schools.* New York: Basic Books.

Lipsitz, George. 1995. The possessive investment in whiteness: Racialized social democracy and the "white" problem in American studies. *American Quarterly 47* (3): 369–87.

Lott, Eric. 1993. *Love and theft: Blackface minstrelsy and the American working class.* New York: Oxford University Press.

MacLeod, Jay. 1987. *Ain't no makin' it.* Boulder, CO: Westview.

McCarthy, Cameron, and Warren Crichlow, eds. 1993. *Race, identity and representation in education.* New York: Routledge.

Morrison, Toni. 1993. *Playing in the dark: Whiteness in the literary imagination.* New York: Random House.

Oakes, Jeannie. 1985. *Keeping track: How schools structure inequality.* New Haven, CT: Yale University Press.

_____. 1994. More than a misapplied technology: A normative and political response to Hallinan on tracking. *Sociology of Education 76* (2): 84–89.

Oakes, Jeannie, and Gretchen Guiton. 1995. Matchmaking: The dynamics of high school tracking decisions. *American Educational Research Journal 32*:3–33.

Perry, Pamela. 1998. Beginning to see the white: A comparative ethnography in two high schools of the racial consciousness and identities of white youth. Ph.D. diss., University of California, Berkeley.

Pfeil, Fred. 1995. *White guys: Studies in postmodern domination and difference.* New York: Verso.

Phoenix, Ann. 1997. "I'm white! So what?" The construction of whiteness for young Londoners. In *Off white: Readings on race and power in society,* edited by Michelle Fine, Linda C. Powell, Lois Weis, and L. Mun Wong, 187–97. New York: Routledge.

Pinderhughes, Howard. 1997. *Race in the hood: Conflict and violence among urban youth.* Minneapolis: Minnesota University Press.

powell, john a. 1997. Reflections on the self: Exploring between and beyond modernity and postmodernity, *Minnesota Law Review 81* (6): 1481–1520.

Roediger, David. 1991. *The wages of whiteness: Race and the making of the American working class.* New York: Verso.

_____. 1994. *Towards the abolition of whiteness.* New York: Verso.

Rosaldo, Renato. 1989. *Culture and truth: The remaking of social analysis.* Boston: Beacon.

Rose, Tricia. 1994. *Black noise: Rap music and black culture in contemporary America.* Hanover, NH: Wesleyan University Press.

Saxton, Alexander. 1990. *The rise and fall of the white republic.* New York: Verso.

Segrest, Mab. 1994. *Memoirs of a race traitor.* Boston: South End.

Steele, Claude M., and Joshua Aronson. 1998. Stereotype threat and the test performance of academically successful African Americans. In *The black-white test score gap,* edited by Christopher Jencks and Meredith Phillips, 401–27. Washington, DC: Brookings Institution.

Thandeka. 1999. The cost of whiteness. *Tikkun 14* (3): 33–38.

Thorne, Barrie. 1993. *Gender play: Girls and boys in school.* New Brunswick, NJ: Rutgers University Press.

Twine, France Winddance. 1997. Brown-skinned white girls: Class, culture, and the construction of white identity in suburban communities. In *Displacing whiteness: Essays in social and cultural criticism,* edited by Ruth Frankenberg, 214–43. Durham, NC: Duke University Press.

Valenzuela, Angela. 1999. *Subtractive schooling: U.S.-Mexican youth and the politics of caring.* Albany: State University of New York Press.

Wallace, Michelle (a project of). 1992. *Black popular culture.* Edited by Gina Dent. Seattle, WA: Bay.

Ware, Vron. 1992. *Beyond the pale: White women, racism and history.* New York: Verso.

Wellman, David. 1977. *Portraits of white racism.* Cambridge, UK: Cambridge University Press.

Williams, David R., James S. Jackson, Tony N. Brown, Myriam Torres, Tyrone A. Forman, and Kendrick Brown. 1999. Traditional and contemporary prejudice and urban whites' support for affirmative action and government help. *Social Problems 46* (4):503–27.

Williams, Raymond. 1976. Base and superstructure in Marxist cultural theory. In *Schooling and capitalism: A sociological reader,* edited by R. Dale, 202–10. London: Routledge and Kegan Paul.

Wray, Matt, and Annalee Newitz, eds. 1997. *White trash: Race and class in America.* New York: Routledge.

NAMING EXPERIENCE

Just as we learn social attitudes and expectations from others, we also learn how to make sense of our experiences through interaction. People learn from one another what to think, feel, and expect from their experiences. Even when we experience something physical, such as illness, we talk with others about these symptoms in order to figure out what is really going on. People are sometimes surprised to learn that we don't just "know" how we are feeling. Socialization includes information for how we are expected to feel in various contexts; for example, we learn that grief is associated with death and funerals. Thus, when our emotions fit with our expectations of the situation, we are more easily able to identify and make sense of them—"My father died recently. That's why I'm feeling so sad." Oftentimes, however, we are not certain what we are feeling or why we feel a particular way that seems out of context for the situation. On these occasions, we usually talk with others (or internally to ourselves) in an effort to make sense of our experiences. It can be instructive to listen carefully to the way people help and coach one another when they are trying to define an experience. This doesn't necessarily imply that our feelings are "real." Rather, the implication is that our experiences, including feelings, only make sense to us when we are able to give them a name and categorize them.

Different groups and cultures place different emphasis on various feelings and experiences. For instance, if you are a member of a religious community, you learn to recognize and pay attention to your inner spiritual feelings. People trained in culinary arts have *learned* how to taste food and drink in more complex ways. There are cultures in which the dream experience is seen as central to social life, and people in these groups can remember and even participate lucidly in their dreams in ways that would astonish most Westerners. One of my students once did a presentation on the way in which funeral directors are trained, or socialized, in the art of guiding other people through the experience of grief while simultaneously helping them to make practical decisions such as selecting a coffin and negotiating with insurance. Each of these examples illustrates that even taken-for-granted feelings have social origins and reflect cultural values and practices. We learn to focus on and attach meaning to certain experiences based on the values of our culture and reference groups.

"Becoming a Marihuana User" is a classic sociological article written by Howard Becker in 1953. Becker observed that people who use marijuana for pleasure have to *learn* how to smoke the drug, identify its effects, and consider the effects to be pleasant. If they don't learn these things, they won't continue smoking. It's an acquired taste—acquired through interaction with others who tell you what to do and feel. This article was a social research milestone in demonstrating that even physiological experiences have to be interpreted before we can understand them and "know" how to feel about them.

"The Development of Feeling Norms Underlying Romantic Love Among Adolescent Females" explores the socialization process of *learning* to be "in love." Being in love is one of the most cherished experiences in Western culture. Yet, as Robin Simon and her

(Continued)

(Continued)

colleagues demonstrate in this article, even seemingly "normal" feelings such as love and attraction have to be learned. Based on interviews with adolescent girls in junior high, Simon and colleagues describe the social learning process through which young girls train one another to look for, recognize, and respond to feelings of attraction. This learning process includes a set of rules for acceptable and unacceptable feelings (e.g., you should only feel attraction for one person at a time and only for someone of the opposite sex).

READING QUESTIONS

1. Consider the expression, "It's a learned taste." Recall an experience in which you tried a food or activity that you didn't like at first, but now enjoy. What led you to try it again and eventually come to like it?

2. Recall an occasion when you were confused about something that happened to you or that you were feeling. With whom did you talk, and what can you remember about how that person defined the situation for you?

3. When children ask adults about sex, common first responses carry an emotional tone of shame and embarrassment. The child usually picks up the attitude that sex is a "big deal," but one that people don't talk about comfortably. Consider your own initial learning experience. When did you first become aware of "sex" (not your own sexuality, just the idea of sex)? What emotions or feelings do you associate with that experience? Were people helpful in their explanations, or did they seem embarrassed and abstract? Have subsequent experiences altered your first impressions, or do you still have the same initial feeling imprint based on your first questions?

4. Think about the last time you felt ill. How did you decide what was wrong with you?

5. Consider an occasion in which your feelings seemed "inappropriate" for the situation. Try to reconstruct the conversation you had with yourself about this experience and identify who or what made you feel your feelings were inappropriate.

20

Becoming a Marihuana User

Howard S. Becker

(1953)

The use of marihuana is and has been the focus of a good deal of attention on the part of both scientists and laymen. One of the major problems students of the practice have addressed themselves to has been the identification of those individual psychological traits which differentiate marihuana users from nonusers and which are assumed to account for the use of the drug. That approach, common in the study of behavior categorized as deviant, is based on the premise that the presence of a given kind of behavior in an individual can best be explained as the result of some trait which predisposes or motivates him to engage in the behavior.[1]

This study is likewise concerned with accounting for the presence or absence of marihuana use in an individual's behavior. It starts, however, from a different premise: that the presence of a given kind of behavior is the result of a sequence of social experiences during which the person acquires a conception of the meaning of the behavior, and perceptions and judgments of objects and situations, all of which make the activity possible and desirable. Thus, the motivation or disposition to engage in the activity is built up in the course of learning to engage in it and does not antedate this learning process. For such a view it is not necessary to identify those "traits" which "cause" the behavior. Instead, the problem becomes one of describing the set of changes in the person's conception of the activity and of the experience it provides for him.[2]

This paper seeks to describe the sequence of changes in attitude and experience which led to *the use of marihuana for pleasure.* Marihuana does not produce addiction, as do alcohol and the opiate drugs; there is no withdrawal sickness and no ineradicable craving for the drug.[3] The most frequent pattern of use might be termed "recreational." The drug is used occasionally for the pleasure the user finds in it, a relatively casual kind of behavior in comparison with that connected with the use of addicting drugs. The term "use for pleasure" is meant to emphasize the noncompulsive and casual character of the behavior. It is also meant to eliminate from consideration here those few cases in which marihuana is used for its prestige value only, as a symbol that one is a certain kind of person, with no pleasure at all being derived from its use.

The analysis presented here is conceived of as demonstrating the greater explanatory usefulness of the kind of theory outlined above as opposed

AUTHOR'S NOTE: This paper was read at the meetings of the Midwest Sociological Society in Omaha, Nebraska, April 25, 1953. The research on which this paper is based was done while I was a member of the staff of the Chicago Narcotics Survey, a study done by the Chicago Area Project, Inc., under a grant from the National Institute of Mental Health. My thanks to Solomon Kobrin, Harold Finestone, Henry McKay, and Anselm Strauss, who read and discussed with me earlier versions of this paper.

to the predispositional theories now current. This may be seen in two ways: (1) predispositional theories cannot account for that group of users (whose existence is admitted)[4] who do not exhibit the trait or traits considered to cause the behavior and (2) such theories cannot account for the great variability over time of a given individual's behavior with reference to the drug. The same person will at one stage be unable to use the drug for pleasure, at a later stage be able and willing to do so, and still later, again be unable to use it in this way. These changes, difficult to explain from a predispositional or motivational theory, are readily understandable in terms of changes in the individual's conception of the drug as is the existence of "normal" users.

The study attempted to arrive at a general statement of the sequence of changes in individual attitude and experience which have always occurred when the individual has become willing and able to use marihuana for pleasure and which have not occurred or not been permanently maintained when this is not the case. This generalization is stated in universal terms in order that negative cases may be discovered and used to revise the explanatory hypothesis.[5]

Fifty interviews with marihuana users from a variety of social backgrounds and present positions in society constitute the data from which the generalization was constructed and against which it was tested.[6] The interviews focused on the history of the person's experience with the drug, seeking major changes in his attitude toward it and in his actual use of it, and the reasons for these changes. The final generalization is a statement of that sequence of changes in attitude which occurred in every case known to me in which the person came to use marihuana for pleasure. Until a negative case is found, it may be considered as an explanation of all cases of marihuana use for pleasure. In addition, changes from use to nonuse are shown to be related to similar changes in conception, and in each case it is possible to explain variations in the individual's behavior in these terms.

This paper covers only a portion of the natural history of an individual's use of marihuana,[7] starting with the person having arrived at the point of willingness to try marihuana. He knows that others use it to "get high," but he does not know what this means in concrete terms. He is curious about the experience, ignorant of what it may turn out to be, and afraid that it may be more than he has bargained for. The steps outlined below, if he undergoes them all and maintains the attitudes developed in them, leave him willing and able to use the drug for pleasure when the opportunity presents itself.

I

The novice does not ordinarily get high the first time he smokes marihuana, and several attempts are usually necessary to induce this state. One explanation of this may be that the drug is not smoked "properly," that is, in a way that ensures sufficient dosage to produce real symptoms of intoxication. Most users agree that it cannot be smoked like tobacco if one is to get high:

> Take in a lot of air, you know, and . . . I don't know how to describe it, you don't smoke it like a cigarette, you draw in a lot of air and get it deep down in your system and then keep it there. Keep it there as long as you can.

Without the use of some such technique[8] the drug will produce no effects, and the user will be unable to get high:

> The trouble with people like that [who are not able to get high] is that they're just not smoking it right, that's all there is to it. Either they're not holding it down long enough, or they're getting too much air and not enough smoke, or the other way around or something like that. A lot of people just don't smoke it right, so naturally nothing's gonna happen.

If nothing happens, it is manifestly impossible for the user to develop a conception of the drug as an object which can be used for pleasure, and use will therefore not continue. The first step in the sequence of events that must occur if the person is to become a user is that he must learn to use the proper smoking technique in order that his use of the drug will produce some effects in terms of which his conception of it can change.

Such a change is, as might be expected, a result of the individual's participation in groups in which marihuana is used. In them the individual learns the proper way to smoke the drug. This may occur through direct teaching:

I was smoking like I did an ordinary cigarette. He said, "No, don't do it like that." He said, "Suck it, you know, draw in and hold it in your lungs till you . . . for a period of time."

I said, "Is there any limit of time to hold it?"

He said, "No, just till you feel that you want to let it out, let it out." So I did that three or four times.

Many new users are ashamed to admit ignorance and, pretending to know already, must learn through the more indirect means of observation and imitation:

I came on like I had turned on [smoked marihuana] many times before, you know. I didn't want to seem like a punk to this cat. See, like I didn't know the first thing about it—how to smoke it, or what was going to happen, or what. I just watched him like a hawk—I didn't take my eyes off him for a second, because I wanted to do everything just as he did it. I watched how he held it, how he smoked it, and everything. Then when he gave it to me I just came on cool, as though I knew exactly what the score was. I held it like he did and took a poke just the way he did.

No person continued marihuana use for pleasure without learning a technique that supplied sufficient dosage for the effects of the drug to appear. Only when this was learned was it possible for a conception of the drug as an object which could be used for pleasure to emerge. Without such a conception marihuana use was considered meaningless and did not continue.

II

Even after he learns the proper smoking technique, the new user may not get high and thus not form a conception of the drug as something which can be used for pleasure. A remark made by a user suggested the reason for this difficulty in getting high and pointed to the next necessary step on the road to being a user:

I was told during an interview, "As a matter of fact, I've seen a guy who was high out of his mind and didn't know it."

I expressed disbelief: "How can that be, man?"

The interviewee said, "Well, it's pretty strange, I'll grant you that, but I've seen it. This guy got on with me, claiming that he'd never got high, one of those guys, and he got completely stoned. And he kept insisting that he wasn't high. So I had to prove to him that he was."

What does this mean? It suggests that being high consists of two elements: the presence of symptoms caused by marihuana use and the recognition of these symptoms and their connection by the user with his use of the drug. It is not enough, that is, that the effects be present; they alone do not automatically provide the experience of being high. The user must be able to point them out to himself and consciously connect them with his having smoked marihuana before he can have this experience. Otherwise, regardless of the actual effects produced, he considers that the drug has had no effect on him: "I figured it either had no effect on me or other people were exaggerating its effect on them, you know. I thought it was probably psychological, see." Such persons believe that the whole thing is an illusion and that the wish to be high leads the user to deceive himself into believing that something is happening when, in fact, nothing is. They do not continue marihuana use, feeling that "it does nothing" for them.

Typically, however, the novice has faith (developed from his observation of users who do get high) that the drug actually will produce some new experience and continues to experiment with it until it does. His failure to get high worries him, and he is likely to ask more experienced users or provoke comments from them about it. In such conversations he is made aware of specific details of his experience which he may not have noticed or may have noticed but failed to identify as symptoms of being high:

> I didn't get high the first time . . . I don't think I held it in long enough. I probably let it out, you know, you're a little afraid. The second time I wasn't sure, and he [smoking companion] told me, like I asked him for some of the symptoms or something, how would I know, you know. . . . So he told me to sit on a stool. I sat on—I think I sat on a bar stool—and he said, "Let your feet hang," and then when I got down my feet were real cold, you know.
>
> And I started feeling it, you know. That was the first time. And then about a week after that, some-time pretty close to it, I really got on. That was the first time I got on a big laughing kick, you know. Then I really knew I was on.

One symptom of being high is an intense hunger. In the next case the novice becomes aware of this and gets high for the first time:

> They were just laughing the hell out of me because like I was eating so much. I just scoffed [ate] so much food, and they were just laughing at me, you know. Sometimes I'd be looking at them, you know, wondering why they're laughing, you know, not knowing what I was doing. [Well, did they tell you why they were laughing eventually?] Yeah, yeah, I come back, "Hey, man, what's happening?" Like, you know, like I'd ask, "What's happening?" and all of a sudden I feel weird, you know. "Man, you're on you know. You're on pot [high on marihuana]." I said, "No, am I?" Like I don't know what's happening.

The learning may occur in more indirect ways:

> I heard little remarks that were made by other people. Somebody said, "My legs are rubbery," and I can't remember all the remarks that were made

because I was very attentively listening for all these cues for what I was supposed to feel like.

The novice, then, eager to have this feeling, picks up from other users some concrete referents of the term "high" and applies these notions to his own experience. The new concepts make it possible for him to locate these symptoms among his own sensations and to point out to himself a "something different" in his experience that he connects with drug use. It is only when he can do this that he is high. In the next case, the contrast between two successive experiences of a user makes clear the crucial importance of the aware-ness of the symptoms in being high and re-emphasizes the important role of interaction with other users in acquiring the concepts that make this awareness possible:

> [Did you get high the first time you turned on?] Yeah, sure. Although, come to think of it, I guess I really didn't. I mean, like that first time it was more or less of a mild drunk. I was happy, I guess, you know what I mean. But I didn't really know I was high, you know what I mean. It was only after the second time I got high that I realized I was high the first time. Then I knew that something different was happening.
>
> [How did you know that?] How did I know? If what happened to me that night would of happened to you, you would've known, believe me. We played the first tune for almost two hours—one tune! Imagine, man! We got on the stand and played this one tune, we started at nine o'clock. When we got fin-ished I looked at my watch, it's a quarter to eleven. Almost two hours on one tune. And it didn't seem like anything. I mean, you know, it does that to you. It's like you have much more time or something. Anyway, when I saw that, man, it was too much. I knew I must really be high or something if anything like that could happen. See, and then they explained to me that that's what it did to you, you had a different sense of time and everything. So I realized that that's what it was. I knew then. Like the first time, I probably felt that way, you know, but I didn't know what's happening.

It is only when the novice becomes able to get high in this sense that he will continue to use marihuana for pleasure. In every case in which use continued, the user had acquired the necessary concepts with which to express to himself the fact that he was experiencing new sensations caused by the drug. That is, for use to continue, it is necessary not only to use the drug so as to produce effects but also to learn to perceive these effects when they occur. In this way marihuana acquires meaning for the user as an object which can be used for pleasure.

With increasing experience the user develops a greater appreciation of the drug's effects; he continues to learn to get high. He examines succeeding experiences closely, looking for new effects, making sure the old ones are still there. Out of this there grows a stable set of categories for experiencing the drug's effects whose presence enables the user to get high with ease.

The ability to perceive the drug's effects must be maintained if use is to continue; if it is lost, marihuana use ceases. Two kinds of evidence support this statement. First, people who become heavy users of alcohol, barbiturates, or opiates do not continue to smoke marihuana, largely because they lose the ability to distinguish between its effects and those of the other drugs.[9] They no longer know whether the marihuana gets them high. Second, in those few cases in which an individual uses marihuana in such quantities that he is always high, he is apt to get this same feeling that the drug has no effect on him, since the essential element of a noticeable difference between feeling high and feeling normal is missing. In such a situation, use is likely to be given up completely, but temporarily, in order that the user may once again be able to perceive the difference.

III

One more step is necessary if the user who has now learned to get high is to continue use. He must learn to enjoy the effects he has just learned to experience. Marihuana—produced sensations are not automatically or necessarily pleasurable. The taste for such experience is a socially acquired one, not different in kind from acquired tastes for oysters or dry martinis. The user feels dizzy, thirsty; his scalp tingles; he misjudges time and distances; and so on. Are these things pleasurable? He isn't sure. If he is to continue marihuana use, he must decide that they are. Otherwise, getting high, while a real enough experience, will be an unpleasant one he would rather avoid.

The effects of the drug, when first perceived, may be physically unpleasant or at least ambiguous:

> It started taking effect, and I didn't know what was happening, you know, what it was, and I was very sick. I walked around the room, walking around the room trying to get off, you know; it just scared me at first, you know. I wasn't used to that kind of feeling.

In addition, the novice's naive interpretation of what is happening to him may further confuse and frighten him, particularly if he decides, as many do, that he is going insane:

> I felt I was insane, you know. Everything people done to me just wigged me. I couldn't hold a conversation, and my mind would be wandering, and I was always thinking, oh, I don't know, weird things, like hearing music different. . . . I get the feeling that I can't talk to anyone. I'll goof completely.

Given these typically frightening and unpleasant first experiences, the beginner will not continue use unless he learns to redefine the sensations as pleasurable:

> It was offered to me, and I tried it. I'll tell you one thing. I never did enjoy it at all. I mean it was just nothing that I could enjoy. [Well, did you get high when you turned on?] Oh, yeah, I got definite feelings from it. But I didn't enjoy them. I mean I got plenty of reactions, but they were mostly reactions of fear. [You were frightened?] Yes, I didn't enjoy it.

I couldn't seem to relax with it, you know. If you can't relax with a thing, you can't enjoy it, I don't think.

In other cases the first experiences were also definitely unpleasant, but the person did become a marihuana user. This occurred, however, only after a later experience enabled him to redefine the sensations as pleasurable:

[This man's first experience was extremely unpleasant, involving distortion of spatial relationships and sounds, violent thirst, and panic produced by these symptoms.] After the first time I didn't turn on for about, I'd say, ten months to a year. . . . It wasn't a moral thing; it was because I'd gotten so frightened, bein' so high. An' I didn't want to go through that again, I mean, my reaction was, "Well, if this is what they call bein' high, I don't dig [like] it." . . . So I didn't turn on for a year almost, accounta that. . . .

Well, my friends started, an' consequently I started again. But I didn't have any more, I didn't have that same initial reaction, after I started turning on again.

[In interaction with his friends he became able to find pleasure in the effects of the drug and eventually became a regular user.]

In no case will use continue without such a redefinition of the effects as enjoyable.

This redefinition occurs, typically, in interaction with more experienced users who, in a number of ways, teach the novice to find pleasure in this experience which is at first so frightening.[10] They may reassure him as to the temporary character of the unpleasant sensations and minimize their seriousness, at the same time calling attention to the more enjoyable aspects. An experienced user describes how he handles newcomers to marihuana use:

Well, they get pretty high sometimes. The average person isn't ready for that, and it is a little frightening to them sometimes. I mean, they've been high on lush [alcohol], and they get higher that way than they've ever been before, and they don't know what's happening to them. Because they think

they're going to keep going up, up, up till they lose their minds or begin doing weird things or something. You have to like reassure them, explain to them that they're not really flipping or anything, that they're gonna be all right. You have to just talk them out of being afraid. Keep talking to them, reassuring, telling them it's all right. And come on with your own story, you know: "The same thing happened to me. You'll get to like that after awhile." Keep coming on like that; pretty soon you talk them out of being scared. And besides they see you doing it and nothing horrible is happening to you, so that gives them more confidence.

The more experienced user may also teach the novice to regulate the amount he smokes more carefully, so as to avoid any severely uncomfortable symptoms while retaining the pleasant ones. Finally, he teaches the new user that he can "get to like it after awhile." He teaches him to regard those ambiguous experiences formerly defined as unpleasant as enjoyable. The older user in the following incident is a person whose tastes have shifted in this way, and his remarks have the effect of helping others to make a similar redefinition:

A new user had her first experience of the effects of marihuana and became frightened and hysterical. She "felt like she was half in and half out of the room" and experienced a number of alarming physical symptoms. One of the more experienced users present said, "She's dragged because she's high like that. I'd give anything to get that high myself. I haven't been that high in years."

In short, what was once frightening and distasteful becomes, after a taste for it is built up, pleasant, desired, and sought after. Enjoyment is introduced by the favorable definition of the experience that one acquires from others. Without this, use will not continue, for marihuana will not be for the user an object he can use for pleasure.

In addition to being a necessary step in becoming a user, this represents an important condition for continued use. It is quite common for experienced users suddenly to have an unpleasant or frightening experience, which they cannot define as pleasurable, either because they have used a larger amount of marihuana than usual or because it turns out to be a higher-quality marihuana than they expected. The user has sensations which go beyond any conception he has of what being high is and is in much the same situation as the novice, uncomfortable and frightened. He may blame it on an overdose and simply be more careful in the future. But he may make this the occasion for a rethinking of his attitude toward the drug and decide that it no longer can give him pleasure. When this occurs and is not followed by a redefinition of the drug as capable of producing pleasure, use will cease.

The likelihood of such a redefinition occurring depends on the degree of the individual's participation with other users. Where this participation is intensive, the individual is quickly talked out of his feeling against marihuana use. In the next case, on the other hand, the experience was very disturbing, and the aftermath of the incident cut the person's participation with other users to almost zero. Use stopped for three years and began again only when a combination of circumstances, important among which was a resumption of ties with users, made possible a redefinition of the nature of the drug:

It was too much, like I only made about four pokes, and I couldn't even get it out of my mouth, I was so high, and I got real flipped. In the basement, you know, I just couldn't stay in there anymore. My heart was pounding real hard, you know, and I was going out of my mind; I thought I was losing my mind completely. So I cut out of this basement, and this other guy, he's out of his mind, told me, "Don't, don't leave me, man. Stay here." And I couldn't.

I walked outside, and it was five below zero, and I thought I was dying, and I had my coat open; I was sweating. I was perspiring. My whole insides were all . . . , and I walked about two blocks away,

and I fainted behind a bush. I don't know how long I laid there. I woke up, and I was feeling the worst, I can't describe it at all, so I made it to a bowling alley, man, and I was trying to act normal, I was trying to shoot pool, you know, trying to act real normal, and I couldn't lay and I couldn't stand up and I couldn't sit down, and I went up and laid down where some guys that spot pins lay down, and that didn't help me, and I went down to a doctor's office. I was going to go in there and tell the doctor to put me out of my misery . . . because my heart was pounding so hard, you know. . . . So then all weekend I started flipping, seeing things there and going through hell, you know, all kinds of abnormal things. . . . I just quit for a long time then.

[He went to a doctor who defined the symptoms for him as those of a nervous breakdown caused by "nerves" and "worries." Although he was no longer using marihuana, he had some recurrences of the symptoms which led him to suspect that "it was all his nerves."] So I just stopped worrying, you know; so it was about thirty-six months later I started making it again. I'd just take a few pokes, you know. [He first resumed use in the company of the same user-friend with whom he had been involved in the original incident.]

A person, then, cannot begin to use marihuana for pleasure, or continue its use for pleasure, unless he learns to define its effects as enjoyable, unless it becomes and remains an object which he conceived of as capable of producing pleasure.

IV

In summary, an individual will be able to use marihuana for pleasure only when he goes through a process of learning to conceive of it as an object which can be used in this way. No one becomes a user without (1) learning to smoke the drug in a way which will produce real effects; (2) learning to recognize the effects and connect them with drug use (learning, in other words, to get high); and (3) learning to enjoy the sensations he perceives. In the course of this process he develops a disposition or motivation to use marihuana which was not and could not have been present when he began use, for it involves and depends on conceptions of the drug which could only grow out of the kind of actual experience detailed above. On completion of this process he is willing and able to use marihuana for pleasure.

He has learned, in short, to answer "Yes" to the question: "Is it fun?" The direction his further use of the drug takes depends on his being able to continue to answer "Yes" to this question and, in addition, on his being able to answer "Yes" to other questions which arise as he becomes aware of the implications of the fact that the society as a whole disapproves of the practice: "Is it expedient?" "Is it moral?" Once he has acquired the ability to get enjoyment out of the drug, use will continue to be possible for him. Considerations of morality and expediency, occasioned by the reactions of society, may interfere and inhibit use, but use continues to be a possibility in terms of his conception of the drug. The act becomes impossible only when the ability to enjoy the experience of being high is lost, through a change in the user's conception of the drug occasioned by certain kinds of experience with it.

In comparing this theory with those which ascribe marihuana use to motives or predispositions rooted deep in individual behavior, the evidence makes it clear that marihuana use for pleasure can occur only when the process described above is undergone and cannot occur without it. This is apparently so without reference to the nature of the individual's personal makeup, or psychic problems. Such theories assume that people have stable modes of response which predetermine the way they will act in relation to any particular situation or object and that, when they come in contact with the given object or situation, they act in the way in which their makeup predisposes them.

This analysis of the genesis of marihuana use shows that the individuals who come in contact with a given object may respond to it at first in a great variety of ways. If a stable form of new behavior toward the object is to emerge, a transformation of meanings must occur, in which the person develops a new conception of the nature of the object.[11] This happens in a series of communicative acts in which others point out new aspects of his experience to him, present him with new interpretations of events, and help him achieve a new conceptual organization of his world, without which the new behavior is not possible. Persons who do not achieve the proper kind of conceptualization are unable to engage in the given behavior and turn off in the direction of some other relationship to the object or activity.

This suggests that behavior of any kind might fruitfully be studied developmentally, in terms of changes in meanings and concepts, their organization and reorganization, and the way they channel behavior, making some acts possible while excluding others.

NOTES

1. See, as examples of this approach, the following: E. Marcovitz & H. J. Meyers (1944, December), "The marihuana addict in the army," *War Medicine, 6,* 382–391; H. S. Gaskill (1945, September), "Marihuana, an intoxicant," *American Journal of Psychiatry, 102,* 202–204; S. Charen & L. Perelman (1946, March), "Personality studies of marihuana addicts," *American Journal of Psychiatry, 102,* 674–682.

2. This approach stems from George Herbert Mead's (1934) discussion of objects in *Mind, self, and society,* Chicago: University of Chicago Press, pp. 277–280.

3. Cf. R. Adams (1942, November), "Marihuana," *Bulletin of the New York Academy of Medicine, 18,* 705–730.

4. Cf. L. Kolb (1938, July), "Marihuana," *Federal Probation, 2,* 22–25; and W. Bromberg (1939, July 1), "Marihuana: A psychiatric study," *Journal of the American Medical Association, 113,* 11.

essential for identifying not only the content of feeling norms that underlie romantic love, but also the processes through which these norms are developed and conveyed in day-to-day interaction. Also, by examining daily speech activities we can examine how emotion norms and beliefs are reflected in actual discourse. Without this level of analysis, it is easy to assume greater conformity to emotion norms than actually exists. Finally, our analysis of field notes helps us identify certain feeling norms which are so taken for granted that they are no longer regarded as constraints.

Although data from all of the groups were analyzed for this paper, some groups of girls were more interested in romance and had more contact with boys than others. Among the girls who had romantic interests, relationships with boys varied considerably. In fact, at this school, the term "going together" was used widely by both girls and boys to refer to a variety of romantic relationships, ranging from those which lasted several months to those which lasted one or two days. In some cases, the girl and the boy spent their lunch period together; in others, the couple had minimal contact at school.* In most cases, the relationships were brief (less than two weeks) and were limited to some social contact at school, which sometimes included expressions of affection such as hand holding and kissing. . . .

FEELING NORMS UNDERLYING ROMANTIC LOVE IN ADOLESCENT FEMALE PEER CULTURE

We begin with the observation that romantic love was a frequent topic of conversation among the female students. By the seventh grade, most of the girls at the school had become concerned with romance and had begun to form relationships with boys. While the girls were obtaining normative information about romantic love, the feelings and behavior that group members considered appropriate were still in the process of negotiation. Some feeling norms were generally accepted; others were not shared by all group members. An examination of the girls' talk about romantic love revealed that they used a variety of discourse strategies to communicate normative information and clarify feeling norms.

Norm 1: Romantic relationships should be important, but not everything in life. Previous research shows that white adolescent females tend to embrace traditional feminine concerns of romance, marriage, and domesticity and to reject both academic and athletic values (Eder 1985; Griffin 1985; Kessler et al. 1985; Lever 1978; McRobbie 1978). Although romance was salient to most of the girls in this study, group members had mixed attitudes about the importance of relationships with boys in relation to their other interests and activities. Some girls thought "they could not live without boys"; others believed that "learning about themselves and their schoolwork" was primary (interview, eighth-grade group, March 30, 1983). Concerns about the relative importance of romantic love required the development of a feeling norm among adolescent females.

One such norm that had begun to emerge in some peer groups was that romantic relationships should be important, but not everything in life. Many seventh- and eighth-grade girls agreed that relationships with boys were important. Group members, however, also were becoming critical of friends who were perceived as "boy-crazy," a term used by adolescents to describe girls who made boys their primary interest and activity. As the following two examples illustrate, this norm still was being negotiated when the girls were in the eighth grade.

---

*Often the best friend of the girl and of the boy arranged these relationships by contacting the interested parties over the telephone, so that the couple might not have had much direct contact either before or after they started "going together."

In the first example, one group of girls debates the relative importance of romantic relationships. This exchange was part of an in-depth group interview about romance novels, which many eighth-grade girls liked to read. Ellen, Hanna, Natalie, Peg, and Tricia* had been discussing why they liked reading romance novels when the researcher asked them how important romantic love was to them. Ellen began by expressing her view that boys are the most important thing in her life, a view that runs counter to the emerging feeling norm.

1.	Ellen:	Boys [are] the most important thing in my life. That's what I
2.		marked on my value chart today.
3.	Hanna:	Yes. I know.
4.	Researcher:	Why? Why are boys the most important / / thing?
5.	Hanna:	Boys, um (pleasure)
6.	Ellen:	You can't live without 'em!
7.	Natalie:	You can't live / / with 'em and you can't live without 'em!
8.	Peg:	You can't live with 'em.
9.	Ellen:	You can too.
10.	Tricia:	That's / / a matter of opinion.
11.	Ellen:	There is no way—there is no way a girl could live her
12.		whole life without a boy.
13.	Tricia:	I can.
14.	Ellen:	You can live your whole life without a boy?
15.	Tricia:	Yeah. / / I'm not goin' to, though.
16.	Peg:	Uh uh!
17.	Ellen:	(be isolated) you never kissed one or nothin'.
18.	Natalie:	Lesbies can.
19.	Researcher:	That's true.
20.	Tricia:	You wouldn't know, Natalie. ((laughing)) (interview, eighth grade, March 30).

*All names are pseudonyms. The following notations are used in the examples from transcripts:

( ) refers to an uncertain or unclear utterance or speaker;

(( )) refers to nonverbal behavior;

// refers to the point at which the next speaker begins talking during someone else's turn;

/1/ first interruption; /2/ second interruption;

refers to a brief pause.

In this example it is clear that group members had conflicting views about the relative importance of romance, and expressed their opinions openly. Yet even though the girls engaged in a normative debate, they expressed conflict in a playful, nonserious way. Rather than responding defensively to Ellen's question in Line 14, Tricia said teasingly that even though she could live without boys, she was not going to do so. In Line 18, Natalie's substitution of the word "lesbies" for lesbians contributes to the playfulness of this exchange.

Whereas normative debates often were carried out in a playful and joking manner, conflict exchanges over normative issues were sometimes quite serious. This was especially true when lighter disputes were unsuccessful at producing normative consensus, as in the next example. The following exchange was part of the same group interview. At this point Ellen not only had stated repeatedly that boys were her central interest, but also had been flirting with some boys at a nearby table.

1.	Researcher:	What about you, Tricia? How do you feel / / about it all?
2.	Peg:	Ellen, / / I'm only teasin', gosh! ((singsong voice))
3.	Tricia:	I feel the same way that Peg does. Especially now when
4.		we're just about to go into high school, our grades are more
5.		important than / / boys.
6.	Natalie:	See, we may be friends / / with them, but we're not sluts.
7.	Researcher:	Um hum, ((to Tricia))
8.	Hanna:	Will you repeat that, please? ((angry voice))
9.	Tricia:	No, /1/ you /2/ don't qualify.
10.	Natalie:	/1/ I know, but we're not sluts.
11.	Ellen:	/2/ ( ) fuck you (you guys))! ((Ellen stomps off, angry
12.		and upset)) (interview, eighth grade, March 30).

In both examples, the girls' openly expressed their conflicting views about the relative importance of romance and clarified this feeling norm to group members. In the second example, however, the conflict escalated and became more serious and more heated. Tricia and Peg became annoyed when the emerging norm was violated repeatedly, and engaged in confrontations when their friends' attitudes and behaviors did not match their expectations. In Lines 6 and 10, for example, Natalie accuses violators of this norm of being "sluts." Responses to norm violations are important ways in which group members develop and communicate knowledge about interpersonal and interactional norms (Eder and Sanford 1986; Mehan 1979). Although conflict was not resolved in either of these exchanges, the girls learned through these debates what their friends viewed as appropriate and inappropriate feeling and behavior with respect to this norm. Romantic love was a salient emotion for most of these girls, but several were concerned with setting some limits on its importance.

The Object of Romantic Feelings

According to Gordon (1981, p. 567), "sentiments," such as romantic love, are feelings that are "organized around a relationship to a social object, usually another person." While the girls were developing a norm about the relative importance of romance, they also were acquiring cultural knowledge about the object of romance. In fact, by the eighth grade, three norms concerning the object of romantic feelings had emerged.

Norm 2: One should have romantic feelings only for someone of the opposite sex. The most basic feeling norm concerning the object of romance was that one should have romantic feelings only for someone of the opposite sex. By the time they had become actively interested in romance, a norm of heterosexuality had developed in these groups of girls. In contrast to the previously discussed feeling norm, there was considerable consensus for this norm. In view of the general negative view of homosexuality at the school and the label attached to alleged norm violators, it is not surprising that this norm was widely accepted. We found that the girls used a variety of discourse strategies to clarify and reinforce the norm of heterosexuality to friends. The way in which this norm was communicated depended upon whether alleged norm violators were nongroup or group members.

One way in which the norm of heterosexuality was communicated was through gossip about nongroup members' deviant affect and behavior. Girls who did not express romantic interest in boys or who had gender-atypical interests often were the targets of gossip. For example, Sandy and Paula were discussing Sandy's sister in the sixth grade, who did not share their romantic interest in boys and who was interested in sports and in becoming a mechanic.

Sandy said her sister is extremely different from her and has absolutely no interest in boys—she considers boys pests. Sandy referred to her sister as a tomboy. She said that since her sister is a tomboy, if she liked boys then she would be queer, but on the other hand, if she liked girls then she would really be queer. Then Paula added jokingly that if she didn't like anyone at all she would still be queer. I [researcher] said, "It sounds like she doesn't have a chance" (field notes, seventh grade, May 24).

This example shows that Sandy and Paula were reinforcing a feeling norm of which they had only limited understanding. Girls at this school were establishing violations of the norm of heterosexuality on the basis of gender-inappropriate behavior. Sandy's sister's outward disinterest in boys as well as her nontraditional interests and behaviors were considered by these group members to be deviant with regard to the norm of heterosexuality. Yet, by establishing violations of this norm on the basis of nonstereotypical gender-role behavior, the girls were reinforcing and reproducing existing gender norms that ultimately constrain their own behavior.

In general, it was not uncommon for girls and boys who were not actively pursuing romantic relationships or who routinely engaged in gender-inappropriate behavior to be labeled homosexual. In fact, children at the school who were perceived to be deviant in other ways were the objects of these allegations as well (Evans and Eder 1989). Unpopular students who were viewed as unattractive and/or unintelligent also were singled out for group discussions in which they were accused indirectly of being homosexual.

Annie said, "I'm gonna beat that girl up someday," referring to twins and a little chubby girl in a green sweater who were sitting at the middle of the table pretty far down. So we all turned to look at her and Marsha agreed that she was really disgusting, that "they're gay" (field notes, seventh grade, February 3).

Rather than relying on the display of romantic feelings toward someone of the same sex as an indication of affective deviance, Annie and Marsha accused these girls of being "gay" solely on the basis of physical appearance.

A second way in which the norm of heterosexuality was communicated was by teasing group members. Humor often was used when the girls confronted their friends about norm violations. Group members frequently teased one another about behaviors that could be interpreted as homosexual, such as close physical contact between friends. Although many girls still viewed close physical contact between friends as acceptable, others were beginning to redefine such expressions of affection as inappropriate.

> The little girl with glasses came over and actually sat on Andrea's lap. She's so tiny that she can do this easily, and Andrea laughed and said, "You're really not my type" (field notes, sixth grade, May 20).

Not only did the girls tease one another about overt expressions of affection, they also chided one another about their actual feelings. Statements concerning both positive and negative affect for females were a frequent source of group humor.

> . . . they were talking about why would somebody like this particular girl. Debby said, "I wouldn't like her!" Melinda said, "Well, I should *hope* not" (field notes, eighth grade, April 20).

In addition to teasing one another about their feelings and behaviors, group members also chided each other about their best-friend relationships. In fact, adolescence is a period in which female friendships are faced with a dilemma. Even while intimate feelings between close friends usually deepen, girls routinely tease one another about the romantic implications of these relationships.

> Julie said something about how Bonnie and somebody were considered her best mates. Right away Mia said, "Ooooh . . ." as this sort of implied that they were gay. Hillary picked up on that and went "Ooooh!" (field notes, eighth grade, April 9).

The final way in which the norm of heterosexuality was communicated was through self-denial.

Self-denials often were used to clarify the nature of intimate female friendships. Although many girls at the school continued to have strong positive feelings for their female friends, verbal and behavioral expressions of affection frequently were followed by a disclaimer. In light of the pressures for heterosexuality from peers and the seriousness of norm violations, it is not surprising that many girls at the school became quite concerned that their own feelings and behaviors towards their close friends might be perceived by others as homosexual.

> Sally was really talkative today, and it was interesting to see her being so talkative. She was going on and on about how somebody would sign her letters "love you queerly." She said, "I always sign my letters 'love you dearly, but not queerly.'" But then she was joking, saying, "I didn't know what that meant," until Mary explained it to her. Then they were joking about how innocent she was and didn't even know what "queer" meant (field notes, seventh grade, March 3).

Whereas self-denials often were humorous, denials of affective deviance with respect to the norm of heterosexuality sometimes were quite serious. The girls were especially self-conscious about expressions of affection that were overt and therefore readily observable. They were concerned that nongroup members would misinterpret these visible signs of affection as romantic.

> Alice told me that she had taken a bunch of photographs recently. She said it was embarrassing because most of the pictures were taken when people happened to be hugging and kissing each other, and that she hoped she got hold of the pictures before her mother did when they got back from being developed. She said, for example, "Natalie and another girl were hugging each other in friendship" (which meant that she wanted me to know that that was differentiated from a romantic hug) (field notes, eighth grade, February 7).

Not only was Alice embarrassed by the hugging and kissing in the photographs, but she also was concerned that if her mother saw the pictures, she might interpret these actions as homosexual. By distinguishing between a "friendship" hug and a "romantic" hug, however, Alice clarified both to herself and to the researcher that this behavior was within the realm of acceptable conduct.

Overall the norm of heterosexuality was communicated among adolescent females through gossip, teasing, and self-denials. In these discussions, group members collectively explored what does and does not constitute homosexual feeling and behavior in order to develop an understanding of this feeling norm and of norm violations. Through these discussions, however, the girls not only expressed their own homophobic concerns but also supported and maintained the broader cultural norm of heterosexuality. Many girls at the school continued to value intimate relationships with females; nevertheless they upheld and reproduced what Rich (1980) called "the norm of compulsory heterosexuality."

Norm 3: One should not have romantic feelings for a boy who is already attached. Another feeling norm that had emerged in regard to the object of romance was that one should not have romantic feelings for a boy who is already attached. A corollary of this norm was that if one had such feelings, they should not be expressed. In most groups, the development of this norm was a direct response to changes in group members' romantic activities.

The norm of exclusivity had only minimal relevance during an earlier phase, when the girls were first becoming interested in romance, but this norm had become highly salient by the time they began to form relationships with boys.

Early in the seventh grade, most of the girls talked about the boys they liked,* but often were shy about letting boys know their feelings. As long as romantic activities consisted of only talking about the objects of their affection, the norm of exclusivity had little significance. In fact, during this stage in the development of their romantic activities, it was not uncommon for many group members to like the same boy. Just as they might have other interests in common, sharing a romantic interest in a particular boy was considered to be acceptable, if not appropriate.

> Interestingly enough, Marsha and Josephine talked about how they both liked this guy Jack. They pointed him out to me and I [researcher] said, "Oh, oh, you both like the same guy?" They said, "Oh yeah, it's okay. We can do that. We always like the same people, but we don't get mad at each other" (field notes, seventh grade, March 30).

In an interview with another group of seventh-grade girls, it became clear that the distinction between *liking* and *going with* the same boy is important. The former is permissible; the latter is not.

1.	Carrie:	They can like, like, like as much as they want, but they
2.		don't / / (go)
3.	Marla:	They don't two-time!
4.	Researcher:	But what?
5.	Carrie:	They can like a person as much as they want.
6.	Researcher:	Can two friends *go* together / / with the same boy?
7.	(Alice):	Oh, they don't have any choice / / (they)
8.	Carrie:	No.
9.	Bonnie:	No (interview, seventh grade, May 24).

---

*Although Zick Rubin's (1970, 1973) research shows that "liking" and "loving" are distinct emotional states, the girls in this study used these emotion words interchangeably, especially when referring to their romantic feelings for boys.

Throughout this year, many girls began to pursue boys openly and to make their feelings more public, often through a friend who served as an intermediary. Once a group member had acted openly on her feelings and formed a relationship with a boy, it was no longer acceptable for other girls either to have or to express romantic feelings for him. At this point in the development of their romantic activities, the norm of exclusivity had become highly salient, and violations began to be perceived as a serious threat. Most of the girls became concerned about violations; they were resentful and jealous of those who did not abide by the norm of exclusivity.

Gossip was one way in which the girls clarified and reinforced this norm. In the following example from a seventh-grade interview, Natalie is accusing Rhoda, an attractive group member, of flirting with her and Tricia's boyfriends.

1.	Natalie:	Rhoda, every time I get a boyfriend or Tricia gets a boyfriend
2.		# or we like somebody, she starts # y'know messing around
3.		with him and everything and # y'know—and everything, she
4.		shows her ass off and so, they start *likin'* her, right? And she
5.		did that, she was trying to do that to Sammy Jones #
6.		Tricia's boyfriend # ya know, the one that broke up with her
7.		after four months (interview, seventh grade, May 24).

Although gossip episodes such as this do not inform norm violators about the deviant nature of their behavior, they communicate normative information to other group members (Eder and Enke 1988; Fine 1986; Goodwin 1980).

The girls considered it inappropriate to have or express romantic feelings not only for a boy who was involved with someone else, but also for a boy whom a group member was in the process of pursuing. Group members sometimes engaged in confrontations with alleged norm violators in order to communicate their inappropriate behavior and affect. In the next exchange, several members of a seventh-grade group directly accuse Carol of flirting with Ted, a boy Betty is pursuing but not currently going with. Although Carol argues initially that she has not done anything wrong, later she agrees to be an intermediary for Betty in order to resolve the dispute.

1.	Mary:	Ted came up to Carol and said she—that he loved her.
2.	Linda:	Who?
3.	Betty:	*Carol!*
4.	Carol:	What?
5.	Betty:	I don't like you no more.
6.	Carol:	What'd I do?

(Continued)

(Continued)

7.	Linda:	Taking Betty's boyfriend.
8.	Carol:	I didn't either! ((pounds table as she half laughs))
9.	Mary:	It wasn't Carol's *fault*, though.
10.	Betty:	*Yes it was!* She *flirts!*
11.	Carol:	I was just walking there / / ( ).
12.	Betty:	You *flirt.* You *flirt.* Yes, you / /
13.	Carol:	I didn't even do nothing. ((laughter))
14.	Betty:	You *flirt*, Carol! You're mean! I don't like you no more.
15.	Carol:	You won't (mind me) after I get done talking # *if* you still
16.		want me to.
17.	Betty:	Huh?
18.	Carol:	If you—do you want me to still talk to him? / / ((Betty
19.		nods)) Alright, shut up. God.
20.	Nancy:	Hell, she called me up, she goes, "Nancy, call Ted and talk to
21.		him."
22.	Betty:	(I sank you) ((silly voice)) (taped conversation, seventh grade, May 5).

This example is interesting because it shows that these girls expect their friends to know not only with whom they are going, but also their *intentions* to become romantically involved with certain boys. Acceptable contact with these boys is limited to behavior that will promote their friends' romantic interests (e.g., serving as intermediaries), and excludes any friendly behavior that might encourage romantic feelings to develop. As shown in the previous example, such behavior makes a girl subject to the negative label "flirt."* It is also noteworthy that group members use confrontations such as this to sanction inappropriate behavior and affect. Because violations of the norm of exclusivity have serious consequences for group members, including the possibility of being in competition with friends over boys, it is not surprising that confrontations sometimes are used to clarify and reinforce this norm.

Although most group members increasingly saw the need for the norm of exclusivity to protect themselves from unpleasant feelings of jealousy, some girls were reluctant to give up the freedom to have or express romantic feelings whenever they desired. Because norm violations were viewed as serious, girls who continued to defy this

---

*The label "flirt" has a double meaning among adolescent females. Whereas the term sometimes is used to describe girls who express romantic feelings toward a group member's boyfriend, it is also used to describe girls who express romantic feelings for more than one boy. In the previous example, the girls used it in the former sense. Like the labels "gay" and "slut," the girls also use the label "flirt" to refer to an emotional social type. Emotional social types are persons who routinely violate emotion norms and who serve as examples in correcting young people's feeling and/or expression. See Gordon (1989) for a discussion of the functions of the emotional social type in childhood emotional socialization.

norm occasionally engaged in playful modes of interaction whereby they could express their "deviant" feelings while acknowledging the norm of exclusivity.

For example, several seventh-grade girls were teasing Mary about "liking" Wally and dragged her over to the ball diamond, where Wally was playing softball. The teasing consisted of trying to get Mary to talk with him and telling Wally that Mary wanted to "go in the stairwell" with him. Mary refused to talk to Wally. This reaction led to some joking exchanges among the other group members, several of whom also had romantic feelings for Wally.

1.	Carol:	I'll take him if you don't.
2.	Elaine:	Whoo! You hear that one, Wally?
3.	Carol:	Well, I don't care.
4.	Elaine:	Wally, Wally, Wally, Wally. She says she'll take
5.		ya if Mary don't want ya. ((Unrelated talk for
6.		five turns.))
7.	Elaine:	She said she'd take ya if Mary don't want ya.
8.	Mary:	What'd you tell him Elaine? Elaine / / ( )
9.	Linda:	Hey you! If Mary don't want ya and Carol don't
10.		want ya, I'll take ya!
11.	Carol:	Uh uh, I will. I'll take him if Mary don't and
12.		then if I don't, you do (taped conversation, seventh grade, April 7).

Here the girls use playful teasing to inform Wally of their romantic feelings, while acknowledging at the same time that they will wait to act on these feelings until Mary no longer "wants" him. The joking nature of this exchange provides these girls with more freedom to express their feelings for Wally and thus to violate the norm of exclusivity.*

This finding suggests that feeling and expression norms do not determine adolescent girls' affect and behavior, but serve as an important cultural resource which is incorporated into their action. Through expressing their knowledge of this norm, in fact, these girls succeed in expressing their feelings for a boy who is being pursued by a friend. At the same time, their ability to transform cultural knowledge into a playful frame gives them an opportunity to violate the norm without negative sanctions.

In brief, when group members began to pursue boys and form romantic relationships, the girls developed the norm of exclusivity to deal with their new concerns. They communicated this norm through gossip and confrontations as well as in more playful modes of discourse. Yet even though norm violations were viewed negatively by most of the girls, several group members did not feel compelled to abide by this norm. Instead they responded with "resistance" by continuing to hold and express romantic feelings for boys who were already "taken." In some cases their resistance was communicated through playful teasing, which

*Although an alternative interpretation of this exchange is that the girls actually are supporting Mary's romantic interest rather than violating the norm of exclusivity, ethnographic data on these girls show that several of them in fact had romantic feelings for Wally. Because Mary was somewhat overweight, the girls did not take her interest in him seriously.

allowed them to express their normatively inappropriate feelings while simultaneously showing their awareness of the norm of exclusivity.

Norm 4: One should have romantic feelings for only one boy at a time. The third feeling norm pertaining to the object of romance was that one should have romantic feelings for only one boy at a time. A corollary was that if one had romantic feelings for more than one boy, these feelings should not be expressed. In some groups, the development of the norm of monogamy reflected the girls' awareness of the societal norm of monogamy. In other groups, however, this norm was developed to deal with the problems created by having multiple boyfriends.

For example, when we asked one group of seventh-grade girls about the possibility of going with more than one person at a time, the reason they gave for avoiding this behavior was the likelihood of creating jealousy among boyfriends. Because jealousy and other forms of conflict among males were expressed frequently in physical fights, the consequences of creating jealousy were considered to be quite serious.

I asked if you could only go with one person at a time and she said, "It depends on who you're talking about." She said that you should only go with one at a time but that some girls went with more than one. I asked why they shouldn't do that, and she said because "then you get a couple of jealous boyfriends on your hands" and they might end up getting into a fight, and that it was best to avoid that (field notes, seventh grade, April 27).

Some girls continued to have multiple boyfriends, but were careful to become involved only with boys who were separated geographically. As long as a boy was unaware of his girlfriend's other romantic involvements, jealousy and its negative consequences could be avoided. For some of these girls, in fact, having multiple boyfriends was a source of status—something they bragged about to their female friends.

Effie and Laura had a long conversation. Laura told Effie that she was going with two guys, one from Royalton and another from California. She said that they were both going to be coming down this summer and she didn't know what to do. She presented this as a dilemma, but she was laughing about it. She really wanted to show that she was popular with boys (field notes, eighth grade, April 6).

Although some groups developed the norm of monogamy to deal with the practical problems associated with having multiple boyfriends, in other groups the development of this norm reflected group members' knowledge of the cultural norm of monogamy. When we asked one group of seventh-grade girls whether two people could go with the same boy, their response turned to the inappropriateness of having multiple romantic partners.

1.	Researcher:	How come two people can't go with the same boy at the same
2.		time? It seems like you could logi—
3.	Ellen:	Because you're only supposed to—when you go with a person
4.		like if you
5.	Natalie:	It's like a bigamist.
6.	Ellen:	Oh . . .
7.	Natalie:	You know, when you
8.	Ellen:	Like a what?
9.	Natalie:	A bigamist. Like when you go with somebody. Like it's, it's
10.	Ellen:	Two-timing.

11.	Natalie:	When you go with each other the same—when you go with each
12.		other it's kinda like gettin' married or somethin', you
13.		know, and like if you're goin' with two people at the same
14.		time it's like a bigamist.
15.	Ellen:	Like Natalie did!
16.	Natalie:	Yeah, I did that once.
17.	Ellen:	Yeah, with Steve and Robert.
18.	Natalie:	I did it twice. ((Natalie and Ellen burst out laughing)) (interview, seventh grade, May 24).

This example illustrates that the girls are drawing on their knowledge of the societal norm of monogamy (which pertains to marriage) in order to develop a feeling norm regarding multiple partners which is relevant to their own romantic relationships. The exchange also shows that even though these girls agreed that it was inappropriate to have romantic feelings for more than one boy at a time, violations of this norm were not perceived as serious.

By the time these girls were in eighth grade, however, having romantic feelings for more than one boy was no longer viewed as acceptable. Moreover, they used different strategies to clarify this norm and to sanction deviant affect and behavior. In the following exchange, Ellen and Hanna are telling the other girls about what happened at church the night before. Because Ellen is already going with Craig, she is first accused and later reprimanded for going to church solely to meet other boys.

1.	Ellen:	We were sittin' there startin' at guys at church last night,
2.		me and Hanna were, and—
3.	Hanna:	And she saw one that looked just like Craig.
4.	Natalie:	But # / / I was—
5.	Ellen:	I wasn't starin' at him.
6.	Hanna:	That was groaty.
7.	(Natalie:)	You're going with Craig.
8.	Ellen:	I know. I stared at Steve. ((laughs))
9.	Hanna:	I know, but he looks like him in the face,
10.	Natalie:	But, um, he just—
11.	Peg:	You / / go to church for a different reason than that, Ellen!
12.	Natalie:	I / / get stuck on one guy.
13.	Peg:	Then you shouldn't of been there (interview, eighth grade, March 30).

Although Peg and Natalie considered this violation to be serious, Ellen continued to view it as humorous, laughing as she acknowledged that she "stared" at another boy. Given Ellen's reluctance to consider the seriousness of her violation, Peg and Natalie used more confrontive strategies to inform her about the inappropriateness of her affect and behavior with respect to this norm.

As girls begin to take this norm seriously, they need to become more aware of their romantic feelings. They may even begin to modify their emotions on certain occasions, changing romantic attractions to nonromantic feelings in order to avoid norm violations. Sometimes the girls explicitly discussed their feelings toward boys, thus showing their close monitoring of these feelings. Awareness of romantic feelings was especially important during times of transition from one boyfriend to another. Because "going together" arrangements typically lasted less than two weeks, these transitions were frequent.

> Gwen and Ellen went "cruising" with some boys over the weekend. The boy Gwen was with asked her to go with him but he broke up with her the next morning because another boy that Gwen went with last week threatened to beat him up. So then the other boy asked her back with him Monday morning and she's going with him again now. She said that "one thing I can say for certain is that I love (the boy she's going with), but I can also say for certain that I really like (the boy she went with on Saturday)" (field notes, eighth grade, March 30).

Through Gwen's claim that she "loves" the boy she is currently going with and "likes" the boy she went with on Saturday, her feelings appear to conform with the norm of monogamy. Although it is not clear whether her current feelings are the result of emotion (or expression) work, it is clear that she pays close attention to her feelings and can discuss them with "certainty."

Other girls expressed more confusion about their emotions. In some cases, their confusion stemmed from the discrepancy between their *actual* feelings and the feelings they thought they *ought* to have. Even though they knew that they *should* have romantic feelings for only one boy at a time, girls sometimes found themselves feeling multiple attractions.

> I heard Karla being teased when a specific boy walked by. Her friends were saying that she had a crush on him and once they yelled it at the boy. Karla acted rather embarrassed and angry about this. When they yelled at the boy, they asked Karla if it was true that she liked him. Karla said that she did like him "for a friend." They said that they had seen her walking with him in the halls. After a long pause Karla asked Laura rather indignantly, "How could I like him when I'm already going with somebody?" Effie said, "Two- timing." Karla was embarrassed and seemed rather mild in her denial (field notes, eighth grade, April 21).

Karla's feelings are creating some discomfort for her because they do not conform readily to this feeling norm. She claims that she likes the other boy only "for a friend," but she expresses embarrassment as well as anger toward her friends, who perceive it to be a stronger attraction. Although we do not know whether Karla subsequently modified her feelings and/or expressions toward this boy, emotion work might be necessary in situations such as this, if girls are to abide by the norm of monogamy.

Norm 5: One should always be in love. The final feeling norm emerged was that one should always be in love. This norm differed from those discussed previously in that it was not devised to deal with group concerns, but was developed largely to deal with the concerns of individuals. Whereas violations of most feeling norms had consequences for other group members and peers (e.g., the norms of heterosexuality, exclusivity, and monogamy), violations of this final norm had consequences only for individual girls. Because such violations did not affect others, this norm was held even less widely than those discussed previously. For many girls at the school, however, this emotion norm was a basic part of their knowledge and understanding of romantic love.

For some girls, the onset of their first romantic attraction was the beginning of a continuous state of being in love, often with frequent changes in the object of their feelings. In fact, simply having romantic feelings may have been more important than the actual boys to whom these feelings were directed. For example, a researcher noticed that a girl had "I love" written on her hand and asked her about it. Although this girl's romantic feelings had no particular target, she explained that she was ready to add the name of a boy as soon as a suitable target was found.

The importance of always being in love became particularly evident when relationships with boys ended. For instance, when girls realized that a boy they had been going with now liked someone else, they often redirected their romantic feelings toward someone new.

> She said that she was just going to go up and ask him if he had any intention of going with her again, and if he didn't, she was just "going to have to find someone else." I don't think she has the concept in her mind that she could possibly not be involved with anyone (field notes, eighth grade, March 23).

The salience of this norm was related to the duration of adolescent romantic relationships. Although it might seem that "long-term" relationships would be preferred because girls would not continually have to seek out new boyfriends, some girls reported that being in a long-term

relationship was a disadvantage because it took them out of circulation.

> Apparently Alice's boyfriend broke up with her today and she was unhappy. She saw him walk by the media center and called to him several times, but he ignored her purposely. She said that the worst of it was that she had gone with him several months, and during that time had progressively cut herself off from contact with other boys so that she didn't even have any male friends left (field notes, eighth grade, March 4).

Within four days Alice had a new boyfriend, but her comments show that replacing her old boyfriend was an important concern.

During the early stage in the development of their romantic activities, when the girls were beginning to have romantic feelings but did not act on them, all group members could adhere easily to this norm. Once they started to form romantic relationships, however, only the girls who were popular with boys could continually attract new boyfriends. In fact, the status associated with being popular with boys contributed to the salience of this norm among the girls at this school. At the same time, group members also had a hand in reinforcing this feeling norm.

> When Nancy came up she asked, "Who do you like now, Carol?" a question which Nancy often asks Carol. Carol said, "Pete." Nancy said, "Oh yeah." Shortly after that Linda said, "Guess who Pete likes?" Betty said, "Carol." Nancy said, "God, you guys get everything you want" (field notes, seventh grade, April 14).

Even though less popular girls could not attract new boyfriends so easily, nevertheless they were able to abide by this norm. One strategy commonly used by these as well as by the more popular girls was to "recycle" the boys with whom they had had a previous relationship.

1.	Ellen:	And then she went with George and then she went to likin' Tom
2.		again.
3.	Natalie:	Yeah. ((pause)) But sometimes it kinda switches on and off, like
4.		s— like you'll like one boy and then you'll get tired of 'im and
5.		you go with somebody else and then you'll like him again. Like
6.		with Bryan and Dale. I used to do that a lot (interview, seventh grade, May 24).

Natalie's comments suggest that her and her friends' feelings for former boyfriends sometimes are re-created for the purpose of conforming to this norm. Natalie's comments also imply that conformity is likely to result in emotion work on the part of these girls, who sometimes evoke romantic feelings for boys they were previously "tired of."

The advantages of conforming to this norm include appearing to be popular with boys as well as providing ongoing evidence of a heterosexual orientation; both are important concerns to girls at this age. At the same time, however, conformity carries several possible costs. One such cost is that emotion work may be necessary in order to always be in love. Although we can only speculate at this point, adolescent girls sometimes may create romantic feelings for boys to whom they are not attracted so they can conform to this norm. Hochschild (1983b) argued that when insincere feelings are created routinely, people lose touch with their actual feelings. Insofar as girls have insincere feelings, it is possible that eventually they will have difficulty in distinguishing between their "real" romantic feelings and their less authentic feelings, which they created in order to satisfy the requirements of this norm.

A second potential cost stems from the dilemma faced by adolescent females as a result of their adherence to this norm. On the one hand, girls consider being continuously in love as socially desirable because it is a way to reaffirm their popularity with boys and thus to increase

their own status in relation to other females. On the other hand, group members who both attract too much attention from males and appear to be indiscriminate in their choice of romantic partners are often criticized by their friends for being "sluts," and ultimately are viewed in a negative manner.

DISCUSSION

In this paper we argue that adolescence is a period during which females acquire cultural knowledge about romantic love, including the social norms that guide romantic feelings. In addition to obtaining normative information about romance, we found that the girls in this study had developed several feeling and expression norms to deal with their own concerns about romantic love. By the seventh and eighth grade, norms concerning the relative importance of romantic relationships as well as the appropriate object of romantic feelings had emerged in these groups of friends. Whereas some of these norms were highly developed and generally accepted (e.g., the norms of heterosexuality, exclusivity, and monogamy), others were not held by all group members and still were being negotiated (e.g., the norm concerning the relative importance of romantic relationships).

We also found that adolescent girls used a variety of discourse strategies to communicate normative information and to reinforce emotion norms to friends. In general, group members informed one another about feeling and expression norms through light and playful language activities, as well as through serious and confrontive modes of discourse. Language that involved humor was one of the more common discourse strategies used by these girls. Through joking and teasing remarks, group members could point out their friends' norm violations in an indirect, nonthreatening manner. Moreover, teasing and joking were ways in which the girls could show their awareness of feeling norms while simultaneously expressing their own normatively inappropriate emotions.

The girls also commonly used gossip and confrontations to clarify and reinforce feeling norms. Although gossip did not directly inform norm violators of their inappropriate affect and behavior, it provided normative information to other group members. Finally, confrontations sometimes were used when indirect strategies were ineffective at producing normative consensus and when norm violations had negative consequences for group members. In these exchanges, girls expressed social disapproval of affective deviance through accusations, insults, and reprimands. Not surprisingly, such exchanges often involved considerable conflict and tension. Overall, through these various language activities and modes of discourse, the girls conveyed what they viewed as appropriate and inappropriate in regard to the group's feeling and expression norms.

Even though girls obtain normative information about romantic love from friends, they do not always abide by emotion norms. Rather, our analysis of discourse revealed that group members sometimes responded with "resistance" and intentionally defied their group's feeling and expression norms. Therefore, feeling and expression norms underlying romantic love constrain but do not determine adolescent females' affect and behavior. Further research is necessary to determine the degree to which girls resist other emotion norms, as well as to identify the full range of emotion management processes used by adolescent females.

Romance is highly salient, however, because having a boyfriend enhances girls' popularity with peers at an age when being popular is important for their self-image. In fact, two norms that emerged in these peer groups reveal the salience of romance to girls during this period: the norms concerning the relative importance of romantic relationships and the importance of being in love continually. It is possible that even after romantic relationships become tied less closely to peer group status, females continue to feel that they always should be in a romantic relationship with a male in order to validate their attractiveness and worth to self and to others.

Although it was not our purpose to examine the actual emotional experiences of adolescent girls, our findings support the view that emotions are in part socially constructed and that feeling and expression are subject to normative influences. By focusing on romantic socialization in adolescent peer groups, we have shown how, in everyday interaction with friends, females obtain normative information about romantic feelings as well as maintaining, reproducing, and recreating one aspect of their society's emotion culture. . . .

References

Berger, Peter L., and Thomas Luckman. 1967. *The Social Construction of Reality: A Treatise in the Sociology of Knowledge.* New York: Anchor.

Cancian, Francesca M. 1985. "Gender Politics: Love and Power in the Private and Public Spheres." Pp. 253–264 in *Gender and the Life Course,* edited by Alice S. Rossi. New York: Aldine.

_____. 1987. *Love in America: Gender and Self Development.* Boston: Cambridge University Press.

Cancian, Francesca M., and Steven L. Gordon. 1988. "Changing Emotion Norms in Marriage: Love and Anger in U.S. Women's Magazines since 1900." *Gender and Society* 2(3):308–342.

Cantor, Muriel. 1987. "Popular Culture and the Portrayal of Women: Content and Control." Pp. 190–214 in *Analyzing Gender,* edited by Beth Hess and Myra Marx Ferree. New York: Sage.

Clark, Candice. 1987. "Sympathy Biography and Sympathy Margin." *American Journal of Sociology* 93:290–321.

Corsaro, William A., and Thomas A. Rizzo. 1988. "Discussione and Friendship: Socialization Processes in the Peer Culture of Italian Nursery School Children." *American Sociological Review* 53:879–894.

Eder, Donna. 1985. "The Cycle of Popularity: Interpersonal Relations Among Female Adolescents." *Sociology of Education* 58:154–165.

_____. 1988. "Teasing Activities among Adolescent Females." Paper presented at conference "Gender Roles through the Life Span," Ball State University, Muncie, IN.

Eder, Donna, and Janet Enke. 1988. "Gossip as a Means of Strengthening Social Bonds." Paper presented at the annual meeting of the American Sociological Association, Atlanta.

Eder, Donna, and Stephanie Sanford. 1986. "The Development and Maintenance of Interactional Norms among Early Adolescents." *Sociological Studies of Child Development* 1:283–300.

Evans, Cathy, and Donna Eder. 1989. "'No Exit': Processes of Social Isolation in the Middle School." Paper presented at the annual meeting of the American Sociological Association, San Francisco.

Fine, Gary Alan. 1986. "The Social Organization of Adolescent Gossip: The Rhetoric of Moral Evaluation." Pp. 405–423 in *Children's Worlds and Children's Language,* edited by Jenny Cook-Gumperz, William Corsaro, and Jurgen Streeck. Berlin: Moulin.

Goodwin, Marjorie H. 1980. "He-Said-She-Said: Formal Cultural Procedures for the Construction of a Gossip Dispute Activity." *American Ethnologist* 7:674–695.

Gordon, Steven L. 1981. "The Sociology of Sentiments and Emotion." Pp. 562–592 in *Social Psychology: Sociological Perspectives,* edited by Morris Rosenberg and Ralph H. Turner. New York: Basic Books.

_____. 1989. "The Socialization of Children's Emotions: Emotional Culture, Competence, and Exposure." Pp. 319–349 in *Children's Understanding of Emotion,* edited by Carolyn Saarni and Paul Harris. New York: Cambridge University Press.

Griffin, Christine. 1985. *Typical Girls?: Young Women from School to Job Market.* London: Routledge and Kegan Paul.

Harris, Paul, and Tjeert Olthof. 1982. "The Child's Concept of Emotion." Pp. 188–209 in *Social Cognition: Studies of the Development of Understanding,* edited by George Butterworth and Paul Light. Chicago: University of Chicago Press.

Hochschild, Arlie R. 1979. "Emotion Work, Feeling Rules, and Social Structure." *American Journal of Sociology* 85(3):551–575.

_____. 1983a. "Attending to, Codifying and Managing Feelings: Sex Differences in Love." Pp. 250–262 in *Feminist Frontiers: Rethinking Sex, Gender, and Society,* edited by Laurel Richardson and Verta Taylor. New York: Addison-Wesley.

_____. 1983b. *The Managed Heart: Commercialization of Human Feeling.* Berkeley: University of California Press.

Holland, Dorothy, and Margaret Eisenhart. 1990. *Educated in Romance: Women, Achievement, and College Culture.* Chicago: University of Chicago Press.

Kessler, S., D. Ashenden, R. Connell, and G. Dowsett. 1985. "Gender Relations in Secondary Schooling." *Sociology of Education* 58:34–47.

Lees, Sue. 1986. *Sexuality and Adolescent Girls.* London: Hutchinson.

Lever, Janet. 1978. "Sex Differences in the Complexity of Children's Play and Games." *American Sociological Review* 43:471–483.

Lofland, Lyn H. 1985. "The Social Shaping of Emotion: Grief in Historical Perspective." *Symbolic Interaction* 8:171–190.

McRobbie, Angela. 1978. "Working Class Girls and the Culture of Femininity." Pp. 96–108 in *Women Take Issue,* edited by The Women's Study Group, Centre for Contemporary Cultural Studies. London: Hutchinson.

Mead, George Herbert. 1934. *Mind, Self, and Society.* Chicago: University of Chicago Press.

Mehan, Hugh. 1979. *Learning Lessons: Social Organization in the Classroom.* Cambridge, MA: Harvard University Press.

Rich, Adrienne. 1980. "Compulsory Heterosexuality and Lesbian Existence." *Signs: Journal of Women in Culture and Society* 5:631–660.

Rosenberg, Florence, and Roberta Simmons. 1975. "Sex Differences in the Self-Concept in Adolescence." *Sex Roles* 1:147–159.

Rubin, Lillian B. 1977. *Worlds of Pain: Life in the Working-Class Family.* New York: Basic Books.

Rubin, Zick. 1970. "Measurement of Romantic Love." *Journal of Personality and Social Psychology* 16: 265–273.

_____. 1973. *Liking and Loving: An Invitation to Social Psychology.* New York: Holt, Rinehart and Winston.

Saarni, Carolyn. 1979. "Children's Understanding of Display Rules for Expressive Behavior." *Developmental Psychology* 15(4):424–429.

Schofield, Janet. 1982. *Black and White in School.* New York: Praeger.

Stearns, Carol Z., and Peter N. Stearns. 1986. *Anger: The Struggle for Emotional Control in America's History.* Chicago: University of Chicago Press.

Swidler, Ann. 1980. "Love and Adulthood in American Culture." Pp. 120–147 in *Themes of Work and Love in Adulthood,* edited by Neil J. Smelser and Erik H. Erickson. Cambridge, MA: Harvard University Press.

Thoits, Peggy A. 1989. "The Sociology of Emotions." *Annual Review of Sociology* 15:317–342.

Waller, Willard. 1937. "The Rating and Dating Complex." *American Sociological Review* 2:727–734.

Wulff, Helena. 1988. *Twenty Girls: Growing Up, Ethnicity and Excitement in a South London Microculture.* Stockholm: University of Stockholm Press.

Youniss, James, and Jacqueline Smollar. 1985. *Parents and Peers in Social Development: A Sullivan-Piaget Perspective.* Chicago: University of Chicago Press.

PART V

PRODUCING SOCIAL ORDER THROUGH INTERACTION

All the world's a stage,

And all the men and women merely players:

They have their exits and their entrances;

And one man in his time plays many parts.

—William Shakespeare, *As You Like It*

We are told on good authority, Callicles, that heaven and earth and their respective inhabitants are held together by the bonds of society and love and order and discipline and righteousness, and that is why the universe is an ordered whole or cosmos and not a state of disorder and license.

—Plato, *Gorgias*

MEANING IS NEGOTIATED THROUGH INTERACTION

Jodi O'Brien

Imagine you are staying in a hotel and return to your room one evening to find a stranger undressed and sitting in the bed. What do you do? A likely first response would be to check your key and the door number to see if you have the wrong room. How the stranger reacts will also give you important cues about the situation. If the person immediately begins to scream, you will likely conclude that you definitely have the wrong room or some mistake has been made. However, what if the person were to wink at you and say, "Hi there, I've been waiting for you." This comment would likely lead to an entirely different scenario playing out in your head. As we've discussed in earlier sections of the book, your response will depend on how you interpret the situation, and in a situation that is ambiguous you will look for clues from the other person to figure out what is going on. Once you have decided what is going on, you will have a better idea of how to respond. Another way of looking at this is that once you know the scene, you'll have an idea of the social identities that are expected for that scene.

WHAT'S GOING ON? PROJECTING A DEFINITION OF THE SITUATION

For the socialized actor, most situations are not this ambiguous. When we enter a situation we immediately name it; we *define the situation*. Some sociologists call this "framing." Once we know the definition of the situation or the frame, we know the scene and what is likely to be expected of us and others. In other words, frames set into motion a series of related categories in our minds that include the appropriate scripts for feeling and acting. Part IV described the process by which we learn these social scripts and identities. In this section, the focus is on the ways in which people signal to another and *negotiate* the definition of the situation. Most social interaction goes so smoothly that we are not aware of the underlying work we are doing as social actors to create a meaningful situation.

This interaction work is obvious in the imaginary play of children who spend a great deal of time defining the situation and negotiating the appropriate roles. "Pretend you are a pirate and this tree is your ship," one child might say. "I am the good guy and this table is my ship and you try to get onboard and we'll have a sword fight with these sticks. Ok?" This scene setting will continue throughout the game, which requires continuous active announcements about what each "prop" stands for, who each player is, and so forth. Fights usually break out when one child wants to be something that is "not appropriate" for the scene. "I'll be a cowboy who comes and ropes the pirate," another child might announce. "There *are no* cowboys in pirates," the other children will explain in exasperation.

As Mead discussed in his theory of self development through play (see Part III, Reading 12), children initially take on different roles and play them without concern for the interactional context: A cowboy, a pirate, and a nurse can all play happily together. In this case, each child is simply practicing the characteristics associated with the respective character. However, as the child becomes more sophisticated and socialized, she begins to associate different characters with specific scenes or frames and becomes more vigilant about populating the play with characters that are appropriate to the scene as she has learned it. For Mead, this form of interactional play is key to becoming fully socialized. One learns to adopt social identities that are specific to the definition of the situation.

Children work actively at establishing the definition of the situation, but for most of us, social life involves a series of moving from one encounter to another in which the situation is more or less defined by cues such as location (church, classroom, grocery store) and event (date, exam, funeral). Through the socialization process, we learn to associate specific social identities—and corresponding behavior and feelings—with specific locations and events. In other words, we have a series of *event schemas* and *place schemas* that trigger associative responses that seem and feel automatic. These schemas include grand events such as a wedding or moments as trivial as an encounter with an old acquaintance while walking down the street. In each case, we define the situation (mostly automatically and mindlessly) and respond accordingly. This seemingly automatic behavior masks the extent to which these patterns are socially learned and *interactionally maintained.*

Erving Goffman (Reading 22) is a sociologist who devoted most of his career to describing and explaining the ways in which we continuously create and recreate social experience through our interactions with one another. Goffman invites us to slow down each frame of interaction and to explore the systematic ways in which, much like children at play, we are constantly making social reality. What seems orderly and routine on the surface is actually the result of *interaction work.* The appearance of order comes from the fact that, as socialized beings, we share similar scripts or expectations of various situations and we work together to *realize*—make real—our own scripts or expectations. Thus, according to Goffman, social life can be usefully analyzed as a form of theater in which each person, knowing the script, does her or his best to enact the appropriate identities for the situation. Goffman also notes that because humans are prone to error, we are always making performance mistakes. But just as the audience waits in suspended animation for an actor to remember his line, we help each other to smooth over the mistakes so that the performance can continue. These actions include *tact, giving accounts* and practicing the *nothing unusual bias.* Let's look more closely at some of Goffman's ideas.

LIFE AS THEATER

"Life as theater" uses the metaphor of *performance* to explain interaction routines. Like any metaphor, it is not a complete description of social reality, but in many ways, our interactions with others do seem to resemble a theatrical performance.

The theater metaphor can be seen in the origins of the word *person,* which comes from the Latin *persona,* meaning a mask worn by actors. We behave differently (play different roles) in front of different people (audiences). We pick out clothing (a costume) that is consistent with the image we wish to project. We enlist the help of friends, caterers, and decorators (fellow actors and stage crew) to help us successfully "stage" a dinner for a friend, a birthday party for a relative, or a rush party for a sorority or fraternity. And if we need to adjust our clothing or wish to say something unflattering about one of our guests, we are careful to do so out of sight from others (backstage).

The presentation of ourselves to others is known as *dramaturgy,* and the use of the theatrical metaphor for analyzing human interaction is known as the *dramaturgical perspective.* Goffman is one of the most noted writers on this subject. In 1959, he published *The Presentation of Self in Everyday Life.* In this classic book, Goffman analyzes everyday "performances." He details the care people take in preparing and presenting their performances—that is, the manner in which people *manage* the impressions others form of them.

Why do people spend so much time and energy thinking about what they should say and how they should look? Some would say that we should simply "be ourselves" and that only those who are deceitful need to worry about managing their image. They would concede that con artists and the insincere have to be concerned about these issues, but what about good, decent people? In fact, however, even saints are concerned with the presentation of self. To tell us to simply "be" ourselves implies that who we are is easily, quickly, and accurately perceived by those with whom we interact. But if we have just met someone or will be interacting with someone for only a short length of time (for example, in a job interview), we certainly can't count on the person to see us as we see ourselves. Dramaturgy can be an issue even when we interact with people who have known us for some time. Who we are may not be obvious to others—most of us do not wear our personal characteristics and convictions tattooed onto our foreheads.

Private Minds, Public Identities: Impression Management

A simple but profound truth about human interaction is that minds are private. Our thoughts, desires, beliefs, and character cannot be directly perceived and evaluated by others. We are not a race of mind readers, and so we must depend on signs and gestures to comprehend one another. Recall the example of the border guard from the essay in Part II. The guard sizes people up and treats them according to their appearance. Therefore, it is in people's best interest to appear in a way that gets them treated as they wish. In this case, they want to appear "law-abiding."

The fact that minds are private doesn't mean that people are obligated to accurately display their thoughts and desires to others, but it does mean that even the most honest people must be concerned about how they come across to others. In Goffman's (1959) words,

Whether an honest performer wishes to convey the truth or whether a dishonest performer wishes to convey a falsehood, both must take care to enliven their performances with appropriate expressions, exclude from their performances expressions that might discredit the impression being fostered, and take care lest the audience impute unintended meanings. (p. 66)

It is crucial to remember that *impression management* is something everyone does in everyday activities. To one degree or another, we all manage others' impressions of us in interactions. We have to "perform" or "project" our intentions and desires, because people can't read our minds.

Because minds are private, people typically behave so as to highlight important facts about themselves that might otherwise go unnoticed. Goffman calls this activity *dramatic realization.* For example, when you are in a job interview, you might describe in great detail a position of responsibility you held in the past. Or if you are in traffic court, you might point out the absence of any past traffic violations to the judge. This feature may be true about you, but you probably wouldn't bring it up as a way to impress a potential date. Instead, you might focus on highlighting your favorite music or activities. Dramatic realization is an attempt to make traits and characteristics "real" and noticeable that might otherwise go unnoticed. If these traits are not noticed, they don't exist as "real" aspects of the performance. It is up to the individual to bring them into play.

Goffman also makes the point that we often try to present ourselves in a favorable light, a process he calls *idealization.* We might simply accent those aspects about ourselves that are positive (for example, mentioning that you are on the varsity team but not mentioning that you have just lost your job), or we might engage in outright deception (saying you are on the varsity team when you are not).

People also have a general tendency to convey the impression that the role they are currently engaged in is their most important role. For example, when an individual walks into a store to buy an expensive suit, she will be interacting with a "salesperson." The salesperson may also be a parent, spouse, community volunteer, jogger, gardener, and so forth, but if that salesperson is good at the job, he will take part in the interaction as if serving customers is the only (or at least the most important) role in his life at that moment.

Before an interaction can proceed successfully, two actors must agree about the sort of situation they are in and the role each is to play. Is it a friendly chat between acquaintances, a seduction between lovers, or a coaching session between subordinate and supervisor? This process is referred to as *identity negotiation.* People in an interaction each project an identity, and their responses to each other indicate whether they accept the projected identity. For example, if you ask your boss how old she is and she doesn't acknowledge the question, she has chosen not to grant you the identity of "familiar acquaintance." When two people agree on the identities they are both going to play in an interaction, they have arrived at what Goffman refers to as a *working consensus.*

Public agreement on identities does not necessarily reflect the actor's *private* beliefs. People often have pleasant chats with coworkers they dislike. There are many possible reasons for doing this—to be polite, to prevent an awkward scene, to ensure good relations in the workplace, or perhaps to stay in the good graces of a person who controls resources that might be needed sometime. Whatever the private reality might be, it is the public, socially agreed upon definition of the situation that will guide the interaction.

Once a public agreement has been reached (whether implicitly or explicitly), it carries the weight of a contract. The working consensus has a moral character to it. Each actor *feels as if* he or she has the right to be treated in a particular way by other actors. The actors also *feel as if* they have an obligation to behave in ways that are consistent with the presented identity. For example, in an interaction between a teacher and a student, the person who is in the role of the teacher expects certain behavior from the person who is the student; these behaviors include being treated respectfully, being treated as a status superior, being treated as an expert on the subject, and so on. At the same time, the person who has claimed the identity of teacher has numerous obligations or duties, such as competently carrying out the teacher's role, being respectful of students, knowing a great deal about the subject, and being able to convey that knowledge to students. The rights and duties associated with an identity that has been publicly accepted must be respected if the expected social order of the interaction is to continue. If a math teacher is unable to solve a problem in front of the class or if a student treats the teacher as a younger sibling, the interaction grinds to an uncomfortable halt.

In sum, interaction has two key elements—publicly defining (and presenting) a personal identity and defining what sort of situation the individual is in with others. There are many possible answers to the questions "Who am I?" "Who are you?" "What's going on?" For successful interaction to occur, these definitions must be projected and negotiated by the participants. The participants jockey to claim identities and to define the situation in ways that will help them accomplish their personal goals. Once identities are established, they must be actively maintained.

Who Are We and What Are We Doing Here?

> When an individual enters the presence of others, they commonly seek to acquire information about him [*sic*] or to bring into play information already possessed. They will be interested in his general socio-economic status, his conception of self, his attitude toward them, his competence, his trustworthiness, etc. (Goffman, 1959, p. 1)

When they come together, people must actively strive to present a definition of the role they wish to play in the interactional moment and the definition of the situation as they see it. Failure to do so may lead to misunderstandings, embarrassment, and the breakdown of the interaction. In a study of gym trainers and their clients, Linda Van Leuven (2001) describes the different definitions that client and trainer may bring to the interaction. Clients sometimes define the situation as a personal friendship or even a romantic encounter. Accordingly, they may enter the situation prepared to act out the identity of "engaging flirt." Trainers, who are aware of this propensity in some clients, develop strategies designed to let the client know immediately what they can expect of the situation—a "workout" and not an occasion to "visit" or to "flirt." For instance, a trainer may grill a potential client about her or his commitment in advance. During the sessions, the trainer might carefully avoid eye contact so as to discourage conversation. These interactional strategies help to establish a frame around the situation and to signal to participants what the boundaries and expectations are.

Goffman notes that there are many skills required to bring off a reasonable interactional performance. Because interaction requires the ongoing cooperation of participants, it is vulnerable and can break down. A situation might be defined in an inappropriate way. Or the identities the participants claim might somehow be discredited (as when a math teacher cannot solve a problem in front of the class). In that case, the result is embarrassment.

From a dramaturgical perspective, embarrassment can be defined as a breakdown in a projected identity. It is striking to note how uncomfortable we are made by embarrassment and how hard we work to avoid it. Indeed, embarrassment makes us so uncomfortable that we usually cooperate to prevent or smooth over other people's embarrassing actions, even if they are strangers. We might look away when someone stumbles clumsily, pretend not to hear the fight the couple is having at a nearby table, or readily and eagerly accept other people's explanations for their unacceptable behavior. Engaging in cooperative support of each other's identities to avoid or repair embarrassment is called *tact*. The presence and prevalence of tact is an extraordinary thing. Humans apparently have a very deep commitment to support each other's identities, even the identities of strangers.

True, there are times when someone might react to an embarrassing moment without tact (or even have engineered the moment, if it involves a rival), but these instances stand out because they are exceptions. Practical jokes that make someone look foolish (that is, those that discredit someone's "face") would not be funny if they were not a deviation from the usual norm of tact.

The mutual obligation to avoid "scenes" and to be who we claim to be means that whenever a situation or identity is threatened, someone must repair the interaction. When the audience helps in the repair work, they are being *tactful*—but, of course, the person whose identity is threatened can also work to repair the interaction. Following behavior that threatens an identity, people usually can offer explanations or give an *account* of the actions.

Offering accounts after an inappropriate act does not guarantee that others will accept ("honor") the account. Not every explanation is acceptable. "I had car trouble" might be a reasonable excuse for failing to get to class on time, but not "Voices told me to come late today." And some explanations are acceptable in some situations but not in others. Burning the stew because "I was distracted by a phone call" is acceptable, but the same excuse would certainly not be honored as an explanation for why someone failed to show up for her wedding. What is judged to be an acceptable account varies from situation to situation. It can also vary tremendously from one culture to another.

Goffman emphasizes just how fragile and potentially disruptable interaction routines really are. His intent is not so much to present people as cynical and calculating as to draw our attention to the tricky interpersonal gymnastics required of social actors. What is remarkable—and Goffman's respectful awe is apparent in his voluminous writings—is that people somehow do manage to project mutually understood definitions of self and situation, despite all the things that could go wrong.

It's important to note that people *learn* acceptable definitions of identity and situation. Some of these learning processes are very explicit. For instance, business schools frequently hold "mock cocktail parties" in order to teach students how to network with clients. Informal social networking is an important factor in successful business encounters. For this reason, business schools provide students with an opportunity to "try on" and practice performing social networking identities. Students learn tips such as "don't have both hands full with drink and food, because you won't be able to shake someone else's hand" and "you have to appear eager but not like you're a 'social climber.'"

Whether one intends to project an identity of competent instructor, capable business-woman, earnest priest, or intimidating thug, we all have to engage in impression management; we have to signal to others our definition of the situation and our intended position.

Negotiating a Working Consensus

The generative quality of social structure is observable in face-to-face encounters. Individuals bring different ideas, goals, and expectations to social encounters. As they strive to achieve a working definition of what is going on, they transcribe their private definitions, as well as their immediate feelings, into a form that they think others will understand and accept. In other words, people manage, despite many differences, to engage in meaningful, sustainable discourses. We all do this through continual negotiation.

The theatrical form most indicative of the generative, negotiated quality of interaction is improvisation. "Theater sports" is a form of entertainment in which the audience calls out a "frame" or "setting"—usually one involving some sort of controversy or misunderstanding—and the actors then improvise their roles within the parameters of the setting. The actors and audience share a general understanding of what the scene or setting consists of, but how it is played out is largely determined by each actor's performance repertoire (that is, each actor's familiarity with how people might react in this situation) and how the other performers respond. If you have participated in theater sports, you know that the fun is in seeing how diverse actors play off one another when they don't know what the others are likely to do.

Everyday interaction is an ongoing series of such moments. The ability to negotiate working understandings of different situations is the genius of human sociability. The fact that everyday encounters feel more or less like comfortable routines—rather than a madcap scramble of miscues, misunderstandings, and maladies—is a testament to the existence of shared social scripts.

The negotiation process becomes apparent in situations that are less familiar and routine. On those occasions, people are likely to be more aware of the potential gap between the private and projected definitions of various participants. These situations are often "precarious."

In a study of interaction between patients and staff in gynecological exams, Joan Emerson illustrates the impression management that must take place when participants have strongly competing definitions of the situation (see Reading 23). The patient is likely to feel that the examination is a violation of her body and her dignity, whereas the medical staff wants to establish an air of professional detachment. The doctors and nurses performing this medical procedure must take care to ensure that the situation continues to be defined as a medical examination, because the exam includes many sensitive behaviors that could threaten this definition. Although most interactions are not as precarious as this situation, any interaction can end up being redefined in a negative light ("I thought you were being helpful. Now I just think you're being patronizing and manipulative!"). Thus, the concerns and dramaturgical activity that are brought out so clearly in the gynecological examination are relevant to many more ordinary settings.

Readings 24, 25, and 26 each highlight different aspects of the self presentation and identity work. In "Smell, Odor, and Somatic Work" (Reading 24), Dennis Waskul and Phillip Vannini focus on something that we usually take for granted or consider too biological to be a matter of interaction: body odor. Yet, as they point out, there are significant social meanings associated with bodily smells, and "somatic work" can be seen as a form of interaction work in which we engage in attempts to convey an appropriately clean and virtuous body and also judge others as social actors according to bodily odors.

Goffman was particularly interested in stigma and its consequences for interaction. According to Goffman, *stigmas* are an aspect of social interaction and reflect particular social statuses and ideals. For instance, certain professions or ethnicities may be stigmatized in some contexts or cultures and not others. Goffman was interested in the way in which people manage stigmatized identities. Panhandling is usually considered a stigmatized or problematic activity in contemporary society, and it is usually associated with identity in that we think of "panhandlers" rather than people who happen to panhandle. Stephen Lankenau (Reading 25) describes aspects of panhandling as a form of interaction routine in which the person is actively engaged in a performance intended to get the "audience" to treat him as a person. The typical script when someone encounters a person panhandling is to act as if nothing unusual is going on and to ignore the person panhandling. Lankenau notes that some people who panhandle are active and creative in performing routines to disrupt the stigma or "nonperson" identity.

Amir Marvasti (Reading 26) uses his personal experiences as well as interviews to describe the interaction work he and other Middle Eastern Americans must engage in as a result of the War in Iraq. Since the outset of the war, Middle Eastern Americans have become stigmatized and often find themselves negotiating interactional "disruptions" that would otherwise be considered rude or unacceptable.

EMOTIONAL LABOR AND EMOTIONAL CAPITAL

Interactional routines lead people to reproduce taken-for-granted cultural patterns. Because minds are private, we all must dramatize (in other words, signal) the identities we wish to claim and our definition of the situation. To be effective in interactions, we select symbolic representations that we know to be reliable signals of our intentions. This selection of culturally typical or expected symbols is a process of *idealization.* You may not like business suits, for instance, but you will put one on for a job interview because you believe it to be the appropriate costume for presenting the identity of an eager and professional potential employee. When you present yourself with the appropriate costume, props, and mannerisms, you effectively reproduce a set of cultural expectations or *ideals*—one of them being that "businesspeople wear suits." In other words, you will be presenting a symbolic *ideal type,* and through your self-presentation, you will be affirming the ideal type. The implications of idealization for perpetuating social norms are significant. Some of the consequences of "dramatizing the ideal" are discussed in Parts VI and VII of this book.

Another aspect of interaction routines that has been the subject of considerable study is *emotional labor.* Because interaction routines require us to adjust our behavior to public expectations, we can reasonably ask, what about the underlying private feelings? What happens when these don't mesh well with public expectations? Most of us have been in situations in which we had to engage in public behavior that required us to "put on a happy face" when we weren't feeling up to it. The ability to engage in appropriate social performance even when you're experiencing inner turmoil or tragedy is sometimes seen as a form of "grace" or maturity. What about situations in which the "happy face" is required as part of the job—that is, part of the idealized or ideal type expectations for a particular social identity? Sociologist Arlie Hochschild was one of the first to explore that aspect of performance, and she called it "emotional labor." Most interaction routines require some degree of emotional labor—i.e., we are often publicly pushing out what is expected of us. People who are in positions of less power or those who suffer from social stigma are likely to be more aware of disparities between how they feel privately and what is expected of them publicly. People who have power are usually able to define the situation according to their desires, and thus are more likely to feel satisfied with the interaction and less aware of the emotional labor. Hochschild is interested in the emotional labor that is required as part of paid employment. In a classic sociological study (*The Managed Heart,* 1983), she looked at the emotional labor that is a required aspect of the performances of flight attendants. In the article included here (Reading 27), Hochschild reports on the ways in which flight attendants are socialized to put on a happy face no matter how rude, drunk, or inappropriate the passengers are. This type of performance requires what Hochschild calls "deep acting," and she asks, what are the costs of this deeply acted emotional labor? How does it affect the flight attendants' ability to accurately gauge how they really feel?

In Reading 28, David Schweingruber and Nancy Berns extend the concept of emotional labor to "emotional capital." They suggest that the emotional labor required to perform certain professional identities can sometimes become a form of *emotional capital* whereby people are better able to make sense of themselves and the job they are doing and to see the performance as a form of emotional development. Schweingruber and Berns follow the experiences of young people who sell encyclopedias door-to-door. The sales training involves a practice called "emotion mining" in which the salespeople are encouraged to look for aspects of their personality that will help them perform better on the job. Schweingruber and Berns suggest that this process results in a form of emotional capital that helps the salesperson create a bridge between the sales identity and other aspects of personal self.

Performing Interaction Rituals

Goffman opens *The Presentation of Self in Everyday Life* (1959) with the following lines from the philosopher George Santayana:

Masks are arrested expressions and admirable echoes of feelings, at once faithful, discreet, and superlative. Living things in contact with the air acquire a cuticle, and it is not urged against cuticles that they are not hearts; yet some philosophers seem to be angry with images for not being things, and with words for not being feelings. Words and images are like shells, no less integral parts of nature than are the substances they cover, but better addressed to the eye and more open to observation. (p. vi)

Through this quotation, Goffman anticipates readers' reactions to his theory that we "perform" ourselves, our ideals, and our beliefs rather than somehow simply exuding them naturally. Some people are inclined to associate "performance" with fakery or trickery. They assume that, behind the stage, there is something "more real."

Goffman and sociologists of his persuasion do not disavow the existence of a physiology, a psyche, and perhaps even a soul that may be independent of social forces, but their theoretical and analytical focus is on *social* relations. "Reality" is in the expression of social meaning achieved through interaction. We are, first and foremost, *expressive* creatures. To express ourselves, we must transform individual urges, amorphous images, and fuzzy ideas into communicable form. We do so through interactional speech and gesture. Thus, "reality" consists of shared forms of expression that, as we have noted, take on patterns. Goffman calls these patterns "interaction rituals."

Producing a shared reality requires give and take, concession, and acknowledgment of others. *Interaction rituals* are enactments of ceremony that reinforce cultural symbols and expectations. The rituals range from simple greeting exchanges (in which people acknowledge the presence of other people) to elaborate ceremonies (such as weddings and funerals). And these interaction rituals have a conservative aspect: Through ritual presentations of the "ideal," people conserve or maintain the status quo.

For Goffman (1959), everyday ceremonies, or rituals, give meaning to our collective existence:

To the degree that a performance highlights the common official values of the society in which it occurs, we may look upon it as a ceremony—as an expressive rejuvenation and reaffirmation of the moral values of the community. . . . To stay in one's room away from the place where the party is being given . . . is to stay away from where reality is being performed. The world, in truth, is a wedding. (pp. 35–36)

REFERENCES AND SUGGESTIONS FOR FURTHER READING

Charon, J. (1989). *Symbolic interactionism* (3rd ed.). Englewood Cliffs, NJ: Prentice Hall.
Goffman, E. (1959). *The presentation of self in everyday life.* Garden City, NY: Doubleday.
Hochschild, A. R. (1983). *The managed heart.* Berkeley: University of California Press. (See also 20th Anniversary Edition, 2003)
Kuhn, M. H., & McPartland, T. S. (1954). An empirical investigation of self-attitudes. *American Sociological Review, 19,* 68–76.
Turner, R. (1976). The real self: From institution to impulse. *American Journal of Sociology, 81,* 989–1016.
Twain, M. (1946). *The adventures of Tom Sawyer.* New York: Grosset & Dunlap. (Original work published 1875)
Van Leuven, L. (2001). What does this service include? In J. O'Brien & P. Kollock (Eds.), *The production of reality* (3rd ed., pp. 254–264). Thousand Oaks, CA: Pine Forge Press.

PROJECTING THE DEFINITION OF THE SITUATION

One of the simplest but most profound aspects of social interaction is that we are not mind readers. Because of this, much of social interaction is a *signaling process* that involves letting each other know what's going on. Our gestures, cues, and conversation are attempts to communicate a definition of the situation. This process includes signaling what kind of moment or event we think we're in: What's the script? Is this a casual conversation at the store, an argument, or a celebration? Through our gestures and remarks, we let people know what our expectations of the situation are and what social role we are trying to play in the moment (flirtatious potential date, hassled shopper, betrayed spouse, etc.). Although most day-to-day behavior seems routine and automatic, we're actually working together all the time to signal to one another. The signaling may be as simple as "I see and acknowledge you as a comrade" or as complex as trying to get a raise from a boss you disrespect. Much human social interaction can be analyzed in terms of the kinds of signaling of expectations that people are doing with one another. When people encounter one another, whether they are strangers or close friends, they have to define their expectations. Social expectations are often taken for granted, and people play out the routines with enough ease that it seems "natural." However, whether we are aware of it or not, we are constantly negotiating a definition of the situation. Hurt feelings, anger, and frustration are often the results of differing expectations that cannot be reconciled.

Erving Goffman is a name that appears repeatedly throughout this book. This selection is excerpted from his book *The Presentation of Self in Everyday Life*. In this now-classic book, Goffman uses the metaphor of the theater to describe everyday encounters. According to Goffman, much of our behavior is an attempt to project social identities to others. Regardless of whether we are trying to manipulate someone, persuade them, or just get their attention, we must "perform" a social role in order to let them know what script we are trying to enact and what our expectations are.

"Behavior in Private Places" is a well-known sociological study of gynecology exams. Joan Emerson highlights the potentially precarious situation between medical staff, who want to define the exam as a sterile medical procedure, and the patient, who may feel violated and embarrassed. In this situation, the patient's cooperation cannot be taken for granted. Thus, the staff uses several strategies designed to keep the patient in her appropriate role so that the exam can be completed in a "routine" manner.

READING QUESTIONS

1. Based on Goffman's article, why do people often behave politely in encounters with someone they privately dislike?

2. Recall an occasion in which you mentally practiced an interaction before going into the situation. What impression were you hoping to convey? What resistance, if any, did you anticipate? Are you more likely to consciously practice a performance if the situation is new or if it's routine?

3. Recall a situation in which you were embarrassed. Was the embarrassment due to playing the wrong role for the situation, or misplaying the expected role for the situation? What's the difference?

4. Use the concepts of interaction routines, idealization, definition of the situation, and negotiating a working consensus to explain why people become so upset when things go wrong at "special events" such as weddings.

5. Why are children not allowed at certain events? Who else might be considered "socially incompetent" in certain settings?

6. Consider other events that involve precarious or "competing" definitions of the situation. In these events, do participants have to be more or less strategic in their performances? Why?

7. Think about someone you know who is just a little bit "off" (for example, the aunt who talks too loudly about sex, the uncle who drinks too much, the classmate who never "gets it"). How is it that you and others "know" this person is "off"? What unspoken interaction rules do you hold in common that the "off" person seems not to get? How do you and others respond to this person? Do the responses preserve the definition of the situation (that is, do you "accommodate" the person), or do you respond in ways that give the person information that he or she is "off"?

PROJECTING THE DEFINITION OF THE SITUATION

22

The Presentation of Self in Everyday Life: Selections

Erving Goffman

(1959)

INTRODUCTION

When an individual enters the presence of others, they commonly seek to acquire information about him or to bring into play information about him already possessed. They will be interested in his general socio-economic status, his conception of self, his attitude toward them, his competence, his trustworthiness, etc. Although some of this information seems to be sought almost as an end in itself, there are usually quite practical reasons for acquiring it. Information about the individual helps to define the situation, enabling others to know in advance what he will expect of them and what they may expect of him. Informed in these ways, the others will know how best to act in order to call forth a desired response from him.

For those present, many sources of information become accessible and many carriers (or "sign-vehicles") become available for conveying this information. If unacquainted with the individual, observers can glean clues from his conduct and appearance which allow them to apply their previous experience with individuals roughly similar to the one before them or, more important, to apply untested stereotypes to him. They can also assume from past experience that only individuals of a particular kind are likely to be found in a given social setting. They can rely on what the individual says about himself or on documentary evidence he provides as to who and what he is. If they know, or know of, the individual by virtue of experience prior to the interaction, they can rely on assumptions as to the persistence and generality of psychological traits as a means of predicting his present and future behavior. . . .

The expressiveness of the individual (and therefore his capacity to give impressions) appears to involve two radically different kinds of sign activity: the expression that he *gives,* and the expression that he *gives off.* The first involves verbal symbols or their substitutes which he uses admittedly and solely to convey the information that he and the others are known to attach to these symbols. This is communication in the traditional and narrow sense. The second involves a wide range of action that others can treat as symptomatic of the actor, the expectation being that the action was performed for reasons other than the information conveyed in this way. As we shall have to see, this distinction has only an initial validity. The individual does of course intentionally convey misinformation by means of both of these types of communication, the first involving deceit, the second feigning.

Taking communication in both its narrow and broad sense, one finds that when the individual is in the immediate presence of others, his activity will have a promissory character. The others are likely to find that they must accept the individual on faith, offering him a just return while he is present before them in exchange for something whose true value will not be established until after he has left their presence. (Of course, the others also live by inference in their dealings with the physical world, but it is only in the world of social interaction that the objects about which they make inferences will purposely facilitate and hinder this inferential process.) The security that they justifiably feel in making inferences about the individual will vary, of course, depending on such factors as the amount of information they already possess about him, but no amount of such past evidence can entirely obviate the necessity of acting on the basis of inferences. As William I. Thomas suggested:

> It is also highly important for us to realize that we do not as a matter of fact lead our lives, make our decisions, and reach our goals in everyday life either statistically or scientifically. We live by inference. I am, let us say, your guest. You do not know, you cannot determine scientifically, that I will not steal your money or your spoons. But inferentially I will not and inferentially you have me as a guest.[1]

Let us now turn from the others to the point of view of the individual who presents himself before them. He may wish them to think highly of him, or to think that he thinks highly of them, or to perceive how in fact he feels toward them, or to obtain no clear-cut impression; he may wish to ensure sufficient harmony so that the interaction can be sustained, or to defraud, get rid of, confuse, mislead, antagonize, or insult them. Regardless of the particular objective which the individual has in mind and of his motive for having this objective, it will be in his interests to control the conduct of the others, especially their responsive treatment of him.[2] This control is achieved largely by influencing the definition of the situation which the others come to formulate, and he can influence this

definition by expressing himself in such a way as to give them the kind of impression that will lead them to act voluntarily in accordance with his own plan. Thus, when an individual appears in the presence of others, there will usually be some reason for him to mobilize his activity so that it will convey an impression to others which it is in his interests to convey. . . .

I have said that when an individual appears before others his actions will influence the definition of the situation which they come to have. Sometimes the individual will act in a thoroughly calculating manner, expressing himself in a given way solely in order to give the kind of impression to others that is likely to evoke from them a specific response he is concerned to obtain. Sometimes the individual will be calculating in his activity but be relatively unaware that this is the case. Sometimes he will intentionally and consciously express himself in a particular way, but chiefly because the tradition of his group or social status require this kind of expression and not because of any particular response (other than vague acceptance or approval) that is likely to be evoked from those impressed by the expression. Sometimes the traditions of an individual's role will lead him to give a well-designed impression of a particular kind and yet he may be neither consciously nor unconsciously disposed to create such an impression. The others, in their turn, may be suitably impressed by the individual's efforts to convey something, or may misunderstand the situation and come to conclusions that are warranted neither by the individual's intent nor by the facts. In any case, insofar as the others act *as if* the individual had conveyed a particular impression, we may take a functional or pragmatic view and say that the individual has "effectively" projected a given definition of the situation and "effectively" fostered the understanding that a given state of affairs obtains. . . .

When we allow that the individual projects a definition of the situation when he appears before others, we must also see that the others, however passive their role may seem to be, will themselves effectively project a definition of the situation by virtue of their response to the individual and by virtue of any lines of action they initiate to him. Ordinarily the definitions of the situation projected by the several different participants are sufficiently attuned to one another so that open contradiction will not occur. I do not mean that there will be the kind of consensus that arises when each individual present candidly expresses what he really feels and honestly agrees with the expressed feelings of the others present. This kind of harmony is an optimistic ideal and in any case not necessary for the smooth working of society. Rather, each participant is expected to suppress his immediate heartfelt feelings, conveying a view of the situation which he feels the others will be able to find at least temporarily acceptable. The maintenance of this surface of agreement, this veneer of consensus, is facilitated by each participant concealing his own wants behind statements which assert values to which everyone present feels obliged to give lip service. Further, there is usually a kind of division of definitional labor. Each participant is allowed to establish the tentative official ruling regarding matters which are vital to him but not immediately important to others, e.g., the rationalizations and justifications by which he accounts for his past activity. In exchange for this courtesy he remains silent or noncommittal on matters important to others but not immediately important to him. We have then a kind of interactional *modus vivendi*. Together the participants contribute to a single overall definition of the situation which involves not so much a real agreement as to what exists but rather a real agreement as to whose claims concerning what issues will be temporarily honored. Real agreement will also exist concerning the desirability of avoiding an open conflict of definitions of the situation.[3] I will refer to this level of agreement as a "working consensus."

It is to be understood that the working consensus established in one interaction setting will be quite different in content from the working consensus established in a different type of setting. Thus, between two friends at lunch, a reciprocal show of affection, respect, and concern for the other is maintained. In service occupations, on the other hand, the specialist often maintains an image of disinterested involvement in the problem of the client, while the client responds with a show of respect for the competence and integrity of the specialist. Regardless of such differences in content, however, the general form of these working arrangements is the same. . . .

. . . Given the fact that the individual effectively projects a definition of the situation when he enters the presence of others, we can assume that events may occur within the interaction which contradict, discredit, or otherwise throw doubt upon this projection. When these disruptive events occur, the interaction itself may come to a confused and embarrassed halt. Some of the assumptions upon which the responses of the participants had been predicated become untenable, and the participants find themselves lodged in an interaction for which the situation has been wrongly defined and is now no longer defined. At such moments the individual whose presentation has been discredited may feel ashamed while the others present may feel hostile, and all the participants may come to feel ill at ease, nonplussed, out of countenance, embarrassed, experiencing the kind of anomy that is generated when the minute social system of face-to-face interaction breaks down. . . .

We find that preventive practices are constantly employed to avoid these embarrassments and that corrective practices are constantly employed to compensate for discrediting occurrences that have not been successfully avoided. When the individual employs these strategies and tactics to protect his own projections, we may refer to them as "defensive practices"; when a participant employs them to save the definition of the situation projected by another, we speak of "protective practices" or "tact." Together, defensive and protective practices comprise the techniques employed to safe-guard the impression fostered by an individual during his presence before others. It should be added that while we may be ready to see that no fostered impression would survive if defensive practices were not employed, we are less ready perhaps to see that few impressions could survive if those who received the impression did not exert tact in their reception of it.

In addition to the fact that precautions are taken to prevent disruption of projected definitions, we may also note that an intense interest in these disruptions comes to play a significant role in the social life of the group. Practical jokes and social games are played in which embarrassments which are to be taken unseriously are purposely engineered.[4] Fantasies are created in which devastating exposures occur. Anecdotes from the past—real, embroidered, or fictitious—are told and retold, detailing disruptions which occurred, almost occurred, or occurred and were admirably resolved. There seems to be no grouping which does not have a ready supply of these games, reveries, and cautionary tales, to be used as a source of humor, a catharsis for anxieties, and a sanction for inducing individuals to be modest in their claims and reasonable in their projected expectations. The individual may tell himself through dreams of getting into impossible positions. Families tell of the time a guest got his dates mixed and arrived when neither the house nor anyone in it was ready for him. Journalists tell of times when an all-too-meaningful misprint occurred, and the paper's assumption of objectivity or decorum was humorously discredited. Public servants tell of times a client ridiculously misunderstood form instructions, giving answers which implied an unanticipated and bizarre definition of the situation.[5] Seamen, whose home away from home is

rigorously he-man, tell stories of coming back home and inadvertently asking mother to "pass the fucking butter."[6] Diplomats tell of the time a near-sighted queen asked a republican ambassador about the health of his king.[7]

To summarize, then, I assume that when an individual appears before others he will have many motives for trying to control the impression they receive of the situation. This report is concerned with some of the common techniques that persons employ to sustain such impressions and with some of the common contingencies associated with the employment of these techniques. It will be convenient to end this introduction with some definitions. . . . For the purpose of this report, interaction (that is, face-to-face interaction) may be roughly defined as the reciprocal influence of individuals upon one another's actions when in one another's immediate physical presence. An interaction may be defined as all the interaction which occurs throughout any one occasion when a given set of individuals are in one another's continuous presence; the term "an encounter" would do as well. A "performance" may be defined as all the activity of a given participant on a given occasion which serves to influence in any way any of the other participants. Taking a particular participant and his performance as a basic point of reference, we may refer to those who contribute the other performances as the audience, observers, or co-participants. The pre-established pattern of action which is unfolded during a performance and which may be presented or played through on other occasions may be called a "part" or "routine."[8] These situational terms can easily be related to conventional structural ones. When an individual or performer plays the same part to the same audience on different occasions, a social relationship is likely to arise. Defining social role as the enactment of rights and duties attached to a given status, we can say that a social role will involve one or more parts and that each of these different parts may be presented by the performer on a series of occasions to the same kinds of audience or to an audience of the same persons. . . .

Performances

Front

I [use] the term "performance" to refer to all the activity of an individual which occurs during a period marked by his continuous presence before a particular set of observers and which has some influence on the observers. It will be convenient to label as "front" that part of the individual's performance which regularly functions in a general and fixed fashion to define the situation for those who observe the performance. Front, then, is the expressive equipment of a standard kind intentionally or unwittingly employed by the individual during his performance. For preliminary purposes, it will be convenient to distinguish and label what seem to be the standard parts of front.

First, there is the "setting," involving furniture, décor, physical layout, and other background items which supply the scenery and stage props for the spate of human action played out before, within, or upon it. A setting tends to stay put, geographically speaking, so that those who would use a particular setting as part of their performance cannot begin their act until they have brought themselves to the appropriate place and must terminate their performance when they leave it. It is only in exceptional circumstances that the setting follows along with the performers; we see this in the funeral cortège, the civic parade, and the dreamlike processions that kings and queens are made of. In the main, these exceptions seem to offer some kind of extra protection for performers who are, or who have momentarily become, highly sacred. . . .

It is sometimes convenient to divide the stimuli which make up personal front into "appearance" and "manner," according to the function performed by the information that these stimuli convey. "Appearance" may be taken to refer to those stimuli which function at the time to tell us of the performer's social statuses. These stimuli also tell us of the individual's temporary ritual state, that is, whether he is engaging in formal social activity, work, or informal recreation, whether or not he is celebrating a new phase in the season cycle or in his life-cycle. "Manner" may be taken to refer to those stimuli which function at the time to warn us of the interaction role the performer will expect to play in the oncoming situation. Thus a haughty, aggressive manner may give the impression that the performer expects to be the one who will initiate the verbal interaction and direct its course. A meek, apologetic manner may give the impression that the performer expects to follow the lead of others, or at least that he can be led to do so. . . .

Dramatic Realization

While in the presence of others, the individual typically infuses his activity with signs which dramatically highlight and portray confirmatory facts that might otherwise remain unapparent or obscure. For if the individual's activity is to become significant to others, he must mobilize his activity so that it will express *during the interaction* what he wishes to convey. In fact, the performer may be required not only to express his claimed capacities during the interaction but also to do so during a split second in the interaction. Thus, if a baseball umpire is to give the impression that he is sure of his judgment, he must forgo the moment of thought which might make him sure of his judgment; he must give an instantaneous decision so that the audience will be sure that he is sure of his judgment.[9] . . .

Similarly, the proprietor of a service establishment may find it difficult to dramatize what is actually being done for clients because the clients cannot "see" the overhead costs of the service rendered them. Undertakers must therefore charge a great deal for their highly visible product—a coffin that has been transformed into a casket—because many of the other costs of conducting a funeral are ones that cannot be readily dramatized.[10] Merchants, too, find that they must charge high prices for things that look intrinsically inexpensive in order to compensate the establishment for expensive things like insurance, slack periods, etc., that never appear before the customers' eyes. . . .

Idealization

. . . I want to consider here another important aspect of this socialization process—the tendency for performers to offer their observers an impression that is idealized in several different ways.

The notion that a performance presents an idealized view of the situation is, of course, quite common. Cooley's view may be taken as an illustration:

> If we never tried to seem a little better than we are, how could we improve or "train ourselves from the outside inward"? And the same impulse to show the world a better or idealized aspect of ourselves finds an organized expression in the various professions and classes, each of which has to some extent a cant or pose, which its members assume unconsciously, for the most part, but which has the effect of a conspiracy to work upon the credulity of the rest of the world. There is a cant not only of theology and of philanthropy, but also of law, medicine, teaching, even of science—perhaps especially of science, just now, since the more a particular kind of merit is recognized and admired, the more it is likely to be assumed by the unworthy.[11]

Thus, when the individual presents himself before others, his performance will tend to incorporate and exemplify the officially accredited values of the society, more so, in fact, than does his behavior as a whole.

To the degree that a performance highlights the common official values of the society in which it occurs, we may look upon it, in the manner of Durkheim and Radcliffe-Brown, as a ceremony—as an expressive rejuvenation and reaffirmation of the moral values of the community. Furthermore, insofar as the expressive bias of performances comes to be accepted as reality, then that which is accepted at the moment as reality will have some of the characteristics of a celebration. To stay in one's room away from the place where the party is given, or away from where the practitioner attends his client, is to stay away from where reality is being performed. The world, in truth, is a wedding.

One of the richest sources of data on the presentation of idealized performances is the literature on social mobility. In most societies there seems to be a major or general system of stratification, and in most stratified societies there is an idealization of the higher strata and some aspiration on the part of those in low places to move to higher ones. (One must be careful to appreciate that this involves not merely a desire for a prestigeful place but also a desire for a place close to the sacred center of the common values of the society.) Commonly we find that upward mobility involves the presentation of proper performances and that efforts to move upward and efforts to keep from moving downward are expressed in terms of sacrifices made for the maintenance of front. Once the proper sign-equipment has been obtained and familiarity gained in the management of it, then this equipment can be used to embellish and illumine one's daily performances with a favorable social style.

Perhaps the most important piece of sign-equipment associated with social class consists of the status symbols through which material wealth is expressed. American society is similar to others in this regard but seems to have been singled out as an extreme example of wealth-oriented class structure—perhaps because in

America the license to employ symbols of wealth and financial capacity to do so are so widely distributed. . . .

Reality and Contrivance

. . . Some performances are carried off successfully with complete dishonesty, others with complete honesty; but for performances in general neither of these extremes is essential and neither, perhaps, is dramaturgically advisable.

The implication here is that an honest, sincere, serious performance is less firmly connected with the solid world than one might first assume. And this implication will be strengthened if we look again at the distance usually placed between quite honest performances and quite contrived ones. In this connection take, for example, the remarkable phenomenon of stage acting. It does take deep skill, long training, and psychological capacity to become a good stage actor. But this fact should not blind us to another one: that almost anyone can quickly learn a script well enough to give a charitable audience some sense of realness in what is being contrived before them. And it seems this is so because ordinary social intercourse is itself put together as a scene is put together, by the exchange of dramatically inflated actions, counteractions, and terminating replies. Scripts even in the hands of unpracticed players can come to life because life itself is a dramatically enacted thing. All the world is not, of course, a stage, but the crucial ways in which it isn't are not easy to specify. . . .

When the individual does move into a new position in society and obtains a new part to perform, he is not likely to be told in full detail how to conduct himself, nor will the facts of his new situation press sufficiently on him from the start to determine his conduct without his further giving thought to it. Ordinarily he will be given only a few cues, hints, and stage directions, and it will be assumed that he already has in his repertoire a large number of bits and pieces of performances that will be required in the new setting. The individual will already have a fair idea of what modesty, deference, or righteous indignation looks like, and can make a pass at playing these bits when necessary. He may even be able to play out the part of a hypnotic subject[12] or commit a "compulsive" crime[13] on the basis of models for these activities that he is already familiar with.

A theatrical performance or a staged confidence game requires a thorough scripting of the spoken content of the routine; but the vast part involving "expression given off" is often determined by meager stage directions. It is expected that the performer of illusions will already know a good deal about how to manage his voice, his face, and his body, although he—as well as any person who directs him—may find it difficult indeed to provide a detailed verbal statement of this kind of knowledge. And in this, of course, we approach the situation of the straightforward man in the street. Socialization may not so much involve a learning of the many specific details of a single concrete part—often there could not be enough time or energy for this. What does seem to be required of the individual is that he learn enough pieces of expression to be able to "fill in" and manage, more or less, any part that he is likely to be given. The legitimate performances of everyday life are not "acted" or "put on" in the sense that the performer knows in advance just what he is going to do, and does this solely because of the effect it is likely to have. The expressions it is felt he is giving off will be especially "inaccessible" to him.[14] But as in the case of less legitimate performers, the incapacity of the ordinary individual to formulate in advance the movements of his eyes and body does not mean that he will not express himself through these devices in a way that is dramatized and performed in his repertoire of actions. In short, we all act better than we know how.

When we watch a television wrestler gouge, foul, and snarl at his opponent we are quite ready to see that, in spite of the dust, he is, and knows he is, merely playing at being the "heavy," and that in another match he may be given the other role, that of clean-cut wrestler, and perform this with equal verve and proficiency. We seem less ready to see, however, that while such details as the number and character of the falls may be fixed beforehand, the details of the expressions and movements used do not come from a script but from command of an idiom, a command that is exercised from moment to moment with little calculation or forethought. . . .

Personality-Interaction-Society

In recent years there have been elaborate attempts to bring into one framework the concepts and findings derived from three different areas of inquiry: the individual personality, social interaction, and society. I would like to suggest here a simple addition to these inter-disciplinary attempts.

When an individual appears before others, he knowingly and unwittingly projects a definition of the situation, of which a conception of himself is an important part. When an event occurs which is expressively incompatible with this fostered impression, significant consequences are simultaneously felt in three levels of social reality, each of which involves a different point of reference and a different order of fact.

First, the social interaction, treated here as a dialogue between two teams, may come to an embarrassed and confused halt; the situation may cease to be defined. Previous positions may become no longer tenable, and participants may find themselves without a charted course of action. The participants typically sense a false note in the situation and come to feel awkward, flustered, and, literally, out of countenance. In other words, the minute social system created and sustained by orderly social interaction becomes disorganized. These are the consequences that the disruption has from the point of view of social interaction.

Secondly, in addition to these disorganizing consequences for action at the moment, performance disruptions may have consequences of a more far-reaching kind. Audiences tend to accept the self projected by the individual performer during any current performance as a responsible representative of his colleague-grouping, of his team, and of his social establishment. Audiences also accept the individual's particular performance as evidence of his capacity to perform the routine and even as evidence of his capacity to perform any routine. In a sense these larger social units—teams, establishments, etc.—become committed every time the individual performs his routine; with each performance the legitimacy of these units will tend to be tested anew and their permanent reputation put at stake. This kind of commitment is especially strong during some performances. Thus, when a surgeon and his nurse both turn from the operating table and the anesthetized patient accidentally rolls off the table to his death, not only is the operation disrupted in an embarrassing way, but the reputation of the doctor, as a doctor and as a man, and also the reputation of the hospital may be weakened. These are the consequences that disruptions may have from the point of view of social structure.

Finally, we often find that the individual may deeply involve his ego in his identification with a particular part, establishment, and group, and in his self-conception as someone who does not disrupt social interaction or let down the social units which depend upon that interaction. When a disruption occurs, then, we may find that the self-conceptions around which his personality has been built may become discredited. These are consequences that disruptions may have from the point of view of individual personality.

Performance disruptions, then, have consequences at three levels of abstraction: personality, interaction, and social structure. While the likelihood of disruption will vary widely from interaction to interaction, and while the social importance of likely disruptions will vary from interaction to interaction, still it seems that there is no interaction in which the participants do not take an appreciable chance of being slightly embarrassed or a slight chance of being deeply humiliated. Life may not be much of a gamble, but interaction is. Further, insofar as individuals make efforts to avoid disruptions or to correct for ones not avoided, these efforts, too, will have simultaneous consequences at the three levels. Here, then, we have one simple way of articulating three levels of abstraction and three perspectives from which social life has been studied.

Staging and the Self

The general notion that we make a presentation of ourselves to others is hardly novel; what ought to be stressed in conclusion is that the very structure of the self can be seen in terms of how we arrange for such performances in our Anglo-American society. . . .

The self, then, as a performed character, is not an organic thing that has a specific location, whose fundamental fate is to be born, to mature, and to die; it is a dramatic effect arising diffusely from a scene that is presented, and the characteristic issue, the crucial concern, is whether it will be credited or discredited.

In analyzing the self then we are drawn from its possessor, from the person who will profit or lose most by it, for he and his body merely provide the peg on which something of collaborative manufacture will be hung for a time. And the means for producing and maintaining selves do not reside inside the peg; in fact these means are often bolted down in social establishments. There will be a back region with its tools for shaping the body, and a front region with its fixed props. There will be a team of persons whose activity on stage in conjunction with available props will constitute the scene from which the performed character's self will emerge, and another team, the audience, whose interpretive activity will be necessary for this emergence. The self is a product of all of these arrangements, and in all of its parts bears the marks of this genesis.

The whole machinery of self-production is cumbersome, of course, and sometimes breaks down, exposing its separate components: back region control; team collusion; audience tact; and so forth. But, well oiled, impressions will flow from it fast enough to put us in the grips of one of our types of reality—the performance will come off and the firm self accorded each performed character will appear to emanate intrinsically from its performer.

Let us turn now from the individual as character performed to the individual as performer. He has a capacity to learn, this being exercised in the task of training for a part. He is given to having fantasies and dreams, some that pleasurably unfold a triumphant performance, others full of anxiety and dread that nervously deal with vital discreditings in a public front region. He often manifests a gregarious desire for teammates and audiences, a tactful considerateness for their concerns; and he has a capacity for deeply felt shame, leading him to minimize the chances he takes of exposure.

These attributes of the individual *qua* performer are not merely a depicted effect of particular performances; they are psychobiological in nature, and yet they seem to arise out of intimate interaction with the contingencies of staging performances.

And now a final comment. In developing the conceptual framework employed in this report, some language of the stage was used. I spoke of performers and audiences; of routines and parts; of performances coming off or falling flat; of cues, stage settings, and backstage; of dramaturgical needs, dramaturgical skills, and dramaturgical strategies. Now it should be admitted that this attempt to press a mere analogy so far was in part a rhetoric and a maneuver. . . .

And so here the language and mask of the stage will be dropped. Scaffolds, after all, are to build other things with, and should be erected with an eye to taking them down.

This report is not concerned with aspects of theater that creep into everyday life. It is concerned with the structure of social encounters—the structure of those entities in social life that come into being whenever persons enter one another's immediate physical presence. The key factor in this structure is the maintenance of a single definition of the situation, this definition having to be expressed, and this expression sustained in the face of a multitude of potential disruptions.

A character staged in a theater is not in some ways real, nor does it have the same kind of real consequences as does the thoroughly contrived character performed by a confidence man; but the *successful* staging of either of these types of false figures involves use of *real* techniques—the same techniques by which everyday persons sustain their real social situations. Those who conduct face to face interaction on a theater's stage must meet the key requirement of real situations; they must expressively sustain a definition of the situation: but this they do in circumstances that have facilitated their developing an apt terminology for the interactional tasks that all of us share.

Notes

1. Quoted in E. H. Volkart, editor, *Social Behavior and Personality,* Contributions of W. I. Thomas to Theory and Social Research (New York: Social Science Research Council, 1951), p. 9.

2. Here I owe much to an unpublished paper by Tom Burns of the University of Edinburgh. He presents the argument that in all interaction a basic underlying theme is the desire of each participant to guide and control the responses made by the others present. A similar argument has been advanced by Jay Haley in a recent unpublished paper, but in regard to a special kind of control, that having to do with defining the nature of the relationship of those involved in the interaction.

3. An interaction can be purposely set up as a time and place for voicing differences in opinion. But in such cases participants *must* be careful to agree not to disagree on the proper tone of voice, vocabulary, and degree of seriousness in which all arguments are to be phrased, and upon the mutual respect which disagreeing participants must carefully continue to express toward one another. This debaters' or academic definition of the situation may also be invoked suddenly and judiciously as a way of translating a serious conflict of views into one that can be handled within a framework acceptable to all present.

4. Goffman, *op. cit.,* pp. 319–27.

5. Peter Blau, "Dynamics of Bureaucracy" (Ph.D. dissertation, Department of Sociology, Columbia University, forthcoming, University of Chicago Press), pp. 127–29.

6. Walter M. Beattie, Jr., "The Merchant Sea-man" (unpublished M.A. report, Department of Sociology, University of Chicago, 1950), p. 35.

7. Sir Frederick Ponsonby, *Recollections of Three Reigns* (New York: Dutton, 1952), p. 46.

8. For comments on the importance of distinguishing between a routine of interaction and any particular instance when this routine is played through, see John van Neumann and Oskar Morgenstern, *The Theory of Games and Economic Behaviour* (2nd ed.) (Princeton: Princeton University Press, 1947), p. 49.

9. See Babe Pinelli, as told to Joe King, *Mr. Ump* (Philadelphia: Westminster Press, 1953), p. 75.

10. Material on the burial business used throughout this report is taken from Robert W. Habenstein, "The American Funeral Director" (unpublished Ph.D. dissertation, Department of Sociology, University of Chicago, 1954). I owe much to Mr. Habenstein's analysis of a funeral as a performance.

11. Charles H. Cooley, *Human Nature and the Social Order* (New York: Scribner's, 1922), pp. 352–53.

12. This view of hypnosis is neatly presented by T. R. Sarbin, "Contributions to Role-Taking Theory. I: Hypnotic Behavior," *Psychological Review,* 57, pp. 255–70.

13. See D. R. Cressey, "The Differential Association Theory and Compulsive Crimes," *Journal of Criminal Law, Criminology and Police Science,* 45, pp. 29–40.

14. This concept derives from T. R. Sarbin, "Role Theory," in Gardner Lindzey, *Handbook of Social Psychology* (Cambridge: Addison-Wesley, 1954), Vol. 1, pp. 235–36.

PROJECTING THE DEFINITION OF THE SITUATION

23

Behavior in Private Places: Sustaining Definitions of Reality in Gynecological Examinations

Joan P. Emerson

(1970)

INTRODUCTION

In *The Social Construction of Reality,* Berger and Luckmann discuss how people construct social order and yet construe the reality of everyday life to exist independently of themselves.[1] Berger and Luckmann's work succeeds in synthesizing some existing answers with new insights. Many sociologists have pointed to the importance of social consensus in what people believe; if everyone else seems to believe in something, a person tends to accept the common belief without question. Other sociologists have discussed the concept of legitimacy, an acknowledgment that what exists has the right to exist, and delineated various lines of argument which can be taken to justify a state of affairs. Berger and Luckmann emphasize three additional processes that provide persons with evidence that things have an objective existence apart from themselves. Perhaps most important is the experience that reality seems to be out there before we arrive on the scene. This notion is fostered by the nature of language, which contains an all-inclusive scheme of categories, is shared by a community, and must be learned laboriously by each new member. Further, definitions of reality are continuously validated by apparently trivial features of the social scene, such as details of the setting, persons' appearance and demeanor, and "inconsequential" talk. Finally, each part of a systematic world view serves as evidence for all the other parts, so that reality is solidified by a process of intervalidation of supposedly independent events.

Because Berger and Luckmann's contribution is theoretical, their units of analysis are abstract processes. But they take those processes to be grounded in social encounters. Thus, Berger and Luckmann's theory provides a framework for making sense of social interaction. In this paper observations of a concrete situation will be interpreted to show how reality is embodied in routines and reaffirmed in social interaction.

Situations differ in how much effort it takes to sustain the current definition of the situation. Some situations are relatively stable; others are precarious.[2] Stability depends on the likelihood of

AUTHOR'S NOTE: Arlene K. Daniels has applied her talent for editing and organizing to several drafts of this paper. Robert M. Emerson, Roger Pritchard, and Thomas J. Scheff have also commented on the material. The investigation was supported in part by a predoctoral fellowship from the National Institute of Mental Health (Fellowship Number MPM-18,239) and by Behavioral Sciences Training Grant MH-8104 from the National Institute of Mental Health, as well as General Research Support Grant I-SOI-FR-05441 from the National Institutes of Health, U.S. Department of Health, Education, and Welfare, to the School of Public Health, University of California, Berkeley.

three types of disconforming events. Intrusions on the scene may threaten definitions of reality, as when people smell smoke in a theater or when a third person joins a couple and calls one member by a name the second member does not recognize. Participants may deliberately decline to validate the current reality, like Quakers who refused to take off their hats to the king. Sometimes participants are unable to produce the gestures which would validate the current reality. Perhaps a person is ignorant of the relevant vocabulary of gestures. Or a person, understanding how he should behave, may have limited social skills so that he cannot carry off the performance he would like to. For those who insist on "sincerity," a performance becomes especially taxing if they lack conviction about the trueness of the reality they are attempting to project.

A reality can hardly seem self-evident if a person is simultaneously aware of a counter-reality. Berger and Luckmann write as though definitions of reality were internally congruent. However, the ordinary reality may contain not only a dominant definition, but in addition counterthemes opposing or qualifying the dominant definition. Thus, several contradictory definitions must be sustained at the same time. Because each element tends to challenge the other elements, such composite definitions of reality are inherently precarious even if the probability of disconfirming events is low.

A situation where the definition of reality is relatively precarious has advantages for the analysis proposed here, for processes of sustaining reality should be more obvious where that reality is problematic. The situation chosen, the gynecological examination,[3] is precarious for both reasons discussed above. First, it is an excellent example of multiple contradictory definitions of reality, as described in the next section. Second, while intrusive and deliberate threats are not important, there is a substantial threat from participants' incapacity to perform.

Dramaturgical abilities are taxed in gynecological examinations because the less convincing reality internalized by secondary socialization is unusually discrepant with rival perspectives taken for granted in primary socialization.[4] Gynecological examinations share similar problems of reality-maintenance with any medical procedure, but the issues are more prominent because the site of the medical task is a woman's genitals. Because touching usually connotes personal intimacy, persons may have to work at accepting the physician's privileged access to the patient's genitals.[5] Participants are not entirely convinced that modesty is out of place. Since a woman's genitals are commonly accessible only in a sexual context, sexual connotations come readily to mind. Although most people realize that sexual responses are inappropriate, they may be unable to dismiss the sexual reaction privately and it may interfere with the conviction with which they undertake their impersonal performance. The structure of a gynecological examination highlights the very features which the participants are supposed to disattend. So the more attentive the participants are to the social situation, the more the unmentionable is forced on their attention.

The next section will characterize the complex composition of the definition of reality routinely sustained in gynecological examinations. Then some of the routine arrangements and interactional maneuvers which embody and express this definition will be described. A later section will discuss threats to the definition which arise in the course of the encounter. Measures that serve to neutralize the threats and reaffirm the definition will be analyzed. The concluding section will turn to the theoretical issues of precariousness, multiple contradictory definitions of reality, and implicit communication.

THE MEDICAL DEFINITION AND ITS COUNTERTHEMES

Sometimes people are in each other's presence in what they take to be a "gynecological examination."

What happens in a gynecological examination is part of the common stock of knowledge. Most people know that a gynecological examination is when a doctor examines a woman's genitals in a medical setting. Women who have undergone this experience know that the examination takes place in a special examining room where the patient lies with her buttocks down to the edge of the table and her feet in stirrups, that usually a nurse is present as a chaperone, that the actual examining lasts only a few minutes, and so forth. Besides knowing what equipment to provide for the doctor, the nurse has in mind a typology of responses patients have to this situation, and a typology of doctors' styles of performance. The doctor has technical knowledge about the examining procedures, what observations may be taken to indicate ways of getting patients to relax, and so on.

Immersed in the medical world where the scene constitutes a routine, the staff assume the responsibility for a credible performance. The staff take part in gynecological examinations many times a day, while the patient is a fleeting visitor. More deeply convinced of the reality themselves, the staff are willing to convince skeptical patients. The physician guides the patient through the precarious scene in a contained manner: taking the initiative, controlling the encounter, keeping the patient in line, defining the situation by his reaction, and giving cues that "this is done" and "other people go through this all the time."

Not only must people continue to believe that "this is a gynecological examination," but also that "this is a gynecological examination going right." The major definition to be sustained for this purpose is "this is a medical situation" (not a party, sexual assault, psychological experiment, or anything else). If it is a medical situation, then it follows that "no one is embarrassed"[6] and "no one is thinking in sexual terms."[7] Anyone who indicates the contrary must be swayed by some nonmedical definition.

The medical definition calls for a matter-of-fact stance. One of the most striking observations about a gynecological examination is the marked implication underlying the staff's demeanor toward the patient: "Of course, you take this as matter-of-factly as we do." The staff implicitly contend: "In the medical world the pelvic area is like any other part of the body; its private and sexual connotations are left behind when you enter the hospital." The staff want it understood that their gazes take in only medically pertinent facts, so they are not concerned with an aesthetic inspection of a patient's body. Their nonchalant pose attempts to put a gynecological examination in the same light as an internal examination of the ear.

Another implication of the medical definition is that the patient is a technical object to the staff. It is as if the staff work on an assembly line for repairing bodies; similar body parts continually roll by and the staff have a particular job to do on them. The staff are concerned with the typical features of the body part and its pathology rather than with the unique features used to define a person's identity. The staff disattend the connection between a part of the body and some intangible self that is supposed to inhabit the body.

The scene is credible precisely because the staff act as if they have every right to do what they are doing. Any hint of doubt from the staff would compromise the medical definition. Since the patient's nonchalance merely serves to validate the staff's right, it may be dispensed with or without the same threat. Furthermore, the staff claim to be merely agents of the medical system, which is intent on providing good health care to patients. This medical system imposes procedures and standards which the staff are merely following in this particular instance. That is, what the staff do derives from external coercion—"We have to do it this way"—rather than from personal choices which they would be free to revise in order to accommodate the patient.

The medical definition grants the staff the right to carry out their task. If not for the medical definition the staff's routine activities could be defined as unconscionable assaults on the dignity of individuals. The topics of talk, particularly inquiries about bodily functioning, sexual experience, and death of relatives might be taken as offenses against propriety. As for exposure and manipulation of the patient's body, it would be a shocking and degrading invasion of privacy were the patient not defined as a technical object. The infliction of pain would be mere cruelty. The medical definition justifies the request that a presumably competent adult give up most of his autonomy to persons often subordinate in age, sex, and social class. The patient needs the medical definition to minimize the threat to his dignity; the staff need it in order to inveigle the patient into cooperating.

Yet definitions that appear to contradict the medical definition are routinely expressed in the course of gynecological examinations. Some gestures acknowledge the pelvic area as special; other gestures acknowledge the patient as a person. These counterdefinitions are as essential to the encounter as the medical definition. We have already discussed how an actor's lack of conviction may interfere with his performance. Implicit acknowledgments of the special meaning of the pelvic area help those players hampered by lack of conviction to perform adequately. If a player's sense of "how things really are" is implicitly acknowledged, he often finds it easier to adhere outwardly to a contrary definition.

A physician may gain a patient's cooperation by acknowledging her as a person. The physician wants the patient to acknowledge the medical definition, cooperate with the procedures of the examination, and acknowledge his professional competence. The physician is in a position to bargain with the patient in order to obtain this cooperation. He can offer her attention and acknowledgment as a person. At times he does so.

Although defining a person as a technical object is necessary in order for medical activities to proceed, it constitutes an indignity in itself. This indignity can be canceled or at least qualified by simultaneously acknowledging the patient as a person.

The medical world contains special activities and special perspectives. Yet the inhabitants of the medical world travel back and forth to the general community where modesty, death, and other medically relevant matters are regarded quite differently. It is not so easy to dismiss general community meanings for the time one finds oneself in a medical setting. The counterthemes that the pelvic area is special and that patients are persons provide an opportunity to show deference to general community meanings at the same time that one is disregarding them.

Sustaining the reality of a gynecological examination does not mean sustaining the medical definition, then. What is to be sustained is a shifting balance between medical definition and counterthemes.[8] Too much emphasis on the medical definition alone would undermine the reality, as would a flamboyant manifestation of the counterthemes apart from the medical definition. The next three sections will suggest how this balance is achieved.

SUSTAINING THE REALITY

The appropriate balance between medical definition and counterthemes has to be created anew at every moment. However, some routinized procedures and demeanor are available to participants in gynecological examinations. Persons recognize that if certain limits are exceeded, the situation would be irremediably shattered. Some arrangements have been found useful because they simultaneously express medical definition and countertheme. Routine ways of meeting the task requirements and also dealing with "normal trouble" are available.

This section will describe how themes and counterthemes are embodied in routinized procedures and demeanor.

The pervasiveness of the medical definition is expressed by indicators that the scene is enacted under medical auspices.[9] The action is located in "medical space" (hospital or doctor's office). Features of the setting such as divisions of space, decor, and equipment are constant reminders that it is indeed "medical space." Even background details such as the loudspeaker calling, "Dr. Morris. Dr. Armand Morris" serve as evidence for medical reality (suppose the loudspeaker were to announce instead, "Five minutes until post time"). The staff wear medical uniforms, don medical gloves, use medical instruments. The exclusion of lay persons, particularly visitors of the patient who may be accustomed to the patient's nudity at home, helps to preclude confusion between the contact of medicine and the contact of intimacy.[10]

Some routine practices simultaneously acknowledge the medical definition and qualify it by making special provision for the pelvic area. For instance, rituals of respect express dignity for the patient. The patient's body is draped so as to expose only that part which is to receive the technical attention of the doctor. The presence of a nurse acting as "chaperone" cancels any residual suggestiveness of male and female alone in a room.[11]

Medical talk stands for and continually expresses allegiance to the medical definition. Yet certain features of medical talk acknowledge a nonmedical delicacy. Despite the fact that persons present on a gynecological ward must attend to many topics connected with the pelvic area and various bodily functions, these topics are generally not discussed. Strict conventions dictate what unmentionables are to be acknowledged under what circumstances. However, persons are exceptionally free to refer to the genitals and related matters on the obstetrics-gynecology service. If technical matters in regard to the pelvic area come up, they are to be discussed nonchalantly.

The special language found in staff-patient contacts contributes to depersonalization and desexualization of the encounter. Scientific-sounding medical terms facilitate such communication. Substituting dictionary terms for everyday words adds formality. The definite article replaces the pronoun adjective in reference to body parts, so that for example, the doctor refers to "the vagina" and never "your vagina." Instructions to the patient in the course of the examination are couched in language which bypasses sexual imagery; the vulgar connotation of "spread your legs" is generally metamorphosed into the innocuous "let your knees fall apart."

While among themselves the staff generally use explicit technical terms, explicit terminology is often avoided in staff-patient contacts.[12] The reference to the pelvic area may be merely understood, as when a patient says: "I feel so uncomfortable there right now" or "They didn't go near to this area, so why did they have to shave it?" In speaking with patients the staff frequently uses euphemisms. A doctor asks: "When did you first notice difficulty down below?" and a nurse inquires: "Did you wash between your legs?" Persons characteristically refer to pelvic examinations euphemistically in staff-patient encounters. "The doctors want to take a peek at you," a nurse tells a patient. Or "Dr. Ryan wants to see you in the examining room."

In one pelvic examination there was a striking contrast between the language of staff and patient. The patient was graphic; she used action words connoting physical contact to refer to the examination procedure: feeling, poking, touching, and punching. Yet she never located this action in regard to her body, always omitting to state where the physical contact occurred. The staff used impersonal medical language and euphemisms: "I'm going to examine you"; "I'm just cleaning out some blood clots"; "He's just trying to fix you up a bit."

Sometimes the staff introduce explicit terminology to clarify a patient's remark. A patient tells the doctor, "It's bleeding now" and the doctor answers, "You? From the vagina?" Such a response indicates the appropriate vocabulary, the degree of freedom permitted in technically oriented conversation, and the proper detachment. Yet the common avoidance of explicit terminology in staff-patient contacts suggests that despite all the precautions to assure that the medical definition prevails, many patients remain somewhat embarrassed by the whole subject. To avoid provoking this embarrassment, euphemisms and understood references are used when possible.

Highly specific requirements for everybody's behavior during a gynecological examination curtail the leeway for the introduction of discordant notes. Routine technical procedures organize the event from beginning to end, indicating what action each person should take at each moment. Verbal exchanges are also constrained by the technical task, in that the doctor uses routine phrases of direction and reassurance to the patient. There is little margin for ad-libbing during a gynecological examination.

The specifications for demeanor are elaborate. Foremost is that both staff and patient should be nonchalant about what is happening. According to the staff, the exemplary patient should be "in play": showing she is attentive to the situation by her bodily tautness, facial expression, direction of glance, tone of voice, tempo of speech and bodily movements, timing and appropriateness of responses. The patient's voice should be controlled, mildly pleasant, self-confident, and impersonal. Her facial expression should be attentive and neutral, leaning toward the mildly pleasant and friendly side, as if she were talking to the doctor in his office, fully dressed and seated in a chair. The patient is to have an attentive glance upward,

at the ceiling or at other persons in the room, eyes open, not dreamy or "away," but ready at a second's notice to revert to the doctor's face for a specific verbal exchange. Except for such a verbal exchange, however, the patient is supposed to avoid looking into the doctor's eyes during the actual examination because direct eye contact between the two at this time is provocative. Her role calls for passivity and self-effacement. The patient should show willingness to relinquish control to the doctor. She should refrain from speaking at length and from making inquiries which would require the doctor to reply at length. So as not to point up her undignified position, she should not project her personality profusely. The self must be eclipsed in order to sustain the definition that the doctor is working on a technical object and not a person.

The physician's demeanor is highly stylized. He intersperses his examination with remarks to the patient in a soothing tone of voice: "Now relax as much as you can"; "I'll be as gentle as I can"; "Is that tender right there?" Most of the phrases with which he encourages the patient to relax are routine even though his delivery may suggest a unique relationship. He demonstrates that he is the detached professional and the patient demonstrates that it never enters her mind that he could be anything except detached. Since intimacy can be introduced into instrumental physical contact by a "loving" demeanor (lingering, caressing motions and contact beyond what the task requires), a doctor must take special pains to ensure that his demeanor remains a brisk, no-nonsense show of efficiency.[13]

Once I witnessed a gynecological examination of a forty-year-old woman who played the charming and scatterbrained Southern belle. The attending physician stood near the patient's head and carried on a flippant conversation with her while a resident and medical student actually performed the examination. The patient completely ignored the examination, except for brief answers to the examining doctor's inquiries. Under these somewhat trying circumstances she attempted to carry off a gay, attractive pose and the attending physician cooperated with her by making a series of bantering remarks.

Most physicians are not so lucky as to have a colleague conversing in cocktail-hour style with the patient while they are probing her vagina. Ordinarily the physician must play both parts at once, treating the patient as an object with his hands while simultaneously acknowledging her as a person with his voice. In this incident, where two physicians simultaneously deal with the patient in two distinct ways, the dual approach to the patient usually maintained by the examining physician becomes more obvious.[14]

The doctor needs to communicate with the patient as a person for technical reasons. Should he want to know when the patient feels pain in the course of examination or information about other medical matters, he must address her as a person. Also the doctor may want to instruct the patient on how to facilitate the examination. The most reiterated instruction refers to relaxation. Most patients are not sufficiently relaxed when the doctor is ready to begin. He then reverts to a primitive level of communication and treats the patient almost like a young child. He speaks in a soft, soothing voice, probably calling the patient by her first name, and it is not so much the words as his manner which is significant. This caressing voice is routinely used by hospital staff members to patients in critical situations, as when the patient is overtly frightened or disoriented. By using it here the doctor heightens his interpersonal relation with the patient, trying to reassure her as a person in order to get her to relax.

Moreover even during a gynecological examination, failing to acknowledge another as a person is an insult. It is insulting to be entirely instrumental about instrumental contacts. Some

acknowledgment of the intimate connotations of touching must occur. Therefore, a measure of "loving" demeanor is subtly injected. A doctor cannot employ the full gamut of loving insinuations that a lover might infuse into instrumental touching. So he indirectly implies a hint of intimacy which is intended to counter the insult and make the procedure acceptable to the woman. The doctor conveys this loving demeanor not by lingering or superfluous contact, but by radiating concern in his general manner, offering extra assistance, and occasionally by sacrificing the task requirements to "gentleness."

In short, the doctor must convey an optimal combination of impersonality and hints of intimacy that simultaneously avoid the insult of sexual familiarity and the insult of unacknowledged identity. The doctor must manage this even though the behavior emanating from each definition is contradictory. If the doctor can achieve this feat, it will contribute to keeping the patient in line. In the next section, we will see how the patient may threaten this precarious balance.

PRECARIOUSNESS IN GYNECOLOGICAL EXAMINATIONS

Threats to the reality of a gynecological examination may occur if the balance of opposing definitions is not maintained as described above. Reality in gynecological examinations is challenged mainly by patients. Occasionally a medical student, who might be considerably more of a novice than an experienced patient, seemed uncomfortable in the scene.[15] Experienced staff members were rarely observed to undermine the reality.

Certain threatening events which could occur in any staff-patient encounter bring an added dimension of precariousness to a gynecological examination because the medical aegis screens so much more audacity at that time. In general, staff expect patients to remain poised and in play like a friendly office receptionist; any show of emotion except in a controlled fashion is objectionable. Patients should not focus on identities of themselves or the staff outside those relevant to the medical exchange. Intractable patients may complain about the pain, discomfort, and indignities of submitting to medical treatment and care. Patients may go so far as to show they are reluctant to comply with the staff. Even if they are complying, they may indirectly challenge the expert status of the staff, as by "asking too many questions."

Failure to maintain a poised performance is a possible threat in any social situation. Subtle failures of tone are common, as when a performer seems to lack assurance. Performers may fumble for their lines: hesitate, begin a line again, or correct themselves. A show of embarrassment, such as blushing, has special relevance in gynecological examinations. On rare occasions when a person shows signs of sexual response, he or she really has something to blush about. A more subtle threat is an indication that the actor is putting an effort into the task of maintaining nonchalant demeanor; if it requires such an effort, perhaps it is not a "natural" response.

Such effort may be indicated, for example, in regard to the direction of glance. Most situations have a common visual focus of attention, but in a gynecological examination the logical focus, the patient's internal organs, is not accessible; and none of the alternatives, such as staring at the patient's face, locking glances with others, or looking out the window are feasible. The unavailability of an acceptable place to rest the eyes is more evident when the presence of several medical students creates a "crowd" atmosphere in the small cubicle. The lack of a visual focus of attention and the necessity to shift the eyes from object to object requires the participants to remain vaguely aware of their directions of glance. Normally the resting

place of the eyes is a background matter automatically managed without conscious attention. Attentiveness to this background detail is a constant reminder of how awkward the situation is.

Certain lapses in patients' demeanor are so common as hardly to be threatening. When patients express pain it can be overlooked if the patient is giving other signs of trying to behave well, because it can be taken that the patient is temporarily overwhelmed by a physiological state. The demonstrated presence of pain recalls the illness framework and counters sexual connotations. Crying can be accredited to pain and dismissed in a similar way. Withdrawing attention from the scene, so that one is not ready with an immediate comeback when called upon, is also relatively innocuous because it is close to the required passive but in play demeanor.

Some threats derive from the patient's ignorance of how to strike an acceptable balance between medical and nonmedical definitions, despite her willingness to do so. In two areas in particular, patients stumble over the subtleties of what is expected: physical decorum (proprieties of sights, sounds, and smells of the body) and modesty. While the staff is largely concerned with behavioral decorum and not about lapses in physical decorum, patients are more concerned about the latter, whether due to their medical condition or the procedure. Patients sometimes even let behavioral decorum lapse in order to express their concern about unappealing conditions of their bodies, particularly discharges and odors. This concern is a vestige of a nonmedical definition of the situation, for an attractive body is relevant only in a personal situation and not in a medical one.

Some patients fail to know when to display their private parts unashamedly to others and when to conceal them like anyone else. A patient may make an "inappropriate" show of modesty, thus not granting the staff the right to view what medical personnel have the right to view and others do not. But if patients act as though they literally accept the medical definition this also constitutes a threat. If a patient insists on acting as if the exposure of her breasts, buttocks, and pelvic area are no different from exposure of her arm or leg, she is "immodest." The medical definition is supposed to be in force only as necessary to facilitate specific medical tasks. If a patient becomes nonchalant enough to allow herself to remain uncovered for much longer than is technically necessary she becomes a threat. This also holds for verbal remarks about personal matters. Patients who misinterpret the license by exceeding its limits unwittingly challenge the definition of reality.[16]

NEUTRALIZING THREATENING EVENTS

Most gynecological examinations proceed smoothly and the definition of reality is sustained without conscious attention.[17] Sometimes subtle threats to the definition arise, and occasionally staff and patient struggle covertly over the definition throughout the encounters.[18] The staff take more preventive measures where they anticipate the most trouble: young, unmarried girls; persons known to be temporarily upset; and persons with reputations as uncooperative. In such cases the doctor may explain the technical details of the procedure more carefully and offer direct reassurance. Perhaps he will take extra time to establish personal rapport, as by medically related inquiries ("How are you feeling?" "Do you have as much pain today?"), personal inquiries ("Where do you live?"), addressing the patient by her first name, expressing direct sympathy, praising the patient for her behavior in this difficult situation, speaking in a caressing voice, and affectionate gestures. Doctors also attempt to reinforce rapport as a response to threatening events.

The foremost technique in neutralizing threatening events is to sustain a nonchalant demeanor even if the patient is blushing with embarrassment, blanching from fear, or moaning in pain. The patient's inappropriate gestures may be ignored as the staff convey, "We're waiting until you are ready to play along." Working to bring the scene off, the staff may claim that this is routine, or happens to patients in general; invoke the "for your own good" clause; counterclaim that something is less important than the patient indicates; assert that the unpleasant medical procedure is almost over; and contend that the staff do not like to cause pain or trouble to patients (as by saying, "I'm sorry" when they appear to be causing pain). The staff may verbally contradict a patient, give an evasive answer to a question, or try to distract the patient. By giving a technical explanation or rephrasing in the appropriate hospital language something the patient has referred to in a nonmedical way, the staff member reinstates the medical definition.

Redefinition is another tactic available to the staff. Signs of embarrassment and sexual arousal in patients may be redefined as "fear of pain." Sometimes sexual arousal will be labeled "ticklishness." After one examination the doctor thanked the patient, presumably for her cooperation, thus typifying the patient's behavior as cooperative and so omitting a series of uncooperative acts which he had previously acknowledged.

Humor may be used to discount the line the patient is taking. At the same time, humor provides a safety valve for all parties whereby the sexual connotations and general concern about gynecological examinations may be expressed by indirection. Without taking the responsibility that a serious form of the message would entail, the participants may communicate with each other about the events at hand. They may discount the derogatory implications of what would be an invasion of privacy in another setting by dismissing the procedure with a laugh. If a person can joke on a topic, he demonstrates to others that he possesses a laudatory degree of detachment.

For example, in one encounter a patient vehemently protests, "Oh, Dr. Raleigh, what are you doing?" Dr. Raleigh, exaggerating his southern accent, answers, "Nothin'." His levity conveys: "However much you may dislike this, we have to go on with it for your own good. Since you know that perfectly well, your protest could not be calling for a serious answer." Dr. Raleigh also plays the seducer claiming innocence, thus obliquely referring to the sexual connotations of where his hand is at the moment. In another incident Dr. Ryan is attempting to remove some gauze which has been placed in the vagina to stop the bleeding. He flippantly announces that the remaining piece of gauze has disappeared inside the patient. After a thorough search Dr. Ryan holds up a piece of gauze on the instrument triumphantly: "Well, here it is. Do you want to take it home and put it in your scrapbook?" By this remark Dr. Ryan ridicules the degree of involvement in one's own medical condition which would induce a patient to save this kind of memento. Later in the same examination Dr. Ryan announces he will do a rectal examination and the (elderly) patient protests, "Oh, honey, don't bother." Dr. Ryan assures her jokingly, "It's no bother, really." The indirect message of all three jokes is that one should take gynecological procedures casually. Yet simultaneously an undercurrent of each joke acknowledges a perspective contrary to the medical definition.

While in most encounters the nurse remains quietly in the background, she comes forward to deal actively with the patient if the definition of reality is threatened. In fact, one of the main functions of her presence is to provide a team member for the doctor in those occasional instances where the patient threatens to get out of line. Team members can create a more convincing reality than one person alone. Doctor and nurse may collude against an uncooperative patient, as by giving each other significant looks. If things reach the point of staff collusion, however, it may mean that only by excluding the patient can the definition of reality be reaffirmed. A more drastic form of solidifying the definition by excluding recalcitrant participants is to cast the patient into the role of an "emotionally disturbed person." Whatever an "emotionally disturbed person" may think or do does not count against the reality the rest of us acknowledge.

Perhaps the major safeguard of reality is that challenge is channeled outside the examination. Comments about the unpleasantness of the procedure and unaesthetic features of the patient's body occur mainly between women, two patients or a nurse and a patient. Such comments are most frequent while the patient gets ready for the examination and waits for the doctor or after the doctor leaves. The patient may establish a momentary "fellow-woman aura" as she quietly voices her distaste for the procedure to the nurse. "What we women have to go through" the patient may say. Or, "I wish all gynecologists were women." Why? "They understand because they've been through it themselves." The patient's confiding manner implies: "I have no right to say this, or even feel it, and yet I do." This phenomenon suggests that patients actually have strong negative reactions to gynecological examinations which belie their acquiescence in the actual situation. Yet patients' doubts are expressed in an innocuous way which does not undermine the definition of reality when it is most needed.

To construct the scene convincingly, participants constantly monitor their own behavior and that of others. The tremendous work of producing the scene is contained in subtle maneuvers in regard to details which may appear inconsequential to the layman. Since awareness may interfere with a convincing performance, the participants may have an investment in being as unself-conscious as possible. But the sociologist is free to recognize the significance of "inconsequential details" in constructing reality.

CONCLUSION

In a gynecological examination the reality sustained is not the medical definition alone, but a dissonance of themes and counterthemes. What is done to acknowledge one theme undermines the others. No theme can be taken for granted because its opposite is always in mind. That is why the reality of a gynecological examination can never be routinized, but always remains precarious.

The gynecological examination should not be dismissed as an anomaly. The phenomenon is revealed more clearly in this case because it is an extreme example. But the gynecological examination merely exaggerates the internally contradictory nature of definitions of reality found in most situations. Many situations where the dominant definition is occupational or technical have a secondary theme of sociality which must be implicitly acknowledged (as in buttering up the secretary, small talk with sales clerks, or the undertaker's show of concern for the bereaved family). In "business entertaining" and conventions of professional associations a composite definition of work and pleasure is sustained. Under many circumstances a composite definition of action as both deviant and unproblematic prevails. For example, while Donald Ball stresses the claim of respectability in his description of an abortion clinic, his material illustrates the interplay of the dominant theme of respectability and a countertheme wherein the illicitness of the situation is acknowledged.[19] Internally inconsistent definitions also are sustained in many settings on who persons are and what their relation is to each other.

Sustaining a sense of the solidness of a reality composed of multiple contradictory definitions takes unremitting effort. The required balance among the various definitions fluctuates from moment to moment. The appropriate balance depends on what the participants are trying to do at that moment. As soon as one matter is dealt with, something else comes into focus, calling for a different balance. Sometimes even before one issue is completed, another may impose itself as taking priority. Further, each balance contains the seeds of its own demise, in that a temporary emphasis on one theme may disturb the long-run balance unless subsequent emphasis on the countertheme negates it. Because the most effective balance depends on many unpredictable factors, it is difficult to routinize the balance into formulas that prescribe a specific balance for given conditions. Routinization is also impractical because the particular forms by which the themes are expressed are opportunistic. That is, persons seize opportunities for expression according to what would be a suitable move at each unique moment of an encounter. Therefore, a person constantly must attend to how to express the balance of themes via the currently available means.

Multiple contradictory realities are expressed on various levels of explicitness and implicitness. Sustaining a sense of solidness of reality depends on the right balance of explicit and implicit expressions of each theme through a series of points in time. The most effective gestures express a multitude of themes on different levels. The advantages of multiple themes in the same gesture are simultaneous qualification of one theme by another, hedging (the gesture lacks one definite meaning), and economy of gestures.

Rational choices of explicit and implicit levels would take the following into account. The explicit level carries the most weight, unless countered by deliberate effort. Things made explicit are hard to dismiss or discount compared to what is left implicit. In fact, if the solidification of explication is judged to be nonreversible, use of the explicit level may not be worth the risk. On the other hand, when participants sense that the implicit level is greatly in use, their whole edifice of belief may become shaken. "I sense that a lot is going on underneath" makes a person wonder about the reality he is accepting. There must be a lot he does not know, some of which might be evidence which would undermine what he currently accepts.

The invalidation of one theme by the concurrent expression of its countertheme must be avoided by various maneuvers. The guiding principle is that participants must prevent a definition that a contradiction exists between theme and countertheme from emerging. Certain measures routinely contribute to this purpose. Persons must try to hedge on both theme and countertheme by expressing them tentatively rather than definitely and simultaneously alluding to and discounting each theme. Theme and countertheme should not be presented simultaneously or contiguously on the explicit level unless it is possible to discount their contradictory features. Finally, each actor must work to keep the implicit level out of awareness for the other participants.

The technique of constructing reality depends on good judgment about when to make things explicit and when to leave them implicit, how to use the implicit level to reinforce and qualify the explicit level, distributing themes among explicit and implicit levels at any one moment, and seizing opportunities to embody messages. To pursue further these tentative suggestions on how important explicit and implicit levels are for sustaining reality, implicit levels of communication must be explored more systematically.

NOTES

1. P. Berger & T. Luckmann (1966), *The social construction of reality*, Garden City, NY: Doubleday.

2. The precarious nature of social interaction is discussed throughout the work of Erving Goffman.

3. The data in this article are based on observations of approximately 75 gynecological examinations conducted by male physicians on an obstetrics-gynecology ward and some observations from a medical ward for comparison. For a full account of this study, see J. P. Emerson (1963), "Social functions of humor in a hospital setting," unpublished doctoral dissertation, University of California at Berkeley. For a sociological discussion of a similar setting, see W. P. Rosengren & S. DeVault (1963), "The sociology of time and space in an obstetrical hospital," in E. Freidson (Ed.), *The hospital in modern society* (pp. 266–292), New York: Free Press of Glencoe.

4. "It takes severe biographical shocks to disintegrate the massive reality internalized in early childhood; much less to destroy the realities internalized later. Beyond this, it is relatively easy to set aside the reality of the secondary internalizations." Berger & Luckmann (1966), p. 142.

5. As stated by Lief and Fox: "The amounts and occasions of bodily contact are carefully regulated in all societies, and very much so in ours. Thus, the kind of access to the body of the patient that a physician in our society has is a uniquely privileged one. Even in the course of a so-called routine physical examination, the physician is permitted to handle the patient's body in ways otherwise permitted only to special intimates, and in the case of procedures such as rectal and vaginal examinations in ways normally not even permitted to a sexual partner." H. I. Lief & R. C. Fox (1963), "Training for 'detached concern' in medical students," in H. I. Lief et al. (Eds.), *The psychological basis of medical practice*, New York: Harper & Row, p. 32. As Edward Hall remarks, North Americans have an inarticulated convention that discourages touching except in moments of intimacy. E. T. Hall (1959), *The silent language*, Garden City, NY: Doubleday, p. 149.

6. For comments on embarrassment in the doctor-patient relation, see M. Balint (1957), *The doctor, his patient, and the illness*, New York: International Universities Press, p. 57.

7. Physicians are aware of the possibility that their routine technical behavior may be interpreted as sexual by the patient. The following quotation states a view

held by some physicians: "It is not unusual for a suspicious hysterical woman with fantasies of being seduced to misinterpret an ordinary movement in the physical examination as an amorous advance." E. Weiss & O. S. English (1949), *Psychosomatic medicine*, Philadelphia: W. B. Saunders; quoted in M. Hollender (1958), *The psychology of medical practice*, Philadelphia: W. B. Saunders, p. 22. An extreme case suggests that pelvic examinations are not without their hazards for physicians, particularly during training: "A third-year student who had prided himself on his excellent adjustment to the stresses of medical school developed acute anxiety when about to perform, for the first time, a pelvic examination on a gynecological patient. Prominent in his fantasies were memories of a punishing father who would unquestionably forbid any such explicitly sexual behavior." S. Bojar (1961), "Psychiatric problems of medical students," in G. B. Glaine, Jr., et al. (Eds.), *Emotional problems of the student*, Garden City, NY: Doubleday, p. 248.

8. Many other claims and assumptions are being negotiated or sustained in addition to this basic definition of the situation. Efforts in regard to some of these other claims and assumptions have important consequences for the fate of the basic definition. That is, in the actual situation any one gesture usually has relevance for a number of realities, so that the fates of the various realities are intertwined with each other. For example, each participant is putting forth a version of himself which he wants validated. A doctor's jockeying about claims about competence may reinforce the medical definition and so may a patient's interest in appearing poised. But a patient's ambition to "understand what is really happening" may lead to undermining of the medical definition. Understanding that sustaining the basic definition of the situation is intertwined with numerous other projects, however, we will proceed to focus on that reality alone.

9. Compare Donald Ball's account of how the medical definition is conveyed in an abortion clinic, where it serves to counter the definition of the situation as deviant. D. W. Ball (1967, Winter), "An abortion clinic ethnography," *Social Problems, 14*, 293–301.

10. Glaser and Strauss discuss the hospital prohibition against examinations and exposure of the body in the presence of intimates of the patient. B. Glaser & A. Strauss (1965), *Awareness of dying*, Chicago: Aldine, p. 162.

11. Sudnow reports that at the county hospital he studied, male physicians routinely did pelvic examinations without nurses being present, except in the emergency ward. D. Sudnow (1967), *Passing on: The social organization of dying*, Englewood Cliffs, NJ: Prentice Hall, p. 78.

12. The following quotation suggests that euphemisms and understood references may be used because the staff often has the choice of using "lewd words" or not being understood. Our popular vocabulary for describing sexual behavior has been compounded of about equal parts of euphemism and obscenity, and popular attitude and sentiment have followed the same duality. Among both his male and female subjects, the interviewers found many who knew only the lewd words for features of their own anatomy and physiology. N. N. Foote (1955), "Sex as play," in J. Himelhock & S. F. Fava, *Sexual behavior in American society*, New York: Norton, p. 239.

13. The doctor's demeanor typically varies with his experience. In his early contacts with patients the young medical student may use an extreme degree of impersonality generated by his own discomfort in his role. By the time he has become accustomed to doctor-patient encounters, the fourth-year student and intern may use a newcomer's gentleness, treating the scene almost as an intimate situation by relying on elements of the "loving" demeanor previously learned in nonprofessional situations. By the time he is a resident and focusing primarily on the technical details of the medical task, the physician may be substituting a competent impersonality, although he never reverts to the extreme impersonality of the very beginning. The senior doctor, having mastered not only the technical details but an attitude of detached concern as well, reintroduces a mild gentleness, without the involved intimacy of the intern.

14. The management of closeness and detachment in professional-client relations is discussed in C. Kadushin (1962, March), "Social distance between client and professional," *American Journal of Sociology, 67*, 517–531. Wilensky and Lebeaux discuss how intimacy with strangers in the social worker-client relation

is handled by accenting the technical aspects of the situation, limiting the relationship to the task at hand, and observing the norms of emotional neutrality, impartiality, and altruistic service. H. L. Wilensky & C. N. Lebeaux (1958), *Industrial society and social welfare,* New York: Russell Sage Foundation, pp. 299–303.

15. For a discussion of the socialization of medical students toward a generally detached attitude, see Lief & Fox (1963), pp. 12–35. See also M. J. Daniels (1960, November), "Affect and its control in the medical intern," *American Journal of Sociology, 66,* 259–267.

16. The following incident illustrates how a patient may exceed the limits. Mrs. Lane, a young married woman, was considered by the physicians a "seductive patient," although her technique was subtle and her behavior never improper. After examining Mrs. Lane, an intern privately called my attention to a point in the examination when he was pressing on the patient's ovaries and she remarked to the nurse: "I have this pain in intercourse until my insides are about to come out." The intern told me that Mrs. Lane said that to the nurse, but she wanted him to hear. He didn't want to know that, he said; it wasn't necessary for her to say that. The intern evidently felt that

Mrs. Lane's remark had exceeded the bounds of decorum. A specific medical necessity makes the imparting of private information acceptable, the doctor's reaction suggests, and not merely the definition of the situation as medical.

17. There is reason to think that those patients who would have most difficulty in maintaining their poise generally avoid the situation altogether. Evidence that some uncool women avoid pelvic examinations is found in respondents' remarks quoted by Rainwater: "I have thought of going to a clinic for a diaphragm, but I'm real backward about doing that. I don't even go to the doctor to be examined when I'm pregnant. I never go until about a month before I have the baby." "I tell you frankly, I'd like a diaphragm but I'm just too embarrassed to go get one." L. Rainwater (1960), *And the poor get children,* Chicago: Quadrangle, pp. 10, 31.

18. An example of such a struggle is analyzed in J. P. Emerson (1970), "Nothing unusual is happening," in T. Shibutani (Ed.), *Human nature and collective behavior. Papers in honor of Herbert Blumer,* Englewood Cliffs, NJ: Prentice Hall.

19. Donald Ball (1967).

IDENTITY WORK, STIGMA, AND SELF PRESENTATION IN INTERACTION

This section builds on the ideas of the previous section on the definition of the situation. Just as we have to project a definition of the situation to those with whom we're interacting, we also have to project definitions of ourselves. Other people can't read our minds or see at a glance how it is that we see ourselves and what definition of the situation we hope to project. Accordingly, we use "ideal types" or known scripts and identities to signal our intentions to others. Goffman calls this "impression management." People put a lot of energy into presenting social identities to others. Regardless of our motives, we have to engage in impression management in order to "dramatize" or highlight the information and impression we want to project. For instance, even when you know you are well qualified for a potential job, you take care to dress appropriately for the situation so that you can signal your worthiness to the potential employer. In this case, your clothing signals that you know the script and can be trusted to perform as a capable employee.

"Identity work" is another concept from Goffman and is closely related to impression management. Identity work refers to the nuanced behavior we engage in as we try to get people to attribute specific identities to us. This can be an identity that is fleeting and situational such as portraying the competent sales clerk at a job, or more stable and enduring such as portraying our best qualities to a potential date. As part of this process, we wear clothing that reflects who we want to be and purchase cars and products that reflect our identification with particular reference groups. Some theorists have even proposed that we choose friends (and dates) based on the extent to which they complement our image of ourselves—friendship as accessorizing, to put it glibly.

Goffman was particularly interested in *stigma*, which he insisted was best understood as a situation rather than an attribute of the person. In other words, someone is potentially stigmatized when her or his image or ability detracts from the idealization of the projected situation. For instance, someone who appears dirty and jobless sleeping in the doorway of a shopping mall detracts from the image of a clean, fun, inviting environment. Thus, the "homeless" identity carries a stigma. The readings in this section illustrate various aspects of identity work and stigma in interactional settings.

In "Smell, Odor, and Somatic Work," Dennis Waskul and Phillip Vannini explore the taken-for-granted sense of smell as it functions in social interaction. They point out the various ways in which body odor is an aspect of self presentation. Appropriate (i.e., little or nicely perfumed) odor is expected and acceptable. Other "strange" odors can be a source of embarrassment or even stigma. People are well aware of the social implications of odor and take great care to manage their own odor impression.

Stephen E. Lankenau conducted interviews and engaged in many hours of observation for his research on impression management among panhandlers. In "Panhandling Repertoires and Routines for Overcoming the Nonperson Treatment," he describes various strategies that panhandlers engage in to manage their stigmatized identities and simply get people to engage in the most fundamental of interaction routines: acknowledging the existence of the other.

"Being Middle Eastern American: Identity Negotiation in the Context of the 'War on Terror'" is based on author Amir Marvasti's personal experiences and interviews. Middle Eastern identities in the United States have become highly stigmatized since the events of September 11, 2001. Marvasti notes that not everyone responds to the stigma in the same way; different people experience the stigma differently depending on the social context and their relative skills for managing their identity as Middle Eastern.

READING QUESTIONS

1. Think about the clothes you wear. What image of self are you conveying by your clothing choices? Who is the audience in your head when you get dressed and feel good about how you look? What clothes would you not be caught dead wearing? Why?

2. Observe the various slogans on T-shirts, and consider the information they provide about the wearer's commitments and values. What T-shirt slogans would you not want to wear? Do you find yourself responding positively to strangers who wear T-shirts that signal something that you identify with?

3. Try an exercise in which you wear clothes that are not expected for the situation (for example, dress poorly to shop in a nice store, or wear a suit on a casual date). Does the clothing seem to have any effect on people's perceptions of the situation and how they respond to you? What is the connection between a "dress code" and a definition of the situation?

4. Make a list of situations in which you are keenly aware of trying to portray a particular image. Discuss situations in which you feel obligated to present a public image that is at odds with your private image of yourself.

5. Think of other social identities that are often stigmatized. How do you react in the presence of these people? In what sort of interactions have you felt stigmatized?

6. Consider the relationship between skillful creativity and successful management of stigmatized identities. Think of examples of "stigmatized" people you know who are able to put others "at ease." How do they do this?

IDENTITY WORK, STIGMA, AND SELF PRESENTATION IN INTERACTION

24

Smell, Odor, and Somatic Work: Sense-Making and Sensory Management

Dennis D. Waskul and Phillip Vannini

(2008)

Flesh and organs bestow the capacity to sense, but they are merely the raw materials by which somatic perception is wrought. The act of perception requires the reflexive faculty to feel or perceive.

To sense, in other words, is to make sense, and sense-making entails what we call "somatic work." We investigate these dynamics in the context of olfaction. We highlight how olfaction intersects with social, cultural, and moral order, thus compelling reflexive forms of somatic work by which people manage smell (as an act) and odor (as signs).

SENSE-MAKING AS SOMATIC WORK

Smell is an *act* (verb); it is something that people *do*. In contrast, odor is a *state* (noun); it is an olfactory condition. Smelling of odor evokes olfactory definitions of the situation by which multiple meanings mediate between the act of smelling and the condition of odor. In this way, odor and smell are conjoined in an interpretive relationship. Inspired by popular sociological concepts such as identity work (Snow and Anderson 1987) and emotional labor (Hochschild 1983), somatic work refers to a diverse range of reflexive symbolic, iconic, and indexical sense-making experiences

and practical activities. Through such experiences and activities individuals produce, extinguish, manage, reproduce, negotiate, interrupt, and/or communicate somatic sensations in order to make them congruent with personal, interpersonal, and/or cultural notions of moral, aesthetic, and/or logical desirability.

SOMATIC RULES: MORAL ORDER AND MORAL ODOR

Somatic work is fashioned in the context of negotiated somatic rules that vary by personal, interpersonal, situational, contextual, cultural, and historical circumstances.

As stated by Largey and Watson (1972:1022), "particular odors, whether real or alleged, are sometimes used as indicants of the moral purity of particular individuals and groups within the social order, the consequences of which are indeed real." Because olfaction and odor are constructions of normative aesthetic and moral code, olfactory rules are enforced and odor is faithfully managed. The management of odor is common and widespread, observable in almost every body, everywhere. In Anglophone North America, odor is traditionally something to be eliminated or produced—on (and in) the body, the home, at work, automobiles, our communities—by use of air fresheners, deodorants, breath mints, fans, ventilation, air purification systems, [and] pollution laws. Even the mere mention of odors in conversation, especially body odors, is a delicate subject and it is not uncommon to find ourselves occasionally ignoring or denying the presence of uncontrollable, bad odors out of both a sense of tactfulness and taboo (cf. Zerubavel 2006). Adherence to the olfaction rules of moral odor/moral order represent more than the folkways of a culture and more than a matter of manners, politeness, and etiquette. As testified by recent "scent free" work and public space regulations, violations of olfaction rules are of potential legal concern and the production of inappropriate odor can be cause for civil litigation (although, given its gaseous consequences, one might wonder if the same logic might result in a bean prohibition—at least for human consumption, and possibly our companion animals).

More than merely "giving off" a creditable odor, olfactory impression management is built of two basic processes identified by Largey and Watson (1972:1024–1032): odor avoidance and odor attraction. Odor avoidance refers to cultural inclinations to avoid individuals, groups, or environments that are considered foul smelling; odor attraction refers to cultural tendencies to approve of individuals, groups, or environments that are considered aromatically pleasing (Largey and Watson 1972). These basic cultural olfactory processes are expressed in deodorizing rituals—culturally grounded practices that entail "the removal of socially discreditable odors through such activities as washing, gargling, and cleansing of teeth" (p. 1027), and odorizing rituals—practices that involve the "presentation of self with accreditable odors through the 'art' of

perfuming" (p. 1027). By means of deodorizing and odorizing rituals, people attempt "to avoid moral stigmatization and present an olfactory identity that will be in accord with social expectations, in turn, gaining moral accreditation: he who smells good is good" (p. 1028).

SOMATIC WORK AS FACE-WORK

Odor is perceived and immediately evaluated in accord with basic olfactory rules. Individuals become sensitive to these rules throughout the process of socialization, a process that refers not only to technical learning, but also to the "moral evaluation of objects and actions—an evaluation that easily conflates with sensory judgments" (Fine 1995:266). Therefore, it is prudent to suggest that olfactory somatic rules are generally enforced and odor is dutifully managed in all instances of social interaction. As Peter (age 57) suggests, "There is a manipulative element to controlling odors."*

Indeed, odor conveys meaning and is, therefore, a significant element of the dramaturgies of everyday life. As we will illustrate, olfactory impression management is often expressed in positive and negative interpersonal rituals, violations of which may be stigmatizing.

Olfactory Impression Management: Positive and Negative Interpersonal Rituals of Olfactory Face-Work

Goffman (1967:45) pointed out that "the general capacity to be bound by moral rules may well belong to the individual, but the particular set of rules which transforms him into a human being derives from requirements established in the ritual organization of social encounters." Likewise, constructions

---

*We collected data through the use of research journals. We asked two cohorts of graduate students enrolled in an applied communication program at Royal Roads Western Canadian University to record their experiences with smell over a period of two weeks.

of odor, olfactory somatic rules, and perceptions of smell directly intersect with the normative dramaturgies of everyday life—as both a part of the processes of presentation of self and a means of bestowing sanctity or stigma unto others. In this way, "the physical and the moral are united in odour" (Synnott 1993:191) and represent a genuine form of somatic surveillance, as evidenced by Nichole (age 40) who wrote, "Personal body odor is something that I prefer to keep under control at all times, regardless of whether I am in public or not."

For these reasons, the participants in this study are "dramaturgically aware" (Brissett and Edgley 1990) of the significance of odor to impression management—and particularly in terms of the implications for "face" (Goffman 1967:5)— "the positive social value a person effectively claims . . . in terms of approved social attributes." "Smelling good is a sign of being good" (Synnott 1993:187)—which is clear to Rose (age 39) who wrote, "Just like looks, smell is tied to impression; if you want to make a good one you need to smell nice." Likewise, Steve (age 56) wrote, "I think you can lose credibility with people if odor is not controlled." Several participants in this study expressed similar sentiments:

> Anytime I expect to be in close proximity to others, like at a Doctor's appointment or church, are times that I pay particular attention to how I smell. (Allison, 32)

> It is important for me to smell good when I am with other people. It makes me feel good about myself and then I can focus on other people rather than worrying about the impression that I am making. (Chandra, 53)

Because odor conveys meaning, it both reflects character and expresses to others an awareness of and commitment to olfactory rules of decorum— precisely what Allison (age 32) suggested when she wrote, "smelling good gives the impression that I take care of myself and have consideration for others who have to spend time with me." Or, in other words,

"just as the member of any group is expected to have self-respect, so also [s]he is expected to sustain a standard of considerate-ness" (Goffman 1967:10).

Olfactory impression management is imperative to the participants in this study and, all the more so, in situations they deem important. In these situations we see most clearly the kind of olfactory somatic work that "serves to counteract 'incidents'—that is, events whose effective symbolic implications threaten face" (Goffman 1967:12). Also in these situations people routinely engage in positive interpersonal rituals (Durkheim 1915; Goffman 1971:63)—rituals that "affirm and support the social relationship" between odors and their source. For example, Amy (age 31) explains why she was especially motivated to smell pleasant on her wedding day.

> I was very conscious of wanting to smell good on my wedding day. Like every bride, I wanted to look beautiful and was afraid that I would get hot and sweaty in my big, heavy dress on a hot August day. I was aware that I would be hugged and kissed a lot on that day and that I would be talking to a lot of people (most of my closest family and friends, in fact) and for that reason was wanting to smell good.

Romantic encounters—or circumstances where romance is possible—were also commonly cited as important moments for acute olfactory dramaturgical awareness and positive interpersonal olfactory ritual.

> The greater the chance of intimacy the more important smelling good is. Walking the dog Saturday morning—don't care about my smell. Going to work—clean and fresh is good enough, no reason to break out the *Baldessarini* [fragrance for men]. Dancing, or any social situation where one is likely to get close to women, one wants to avoid being repugnant. (Peter, 57)

> I like to smell good by applying perfume when I go out with my husband on a rare dinner date or to the movies. (Allison, 32)

In addition to personal odor, the participants in this study were also dramaturgically aware of the significance of environmental olfactory impression management. Nearly all expressed concern about managing odor in places that people inhabit. Ashley (age 48) previously explained that the smell of a home reflects on its residents, and others expressed similar sentiments. As Jenna (age 33) wrote:

> A home must have controlled smells. No one wants to be in a home with offensive or too strong smells. No one would visit a smelly home and the occupants might carry the smells outside of the home with them making them unpleasant to be around (i.e., mold, cigarette smoke, crazy strong perfume).

Respondents also identified work environments as important places for the management of odor, and not only in terms of previously mentioned olfactory political correctness. Thus, it is not surprising that Susan (age 25) was especially dramaturgically aware of her olfactory impression management during important work-related meetings and interactions with clients.

> It is particularly important for me to smell good when I am meeting clients—especially for the first time. Smell is such an important part of a person, whether you realize it or not, that a bad odor can break what could have been a great relationship! Before a meeting, I usually eat a mint, and wash my hands so I can be sure that I am presenting myself in the best way possible. Also, wearing clean clothes, bathing, and not going out the night before helps too!! . . . I don't want to be remembered by a stench!

Restaurants were also identified as important environments for the control of odor. Kate (age 29) claims that "food is so tied with smells." Melissa (age 28) wrote, "Smell definitely impacts the sense of taste," and therefore:

> The sense of smell is being used to its fullest in a restaurant with all the culinary smells about. . . . Good smells seem to enhance taste, and bad smells can just ruin the whole experience. Food establishments control smell also by putting familiar smells out to the public: popcorn at movies, fries from McDonald's (I've heard they fan it into the air outside). Smell is very important to sales I would imagine.

The participants in this study cited bathrooms as among the most important environments for the control and manipulation of odor. Just as the smell of flatulence, urine, and feces contaminates the moral and aesthetic character of the olfactory offender, so too can it pollute an entire environment. As Cahill (1985:43) explains, "because the profaning power of odor operates over a distance and in all directions, moreover, individuals who defecate in . . . bathrooms not only temporarily profane themselves but also risk profaning the entire setting." However, because bathrooms are the designated place for "creature releases" (Goffman 1963:69)—and all creatures must release—they are also social environments rife with negative interpersonal rituals (Durkheim 1915; Goffman 1971:62) that involve an honoring of the "individual's right to private 'preserves' and 'to be let alone'" (Cahill 1985:39). But adherence to this negative interpersonal ritual—especially in private bathrooms—entails a "dual set of issues for the offender and the offended" (Goffman 1971:100). On one hand, those who encounter the smells that emulate from a bathroom dutifully honor the negative ritual through "tactful blindness" (Goffman 1955:219). On the other hand, those who produce the smell are "responsible for trying to make amends for his [or her] offense and for showing proper regard for the process of correction" (Goffman 1971:100). Therefore, as Nichole (age 40) suggests: "Like many people, I feel the need to remedy bathroom odors when they occur. Although everybody experiences and contributes to these odors, it seems important to hide them when they happen."

"In our society, defecation involves an individual in activity which is defined as inconsistent with the cleanliness and purity standards expressed in many of our performances"—writes Goffman (1959:181), and even its odor is a possible expressive and impressive hazard. As numerous participants in this study suggest, failure to control the odors of flatulence, feces, and urine in the bathroom is a potential dramaturgical catastrophe—a source of looming prospective embarrassment, regardless of whether the bathroom is in a home or a work environment, for public or private use.

[It is important to control odor in] The bathroom: because it is a publicly used space and is often associated with negative smells resulting from bodily elimination. I leave a box of matches in the bathroom for guests or family members to light after using the toilet. I find the smell of burnt sulphur more appealing than artificial sprays. If odor is not controlled in these places then it may leave a bad impression for guests who visit our home. It is almost as if when a person uses the bathroom they want to feel as if they were the first and only ones to use it. It is unpleasant to be reminded that anyone visited the space before them. (Allison, 32)

We found an especially incisive illustration of negative interpersonal olfactory rituals among our female respondents, who expressed a surprisingly recurring concern about their perception of body odor during menstruation. As Cindy (age 36) wrote, "Sometimes when on my menstrual cycle I think I smell bad and I feel quite worried at times, using perfume to cover it up." Cindy's use of perfume to cover, "pass" (Goffman 1963), or otherwise distance herself from the perceived odor of her menstruating body is a clear example of negative olfactory interpersonal ritual. It also provocatively suggests the significance of moral and aesthetic assessments as they intersect with the politics of everyday life. "Women are suspected of being naturally foul, reeking of unpleasant body fluids, such as menstrual blood" (Classen, Howes, and Synnott 1994:164). Indeed the ideology of aroma is often gendered:

I find that I am very self conscious about odor when I am on my period. I am just never sure if I smell "unfresh." It seems important for me to hide the fact that it is that time of the month. (Nichole, 40)

Am entire feminine hygiene industry is built on the dubious contention that women's bodies naturally stink and thus require potent remedies—remedies that are "necessary" and expected if women are to adhere to normative negative olfactory rituals. More generally, what is also implicit is a perceived odiferous abjection, which may be sanctioned by olfactory stigma.

Olfactory Stigma

"I don't want to smell in public! I think it is humiliating to smell bad"—vividly remarks Beth (age 31). She is not the only one in our sample who feels this way. As several participants in this study have suggested in their own words, "particular odors, whether real or alleged, are sometimes used as indicants of the moral purity of particular individuals and groups within the social order, the consequences of which are indeed real" (Largey and Watson 1972:1022). In short, an odorous body is an offensive body (Hyde 2006), and failure to adhere to somatic rules and maintain expected olfactory impressions is potentially stigmatizing. Numerous participants in this study admit to judging people on the basis of their odor. And, as Susan (age 25) confesses, unpleasant odor results in olfactory stigma: "I find myself judging people negatively when they smell bad in some way—be it their breath, or something else. I don't usually notice if their smell is just normal or pleasant, but I definitely notice when it isn't."

Susan's sentiments might well explain why some people, like Amy (age 31), are not so concerned about smelling fragrant but are quite concerned about the possibility of smelling awful: "While it's not necessarily important that I smell *good*, I am very conscious of not wanting to smell bad" (emphasis in original). For the participants in this study, class was commonly associated with olfaction. Odor is literally "classy" in that "smell provides a potent symbolic means for creating and enforcing class . . . boundaries" (Classen et al. 1994:169).

> The most offensive odor I recall is the odor unwashed people give off. It's not even really body odor—it's more of an all-encompassing, greasy, unclean smell. I associate this with the rough-looking (probably homeless) people I pass on the street. I actually find this odor more offensive than plain body odor. While not pleasant either, body odor is something I associate more with an occasional hygiene problem. This unwashed smell is worse because I associate it with a thoroughly unclean person. (Amy, 31)

Considering the significance of olfactory impression management and the potentially stigmatizing implications of odor, it is not surprising that the participants in this study vividly recall circumstances of somatic abjection, moments when they found themselves embarrassingly rank. Indeed, "the individual is always in jeopardy because of the adventitious linking of events, the vulnerability of his body, and the need in social situations to maintain the proprieties" (Goffman 1967:169); failure leads to embarrassment—a deficit in projecting an acceptable self before others (Goffman 1967). Some of these recollections of olfactory abjection owe to accidental circumstances. For example, Frank (age 45) recalls falling into an abandoned latrine pit.

> I remember a summer in Peachland when me and a couple of buddies were exploring an old abandoned campsite. . . . I was not noticing where I was walking and stepped into an abandoned pit toilet. It took my two friends 20 minutes to get me out as they were laughing so hard as to make rescue that much more difficult. I stank really bad, as you may imagine, even after a "bath" in the lake. They made me ride in the stern of the boat on the way back to the cabin and I ended up showering at the camp site for 1/2 an hour and burning my shorts.

However, the embarrassment of somatic abjection is easily "excused" (Scott and Lyman 1968) in accidental circumstances where one is "victimized" by the fickle hand of fate. More mortifying are moments of olfactory abjection that owe to one's own carelessness or inattentiveness. It is notable that many of these moments of olfactory abjection were merely perceived; people believed they stunk—no one necessarily shared that definition of the situation and abjection (as well as its social consequence) was self-inscribed.

> I was at work one day, and I had been out too late the night before. Not only did I not have time to shower, but I was convinced they could smell the beer on me from a mile away! Between that and the fact that I could not stop sweating—I was a TREAT to work with, I'm sure! I felt disgusting, and tried to avoid people the whole day. Even though my coworkers are in very close proximity to me, I sent them emails instead of talking to them face to face. I spent all day staring at my computer, trying not to wave my arms around or "waft" any of my smell in their general direction. I drank a lot of water, and washed my hands a lot to try and compensate for my stinkiness! I was SO glad to go home! I don't know that anyone reacted to it, to be honest, but I kept thinking that people were shying away from me. I just felt so unprofessional and gross, that it ruined even my phone calls that day! (Susan, 25, emphasis in original)

It is difficult to tell if these memories of olfactory abjection were truly "discreditable" (Goffman 1963:4). It is impossible to know if other people noticed the rank odor; as loyal citizens of expressive order, those who smell the abject stench of another person may simply respond with polite "tactful blindness" (Goffman 1955:219). Tact is common and expected, but certainly not universal—some people are "discredited" (Goffman 1963:4), and all olfactory abjection risks possible sanction.

> One time I was trying on a wet suit in a diving store and it was a very hot day. I had just come from work and was wearing my work clothes. The wet suit I was

trying on was extremely tight and it was really a lot of effort to get it on. I was sweating but what was worse was that my feet really smelled from the dress shoes that I was wearing. I needed the guy's help to get this wet suit on—he was very attractive and it was very embarrassing to ask for his help with such a horrible smell wafting through my dressing room. He said, "What's that peculiar smell?" in a joking sort of way. I was mortified but stuck to the task at hand and got out of there quickly. (Rose, 39)

CONCLUSIONS

"That which we call a rose by any other word would smell as sweet," or so muses Juliet in Shakespeare's famous tragedy (Act II, Scene 2). However, not withstanding romance—in fact, quite to the contrary—our analysis suggests olfactory perception is not so simple. Through smell, meaning is reflexively bestowed unto odor in the context of negotiated somatic rules. For this reason, odor is a "sign vehicle" (Goffman 1959) we thus manipulate and manage on bodies and in environments in an effort to convey desired impressions. Clearly, odor is a subtle but significant component of the culturally normative and aesthetic rituals of expressive and impressive everyday life.

REFERENCES

Brissett, Dennis and Charles Edgley. 1990. *Life as Theater: A Dramaturgical Sourcebook.* New York: Aldine.

Cahill, Spencer. 1985. "Meanwhile Backstage: Public Bathrooms and Interaction Order." *Urban Life* 14:33–58.

Classen, Constance, David Howes, and Anthony Synnott. 1994. *Aroma: The Cultural History of Smell.* New York: Routledge.

Durkheim, Emile. 1915. *The Elementary Forms of Religious Life: A Study in Religious Sociology.* New York: MacMillan.

Fine, Gary A. 1995. "Wittgenstein's Kitchen: Sharing Meaning in Restaurant Work." *Theory and Society* 24:245–269.

Fine, Gary A. and Tim Hallett. 2003. "Dust: A Study in Sociological Miniaturism." *Sociological Quarterly* 44:1–15.

Goffman, Erving. 1955. "On Face-Work: An Analysis of Ritual Elements in Social Interaction." *Psychiatry: Interpersonal and Biological Processes* 18:213–231.

____. 1959. *The Presentation of Self in Everyday Life.* Garden City, NY: Doubleday.

____. 1963. *Stigma: Notes on the Management of Spoiled Identity.* Englewood Cliffs, NJ: Prentice Hall.

____. 1967. *Interaction Ritual: Essays in Face-to-Face Behavior.* Chicago, IL: Aldine.

____. 1971. *Strategic Interaction.* Philadelphia, PA: University of Pennsylvania Press.

Hochschild, Arlie. 1983. *The Managed Heart: Commercialization of Human Feeling.* Berkeley: University of California Press.

Hyde, Alan. 2006. "Offensive Bodies." Pp. 95–112 in *The Smell Culture Reader,* edited by Jim Drobnick. New York: Berg.

Largey, Gale P. and David R. Watson. 1972. "The Sociology of Odours." *American Journal of Sociology* 77:1021–1034.

Scott, Marvin and Stanford Lyman. 1968. "Accounts." *American Sociological Review* 33:42–62.

Snow, David and Leon Anderson. 1987. "Identity Work Among the Homeless: The Verbal Construction and Avowal of Personal Identities." *American Journal of Sociology* 92:1336–1371.

Synnott, Anthony. 1993. *The Body Social: Symbolism, Self, and Society.* London: Routledge.

Zerubavel, Eviatar. 2006. *The Elephant in the Room: Silence and Denial in Everyday Life.* New York: Oxford University Press.

IDENTITY WORK, STIGMA, AND SELF PRESENTATION IN INTERACTION

25

Panhandling Repertoires and Routines for Overcoming the Nonperson Treatment

Stephen E. Lankenau

(1999)

Some of the people just walk by and don't say nothin'. I call them zombies [laughs]. You ask them for change and they don't say "yes," "no," or "maybe I be back." They just walk by you like they don't even see you—it's like I'm not even sitting there. They could say "I ain't got none" or "no" or something. They just walk by.

—Alice, a homeless panhandler*

We use a variety of ploys to avoid the gaze or overtures extended by panhandlers—we avert our eyes, quicken our pace, increase the volume on our headphones. Some panhandlers manage to capture our attention, less frequently our money, using humor, offering services, telling stories, or by using other dramatic devices. A close examination of the exchanges between panhandler and passersby reveals that these interactions occur within a multilayered, theatrical context; dramas are enacted at the face-to-face level yet display the larger social relations among the poor and nonpoor.

Goffman's (1959) dramaturgical perspective presents social life as a play in which persons or actors conduct themselves before various audiences according to scripted roles. Compared with the exchanges among everyday persons, however, interactions between panhandler and pedestrian more closely resemble the basic structural features of a play. The panhandler, who is the main actor, is like an improvisational performer who uses a repertoire of pieces or routines to accomplish the act of panhandling. I refer to a panhandler's collection of these actions as his or her panhandling repertoire. Similarly, in reaction to the performer, pedestrians serve as the audience and respond to the panhandling routine by selecting from a menu of responses, like engaging or ignoring the panhandler. Being ignored by a passerby, which Goffman (1963) referred to as the "nonperson treatment," is a primary problem confronted by panhandlers, but one that is directly addressed through a repertoire of panhandling routines. The

---

*All quotations in this article are by persons who gave their informed consent to participate in this research. All names in this study are pseudonyms, and certain biographical details have been deleted or altered to protect anonymity.

fact that I am categorizing panhandlers according to various routines, however, does not necessarily imply that certain individuals are acting or feigning need and distress. Rather, panhandling repertoires are one way of describing the public drama between panhandler and passersby.

A PRIMARY PROBLEM FACING PANHANDLERS—THE NONPERSON TREATMENT

Negative stereotypes of homeless persons, such as being dangerous, dirty, diseased, and mentally ill, are often connected to panhandlers, which then fuels a fearful desire to maintain a certain physical distance from panhandlers (Liebow 1993; Wagner 1993). Similarly, owing to the common associations between poverty and crime in the minds of middle-class persons (Reiman 1970), panhandlers are often merged into the "dangerous class." Additionally, race and gender differences also add strangeness as the great majority of panhandlers in this study are Black and male, whereas the pedestrian population in contact with the panhandling population is much more racially diverse and gender balanced.

These attitudes and perspectives among passersby typically prompt a particular response toward panhandlers and their overtures for money or food—the nonperson treatment. A person withholding glances or close scrutiny of another and effectively treating the other as though he or she did not exist characterizes the nonperson treatment.

In general, the nonperson treatment is one type of interaction occurring among unfamiliar persons in public places. When approaching a stranger in public, one typically ignores the other completely; provides the other with a subtle, noninvasive form of acknowledgment; or explicitly engages the other in some fashion. Goffman (1963) referred to these three types of interactions, respectively, as the nonperson treatment, civil inattention, and encounter or face engagement.

As suggested earlier by Alice, passersby commonly direct the nonperson treatment toward panhandlers. Pedestrians accomplish the nonperson treatment by effectively using props to pretend that the panhandler is neither seen nor heard or by simply looking down or straight ahead as though the panhandler were an inanimate object, like a tree or statue. From a panhandler's perspective, passersby using these variations of the nonperson treatment appear then as "zombies." Such explicit attempts to avoid and ignore reveal that the nonperson treatment is sometimes a conscious form of interaction rather than a passive or default disposition.

I propose that panhandlers devise a repertoire of panhandling routines to break out of the role of stranger or to awaken pedestrians from the blasé state; these dramaturgical actions then minimize the nonperson treatment and pave the way for encounters. Framing panhandling as a theatrical exchange between two classes of actors with dissimilar material resources, different interactional objectives, and contrasting viewpoints, however, is a critical factor toward understanding the repertoire of routines enacted by panhandlers. Despite these inequalities, this analysis shows that panhandling repertoires lead to exchanges between the zombie and the stranger and thereby foster greater understanding among both classes of actors.

PANHANDLING REPERTOIRES

Panhandlers overcome the nonperson treatment by initiating encounters through the use of dramaturgical techniques, routines, acts, pieces, or routines, which I collectively call panhandling repertoires. Often enacted in a performancelike manner, repertoires capture the attention and interest of passersby by appealing to a range of emotional qualities, such as amusement, sympathy, and fear.

On the basis of ethnographic research conducted on the streets of Washington, D.C., I have conceptualized five primary panhandling routines: the entertainer, the greeter, the servicer, the storyteller, and the aggressor, along with strategies within certain routines. The entertainer offers music or humor, the greeter provides cordiality and deference, the servicer supplies a kind of service, the storyteller presents a sad or sympathetic tale, and the aggressor deals in fear and intimidation. Generally, the entertainer and greeter attempt to produce enjoyment or good feelings, whereas the storyteller and aggressor elicit more serious or hostile moods. The servicer, who occupies a more neutral position, is focused on providing some sort of utility. Fundamentally, the moods or impressions created by the routines are largely attempts to attenuate strangeness or awaken pedestrians from their blasé condition, which then paves the way for an encounter and possible contributions.

Storyteller

Of all the panhandling routines, the storyteller approach most clearly conveys the dramaturgical nature of panhandling. The storyteller routine is based on using stories to evoke understanding, pity, or guilt from pedestrians. The primary message is need in virtually all cases. Stories consist of various signs, appearances, lines, or narratives that focus on shaking pedestrians from their blasé state. The storyteller routine is then accomplished by means of one or more specific subroutines: the silent storyteller, the sign storyteller, the line storyteller, and the hard luck storyteller. Here, Duane, a long-time homeless panhandler, points to the tactics or arts of capturing the sympathy of passersby with a good story:

> What makes my panhandlin' successful and any other panhandlin' successful is the emotions. Now if you were reared in a good moral background and I come up to you [he pulls his face close—about six inches away], "Excuse me sir, I'm really tired. I just moved in and I've got five kids. Me and my wife—we can't get jobs." Now when you say the word

kids—"Forget me—I've got babies I'm tryin' to feed." Or sickness—"I'm dyin'" or "my wife, my mother." More than just I'm givin' them money to get something to eat. These things are tactics. They'll be touched. [Duane gets up and demonstrates by calling out onto the sidewalk.] "Ma'am, my wife only has one hour to live! I'm tryin' to raise money. Please, someone help!" [He returns to the table] Now, did you catch some of the arts? There's an appeal to your emotions. And you got those regulars who are sittin' down, "Hey, I'm homeless. Can you spare some change sir?" And you see the same jerk on the same corner every day. And then you get into a habit, "Well here's a dollar." But the real money comes from the emotions.

In addition to narratives, stories are conveyed symbolically through down-and-out facial expressions, as Ray indicates:

> People look at me—the way I talk—and you know, feel sorry for me. They know I'm homeless by the way I'm lookin'! And I give them a sad little look.

Clothing, appearances, and presentation of self may also be manipulated or used to tell the desired story. In fact, becoming a successful storyteller is contingent on developing a look that works, as Fox suggests:

> When I first started panhandling I couldn't understand why people weren't giving me money—I looked too clean. So I grew this ratty beard and figured so that's the trick of the trade. As long as I was looking presentable like I was doing a 9-to-5 job—say working as a computer specialist—I wasn't getting a dime [laughs].

Hence, storytellers may have to consciously manage their appearance more than others to foster the impression of need. On buying or receiving new or secondhand clothes and shoes, for instance, storytellers find themselves in the difficult position of negotiating those symbols that do not suggest need, as compared with other routines that rely less on a sympathetic or pitiful appearance or story. I now discuss the four storyteller subroutines in greater detail.

The silent storyteller relies primarily on symbolic communication rather than verbal exchanges to gain the attention of passersby. The silent storyteller uses attire, expressions, movements, and other props to advertise his or her situation and needs. Movements might entail limping down the street or shivering unprotected in the rain and cold. Props may include crutches, a wheelchair, or other symbols of disability; bags of belongings; or children. Generally, silent storytellers, who often sit with their cup on the sidewalk and refrain from unnecessary interactions, are the most passive of all panhandlers. Harlan, a panhandler for the past six years, explains his silent approach:

> Over the years I've looked at all the guys' styles and when I first started some of the guys used signs and some of the guys talked, some the guys sing, some of the guys danced, some of the guys do everything—I mean I can do all that too. I don't like to ask people for money so when I first started I used to say "Excuse me sir, can you spare some change?" Then I started to develop my own thing—something told me not to say anything. In other words, I let my cup do the talking. People used to tell me a long time ago, if anyone wants you to have anything they'll give it to you. You know, you don't have to ask. I'm not gonna ask everybody that comes up and down the street to give me a nickel [laughs]. I've tried it, I've done it. You know, I just let my cup do the talking.

Like the silent storyteller, the sign storyteller typically waits passively for a pedestrian to initiate an encounter. A sign is a tool that effectively creates interest and concern within passersby with minimal effort exerted by the panhandler. A sign, as compared with a verbal exchange, reduces the likelihood of being subjected to a negative or humiliating interaction, as explained by Walt:

> I let the sign do the talking. I don't speak unless I'm spoken to or unless to say "good morning" or

something like that or "good afternoon." I just hold a sign and if people want to give me money they give me money and if they don't they walk by and nothing is ever said. There's no dirty looks, no nothin' because you can't look nasty to everyone that doesn't give you money because you'd be looking nasty to 90 percent of the world [chuckles].

Lou also uses a cardboard sign that reads, "Homeless and Hungry. Please Help. Thank you. God Bless All." He includes his name in the lower right corner of the sign. Lou sits on the sidewalk with his back against a building, his belongings on either side, and his sign and cup positioned in front of him. For Lou, the sign removes the uncomfortable process of verbally soliciting money and minimizes negative exchanges:

> I don't like asking people for money straight out—that's why I use my sign. And incidentally, I don't feel as bad because I'm not asking people. A lot of people are afraid of me if I ask. With the sign they have the option of walking by or not walking by.

Thus, sign storytellers view the sign as an unobtrusive, non-threatening device but one that still conveys a message of need. Generally, signs protect panhandlers from degrading interactions by allowing agreeable donors to initiate an exchange without compulsion or intimidation.

The line storyteller is the most common among all storytellers and possibly the most ubiquitous routine in the panhandling repertoire. The line storyteller typically remains stationary and simply presents a line to pedestrians as they pass. Almost all lines focus on money in one form or another. The most basic, unadorned money line is "Can you spare some change?" but specific higher amounts, such as a quarter or a dollar are often inserted in place of *change*. Another variation on the money line is to ask for very little money, such as "Can you help me out? Pennies will do" or an odd amount of money, such as "Can you spare 27 cents?"

Other lines may refer to "help" rather than money while specifying how the help would be put to good use. In these instances, food is a typical theme, such as "Can you help me get something to eat?" or "Can you spare some change to get a burrito?" In addition to food, transportation needs are another common theme used by line storytellers, such as "Can you spare two or three dollars for bus fare?" Lines invoking transportation may also include a destination and purpose, like returning to the shelter for the evening, buying medication at a hospital, or going to a job interview. Lines also focus on the return from unintended destinations, such as a hospital or jail, which may involve displaying evidence of a stay, like an institutionally marked identification wristband. Beyond money, food, transportation, and destinations, line storytellers focus on innumerable topics, but lines typically center on subjects that a homeless or poor person might realistically need.

The hard luck storyteller uses a more direct approach than the teller of a line story and offers an in-depth narrative focusing on difficult or unusual circumstances. On gaining the person's attention, the hard luck storyteller then presents an extended narrative to elicit sympathy and a contribution. Often, hard luck storytellers elaborate and combine themes used by line and sign storytellers. Here is an example of a hard luck story told to me one afternoon:

> I know this is a little unusual but I need you to save me. God told me to approach the man with the pink shirt. [I was wearing a pink shirt.] I almost just committed suicide by jumping off the bridge. You need to help me and my two daughters. We're trying to get a bus ticket to Philadelphia. I've been in prison for the past five years and I've been out a month and I'm broke. When I was in prison my wife was raped and murdered. I need $15—Travelers Aid is going to pay the rest of the ticket. [I gave him a dollar from my wallet.] Can you help me get something to eat from Roy Rogers then? I'll put that dollar towards the bus but I need some money for food as well.

In sum, storytellers attempt to negate the blasé state by emphasizing the apparent disparities between themselves and pedestrians. These differences then create feelings of sympathy or pity within passersby and often lead to encounters and contributions. The storyteller's dramatized tales or physical appearance, however, may actually exacerbate the level of strangeness between panhandler and pedestrian—a result that is in contrast to more positive routines that neutralize strangeness, such as the entertainer, greeter, and servicer routines. Aggravating strangeness through stories or appearances, though, places storytellers in the "sick role" (Parsons 1951) or a position of alienated dependency, which then paves the way for sympathy and contributions.

Aggressor

The aggressor technique is premised on evoking guilt and fear in pedestrians by using either real or feigned aggression. Compared with the storyteller, the aggressor captures the attention of a pedestrian in a more pointed and dramatic fashion. Like the storyteller routine, however, the aggressor increases feelings of strangeness by highlighting disparities and differences. Primarily, the aggressor obtains food, money, and other items through intimidation, persistence, and shame.

Intimidation is accomplished through sarcastic and abusive comments, or fearful movements, like walking alongside, grabbing hold of the pedestrian, or silently using intimidating looks or stares. For instance, I encountered an unidentified panhandler using a kind of physical intimidation by standing in front of an ATM machine and then darting and lunging at pedestrians as they passed. Finally, a woman who initially refused his overtures gave him some money after completing her transaction at the ATM machine.

Persistence entails doggedly pursuing a contribution after it has been refused or seeking more money after an initial donation. Rita, for example, displayed this kind of persistence, though politely, during our hour-long encounter. After meeting her in front of McDonald's and buying her lunch, she then requested the change from lunch, asked for additional money to help her pay rent, and then asked for any old articles of clothing. During our meeting, Rita clearly displayed need especially after describing how she had been partially disabled by a stroke. Her method of asking, however, conveyed this element of aggressiveness and persistence.

Shame is evoked by making the donor feel that his or her quarter or dollar donation is insufficient and cheap given the vast material discrepancies between donor and panhandler. For example, my first encounter with Mel incorporated a sad tale with a shameful admonishment. After meeting him on the street, he lifted his shirt with his left hand revealing a long scar extending from his sternum to his belly button. The scar was folded over like it had recently been sewn up. "See this," he said, pointing to the scar with his right hand, "I need to eat right now. It's also about time for me to take my insulin. I'm a diabetic." I responded by giving him a dollar. "Can you tell me what I can get with that?" he returned somewhat indignantly.

Any of these prior examples may have constituted a form of aggressive panhandling under the District of Columbia's Panhandling Control Act, enacted in 1993. This act prohibits panhandling in an aggressive manner, which includes "approaching, speaking to, or following a person in a manner as would cause a reasonable person to fear bodily harm" and "continuously asking, begging, or soliciting alms from a person after the person has made a negative response."

Most panhandlers are well aware of this law and the prohibitions surrounding aggressive panhandling. Consequently, panhandlers often distinguish themselves from other panhandlers who act in an aggressive fashion, as Lou suggests:

You have people out there with the cup going right up to people and saying "Help me out." That's what they call aggressive panhandling. That makes a bad name for me because I use a sign. And I mean that says it all. I'm not in people's face. I'm just off on the side. That's how I do it.

Up until now, I have described the aggressor routine as one that is consciously initiated by the panhandler. However, it also is clear that due to the many negative comments and interactions panhandlers report receiving from passersby, at least some of the time behaving aggressively is a reaction rather than a role, as suggested by Vern:

I have no problem [with] people askin' for change because you can always say no. Some people have attitudes but you got to keep a good mind because I've been through it with people: "You got some spare change?" "Get the hell out of my face." You can't lose your spot over that because as soon as you get aggressive [makes police siren noise]. Don't let one dollar mess you up from a hundred dollars. They [fellow panhandlers] tell me that four or five times a night.

Hence, panhandlers generally understand the economic and legal imperatives behind remaining silent when publicly humiliated. Although easier said than done, managing one's emotions in the face of rejection or abusive comments is part of the job, as suggested by Ray:

I don't do aggressive panhandling. I don't harass nobody. If you have a problem with me I have nothin' to say to you—I'm a panhandler. If people have something to say I just let it go—words are words.

Whereas the aggressor routine is often good at stirring pedestrians from their blasé condition, such action runs the risk of furthering strangeness and alienating potential donors. Particularly among panhandlers who are tempted to react aggressively to humiliating interactions with passersby or police, the job of panhandling is akin to service occupations that require emotional labor (Hochschild 1983) or publicly managing one's feelings.

Servicer

In contrast to all other routines, the servicer provides specific services to stimulate social interaction and exchange. Using various dramaturgical techniques, the servicer transforms the exchange into something different than merely giving money to a panhandler. The servicer dispels the blasé attitude by ostensibly offering a service while lessening the sense of strangeness by converting the interaction into a kind of business transaction. In other words, giving money to a stranger in public is an unfamiliar practice, whereas being engaged by a salesperson offering a service is a familiar ritual. Regardless of whether a service is desired or not, however, providing a service dampens strangeness by establishing a sense of obligation and reciprocity between panhandler and pedestrian. Although this rapport may be contrived in some cases and more akin to "counterfeit intimacy" (Enck and Preston 1988), that is, interaction supporting the illusion that a legitimate service is being performed when both parties know this to be false.

The servicer repertoire consists of a formal, proactive component and an informal, reactive aspect. The formal servicer consciously seeks out situations to provide a service in exchange for a tip, much like a bellhop or bathroom attendant. Roaming the streets in search of an opportunity is a particular characteristic of the formal servicer; in contrast, the informal servicer is more typically sought out by virtue of possessing something desirable, such as information. Additionally, the informal servicer can be viewed as a secondary type of routine that emerges owing to the failure of a primary one or arises when a panhandler is in the right place at the right time.

Car parking, that is, pointing out parking spaces to drivers in exchange for a tip, is the most prevalent type of formal service. This practice, however, is illegal under the Panhandling Control Act. The maximum penalties for violating the statute are a $300 fine and 90 days in jail. Despite its illegality and potential costs, parking cars remains a booming business in certain neighborhoods.

I gained a sense of the car-parking routine one evening by observing Spike, who is one of among a half-dozen car parkers that work a certain neighborhood. As we spoke alongside a busy street, Spike motioned to an approaching luxury sedan that a spot would be vacant. As the vehicle backed diagonally into the space, Spike stood behind and yelled out directions: "Turn your wheel to the left. You're OK. Come on." The driver—a tall, professionally dressed man—took several minutes to emerge. Spike noted the car's Georgia license plate and asked the man as he opened his door what part of Georgia he was from. "I'm from Atlanta," the car owner said. "Oh yeah, I'm from Statesboro," Spike responded. The man then gave Spike some change. During this exchange, Spike's friendly demeanor also demonstrates how car parkers often integrate the greeter rap into their parking routine.

In terms of earnings, car parking appears to be the most lucrative of all the panhandling routines. [Because] most car parkers panhandle in addition to parking cars, it is difficult to gain an accurate understanding of the payoffs of car parking alone. In any case, regular car parkers report a minimum of $40 of total earnings on a good evening compared with the median level of $35 among all panhandlers. However, earnings reportedly can exceed $100 if a car parker encounters extra generous drivers who give $10 or $20 at a time.

The increased earnings netted by car parkers may stem from any one of numerous factors, including drivers giving out of fear, generosity, appreciation, a desire to impress friends or dates, or inebriation. However, Mel, a long-time car parker, offers his own explanation for why car parkers earn such relative high earnings:

> It's free money out there. I don't ask for nothing. I just direct cars into parking spaces and people give

me money—some change, one dollar, five dollars, ten dollars, twenty dollars. Sometimes they're so happy to give me money even though they could've paid for an actual space in a parking lot for less. If you ever get hard up for money, go over there and try it. It's almost like they're trained. They expect it when they come into the neighborhood.

In contrast to the formal servicer, such as the car parker, the informal servicer provides services to pedestrians, vendors, storeowners, and the police. These services, which result from a pan-handler's propensity for being in the right place at the right time, include offering an umbrella to a soaked pedestrian; giving directions to specific street addresses; escorting unchaperoned, some-times inebriated persons to their final destina-tions; or hailing a taxi for the less streetwise or infirm. These exchanges convert the panhandler into an informal service provider.

Beyond informally offering everyday informa-tion and help, panhandlers occasionally encounter more significant and valued news. Owing to their near omnipresence on the streets, panhandlers are frequently knowledgeable of many important hap-penings. Information absorbed by panhandlers, particularly facts about persons relating to crimes, are sought after by storeowners and police, as explained by Vance:

We provide services to some of the storeowners. If there's a break-in or vandalism, we usually know who did it within a 24–48 hour period, whereas it might take the police several days to a week to find out the same information.

However, not all panhandlers capitalize on the opportunity to provide information to the powers that seek it. Each panhandler may have personal reasons for not offering up important information, such as fear of retaliation, a code of silence among street people, not knowing the desired facts, or not trusting the police. Hence, a witness who fails to cooperate with the police when the stakes are high

may feel the stick rather than being handed a carrot, as Mel explains:

I went to jail because I wouldn't open my mouth. So they said I was in contempt of court. I was the wit-ness of a murder and they all pointed their fingers at me man—I'm telling you Joe—"He saw it. He was there." I was just walking past. I didn't see who was blowing who away. I be everywhere. I see a whole lot of things—and that be my business. I hear the gun-shot goin' off, but do you think I looked around to see what time it was? I keep with my straight steady walk—outta there—caught a cab.

In sum, the servicer captures a pedestrian's attention by creating the impression that he or she has some valuable utility to offer in exchange for payment, much like the relationship between sales-clerk and patron. Although intimacy or familiarity may increase the likelihood of a pedestrian giving money to a servicer, the quality of strangeness is attenuated by the panhandler's ability to turn the interaction into a kind of neutral business exchange. Because of their presence on the streets, overcoming the nonperson treatment is occasion-ally a moot point as panhandlers are sometimes actively approached for information or assistance. As indicated, however, panhandlers must intermit-tently use other dramaturgical routines to avoid encounters (and thereby foster strangeness) with more powerful persons, such as the police, who seek to develop exchanges that may be disadvantageous or detrimental to their existence on the streets.

Greeter

The greeter offers friendliness, respect, flattery, and deference to passersby in exchange for contri-butions and cordial responses. This routine largely revolves around polite behavior, such as greeting pedestrians with a "hello" or "good morning," quite like department store employees who welcome customers at store entrances. Like these service occupations, the greeter routine is firmly rooted in dramaturgically managing emotions. Additionally, the routine is enhanced when a panhandler becomes familiar with a panhandling locale and then remembers faces, names, and biographical facts about contributors. Hence, a command of these more intimate details about passersby allows the greeter to personalize each greeting and devise a more comprehensive panhandling repertoire.

Sanford personifies the greeter routine. During numerous observations and encounters, Sanford always offered a pleasant greeting and a distinctive, friendly smile. Sanford typically stands at the top of the Metro (subway) or along a busy side street greeting passersby during their commute or afternoon stroll. As he explains,

> I greet people in the morning—say "good morning" to them—say "hello." I try to make people happy and everything. I generally get a good response—a happy greeting in a happy way especially with a smile. They always like my smile. Everybody has their own different style. My style is my smile. That's how a lot of people remember me you know.

Whereas Sanford capitalizes on his friendly smile and good nature, Lonnie, a 40-year-old native of the West Indies, appeals to pedestrians through his pleasing Caribbean accent and interactional flair:

> I just talk to people because I'm gifted. I know that I'm gifted, ok. It doesn't matter what you have on as long as you are a gentle person and your mind is proper. As long as you have a pleasant personality it doesn't matter [exclaimed] what you have on—how stinky you feel or whatever. If you are nice to people, people will give.

Although some panhandlers possess specific attributes that facilitate the greeter routine, such as a friendly smile or a courteous manner, a certain amount of on-the-job learning is usually involved. Wally implicitly describes his evolution from the

aggressor to the greeter, which required emotion management skills:

> I always say "good morning" to the people. It makes them feel real good. And most of the time I'm good at it but I was a nasty motherfucker when I came here. But now I've learned my lesson—I've learned from my mistakes. Now that I'm so nice to the people I can get anything I want. When I was nasty and dirty I used the "f" word. Now I think things have changed. Now I just like being friendly with my cup in hand—"Hey, how are you doin'!"

Just as a panhandler's repertoire may undergo an evolution, city commuters often require a breaking-in period before moving from the non-person treatment toward being open to encounters with panhandlers new to their daily schedule. As Sanford explains, pedestrians were generally skeptical of him and his routine until he developed a presence in the neighborhood:

> When I first came up here [to this neighborhood] people didn't really know me or nothin' and I didn't get no friendly greetin'. I got a couple right. But then they saw what kind of guy I was, right. There's a lot of stereotypes—guys who are homeless panhandlin'—cussin' people out bein' disrespectful to people and everything. Or they feel a lot of them are alcoholics or crack addicts or whatever. So you know, they saw that it wasn't like that with me so as soon as they got to know me I got a better greetin'. Cause I couldn't even get a dollar when I first got here [laughs].

Once a panhandler is known in a certain area and rapport is established with a group of regular contributors, the greeter may be emboldened to mix compliments, such as "You're looking good today," with more conservative salutations, like "good morning." Alternatively, a more confidant, forward greeter may deal largely in compliments.

In sum, the greeter deploys pleasantries to maintain friendships with regular contributors or displays politeness and deference to newcomers.

Given its versatility, it is a routine used by nearly all panhandlers. Although some use it as a primary part of their repertoire when dealing with large processions of anonymous crowds, storytellers and others typically use it as a secondary routine on encountering persons who give regularly.

Entertainer

The entertainer provides humor and enjoyment and encompasses two more specific routines: the joker and the musician. Both typically awaken pedestrians from their blasé state through a benign or positive offering, such as a joke or a song. Strangeness is then reduced by creating rapport or intimacy by performing a familiar tune or by developing an ongoing presence in a particular neighborhood. Generally, the entertainer routine most clearly resembles an actor staging a performance before an audience.

The joker entertains by telling funny stories, making irreverent comments, or offering bizarre appearances. Minimally, the joker's goal is to make an unsuspecting pedestrian smile or laugh. Once the pedestrian is loosened up, it is hoped that a contribution will follow.

For instance, Yancy demonstrates the joker by presenting a strange appearance in conjunction with humorous lines. One evening, I observed Yancy walking along a crowded sidewalk with the collar of his blue shirt pulled over his forehead, exposing only his face and a green leaf drooping over his left eye and cheek. Donning this clownish look and occasionally saying, "Can you help me out? I'm trying to get on the Internet," he moved about holding out an upturned baseball cap. During an interview, Yancy explained how confronting a weary afternoon commuter with a humorous scenario, like the incongruity between a homeless panhandler and the Internet, is a good antidote for the nonperson treatment:

A certain line can make their day or a little bit of laughter. If a person may have his briefcase or purse and whatnot and they may have two bags of groceries from Sutton Place Gourmet and a bottle of beaujolais nouveau. They want to go home and smoke a cigarette and watch cable and you're telling them that you're panhandling and trying to get on the Internet.

Humor sometimes emerges spontaneously, seemingly without any instrumental intentions. For instance, while standing outside the Metro late one quiet evening, Ralph called out to a Metro system repairman riding up the escalator: "Hey, I caught my foot in the escalator last week." While walking away, the repairman sarcastically replied, "Sue Metro." Ralph then excitedly responded, "But you're the Metro man!" And then to the cadence of the Village People's song "Macho Man," Ralph sang "Metro, Metro man, I'd like to be a Metro man." No money was exchanged, but all parties within earshot appeared amused.

The musician is another variation on the entertainer routine and covers a range of musical acts from polished saxophonist to struggling crooner. Often, musicians play familiar and fun tunes to maximize appeal. Likewise, singers frequently enhance their act by interspersing humorous lines or jokes into songs.

For instance, a companion and I were abruptly accosted one evening by a man standing five-and-a-half-feet tall with long sideburns and cowboy boots who introduced himself as "Blelvis"—Black Elvis. Blelvis announced that he could sing over 1,000 Elvis songs and could relate any word to an Elvis song. As we continued walking toward our destination, I mentioned the word *cat* and Blelvis began singing a tuneful Elvis melody containing the word *cat*. Eventually, Blelvis asked for $1.50 for his performance.

This encounter with Blelvis, though largely promoted as a musical/comedy act, also contained elements of the aggressor technique. After initiating the encounter, Blelvis followed close behind and offered us little choice but to engage him. When my companion produced only $0.50 in response to his solicitation, Blelvis deftly grabbed a bottle of beer from the bag I was carrying.

Because many street performers are less aggressive than Blelvis or lack genuine musical talent, contributions may be more linked to sympathy and respect than to performing abilities. For example, late one afternoon, Alvin sat on a milk crate and played a Miles Davis tune, "Solar," on his worn clarinet. Several moments after Alvin ceased his playing, which was inspired but not exceptional, a group of young men walked past, and one dropped a handful of coins into Alvin's green canvas bag. Alvin responded to the contributions by pulling the bag next to his side and reasserting his identity as a musician: "Sometimes people hear me when I'm playing good but give me money when I'm playing bad or just warming up. They might give me money now or later. But I don't want anyone to think I'm a panhandler."

Hence, some ambiguous performers, like Alvin, occasionally struggle to prevent one routine, such as the musician, from being misinterpreted for another act that may be more degrading to the self, like the storyteller.

In sum, entertainers awaken pedestrians from their blasé state through benign or positive offerings, such as a song or a joke. Strangeness is reduced by performing familiar tunes or developing a welcoming presence in a particular neighborhood. Many panhandlers devise a coherent repertoire based largely on the entertainer and greeter routines, given the affinity between these two routines.

CONCLUSION

I have shown that dramaturgical routines are a useful way of describing and theorizing about the interactions and exchanges that constitute panhandling. From this symbolic interactionist perspective, sidewalks serve as stages on which panhandlers confront and overcome the nonperson treatment. Given the numerous contingencies facing panhandlers, the most successful panhandlers devise a repertoire of several routines to stir the blasé attitude, to minimize strangeness, and to maximize contributions.

Fundamentally, however, panhandling and panhandling routines are a response to economic and social marginality. After years of homelessness, joblessness, or health problems, few panhandlers possess the resources or skills necessary to gain stable jobs in the formal economy. Rather than relying exclusively on programs designed for the poor and homeless, such as food stamps, soup kitchens, or shelters (which many view as controlling, humiliating institutions), the individuals described here support themselves by creatively, sometimes desperately, engaging the consciences of passersby. Surviving in this manner is an accomplishment given that the majority of Americans do not believe the homeless should be allowed to panhandle publicly (Link et al. 1995).

In a broader sense, panhandling routines represent general strategies that any person might use to get what he or she wants from reluctant others. For instance, the salesperson who humors her clients to facilitate sales is being the entertainer, whereas the minister who dramatizes the church's financial status to increase contributions is playing the storyteller. Viewed in this manner, panhandler routines perform the same function as those deployed by the salesperson or the minister. When enacted by a panhandler, however, the entertainer, the storyteller, and the other routines appear in their boldest terms; that is, the performing and staging are done in the most unadorned settings and without the protection of position or prestige. In light of such difficulties, panhandlers who devise routines to overcome the nonperson treatment demonstrate a certain resiliency and fortitude, qualities that, were it not for their position as a poor panhandler, might have earned them raises and promotions rather than leftovers and spare change.

REFERENCES

Enck, Graves E. and James D. Preston. 1988. "Counterfeit Intimacy: A Dramaturgical Analysis of an Erotic Performance." *Deviant Behavior* 9:369–81.

Goffman, Erving. 1959. *The Presentation of Self in Everyday Life.* New York: Anchor/Doubleday.

———. 1963. *Behavior in Public Places.* New York: Free Press.

———. 1974. *Frame Analysis: An Essay on the Organization of Experience.* New York: Harper & Row Colophon.

Liebow, Elliot. 1993. *Tell Them Who I Am: The Lives of Homeless Women.* New York: Free Press.

Link, Bruce G., Sharon Schwartz, Robert Moore, Jo Phelan, Elmer Struening, Ann Stueve, and Mary Ellen Colten. 1995. "Public Knowledge, Attitudes, and Beliefs About Homeless People: Evidence for Compassion Fatigue." *American Journal of Community Psychology* 23(4): 533–55.

Parsons, Talcott. 1951. *The Social System.* New York: Free Press.

Reiman, Jeffrey. 1970. *The Rich Get Richer and the Poor Get Prison.* New York: Simon & Schuster.

Wagner, David. 1993. *Checkerboard Square: Culture and Resistance in a Homeless Community.* Boulder, CO: Westview Press.

IDENTITY WORK, STIGMA, AND SELF PRESENTATION IN INTERACTION

26

Being Middle Eastern American: Identity Negotiation in the Context of the "War on Terror"

Amir Marvasti

(2006)

About a year after September 11, 2001, I was in a shopping mall in a northeastern [U.S.] city. For the last thirty minutes, I had been acutely aware of a security guard who had been following me around the mall. I was not completely surprised to see him follow me into the restroom. I was, however, taken aback when he moved closer to me near the urinal and looked over my shoulder as I was urinating. I was not sure what to say or do. I thought, "Is he worried that I am going to contaminate the city's water supply with my toxic urine?" I felt violated but did not want to cause a scene. So I started singing, "Chances are, 'cause I wear a silly grin the moment you come into view . . ." I had learned the lyrics from a Taco Bell toy that played the song when you squeezed it. I did not really know the rest of the song, but it did not matter; crowing in English seemed to have done the job. The security guard backed off and left me alone for the rest of my time at the mall.

As this story from my own life shows, September 11th and the ensuing period that has been named "the War on Terror" have significantly changed the daily lives of Middle Eastern Americans. For members of this ethnic group, it was indeed "the day that changed everything." In the days following September 11th, anything seemed possible, even mass detentions on a scale similar to what Japanese Americans were subjected to after Pearl Harbor. Such fears were so real that on the night of September 11th, I actually packed some of my belongings and essential documents in a small suitcase in preparation for mass detentions. I was, after all, born in Iran and physically resembled the terrorists, whose images were relentlessly displayed in all the mass media.

The extreme measures I feared did not materialize in the aftermath of the terrorist attacks; however, our lives have, in many ways, changed for the worse. In particular, Middle Eastern Americans experience more stereotyping more frequently than before. We are asked to explain our intentions, politics, and personal beliefs, even in the course of the mundane routines of everyday life, such as shopping at a mall. Although prejudice and discrimination against this ethnic group existed for decades before September 11th, the recent intensity and regularity of these demands are unprecedented. As one of my respondents put it, it happened before, "but not with this magnitude, and not with the accusatory tone. . . . Before it was just out of curiosity, and it was incidental, but this is an even more demanding tone of 'Who are you? And why did your people do this?'" In this article, I investigate how Middle Eastern Americans respond to these disruptions of their daily routines.

STIGMA AND THE MANAGEMENT OF SPOILED IDENTITY

Numerous studies have highlighted how stigmatized individuals employ various resistance and management strategies in response to negative labels. Much of the scholarship is inspired by Goffman's seminal work *Stigma* (1963), in which he states:

[When a stranger] is present before us, evidence can arise of his possessing an attribute that makes him different from others. . . . He is thus reduced in our minds from a whole and usual person to a tainted, discounted one. Such an attribute is a stigma. (Pp. 2–3)

For Goffman, stigma is a variable social construct and not a fixed characteristic of the person. Stigma is bound by social roles and expectations and derives its meaning from particular social contexts. An ascribed status or attribute, such as one's race or ethnicity, is not inherently stigmatizing, but becomes so under a specific set of social rules and social conditions.

In this article, I am most interested in the "obtrusiveness" of stigma (Goffman 1963:129) and its "disruption" of daily routines (Harvey 2001). Specifically, I focus on encounters that become "incidents" or "scenes" (Goffman 1959:210–12). In such situations, as the norms of "audience tact" and "disattention" are suspended, the stigmatized individuals find themselves caught in the interactional spotlight, forced to explain themselves to others. From the perspective of the stigmatized, these disruptions are especially significant for their "moral careers"—or how they judge themselves and others over time (Goffman 1962:128). As one respondent put it, in such moments "the thin veneer of civility" is stripped away and negative labels are openly applied and contested.

This article examines stigma-related accounts as performances that involve both the substance of everyday experience (i.e., *what* is being contested or questioned and under *what* conditions) and the social construction of reality (i.e., *how* it is presented). This view of stigma is consistent with the symbolic interactionist premise that objects are not inherently meaningful; rather, individuals assign meanings in general, and identities in particular, through interaction. Stigma is realized in the reflexive interplay between social conditions and self presentation. The meaning and practical significance of stigma is interactionally achieved in everyday encounters.

Following this approach, stigmatizing encounters involve both concrete realities and fluid practices in which actors use language to settle identity disputes. In this sense, stigma becomes a locally circumscribed achievement. Applying these insights to Middle Eastern Americans' encounters with those who question their identities, specific cultural resources (i.e., racist stereotypes and fear of terrorism perpetuated by the media) provide the social context for inquiries about Middle Eastern people.

SOCIAL CONTEXT AND HISTORY

In many ways, the case of Middle Eastern Americans is similar to that of Japanese Americans in the first half of the twentieth century. Political turmoil in the Middle East and terrorism have created an identity crisis for those with ancestral ties to that part of the world. The negative stereotypes of Middle Eastern Americans ("Arabs" in particular) predate the September 11th tragedies.

In fact, negative opinions toward Middle Eastern Americans date back at least to the hostage crisis of 1972 in which Palestinian militants took eleven Israeli athletes hostage during the Olympic Games in Munich. The German authorities' attempt to rescue the hostages ended in a massacre that claimed the lives of all eleven hostages and five of the eight terrorists. Shortly after this event, the Federal Bureau of Investigation launched one of its first national campaigns to interview and deport Arab Americans (Marvasti and McKinney 2004:56). Later, the Iranian hostage crisis in 1979, the first Gulf War in 1991, and the 1993 bombing of the World Trade Center all reinforced negative stereotypes of Middle Eastern Americans. Each conflict was followed by a wave of

hate crimes and discrimination. Mosques were vandalized, and people were fired from jobs and assaulted on the streets (Feagin and Feagin 2003:327–30; Marvasti and McKinney 2004:53–60; Schaefer 2006:299–302; U.S. Congress 1986).

These backlashes were relatively isolated and episodic until September 11, 2001, when systematic discrimination against Middle Eastern Americans received considerable public support. A *Newsweek* poll conducted shortly after the terrorist attacks, on September 14–15, 2001, indicated that "32% of Americans think Arabs living in this country should be put under special surveillance as Japanese Americans were" (Jones 2001:3–4). Similarly, in June 2002 a Gallup survey of 1,360 American adults showed that "of the five immigrant groups tested [Arabs, Hispanics, Asians, Africans, and Europeans], the public is least accepting of Arab immigrants, as 54% say there are too many entering the United States" (Jones 2002:3).

Since September 11, 2001, accountability has become an everyday reality for Middle Eastern Americans in light of official policies that systematically demand that they explain their every action. Furthermore, the current terror warning system, which is intended to alert the public about potential terrorist attacks, acts as an accounting catalyst. As the level of terror is "elevated," for example, from yellow to orange, public fears and suspicions are equally increased, and subsequently more Middle Eastern people are forced into the position of account-givers. At the same time, terror warnings call on ordinary citizens to be "alert" and report anything "suspicious"—in a sense, deputizing them as semiofficial account-takers. In essence, the terror alert system encourages the suspension of tact and disattention, especially to the detriment of "Middle Eastern–looking" people. To borrow from Goffman (1963), Middle Eastern Americans are suffering "ill-fame" perpetuated by the mass media. In his words, their "public image . . . seems to be constituted from a small selection of facts which . . . are inflated into dramatic news-worthy appearance, and then used as a full picture [of their identity]" (p. 71). Under these circumstances, aspects of one's life that would ordinarily be considered private are routinely subjected to public and official scrutiny in everyday encounters.

METHODS AND DATA

From May 2002 to May 2004, my wife (a white woman from the southern United States) and I conducted twenty in-depth interviews with twelve male and eight female respondents, whose age ranged from eighteen to fifty-five years. All were either enrolled in college or had earned a four-year degree (at minimum), and lived in one of three different states (Florida, Pennsylvania, and Virginia). Eighteen were naturalized citizens and two were long-time immigrants who had lived and worked in the United States for over ten years and planned to become citizens. In our interviews, we asked respondents how they managed being Middle Eastern, particularly when facing discrimination. The interview data was supplemented with autoethnographic data from my experience as an Iranian immigrant who has lived in the United States since 1983.

Encounter narratives are the norm in the sociology of stigma for both practical and theoretical reasons. Practically, it is difficult to position oneself as a researcher to observe stigma management firsthand. Researchers would have to shadow the stigmatized through their daily routines to isolate specific stigma-related encounters. Theoretically, a person defines stigmatization experiences largely in retrospect. It is after reflecting on an encounter that a person might say, "I am/was stigmatized" or "I resist/resisted stigma in this way." Additionally, similarities between my respondents' accounts suggest that their narratives are not random fictions but reflections of a patterned experience.

Middle Eastern individuals presented or accounted for their selves in disrupted social encounters or "incidents" (Goffman 1959:212). Accounting practices took mainly five forms: humorous accounting, educational accounting, defiant accounting, cowering, and passing. Analyzing these accounting strategies enables us to vividly grasp the interplay between artful self presentations and obdurate social conditions. Each constitutes a different interpretive practice individuals use to establish a situationally practical and useful Middle Eastern self.

Humorous Accounting

When questioned about their ethnic identity, respondents sometimes use humor as a way of shifting attention away from the stereotypes that threaten their identities. In this way, they use humor as a diversion technique (Taub, McLorg, and Fanflik 2004). Consider, for example, how Ali accounted for his Middle Eastern–sounding name.

AM: Do you get any reactions about your name? Like people asking you what kind of name is that?

Ali: Sometimes they do; sometimes they don't. Sometimes, if they haven't met me or if they are sending me correspondence, they think it's a lady's name and a lot of correspondence comes in Ms. Ali [last name]. They think I'm either Alison or something like that. Nowadays, when my name comes up [in face-to-face contacts with clients], I use my sense of humor. For example, when they can't spell my name or ask questions about it, I say, "I'm the brother of Muhammad Ali, the boxer."

Ali's deliberate use of associations with the famed boxer places his name in a cultural context his account-takers are familiar with. In this type of accounting, individuals use humor to establish a common ground or "facilitating normalized role-taking" (Davis 1961:128).

Another respondent, whose first name, Ladan (the name of a flower in Persian), brings up unwelcome and troubling associations with the notorious terrorist Osama Bin Laden, tells this story about how she used humor with an inquisitive customer.

AM: With the name Ladan, do you run into any problems?

Ladan: Where I work [at a department store] we all wear nametags, with the name Ladan very clearly spelled out LADAN. And this old couple, they approached me and I was very friendly with them—I usually chitchat with my customers. And he started asking me all these questions like, "You're so pretty, where're you from?" [I respond,] "I'm from Iran." [He says,] "What?" [I repeat,] "I'm from Iran." So he asks, "What's your name?" And I say, "Ladan." So he bent down to read my nametag and he just looked at me with a funny face and asked, "Are you related to Bin Laden?"

AM: Was he joking?

Ladan: No, he was not. But I did joke back to him and I said, "Yes, he's my cousin and actually he's coming over for dinner tonight." [She chuckles.]

AM: So, when this sort of thing happens, you use humor to deal with it?

Ladan: Yeah, I do, because otherwise, if I don't turn it into a joke or a laughing mood, I get upset. I get really, really offended.

AM: So what was this guy's reaction? Did he laugh with you?

Ladan: When this guy realized my name is Ladan and I'm from Iran, he changed his attitude. He became reserved and he even went one step backward. When I noticed he was uncomfortable, I completed the transaction with his wife and let them leave as soon as they wanted.

In this case, Ladan's use of humor does not necessarily result in the proverbial "happy ending," or a clearly discernible resolution. The customer turned away and ended the interaction. Whether Ladan remained stigmatized by this encounter or whether the customer walked away feeling that he successfully applied the stigma is unknown, perhaps even for the participants involved in the interaction. What is clearer is that Ladan's account allowed her to highlight the ludicrousness of the account-taker's assumptions and his right to solicit an account. Here, the way of speaking shapes the substance of the identity. Ladan is not giving a specific and accurate account of who she "really" is, but is using humor to construct an encounter-specific account that implicitly questions the account-taker's right to ask her questions about her identity.

I also use humor to account for my name. The following encounter took place on election day (November 14, 2002) at a voting precinct in a small town in Pennsylvania where I went to cast my vote in the midterm elections. The encounter begins with the examination of my photo identification.

Election Supervisor: Okay . . . this is a hard one! [squinting at my driver's license] You're ready? [alerting her coworker] It says Amar. . . . It's A . . .

I wait, silent and motionless, as the three [elderly] women probe my ID. I fear that any sudden movement might send people running out of the building screaming for help. "Speak!" I scream in my head. The words finally roll out of my mouth:

AM: You know, my dad gave me a long name, hoping that it would guarantee my success in life. [They laugh.]

Election Supervisor: Well, you must be a doctor because you sure sign your name like one.

AM: [I cannot resist] Actually, I am a doctor. . . . So maybe my dad had the right idea after all.

In this case, I use humor as a method of introduction, a way of constructing an identity for the occasion that gives more weight to *how* one speaks rather than *what* one speaks. It was not clear to me what they thought about me, but I sensed that they were still puzzled—I had to account for who I am. The immediate substance of my identity was not in question—they had my photo identification in front of them and most likely could tell from my swarthy appearance that I was not a native Pennsylvanian. Instead, humorous accounting allowed me to shape the broad contours of my identity for the occasion. Namely, I was able to communicate that I come from a "normal" family that aspires to the universal notion of "success in life," that I am aware that there are concerns about my identity, and am capable of responding to them in a sensible way.

In humorous accounting, the substance of the account is incidental and is deliberately trivialized. The account-giver acknowledges the demands of the encounter while simultaneously undermining the legitimacy and the urgency of the request for an account. How the account-giver handles the substance of the matter shapes the identity in question.

Educational Accounting

Sometimes accounting takes on a deliberate pedagogical form. In such cases, the account-giver assumes the role of an educator, informing and instructing the account-taker about relevant topics. This strategy of "normalization" (Goffman 1963) combats stigma by correcting stereotypes. Unlike humorous accounting, educational accounting centers on the informational substance of the account.

In response to suspicions and antagonism from his neighbors, a Pakistani Muslim, Hassan, conducted a sort of door-to-door educational accounting:

After September 11th, I walked the street the whole week and talked to every single one of my neighbors. . . . And one of my neighbors—his brother was in Tower Two and he got out, and his mother was there and she was *furious* with Muslims and me. And we were there for three hours, my wife, my kids, her [the neighbor], her son and her other son that came out of the World Trade Center—he had come down by the time the buildings came down. And I was like, "Look, that's not Islam. That's not who Muslims are. Ask your son, what type of person am I? What type of person is my wife? Do I oppress my wife? Do I beat my wife? Have you ever heard me say anything extreme before?" . . . They all know I don't drink, they all know that I pray five times a day, they all know I fast during the month of Ramadan. At the end of Ramadan, we have a big party and invite everyone over to help celebrate the end of fast. This year, they'll all probably fast one day with me so they can feel what it's like.

Hassan's approach is proactive; it addresses potential questions before they are explicitly asked. In some ways, this form of educational accounting is similar to what Hewitt and Stokes (1975:1–3) call "disclaimers" or a "prospective construction of meaning" that individuals use in an attempt to avoid being categorized in an undesirable way. In this example, Hassan tries to transform the relationship between him, as an account-giver, and the account-takers who suspect him of being an "evildoer." Unlike humorous accounting, where account-givers deliberately trivialize cultural stereotypes, educational accounting explicitly and diligently addresses them in order to debunk them.

Account-givers have to give considerable attention to deciding which inquiries are worthy of an educational account. For example, an Iranian respondent, Mitra, indicates that she filters inquiries about her culture and identity before answering them:

> If they ask about the government or the senate over there [Iran], I don't know anything about it. I know who the president is, but they ask me about the senate or the name of the senator over there, I don't know. Since I don't know I'm not going to get involved. I'll say I don't know or I'm not interested. If they say, "Oh, you are from *that* country!" or "You are from the Middle East and you are a terrorist," those kinds of comments I'm not going to get into. I'll just say, *"No,* I'm not." But if they ask me about the culture I'll tell them, "Alright," and inform them about it—as much as I know.

Although inclined to assume the role of an educator, Mitra is unwilling or unprepared to respond to every question. Part of her educational accounting strategy involves evaluating the degree of her expertise on the subject and the tone of the questions. As she says, if the account-taker begins with accusations, such as "you are a terrorist," the only reasonable reply might be to deny the accusation and end the interaction.

Educational accounting was a common strategy for Middle Eastern Muslim women in my sample, especially those who wear the *hijab.* Many of them were approached by strangers who asked questions such as "Isn't it hot under there?" "Does that come in many colors?" "Why do you wear that?" "Are you going to make *them* [referring to the ten- and twelve-year-old girls who

were standing in a grocery store line with their mother] wear it too?" These women were literally stopped on the street by strangers who asked questions about the *hijab,* sometimes so directly as to constitute rudeness. My respondents reported that whenever time and circumstances allowed, they provide accounts of their religious practices and beliefs. Some of these answers include "I wear it because it is my culture," "I wear it so that you won't stare at my body when you are talking to me," or a more flippant response such as, "It's cooler under my scarf than you think."

Defiant Accounting

When prompted to provide an account, Middle Eastern Americans sometimes express righteous indignation. I call this defiant accounting. Similar to humorous accounting, the account-giver exerts agency by challenging the other's right and the rationale to request the account. However, whereas humorous accounting entails indirect and fairly conciliatory objections to stigma, in defiant accounting the stigmatized make explicit demands for counter-explanations from the "normals." For example, consider how Alham, a young Iranian woman, describes her experiences with a coworker.

> She [the coworker] would tell me, "I don't know which country you come from but in America we do it like this or that." I let it go because I was older than her and we had to work together. . . . But one day I pulled her aside and I told her, "For your information, where I come from has a much older culture. And what I know, you can't even imagine. So why don't you go get some more education. And if you mention this thing again—'my country is *this,* your country is *that'*—I'm going to take it to management and they're going to fire you or they're going to fire me." And that was it.

Alham does not provide an account to repair the interaction or to restore it to a state of equilibrium. On the contrary, she explicitly seeks to challenge the conventional format of the encounter. Instead of aiming for consensus, defiant accounting foregrounds conflicting viewpoints and signals the account-giver's objection to the entire affair. The interaction is explicitly focused on the fairness of the exchange between the account-giver and the account-taker.

Account-givers are especially likely to use defiant strategies when they find the request for an account unfair. Specifically, ethnic minorities who are subjected to profiling may become defiant in response to the practice. For example, when I learned that, unlike myself, my white colleagues were not asked to show ID cards upon entering the campus gym, I felt justified in becoming defiant. In one instance, while pulling out my ID card from my wallet, I asked the woman at the front counter why my white faculty friend, who had just walked in ahead of me, was not asked to present an ID. She explained that she had not noticed the other person entering or she would have asked him to do the same.

This encounter highlights the unpredictability of defiant accounting for both parties involved in the interaction. At its core, this strategy counters an account request with another: They ask for my ID and I ask why I should be the only one subjected to this rule. In turn, the other side presents its account and so on. This chain of accounts and counter-accounts could result in a formal dispute. Though it is possible that in some cases, when confronted, the account-takers simply back down and cease their efforts, it is just as likely that they intensify their demands, especially when they are backed by policies or other public mandates.

Defiant accounting is a risky approach that can either shield the account-giver from a potentially humiliating process or generate additional requests and demands. In some cases, defiant accounting can become a type of mass resistance, as with African Americans and the passive resistance component of the civil rights movement of the 1960s.

Cowering

Stigma, particularly when endured for a long period, can cause a person to engage in what Goffman (1963:17) calls "defensive cowering": The stigmatized simply go along with the stereotypical demands of the setting in order to avoid greater harm. With cowering, artful practice and agency take a backseat to external conditions. In encounters of this type, the stigmatized person is virtually powerless in the face of rigid demands of the setting.

Since September 11th, I have been very conscious of this fact when flying. Although I am certain that I have been singled out for security checks, I fear that objecting and confronting these practices would lead to additional hardships (i.e., a direct confrontation with law enforcement agents in which they have the greater authority and likelihood to win). For example, while traveling domestically, my thirteen-year-old daughter (whose mother is white American but has my Middle Eastern–sounding last name) and I were sent to a separate security line for a "random" screening. From my daughter's perspective this was "a good thing" because it meant going to a shorter line, but for me being searched was both humiliating and threatening.

During this incident, I assumed any kind of "talking back" would draw further unwanted attention and possibly result in hours of interrogation—and a missed flight. I later asked an airline representative at the ticket counter why my daughter and I were so frequently selected for "random" screenings. She responded that we were in fact profiled by a computer program and, for reasons of national security, the airline could not tell us what specific criteria were used for singling us out. After hearing this, I replied, "Thank you for taking the time to speak with me. I am not trying to be difficult, but I think the system is flawed . . . but I am happy to help with whatever it takes to make everyone feel safe. Thanks again."

In another incident, shortly after September 11th, my wife and I were browsing in a video store in Florida. A little boy (maybe about five years old) who was walking in front of us with his parents began frantically tugging at his mother's shirttail with his eyes firmly fixed on me. When his mother finally looked down at him and asked, "What?" the boy said, "Mommy . . . I thought they were all in jail." The boy's parents looked at me and pulled their child away. I tried very hard to smile, but my wife was outraged and wanted to confront the parents. I advised against it, fearing that a full-blown confrontation would only highlight and give credibility to the stereotype expressed by the boy.

Similarly, when a man driving by in his truck yelled at me, "Ragheads go home!" I had no opportunity to account or choose an accounting strategy. The incident was too shocking, too threatening, and too quick for me to rationally decide on an accounting strategy. I just cowered and tried to make sure the driver did not have the chance to run over me.

My interviewees spoke of similar incidents when they were dumbfounded by the sheer incivility of the attack. For example, a Pakistani man recalled being thrown out of an elevator on a college campus by a student who stated he did not want to be in the same space "with people like him." Several female respondents reported being verbally harassed or physically attacked. One was pelted with spitballs when she was in high school, another reported that her friend's scarf was pulled off by a teenage boy at a grocery store, and another was repeatedly yelled at—"Go home!"—by people in passing cars as she walked to her office on campus.

What these incidents have in common is that they severely limit the agency of the stigmatized; in most cases, the best possible performance is cowering, which is more about "saving body," or

one's physical safety, than "saving face" (Goffman 1959, 1963). In the biographies of the stigmatized, such overt acts of discrimination, however isolated, have great significance as "turning points" or "epiphanies" (Denzin 1989) that define the self as deviant and powerless in relation to normal others.

Passing

The goal of passing (Goffman 1963) is information control and the concealment of stigmatizing attributes from "normals." As an accounting strategy, passing means eliminating the need for an account (see Lyman and Scott 1989:126–27). How individuals present their identity can potentially eliminate the need for accounting altogether. My respondents accomplished passing by manipulating their appearance. The stereotypical image of a Middle Eastern person roughly translates into someone with dark hair, large facial features, swarthy skin, non-European foreign accent, facial hair on men, and veils and scarves on women. Faced with these stereotypes, some respondents consciously altered their looks to avoid any outside marker that might associate them with these stereotypes. Self-presentation (Goffman 1959), especially attention to clothes and grooming, is an equally important consideration for successful passing. For example, wearing jeans and being clean-shaven draws less attention and leads to fewer occasions for accounting.

Some Middle Eastern Americans try to pass by trading their own ethnic identity for a less controversial one. The simplest way to do this is to move to an ethnically diverse region. The respondents who live in South Florida stated that one reason they did not experience negative episodes of ethnic accounting is because they are perceived as Hispanic. For example, an Iranian woman was asked what kind of Spanish she was speaking when she was having a conversation with her teenage daughter in Farsi at the mall. Another Iranian man tried to pass as Italian by placing an Italian flag vanity license plate on his car. As a general rule, my respondents displayed Western or patriotic symbols (e.g., an American flag) at work, in front of their homes, or on their cars to avoid ethnic accounting. After September 11th, my neighbor gave me an American flag to place outside my apartment. As he put it, "This is for your own safety." In a sense, patriotic symbols are accounting statements in their own right and act as "disidentifiers" (Goffman 1963:93) that help separate "loyal Americans" from suspected terrorists.

Another strategy for passing is to give an ambiguous account in response to ethnic identity questions. For example, asked about his country of origin, an Egyptian man stated that he was Coptic (a pre-Islamic Egyptian culture). He noted that uninformed account-takers typically find it too embarrassing to ask follow-up questions, pretend to know what "Coptic" means, and drop the subject altogether. Iranians create this kind of ambiguity by stating that they are Persians (the designation of ancient Iran). Another way to circumvent accounts is to name one's city of birth instead of country of birth. I once told a college classmate that I was from Tehran. To my astonishment, he asked, "Is that near Paris?"

Changing one's name is another way to pass. Some respondents change their Muslim names (e.g., Akbar) to typical American names (e.g., Michael). When asked why he changed his name, Ahmad explained that he was tired of people slamming down the phone when he made inquiries about jobs. Some change from widely known ethnic-sounding names to lesser known ones as in the change from Hossein to Sina.

Passing strategies pose their own risks for the stigmatized. In particular, the media have constructed passing among Middle Eastern Americans as an extension of the "evil terrorist plot." After September 11th, it was widely reported that the hijackers were specifically instructed to wear jeans and shave their faces to pass as native-born ethnics. Therefore, rather than being viewed as a sign of cultural assimilation, Middle Eastern Americans' conspicuous attempts at passing can be cast as a diabolical plan to form a "sleeper cell" or to disguise "the wolves among us." These days, when I go to an airport, I am very conscious of how much passing would be considered legitimate. Trying to conceal too much information about oneself can arouse suspicion. In fact, I sometimes wear my gold medallion with its Allah (Arabic for "God") inscription conspicuously on the outside of my shirt to indicate that I am not attempting to "misrepresent" myself or deceive anyone.

CONCLUSIONS

The interpretive model used in this study combines the interactionist concepts of accounts and stigma management with the structural emphasis on concrete social condition. The analysis focuses on accounting as an interpretive process for establishing situationally specific ethnic identities. Rather than being a case of stigma as objective reality, the case of Middle Eastern Americans' spoiled identities suggests that stigma, the stigmatized, and stigmatizers become meaningful within specific social interactions under certain social or political conditions.

In this case, the conditions include the reality of the so-called "War on Terror" and a pervasive fear of terrorism, both of which have made Middle Eastern Americans "legitimate" targets of scrutiny in everyday life. The political turmoil in the Middle East directly affects their lives in the United States, so much so that there is almost a direct correspondence between the volatility of the region and the instability of Middle Eastern identities in the United States. Every terrorist attack, every hostage taking, and every virulent speech issued from the Middle East triggers a corresponding wave of public scrutiny in the

United States. These are the conditions, but how do we get at everyday practices? How do Middle Eastern Americans cope in real-life situations? Answering these questions requires wearing a different analytic hat, so to speak, the interpretive interactionist hat.

One way my respondents and I cope with these conditions is by being adaptable and fluid with our self presentations. We do not enter daily interaction as members of a stigmatized group. Many of us are devout Muslims who practice our religion proudly despite stereotypes and the negative press. To suggest that we are narrowly defined by the stigma of being Middle Eastern is an empirically unfounded claim. It is equally problematic to imply that the majority of Americans are engaged in a mass stigmatization campaign. On a general level, my analysis is informed by the idea that ethnic difference is variable and interactionally achieved (Garfinkel 1967), and suggests that Middle Eastern Americans use a range of interpretive practices to define their ethnic-national identities in the context of everyday life during the War on Terror.

My respondents and I experience being forced into positions where we have to account for our ethnic identities. What triggers these accounting encounters (e.g., genuine interest, fear, or malice) is of secondary relevance. As C. Wright Mills (1939) suggests, the motives for these encounters are themselves situated and discerned in the course, and in the language, of the interaction. In these encounters, account-givers and account-takers monitor each other at every turn and respond accordingly. I have labeled this type of interaction *accounting encounters,* and have underlined some of the self-presentation strategies Middle Eastern Americans use as they account for their identity (humorous, educational, and defiant accounting, cowering, and passing).

What these accounting strategies share is that they are all attempts at salvaging spoiled identities in disrupted routine interactions. My respondents indicated that they measure the quality of their lives by the number of disruptions they face (i.e., a good day means not receiving unwanted attention). It is true that most people experience some type of "incident" or "scene" in their daily lives, but it is also true that most find "their predicament . . . much less charged and more easily set to rights" (Davis 1961:132).

At a different level, this article also hints at the onerous "emotional labor" (Hochschild 1983) unwilling account-givers have to perform in order to cope with stigma. I believe that examining stigma as interpretive practice has clear political implication. Like most studies of deviance and stigma, my work is intended to humanize myself and my respondents, but beyond that, I hope for social change. By voicing my own and my respondents' perspectives, I want to inspire my readers to initiate new interpretive practices. Ultimately, this article is a purposeful account in its own right that aims to change negative perceptions and hurtful practices.

REFERENCES

Biernacki, Patrick and Dan Waldorf. 1981. "Snowball Sampling: Problems and Techniques of Chain Referral Sampling." *Sociological Method & Research* 10:141–63.

Brown, Anthony. 2001. "Nervous Pilots Order Off 'Arab' Passengers." *The Observer,* September 23, p. 2.

Davis, Fred. 1961. "Deviance Disavowal: The Management of Strained Interaction by the Visibly Handicapped." *Social Problems* 9:121–32.

Denzin, Norman. 1989. *Interpretive Biography.* Newbury Park, CA: Sage.

Feagin, Joe and Clairece Feagin. 2003. *Racial and Ethnic Relations,* 7th ed. Upper Saddle River, NJ: Prentice Hall.

Garfinkel, Harold. 1967. *Studies in Ethnomethodology.* Englewood Cliffs, NJ: Prentice Hall.

Goffman, Erving. 1959. *The Presentation of Self in Everyday Life.* Garden City, NY: Doubleday Anchor Books.

———. 1962. *Asylums: Essays on the Social Situation of Mental Patients and Other Inmates.* Garden City, NY: Doubleday Anchor Books.

———. 1963. *Stigma: Notes on the Management of Spoiled Identity.* Englewood Cliffs, NJ: Prentice Hall.

Harvey, Richard D. 2001. "Individual Differences in the Phenomenological Impact of Social Stigma." *The Journal of Social Psychology* 14:174–89.

Hewitt, John P. and Randall Stokes. 1975. "Disclaimers." *American Sociological Review* 40:1–11.

Hochschild, Arlie. 1983. *The Managed Heart: Commercialization of Human Feeling.* Berkeley: University of California Press.

———. 2002. "Effects of September 11th on Immigration Attitudes Fading but Still Evident." *The Gallup Organization* (www.gallup.com).

Jones, Jeffrey M. 2001. "Americans Felt Uneasy Toward Arabs Even Before September 11th." *The Gallup Organization* (www.gallup.com).

———. 2002. "Effects of September 11th on Immigration Attitudes Fading but Still Evident." *The Gallup Organization* (www.gallup.com).

Lyman, Stanford and Marvin Scott. 1989. *A Sociology of the Absurd.* Dix Hills, NY: General Hall.

Marvasti, Amir and Karyn McKinney. 2004. *Middle Eastern Lives in America.* New York: Rowman & Littlefield.

Mills, C. Wright. 1939. "Situated Actions and Vocabularies of Motive." *American Sociological Review* 5:904–13.

Schaefer, Richard T. 2006. *Racial and Ethnic Groups,* 10th ed. Upper Saddle River, NJ: Prentice Hall.

Taub, D. E., P. A. McLorg, and P. L. Fanflik. 2004. "Stigma Management Strategies Among Women With Physical Disabilities: Contrasting Approaches of Downplaying or Claiming a Disability Status." *Deviant Behavior* 25:169–190.

U.S. Congress, House of Representatives, Subcommittee on Criminal Justice of the House Judiciary Committee. July 16, 1986. *Ethnically Motivated Violence Against Arab Americans.* 99th Cong., 2nd sess. Serial no. 135. Washington, DC: U.S. Government Printing Office.

EMOTIONAL LABOR AND EMOTIONAL CAPITAL

The previous sections deal with the interactional processes of "impression management" and "identity work." Similar to acting in the theater, this social performativity is intended to induce particular understandings and responses in others, or the "audience." There are many occasions when portraying an identity that is consistent with the expected definition of the situation can be a lot of work for the person. For instance, if you do not like your spouse's parents but feel you must make a good impression to "keep the peace," you may find yourself working hard to maintain a smiling, friendly demeanor when you're actually feeling irritated and resentful. This kind of emotion work is not uncommon in everyday interaction and illustrates the distinction between private experiences and public performance (and the ability to be aware of both). "Emotional labor" refers to the ways in which we regulate our private feelings and bring them into line with social expectations. In particular, the concept refers to situations in which people are *required* to perform certain emotions as part of their job. Depending on the job and the circumstances, emotional labor can be very challenging and personally costly.

Emotional labor as an aspect of impression management has been a subject of extensive study in recent years. "Emotional capital" is a relatively new concept that refers to the process whereby certain impression management situations provide us with greater self-insight and a wide repertoire of emotions to use in subsequent interactions. For example, the boss who learns that employees respond better to criticism when she makes an attempt to engage with them on friendly terms has expanded her emotional capital. In other words, there is more than one way to manage impressions in a given situation. The person with the greater emotional capital is more likely to approach the situation creatively and effectively.

Sociologist Arlie Russell Hochschild was one of the first sociologists to discuss emotion management and emotional labor. The selection here is from her book *The Managed Heart.* This excerpt is based on a study of flight attendants and their interactions with the public. One of the services airlines try to provide in a highly competitive industry is a "friendly" experience. Flight attendants must present a friendly face despite the fact that the situation is often tense and passengers may be frightened, rude, and sometimes drunk. What do flight attendants do to "signal" a friendly situation, and how does this "emotion work" affect them personally? These are some of the questions Hochschild addresses in this reading.

In "Shaping the Selves of Young Salespeople Through Emotion Management," David Schweingruber and Nancy Berns chronicle the experience of young people who work summer jobs as door-to-door book salespeople. The company they work for has a very intense training program, much of which is oriented around emotion management with the intent of creating and performing a certain "go-getter" impression. Schweingruber and Berns discuss the emotional labor involved in the job, but also point out that salespeople gain some unexpected emotional capital as they learn to navigate the precarious and unpredictable terrain of this particular job.

READING QUESTIONS

1. Make a list of jobs that require "emotional labor." What are some of the activities that constitute emotional labor in specific jobs?

2. When does emotional communication feel like work, and when does it feel like "authentic" self-expression? What's the difference?

3. Recall an experience in which you learned some new skills for emotion management. Describe this emotional capital and how it has been of benefit to you.

4. One of the consequences of emotional labor is disassociation—the inability to have "authentic" emotional engagement. Consider the circumstances through which this might occur?

5. Use Goffman to explain why people "go along" with emotional labor? If we know the flight attendant or salesperson is being "friendly" as part of an impression management process, why do we continue to expect this behavior? What happens when an employee or service provider doesn't engage in the impression management that we expect?

6. Why do some emotional labor performances seem more "genuine" than others?

EMOTIONAL LABOR AND EMOTIONAL CAPITAL

27

The Managed Heart: Commercialization of Human Feeling

Arlie Russell Hochschild

(1983)

BEHIND THE SUPPLY OF ACTING: SELECTION

... Even before an applicant for a flight attendant's job is interviewed, she is introduced to the rules of the game. Success will depend in part on whether she has a knack for perceiving the rules and taking them seriously. Applicants are urged to read a preinterview pamphlet before coming in. In the 1979–1980 *Airline Guide to Stewardess and Steward Careers,* there is a section called "The Interview." Under the subheading "Appearance," the manual suggests that facial expressions should be "sincere" and "unaffected." One should have a "modest but friendly smile" and be "generally alert, attentive, not overly aggressive, but not reticent either." Under "Mannerisms," subheading "Friendliness," it is suggested that a successful candidate must be "outgoing but not effusive," "enthusiastic with calm and poise," and "vivacious but not effervescent." As the manual continues: "Maintaining eye contact with the interviewer demonstrates sincerity and confidence, but don't overdo it. Avoid cold or continuous staring." Training, it seems, begins even before recruitment.

Like company manuals, recruiters sometimes offer advice on how to appear. Usually they presume that an applicant is planning to put on a front; the question is which one. In offering tips for success, recruiters often talked in a matter-of-fact way about acting, as though assuming that it is permissible if not quite honorable to feign. As one recruiter put it, "I had to advise a lot of people who were looking for jobs, and not just at Pan Am. . . . And I'd tell them the secret to getting a job is to imagine the kind of person the company wants to hire and then become that person during the interview. The hell with your theories of what you believe in, and what your integrity is, and all that other stuff. You can project all that when you've got the job." . . .

The trainees, it seemed to me, were also chosen for their ability to take stage directions about how to "project" an image. They were selected for being able to act well—that is, without showing the effort involved. They had to be able to appear at home on stage.

* * *

TRAINING

The training at Delta was arduous, to a degree that surprised the trainees and inspired their respect. Most days they sat at desks from 8:30 to 4:30 listening to lectures. They studied for daily exams in the evenings and went on practice flights on weekends. There were also morning speakers to be heard before classes began. One morning at 7:45 I was with 123 trainees in the Delta Stewardess Training Center to hear a talk from the Employee Representative, a flight attendant whose regular job was to communicate rank-and-file grievances to management and report back. Her role in the training process was different, however, and her talk concerned responsibilities to the company:

> Delta does not believe in meddling in the flight attendant's personal life. But it does want the flight attendant to uphold certain Delta standards of conduct. It asks of you first that you keep your finances in order. Don't let your checks bounce. Don't spend more than you have. Second, don't drink while in uniform or enter a bar. No drinking twenty-four hours before flight time. [If you break this rule] appropriate disciplinary action, up to and including dismissal, will be taken. While on line we don't want you to engage in personal pastimes such as knitting, reading, or sleeping. Do not accept gifts. Smoking is allowed if it is done while you are seated.

The speaker paused and an expectant hush fell across the room. Then, as if in reply to it, she concluded, looking around, "That's all." There was a general ripple of relieved laughter from the trainees: so that was *all* the company was going to say about their private lives.

Of course, it was by no means all the company was going to say. The training would soon stake out a series of company claims on private territories of self. First, however, the training prepared the trainees to accept these claims. It established their vulnerability to being fired and their dependence on the company. Recruits were reminded day after day that eager competitors could easily replace them. I heard trainers refer to their "someone-else-can-fill-your-seat" talk. As one trainee put it, "They stress that there are 5,000 girls out there wanting *your* job. If you don't measure up, you're out."

Adding to the sense of dispensability was a sense of fragile placement vis-à-vis the outside world. Recruits were housed at the airport, and during the four-week training period they were not allowed to go home or to sleep anywhere but in the dormitory. At the same time they were asked to adjust to the fact that for them, home was an idea without an immediate referent. Where would the recruit be living during the next months and years? Houston? Dallas? New Orleans? Chicago? New York? As one pilot advised: "Don't put down roots. You may be moved and then moved again until your seniority is established. Make sure you get along with your roommates in your apartment."

Somewhat humbled and displaced, the worker was now prepared to identify with Delta. . . . Training seemed to foster the sense that it was safe to feel dependent on the company. Temporarily rootless, the worker was encouraged to believe that this company of 36,000 employees operated as a "family." The head of the training center, a gentle, wise, authoritative figure in her fifties, appeared each morning in the auditorium; she was "mommy," the real authority on day-to-day problems. Her company superior, a slightly younger man, seemed to be "daddy." Other supervisors were introduced as concerned extensions of these initial training parents. (The vast majority of trainees were between nineteen and twenty-two years old.) As one speaker told the recruits: "Your supervisor is your friend. You can go to her and talk about anything, and I mean *anything*." The trainees were divided up into small groups; one class of 123 students (which included three males and nine blacks) was divided into four subgroups, each yielding the more intimate ties of solidarity that were to be the prototype of later bonds at work.

* * *

The company claim to emotion work was mainly insinuated by example. As living illustrations of the right kind of spirit for the job, trainers maintained a steady level of enthusiasm despite the long hours and arduous schedule. On Halloween, some teachers drew laughs by parading through the classroom dressed as pregnant, greedy, and drunk passengers. All the trainers were well liked. Through their continuous cheer they kept up a high morale for those whose job it would soon be to do the same for passengers. It worked all the better for seeming to be genuine.

Trainees must learn literally hundreds of regulations, memorize the location of safety equipment on four different airplanes, and receive instruction on passenger handling. In all their courses, they were constantly reminded that their own job security and the company's profit rode on a smiling face. A seat in a plane, they were told, "is our most perishable product—we have to keep winning our passengers back." How you do it is as important as what you do. There were many direct appeals to smile: "Really work on your smiles." "Your smile is your biggest asset—use it." In demonstrating how to deal with insistent smokers, with persons boarding the wrong plane, and with passengers who are sick or flirtatious or otherwise troublesome, a trainer held up a card that said "Relax and smile." By standing aside and laughing at the "relax and smile" training, trainers parried student resistance to it. They said, in effect, "It's incredible how much we have to smile, but there it is. We know that, but we're still doing it, and you should too."

HOME IN THE SKY

Beyond this, there were actual appeals to modify feeling states. The deepest appeal in the Delta training program was to the trainee's capacity to act as if the airplane cabin (where she works) were her home (where she doesn't work). Trainees were asked to think of a passenger *as if* he were a "personal guest in your living room." The workers' emotional memories of offering personal hospitality were called up and put to use. . . . As one recent graduate put it:

You think how the new person resembles someone you know. *You see your sister's eyes in someone sitting at that seat.* That makes you want to put out for them. I like to think of the cabin as the living room of my own home. When someone drops in [at home], you may not know them, but you get something for them. You put that on a grand scale—thirty-six passengers per flight attendant—but *it's the same feeling.*

On the face of it, the analogy between home and airplane cabin unites different kinds of experiences and obscures what is different about them. It can unite the empathy of friend for friend with the empathy of worker for customer, because it assumes that empathy is the *same sort of feeling* in either case. Trainees wrote in their notebooks, "Adopt the passenger's point of view," and the understanding was that this could be done in the same way one adopts a friend's point of view. The analogy between home and cabin also joins the worker to her company; just as she naturally protects members of her own family, she will naturally defend the company. Impersonal relations are to be seen *as if* they were personal. Relations based on getting and giving money are to be seen *as if* they were relations free of money. The company brilliantly extends and uses its workers' basic human empathy, all the while maintaining that it is not interfering in their "personal" lives.

* * *

By the same token, the injunction to act "as if it were my home" obscured crucial differences between home and airplane cabin. Home is safe. Home does not crash. It is the flight attendant's task to convey a sense of relaxed, homey coziness while at the same time, at takeoff and landing, mentally rehearsing the emergency announcement, "Cigarettes out! Grab ankles! Heads down!" in the appropriate languages. Before takeoff, safety equipment is checked. At boarding, each attendant secretly picks out a passenger she can call on for help in an emergency evacuation. Yet in order to sustain the *if,* the flight attendant must shield guests from this unhomelike feature of the party. As one flight attendant mused:

> . . . If we were going down, if we were going to make a ditching in water, the chances of our surviving are slim, even though we [the flight attendants] know exactly what to do. *But I think I would probably*—and I think I can say this for most of my fellow flight attendants—*be able to keep them from being too worried about it.* I mean my voice might quiver a little during the announcements, but somehow I feel we could get them to believe . . . the best.

Her brave defense of the "safe homey atmosphere" of the plane might keep order, but at the price of concealing the facts from passengers who might feel it their right to know what was coming.

Many flight attendants spoke of enjoying "work with people" and adopted the living room analogy as an aid in being as friendly as they wanted to be. . . . Others spoke of being frustrated when the analogy broke down, sometimes as the result of passenger impassivity. One flight attendant described a category of unresponsive passengers who kill the analogy unwittingly. She called them "teenage execs." . . .

> Teenage execs are in their early to middle thirties. Up and coming people in large companies, computer people. They are very dehumanizing to flight attendants. You'll get to their row. You'll have a full cart of food. They will look up and then look down and keep on talking, so you have to interrupt them. They are demeaning . . . you could be R2-D2 [the robot in the film *Star Wars*]. They would like that better. . . .

It is when the going gets rough—when flights are crowded and planes are late, when babies bawl and smokers bicker noisily with nonsmokers, when the meals run out and the air conditioning fails—that maintaining the analogy to home, amid the Muzak and the drinks, becomes truly a monument to our human capacity to suppress feeling.

Under such conditions some passengers exercise the privilege of not suppressing their irritation; they become "irates." When that happens, back-up analogies are brought into service. In training, the recruit was told: "Basically, the passengers are just like children. They need attention. Sometimes first-time riders are real nervous. And some of the troublemakers really just want your attention." The passenger-as-child analogy was extended to cover sibling rivalry: "You can't play cards with just one passenger because the other passengers will get jealous." To think of unruly passengers as "just like children" is to widen tolerance of them. If their needs are like those of a child, those needs are supposed to come first. The worker's right to anger is correspondingly reduced; as an adult he must work to inhibit and suppress anger at children.

Should the analogy to children fail to induce the necessary deep-acting, surface-acting strategies for handling the "irate" can be brought into play. Attendants were urged to "work" the passenger's name, as in "Yes, Mr. Jones, it's true the flight is delayed." This reminds the passenger that he is not anonymous, that there is at least some pretension to a personal relation and that some emotion management is owed. Again, workers were told to use terms of empathy. As one flight attendant, a veteran of fifteen years with United, recalled from her training: "Whatever happens, you're supposed to say, I know just how you feel. Lost your luggage? I know just how you feel. Late for a connection? I know just how you feel. Didn't get that steak you were counting on? I know just how you feel." Flight attendants report that such expressions of empathy are useful in convincing passengers that they have misplaced the blame and misaimed their anger. . . .

* * *

RESPONSES TO THE CONTRADICTION

The slowdown is a venerable tactic in the wars between industrial labor and management. Those whose work is to offer "personalized service" may also stage a slowdown, but in a necessarily different way. Since their job is to act upon a commercial stage, under managerial directors, their protest may take the form of rebelling against the costumes, the script, and the general choreography. . . .

For a decade now, flight attendants have quietly lodged a counter-claim to control over their own bodily appearance. Some crews, for example, staged "shoe-ins." ("Five of us at American just walked on the job in Famolares [low-heeled shoes] and the supervisor didn't say anything. After that we kept wearing them.") Others, individually or in groups, came to work wearing an extra piece of jewelry, a beard a trifle shaggier, a new permanent, or lighter makeup. . . . Sometimes, as in the case of body-weight regulations, the issue was taken to court. . . .

Workers have also—in varying degrees—reclaimed control of their own smiles, and their facial expressions in general. According to Webster's Dictionary, "to smile" is "to have or take on a facial expression showing pleasure, amusement, affection, friendliness, irony, derision, etc., and characterized by an upward curving of the corners of the mouth and a sparkling of the eyes." But in the flight attendant's work, smiling is separated from its usual function, which is to express a personal feeling, and attached to another one—expressing a company feeling. The company exhorts them to smile more, and "more sincerely," at an increasing number of passengers. The workers respond to the speed-up with a slowdown: they smile less broadly, with a quick release and no sparkle in the eyes, thus dimming the company's message to the people. It is a war of smiles.

* * *

The smile war has its veterans and its lore. I was told repeatedly, and with great relish, the story of one smile-fighter's victory, which goes like this. A young businessman said to a flight attendant, "Why aren't you smiling?" She put her tray back on the food cart, looked him in the eye, and said, "I'll tell you what. You smile first, then I'll smile." The businessman smiled at her. "Good," she replied. "Now freeze, and hold that for fifteen hours." Then she walked away. In one stroke, the heroine not only asserted a personal right to her facial expressions but also reversed the roles in the company script by placing the mask on a member of the audience. She challenged the company's right to imply, in its advertising, that passengers have a right to her smile. This passenger, of course, got more: an expression of her genuine feeling.

The slowdown has met resistance from all quarters and not least from passengers who "misunderstand." Because nonstop smiling had become customary before the speed-up occurred, the absence of a smile is now cause for concern. Some passengers simply feel cheated and consider unsmiling workers facial "loafers." Other passengers interpret the absence of a smile to indicate anger. As one worker put it: "When I don't smile, passengers assume I'm angry. But I'm not angry when I don't smile. I'm just not smiling." . . .

What is distinctive in the airline industry slowdown is the manner of protest and its locus. If a stage company were to protest against the director, the costume designer, and the author of a play, the protest would almost certainly take the form of a strike—a total refusal to act. In the airline industry the play goes on, but the costumes are gradually altered, the script is shortened little by little, and the style of acting itself is changed—at the edge of the lips, in the cheek muscles, and in the mental activities that regulate what a smile means.

The general effect of the speed-up on workers is stress. As one base manager at Delta frankly explained: "The job is getting harder, there's no question about it. We see more sick forms. We see more cases of situational depression. We see more alcoholism and drugs, more trouble sleeping and relaxing." The San Francisco base manager for United Airlines commented:

I'd say it's since 1978, when we got the Greyhound passengers, that we've had more problems with drug and alcohol abuse, more absenteeism, more complaints generally.

It's mainly our junior flight attendants and those on reserve—who never know when they will be called up—who have the most problems. The senior flight attendants can arrange to work with a friend in first class and avoid the Friendship Express altogether.

There are many specific sources of stress—notably, long shifts, disturbance in bodily rhythms, exposure to ozone, and continual social contact with a fairly high element of predictability. But there is also a general source of stress, a thread woven through the whole work experience: the task of managing an estrangement between self and feeling and between self and display.

EMOTIONAL LABOR AND EMOTIONAL CAPITAL

28

Shaping the Selves of Young Salespeople Through Emotion Management

David Schweingruber and Nancy Berns

(2005)

Although Arlie Hochschild (1983), in her seminal *The Managed Heart,* emphasized the negative effects of emotional labor (emotion management for a wage), several scholars since then have shown that emotional labor can be satisfying for some service workers—particularly if a person's work role is central to his or her personal identity. Spencer Cahill (1999) made an important contribution to understanding the connection between the self and emotional labor by introducing the concept of "emotional capital." In his study of mortuary science students, Cahill found that all the students who could handle the emotional difficulties of working with the dead had "lived, played, and/or worked in and around funeral homes" (p. 111), most as children of funeral directors. No one without this emotional capital was able to successfully deal with the sights and smells of working with human cadavers.

In this article, we explore some of the complexities of emotional capital with a case study of the Enterprise Company, which trains and organizes college students to sell educational books door-to-door during their summer breaks. We used ethnographic and other research methods to examine the training and organization of salespeople over the course of a year. Managers at the company believe that the most difficult task for their student dealers is learning how to overcome negative emotions; thus, they speak of their training program as "emotional training." Importantly for our study, they train with students from a variety of backgrounds and work with these students to develop what are called *emotional purposes*—anything that students feel strongly about and can be used to sell books. One significant example of an emotional purpose is an *emotional other*, a term we derived from Mead's (1934) "generalized other." An emotional other is a person for whom a salesperson has strong feelings and who can be used, such as through imagined conversations, to motivate the salesperson to continue selling books. We introduce two other terms that describe how managers and salespersons work with emotional capital. We use the term *emotion mining* to refer to the search for and development of potential emotional capital in workers' experiences that had not been previously recognized by the workers as related to their job. We use the term *emotional bridge* to describe how this new emotional capital is used to connect the worker's previous self to the new self that is being developed on the job. We emphasize the reflexive relationship between emotion management and the self. Workers manage their emotions in an attempt to develop a new, better self, which in turn will be better equipped to do emotion management.

STUDY OVERVIEW: THE ENTERPRISE COMPANY

The focus of this study is the Enterprise Company, the oldest extant door-to-door sales company in the United States. Its student sales program began following the Civil War to help young Southern men earn money for college by selling Bibles and other religious books during the summer. Many of the contemporary features of the program were already in place by the 1910s. These included students selling in territories far from their hometowns, selling throughout the summer and delivering books shortly before returning to school, working six days a week and meeting in groups on Sundays, and having experienced student dealers recruit their friends and supervise them in the field. Although the company still offers some religious books, its main product line now consists of educational books designed to help elementary and high school students with their school work. Potential student dealers are recruited on their college campuses, often by other students. Following the end of the school year, student dealers travel to company headquarters for a week-long training session. Dealers are then sent with a team, which usually includes other students from their school, to an assigned sales area somewhere in the United States. Student dealers are expected to work at least thirteen and a half hours a day, six days a week, in all weather. Sundays they meet with their team for additional training and management and engage in some recreation.

Since salespeople work alone and are technically independent contractors (not employees), Enterprise is limited in its worker-control strategies. The company relies primarily on what Perrow (1986) calls "premise control" or "unobtrusive control," a worker-control strategy that focuses on changing the way workers think. Salespersons learn how to think about their products, their work routines, their potential customers, the company, and themselves. The goal of company managers is for students to successfully learn this new way of thinking—what we call "Enterprise Thinking"—so they will be able to make sense of and be committed to the sales job.

EMOTIONAL TRAINING

Teaching emotion management is central to the Enterprise training program. In fact, Enterprise managers use the term "emotional training" (or "emotional preparation") to refer to the focus of its training program. Emotional training is the process of changing the way dealers think and feel so that they will be able to succeed in the book field. Enterprise managers contrast emotional training with "technical training," which consists of learning sales scripts and other work routines. Managers typically claim that training should be 80 percent emotional and 20 percent technical.

Managers stress the importance of emotional training because the job is viewed as one that produces strong emotions. The Enterprise sales job is often described as an "emotional roller coaster." Because the job is so physically, socially, and emotionally difficult, around a third of dealers each summer quit the job before finishing their twelve weeks of selling. Many others remain in the book field but fall "off-schedule," a negative designation that includes knocking on the first door after 8 a.m., quitting before 9:30 p.m., or taking breaks in between. Enterprise dealers regularly experience such emotional challenges as negative social interactions with prospects, loneliness, failure to sell, and fatigue. However, most dealers define the hardest part of the job in terms of their selves. This is the intention of their managers. Copp (1998) suggests that "people may fail to control their emotions when they interact in situations that seem beyond their control" (p. 325). Enterprise's strategy is to teach salespersons that everything is within their control: proper attitude and work habits will inevitably lead to success. Narratives suggesting that salespersons' circumstances, for example, their sales territory, might affect their sales performance are discouraged. According to the sales manual, "You see, it is not the circumstances that happen to you in life; it is the ATTITUDE toward those circumstances that determines the kind of person you are going to be." Thus, dealers talk about the difficulties of "keeping on schedule," "staying positive," "staying motivated," "keeping focused," and "controlling emotions." These salespersons are attempting to build a self that will allow them to manage the emotions of the book field.

Emotional training involves storytelling. Managers tell stories to student dealers, and dealers share stories with each other. Stories within the company's official discourse attempt to make sense of the Enterprise sales job and the selves of the people working there. Some of these stories may then become part of a dealer's repertoire that she or he can use to make sense of her or his experience in the book field. Managers also attempt to help dealers develop their own stories that can be used in their work. They engage in emotion mining, the search for and development of potential emotional capital, to discover what personal experiences and attributes can become reasons to sell books.

At the heart of this training is the assertion that selling books door-to-door will make you a better person. Or, in the words of the company's motto, the sales program is about "building character in young people." This master narrative is described in the company sales manual:

> What kind of person do you want to be a year from now? Or two years from now? Or five years from now? Or 10? Or 20? Right now you are in the process of becoming the person you will be in a year, or two, or five, or 10 or 20 years from now. The habits you have now will determine the kind of person you will become unless you change those habits now.

Although it does not hold true for everyone, the promise of a better self through door-to-door sales is not a fabrication. The company's managers, who all began as Enterprise door-to-door salespersons, are true believers. Many dealers do report a transforming experience, as this dealer told us: "It was definitely the best experience of my life. You learn so much about yourself and other people, how to deal with people and problems. It's a great thing: you learn so much and then you can come back the next year as a student manager and learn even more" (white male, first-year dealer).

These dealers claim the job teaches them to better experience adversity, learn more about themselves, improve their "self-motivation," gain increased knowledge about the world and human behavior, and improve their interpersonal skills. Their growth in the book field, they believe, will carry over to other aspects of their life. Although not all student dealers experience this personal transformation, this master narrative is dominant in managers' and dealers' institutional talk.

Emotional Purposes: Personalized Narratives

Mandy, one of the Midwestern University full-timers, gathered her team in her motel room around 10 p.m., after a busy day of sales school, to share stories about the people who inspired them the most. Students discussed a grandfather who had risen from teller to bank president, a sister whose husband was killed, a grandmother who raised the student and her siblings after the death of their mother, and other relatives who had sacrificed for their families. Mandy told her team about her parents' sneaking out of Laos and living for months in refugee camps in Thailand and the Philippines. They eventually made it to the United States. Mandy said she learned while living in the camps that when you have an opportunity, you can't let go. "Don't give up on anything you do," she said. "Don't take anything for granted." After everyone had shared their stories, Mandy told them that as they go through hardship, they should keep these admired people in mind.

It was not obvious to college students beginning their sales training that an inspirational relative or a dramatic experience like escaping your native country in disguise can become a reason to sell books door-to-door. Enterprise managers help dealers turn these sorts of experiences into "emotional purposes" (also called "emotional incentives") that can be used to sell books. Dealers describe the book field as a world of deep negative emotions that must be dealt with emotionally, not rationally. They believe, in fact, that money is an insufficient reason to sell books (Schweingruber and Berns 2003).

Instead, company managers recommended they focus on "something more" than money. The term "emotional purpose" describes a personalized, non-monetary reason to sell books. According to Robert, a popular sales manager, "an emotional purpose has a physical effect on you because it is so important to you. . . . It is something important enough to you that when you think about it, it's a big deal. It makes your throat tighten and your eyes water."

During spring training meetings, Enterprise managers meet with their recruits and attempt to learn what motivates them. During this process of emotion mining, the manager and dealer attempt to develop a personalized narrative of what is important to the dealer and how that will get him or her through the summer. Although each dealer's narrative may be unique, the manager does not start from scratch in helping to develop this narrative. The manager has a standard list of possible emotional incentives in mind and tries to find out which ones will work for each dealer. An ideal narrative should describe how the Enterprise sales job will transform the student's self.

One type of emotional purpose focuses on creating a better self that can be carried into many future situations. These include becoming a "finisher" and a "professional" and developing a "positive mental attitude." For instance,

> My purpose before I started this job was that I was . . . just afraid of responsibility, you know what I mean? But taking on this job you have to be very responsible and very committed. . . . You're doing this because you are helping yourself out or just becoming a better person. (Black male, first-year dealer)

A second type of emotional purpose involves transforming a relationship with another person, whom we call an emotional other. These emotional others may include parents, friends, Enterprise teammates or managers, sales prospects, or people in the dealers' imagined futures, such as future employers or spouses. We describe these emotional others in more detail below.

A salesperson's personalized set of emotional purposes forms an emotional bridge between his or her old self and a new self who will be able to work hard in the book field and, salespeople are told, will serve them well in their future jobs and families. As managers learn about their salespeople, they find emotional capital that can be used to assemble the new self. Rejecting some of the possible emotional incentives is not a problem. If a dealer says he's not competitive, his student manager does not need to convince him to care about competitions, but if he is competitive, he can learn to be competitive about selling books. If a dealer's family supports her decision to work for Enterprise, she may dedicate her summer to them. If they do not, she can focus on proving to these "skeptics" that they are wrong. The emotional purposes that a dealer chooses are reinforced through a variety of practices, including writing them down, sharing them with other dealers, repeating them aloud while going door-to-door, and incorporating them into ceremonies, competitions, and other social events.

Mr. Mediocrity and "What-Ifs": Generic Narratives

The evening before the start of sales school, the team from Midwestern University lined up in a classroom to practice their "approach" with Dan, their regional sales manager. They had been practicing with the full-timers throughout the spring, but with better results. Dan was brutal with them, yelling at them to get off his porch and kicking their book bags. The next morning, the students walked to a large municipal auditorium for the official start of sales school. Rich, the company's vice president of marketing, greeted them by acting out, with great energy and humor, the day they had signed up to be a door-to-door salesperson and impersonating all the people—their roommate, their parents, and everyone at their college—who thought they were crazy to

sell books door-to-door. The audience laughed in recognition of their experience. Then Rich spoke of the doubts that the salespersons themselves had and personified them as Mr. Mediocrity (or Mr. M.), who appears in company materials as a little green man and sits on students' shoulders. "On your first day," said Rich, "at your first door, [Mr. Mediocrity] will say, 'This isn't working out, is it?'" Rich instructs student dealers to knock Mr. M. off their shoulders and stomp on him. He stomps loudly and repeatedly on the ground and announces, "This will stun him."

Although much of sales school resembles a pep rally emphasizing the joys of the company, its products, and the sales job, many sessions are aimed at informing student dealers of everything that can go wrong in the book field—and how they are supposed to react to it and feel about it. Enterprise managers, like Dan and Rich, engage in this preemptive emotional training because they believe if dealers are prepared for a negative experience, they are more likely to handle it correctly and less likely to quit the job. Managers use generic narratives to describe events that have happened to dealers (like getting made fun of for joining the company) and that are likely to happen to them. Although generic in the sense that they could apply to anyone, these narratives are told or enacted with humor, pathos, or dramatized hostility (as in the practice approaches).

One technique for discussing potential problems and rehearsing emotion work is a storytelling exercise called "what-ifs." For each what-if, the manager describes in great detail a situation that will be encountered in the book field. One manager's description of rain included shoes that do not ever dry, socks fallen down to the middle of your feet, feet hurting from the wetness, and no one letting you in his or her house. The manager and dealers then discuss how dealers can manage emotions during this circumstance and continue selling. By the end of training, the student dealers are supposed to be able to finish the story themselves. The goal of the exercise is for the dealers to be able to repeat the story to themselves when they actually encounter the situation. Another variation is to have student dealers come up with three positive things about any problem. For example, a flood in the sales territory means that (1) people will need new books, (2) more people may be home, and (3) people will admire that you are out selling during a flood.

Motivational Talks: Sharing Narratives

Perhaps the most moving story the Midwestern University students heard at sales school was Robert's description of being orphaned as a seventh grader and taken in by an aunt and uncle. Robert told his audience that he was a "confused young man" who did not get along with his uncle very well. During his first summer of selling books, however, he learned "things Uncle Frank was trying to teach me." After a summer in the book field, Robert could appreciate for the first time his uncle's hard work and the sacrifice he had made to take in Robert and his siblings. His uncle had a new respect for Robert after his hard work in the book field and could see the transformation he had undergone. The topic of Robert's testimonial was the "Success Coin," an award dealers can win by putting in seventy-five hours a week during their first two weeks in the book field. His talk was not uncommon in connecting an emotional personal story to whatever Enterprise award, principle, or work routine is being promoted.

During sales school, student dealers are exposed to numerous "motivational talks" that contain stories about selling books door-to-door or overcoming other great challenges. Former dealers at sales school describe how sticking with Enterprise resulted in personal growth, self-confidence, money, success in future jobs, and healing of family conflict. Any claims Enterprise makes about its sales program can be incorporated into these narratives, which are also found in motivational books

and tapes supplied by the company. These stories are intended to provide model narratives that student dealers can draw upon to make sense of their experiences in the book field and manage their emotions.

EMOTION MANAGEMENT IN THE BOOK FIELD

Stories that student dealers hear during training only guide their actions to the extent that they are able to repeat them to themselves in the book field—or create their own stories that are shaped by those provided to them. In this section, we examine how student dealers make use of these stories to perform emotion management while going door-to-door. There are two aspects of this process. First, student dealers use these narratives in the book field because they are useful—or dealers hope they will be useful—in dealing with their practical concerns. Second, the use of these narratives function as a form of "premise control." Salespersons are supposed to engage in "a constant and intense self-scrutiny, a continual evaluation of [their] personal experiences, emotions, and feelings" (Rose 1990, p. 254) in relation to the narratives of self-actualization and autonomy endorsed by the company.

Service-Mindedness as an Emotional Purpose

The idea of "service-mindedness," one of the most common emotional purposes, reframes the job as providing a service. Salespersons who adopt this definition of the job can feel positive about the services they provide in the book field—even if they are not selling books. Successfully defining the job this way can act as a hedge against negative feelings resulting from rejection by prospects as well as many salespersons' previously held beliefs that door-to-door sales is an impolite activity. One type of service dealers claim to provide is helping students by selling them educational books that would aid them in school. Student dealers believed in their products. Although we heard them complain about almost every aspect of the job, rarely was a bad word ever said about the company's line of educational books. One student dealer described to us the importance of service-mindedness and how he incorporated it into an affirmation he repeated to himself.

> My big thing is I'd just tell myself I'm going to show this to thirty families a day. I've had so many people, especially this summer, [who] are just like, "Steve, thanks so much for stopping by and showing us books because my kids just need help in math and these books look like they're really going to help." And so then I just drive around all day saying, "So many people out here want books. I just have to find them. So many people out here want books. My job is just to find them." Just takes the pressure off because I know I'm supposed to be doing what I'm doing and I really am helping people out. People are excited about me stopping by. (White male, third-year dealer)

However, student dealers also believe they can provide services even to prospects who do not buy any books. One of these services was simply to have a talk with the family about the importance of education, a theme of the official sales talk. Enterprise managers encouraged dealers to think of themselves as "professional educational consultants." Dealers were also taught they could serve prospects by being the most positive person they would encounter all summer. Thus, the dealers' positive emotions can rub off on the prospects. This idea was expressed in a popular positive affirmation, which is printed on a large red card included in dealers' sales kits: "This is the best day I've ever had! I can, I will, and I'm going to help 30 people today live a richer, fuller, more meaningful life because I stopped by and showed them my books." Focusing on creating positive emotions for sales prospects can lift dealers' own spirits, as with

this dealer who connected service-mindedness with her larger emotional purpose of regaining her confidence:

> My emotional purpose was to, like, regain [my confidence]. I had a really rough school year and I lost a lot of my confidence. And that was really my main purpose, was to go out there and to get something nontangible for Mrs. Jones and to give her something. So that kinda served as my attitude too, but just, you know, I wanted people when I walked in the room to feel happy that I was there. . . . I wanted that confidence. (Asian female, second-year dealer)

Emotional Others

Another popular type of emotional purpose involves an emotional other. Mead (1934) argued that people carry on internal conversations with a "generalized other" which is a mental representation of a community with which each person interacts. Likewise, an Enterprise dealer visualizes conversations with emotional others and otherwise incorporates them into his or her thoughts as part of emotion management. Emotional others can be specific people from salespersons' pre-Enterprise network; other Enterprise workers; or imagined future others, like employers, spouses, and children (since the sales job will make salespersons better employees, husbands, wives, and parents). Service-mindedness can be thought of as making sales prospects into emotional others. Perhaps the most popular emotional others are a salesperson's parents, who can be symbolically "sold for" as part of a "dedication." To help keep Mom and Dad in mind, dealers may post a picture of them in their car or even call them in the morning to tell them they will be selling for them that day. Some pretend the recipient of the dedication is present and have imaginary conversations with him or her, as this dealer reported: "When I choose somebody to work for on a certain day . . . I would talk to them in the car, I would call them on the [toy] cell phone [he had won in a contest] when

I was walking down the sidewalk, I would pretend like they were there" (white male, first-year dealer). These supportive family members also receive training. Managers coach parents on the proper narratives to use when talking to their children during the summer. Managers warn parents that their son or daughter will call them at some point in the summer saying they hate the job and want to quit. Parents are offered some suggestions for how to respond—all of which end in the parents' encouraging their children to stay with the job. Narratives for making sense of the sales job are often provided by parents of experienced or former dealers, whom managers arrange to meet with parents of rookie dealers with the expectation that they will talk about their own skepticism and fear about the company and their current understanding of what a wonderful experience selling books actually was for their child.

Parents and others in a salesperson's pre-Enterprise network can be transformed into another type of emotional other, the skeptic. Skeptics are a salesperson's emotional others who believe that selling books door-to-door is a mistake. During the summer, the salesperson can visualize interactions with these skeptics when he tells them how much money he made. According to one salesperson, "I think skeptics motivate me. . . . I want to be able to tell these people, yeah, it was a pretty good summer. I made about $14,000 but I'm coming back next summer. I want to rub it in" (white male, second-year dealer).

Student dealers use other salespersons as emotional others. Dealers may focus on beating friendly rivals (a practice promoted by publishing sales statistics from around the country in a weekly newsletter) or on demonstrating their commitment to their managers and teams, which they may have made in a sales school commitment ceremony or put into writing. Student managers may attempt to set a good example for the rookies in their organization. Finally, student dealers who are religious may focus on God as an emotional other who wants

to "sculpt" them through the challenges of the book field (Schweingruber 2006a).

Letters From One Self to Another Self

Earlier we described how salespeople can draw on their pre-Enterprise selves to create new and improved selves that will serve them well in the book field and beyond. Emotional capital discovered and developed through emotion mining forms an emotional bridge between the old and new selves. Enterprise managers have developed techniques allowing communication from one self to the other. As student dealers develop personalized emotional purposes and goals during sales school, they put them into writing. This allows a student dealer's sales school self to communicate with her book field self. Sales school is a bridge between the pre-Enterprise self and the book field self. Students at sales school are learning Enterprise Thinking, but they have no actual experience on the job. Thus, the book field self might be assumed to be more informed about being a door-to-door salesperson. However, Enterprise managers tell dealers that their thoughts during sales school are clear and rational because they are not contaminated by the negative emotions of the book field. They are also in regular contact with managers and teammates who can help them maintain the company's official definition of the situation. Messages from this "rational" sales school self can then be used by salespersons to manage their emotions in the book field. One manager, for instance, had dealers fill out a "persistence card," which was to begin with the lines, "Dear X, I wrote this when my head was clear. This is what I want to get out of this summer." This letter was given to the sales manager at sales school and then mailed to the salesperson during the fourth week of the summer. Another manager had student dealers write letters to themselves that they were to open only when they were about to quit the job.

Dealers also make lists that are used similarly to the letters in emotionally bridging the two selves.

The dealer and his or her sales manager refer to the lists during the summer to help the dealer stay motivated. According to one dealer, "We wrote out a list of emotional purposes and then whenever I got to the point—why am I doing this?—then you go back to the list and think: there's twenty-five reasons I'm doing this job. I need to do this job. I want to do this job for these reasons" (white female, second-year dealer).

Positive Affirmations

Julie, one of the dealers followed by the first author, had twenty "positive phrases" taped to the dashboard, ceiling, sun shade, and steering wheel of her car. These included

Don't think—just put your head down and work!

Winners perform consistently regardless of how they feel!

Success is measured by what you do compared to what you're *capable* of!

You good lookin' thing, don't you ever die.

Throughout the day, Julie commented on how "positive" things are. These included things that seemed positive, like drinking ice water or a sale, but Julie also used "positive" to note, for instance, a pile of dead worms and a sales prospect wearing a swimsuit in her backyard. After accidentally turning the wrong way onto a one-way street, she announced, "That's the most positive thing to happen to me today."

Enterprise managers promote the use of positive phrases and positive self-talk as a way for student dealers to discipline their thoughts. Many sales managers and dealers claimed that it is impossible to think a negative thought if you are saying something positive out loud. Because of this belief, student dealers are advised to repeat positive phrases aloud as they go between doors.

Undisciplined thinking can be counterproductive to maintaining proper emotions in the book field.

Some positive phrases focus on dispelling negative emotions, such as "Feel fear and do it anyway" and "This too shall pass." Others focus on creating positive emotions, like "I'm a powerhouse of enthusiasm" and "I love people and I love my job." Other positive phrases were used just because they sound funny. One dealer claimed to use the phrase "I feel like I just ate a bagel" because "it's just so corny it makes me smile." Many positive phrases simply describe future success in the book field, such as "Everyone's getting them," "Who's next?" and "Get your checkbook ready—here I come."

Positive phrases can also be tailored to a dealer's particular emotional purposes. For instance, a dealer focusing on service-mindedness may use phrases like "The kids out here need me to work" and "I'm so excited about helping families and helping children. "During "Dad's Week," dealers may work Dad into their positive self-talk. While most positive phrases were short, other dealers used longer ones, such as "It doesn't matter if I have one customer a day, it doesn't matter if I have ten customers a day. One customer isn't going to break my summer and ten customers [aren't] going to make my summer. It's the work habits and the attitude that I'm forming today that are going to last me forever. That's why I sell books."

DISCUSSION AND CONCLUSION

The people of the Enterprise Company are storytellers, and the ability to tell a good story is held in high regard. Storytelling is important, of course, to make sales (which has not been the focus of this article). But Enterprise salespersons also tell stories to each other and to themselves as part of building and maintaining new selves. In this article, we have shown the interconnections between the narrative selves of the salespersons and their emotion management. In this section, we summarize our argument and suggest how the concepts we have developed may sensitize researchers to similar processes in other settings.

Cahill's (1999) discussion of "emotional capital" focused on one type of emotional experience that was useful for people entering a specific profession. Our concept of emotion mining is an extension of Cahill's concept. We suggest that emotional capital is not just something that people own but something they produce and use. The process of emotion mining is akin to the attempt of "method" actors to tap into previous emotional experience to create performances. Rookie salespersons at Enterprise do not have any idea that their relationships with their parents, their religious faith, or their competitiveness can become potent reasons to sell books. Working in conjunction with their managers, they discover which of their attributes and experiences can become "emotional purposes" and how to use these purposes in the book field. Through conversations with managers and other dealers, positive phrases posted on dashboards and repeated aloud between doors, and other techniques, dealers turn this emotional capital into immediate reasons to knock on the next door.

Our analysis also highlights the importance of storytelling in emotional socialization. Emotional training at Enterprise consists largely of storytelling. Managers use a variety of storytelling techniques to provide narratives that make sense of life in the book field. Managers also help student dealers develop their own narratives through emotion mining. Dealers then attempt to use their narratives during their work, sometimes repeating abbreviated versions of them aloud while going door-to-door. Nonapproved narratives are corrected or limited to times, like personal conferences, when the audience is small and trained to reinterpret them. As suggested by scholars like Holstein and Gubrium (2000), the Enterprise Company provides a set of narrative materials for assembling selves. The primary purpose of this process at Enterprise is emotional socialization—the creation of selves who can handle the emotions of the book field.

REFERENCES

Abiala, K. 1999. Customer orientation and sales situations: Variations in interactive service work. *Acta Sociologica* 42:207–22.

Arluke, A. 1994. Managing emotions in an animal shelter. In *Animals and society: Changing perspectives,* edited by A. Manning and J. Serpell. London: Routledge.

Ashforth, B. E., and R. Humphrey. 1993. Emotional labor in service roles: The influence of identity. *Academy of Management Review* 18:88–115.

Blumer, H. 1969. *Symbolic interactionism.* Englewood Cliffs, NJ: Prentice Hall.

Bulan, H.F., R. J. Erickson, and A. S. Wharton. 1997. Doing for others on the job: The affective requirements of service work, gender, and emotional well-being. *Social Problems* 44:235–56.

Cahill, S. E. 1999. Emotional capital and professional socialization: The case of mortuary science students (and me). *Social Psychology Quarterly* 62:101–16.

Cahill, S. E., and R. Eggleston. 1994. Managing emotions in public: The case of wheel chair users. *Social Psychology Quarterly* 57:300–12.

Copp, M. 1998. When emotion work is doomed to fail: Ideological and structural constraints on emotion management. *Symbolic Interaction* 21:299–328.

Drew, P., and J. Heritage. 1992. *Talk at work.* Cambridge, UK: Cambridge University Press.

Ehrenreich, B. 2001. *Nickel and dimed.* New York: Henry Holt.

Etzioni, A. 1961. *A comparative analysis of complex organizations.* New York: Free Press.

Ezzy, D. 1998. Theorizing narrative identity: Symbolic interactionism and hermeneutics. *Sociological Quarterly* 39:239–52.

Fine, G. A. 1991. On the macrofoundations of microsociology: Constraint and the exterior reality of structure. *Sociological Quarterly* 32:161–77.

Fineman, S. 1993. Organizations as emotional arenas. In *Emotions in organizations,* edited by S. Fineman, 9–35. Thousand Oaks, CA: Sage.

Fox, K. J. 2001. Self-change and resistance in prison. In *Institutional selves: Troubled identities in a postmodern world,* edited by J. F. Gubrium and J. A. Holstein. New York: Oxford University Press.

Francis, L. 1997. Ideology and interpersonal emotion management: Redefining identity in two support groups. *Social Psychology Quarterly* 60:153–71.

Garot, R. 2004. "You're not a stone": Emotional sensitivity in a bureaucratic setting. *Journal of Contemporary Ethnography* 33:735–66.

Goffman, E. 1961. *Encounters.* Indianapolis, IN: Bobbs-Merrill.

Gubrium, J. F., and J. A. Holstein. 2001. *Institutional selves: Troubled identities in a postmodern world.* New York: Oxford University Press.

Hall, E. J. 1993. Smiting, deferring, and flirting: Doing gender by giving "good service." *Work and Occupations* 20:452–71.

Hochschild, A. 1983. *The managed heart.* Berkeley: University of California Press.

Holstein, J. A., and J. F. Gubrium. 2000. *The self we live by: Narrative identity in a postmodern world.* Oxford, UK: Oxford University Press.

Irvine, L. 2000. "Even better than the real thing": Narratives of the self in codependency. *Qualitative Sociology* 23:9–28.

Jacoy, C. L. 2003. Vying for heart and minds: Emotional labour as management control. *Labour & Industry* 13:51–71.

James, N. 1993. Divisions of emotional labour: Disclosure and cancer. In *Emotion in organizations,* edited by S. Fineman, 94–117. London: Sage.

Kunda, G. 1992. *Engineering culture: Control and commitment in a high-tech corporation.* Philadelphia: Temple University Press.

Leidner, R. 1993. *Fast food, fast talk: Service work and the routinization of everyday life.* Berkeley: University of California Press.

———. 1999. Emotional labor in service work. In *Emotional labor in the service economy (Annals of the American Academy of Political and Social Science),* edited by R. J. Steinberg and D. M. Figart. Thousand Oaks, CA: Sage.

Lively, K. J. 2000. Reciprocal emotion management: Working together to maintain stratification in private law firms. *Work and Occupations* 27:32–63.

Lois, J. 2001a. Managing emotions, intimacy, and relationships in a volunteer search and rescue group. *Journal of Contemporary Ethnography* 30:131–79.

———. 2001b. Peaks and valleys: The gendered emotional culture of edgework. *Gender & Society* 15:381–406.

Martin, J., K. Knopoff, and C. Beckman. 1998. An alternative to bureaucratic impersonality and emotional labor: Bounded emotionality at the body shop. *Administrative Science Quarterly* 43:429–69.

Mead, G. H. 1934. *Mind, self, and society.* Chicago: University of Chicago Press.

Olesen, V., and D. Bone. 1998. Emotions in rationalizing organizations: Conceptual notes from professional nursing in the USA. In *Emotions in social life: Critical themes and contemporary issues,* edited by G. Bendelow and S. J. Williams. London: Routledge.

Parkinson, B. 1996. *Changing moods: The psychology of mood and mood regulation.* New York: Addison-Wesley Longman.

Paules, G. F. 1996. Resisting the symbolism of service among waitresses. In *Working in the service society,* edited by C. L. Macdonald and C. J. Sirianni. Philadelphia: Temple University Press.

Perrow, C. 1986. *Complex organizations: A critical essay.* New York: Random House.

Pierce, J. L. 1995. *Gender trials: Emotional lives in contemporary law firms.* Berkeley: University of California Press.

Rafaeli, A., and R. I. Sutton. 1990. Busy stores and demanding customers: How do they affect the display of positive emotion? *Academy of Management Journal* 33:623–37.

———. 1991. Emotional contrast strategies as means of social influence: Lessons from criminal interrogators and bill collectors. *Academy of Management Journal* 34:749–75.

Randell, W. L. 1995. *The stories we are: An essay on self-creation.* Toronto, Canada: University of Toronto Press.

Rose, N. 1990. *Governing the soul: The shaping of the private self.* London: Routledge.

_____. 1996. *Inventing ourselves: Psychology, power, and personhood.* Cambridge, UK: Cambridge University Press.

Schweingruber, D. 2006a. Success through a positive mental attitude? The role of positive thinking in door-to-door sales. *Sociological Quarterly* 47(1):41–68.

_____. 2006b. The why, what and how of selling door-to-door: Levels of purpose and perception in a sales company. In *Purpose, meaning, and action: Control theory in sociology,* edited by K. McClelland and T. J. Fararo. New York: Palgrave Macmillan.

Schweingruber, D., and N. Berns. 2003. Doing money work in a door-to-door sales organization. *Symbolic Interaction* 26:447–71.

Sharma, U., and P. Black. 2001. Look good, feel better: Beauty therapy as emotional labour. *Sociology* 35:913–31.

Smith, A. C., and S. Kleinman. 1989. Managing emotions in medical school: Student's contact with the living and the dead. *Social Psychology Quarterly* 52: 56–69.

Snow, D. A., and L. Anderson. 1993. *Down on their luck: A study of homeless street people.* Berkeley: University of California Press.

Snow, D. A., E. B. Rochford, Jr., S. K. Worden, and R. D. Benford. 1986. Frame alignment processes, micromobilization, and movement participation. *American Sociological Review* 51:464–81.

Strauss, A., and J. Corbin. 1998. *Basics of qualitative research.* Thousand Oaks, CA: Sage.

Sutton, R. I. 1991. Maintaining norms about expressed emotions: The case of bill collectors. *Administrative Science Quarterly* 36:245–68.

Sutton, R. I., and A. Rafaeli. 1988. Untangling the relationship between displayed emotions and organizational sales: The case of convenience stores. *Academy of Management Journal* 31:461–87.

Taylor, S., and M. Tyler. 2000. Emotional labour and sexual difference in the airline industry. *Work, Employment and Society* 14:77–95.

Thoits, P. A. 1996. Managing the emotions of others. *Symbolic Interaction* 19:85–109.

Tolich, M. 1993. Alienating and liberating emotions at work: Supermarket clerks' performance of customer service. *Journal of Contemporary Ethnography* 22:361–81.

Wharton, A. S. 1993. The affective consequences of service work. *Work and Occupations* 20:205–32.

Williams, C. 1998. *Blue, white, and pink collar workers in Australia: Technicians, bank employees, and flight attendants.* Sydney, Australia: Allen & Unwin.

_____. 2003. Sky service: The demands of emotional labour in the airline industry. *Gender, Work and Organization* 10:513–50.

PART VI

THE SOCIAL PRODUCTION OF REALITY

If [people] define situations as real, they are real in their consequences.

—W. I. Thomas and Dorothy Thomas (1928), *The Child in America*

[People] make their own history, but they do not make it just as they please; they do not make it under circumstances chosen by themselves, but under circumstances directly encountered, given and transmitted from the past. The tradition of all the dead generations weighs like a nightmare on the brain of the living.

—Karl Marx (1852/1963), *The 18th Brumaire of Louis Bonaparte*

BUILDING AND BREACHING REALITY

Jodi O'Brien

STORIES WE LIVE BY

Writer and philosopher Antonin Artaud once remarked that humans are beasts with stories on their backs. Interactional routines and the coherent realities through which these routines take on meaning can be analyzed as stories. We use these stories to organize and give meaning to our lives. Stories have an organizational logic to them. They are contextual realities that provide the scripts for defining the situation and the identities appropriate to the situation. One question you might ask is what the connection is between the "performance scripts" described in Parts IV and V and "stories" or "realities." Think of scripts as possible lines of action that can take place within a particular type of story. Types of stories are referred to as *genres*. For instance, you are probably familiar with the differences between the horror genre and the romance genre. There are many different scripts that can be written within the horror genre, but you recognize each of them as a manifestation of the particular genre, because it has familiar characters, plots, and story lines.

Similarly, social realities can be recognized in the ways in which people share expectations about the story line, the types of characters, and associated behaviors and feelings. These story lines, or realities, are often taken for granted until someone steps out of character or violates expected routines. These disruptions may cause us to stop and momentarily reflect on the expected story line. We then respond to the disruptions in ways that end up either changing the routine or reinforcing it. One of the most common (but also most taken-for-granted) realities or stories in contemporary U.S. culture comes in the form of a "romance genre." According to this story, our main life quest is to find our "true mate," form a union together, produce biological offspring, and live happily ever after. Even persons who have chosen not to pursue this quest are implicated in the story to the extent that they are constantly asked by others to justify or make sense of their nonparticipation. This story is so prevalent that we tend to think it is "natural" for all humans to want to do this, even though the emergence of (heterosexual) romantic love as a basis for family organization is a relatively recent historical development.

The prevalence of this "marriage" cultural reality, or story, is revealed in the fact that persons who are of marrying age, but who are not married, are expected to give "accounts." In other words, they are expected to provide an explanation for why they are not participating in the cultural story as expected. Some accounts are more acceptable than others. Explaining that you have chosen to devote your life to the Roman Catholic priesthood is acceptable. Announcing that you are gay may not be entirely culturally desirable, but it makes sense in this particular context and is acceptable as an explanation. It is less acceptable, especially for women, to simply say "marriage doesn't interest me." Such a response is likely to raise suspicion among friends and family. "What is wrong with that girl?" they might wonder. They may even begin to speculate that "she is hiding something." Simply not wanting to participate is a behavior that disrupts the taken-for-granted expectation that "everyone wants to get married." Being a priest or being gay is an individual deviation from the expectation that *makes sense* and also reinforces the general expectation: "If he weren't a priest, he would probably be married." Conversely, having no interest at all in the cultural practice of marriage is a "breach" or disruption that leads people to press for more of an explanation, an explanation that "makes sense" within the existing story line that dictates that everyone must be interested in marriage.

When people feel compelled either to go along with a cultural practice or to provide a "reasonable" explanation for their deviation, the practice can be said to be "normative" or even "compulsory." In contemporary U.S. culture, most socialized individuals feel compelled either to consider marriage or to provide themselves and others with an explanation for their nonparticipation. It's important to understand that *both* the act of marrying and the act of providing explanations are "performances" that highlight and reinforce the significance of marriage as a cultural practice.

Other "compulsory" practices include being employed. One of the most common ways that strangers in the United States begin conversations with one another about their own stories is through the question, "What do you do?" Presumably, this is one of those questions that everyone understands. Even young children learn early how to respond to the question, "What does your daddy or mommy do?" If you take the question "What do you do?" literally, you could have a lot of fun with people by responding in ways that do not assume the question is connected to employment: "I do yoga," "I do a lot of lunches," "I do my daily prayers," and so on. If you did this, chances are people would look at you as if you were a bit crazy.

Think of other cultural expectations that are taken for granted and considered "just something everyone knows." Consider the underlying cultural stories that hold these expectations together, for instance, the idea that self-worth is reflected in type of employment. Recall the discussion of the *generalized other* in Part III. Cultural stories are reflected in the stories we tell ourselves about who and what we can and should be. Whenever you find yourself judging or assessing yourself in terms of a "should," you are in conversation with external expectations that you have internalized into your own self-story.

This section of the book explores the way in which people collectively participate in writing, rewriting, and performing various cultural routines or stories. If you view human behavior as a form of living through story, it may be easier to comprehend how and why people disregard or reinterpret contradictory evidence and behave in a way that results in self-fulfilling prophecies. Cognitively, we tend to pay attention to things that resonate with the situational story that is unfolding in any given moment. Behaviors and experiences that disrupt the story line tend to be ignored or "explained away." By acting as if nothing unusual is going on, we are able to maintain the impression that everything is going as expected. In this way, realities become self-sealing. We either find some way to incorporate our experiences into mutually understood stories, or we disregard the experiences as much as possible. This amazing feat of collective reality making is described in detail in this essay.

MAKING SENSE

It has been suggested throughout this book that humans are meaning makers. We make sense of our experiences by naming them. The way in which we define experiences and situations carries with it cues for how we should feel and behave. An aspect of meaning making that is important to the process of constructing realities is the way in which humans create *theories*. We don't just assign meaning to situations; the meaning holds an underlying logic and coherency, a working theory for what is going on. When things don't go as expected, we search our stockpile of working theories for the situation and make sense of things accordingly. For example, if you have a friend who is "always late," then you probably have a working theory to apply when he doesn't show up to meet you at the movies as planned. "That's typical," you say to yourself, shrugging it off. And the situation is resolved. Your friend may call you later to apologize ("I'm so sorry; I got held up"). This apology reinforces the general working story (you did have a date, and that carries certain expectations) as well as making sense of the disruption of the general working story. Imagine instead that you believed you had made appointments with several different people for various things, but none of them showed up. And no one called to apologize or explain. Later, you encounter one of these people, and the person acts as if nothing occurred, saying nothing about having stood you up. At this point, you would probably be confused and begin to wonder what was going on. You would search back and try to apply a working theory to make sense of this "breach" in expectations. It would probably continue to nag at you until you were able to make sense of the situation in a way that was consistent with your general expectations—people make appointments and follow through. Eventually, someone might explain to you that in this particular subculture, people say things all the time such as "let's do lunch," but never actually mean it. "Ah," you might say to yourself, "now I get it. People here are just rude." By deciding that people are "rude," you have reinforced your original cultural expectations and also found a way to make sense of the breach.

All human interaction is grounded in story lines for what is going on and underlying theories for making sense of things when they don't go as expected. These working theories are a central aspect of social realities. Even something as simple as the "Hi, how's it going?" acknowledgment routine reflects very specific cultural expectations and underlying theories. The actual words spoken are completely incongruent with the expected response. If you speak the greeting to someone and she doesn't respond, you have a working theory for why. The theory might include the possibilities "she didn't see me," "she's distracted," or perhaps even "she's annoyed with me." However, it's not likely that you would wonder if, perhaps today, you're invisible. This explanation is simply not part of your working theory.

An unquestioned assumption in the greeting ritual is that people can see one another. Similar to the assumption that people can see you if you're in their presence, there is an assumption that people can hear you. When someone doesn't respond immediately to a statement "obviously" directed at him, we file through several explanations, including "he's just being a jerk," before we hit on the possibility that "hey, maybe he can't hear me." Deaf people report that this is a common experience in encounters with hearing people. When someone finally does get the attention of a deaf person, he or she tends to be annoyed because it has taken awhile to realize what otherwise might seem obvious: This person can't hear me. Instead he or she has been operating with assumptions that include "the person is purposely ignoring me, is rude, etc." Working theories, like other ways of making sense, are also a combination of individual experience and cultural information about how to make sense of those experiences. One of the features of socially constructed realities is that we have working theories that enable us to *generate* a vast number of explanations for situations that don't make sense, but even these theories are a product of social interaction.

Another feature of socially constructed realities is that they contain a great deal of information that "everyone just knows." However, taken literally, this knowledge may seem strange and contradictory when viewed out of context. In the acknowledgment routine described above, most people know that in response to this greeting, they are not supposed to actually go into detail about "how it's going." Someone who did so might be considered a little "off." In contrast, many people who are new to U.S. culture find this greeting routine perplexing: Why would you ask someone how they are and then not stop to hear the answer?

COMMON SENSE

This basic "what everyone knows" knowledge of "reality" is called common sense. *Common sense* is a set of shared cultural rules for making sense of the world. These rules are so well established and taken for granted that they often require no justification. To the question "How did you know that?" or "Why did you do that?" one can reply simply, "It's just common sense." These rules are the bedrock of cultural knowledge; they seem obviously true.

One of the most powerful ways of demonstrating that reality is a social construction is to show the limitations and arbitrariness of common sense, either by pointing out inconsistencies or by contrasting one culture's common sense to another's. One very popular counterculture book in the 1960s was written by two sociologists, Peter Berger and Thomas Luckmann (1966). In this book, *The Social Construction of Reality,* Berger and Luckmann describe the ways in which people create organizing systems with the intent of making their lives orderly and predictable. Eventually, they forget they were the creators of these systems, and, thus reified, the systems take on a life of their own. What were once useful recipes for living become calcified into "commonsense" beliefs that "everyone knows."

There are several profound implications of "commonsense" or socially constructed realities. Self-fulfilling prophecies and the (re)creation of the cultural status quo are two that are worth extensive discussion. Before turning to those implications, let's look in detail at some of the ways in which people actively work together, usually unknowingly, to create and re-create the stories and theories that we use for making sense.

A Theory of Reality

Ethnomethodology is a research area in sociology that explores the folk methods ("ethno methods") that people use to construct systems of meaning and reality. Ethnomethodologists make visible the often invisible or unseen features of reality construction. Hugh Mehan and Houston Wood are two such ethnomethodologists. They have assembled a framework for analyzing collective reality construction. As part of this framework, they have identified five features that underlie all cultural realities (see Reading 30). These five key features of reality are that they are reflexive, coherent, interactional, fragile, and permeable. You can read about each of the features in their article, but let's look at a few examples here.

Reflexive

Realities are *reflexive*. This means that all realities contain self-sealing beliefs—unquestioned beliefs that cannot be proven wrong. For example, if you place your pencil on your desk while you go for a snack and cannot find the pencil when you return, you will assume that you somehow misplaced it. If it reappears where you left it, you will assume that you just overlooked it the first time. In many cultures, people hold an unquestioned belief regarding the immobility of "inanimate" objects, so it's unlikely that you would entertain the notion that your pencil left by itself and then returned. In other words, your working theory of reality does not include the possibility that inanimate objects move around on their own. This is just something everyone knows.

One of the interesting things about realities is that they often contain contradictions and inconsistencies. For instance, imagine a small child who fears monsters under her bed. Her parents might attempt to calm her by saying there are no such things as monsters, so they're not real. "But I can *see* them," she might insist. "I know they're real." Later, she may come down with the flu and ask what is making her so ill. "Germs," a parent might say. "Germs are little bugs that live inside you and make you sick, but you can't see them." How confusing is this information?! Tiny things that you can't see but that live in you and make you sick versus huge monsters you know you can see but apparently, you're told, are not real. All realities contain a series of working theories about how to deal with contradictory information. These working theories are called *secondary elaborations*. In response to information that may appear to contradict a taken-for-granted assumption, we explain away the contradiction with a secondary elaboration: "That girl actually answered the 'how's it going?' question because she's so weird. Everyone knows that you don't really answer that question."

Consider this illustration: Do you watch the 5-day weather forecast? A newcomer to U.S. culture might assume that one needed to watch the forecast only once every 5 days: Presumably, a 5-day forecast will give useful weather information for the next 5 days. Right?

"No!" you exclaim. "You need to watch it every day." The newcomer looks at you, puzzled. "Because the forecast changes," you continue. Now the newcomer is really confused. Why watch a "forecast" if you already know it will not be accurate? Think about this: You watch weather forecasts because you want to know what the weather will be, but you also recognize that the predictions are often inaccurate. So you watch the forecast again to see how it has changed. Does the frequent inaccuracy of the predictions make you doubt the "reality" that we can forecast the weather? No. Instead of questioning the validity of forecasting the weather, you probably explain away the inaccuracies as human error or the inadequacy of present meteorological technology. What you are not likely to do is question the taken-for-granted assumption that there is a pattern to nature, and that, with the right theories and technology, we can know this pattern and make predictions based on it. In other words, you are not likely to assume that the weather is actually random. An unquestioned belief of modern Western thought is that there is order in nature. The cultural enterprise of predicting weather is based on this assumption.

In one famous (and also controversial) study, a psychiatrist, David Rosenhan (1973), conducted a casual but effective experiment intended to determine whether the sane can be reliably distinguished from the insane. His hypothesis was that psychiatric practitioners were so entrenched in their own system of diagnosing patients that they would assume *anyone* who came for treatment was insane. Rosenhan sent several students to psychiatric admitting rooms and instructed them to say they were hearing voices but otherwise to show no symptoms of abnormality. All of the student posers were evaluated and judged to be in need of psychiatric hospitalization. Rosenhan concluded that psychiatric staff work in a context in which they *expect* patients to be insane, so they interpret the behavior of any person presumed to be a patient, even the behavior of "normal" researchers, as insane.

Unquestioned beliefs are often more easily noticed when examining a culture different from our own. In many cases, others' beliefs are described as superstitious or magical. However, Mehan and Wood demonstrate that any culture, including ours, is filled with unquestioned beliefs. When challenged with contradictions and inconsistencies, we reflexively "seal up" the contradiction with a secondary elaboration. This leads Mehan and Wood to conclude that "all people are equally superstitious." People continue to hold certain unquestioned beliefs in the face of contradictory evidence.

Coherent

A second feature of realities is that they have an order and structure to them; realities are *coherent*. Even realities that seem nonsensical and anarchical to outsiders reveal their own order and logic when carefully examined. Coherency is an outcome of the apparent human need to make order out of chaos. If things are orderly, then they are predictable. If you actually had to contemplate and question everything in your environment anew every day, you'd never make it out of the house. One interesting aspect of human life is that we create systems of order and theories for making sense and then tend to believe that these systems or theories reflect a general or real pattern.

Noncontingencies

Psychologists have conducted a series of intriguing studies called "noncontingency" experiments. *Noncontingent* means that there is *no connection* between an outcome and something else in the environment. For instance, you may have a headache right now, but you know it is not contingent on (not connected to) having stubbed your toe earlier. Humans create working theories by formulating connections between what they perceive to be the cause and effect. If I drink too much, I am likely to be hungover; feeling hungover is contingent on drinking too much. Or, my getting into graduate school is contingent on getting good grades.

Noncontingency experiments reveal some very interesting things about the construction of coherency. One is that we form "superstitious" or "neurotic" theories. A horse that receives a mild electric shock in its foot at the same time that a bell is rung will continue to raise its foot every time the bell rings even after the shocks have ceased. The horse associates the shock (and corresponding urge to lift its foot) with the bell, even though the shock is not connected to the bell. Similarly, humans who experience a strong emotion, such as shock or fear due to a particular event, may continue to experience that emotion in similar situations, even if the threat is no longer present. For example, someone who has been traumatized by a dog bite may panic in the presence of all dogs. This associative-emotive pattern is sometimes referred to as a *phobia*.

Even more interesting is an experiment in which a group of students was asked to develop a system for identifying "sick" versus "healthy" cells. It turns out that this is not a very difficult task if you already know the theory. However, if you don't have a working theory, you have to rely on trial and error. Students were shown slides and with each slide, they were asked to push a button indicating "sick" or "healthy." Lights on their panels then lit up indicating either a wrong choice or a right choice. Based on this information, the students studied the slide, trying to come up with a working hypothesis (for example, on the sick cells, "the nucleus looks broken"). When another slide was flashed, they could try out their hypothesis. The indicator lights letting them know their guesses were right or wrong provided the feedback they needed to revise and refine their working theories. Given correct feedback, cell identification turned out to be a simple task for most students. All of these students emerged from the task with a "theory," and their theories were very similar. They'd created a coherent way of cataloging the cells based on trial and error and feedback.

The interesting finding concerned another group that was participating in the same experiment, with one small difference: They were being given random feedback. In other words, their "right" and "wrong" buttons had no connection to their guesses. They, too, were trying to develop a theory of cell identification based on trial and error and feedback, but in this case, the feedback was not contingent on their guesses. Were they able to devise a theory? Yes! Not only did they develop theories, but the theories were very elaborate and complex. In an insightful conclusion, the researchers invited the student groups to talk with each other about their theories. The contingency group had very simple theories (based on the fact that they had received correct feedback), and when they questioned the noncontingency group about their more complicated theories, these students provided responses that were so compelling that the former group began to doubt their own theories and wonder if they were "missing something."

This experiment, and others like it, reveals several fascinating features of reality construction. Most significantly, we are able and inclined to create coherent theories out of even *random* information. It never occurred to the noncontingency group that there was no connection between their answers and the "feedback" they received. Further, when they were informed of this later, several of them insisted that, regardless of the randomness, their theories reflected "correct" assessments.

As you ponder this material, consider some of the ways in which you get the "feedback" that enables you to create coherent theories in your own life. It's a useful "reality check" to examine your sources of information, especially whether these are connected to outcomes in the ways that you believe them to be.

"It Makes Sense to Us!"

In discussing *coherency,* Mehan and Wood are particularly interested in the ways in which realities that may seem preposterous to outsiders are quite ordinary and plausible to insiders. Regardless of the ways in which a system of belief and expectations arose (that is, in spite of the noncontingencies and inconsistencies), it appears coherent to those who share the system of understanding. Persons of different religious or political persuasions often try to "poke holes" in one another's beliefs by pointing out what seem to be "obvious" contradictions. From an ethnomethodological perspective, this is a fruitless exercise and serves only to demonstrate the extent to which all belief systems have a coherency that includes secondary elaborations, or ways for explaining away inconsistencies. When the feature of *reflexivity* is added to *coherency,* we begin to see just how firmly entrenched belief systems can be. Challenges in the form of contradictions may actually serve to strengthen the original belief, especially as a person articulates the secondary elaborations that extend the coherency to cover all possible disruptions.

Interactional and Fragile

The process of creating and maintaining realities is *ongoing and interactional.* As noted in the example about greetings, we work together to create even the simplest realities such as the belief that we are seen by others as distinct and notable persons. Because realities are based on ongoing interactions, they are subject to performance breakdowns (recall the discussion in Part V). In this way, realities are *fragile.* We rely on one another to perform the expected roles and routines that make up significant cultural stories. One of the reasons that grand ceremonies, such as weddings, are a source of so much stress is because the participants are dependent on the actions of others in order for the event to go off well. This is why there are rehearsals for important events: We recognize that these ceremonies require us to perform roles that are highly significant, but for which people don't have much firsthand experience.

Cultural realities actually break down much more than people acknowledge. In our day-to-day lives, we encounter numerous disruptions that threaten to bring smooth interactions to an embarrassed halt. The reflexive and coherent features of reality are reflected in the ways in which people work together to repair these disruptions. *Tact* is one interactional strategy for repairing disrupted routines. Accounts are another. As was discussed in Part V, these strategies reflect a consensus about what the expected routine should be and a willingness to help restore it to a working definition. When disruptions in the expected routine occur, people often have no idea what to do next. They simply don't have a script for the situation. Such situations occur more frequently than we tend to realize. However, we're inclined to overlook the fragility of reality maintenance, in part because we have strategies for continuing on *as if* nothing unusual is happening.

Breaching

Imagine you attend a dinner party given by a friend, and you invite your girlfriend, who has never met the friend, to join you. Upon your arrival, your host takes your coats and says pleasantly, "Make yourself at home." Your girlfriend replies, "Thank you, I will," and proceeds to take off her shoes and socks, turn on the television, and put her feet on the coffee table. Your friend is likely to look at you for an explanation of this seemingly bizarre behavior. You can only shrug and look on in dismay. Your shrug and look of dismay are cues to your friend that you share his view of reality: The girlfriend is behaving strangely and has violated the expected interaction rules for polite company behavior. Imagine further that you approach your girlfriend and ask what's going on. She replies, "He said I could make myself at home." In response to this, you try to explain that he didn't really mean for her to act like she was in her own home. She gives you a wilting look that suggests you're the crazy one and turns up the television.

In an article titled "A Conception of and Experiments With 'Trust' as a Condition of Concerted Stable Actions" (Reading 31), one of the founders of ethnomethodology, Harold Garfinkel, describes social "breaching experiments." Garfinkel achieved great fame and notoriety with the breaching experiments he and his students conducted at the University of California, Los Angeles (UCLA) in the 1960s. Breaching entails making the underlying structure of reality explicit by acting in a manner that is inconsistent with the taken-for-granted rules of interaction that maintain the reality. When reality is breached, interaction often comes to a confused halt. Garfinkel describes a variety of breaching experiments as well as people's reactions to these experiments. According to Garfinkel, we enter into interactional moments "trusting" that others share our expectations and definitions of reality. It is this trust that enables us to engage in stable, coherent, and meaningful interactions.

The situation described above is a "breach." In this case, the woman has breached the expectation that certain phrases are intended as polite and are not meant to be taken literally. The host "trusts" his guests to know the appropriate "visitor" behavior. Otherwise, he would not have made a statement such as "make yourself at home." This example is based on an actual breach conducted by one of my students. She had put off doing the assignment until the last minute and didn't know what to do. As she explained later in her written paper, when the host said "make yourself at home," she recalled reading in Garfinkel about taking statements literally and decided to give it a try. She actually went so far the evening of the party as to take a shower at her host's home.

Breaches reveal just how fragile and interactional (and meaningful) cultural realities are. Confronted with a breach, observers usually try first to ignore it (the "nothing unusual" bias).

We do this whenever we walk away from people on the street who strike us as "off." If it is not possible to ignore the breach, such as someone in an elevator asking you to examine the cut on her arm (another breach carried out by one of my students), people look to others to reaffirm that the breacher is "weird." This usually takes the form of strangers looking at one another, smiling knowingly, and perhaps rolling their eyes. This subtle communication is an effective interactional strategy for signaling that "normal people know the routine, and this person is not normal." Another strategy when confronted with a breach that cannot easily be ignored is to treat it as a joke. If the other person (the breacher) also laughs, then the expected reality is quickly restored, and all participants can sigh in the relief of knowing that they all share the same expectations of the situation.

In the breaching experiments designed by Garfinkel, students conducting breaches were instructed not to let the person repair the breach by treating it as a joke or something that could be ignored. When people do not find interactional support for repairing the situation, they tend to become agitated, in some cases even angry. They look for information that will help them make sense of the situation in ways that are consistent with their working definition of it. If they cannot do so, they become flustered and confused. The boyfriend of the woman who "made herself at home" was furious with her for days afterward. From his perspective, she had violated his "trust" by not behaving as expected and by making him look bad in front of his friends. This response, which is very understandable, illustrates just how much we depend on others to maintain basic definitions of reality, such as "this is just a nice, friendly party." Her behavior resulted in a cascade of consequences that toppled several aspects of the taken-for-granted reality of the occasion and who these friends were to one another.

In another example from one of my own classes, students devised a breach in which they "shopped" from others' carts in a grocery store. The taken-for-granted routine is that once you have placed an item in your cart, it belongs to you. The students who performed this breach matter-of-factly took items from the carts of others. When questioned, they responded simply that the item in the cart had been more convenient to reach than the one on the shelf. When assumptions are breached, people look for a "reasonable" explanation—something that reaffirms the underlying assumptions. "Oh, I'm sorry, I thought that was my cart" is an example of a reasonable explanation for taking something from someone else's cart. But to act as if there is nothing wrong with doing so confuses the other person and makes her or him question, just for a moment, the reality of the situation.

In another breaching experiment, a student cheerfully asked a McDonald's clerk for a Whopper, a menu item at rival Burger King. Rather than saying, "We don't carry that," the McDonald's clerk asked the student to repeat the order. When the request for a Whopper was repeated, the clerk looked around to see if fellow employees had heard this "bizarre" request. In other words, he searched for interactional corroboration of his reality that "everyone knows" the McDonald's menu, and anyone who doesn't is obviously weird. Something as simple as a sideways glance and raised eyebrows from a coworker can indicate that one's reality is intact and that the momentary experience is merely an aberration that can be ignored. In this case, however, the students were particularly tenacious in testing reactions to breaching. After the first person breached the fast-food-order routine, another classmate stepped up and ordered a slice of pizza, which, of course, McDonald's restaurants don't serve.

Caveat Regarding Breaching Experiments

Occasionally, students using previous editions of this text have raised the concern that breaching experiments are a violation of social trust. This concern indicates an excellent insight regarding the theories of Goffman (1959; discussed in Part V) and Garfinkel—both are saying that social order is based on trust and that it occurs in the form of expected interaction routines. We *trust* one another to know the routines and to follow them through. In this way, we are able to carry on interactions with one another without the fear of being hurt or violated. I cannot speak directly for Goffman or Garfinkel, but the following is my own response to students and instructors who have concerns about breaching experiments.

Recall that one of the lessons in Part II is the extent to which we all participate in acts of categorization (stereotyping) that we may not be aware of. Much of our behavior is "mindless." Similarly, many of our interaction routines are mindless and taken for granted. I would never advocate the senseless disruption of another person's routine or status quo just for the sake of doing it. However, breaching experiments, handled with care and sensitivity, can be a way to raise consciousness and to invite others to think critically about their own participation in mindless routines. It's important to note that there are many forms of breaching, and you do not have to involve someone else directly if this feels wrong or uncomfortable. Just thinking up the experiments can be a great exercise in mindfulness. If you do decide to implicate others, consider situations in which the others are also likely to be able to learn something useful from the encounter. Breaching is not the equivalent of being mean or cruel. Most of the students in my classes who experiment with breaching discover that once people settle down and recover from the breach, they are often eager to discuss and learn from the experiment.

The important feature is that persons performing these experiments take the time to debrief their subjects and to engage with them in a discussion of what occurred. This can be an opportunity to practice "interpersonal ethics"—that is, to use the situation to gain greater understanding among all parties involved. Remember, the point is to define and make explicit routines that reflect taken-for-granted assumptions about reality—not to hurt someone or make them needlessly uncomfortable. The best breaching experiments are those in which the person doing them is able to recognize her or his own participation in a taken-for-granted status quo.

Permeable

The fifth feature described by Mehan and Wood is that realities are *permeable*. We are constantly moving between different realities. In doing so, we alter our attitudes and behavior to bring them into line with the expectations of the reality of the moment. People who participate in nudist communities, for example, successfully maintain the reality while on their holidays that nudity is healthy and a source of family fun that is not associated with sexuality. They then return easily to work life, where it is commonly known that public nudity is not acceptable.

If the conditions are right, one can even move into a radically different reality. For example, soldiers move between a reality in which they are trained to kill other humans and another in which killing is defined as murder. The permeability of realities implies that we carry a variety of scripts for various routines, including routines that may seem contradictory, as well as rules and beliefs for bridging the gaps between the realities. In order to make a successful transition between the reality systems of war and civil society, soldiers have to learn and accept a cultural story that designates some people as "the enemy" and others as "those who need protection." One (among many) of the tragedies of war is the fragility of this particular system of belief. Hospitals and social service agencies are filled with men (and increasingly women) who find it difficult to maintain such distinct realities. Their psyches and spirits have broken down as a consequence. Soldiers who fought in Vietnam returned to a civil society that did not necessarily share the reality of the "enemy" these soldiers had been trained to fight and kill. One way to look at the post-Vietnam experience for veterans is to consider that they did not receive interactional support from the society they thought they had been protecting. This lack of support made it difficult for many of these veterans to maintain the belief that the killing they had done in one reality was indeed "honorable."

BELIEVING MAKES IT SO: SELF-FULFILLING PROPHECIES

Imagine an elementary school teacher who is told by school personnel that one group of children in his classroom are "gifted" and likely to be high achievers. Imagine another classroom where a teacher is told that some of her students have tested as "underachievers." An experiment similar to this scenario was conducted in the 1970s by Robert Rosenthal and Lenore Jacobson (1974). Rosenthal and Jacobson wanted to study the effects of preconceived beliefs about intelligence on the performance of schoolchildren. The study took place in an elementary school. The teachers in Grades 1–6 were led to believe that a previously administered "aptitude test" indicated that some of the students in each class were likely to show significant academic improvement over the course of the year. In fact, the researchers had simply identified "gifted" students randomly. However, by the end of the year, students who were seen as gifted and expected by their teachers to improve significantly had indeed improved (as measured by a standard IQ test). Rosenthal and Jacobson's study became famous and is known as the "Pygmalion in the Classroom" study.

Several aspects of the study are noteworthy, and the findings have been supported by many related studies done by other researchers. However, in recent years, this form of research has been criticized, both because of the use of standard IQ tests to measure student improvement and especially because of the ethical implications of labeling the students as "over-" or "under-achievers." Paradoxically, without the research documenting the effects of labeling and self-fulfilling prophecies, the current ethical concerns wouldn't have been noted. Without this research, which today we do understand as unethical, we wouldn't be aware of the potentially damaging effects of labeling expectations held by people in positions of authority.

Rosenthal and Jacobson hypothesized that student performance was shaped, in part, by the way the teachers *treated* students. Subsequent studies of teacher behavior in the classroom indicate that teachers respond differently to students they perceive to be especially bright. They take more time with these students, encourage them to work on more complicated problems, and invite them to participate and share more with other students. In contrast, teachers are likely to "give up" quickly on students whom they perceive to be underachievers. Obviously, the beliefs and actions of elementary school teachers are not the only factors that influence student performance, but the research of Rosenthal and Jacobson highlights one important element that has been repeatedly shown to be significant in influencing performance: the power of beliefs to shape behavior.

A *self-fulfilling prophecy* is an event that becomes true because we act in a way that brings about our initial expectations. In this case, if teachers perceive a child to be especially bright, the belief may set in motion a related set of actions that serves to make the expectation true. The teacher may treat the child differently, which may give the child more chances to develop academic skills. The child, upon recognizing that she is being treated as if she were very bright, may adjust her behavior to try to live up to that expectation. She may begin doing more homework, asking more questions, and generally behaving as if she were gifted. These actions are likely to result in increased performance over time.

Self-Fulfilling Prophecies and Interactional Expectations

Children (as well as adults) who are exposed to high-performance expectations *and* repeatedly told that they are capable of meeting these expectations as well as being given the means to do so, are likely to meet the expectations. This is similar to the process of "possible selves" discussed in the essay in Part III. As described in the work of Nurius and Markus (1986), possible selves involves the internal practice of envisioning a particular outcome and then engaging in the behavior that brings about the envisioned outcome. When others express expectations for us, and especially when they "model" those expectations through emotional and behavioral cues, our internal or "possible self" process is triggered, and the result is likely to be self-fulfilling.

Conversely, people can become stuck in mental loops of despair in which they conjure up conversations and experiences that trigger a chain of negative expectations and the assumption that things are likely to turn out badly. Psychologist Paul Watzlawick (1984) tells us that this kind of negative-expectation thinking can also result in self-fulfilling outcomes (see Reading 32). He uses the example of a couple in which the husband believes that his wife is a nag, and the wife believes that her husband is withdrawn. These beliefs lead each to imagine that the other is going to behave as expected (nag/withdraw). When they encounter one another, each sees what he or she expects to see and is therefore poised to react in such a way that the expectations are made real. For instance, the husband, anticipating that his wife is going to nag him, comes home grumpy and withdrawn. This reinforces her perception ("He's withdrawn"), and she picks up with her nagging. It's an ongoing cycle that is difficult to break because each person perceives the other in terms of preconceived expectations, and here's the important point: The expectations are *confirmed* by the other person's reactions, and thus each person feels justified in her or his initial impressions of the other. "She *really is* a nag; he *really is* withdrawn." Both are quick to see and feel confirmed by the behavior of the other, but neither sees how her or his initial expectations may have actually triggered that behavior.

Self-fulfilling prophecies illustrate an important point made throughout this book: Often, what is important is not what is factually correct, but rather what is defined as real. People's actions are based on their *definitions* of what is real. That is, we respond not to the direct event but to our interpretation of it. This is especially true in interactional dynamics: People behave in ways that correspond to our expectations of them. As one old adage says, treat people like kings and they will behave like kings; treat them like rogues and they will behave like rogues.

Although the saying may seem simple, the process is a bit more complicated and involves threading together the lessons learned from previous sections, especially Parts II and III. In Part II, the power of language is emphasized, expressed in the form of concepts and categories that trigger feelings, expectations, and scripts for action. These categories and scripts are especially significant when we internalize them as self concepts and guide and judge our behavior accordingly. When you put it all together, you see that your own or others' beliefs function as expectations that trigger categorical—often mindless—responses. In turn, these responses reinforce the original categorical ideas or beliefs. Recall Reading 13 (Part III), "A Theory of Genius," in which the author points out that children pick up on our expectations for them in the form of "reflected appraisals" (see Reading 12). These appraisals convey beliefs or expectations about the child's ability to learn. For instance, we expect children to be able to learn to talk, even though this is actually a profoundly complicated task. Rather than shame the child when she makes a mistake, we praise her as if she were a genius and, accordingly, she masters the difficult task of language acquisition. Unfortunately, we're often not as patient or hopeful in our expectations for the acquisition of other skills such as learning a musical instrument or a sport. As a result, the child may pick up on this expectation of failure, experience shame, and give up, thus making the initial expectation self-fulfilling.

An important message in Watzlawick's article is that, by becoming aware of self-fulfilling prophecies, we will be better able to recognize and resist potentially damaging outcomes brought about by our own beliefs (and subsequent behavior in line with these beliefs). For instance, imagine what might happen in the earlier example of husband and wife if one or the other were to intervene in her or his own preconceived expectations and think something radically different such as, "My partner is so loving and supportive." How might these altered expectations result in a different "reflected appraisal." If you look into the "looking glass" (Part III, Reading 12) of another and expect to see love and support instead of nagging and resentment, what do you suppose might happen over time?

Self-Fulfilling Expectations and Stereotypes

Socially held beliefs about the characteristics of groups of people—in other words, stereotypes—often result in self-fulfilling outcomes. Another psychologist, Mark Snyder, studies the relationship between stereotypes and attraction (see Reading 33). Snyder has conducted experiments that demonstrate that the stereotypes about attractive versus unattractive people can be self-fulfilling. In one such study, participants speak on the phone with someone they perceive to be either "traditionally attractive" or "unattractive" based on pictures they've been shown. When speaking with a presumably attractive individual, participants tend to be more upbeat and friendly. This behavior induces similar responses in the person on the phone such that they are likely to be very friendly and outgoing. Participants usually conclude that the attractive people are also more friendly. Snyder points out that this stereotypical belief may be self-fulfilling, because we are likely to treat attractive people as if they are friendly and outgoing. In so doing, we elicit a friendly response.

Together, the features of reality yield a theory explaining why people pursue certain lines of action without noticing alternatives (reflexivity) and how these routines eventually take on the status of cultural stories or belief systems that are assumed to be natural and real. Through ongoing interaction, we reinforce these belief systems and bring about preconceived outcomes by acting on our preconceived beliefs. Stereotypes are especially powerful in this process. Even disruptions and deviations serve to reinforce the original belief or stereotype to the extent that we use secondary elaborations and behaviors to repair the breach and explain away inconsistencies. This theory is a powerful tool for understanding the maintenance of the status quo as a product of everyday beliefs and interaction. It provides an explanation for the persistence of social patterns and the behaviors that sustain those patterns, even among people who may think they are opposed to the status quo.

THE SOCIAL CONSTRUCTION OF THE STATUS QUO

Some cultural stories and routines are better established than others—that is, a large percentage of the population is likely to take them for granted and consider them as a source of authority for organizing social life. Well-established cultural practices that have widely recognized authority can be called *cultural institutions.* These institutions and practices constitute a cultural status quo. How are these institutional beliefs and practices enacted and maintained over time? This is the question we look at in this section. The theory of reality as a social construction can be used to address this question. As you read this material, another useful question to ask about these "dominant" cultural patterns is what alternatives might exist and how the situation might be defined and approached differently if others were in charge of the cultural definition of the situation.

One of the most well-established and least-questioned institutions in this country is the medical profession. Medicine is one of the relatively undisputed sources of authority regarding what constitutes "acceptable" behavior. Those who exhibit unusual or inappropriate behaviors are often referred for medical treatment. Both the determined cause and treatment of these behaviors are part of the body of organized knowledge that constitutes medicine. One feature of this form of knowledge is that certain types of actions and feelings are considered "natural." Deviations from the "natural" patterns are considered "pathological."

Medicalization

Sociologists Peter Conrad and Joseph Schneider (1992) have written extensively about the medicalization of behavior. They use the term *medicalization* to refer to behavior that has been defined as a medical problem or illness and, as such, mandates the medical profession to provide some type of treatment for it. Our culture has a pervasive tendency to define everything from depression to alcoholism as a physiological disease. One behavior Conrad and Schneider examined closely is "hyperkinesis," or hyperactivity. In this study, they explore the emergence of a medical name (hyperkinesis) for hyperactivity in children—behavior that is considered distracting and "out of control" in everyday interactions. Hyperkinesis is particularly interesting because it exhibits none of the usual physiological correlates of disease (for example, fever, bacteria, viruses, changes in blood chemistry), and the symptomatic behaviors—rebelliousness, frustration, excitability— seem to have as much to do with social protest as with organic disease. Conrad and Schneider's thesis is that the increasingly high rates of diagnosed cases of hyperkinesis may indicate a social problem rather than individual behavioral disorders. This is a very controversial statement, but it's worth considering the point that parents and educators tend to look first at the child who appears to be disrupting the classroom status quo, rather than examining the underlying patterns of contemporary education. Such an examination might reveal factors such as extreme boredom, behavioral expectations that are not conducive to learning in small children, and so forth. Culturally, however, we tend to assume the infallibility of medicine and its ability to make the symptoms disappear, rather than examine underlying social patterns.

Conrad and Schneider (1992) also have written extensively on the medicalization of deviant behaviors. For example, all cultures have people who are perceived to be "mad"— that is, people who violate behavioral boundaries that are maintained by the majority. Beliefs about what these people should be called, who should deal with them, and how they should be handled differ remarkably, however. Certain cultures see their "mad" as divinely inspired. In these cultures, madness is attributed to spiritual possession rather than natural pathology. For example, in ancient Hebrew, the term for *madness* is defined variously as "to rave," "to act beside oneself," and "to behave like a prophet." "Mad" people were considered to be so filled with spirits that they could not harness themselves to the chains of worldly conduct. Prophets and the mad were both "raving lunatics" who were thought to be outside society. An interesting question is what social definitions distinguished one from the other.

One social-psychological alternative to the medical model of madness and other forms of asocial conduct is based on the theory that those people who are unusually bright and creative experience an overload of contradictions when they try to meet standard expectations for behavior. These people are thought to be responding to a very complex and contradictory set of "generalized others," reacting rapidly to strong creative passions and urges. This complex creativity manifests as a resistance to socialization. Further, those who have the necessary interpersonal skills and material resources may avoid medical labeling and may become significant contributors in areas such as the arts. Because of their contributions, their "inappropriate" behavior is sometimes labeled "eccentric" rather than "mentally ill."

If you are interested in exploring this topic more, you might begin with some of the writings of one of the framers of this alternative perspective, Thomas Szasz. In a 1971 article,

Szasz describes an extreme, even horrific, example of the medicalization of a "deviant" behavior. This historical case, reported in a prestigious medical journal in 1851, concerned a disease manifest among slaves. The primary symptom of the ominous-sounding disorder called "drapetomania" was running away from plantations!

Despite the increasing cultural awareness of the limitations and misapplications of the medical model of deviance, many medical practitioners continue to treat "conditions" such as transgendered behavior, homosexuality, and "female emotion" as symptoms of pathology. There are still respected scientists who use the medical model to claim that certain people may be more inclined to "social pathology" than others based on racial ethnicity. Medicine is a powerful and influential cultural institution that has done much to improve our quality of life, but it also warrants careful scrutiny. Be aware of its limitations and untold stories.

The media is another influential social institution with tremendous power to define situations in ways that either question or reinforce taken-for-granted cultural stories. In "Consuming Terrorism," (Reading 34) sociologist David Altheide investigates the ways in which media coverage of the Iraq War constructs a particular reality about "terror" and the "enemy." Similar to the work of Conrad and Schneider, Altheide demonstrates the power of a cultural institution, in this case the news media, to define right and wrong, good and evil, and so forth, and to tell a particular story about war in a way that reinforces socially constructed theories about U.S. "goodness." As people begin to take this cultural reality for granted, they find it easier to "explain away" the consequences of war such as "collateral damage" and the proliferation of increased surveillance of ordinary citizens. Government activities that, in another context, would seem atrocious and unacceptable begin to seem reasonable when considered in the context of a media-constructed "culture of terrorism."

Science, medicine, and the media are useful areas for investigating cultural stories that shape the everyday status quo in ways that we often take for granted, even though these realities have a significant impact on our lives. Additional institutional sources of cultural realities include religion, education, and law. Each of these areas can be fruitfully analyzed using the tools from this section to reveal underlying cultural ideals and practices that have a powerful influence on what we think is real and right and good. In a particularly interesting twist on this logic, sociologists Patricia Ewick and Susan Sibley (Reading 35) are interested in the consequences of the "common knowledge" belief that "the 'haves' come out ahead" in legal proceedings. Earlier research suggests that people who do well in the legal system in terms of filing complaints, law suits, and so on tend to be those with "repeat" experience. Furthermore, those with repeat experience also tend to be people with more cultural and social capital. In other words, the "haves" tend to be more likely to use the legal system for their own gain when they feel they have encountered injustice, and the more they use the system, the more experience they gain in being able to navigate it successfully. Consistent with the theories in this section, Ewick and Sibley are interested in the extent to which there is a "commonsense" belief that the "haves" do better in the legal system (it turns out there is), and how this belief works to either encourage or discourage people from seeking legal help or responding to legal inquiries. As they discuss in the article, the belief that the legal system is "too difficult" or "beyond my understanding" works to discourage many deserving people from gaining adequate legal advice and, in consequence, reinforces the cultural status quo that the law is mysterious and too difficult for most people to comprehend.

The Maintenance of Social Hierarchies

One aspect of the cultural status quo that deserves special attention is the maintenance of social hierarchies, or differences and inequalities. *Differences and inequalities* are a prevailing feature of most cultures, but the basis on which they are constructed differs from culture to culture. For instance, in some societies, religious tradition is the basis for extreme prejudice or privilege, whereas in the United States, social class, gender, race/ethnicity, age, and—increasingly—sexual orientation tend to be bases of prejudicial difference and inequality. The social sciences are filled with theories that attempt to explain the dynamics of prejudice. As you will see, the material in this book provides an especially useful set of tools for making sense of how we categorize people and then, through the processes of social construction discussed in this section, reinforce and maintain these patterns of discrimination—even when we may not intend to. Let's take socioeconomic class as an example.

Social class is a powerful influence in U.S. culture, but part of the script or routine connected to social class is the expectation that we should pretend it doesn't matter. This makes it particularly difficult to disrupt the underlying patterns of discrimination. Candace Perin (1988) is an anthropologist who did her dissertation field research in the suburbs of Minneapolis. Instead of going to a foreign country, she decided that the "suburbs" were rich with cultural practices worth studying from an anthropological perspective. Her book on the subject, *Belonging in America,* is an insightful examination of the day-to-day routines of suburbanites who attempt to maintain an image of middle-class wealth, prosperity, and the impression that "everything is always fine." One central suburban expectation is that it is "impolite" to directly confront neighbors about infractions and trespasses. As Perin points out, crabgrass does not respect property boundaries; if your neighbor does not maintain a crabgrass-free lawn, it's likely that some of the stuff will creep onto yours. Neighbors engage in all kinds of roundabout ways of trying to address these infractions without actually confronting the neighbor directly. Larger infractions—garbage cans left at the curb too long, rusty cars left sitting around for a period of time—are reported to the police. Perin noted that the majority of the calls received by police in the greater Minneapolis region during her months of fieldwork were from *anonymous* suburban callers "tattling" on their neighbors. Perin concludes that the interaction routines in the suburbs preserve the impression that all is rosy and well and conflict free. Meanwhile, suburbanites use many "backdoor" strategies to resolve conflict. This perpetuates an image of the suburbs as safe and problem free and may also explain some of the differences in urban versus suburban tolerance for conflict in group interaction.

One additional example illustrates the perpetuation of middle-class norms in mixed-class settings. Most people are aware of middle-class expectations, regardless of their own economic background. Students and faculty from working-class backgrounds can tell many stories about situations in which they have felt out of place with other students and faculty from middle-class backgrounds. Colleagues may suggest social gatherings that are beyond the price range of some of the members of the group, or they may engage in a lot of social con-versation about the price of real estate in the area, their mortgages, and other class-related issues such as fancy vacation destinations and restaurants. What's interesting is that in such instances, people from working-class backgrounds rarely say anything that might indicate that they are unfamiliar or uncomfortable with the discussion. There is a tacit agreement to let the conversation continue on its own terms. Once in a while, someone may say, "I wouldn't know about that, I've never been able to afford to eat in such places." This usually brings the conversation to an awkward halt, leaving the speaker feeling as if he or she sticks out. Those whose taken-for-granted class reality has just been disrupted may, in theory, be aware of the class differences—some of us even teach this material—but in the interactional moment may just feel resentful about the awkwardness. The class norm "nice people don't talk about money" operates to maintain a cultural status quo in which profound class differences are never brought to the social stage.

The final two readings in this section look at the socially constructed process of inequal-ity in detail. When reading these articles, try to apply the principles you've learned from this section to understand how people, often unintentionally, end up reinforcing the cultural status quo through everyday beliefs and related interaction routines. What happens to friends working together in a similar rank when one of them gets promoted to a position of authority over the others? Sociologist Scott Harris describes how friends handle the awk-wardness in the interaction routines that occurs as a result of the change of one person's sta-tus (Reading 36). In Reading 37, sociologist Cecilia Ridgeway describes a theory that she has developed to explain the perpetuation of gender inequality in employment. Despite many formal legal changes in the past three decades that have made it unlawful to dis-criminate against women in employment, women still lag significantly behind men in pro-motions and raises. Ridgeway explains this lag as a manifestation of a particular status quo in which both men and women *perceive* women as being less competent than men in cer-tain employment situations. According to prevailing cultural scripts and stereotypes, women just aren't as effective as men. This perception results in management decisions that may make the expectation self-fulfilling. This interactional explanation is an important contribution to understanding how gender inequality is perpetuated even when people intend to be fair.

Conclusions

The quotation from Karl Marx (1852/1963) at the beginning of this essay suggests that people make their own history, but that they do so within the confines of the circumstances they encounter from others. When he spoke of "circumstances encountered from the past," Marx had in mind the economic conditions—the "mode of production"—that shaped the existence of a group of people. But the idea can be extended to the broader systems of belief that groups of people use to structure and make sense of their shared reality. The definitions that people use to organize and direct their own lives are generally based on, in Marx's terms, "the tradi-tions of the dead generations."

As we discussed in Part II, language-based knowledge systems shape our perceptions. Hence, although several definitions of a situation may be possible, people actually work within a system of beliefs inherited from social ancestors. "Commonsense" stories and theories provide us with a means of making sense of our lives. These stories and theories are often useful and meaningful. However, commonsense theories can also limit certain lines of action and confirm arbitrary "truths" that hinder our capacity to make alternative or new sense of a situation. In this regard, it can be said that these traditions "weigh like a nightmare" on our existence. In acting out these traditions of thought uncritically, we both create and re-create the circumstances of the past.

The social construction of reality is perhaps the most central and profound topic treated in this book. The phrase deserves careful attention. Note first the claim that reality is a *construction*. This idea in itself can seem counterintuitive or even nonsensical. Surely reality is simply the objective world that exists "out there," the subject of study of our sciences. But the alternative claim is that reality is malleable. Different groups, different cultures, or different historical epochs may hold completely different (even diametrically opposed) beliefs about what is "real," what is "obviously true," what is "good," and what is "desired." The second noteworthy element in the title is that reality is a *social* construction. That is, the created realities are the product, not of isolated individuals, but of relationships, communities, groups, institutions, and entire cultures.

I have a colleague who had grown weary of a question constantly posed to her by other faculty: "Do you rent or own?" This seemingly innocent conversation starter is only innocent for those who are able to answer, "I own." The question itself implies a social hierarchy, and one has little choice in response but to affirm the hierarchy ("owning is a pinnacle of success in American life") and one's place in it ("I've arrived," or "I haven't"). Renters usually feel compelled to provide some account that indicates that they share the same class values but just haven't found the right place yet. In her private thoughts, my colleague was frustrated about her situation: She had worked hard most of her life but still couldn't afford to buy a home in her area. She also knew that most homeowners in her generation had been assisted by parents, spouses, or other sources of income. Mostly, she resented being put on the spot with an insensitive question. One day, she startled a group of people by responding to the question, "Do you rent or own?" with a raised eyebrow and glare at the person who asked. Then, in her best slow drawl she exclaimed, "Honey, I don't do mortgages. They are soooo bourgeois!" People actually gasped. With this single utterance, she had reframed the situation. Her answer turned the presumed status of the inquirer on its head and elevated her to a position of "interesting" and beyond the norm. My friend still wants to own a home, but she's found a provocative way to disrupt the taken-for-granted conversational routine that serves only to spotlight the status of the "haves" at the expense of the "have-nots."

Reality can be an amazingly malleable thing, but there are limits to how reality can be constructed. These limits include existing patterns of interaction and the taken-for-granted assumptions that underlie realities. Most of the time, expected definitions of the situation will prevail, because most of us know the routine and either follow it mindlessly or do not (cannot) risk deviation. Power, in a symbolic interactionist sense, is the ability to define a situation in a particular way and to have others act in accordance with this definition. Reality may be a social construction, but we are not all equal participants in this construction.

Stories are a useful epistemology through which to understand how collective life comes to have recognizable patterns. Realities, like stories, do not exist unless people tell them to themselves and to others. Some realities, like some stories, are more comprehensible to the group than are others. Certain stories, and ways of telling them, are considered more or less acceptable. As you ponder the material in this part of the book, ask yourself what story line underlies each of the different realities described: What sort of meaning is attached to persons, situations, and events in each of these stories? Who has the power to write and rewrite stories? How conscious are you of the stories that constitute your realities? The concept of stories illustrates how realities continue and how they change.

REFERENCES AND SUGGESTIONS FOR FURTHER READING

Berger, P., & Luckmann, T. (1966). *The social construction of reality*. Garden City, NY: Doubleday.

Conrad, P., & Schneider, J. (1992). *Deviance and medicalization: From badness to sickness.* Philadelphia: Temple University Press.

Coupland, D. (1991). *Generation X*. New York: St. Martin's Press.

Goffman, E. (1959). *The presentation of self in everyday life*. Garden City, NY: Doubleday.

Marx, K. (1963). *The 18th Brumaire of Louis Bonaparte*. New York: International Publishing Company. (Original work published 1852)

Nurius, P., & Markus, H. (1986). Possible selves. *American Psychologist, 41,* 954–969.

Perin, C. (1988). *Belonging in America*. Madison: University of Wisconsin Press.

Pollner, M., & Goode, D. (1990). Ethnomethodology and person-centering practices. *Person-Centered Review, 5,* 213–220.

Rosenhan, D. (1973). On being sane in insane places. *Science, 179,* 250–258.

Rosenthal, R., & Jacobson, L. (1974). Pygmalion in the classroom. In Z. Rubin (Ed.), *Doing unto others* (pp. 41–47). Englewood Cliffs, NJ: Prentice Hall.

Szasz, T. (1971). The sane slave: An historical note on medical diagnosis as justificatory rhetoric. *American Journal of Psychotherapy, 25,* 228–239.

Thomas, W. I., & Thomas, D. (1928). *The child in America*. New York: Knopf.

Watzlawick, P. (Ed.). (1984). *The invented reality*. New York: Norton.

A THEORY OF REALITY

This section focuses on the ways in which people create and maintain shared systems of belief. These belief systems or paradigms can be thought of as cultural stories that focus our attention, shape our perspectives, and provide guidelines about what is "real" and important. Culturally shared "realities" also provide the basis for making decisions and deciding what is true and right and good. Most inhabitants of a particular reality tend to think that their reality is the only "true" or "real" worldview. Humans have numerous strategies for maintaining belief in particular cultural realities, despite considerable experience that seems to threaten the infallibility of the reality. This is why, despite advances in technology and other developments, human societies change relatively slowly and require major paradigm shifts for doing so. The readings in this section provide examples of the ways in which humans maintain their cultural realities.

"Conceptual Machineries of Universe Maintenance" is another selection from Berger and Luckmann's influential book, *The Social Construction of Reality* (see Reading 17). In this reading, Berger and Luckmann discuss the fact that socially constructed realities are always vulnerable to alternative ideas and belief systems. "Conceptual machineries of universe maintenance" are strategies used to fend off threats to the "official" reality. According to Berger and Luckmann, two of the strategies include therapy and nihilation. *Therapy* is used to convince the "deviant" person that her or his reality is out of line. The therapeutic intent is to bring the person back online with the official or expected reality. *Nihilation* is a tactic used against groups whose ideals are inconsistent with or threatening to the dominant reality. Nihilation tactics involve presenting the alternative reality as foolish or mistaken or unnatural.

In "Five Features of Reality," Mehan and Wood describe five processes that combine to form socially shared systems of belief. Together, these features enable us to maintain dominant systems of belief even when faced with contradictory experiences. As you read the remaining articles in Part VI, consider how each of the five features is illustrated.

Harold Garfinkel's work is well known in sociology. The title of this selection, "A Conception of and Experiments With 'Trust' as a Condition of Concerted Stable Actions," sounds technical, but the idea is less complicated than it sounds. Garfinkel proposes that much of social action is based on shared and taken-for-granted expectations. We use a lot of social "shorthand" in our encounters with one another. We're able to do this because we share common beliefs about how the world works, and we "trust" others to do their part to maintain these beliefs. Garfinkel and his students at UCLA performed social experiments designed to demonstrate that realities actually require a great deal of interactional work and can be easily broken if one party "breaches" the expectations of the situation.

(Continued)

(Continued)

READING QUESTIONS

1. Consider how the "machineries" of therapy and nihilation operate in contemporary U.S. society. Give some examples of alternative belief systems or ways of living that are seen as a threat to the dominant reality. How are these dealt with?

2. Find examples of each of the five features of reality in the essay for Part VI. Make a list of your own examples of each of the five features.

3. Discuss the experiments described in Garfinkel's article and identify exactly what interactional expectation was breached in each one. Garfinkel states that people often respond to breaching with anger. Consider how this is connected to his use of "trust."

4. Think up other examples of "breaching" experiments that you could do. Do you find it easy or difficult to come up with ideas? How would you feel about doing a breaching experiment? What does this tell you about how the status quo is maintained?

5. Some students think that breaching experiments are unethical. Explain why they might think so. What does this indicate about social norms and how they are maintained?

6. Based on their theories, where would Goffman (see Part V) and Garfinkel say "society" is located?

29

Conceptual Machineries of Universe Maintenance

Peter L. Berger and Thomas Luckmann

(1966)

[A] symbolic universe is . . . [a] matrix of all socially objectivated and subjectively real meanings; the entire historic society and the entire biography of the individual are seen as events taking place *within* this universe. . . . [However,] an intrinsic problem . . . presents itself with the process of transmission of the symbolic universe from one generation to another. Socialization is never completely successful. Some individuals "inhabit" the transmitted universe more definitely than others. Even among the more or less accredited "inhabitants," there will always be idiosyncratic variations in the way they conceive of the universe. . . .

This intrinsic problem becomes accentuated if deviant versions of the symbolic universe come to be shared by groups of "inhabitants." In that case . . . the deviant congeals into a reality in its own right, which, by its existence within the society, challenges the reality status of the symbolic universe as originally constituted. . . . [This sets] in motion various conceptual machineries designed to maintain the "official" universe against the heretical challenge. . . .

It goes without saying that the types of conceptual machinery appear historically in innumerable modifications and combinations. . . . But [there are] two general applications of universe-maintaining conceptual machinery: therapy and nihilation.

Therapy entails the application of conceptual machinery to ensure that actual or potential deviants stay within the institutionalized definitions of reality, or, in other words, to prevent the "inhabitants" of a given universe from "emigrating." . . . Since . . . every society faces the danger of individual deviance, we may assume that therapy in one form or another is a global social phenomenon. Its specific institutional arrangements, from exorcism to psychoanalysis, from pastoral care to personnel-counseling programs, belong, of course, under the category of social control. What interests us here, however, is the *conceptual* aspect of therapy. Since therapy must concern itself with deviations from the "official" definitions of reality, it must develop a conceptual machinery to account for such deviations and to maintain the realities thus challenged. This requires a body of knowledge that includes a theory of deviance, a diagnostic apparatus, and a conceptual system for the "cure of souls."

For example, in a collectivity that has institutionalized military homosexuality, the stubbornly heterosexual individual is a sure candidate for therapy, not only because his sexual interests constitute an obvious threat to the combat efficiency of his unit of warrior-lovers, but also because his deviance is psychologically subversive to the others' spontaneous virility. After all, some of them, perhaps "subconsciously," might be tempted to follow his example. On a more fundamental level, the deviant's conduct challenges the societal reality as such, putting in question its taken-for-granted cognitive ("virile men by nature love one another") and normative ("virile men *should* love one another") operating procedures. Indeed, the deviant probably stands as a living insult to the gods, who love one another in the heavens as their devotees do on earth. Such radical deviance requires therapeutic practice soundly grounded in therapeutic theory. There must be a theory of deviance (a "pathology," that is) that accounts for this shocking condition (say, by positing demonic possession). There must be a body of diagnostic concepts (say, a symptomatology, with appropriate skills for applying it in trials by ordeal), which optimally not only permits precise specification of acute conditions, but also detection of "latent heterosexuality" and the prompt adoption of preventive measures. Finally, there must be conceptualization of the curative process itself (say, a catalogue of exorcising techniques, each with an adequate theoretical foundation).

Such a conceptual machinery permits its therapeutic application by the appropriate specialists, and may also be internalized by the individual afflicted with the deviant condition. Internalization in itself will have therapeutic efficacy. In our example, the conceptual machinery may be so designed as to arouse guilt in the individual (say, a "heterosexual panic"), a not too difficult feat if his primary socialization has been even minimally successful. Under the pressure of this guilt, the individual will come to accept subjectively the conceptualization of his condition with which the therapeutic practitioners confront him; he develops "insight," and the diagnosis becomes subjectively real to him. The conceptual machinery may be further developed to allow conceptualization (and thus conceptual liquidation) of any doubts regarding the therapy felt by either therapist or "patient." For instance, there may be a theory of "resistance" to account for the doubts of the latter and a theory of "countertransference" to account for those of the former. Successful therapy establishes a symmetry between the conceptual machinery and its subjective appropriation in the individual's consciousness; it resocializes the deviant into the objective reality of the symbolic universe of the society.

There is, of course, considerable subjective satisfaction in such a return to "normalcy." The individual may now return to the amorous embrace of his platoon commander in the happy knowledge that he has "found himself," and that he is right once more in the eyes of the gods.

Therapy uses a conceptual machinery to keep everyone within the universe in question. Nihilation, in its turn, uses a similar machinery to liquidate conceptually everything *outside* the same universe. . . . This procedure may also be described as a kind of negative legitimation. Legitimation maintains the reality of the socially constructed universe; nihilation *denies* the reality of whatever phenomena or interpretations of phenomena do not fit into that universe. This may be done in two ways. First, deviant phenomena may be given a negative [reality] status, with or without a therapeutic intent. The nihilating application of the conceptual machinery is most often used with individuals or groups foreign to the society in question and thus ineligible for therapy. The conceptual operation here is rather simple. The threat to the social definitions of reality is neutralized by assigning an inferior [reality] status, and thereby a not-to-be-taken-seriously cognitive status, to all definitions existing outside the symbolic universe. Thus, the threat of neighboring anti-homosexual groups can be conceptually liquidated for our homosexual society by looking upon these neighbors as less than human, congenitally befuddled about the right order of things, dwellers in a hopeless cognitive darkness. The fundamental syllogism goes as follows: The neighbors are a tribe of barbarians. The neighbors are anti-homosexual. Therefore, their anti-homosexuality is barbaric nonsense, not to be taken seriously by reasonable men. The same conceptual procedure may, of course, also be applied to deviants within the society. Whether one then proceeds from nihilation to therapy, or rather goes on to liquidate physically what one has liquidated conceptually, is a practical question of policy. The material power of the conceptually liquidated group will be a not insignificant factor in most cases. Sometimes, alas, circumstances force one to remain on friendly terms with barbarians.

Second, nihilation involves the more ambitious attempt to account for all deviant definitions of reality *in terms of* concepts belonging to one's own universe. . . . The deviant conceptions are not merely assigned a negative status, they are grappled with theoretically in detail. The final goal of this procedure is to *incorporate* the deviant conceptions within one's own universe, and thereby to liquidate them ultimately. The deviant conceptions must, therefore, be *translated* into concepts derived from one's own universe. In this manner, the negation of one's universe is subtly changed into an affirmation of it. The presupposition is always that the negator does not really know what he is saying. His statements become meaningful only as they are translated into more "correct" terms, that is, terms deriving from the universe he negates. For example, our homosexual theoreticians may argue

that all men are by nature homosexual. Those who deny this, by virtue of being possessed by demons or simply because they are barbarians, are denying their own nature. Deep down within themselves, they know that this is so. One need, therefore, only search their statements carefully to discover the defensiveness and bad faith of their position. Whatever they say in this matter can thus be translated into an affirmation of the homosexual universe, which they ostensibly negate. In a theological frame of reference, the same procedure demonstrates that the devil unwittingly glorifies God, that all unbelief is but unconscious dishonesty, even that the atheist is *really* a believer.

The therapeutic and nihilating applications of conceptual machineries are inherent in the symbolic universe as such. If the symbolic universe is to comprehend all reality, nothing can be allowed to remain outside its conceptual scope. In principle, at any rate, its definitions of reality must encompass the totality of being. . . .

30

Five Features of Reality

Hugh Mehan and Houston Wood

(1975)

REALITY AS A REFLEXIVE ACTIVITY

When the Azande of Africa are faced with important decisions, decisions about where to build their houses, or whom to marry, or whether the sick will live, for example, they consult an oracle. They prepare for these consultations by following

a strictly prescribed ritual. First, a substance is gathered from the bark of a certain type of tree. Then this substance is prepared in a special way during a seancelike ceremony. The Azande then pose the question in a form that permits a simple yes or no answer, and feed the substance to a small chicken. The Azande decide beforehand whether the death of the chicken will signal an affirmative or negative response, and so they always receive an unequivocal answer to their questions.

For monumental decisions, the Azande add a second step. They feed the substance to a second chicken, asking the same question but reversing the import of the chicken's death. If in the first consultation sparing the chicken's life meant the oracle had said yes, in the second reading the oracle must now kill the chicken to once more reply in the affirmative and be consistent with its first response.

Our Western scientific knowledge tells us that the tree bark used by the Azande contains a poisonous substance that kills some chickens. The Azande have no knowledge of the tree's poisonous qualities. They do not believe the tree plays a part in the oracular ceremony. The ritual that comes between the gathering of the bark and the administration of the substance to a fowl transforms the tree into an oracle. The bark is but a vessel for the oracle to enter. As the ritual is completed the oracle takes possession of the substance. The fact that it was once a part of a tree is irrelevant. Chickens then live or die, not because of the properties of the tree, but because the oracle "hears like a person and settles cases like a king" (Evans-Pritchard, 1937, p. 321).

The Westerner sees insuperable difficulties in maintaining such beliefs when the oracle contradicts itself. Knowing the oracle's bark is "really" poison, we wonder what happens when, for example, the first and second administration of the oracle produces first a positive and then a negative answer? Or, suppose someone else consults the oracle about the same question, and contradictory answers occur? What if the oracle is contradicted by later events? The house site approved by the oracle, for example, may promptly be flooded; or the wife the oracle selected may die or be a shrew. How is it possible for the Azande to continue to believe in oracles in the face of so many evident contradictions to this faith?

What I have called contradictions are not contradictions for the Azande. They are only contradictions because these events are being viewed from the reality of Western science. Westerners look at oracular practices to determine if in fact there is an oracle. The Azande *know* that an oracle exists. That is their beginning premise. All that subsequently happens they experience from that beginning assumption.

The Azande belief in oracles is much like the mathematician's belief in certain axioms. Gasking (1955) has described such unquestioned and unquestionable axioms as *incorrigible propositions*:

> An incorrigible proposition is one which you would never admit to be false whatever happens: it therefore does not tell you what happens. . . . The truth of an incorrigible proposition . . . is compatible with any and every conceivable state of affairs. (For example: whatever is your experience on counting, it is still true that 7 + 5 = 12.) (p. 432)

The incorrigible faith in the oracle is "compatible with any and every conceivable state of affairs." It is not so much a faith about a fact in the world as a faith in the facticity of the world itself. It is the same as the faith many of us have that 7 + 5 always equals 12 (cf. Polanyi, 1958, pp. 190–193, 257–261).

Just as Gasking suggests we explain away empirical experiences that deny this mathematical truth, the Azande too have available to them what Evans-Pritchard (1937) calls "secondary elaborations of belief" (p. 330). They explain the failure of the oracle by retaining the unquestioned absolute reality of oracles. When events occurred that revealed the inadequacy of the mystical faith in oracles, Evans-Pritchard tried to make the Azande understand these failures as he did. They only laughed, or met his arguments:

> sometimes by point-blank assertions, sometimes by one of the evasive secondary elaborations of

belief . . . sometimes by polite pity, but always by an entanglement of linguistic obstacles, for one cannot well express in its language objections not formulated by a culture. (p. 319)

Evans-Pritchard goes on to write:

Let the reader consider any argument that would utterly demolish all Zande claims for the power of the oracle. If it were translated into Zande modes of thought it would serve to support their entire structure of belief. For their mystical notions are eminently coherent, being interrelated by a network of logical ties, and are so ordered that they never too crudely contradict sensory experience, but, instead, experience seems to justify them. *The Zande is immersed in a sea of mystical notions, and if he speaks about his poison oracle he must speak in a mystical idiom* [italics added]. (pp. 319–320)

Seeming contradictions are explained away by saying such things as a taboo must have been breached, or that sorcerers, witches, ghosts, or gods must have intervened. These "mystical" notions reaffirm the reality of a world in which oracles are a basic feature. Failures do not challenge the oracle. They are elaborated in such a way that they provide evidence for the constant success of oracles. Beginning with the incorrigible belief in oracles, all events *reflexively* become evidence for that belief.[1]

The mathematician, as Gasking suggests, uses a similar process:

But it does lay it down, so to speak, that if on counting 7 + 5 you do get 11, you are to describe what has happened in some such way as this: Either "I have made a mistake in my counting" or "Someone has played a practical joke and abstracted one of the objects when I was not looking" or "Two of the objects have coalesced" or "One of the objects has disappeared," etc. (Gasking, 1955; quoted in Pollner, 1973, pp. 15–16)

Consider the analogous case of a Western scientist using chloroform to asphyxiate butterflies.

The incorrigible idiom called chemistry tells the scientist, among other things, that substances have certain constant properties. Chloroform of a certain volume and mix is capable of killing butterflies. One evening the scientist administers the chloroform as usual, and is dismayed to see the animal continue to flutter about.

Here is a contradiction of the scientist's reality, just as oracle use sometimes produces contradictions. Like the Azande, scientists have many secondary elaborations of belief they can bring to bear on such occurrences, short of rejecting the Western causal belief. Instead of rejecting chemistry they can explain the poison's failure by such things as "faulty manufacturing," "mislabeling," "sabotage," or "practical joke." Whatever the conclusion, it would continue to reaffirm the causal premise of science. This reaffirmation reflexively supports the reality that produced the poison's unexpected failure in the first place.

The use of contradictions to reaffirm incorrigible propositions can be observed in other branches of science. In the Ptolemaic system of astronomy, the sun was seen as a planet of the earth. When astronomers looked at the sun, they saw it as an orb circling the earth. When the Copernican system arose as an alternative to this view, it offered little new empirical data. Instead, it described the old "facts" in a different way. A shift of vision was required for people to see the sun as a star, not a planet of the earth.

Seeing the sun as a star and seeing it as a planet circling the earth are merely alternatives. There is no a priori warrant for believing that either empirical determination is necessarily superior to the other.

How is a choice between equally compelling empirical determinations made? The convert to the Copernican system could have said: "I used to see a planet, but now I see a star" (cf. Kuhn, 1970, p. 115). But to talk that way is to allow the belief that an object can be both a star and a planet at the same time. Such a belief is not allowed in Western science. So, instead, the Copernican concludes that the sun was a star all along. By so concluding, the astronomer exhibits an incorrigible proposition of Western thought, the *object constancy assumption*.[2] This is the belief that objects remain the same over time, across viewings from different positions and people. When presented with seemingly contradictory empirical determinations, the convert to Copernicanism does not consider that the sun changes through time. Instead he says: "I once took the sun to be a planet, but I was mistaken." The "discovery" of the sun as a star does not challenge the object constancy belief any more than an oracular "failure" challenges the ultimate reality of Azande belief.

The reaffirmation of incorrigible propositions is not limited to mystical and scientific ways of knowing. This reflexive work operates in commonsense reasoning as well. Each time you search for an object you knew was "right there" the same reflexive process is operating. Say, for example, you find a missing pen in a place you know you searched before. Although the evidence indicates that the pen was first absent and then present, that conclusion is not reached. To do so would challenge the incorrigibility of the object constancy belief. Instead, secondary elaborations—"I must have overlooked it," "I must not have looked there"—are invoked to retain the integrity of the object constancy proposition.

Without an object constancy assumption, there would be no problems about alternative determinations. But, with this assumption as an incorrigible proposition, the person faced with alternative seeings must choose one and only one as real. In choosing one, the other is automatically revealed as false. The falsehood of the rejected alternative may be explained in various ways. It may be due to a defective sensory apparatus, or a cognitive bias, or idiosyncratic psychological dynamics. We explain the inconstancy of the experienced object by saying that inconstancy is a product of the experiencing, not a feature of the object itself.[3]

Once an alternative seeing is explained away, the accepted explanation provides evidence for the object constancy assumption that made the explanation necessary in the first place. By demanding that we dismiss one of two equally valid empirical determinations, the object constancy assumption leads to a body of work that validates that assumption. The work then justifies itself afterward, in the world it has created. This self-preservative reflexive process is common to oracular, scientific, and common sense reasoning.

So far I have approached the reflexive feature of realities as if it were a form of reasoning. But reflexivity is not only a facet of reasoning. It is a recurrent fact of everyday social life. For example, *talk itself is reflexive* (cf. Garfinkel, 1967; Cicourel, 1973). An utterance not only delivers some particular information, it also creates a world in which information itself can appear.

Zimmerman (1973, p. 25) provides a means for understanding the reflexivity of talk at the level of a single word. He presents three identical shapes:

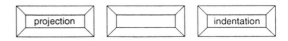

The first and third differ from the second: They each contain single words. These words interact with the box in which they appear so as to change the nature of that box. In so doing, they reflexively illumine themselves. For example, the word "projection," appearing in some other setting, would not mean what it does here. For me it means that I am to see the back panel and the word "projection" as illustrative of a projection. The word "projection" does not merely appear in the scene reporting on that scene. It creates the scene in which it appears as a reasonable object.

Similarly, the word "indentation" not only takes its meaning from the context in which it appears, it reflexively creates that very context. It creates a reality in which it may stand as a part of that reality.

These examples only hint at the reflexivity of talk. . . . Actual conversations are more complex than single words. The social context in which talk occurs, while analogous to one of these static boxes, is enormously ambiguous and potentially infinitely referential. Nonetheless, conversation operates like the printed "projection" and "indentation." An analysis of greetings can be used to show how talk partially constitutes the context and then comes to be seen as independent of it.[4]

To say "hello" both creates and sustains a world in which persons acknowledge . . . (1) [that] they sometimes can see one another; [and] (2) a world in which it is possible for persons to signal to each other, and (3) expect to be signaled back to, by (4) some others but not all of them. This is a partial and only illustrative list of some of the things a greeting accomplishes. Without the superstitious use of greetings, no world in which greetings are possible "objects" would arise. A greeting creates "room" for itself. But once such verbal behaviors are regularly done, a world is built up that can take their use for granted (cf. Sacks, Schegloff, & Jefferson, 1974).

When we say "hello" and the other replies with the expected counter greeting, the reflexive work of our initial utterance is masked. If the other scowls and walks on, then we are reminded that we were attempting to create a scene of greetings and that we failed. Rather than treat this as evidence that greetings are not "real," however, the rejected greeter ordinarily turns it into an occasion for affirming the reality of greetings. He formulates "secondary elaborations" of belief about greetings. He says, "He didn't hear me," "She is not feeling well," "It doesn't matter anyway."

Reflexivity provides grounds for absolute faith in the validity of knowledge. The Azande takes the truth of the oracle for granted, the scientist assumes the facticity of science, the layman accepts the tenets of common sense. The incorrigible propositions of a reality serve as criteria to judge other ways of knowing. Using his absolute faith in the oracle, the Azande dismisses Evans-Pritchard's Western science contradictions. Evans-Pritchard, steeped in the efficacy of science, dismissed the oracle as superstitious. An absolute faith in the incorrigibility of one's own knowledge enables believers to repel contrary evidence. This suggests that all people are equally superstitious.

REALITY AS A COHERENT BODY OF KNOWLEDGE

The phenomenon of reflexivity is a feature of every reality. It interacts with the coherence, interactional, fragility, and permeability features I describe in the rest of this chapter. These five features are incorrigible propositions of the reality of ethnomethodology. They appear as facts of the external world due to the ethnomethodologist's unquestioned assumption that they constitute the world. In other words, these features themselves exhibit reflexivity.

This reflexive loop constitutes the interior structure of ethnomethodology. This will become clearer as I describe the second feature of realities, their exhibition of a coherent body of knowledge. To illustrate this feature I will extrapolate from the work of Zimmerman and Wieder (n.d.), who investigated the life of a number of self-named "freaks," frequent drug users within America's counterculture. Both freaks and their academic ethnographers (e.g., Reich, 1970; Roszack, 1969) describe freaks as radical opponents of the straight culture from which they sprang. As Zimmerman and Wieder (n.d.) write:

From the standpoint of the "straight" members of society, freaks are deliberately irrational. . . . They disavow an interest in efficiency, making long-range plans, and concerns about costs of property (etc.) which are valued by the straight members of American society and are understood by them as indicators of rationality. (p. 103)

On first appearance, here is a reality that seems anarchical. Nonetheless, Zimmerman and Wieder found that

> when it comes to those activities most highly valued by freaks, such as taking drugs, making love, and other "cheap thrills," there is an elaborately developed body of lore. Freaks and others use that knowledge of taking drugs, making love, etc., reasonably, deliberately, planfully, projecting various consequences, predicting outcomes, conceiving of the possibilities of action in more or less clear and distinct ways, and choosing between two or more means of reaching the same end. (pp. 102–103)

The most vivid illustration that freaks use a coherent body of knowledge comes from Zimmerman's and Wieder's discoveries about the place of drugs in the everyday freak life. At first glance such drug use appears irrational. Yet, among freaks, taking drugs "is something as ordinary and unremarkable as their parents regard taking or offering a cup of coffee" (p. 57). Freak behavior is not a function of the freaks' ignorance of chemical and medical "facts" about drugs. The freaks studied knew chemical and medical facts well. They organized these facts into a different, yet coherent corpus of knowledge.

One of the team's research assistants, Peter Suczek, was able to systematize the freaks' knowledge of drugs into a taxonomic schemata (see Table 1).

What the freak calls "dope," the chemist calls "psychotropic drugs." Within the family of dope, freaks distinguish "mind-expanding" and "body" dope. Freaks further subdivide each of these species. In addition, freaks share a common body

Table 1 The Folk Pharmacology for Dope

Types of Dope	Subcategories
Mind-expanding dope	(Untitled)
	"grass" (marijuana)
	"hash" (hashish)
	"LSD" or "acid"
	(lysergic acid)
	Psychedelics
	mescaline
	synthetic
	organic
	natural, peyote
	psilocybin
	synthetic
	organic
	natural, mushrooms
	"DMT"
	miscellaneous
	(e.g., Angel's Dust)
Body dope	"speed" (amphetamines)
	"downers" (barbiturates)
	"tranks" (tranquilizers)
	"coke" (cocaine)
	"shit" (heroin)

Source: Zimmerman and Wieder (n.d.), p. 107.

of knowledge informing them of the practicalities surrounding the use of each type of dope. All knowledge of dope use is grounded in the incorrigible proposition that dope is to be used. One must, of course, know how to use it.

Zimmerman and Wieder (n.d.) found the following knowledge about "psychedelic mind-expanding dope" to be common among freaks:

> The folk pharmacology of psychedelic drugs may be characterized as a method whereby drug users rationally assess choices among kinds of drugs, choices among instances of the same kind of drug,

the choice to ingest or not, the time of the act of ingestion relative to the state of one's physiology and relative to the state of one's psyche, the timing relative to social and practical demands, the appropriateness of the setting for having a psychedelic experience, the size of the dose, and the effectiveness and risk of mixing drugs. (p. 118)

Freaks share similar knowledge for the rest of the taxonomy. Being a freak means living within the auspices of such knowledge and using it according to a plan, as the chemist uses his. Both the freaks' and the scientists' realities are concerned with "the facts." Though the facts differ, each reality reflexively proves its facts as absolute.

Consider how the freak assembles the knowledge he uses. He is not loath to borrow from the discoveries of science. But before accepting what the scientist says, he first tests scientific "facts" against the auspices of his own incorrigible propositions. He does not use the scientists' findings to determine the danger of the drug, but rather to indicate the particular dosage, setting, etc., under which a drug is to be taken.

Scientific drug researchers frequently attend to the experiences of freaks in a comparable way. They incorporate the facts that freaks report about dope into their coherent idiom. The two then are like independent teams of investigators working on the same phenomenon with different purposes. They are like artists and botanists who share a common interest in the vegetable kingdom, but who employ different incorrigibles.

The freak's knowledge, like all knowledge, is sustained through reflexive interactional work. For example, the knowledge contained in the drug taxonomy (Table 1) sometimes "fails," that is, it produces not a "high" but a "bummer." The incorrigible propositions of freak pharmacology are not then questioned. Instead, these propositions are invoked to explain the bummer's occurrence. "For example," Zimmerman and Wieder (n.d.) write:

A "bad trip" may be explained in such terms as the following: it was a bad time and place to drop; my head wasn't ready for it; or it was bad acid or mescaline, meaning that it was cut with something impure or that it was some other drug altogether. (p. 118)

The reflexive use of the freak taxonomy recalls my previous discussion of the Azande. When the oracle seemed to contradict itself, the contradiction became but one more occasion for proving the oracular way of knowing. The reality of oracles is appealed to in explaining the failure of the oracle, just as the reality of freak pharmacology is used to explain a bad trip. It would be as futile for a chemist to explain the bad trip scientifically to a freak as it was for Evans-Pritchard to try to convince the Azande that failures of the oracle demonstrated their unreality.

The coherence of knowledge is a reflexive consequence of the researcher's attention. Zimmerman and Wieder, in the best social science tradition, employed many methods to construct the freak's taxonomy. Freaks were interviewed by sociology graduate students and by their peers. These interviewers provided accounts of their own drug experiences as well. Additional freaks not acquainted with the purposes of the research were paid to keep personal diaries of their day-to-day experiences. Zimmerman and Wieder used a portion of this massive data to construct the freak taxonomy, then tested its validity against further portions of the data.

Such systematizations are always the researcher's construction (Wallace, 1972). To claim that any reality, including the researcher's own, exhibits a coherent body of knowledge is but to claim that coherence can be found *upon analysis*. The coherence located in a reality is found there by the ethnomethodologist's interactional work. The coherence feature, like all features of realities, operates as an incorrigible proposition, reflexively sustained.

Consider the analogous work of linguists (e.g., Chomsky, 1965). Within language-using communities, linguists discover the "rules of grammar." Although the linguist empirically establishes these grammatical rules, speaker-hearers of that language cannot list them. Rules can be located in their talk, upon analysis, but language users cannot describe them.

Similarly, freaks could not supply the taxonomy Zimmerman and Wieder claim they "really" know. It was found upon analysis. It is an imposition of the researcher's logic upon the freak's logic.

Castañeda's (1968, 1971) attempts to explain the reality of Yaqui sorcery further illustrates the reflexity of analysis. In his initial report, *The Teachings of Don Juan,* Castañeda (1968) begins with a detailed ethnography of his experiences of his encounter with a Yaqui sorcerer, Don Juan. In this reality it is common for time to stop, for men to turn into animals and animals into men, for animals and men to converse with one another, and for great distances to be covered while the body remains still.

In the final section of his report, Castañeda systematizes his experiences with the sorcerer. He presents a coherent body of knowledge undergirding Don Juan's teachings. Thus Castañeda, like Zimmerman and Wieder, organizes a "nonordinary" reality into a coherent system of knowledge.

In a second book Castañeda (1971) describes Don Juan's reaction to his systematization of a peyote session, a "mitote." Castañeda told Don Juan he had discovered that mitotes are a "result of a subtle and complex system of cueing." He writes:

> It took me close to two hours to read and explain to Don Juan the scheme I had constructed. I ended by begging him to tell me in his own words what were the exact procedures for reaching agreement.
>
> When I had finished he frowned. I thought he must have found my explanation challenging; he appeared to be involved in deep deliberation. After a reasonable silence I asked him what he thought about my idea.

My question made him suddenly turn his frown into a smile and then into roaring laughter. I tried to laugh too and asked nervously what was so funny.

"You're deranged!" he exclaimed. "Why should anyone be bothered with cueing at such an important time as a mitote? Do you think one ever fools around with Mescalito?"

I thought for a moment that he was being evasive; he was not really answering my question.

"Why should anyone cue?" Don Juan asked stubbornly. "You have been in mitotes. You should know that no one told you how to feel, or what to do; no one except Mescalito himself."

I insisted that such an explanation was not possible and begged him again to tell me how the agreement was reached.

"I know why you have come," Don Juan said in a mysterious tone. "I can't help you in your endeavor because there is no system of cueing."

"But how can all those persons agree about Mescalito's presence?"

"They agree because they *see,*" Don Juan said dramatically, and then added casually, "Why don't you attend another mitote and see for yourself?" (pp. 37–38)

Don Juan finds Castañeda's account ridiculous. This rejection is not evidence that Castañeda's attempt at systematization is incorrect. It indicates that the investigator reflexively organizes the realities he investigates. All realities may *upon analysis* exhibit a coherent system of knowledge, but knowledge of this coherence is not necessarily part of the awareness of its members.

Features emerging "upon analysis" is a particular instance of reflexivity. These features exist only within the reflexive work of those researchers who make them exist. This does not deny their reality. There is no need to pursue the chimera of a presuppositionless inquiry. Because all realities are ultimately superstitious the reflexive location of reflexivity is not a problem within ethnomethodological studies. Rather, it provides them with their most intriguing phenomenon.

My discussion of these first two features of realities also shows that any one feature is separate from the other only upon analysis. In my description of reflexivity, I was forced to assume the existence of a coherent body of knowledge. Similarly, in the present discussion I could not speak about the existence of coherent systems of knowledge without introducing the caveat of "upon analysis," an implicit reference to reflexivity. This situation will continue as I discuss the remaining three features. Though I attempt to keep them separate from one another, I will only be partially successful, since the five are inextricably intertwined. Nevertheless, I will continue to talk of them as five separate features, not as one. I acknowledge that this talk is more heuristic than literal—it provides a ladder with five steps that may be climbed and then thrown away (cf. Wittgenstein, 1921/1961).

REALITY AS INTERACTIONAL ACTIVITY

Realities are also dependent upon ceaseless social interactional work. Wood's study of a mental hospital illustrates the reality of this reality work. He discovered that psychiatric attendants shared a body of knowledge. Wood's (1968) analysis of the attendants' interaction with the patients uncovered labels like: "baby," "child," "epileptic," "mean old man," "alcoholic," "lost soul," "good patient," "depressive," "sociopath," and "nigger" (p. 36). Though borrowed from psychiatry, these terms constitute a corpus of knowledge which reflects the attendants' own practical nursing concerns. These terms can be arranged in a systematic taxonomy (see Table 2). Each is shown to differ from the others according to four parameters of nursing problems.

Wood's study explored how the attendants used this taxonomy to construct meanings for the mental patients' behavior. One explanation of label use is called a "matching procedure." The matching model of labeling patient behavior is essentially a psychological theory. It treats behavior as a private, internal state, not influenced by social dimensions. The matching model assumes the patients' behavior has obvious features. Trained personnel monitor and automatically apply the appropriate label to patients' behavior.

Wood presents five case histories that show that labels are not applied by a simple matching process. They are molded in the day-to-day interaction of

Table 2   The Meaning of the Labels

Psychiatric Attendant Label	Nursing Trouble				
	Work	Cleanliness	Supervisory	Miscellaneous	Frequency × 60
Mean old man	yes	yes	yes	yes	2
Baby	yes	yes	yes	—	20
Child	yes	yes	—	yes	4
Nigger	yes	—	yes	yes	1
Epileptic	—	yes	—	yes	4
Sociopath	yes	—	—	yes	3
Depressive	—	—	—	yes	2
Alcoholic	—	—	yes	—	8
Lost soul	yes	—	—	—	12
Good patient	—	—	—	—	6

Source: Wood (1968), p. 45.

the attendants with one another and with the patients. The labeling of patients is a social activity, not a psychological one.

Wood (1968, pp. 51–91) describes the labeling history of patient Jimmy Lee Jackson. Over the course of his three-month hospitalization, Jackson held the same official psychiatric label, that of "psychoneurotic reaction, depressive type." However, the ward attendants saw Jackson within the web of their own practical circumstances. For them, at one time he was a "nigger," at another a "depressive," and at yet another a "sociopath." These seeings reflected a deep change in the meaning Jackson had for the attendants. When he was seen as a "nigger," for example, it meant that the attendants considered he was "lazy, and . . . without morals or scruples and . . . that the patient is cunning and will attempt to ingratiate himself with the attendants in order to get attention and 'use' them for his own ends" (p. 52). When Jackson became a depressive type, all these negative attributes were withdrawn. The change in attribution, Wood shows, cannot be explained by a matching procedure. The attendants' social interactional work produced the change, independent of Jackson's behavior. This suggests that realities are fundamentally interactional activities.

One evening Jackson was suffering from a toothache. Unable to secure medical attention, he ran his arm through a window pane in one of the ward's locked doors. He suffered a severe laceration of his forearm which required stitches. When the attendants who were on duty during this episode returned to work the following afternoon, they discovered that the preceding morning shift had decided that Jackson had attempted suicide. Jackson was no longer presented to them as a nigger. The morning shift found that persons who had not even witnessed the event had given it a meaning they themselves had never considered. Nevertheless, the evening shift accepted the validity of this label change.

The label change indexed a far larger change. Jackson's past history on the ward was reinterpreted. He now was accorded different treatment by attendants on all shifts. He was listened to sympathetically, given whatever he requested, and no longer exhorted to do more ward work. All the attendants came to believe that he had always been a depressive and that they had always seen him as such.

A few weeks later Jackson became yet another person, a "sociopath." The attendants no longer accepted that he was capable of a suicide attempt. The new label was once again applied retrospectively. Not only was Jackson believed to be incapable of committing suicide now, he was thought to have always been incapable of it. The attendants agreed that the window-breaking incident had been a "fake" or "con"—just the sort of thing a sociopath would do. Attendants who had praised Jackson as a hard worker when he was labeled a depressive now pointed to this same work as proof he was a "conniver." Requests for attention and medicine that had been promptly fulfilled for the depressive Jackson were now ignored for the sociopath Jackson, or used as occasions to attack him verbally.

Yet, as Wood describes Jackson, he remained constant despite these changes in attendant behavior. He did the same amount of work and sought the same amount of attention and medicine whether he was labeled a nigger or a depressive or a sociopath. What Jackson was at any time was determined by the reality work of the attendants.

In the final pages of his study, Wood (1968) further illustrates the power of interactional work to create an external world:

> The evening that he [Jackson] cut his arm, I, like the PAs [psychiatric attendants], was overcome by the blood and did not reflect on its "larger" meaning concerning his proper label. The next day, when I heard all of the morning shift PAs refer to his action as a suicide attempt, I too labeled Jackson a

"depressive" and the cut arm as a suicide attempt. When the label changed in future weeks I was working as a PA on the ward up to 12 hours a day. It was only two months later when I had left the ward, as I reviewed my notes and my memory, that I recognized the "peculiar" label changes that had occurred. While I was on the ward, it had not seemed strange to think that cutting an arm in a window was a serious attempt to kill oneself. Only as an "outsider" did I come to think that Jackson had "really" stayed the same through his three label changes. (pp. 137–138)

As Wood says, Jackson could never have a meaning apart from *some* social context. Meanings unfold only within an unending sequence of practical actions.[5]

The *matching* theory of label use assumes a correspondence theory of signs (cf. Garfinkel, 1952, pp. 91ff.; Wieder, 1970). This theory of signs has three analytically separate elements: ideas that exist in the head, signs that appear in symbolic representations, and objects and events that appear in the world. Meaning is the relation among these elements. Signs can stand on behalf of the ideas in the head or refer to objects in the world. This theory of signs implies that signs stand in a point-by-point relation to thoughts in one's mind or objects in the world. Meanings are stable across time and space. They are not dependent upon the concrete participants or upon the specific scenes in which they appear.

Wood's study indicates that labels are not applied in accordance with correspondence principles. Instead, labels are *indexical expressions*. Meanings are situationally determined. They are dependent upon the concrete context in which they appear. The participants' interactional activity structured the indexical meaning of the labels used on the ward. The relationship of the participants to the object, the setting in which events occur, and the circumstances surrounding a definition determine the meaning of labels and of objects.

The interactional feature indicates that realities do not possess symbols, like so many tools in a box. A reality and its signs are "mutually determinative" (Wieder, 1973, p. 216). Alone, neither expresses sense. Intertwining through the course of indexical interaction, they form a life.

THE FRAGILITY OF REALITIES

Every reality depends upon (1) ceaseless reflexive use of (2) a body of knowledge in (3) interaction. Every reality is also fragile. Suppression of the activities that the first three features describe disrupts the reality. Every reality is equally capable of dissolution. The presence of this fragility feature of realities has been demonstrated by studies called "incongruity procedures" or "breaching experiments."

In one of the simplest of these, Garfinkel used 67 students as "experimenters." These students engaged a total of 253 "subjects" in a game of tick-tack-toe. When the figure necessary for the game was drawn, the experimenters requested the subject to make the first move. After the subject made his mark, the experimenter took his turn. Rather than simply marking another cell, the experimenter erased the subject's mark and moved it to another cell. Continuing as if this were expected behavior, the experimenter then placed his own mark in one of the now empty cells. The experimenters reported that their action produced extreme bewilderment and confusion in the subjects. The reality of the game, which before the experimenter's move seemed stable and external, suddenly fell apart. For a moment the subjects exhibited an "amnesia for social structure" (Garfinkel, 1963, p. 189).

This fragility feature is even more evident in everyday life, where the rules are not explicit. People interact without listing the rules of conduct. Continued reference is made to this knowledge nonetheless. This referencing is not ordinarily available as long as the reality work continues normally. When the reality is disrupted, the interactional activity structuring the reality becomes visible. This is what occurred in the tick-tack-toe game. A usually unnoticed feature of the game is a "rule" prohibiting erasing an opponent's mark. When this unspoken "rule" is broken, it makes its first public appearance. If we were aware of the fragility of our realities, they would not seem real.

Thus Garfinkel (1963) found that when the "incongruity-inducing procedures" developed in games

> were applied in "real life" situations, it was unnerving to find the seemingly endless variety of events that lent themselves to the production of really nasty surprises. These events ranged from . . . standing very, very close to a person while otherwise maintaining an innocuous conversation, to others . . . like saying "hello" at the termination of a conversation. . . . Both procedures elicited anxiety, indignation, strong feelings on the part of the experimenter and subject alike of humiliation and regret, demands by the subjects for explanations, and so on. (p. 198)

Another of the procedures Garfinkel developed was to send student experimenters into stores and restaurants where they were told to "mistake" customers for salespersons and waiters. . . . (see Reading 31, this volume, for details of one such experiment).

The breaching experiments were subsequently refined, such that:

> The person [subject] could not turn the situation into a play, a joke, an experiment, a deception, and the like . . . ; that he have insufficient time to work through a redefinition of his real circumstances; and that he be deprived of consensual support for an alternative definition of social reality. (Garfinkel, 1964; in 1967, p. 58)

This meant that subjects were not allowed to reflexively turn the disruption into a revalidation of their realities. The incorrigible propositions of their social knowledge were not adequate for the present circumstances. They were removed from the supporting interactional activity that they possessed before the breach occurred.

These refinements had the positive consequence of increasing the bewilderment of the subjects, who became more and more like desocialized schizophrenics, persons completely devoid of any social reality. These refinements produced a negative consequence. They were immoral. Once subjects had experienced the fragility, they could not continue taking the stability of realities for granted. No amount of "cooling out" could restore the subject's faith.

But what is too cruel to impose on others can be tried upon oneself. . . .

THE PERMEABILITY OF REALITIES

Because the reflexive use of social knowledge is fragile and interaction dependent, one reality may be altered, and another may be assumed. Cases where a person passes from one reality to another, dramatically different, reality vividly displays this permeability feature.

Tobias Schneebaum, a painter who lives periodically in New York, provides an example of a radical shift in realities in his book, *Keep the River on Your Right* (1969). Schneebaum entered the jungles of Peru in 1955 in pursuit of his art. During the trip the book describes, he gradually lost interest in painterly studies. He found himself drawn deeper and deeper into the jungle. Unlike a professional anthropologist, he carried no plans to write about his travels. In fact, the slim volume from which I draw the following discussion was not written until 13 years after his return.

He happened upon the Akaramas, a stone age tribe that had never seen a white man. They accepted him quickly, gave him a new name, "Habe," meaning "ignorant one," and began teaching him to be as they were.

Schneebaum learned to sleep in "bundles" with the other men, piled on top of one another for warmth and comfort. He learned to hunt and fish with stone age tools. He learned the Akaramas' language and their ritual of telling stories of their hunts and hikes, the telling taking longer than the doing. He learned to go without clothing, and to touch casually the genitals of his companions in play.

When one of the men in Schneebaum's compartment is dying of dysentery, crying out at his excretions of blood and pain, the "others laugh and he laughs too" (p. 109). As this man lies among them whimpering and crying in their sleeping pile at night, Schneebaum writes: "Not Michii or Baaldore or Ihuene or Reindude seemed to have him on their minds. It was as if he were not there among us or as if he had already gone to some other forest" (p. 129). When he dies, he is immediately forgotten. Such is the normal perception of death within the Akarama reality. As Schneebaum describes another incident: "There were two pregnant women whom I noticed one day with flatter bellies and no babies on their backs, but there was no sign of grief, no service . . ." (p. 109).

Gradually, Schneebaum absorbed even these ways and a new sense of time. At one point he left the Akaramas to visit the mission from which he had embarked. He was startled to find that seven months had passed, not the three or four he had supposed. As he was more and more permeated by the stone age reality, he began to feel that his "own world, whatever, wherever it was, no longer was anywhere in existence" (p. 69). As the sense of his old reality disappears, he says, "My fears were not so much for the future . . . but for my knowledge. I was removing my own reflection" (pp. 64–65).

One day, a day like many others, he rises to begin a hunting expedition with his sleeping companions. This day, however, they go much farther than ever before. They paint themselves in a new way and repeat new chants. Finally they reach a strange village. In they swoop, Schneebaum too, shouting their sacred words and killing all the men they can catch, disemboweling and beheading them on the spot. They burn all the huts, kidnap the women and children. They then hike to their own village, without pause, through an entire night. At home, a new dance is begun. The meat of the men they have murdered and brought back with them is cooked. As a new movement of the dance begins, this meat is gleefully eaten. Exhausted at last, they stumble together on the ground. Then the last of the meat is put to ceremonious use:

> We sat or lay around the fires, eating, moaning the tones of the chant, swaying forward and back, moving from the hip, forward and back. Calm and silence settled over us, all men. Four got up, one picked a heart from the embers, and they walked into the forest. Small groups of others arose, selected a piece of meat, and disappeared in other directions. We three were alone until Ihuene, Baaldore, and Reindude were in front of us, Reindude cupping in his hand the heart from the being we had carried from so far away, the heart of he who had lived in the hut we had entered to kill. We stretched out flat upon the ground, lined up, our shoulders touching. Michii looked up at the moon and showed it to the heart. He bit into it as if it were an apple, taking a large bite, almost half the heart, and chewed down several times, spit into a hand, separated the meat into six sections and placed some into the mouths of each of us. We chewed and swallowed. He did the same with the other half of the heart. He turned Darinimbiak onto his stomach, lifted his hips so that he crouched on all fours. Darinimbiak growled, Mayaarii-ha! Michii growled, Mayaari-ha!, bent down to lay himself upon Darinimbiak's back and entered him. (pp. 106–107)

Mass murder, destruction of an entire village, theft of all valuable goods, cannibalism, the ritual eating of the heart before publicly displayed homosexual acts—these are some of the acts Schneebaum participated in. He could not have done them his first day in the jungle. But after his gradual adoption of the Akarama reality, they had become natural. It would have been as immoral for him to refuse to join his brothers in the raid and its victory celebration as it would be immoral for him to commit these same acts within a Western community. His reality had changed. The moral facts were different.

Schneebaum's experience suggests that even radically different realities can be penetrated.[6] We would not have this account, however, if the stone age reality had completely obliterated Schneebaum's Western reality. He would still be with the tribe. The more he permeated the Akaramas' reality, the more suspect his old reality became. The more he fell under the spell of the absolutism of his new reality, the more fragile his old reality became. Like the cannibals, Schneebaum says: "My days are days no longer. Time had no thoughts to trouble me, and everything is like nothing and nothing is like everything. For if a day passes, it registers nowhere, and it might be a week, it might be a month. There is no difference" (p. 174).

As the vision of his old reality receded, Schneebaum experienced its fragility. He knew he must leave soon, or there would be no reality to return to. He describes his departure:

> A time alone, only a few weeks ago, with the jungle alive and vibrant around me, and Michii and Baaldore gone with all the other men to hunt, I saw within myself too many seeds that would grow a fungus around my brain, encasing it with mold that could penetrate and smooth the convolutions and there I would remain, not he who had travelled and arrived, not the me who had crossed the mountains in a search, but another me living only in ease and pleasure, no longer able to scrawl out words on paper or think beyond a moment. And days later, I took myself up from our hut, and I walked on again alone without a word to any of my friends and

family, but left when all again were gone and I walked through my jungle. . . . (p. 182)

The Akaramas would not miss him. They would not even notice his absence. For them, there were no separate beings. Schneebaum felt their reality obliterating "the me who had crossed the mountains in a search." Schneebaum was attached to this "me," and so he left.

In the previous section, I listed three conditions necessary for successful breaches: There can be no place to escape. There can be no time to escape. There can be no one to provide counter evidence. The same conditions are required to move between realities. That is, as Castañeda's (1968, 1971, 1972) work suggests, in order to permeate realities, one must first have the old reality breached. Castañeda has named this necessity the establishment "of a certainty of a minimal possibility," that another reality actually exists (personal communication). Successful breaches must establish that another reality is available for entry. Thus, as Don Juan attempted to make Castañeda a man of knowledge, he first spent years trying to crack Castañeda's absolute faith in the reality of Western rationalism.

Castañeda's work suggests many relations between the fragility and permeability features. It is not my purpose to explore the relations of the five features in this book. But I want to emphasize that such relations can be supposed to exist.

I relied on the "exotic" case of a person passing from a Western to a stone age reality to display the permeability feature of realities. However, any two subsequent interactional encounters could have been used for this purpose. All such passages are of equal theoretic import. Passages between a movie and freeway driving, between a person's reality before and after psychotherapy, between a "straight" acquiring membership in the reality of drug freaks, or before and after becoming a competent religious healer, are all the same. The differences are "merely" methodological, not theoretical.

Studying each passage, I would concentrate on how the reflexive, knowledge, interactional, and fragility features affect the shift.

All realities are permeable. Ethnomethodology is a reality. This book is an attempt to breach the reader's present reality by introducing him to the "certainty of a minimal possibility" that another reality exists.

ON THE CONCEPT OF REALITY

Many ethnomethodologists rely on Schutz's concept of reality (e.g., 1962, 1964, 1966). . . . My use of "reality" contrasts with Schutz's view. For Schutz (e.g., 1962, pp. 208ff.), the reality of everyday life is the *one* paramount reality. Schutz says that this paramount reality consists of a number of presuppositions or assumptions, which include the assumption of a tacit, taken for granted world; an assumed practical interest in that world; and an assumption that the world is intersubjective (e.g., 1962, p. 23). Schutz argues that other realities exist, but that they derive from the paramount reality. For example, he discusses the realities of "scientific theorizing" and of "fantasy." These realities appear when some of the basic assumptions of the paramount reality are temporarily suspended. The paramount reality of everyday life has an elastic quality for Schutz. After excursions into other realities, we snap back into the everyday.

My view of realities is different. I do not wish to call one or another reality paramount. It is my contention that every reality is equally real. No single reality contains more of the truth than any other. From the perspective of Western everyday life, Western everyday life will appear paramount, just as Schutz maintains. But from the perspective of scientific theorizing or dreaming, or meditating, each of these realities will appear just as paramount. Because every reality exhibits the absolutist tendency I mentioned earlier, there is no way to look from the window of one reality at others without

seeing yourself. Schutz seems to be a victim of this absolutist prejudice. As a Western man living his life in the Western daily experience, he assumed that this life was the touchstone of all realities.

My concept of reality, then, has more in common with Wittgenstein (1953) than with Schutz. Wittgenstein (e.g., 1953, pp. 61, 179) recognizes that human life exhibits an empirical multitude of activities. He calls these activities language games. Language games are forever being invented and modified and discarded. The fluidity of language activities do not permit rigorous description. Analysts can discover that at any time a number of language games are associated with one another. This association, too, is not amenable to rigorous description. Instead, language games exhibit "family resemblances." One can recognize certain games going together. But one could no more articulate *the* criteria for this resemblance than one could predict the physical characteristics of some unseen member of a familiar extended family. Wittgenstein (1953, pp. 119, 123) calls a collection of language games bound together by a family resemblance, a *form of life.*[7] Forms of life resemble what I call "realities." Realities are far more as warm than Schutz's terms "finite" and "province" suggest. Forms of life are always forms of life forming.[8] Realities are always realities becoming.

NOTES

1. See Pollner's (1970, 1973) discussions of the reflexive reasoning of the Azande and Polanyi's (1958, pp. 287–294) examination of the same materials. In the Apostolic Church of John Marangue, illness is not bodily malfunction, it is sin. Sin is curable not by medicine, but by confessional healing. When evangelists' attempts to heal church members were not accompanied by recovery, Jules-Rosette (1973, p. 167) reports that church members did not lose their faith in the confessional process. They looked to other "causes" of the "failure." They said things like: Other persons must have been implicated in the sin, and untrue confession must

have been given. Once again, contradictions that could potentially challenge a basic faith do not, as the basic faith itself is not questioned.

2. See Gurwitsch (1966) for a more technical discussion of the object constancy assumption. . . .

3. The . . . planet-star example [is] adapted from Pollner (1973). Much of this discussion of reflexivity derives from Pollner's thinking on these matters.

4. Riel (1972) illustrates how talk reflexively constitutes the context it then seems to independently reference. Trying to make a certain point, she reports turning away from an inadequate sentence she had written to explore notes and texts again. Forty-five minutes later she wrote the now-perfect sentence, only to discover it was exactly the same sentence she had rejected before.

5. Cicourel (1968) examines the interactional work that accomplishes external objects in greater detail. He shows that juvenile delinquents and crime rates are constituted by the social activities of law enforcement personnel.

6. For an account of a reality shift in the other direction, from the stone age to industrial Western society, see Kroeber's *Ishi in Two Worlds* (1961). Again the transition was never total, but this was a result of a political decision on the part of the author's husband. As Ishi's official keeper, he wished to keep him primitive for his own and anthropology's benefit.

7. Blum (1970) has previously explored the importance of Wittgenstein's notion of "form of life" for social science.

8. This phrase, like much of this chapter, has been adapted from the unpublished lectures of Pollner. For Pollner's published writings see Zimmerman and Pollner, 1970; and Pollner, 1970, 1973, 1974.

References

Blum, A. (1970). Theorizing. In J. D. Douglas (Ed.), *Understanding everyday life.* Chicago: Aldine.

Castañeda, C. (1968). *The teachings of Don Juan.* Berkeley: University of California Press.

Castañeda, C. (1971). *A separate reality.* New York: Simon & Schuster.

Castañeda, C. (1972). *A journey to Iztlan.* New York: Simon & Schuster.

Chomsky, N. (1965). *Aspects of the theory of syntax.* Cambridge: MIT Press.

Cicourel, A. V. (1968). *The social organization of juvenile justice.* New York: John Wiley.

Cicourel, A. V. (1973). *Cognitive sociology.* London: Macmillan.

Evans-Pritchard, E. E. (1937). *Witchcraft, oracles and magic among the Azande.* London: Oxford University Press.

Garfinkel, H. (1952). *Perception of the other.* Unpublished Ph.D. dissertation, Harvard University.

Garfinkel, H. (1963). A conception of and experiments with "trust" as a condition of concerted stable actions. In O. J. Harvey (Ed.), *Motivation and social interaction.* New York: Ronald.

Garfinkel, H. (1964). Studies of the routine grounds of everyday activities. *Social Problems, 11,* 225–250 (Chapter 2 in Garfinkel, 1967).

Garfinkel, H. (1967). *Studies in ethnomethodology.* Englewood Cliffs, NJ: Prentice Hall.

Gasking, D. (1955). Mathematics and the world. In A. Flew (Ed.), *Logic and language.* Garden City, NY: Doubleday.

Gurwitsch, A. (1966). *Studies in phenomenology and psychology.* Evanston, IL: Northwestern University Press.

Jules-Rosette, B. (1973). *Ritual context and social action.* Unpublished Ph.D. dissertation. Harvard University.

Kroeber, T. (1961). *Ishi in two worlds.* Berkeley: University of California Press.

Kuhn, T. S. (1970). *The structure of scientific revolutions.* Chicago: University of Chicago Press.

Polanyi, M. (1958). *Personal knowledge.* Chicago: University of Chicago Press.

Pollner, M. (1970). *On the foundations of mundane reason.* Unpublished Ph.D. dissertation. University of California, Santa Barbara.

Pollner, M. (1973). *The very coinage of your brain: The resolution of reality disjunctures.* Unpublished manuscript.

Pollner, M. (1974). Mundane reasoning. *Philosophy of social sciences, 4*(1), 35–54.

Reich, C. A. (1970). *The greening of America.* New York: Random House.

Riel, M. M. (1972). *The interpretive process.* Paper presented to a seminar led by Paul Filmer, University of California, San Diego.

Roszak, T. (1969). *The making of a counter culture.* Garden City, NY: Doubleday.

Sacks, H., Schegloff, E., & Jefferson, G. (1974). A simplest systematics for the analysis of turn taking in conversation. *Language, 50,* 696–735.

Schneebaum, T. (1969). *Keep the river on your right.* New York: Grove.

Schutz, A. (1962). *Collected papers I: The problem of social reality.* The Hague: Martinus Nijhoff.

Schutz, A. (1964). *Collected papers II: Studies in social theory.* The Hague: Martinus Nijhoff.

Schutz, A. (1966). *Collected papers III: Studies in phenomenological philosophy.* The Hague: Martinus Nijhoff.

Wallace, H. T. (1972). *Culture and social being.* Unpublished master's thesis, University of California, Santa Barbara.

Wieder, D. L. (1970). Meaning by rule. In J. D. Douglas (Ed.), *Understanding everyday life.* Chicago: Aldine.

Wieder, D. L. (1973). *Language and social reality.* The Hague: Mouton.

Wittgenstein, L. (1953). *Philosophical investigations.* London: Basil Blackwell & Mott.

Wittgenstein, L. (1961). *Tractatus logico-philosophicus.* London: Basil Blackwell & Mott. (Original work published in 1921)

Wood, H. (1968). *The labelling process on a mental hospital ward.* Unpublished master's thesis. University of California, Santa Barbara.

Zimmerman, D. H. (1973). Preface. In D. L. Wieder, *Language and social reality.* The Hague: Mouton.

Zimmerman, D. H., & Pollner, M. (1970). The everyday world as a phenomenon. In J. D. Douglas (Ed.), *Understanding everyday life.* Chicago: Aldine.

Zimmerman, D. H., & Wieder, D. L. (n.d.). *The social bases for illegal behavior in the student community: First year report.* San Francisco and Santa Barbara: Scientific Analysis Corporation.

A THEORY OF REALITY

31

A Conception of and Experiments With "Trust" as a Condition of Concerted Stable Actions

Harold Garfinkel

(1963)

SOME PRELIMINARY TRIALS AND FINDINGS

Since each of the presuppositions that make up the attitude of daily life assigns an expected feature to the actor's environment, it should be possible to induce experimentally a breach of these expectancies by deliberately modifying scenic events so as to disappoint these attributions. By definition, surprise is possible with respect to each of these expected features. The nastiness of surprise should vary directly with the extent to which the actor complies with the constitutive order of events of everyday life as a scheme for assigning witnessed appearances their status of events in a perceivedly normal environment.

Procedures were used to see if a breach of these presuppositions would produce anomic effects and increase disorganization. These procedures must be thought of as demonstrations rather than as experiments. "Experimenters" were upper division students in the author's courses. Their training consisted of little more than verbal instructions about how to proceed. The demonstrations were done as class assignments and were unsupervised. Students reported their results in anecdotal fashion with no controls beyond the fact that they were urged to avoid interpretation in favor of writing down what was actually said and done, staying as close as possible to a chronological account.

Because the procedures nevertheless produced massive effects, I feel they are worth reporting. Obviously, however, caution must be exercised in assessing the findings.

Demonstration 1: Breaching the Congruency of Relevances

This expectancy consists of the following. The person expects, expects that the other person does the same, and expects that as he expects it of the other the other expects the like of him that the differences in their perspectives that originate in their particular individual biographies are irrelevant for the purposes at hand of each and that both have selected and interpreted the actually and potentially common objects in an "empirically identical" manner that is sufficient for the purposes at hand. Thus, for example, in talking about "matters just known in common" persons will discuss them using a course of utterances that are governed by the expectation that the other person *will* understand. The speaker expects that the other person will assign to his remarks the sense intended by the speaker and expects that thereby the other person will permit the speaker the assumption that both know what he is talking about without any requirement of a check-out. Thus the sensible character of the matter that is being discussed is settled by a fiat assignment that each expects to make, and expects the other to make in reciprocal fashion, that as a condition of his right to decide without interference that he knows what he is talking about and that what he is talking about is so, each will have furnished whatever unstated understandings are required. Much therefore that is being talked about is not mentioned, although each expects that the adequate sense of

the matter being talked about is settled. The more so is this the case, the more is the exchange one of commonplace remarks among persons who "know" each other.

Students were instructed to engage an acquaintance or friend in an ordinary conversation and, without indicating that what the experimenter was saying was in any way out of the ordinary, to insist that the person clarify the sense of his commonplace remarks. Twenty-three students reported twenty-five instances of such encounters. The following are typical excerpts from their accounts.

Case 1. The subject was telling the experimenter, a member of the subject's car pool, about having had a flat tire while going to work the previous day.

(S): "I had a flat tire."

(E): "What do you mean, you had a flat tire?"

She appeared momentarily stunned. Then she answered in a hostile way: "What do you mean? What do you mean? A flat tire is a flat tire. That is what I meant. Nothing special. What a crazy question!"

Case 2. (S): "Hi, Ray. How is your girl friend feeling?"

(E): "What do you mean, how is she feeling? Do you mean physical or mental?"

(S): "I mean how is she feeling? What's the matter with you?" (He looked peeved.)

(E): "Nothing. Just explain a little clearer, what do you mean?"

(S): "Skip it. How are your Med School applications coming?"

(E): "What do you mean, 'How are they?'"

(S): "You know what I mean."

(E): "I really don't."

(S): "What's the matter with you? Are you sick?"

Case 3. On Friday night my husband and I were watching television. My husband remarked that he was tired. I asked, "How are you tired? Physically, mentally, or just bored?"

(S): "I don't know, I guess physically, mainly."

(E): "You mean that your muscles ache, or your bones?"

(S): "I guess so. Don't be so technical."

(S): (After more watching) "All these old movies have the same kind of old iron bedstead in them."

(E): "What do you mean? Do you mean all old movies, or some of them, or just the ones you have seen?"

(S): "What's the matter with you? You know what I mean."

(E): "I wish you would be more specific."

(S): "You know what I mean! Drop dead!"

Case 4. During a conversation (with the male *E*'s fiancee) the *E* questioned the meaning of various words used by the subject. For the first minute and a half the subject responded to the questions as if they were legitimate inquiries. Then she responded with "Why are you asking me these questions?" and repeated this two or three times after each question. She became nervous and jittery, her face and hand movements . . . uncontrolled. She appeared bewildered and complained that I was making her nervous and demanded that I "Stop it!" . . . The subject picked up a magazine and covered her face. She put down the magazine and pretended to be engrossed. When asked why she was looking at the magazine, she closed her mouth and refused any further remarks.

Case 5. My friend said to me, "Hurry or we will be late." I asked him what did he mean by late and from what point of view did it have reference. There was a look of perplexity and cynicism on his face. "Why are you asking me such silly questions? Surely I don't have to explain such a statement. What is

wrong with you today? Why should I have to stop to analyze such a statement. Everyone understands my statements and you should be no exception."

Case 6. The victim waved his hand cheerily.

(S): "How are you?"

(E): "How am I in regard to what? My health, my finance, my school work, my peace of mind, my . . ."

(S): (Red in the face and suddenly out of control.) "Look! I was just trying to be polite. Frankly, I don't give a damn how you are."

Case 7. My friend and I were talking about a man whose overbearing attitude annoyed us. My friend expressed his feeling.

(S): "I'm sick of him."

(E): Would you explain what is wrong with you that you are sick?"

(S): "Are you kidding me? You know what I mean."

(E): "Please explain your ailment."

(S): (He listened to me with a puzzled look.) "What came over you? We never talk this way, do we?" . . .

Case 8. Apparently as a casual afterthought, my husband mentioned Friday night, "Did you remember to drop off my shirts today?"

Taking nothing for granted, I replied, "I remember that you said something about it this morning. What shirts did you mean, and what did you mean by having them 'dropped' off?" He looked puzzled, as though I must have answered some other question than the one asked.

Instead of making the explanation he seemed to be waiting for, I persisted, "I thought your shirts were all in pretty good shape; why not keep them a little longer?" I had the uncomfortable feeling I had overplayed the part.

He no longer looked puzzled, but indignant. He repeated, "A little longer! What do you mean, and what have you done with my shirts?"

I acted indignant too. I asked, "What shirts? You have sport shirts, plain shirts, wool shirts, regular shirts, and dirty shirts. I'm no mind reader. What exactly did you want?"

My husband again looked confused, as though he was trying to justify my behavior. He seemed simultaneously to be on the defensive and offensive. He assumed a very patient, tolerant air, and said, "Now, let's start all over again. Did you drop off my shirts today?"

I replied, "I heard you before. It's your meaning I wish was more clear. As far as I am concerned dropping off your shirts—whichever shirts you mean—could mean giving them to the Goodwill, leaving them at the cleaners, at the laundromat, or throwing them out. I never know what you mean with those vague statements."

He reflected on what I said, then changed the entire perspective by acting as though we were playing a game, that it was all a joke. He seemed to enjoy the joke. He ruined my approach by assuming the role I thought was mine. He then said, "Well, let's take this step by step with 'yes' or 'no' answers. Did you see the dirty shirts I left on the kitchenette, yes or no?"

I could see no way to complicate his question, so felt forced to answer "Yes." In the same fashion, he asked if I picked up the shirts; if I put them in the car; if I left them at the laundry; and if I did all these things that day, Friday. My answers were "Yes."

The experiment, it seemed to me, had been cut short by his reducing all the parts of his previous question to their simplest terms, which were given to me as if I were a child unable to handle any complex questions, problems, or situations.

Demonstration 2: Breaching the Interchangeability of Standpoints

In order to breach the presupposed interchangeability of standpoints, students were asked to enter a store, to select a customer, and to treat the customer as a clerk while giving no recognition that the subject was any other person than the experimenter

took him to be and without giving any indication that the experimenter's treatment was anything other than perfectly reasonable and legitimate.

Case 1. One evening, while shopping at Sears with a friend, I (male) found myself next to a woman shopping at the copper-clad pan section. The store was busy . . . and clerks were hard to find. The woman was just a couple of feet away and my friend was behind me. Pointing to a tea kettle, I asked the woman if she did not think the price was rather high. I asked in a friendly tone. . . . She looked at me and then at the kettle and said "Yes." I then said I was going to take it anyway. She said, "Oh," and started to move sideways away from me. I quickly asked her if she was not going to wrap it for me and take my cash. Still moving slowly away and glancing first at me, then at the kettle, then at the other pans farther away from me, she said the clerk was "over there" pointing off somewhere. In a harsh tone, I asked if she was not going to wait on me. She said, "No, No, I'm not the saleslady. There she is." I said that I knew that the extra help was inexperienced, but there was no reason not to wait on a customer. "Just wait on me. I'll be patient." With that, she flushed with anger and walked rapidly away, looking back once as if to ask if it could really be true.

The following three protocols are the work of a forty-year-old female graduate student in clinical psychology.

Case 2. We went to V's book store, noted not so much for its fine merchandise and its wide range of stock as it is in certain circles for the fact that the clerks are male homosexuals. I approached a gentleman who was browsing at a table stacked neatly with books.

(E): "I'm in a hurry. Would you get a copy of *Sociopathic Behavior* by Lemert, please?"

(S): (Looked *E* up and down, drew himself very straight, slowly laid the book down, stepped back slightly, then leaned forward and in a low voice said) "I'm interested in sociopathic

behavior, too. That's why I'm here. I study the fellows here by pretending to be . . ."

(E): (Interrupting) "I'm not particularly interested in whether you are or are only pretending to be. Please just get the book I asked for."

(S): (Looked shocked. More than surprised, believe me. Stepped around the display table, deliberately placed his hands on the books, leaned forward and shouted) "I don't have such a book. I'm not a clerk! I'm—Well!" (Stalked out of the store.)

Case 3. When we entered I. Magnin's there was one woman who was fingering a sweater, the only piece of merchandise to be seen in the shop. I surmised that the clerk must be in the stockroom.

(E): "That is a lovely shade, but I'm looking for one a little lighter. Do you have one in cashmere?"

(S): "I really don't know, you see I'm . . .

(E): (Interrupting) "Oh, you are new here? I don't mind waiting while you look for what I want."

(S): "Indeed I shall not!"

(E): "But aren't you here to *serve* customers?"

(S): "I'm not! I'm here to . . ."

(E): (Interrupts) "This is hardly the place for such an attitude. Now please show me a cashmere sweater a shade or two lighter than this one."

(The clerk entered.)

(S): (To clerk) "My dear, this—(pointed her face toward *E*)—*person* insists on being shown a sweater. Please take care of her while I compose myself. I want to be certain this (sweater) will do, and she (pointed her face again at *E*) is so *insistent.*" (*S* carried the sweater with her, walked haughtily to a large upholstered chair, sat in it, brushed her gloved hands free from imaginary dirt, jerked her shoulders, fluffed her suit jacket, and glared at *E*).

Case 4. While visiting with a friend in Pasadena, I told him about this being-taken-for-the-clerk experiment. The friend is a Professor Emeritus of Mathematics at the California Institute of Technology and the successful author of many books, some technical, some fictional, and he is most satirical in his contemplations of his fellow man. He begged to be allowed to accompany me and to aid me in the selection of scenes. . . . We went first to have luncheon at the Atheneum, which caters to the students, faculty, and guests of Cal Tech. While we were still in the lobby, my host pointed out a gentleman who was standing in the large drawing room near the entrance to the dining room and said, "Go to it. There's a good subject for you." He stepped aside to watch. I walked toward the man very deliberately and proceeded as follows. (I will use *E* to designate myself; *S*, the subject.)

(E): "I should like a table on the west side, a quiet spot, if you please. And what is on the menu?"

(S): (Turned toward *E* but looked past and in the direction of the foyer) said, "Eh, ah, madam, I'm sure." (looked past *E* again, looked at a pocket watch, replaced it, and looked toward the dining room).

(E): "Surely luncheon hours are not over. What do you recommend I order today?"

(S): "I don't know. You see, I'm waiting . . ."

(E): (Interrupted with) "Please don't keep me standing here while you wait. Kindly show me to a table."

(S): "But Madam,—" (started to edge away from door, and back into the lounge in a slightly curving direction around *E*)

(E): "My good man—" (At this *S*'s face flushed, his eyes rounded and opened wide.)

(S): "But—you—I—oh dear!" (He seemed to wilt.)

(E): (Took *S's* arm in hand and propelled him toward the dining room door, slightly ahead of herself.)

(S): (Walked slowly but stopped just within the room, turned around and for the first time looked directly and very appraisingly at *E*, took out the watch, looked at it, held it to his ear, replaced it, and muttered) "Oh dear."

(E): "It will take only a minute for you to show me to a table and take my order. Then you can return to wait for your customers. After all, I am a guest and a customer, too."

(S): (Stiffened slightly, walked jerkily toward the nearest empty table, held a chair for *E* to be seated, bowed slightly, muttered "My pleasure," hurried toward the door, stopped, turned, looked back at *E* with a blank facial expression.)

At this point *E's* host walked up to *S*, greeted him, shook hands, and propelled him toward *E's* table. *S* stopped a few steps from the table, looked directly at, then through *E*, and started to walk back toward the door. Host told him *E* was the young lady whom he had invited to join them at lunch (then introduced me to one of the big names in the physics world, a pillar of the institution!). *S* seated himself reluctantly and perched rigidly on his chair, obviously uncomfortable. *E* smiled, made light and polite inquiries about his work, mentioned various functions attended which had honored him, then complacently remarked that it was a shame *E* had not met him personally before now, so that she should not have mistaken him for the maître-d'. The host chattered about his long-time friendship with me, while *S* fidgeted and looked again at his pocket watch, wiped his forehead with a table napkin, looked at *E* but avoided meeting her eyes. When the host mentioned that *E* is studying sociology at UCLA, *S* suddenly burst into loud laughter, realized that everyone in the room was looking in the direction of our table,

abruptly became quiet, then said to *E* "You mistook me for the maître-d', didn't you?"

(E): "Deliberately, sir."

(S): "Why deliberately?"

(E): "You have just been used as the unsuspecting subject in an experiment."

(S): "Diabolic. But clever, I must say (To our host) I haven't been so shaken since _____ denounced my theory _____ of _____ in 19 _____. And the wild thoughts that ran through my mind! Call the receptionist from the lobby, go to the men's room, turn this woman to the first person that comes along. Damn these early diners, there's nobody coming in at this time. Time is standing still, or my watch has stopped. I will talk to _____ about this, make sure it doesn't happen to 'somebody.' Damn a persistent woman. I'm not her 'good man!' I'm Dr. _____, and not to be pushed around. This can't be happening. If I do take her to that damned table she wants, I can get away from her, and I'll just take it easy until I can. I remember _____ (hereditary psychopath, wife of one of the 'family' of the institution) maybe if I do what *this* one wants she will not make any more trouble than this. I wonder if she is 'off.' She certainly looks normal. Wonder how you can really tell?"

Demonstration 3: Breaching the Expectancy That a Knowledge of a Relationship of Interaction Is a Commonly Entertained Scheme of Communication

Schutz proposed that from the member's point of view, an event of conduct, like a move in a game, consists of an event-in-a-social-order. Thus, for the member, its recognizably real character is furnished by attending its occurrence with respect to a corpus of socially sanctioned knowledge of the social relationships that the member uses and assumes that others use as the same scheme of expression and interpretation.

It was decided to breach this expectancy by having students treat a situation as something that it "obviously" and "really" was not. Students were instructed to spend from fifteen minutes to an hour in their own homes acting as if they were boarders. They were instructed to conduct themselves in a circumspect and polite fashion: to avoid getting personal; to use formal address; to speak only when they were spoken to.

In nine of forty-nine cases students either refused to do the assignment (five cases) or the try was "unsuccessful" (four cases). Four of the "no try" students said they were afraid to do it; a fifth said she preferred to avoid the risk of exciting her mother who had a heart condition. In two of the "unsuccessful" cases the family treated it as a joke from the beginning and refused, despite the continuing actions of the student experimenter, to change. A third family took the view that something of an undisclosed sort was the matter, but what it might be was of no concern to them. In the fourth family the father and mother remarked that the daughter was being "extra nice" and undoubtedly wanted something that she would shortly reveal.

In the remaining four-fifths of the cases family members were stupefied, vigorously sought to make the strange actions intelligible, and to restore the situation to normal appearances. Reports were filled with accounts of astonishment, bewilderment, shock, anxiety, embarrassment, and anger as well as with charges by various family members that the student was mean, inconsiderate, selfish, nasty, and impolite. Family members demanded explanations: "What's the matter?" "What's gotten into you?" "Did you get fired?" "Are you sick?" "What are you being so superior about?" "Why are you mad?" "Are you out of your mind or are you just stupid?" One student acutely embarrassed his mother in front of her friends by asking if she minded if he had a snack from the refrigerator. "Mind if you have a little snack? You've been eating little snacks around here for years

without asking me. What's gotten into you?" One mother, infuriated when her daughter spoke to her only when she was spoken to, began to shriek in angry denunciation of the daughter for her disrespect and insubordination and refused to be calmed by the student's sister. A father berated his daughter for being insufficiently concerned for the welfare of others and for acting like a spoiled child.

Occasionally family members would first treat the student's action as a cue for a joint comedy routine which was soon replaced by irritation and exasperated anger at the student for not knowing "when enough was enough." Family members mocked the "politeness" of the students— "Certainly Mr. Dinerberg!"—or charged the student with acting like a wise guy and generally reproved the "politeness" with sarcasm.

Explanations were sought in terms of understandable and previous motives of the student: the accusation that the student was covering up something important that the family should know; that the student was working too hard in school; that the student was ill; that there had been "another fight" with a fiancée.

Unacknowledged explanations were followed by withdrawal of the offended member, attempted isolation of the culprit, retaliation, and denunciation. "Don't bother with him, he's in one of his moods again." "Pay no attention but just wait until he asks me for something." "You're cutting me, okay. I'll cut you and then some." "Why must you always create friction in our family harmony?" A father followed his son into the bedroom. "Your mother is right. You don't look well and you're not talking sense. You had better get another job that doesn't require such late hours." To this the student replied that he appreciated his consideration, but that he felt fine and only wanted a little privacy. The father responded in high rage, "I don't want any more of *that* out of *you*. And if you can't treat your mother decently, you'd better move out!"

There were no cases in which the situation was not restorable upon the student's explanation.

Nevertheless, for the most part, family members were not amused and only rarely did they find the experience instructive, as the student argued that it was supposed to have been. After hearing the explanation, a sister replied coldly on behalf of a family of four, "Please, no more of these experiments. We're not rats you know." Occasionally an explanation was accepted and still it added offense. In several cases students reported that the explanation left them, their families, or both wondering how much of what the student had said was "in character" and how much the student "really meant."

Students found the assignment difficult to complete because of not being treated as if they were in the role that they are attempting to play and of being confronted with situations to which they did not know how a boarder would respond.

There were several entirely unexpected results. (1) Although many students reported extensive rehearsals in imagination, very few of those that did it mentioned anticipatory fears or embarrassment. (2) Although unanticipated and nasty developments frequently occurred, in only one case did a student report serious regrets. (3) Very few students reported heartfelt relief when the hour was over. They were much more likely to report a partial relief. They frequently reported that in response to the anger of others they became angry in return and slipped easily into subjectively recognizable feelings and actions.

Demonstration 4: Breaching the Grasp of "What Anyone Knows" to Be Correct Grounds of Action of a Real Social World

Among the possibilities that a premedical student could treat as correct grounds for his further inferences and actions about such matters as how a medical school intake interview is conducted or how an applicant's conduct is related to his chances of admission, certain ones (e.g., that deferring to the interviewer's interests is a condition for making a favorable impression) he treats as matters that he is required to know and act upon as a condition of his competence as a premedical

candidate. He expects others like him to know and act upon the same things; and he expects that as he expects others to know and act upon them, the others in turn expect the like of him.

A procedure was designed to breach the constitutive expectancies attached to "what-any-competent-premedical-candidate-knows" while satisfying the three conditions under which their breach would presumably produce confusion.

Twenty-eight premedical students of the University of California in Los Angeles were run individually through a three-hour experimental interview. As part of the solicitation of subjects, as well as the beginning of the interview, *E* identified himself as a representative of an Eastern medical school who was attempting to learn why the medical school intake interview was such a stressful situation. It was hoped that identifying *E* as a person with medical school ties would minimize the chance that students would "leave the field" once the accent breaching procedure began. How the other two conditions of (a) managing a redefinition in insufficient time and (b) not being able to count on consensual support for an alternative definition of social reality were met will be apparent in the following description.

During the first hour of the interview, the student furnished the facts-of-life about interviews for admission to medical school by answering for the "representative" such questions as "What sources of information about a candidate are available to medical schools?" "What can a medical school learn about a candidate from these sources?" "What kind of a man are the medical schools looking for?" "What should a good candidate do in the interview?" "What should he avoid?" With this much completed, the student was told that the "representative's" research interests had been satisfied. The student was asked if he would care to hear a recording of an actual interview. All students wanted very much to hear the recording.

The recording was a faked one between a "medical school interviewer" and an "applicant." The applicant was depicted as being a boor; his language was ungrammatical and filled with colloquialisms; he was evasive; he contradicted the interviewer; he bragged; he ran down other schools and professions; he insisted on knowing how he had done in the interview and so on.

Detailed assessments by the student of the recorded applicant were obtained immediately after the recording was finished. The following edited assessment is representative:

> I didn't like it. I didn't like his attitude. I didn't like anything about him. Everything he said grated the wrong way. I didn't like his smoking. The way he kept saying "Yeah-h!" He didn't show that he realized that the interviewer had his future in his hands. I didn't like the vague way he answered questions. I didn't like the way he pressed at the end of the interview. He was disrespectful. His motives were too obvious. He made a mess of it. He finished with a bang to say the least. . . . His answers to questions were stupid. I felt that the interviewer was telling him that he wasn't going to get in. I didn't like the interview. I felt it was too informal. To a degree it's good if it's natural but . . . the interview is not something to breeze through. It's just not the place for chit-chat. He had fairly good grades but . . . he's not interested in things outside of school and didn't say what he did *in* school. Then he didn't *do* very much— outside of this lab. I didn't like the man at all. I never met an applicant like that! "My pal"—Just one of these little chats. I never met anybody *like* that. Wrong-way Corrigan.

The student was then given information from the applicant's "official record." This information was deliberately contrived to contradict the principal points in the student's assessment. For example, if the student said that the applicant must have come from a lower-class family, he was told that the applicant's father was vice president of a firm that manufactured pneumatic doors for trains and buses. If the applicant had been thought to be ignorant, he was described as having excelled in courses like The Poetry of Milton and Dramas of Shakespeare. If the student said the applicant did not know how to get along with people, then the applicant was pictured as

having worked as a voluntary solicitor for Sydenham Hospital in New York City and had raised $32,000 from thirty "big givers." The belief that the applicant was stupid and would not do well in a scientific field was met by citing A grades in organic and physical chemistry and graduate level performance in an undergraduate research course.

The *Ss* wanted very much to know what "the others" thought of the applicant, and had he been admitted? The "others" had been previously and casually identified by the "representative" as "Dr. Gardner, the medical school interviewer," "six psychiatrically trained members of the admissions committee who heard only the recorded interview," and "other students I talked to."

The *S* was told that the applicant had been admitted and was living up to the promise that the medical school interviewer and the "six psychiatrists" had found and expressed in the following recommendation of the applicant's characterological fitness.

> Dr. Gardner, the medical school interviewer, wrote, "A well-bred, polite young man, poised, affable, and self-confident. Capable of independent thinking. Interests of a rather specialized character. Marked intellectual curiosity. Alert and free of emotional disturbances. Marked maturity of manner and outlook. Meets others easily. Strongly motivated toward a medical career. Definite ideas of what he wants to achieve which are held in good perspective. Unquestioned sincerity and integrity. Expressed himself easily and well. ecommend favorable consideration." The six psychiatric members of the admissions committee agreed in all essentials.

Concerning the views of "other students," *S* was told that he was, for example, the thirtieth student I had seen; that twenty-eight before him were in entire agreement with the medical school interviewer's assessment; and that the remaining two had been slightly uncertain but at the first bit of information had seen him just as the others had.

Following this, *Ss* were invited to listen to the record a second time, after which they were asked to assess the applicant again.

Results. Twenty-five of the twenty-eight subjects were taken in. The following does not apply to the three who were convinced there was a deception. Two of these are discussed at the conclusion of this section.

Incongruous materials, presented to *S* in the order indicated, were performance information, and characterological information. Performance information dealt with the applicant's activities, grades, family background, courses, charity work, and the like. Characterological information consisted of character assessments of him by the "medical school interviewers," the "six psychiatrically trained members of the admissions committee," and the "other students."

Subjects managed incongruities of performance data with vigorous attempts to make it factually compatible with their original assessments. For example, when they said that the applicant sounded like a lower-class person, they were told that his father was vice president of a national corporation that manufactured pneumatic doors for trains and buses. Here are some typical replies:

"He should have made the point that he *could* count on money."

"That explains why he said he had to work. Probably his father made him work. That would make a lot of his moans unjustified in the sense that things were really not so bad."

"What does that have to do with values?!"

"You could tell from his answers. You could tell that he was used to having his own way."

"That's something the interviewer knew that *I* didn't know."

"Then he's an out and out liar!"

When *Ss* said that the applicant was selfish and could not get along with people, they were told that he had worked as a volunteer for Sydenham Hospital and had raised $32,000 from thirty "big givers."

"He seems to be a good salesman. So possibly he's missing his profession. I'd say *definitely* he's missing his profession!"

"They probably contributed because of the charity and not because they were solicited."

"Pretty good. Swell. Did he know them personally?"

"It's very fashionable to work, for example, during the war for Bundles for Britain. So that doesn't—definitely!—show altruistic motives at all. He is a person who is subject to fashion and I'm very critical of that sort of thing."

"He's so forceful he might have shamed them into giving."

"People who are wealthy—his father would naturally see those people—big contributions—they could give a lot of money and not know what they're giving it for."

That he had a straight A average in physical science courses began to draw bewilderment.

"He took quite a variety of courses . . . I'm baffled.— Probably the interview wasn't a very good mirror of his character."

"He did seem to take some odd courses. They seem to be fairly normal. Not normal—but—it doesn't strike me one way or the other."

"Well! I think you can analyze it this way. In psychological terms. See—one possible way—now I may be all *wet* but this is the way I look at *that*. He probably suffered from an inferiority complex and that's an overcompensation for his inferiority complex. His *great* marks—his *good* marks are a compensation for his failure—in social dealings perhaps, I don't know."

"Woops! And only third alternate at Georgia. (Deep sigh) I can see why he'd feel resentment about not being admitted to Phi Bet."

(Long silence) "Well! From what—that leads me to think he's a grind or something like that."

Attempts to resolve the incongruities produced by the character assessment of "Gardner" and "the other six judges" were much less frequent than normalizing attempts with performance information. Open expressions of bewilderment and anxiety interspersed with silent ruminations were characteristic.

(Laugh) "Golly!" (Silence) "I'd think it would be the other way around."—(Very subdued) "Maybe I'm all wro—My orientation is all off. I'm completely baffled."

"Not polite. Self-confident he certainly was. But not polite—I don't know. Either the interviewer was a little crazy or else I am." (Long pause) "That's rather shocking. It makes me have doubts about my own thinking. Perhaps my values in life are wrong. I don't know."

(Whistles) "I—I didn't think he sounded well bred at all. That whole tone of voice!!—I—Perhaps you noticed though, when he said 'You should have said in the first place' before he took it with a smile.— But even so! No, no I can't see that. 'You should have said that before.' Maybe he was being funny though. Exercising a—No! To me it sounded impertinent!"

"Ugh—Well, that certainly puts a different slant on my conception of interviews. Gee—that— confuses me all the more."

"Well—(laugh)—Hhh!—Ugh! Well, maybe he looked like a nice boy. He did—he did get his point across.—Perhaps—seeing the person would make a big difference.—Or perhaps I would never make a good interviewer." (Reflectively and almost inaudibly) "They didn't mention any of the things I mentioned." (HG: Eh?) (Louder) "They didn't mention any of the things I mentioned and so I feel like a complete failure."

Soon after the performance data produced its consternation, an occasional request would be made: "What did the other students make of him?" Only after Gardner's assessment, and the responses to it had been made were the opinions of the "other students" given. In some cases the subject was told "34 out of 35 before you," in others 43 out of 45, 19 out of 20, 51 out of 52. All the numbers were large. For 18 of the 25 students the delivery hardly varied from the following verbatim protocols:

[34 out of 35] I don't know.—I still stick to my original convictions. I—I—Can you tell *me* what—I saw wrong. Maybe—I—I had the wrong idea—the wrong attitude all along. (Can you tell me? I'm interested that there should be such a disparity.) Definitely.—I—think—it would be definitely the other way—I can't make sense of it. I'm completely baffled, believe me.—I—I don't understand how I could have been so wrong. Maybe my ideas—my evaluations of people are—just twisted. I mean maybe I had the wrong—maybe my sense of

values—is—off—or—different—from the other 33. But I don't think that's the case—because usually— and in all modesty I say this—I—I can judge people. I mean in class, in organizations I belong to—I usually judge them right. So therefore I don't understand at *all* how I could have been so wrong. I don't think I was under any stress or strain— here—tonight but—I don't understand it.

[43 out of 45] [Laugh] I don't know what to say now.—I'm troubled by my inability to judge the guy better than that. [Subdued] I shall sleep tonight, certainly—[Very subdued] but it certainly bothers me.—Sorry that I didn't— *Well!* One question that arises—I may be wrong—(Can you see how they might have seen him?) No. No, I can't see it, no.— Sure with all that background material, yes, but I don't see how Gardner did it without it. Well, I guess that makes Gardner, Gardner, and me, me. (The other 45 students didn't have the background material.) Yeah, yeah, yeah. I mean I'm not denying it at all. I mean for myself, there's no sense saying—Of course! With their background they would be accepted, especially the second man, good God!—Okay, what else?

[23 out of 25] [Softly] Maybe I'm tired. (HG, "Eh?") [Burst of laughter.] Maybe I didn't get enough sleep last night.—Uhh!—Well—I might not have been looking for the things that the other men were looking for.—I wasn't—Huh!—It puts me at a loss, really.

[10 out of 10] So I'm alone in my judgment. I don't know, sir! I don't know, sir!!—I can't explain it. It's senseless.—I tried to be impartial at the beginning. I admit I was prejudiced immediately.

[51 out of 52] You mean that 51 others stuck to their guns, too? (Stuck to their guns in the sense that they saw him just as the judges saw him.) Uh huh. [Deep sigh] I still don't—Yeah! I see. But just listening I don't think he was a—very good chance. But in light of his other things I feel that the interview was not—showing—the real—him.—Hhh!

[36 out of 37] I would go back on my former opinion but I wouldn't go back too far. I just don't see it.— Why should I have these different standards? Were my opinions more or less in agreement on the first man? (No.) That leads me to think.—That's funny. Unless you got 36 unusual people. I can't understand it. Maybe it's my personality. (Does it make any difference?) It *does* make a difference if I assume they're correct. What

I consider is proper, they don't.—It's my attitude—Still in all a man of that sort would alienate me. A wise guy type to be avoided. Of course you can talk like that with other fellows—but in an interview? . . . Now I'm more confused than I was at the beginning of the entire interview. I think I ought to go home and look in the mirror and talk to myself. Do you have any ideas? (Why? Does it disturb you?) Yes it *does* disturb me! It makes me think my abilities to judge people and values are way off from normal. It's not a healthy situation. (What difference does it make?) If I act the way I act it seems to me that I'm just putting my head in the lion's mouth. I did have preconceptions but they're shattered all to hell. It makes me wonder about myself. Why should I have these different standards? It all points to me.

Of the twenty-five Ss who were taken in, seven were unable to resolve the incongruity of having been wrong about such an obvious matter and were unable to "see" the alternative. Their suffering was dramatic and unrelieved. Five more resolved it with the view that the medical school had accepted a good man; five others with the view that it had accepted a boor. Although they changed, they nevertheless did not abandon their former views. For them Gardner's view could be seen "in general," but the grasp lacked convincingness. When attention was drawn to particulars, the general picture would evaporate. These Ss were willing to entertain and use the "general" picture, but they suffered whenever indigestible particulars of the same portrait came into view. Subscription to the "general" picture was accompanied by a recitation of characteristics that were not only the opposite of those in the original view but were intensified by superlative adjectives like "supremely" poised, "very" natural, "most" confident, "very" calm. Further, they saw the new features through a new appreciation of the way the medical examiner had been listening. They saw, for example, that the examiner was smiling when the applicant had forgotten to offer him a cigarette.

Three more Ss were convinced that there was deception and acted on the conviction through the interview. They showed no disturbance. Two of these showed acute suffering as soon as it appeared that the interview was finished, and they were being dismissed with no acknowledgment of a deception. Three others inadvertently suffered in silence and confounded E. Without any indication to E, they regarded the interview as an experimental one in which they were being asked to solve some problems and therefore were being asked to do as well as possible and to make no changes in their opinions, for only then would they be contributing to the study. They were difficult for me to understand during the interview because they displayed marked anxiety, yet their remarks were bland and were not addressed to the matters that were provoking it. Finally three more Ss contrasted with the others. One of these insisted that the character assessments were semantically ambiguous and because there was insufficient information a "high correlation opinion" was not possible. A second, and the only one in the entire series, found, according to his account, the second portrait as convincing as the original one. When the deception was revealed, he was disturbed that he could have been as convinced as he was. The third one, in the face of everything, showed only slight disturbance of very short duration. However, he alone among the subjects had already been interviewed for medical school, had excellent contacts, despite a grade point average of less than C he estimated his chances of admission as fair, and finally he expressed his preference for a career in the diplomatic service over a career in medicine.

As a final observation, twenty-two of the twenty-eight Ss expressed marked relief—ten of them with explosive expressions—when I disclosed the deception. Unanimously they said that the news of the deception permitted them to return to their former views. Seven Ss had to be convinced that there had been a deception. When the deception was revealed, they asked what they were to believe. Was I telling them that there had been a deception in order to make them feel better? No pains were spared, and whatever truth or lies that had to be told were told in order to establish the truth that there had been a deception.

SELF-FULFILLING PROPHECIES

Self-fulfilling prophecies are events that come true because of actions taken based on the belief that they would come true. For instance, if many people believe a gas shortage is going to occur and they all rush to get gas at the same time, they may, in fact, cause a gas shortage. Self fulfilling prophecies illustrate the features of reality that Mehan and Wood call "reflexive" and "interactional." Understanding self-fulfilling prophecies can be very useful for determining how to intervene in behavioral loops that seem to be self-perpetuating. This process also helps explain the power of labels and preconceived expectations for bringing about the actions that seem to justify the original stereotype.

In his article "Self-Fulfilling Prophecies," Paul Watzlawick develops the definition of the self-fulfilling process and gives several examples of how it works. Each of these examples highlights the "reflexivity" and "interactional" features of reality. People form beliefs and expectations and then behave in a way that generates an interactional chain of events that fulfills their expectations. This reaffirms the initial belief and further entrenches it.

"When Belief Creates Reality" is a study based on the concept of self-fulfilling prophecies. Mark Snyder designed a study in which he observed the way people interacted with those persons perceived to be attractive and those perceived not to be attractive. He noticed that when people perceive someone to be attractive, they tend to act more friendly and engaged with the person, thus giving the other person more opportunity to be engaging in response. According to Snyder, this kind of behavior perpetuates the stereotype that attractive people are more friendly and engaging.

READING QUESTIONS

1. Watzlawick gives examples of self-fulfilling prophecies at both the individual and the collective levels. Discuss examples of contemporary world politics that can be explained in terms of self-fulfilling prophecies.

2. Make a list of behavioral stereotypes and consider how these stereotypes might become real and persistent as a result of self-fulfilling interactional expectations.

3. If someone has a preconceived notion and acts in a way that makes it real in the outcome, will the person ever know that it was her or his own behavior that caused the expected outcome? Does it matter? What feature of reality does this process describe?

32

Self-Fulfilling Prophecies

Paul Watzlawick

(1984)

A self-fulfilling prophecy is an assumption or prediction that, purely as a result of having been made, causes the expected or predicted event to occur and thus confirms its own "accuracy." For example, if someone assumes, for whatever reason, that he is not respected, he will, because of this assumption, act in such a hostile, overly sensitive, suspicious manner that he brings about that very contempt in others which "proves" again and again his firmly entrenched conviction. This mechanism may be commonplace and well known, but it is based upon a number of facts that are by no means part of our everyday thinking and which have a profound significance for our view of reality.

In our traditional cause-and-effect thinking we usually see event B as the result of a preceding, causal event (A)—which in turn has, of course, its own causes, just as the occurrence of B produces its own sequel of events. In the sequence $A \rightarrow B$, A is therefore the cause and B its effect. The causality is *linear* and B follows A in the course of time. Accordingly, in this causality model, B can have no effect on A, because this would mean a reversal of the flow of time: The present (B) would have to exert a backward effect on the past (A).

Matters stand differently in the following example: In March 1979, when the newspapers in California began to publish sensational pronouncements of an impending, severe gasoline shortage, California motorists stormed the gas stations to fill up their tanks and to keep them as full as possible. This filling up of 12 million gasoline tanks (which up to this time had on the average been 75% empty) depleted the enormous reserves and so brought about the predicted shortage practically overnight. The endeavor to keep the fuel containers as full as possible (instead of getting gas when the tank was almost empty, as had been done before) resulted in endless lines and hours of waiting time at the gas stations, and increased the panic. After the excitement died down, it turned out that the allotment of gasoline to the state of California had hardly been reduced at all.

Here the customary cause-and-effect thinking breaks down. The shortage would never have occurred if the media had not predicted it. In other words, an event that had not yet taken place (i.e., an event in the future) created an effect in the present (the storming of the gas stations), which in turn caused the predicted event to become reality. In this sense it was the future—not the past—that determined the present.

The objection could be raised that all of this is neither astonishing nor unheard of. Are not almost all human decisions and actions largely dependent on the evaluation of their probable effects, advantages, and dangers (or at least should they not be)? Does not the future therefore always play a part in the present? Significant as these questions may be, they do not seem to make much sense here. Whoever tries, usually on the basis of earlier experience, to evaluate the future effect of his decision normally intends the best possible outcome. The specific action tries to take the future into consideration, and subsequently proves to be true or false, correct or incorrect; but it does not have to have any influence whatever on the course of events. However, an action that results from a self-fulfilling prophecy itself produces the requisite conditions for the occurrence of the expected event, and in this sense *creates* a reality which would not have arisen without it. The action that is at first neither true nor false produces a fact, and with it its own "truth."

Here are examples of both perspectives: If someone begins to suffer from headaches, sneezes, and shivers, he will, on the basis of past experience, assume that he is coming down with a cold; and if his diagnosis is correct, he can, with aspirin, hot drinks, and bedrest, favorably influence the (future) course of the illness by these means in the present. By doing so, he has correctly grasped a causal sequence that had at first been totally independent of him, and exerted a partial influence on it.

A fundamentally different sequence results from the practice of collecting taxes in certain countries. Since the revenue agency assumes a priori that no citizen will ever truthfully declare his income, the tax rate is dictated more or less arbitrarily. The revenue offices rely largely on the information of their assessment agents, who take into consideration such vague factors as a person's standard of living, his real estate property, the fur coats of his wife, the make of his car, and so forth. To the income, "ascertained" in this way, there is then added a certain percentage that is supposed to make up for any undeclared income, because—as we said—it is assumed a priori that the taxpayer cheats. This assumption, however, produces the situation in which a truthful declaration of income becomes unacceptable even for an honest taxpayer, and in which dishonesty

is practically made a necessity if one wants to escape unfair taxes. Again an assumption believed to be true creates the assumed reality, and again it is irrelevant whether the assumption was originally true or false. And so we see that the difference lies in the fact that, in the example of the head cold, a development that is already taking place in the present is acted upon as best as is possible, and its course is influenced in this way in the present; whereas in the examples of the gasoline shortage and the income tax the course of events is induced by the very measures which are undertaken as a (supposed) reaction to the expected event in question. Therefore what is supposed to be a *reaction* (the effect) turns out to be an action (the cause); the "solution" produces the problem; the prophecy of the event causes the event of the prophecy.

This singular reversal of cause and effect is particularly obvious in interpersonal conflicts, where the phenomenon of the so-called *punctuation* of a sequence of events is invariably present. Making use of an example that has already been employed elsewhere (Watzlawick, Bavelas, & Jackson, 1967, pp. 56–58), we will imagine a married couple struggling with a conflict that they both assume to be basically the other's fault, while their own behavior is seen only as a *reaction* to that of their partner. The woman complains that her husband is withdrawing from her, which he admits, but because he sees his silence or his leaving the room as the only possible reaction to her constant nagging and criticizing. For her this reasoning is a total distortion of the facts: His behavior is the *cause* of her criticism and her anger. Both partners are referring to the same interpersonal reality but assign to it a diametrically opposed causality. The diagram, Figure 1, may illustrate this discrepancy, although it postulates—unavoidably but wrongly—a starting point that does not really exist, because the behavior pattern between the two people has been repeating itself for a long time, and the question of who started it has long since become meaningless.

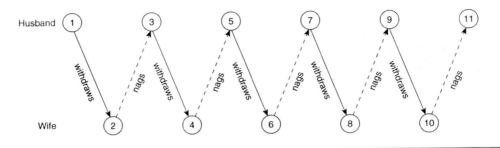

Figure 1

The arrows with the solid lines represent the behavior of the husband ("withdraws"), and the dotted lines that of the wife ("nags"). The husband dissects ("punctuates") the whole of the pattern into the triads 2–3–4, 4–5–6, 6–7–8, and so on, and so sees the interpersonal reality as one in which his wife nags (cause) and he *therefore* withdraws from her (effect). From her point of view, however, it is his cold passivity (cause) that causes her nagging (effect); she criticizes him *because* he withdraws from her, and therefore punctuates the pattern into the triads 1–2–3, 3–4–5, 5–6–7, and so on. With this opposed punctuation, both have literally brought about two contradictory realities and—what is perhaps even more important—two self-fulfilling prophecies. The two modes of behavior, which are seen subjectively as a reaction to the behavior of the partner, cause this very behavior in the other and "therefore" justify one's own behavior.

It goes without saying that self-fulfilling prophecies in an interpersonal context can also be used deliberately and with a specific intent. The dangers of this practice will be discussed later on. As an example here let me only mention the well-known method of former matchmakers in patriarchal societies, who had the thankless task of awakening a mutual interest in two young people, who possibly cared nothing for each other, because their families had decided that for financial reasons, social standing, or other similarly impersonal motives, the two would make a good

couple. The matchmaker's usual procedure was to talk with the young man alone and ask him whether he had not noticed how the girl was always secretly watching him. Similarly, he would tell the girl that the boy was constantly looking at her when her head was turned. This prophecy, disguised as a fact, was often quickly fulfilled. Skilled diplomats also know this procedure as a negotiating technique.[1]

Everyday experience teaches us that only few prophecies are self-fulfilling, and the above examples should explain why: Only when a prophecy is believed, that is, only when it is seen as a fact that has, so to speak, already happened in the future, can it have a tangible effect on the present and thereby fulfill itself. Where this element of belief or conviction is absent, this effect will be absent as well. To inquire how the construction or acceptance of such a prophecy comes to be would go far beyond the scope of this essay. (An extensive study of the social, psychological, and physiological effects of self-fulfilling prophecies was published in 1974 by Jones.) Too numerous and various are the factors involved—from the realities one fabricates for oneself during the course of the so-called noncontingent reward experiments (Watzlawick, 1976, pp. 45–54) . . . , to such oddities as the (perhaps unverified, but not improbable) assertion that since Bernadette had a vision of the Virgin Mary in February of 1858, only pilgrims, but not a single inhabitant of Lourdes, found a miraculous cure there.

Of this story one can say, *se non è vero, è ben trovato,*[2] since it helps to build a bridge from our previous, somewhat trivial reflections to manifestations of self-fulfilling prophecies that have a deeper human as well as scientific significance.

The oracle had prophesied that Oedipus would kill his father and marry his mother. Horrified by this prediction, which he undoubtedly believed to be true, Oedipus tries to protect himself from the impending doom, but the precautionary measures themselves lead to the seemingly inescapable fulfillment of the oracle's dictum. As is known, Freud used this myth as a metaphor for the incestuous attraction for the opposite sex inherent in every child, and the consequent fear of retaliation on the part of the parent of the same sex; and he saw in this key constellation, the Oedipus conflict, the fundamental cause of later neurotic developments. In his autobiography the philosopher Karl Popper (1974) refers back to a self-fulfilling prophecy that he had already described two decades earlier and which he called the Oedipus *effect:*

> One of the ideas I had discussed in *The Poverty* [*of Historicism*] was the influence of a prediction upon the event predicted. I had called this the "Oedipus effect," because the oracle played a most important role in the sequence of events which led to the fulfillment of its prophecy. (It was also an allusion to the psychoanalysts, who had been strangely blind to this interesting fact, even though Freud himself admitted that the very dreams dreamt by patients were often coloured by the theories of their analysts; Freud called them "obliging dreams.")

Again we have the reversal of cause and effect, past and future; but here it is all the more critical and decisive because psychoanalysis is a theory of human behavior that hinges on the assumption of a linear causality, in which the past determines the present. And Popper points to the significance of this reversal by explicating further:

For a time I thought that the existence of the Oedipus effect distinguished the social from the natural sciences. But in biology too—even in molecular biology—expectations often play a role in bringing about what has been expected.

Similar quotations, referring to the effect of such "unscientific" factors as simple expectations and assumptions in the sciences, could be collated in abundance—[*The Invented Reality*] is itself intended as such a contribution. In this connection one might recall, for instance, Einstein's remark in a talk with Heisenberg: "It is the theory that determines what we can observe." And in 1958 Heisenberg himself says, "We have to remember that what we observe is not nature in itself, but nature exposed to our method of questioning." And more radical still, the philosopher of science Feyerabend (1978): "Not conservative, but anticipatory suppositions guide research."

Some of the most carefully documented and elegant investigations of self-fulfilling prophecies in the area of human communication are associated with the name of the psychologist Robert Rosenthal of Harvard University. Of particular interest here is his (1968) book with the appropriate title *Pygmalion in the Classroom,* in which he describes the results of his so-called Oak School experiments. They concerned a primary school with 18 women teachers and over 650 students [see Reading 38]. The self-fulfilling prophecy was induced in the members of the faculty at the beginning of a certain school year by giving the students an intelligence test whereby the teachers were told that the test could not only determine intelligence quotients, but could also identify those 20% of the students who would make rapid and above-average intellectual progress in the coming school year. After the intelligence test had been administered, but before the teachers had met their new students for the first time, they received the names (indiscriminately picked from the student list) of those students who supposedly, on the basis of the test, could be expected with certainty to perform unusually well. The difference between these children and the others thus existed solely in the heads of their particular teacher. The same intelligence test was repeated at the end of the school year for all students and showed *real* above-average increases in the intelligence quotients and achievements of these "special" students, and the reports of the faculty proved furthermore that these children distinguished themselves from their fellow students by their behavior, intellectual curiosity, friendliness, and so on.

Saint Augustine thanked God that he was not responsible for his dreams. Nowadays we do not have this comfort. Rosenthal's experiment is only one, although an especially clear example of how deeply and incisively our fellow human beings are affected by our expectations, prejudices, superstitions, and wishful thinking—all purely mental constructions, often without the slightest glimmer of actuality—and how these discoveries erode our comfortable conviction of the surpassing importance of heredity and innate characteristics. For it hardly needs to be expressly emphasized that these constructions can have negative as well as positive effects. We are not only responsible for our dreams, but also for the reality created by our hopes and thoughts.

It would, however, be a mistake to assume that self-fulfilling prophecies are restricted to human beings. Their effects reach deeper, into prehuman stages of development, and are in this sense even more alarming. Even before Rosenthal carried out his Oak School experiment, he reported in a book published in 1966 a similar experiment with rats that was repeated and confirmed by many scholars in the following years. Twelve participants in a laboratory course in experimental psychology were given a lecture on certain studies that purported to prove that good or bad test achievements of rats (for instance, in learning experiments in labyrinth cages) can become innate by selective breeding. Six of the students then received thirty rats whose genetic constitution allegedly made them especially good, intelligent laboratory subjects, while the other six students were assigned thirty rats of whom they were told the opposite, namely, that they were animals whose hereditary factors made them unsuitable for experiments. In fact and truth, the sixty rats were all of the same kind, the one that has always been used for such purposes. All sixty animals were then trained for exactly the same learning experiment. The rats whose trainers believed them to be especially intelligent did not just do better from the very outset, but raised their achievements far above that of the "unintelligent" animals. At the end of the five-day experiment the trainers were asked to evaluate their animals subjectively, in addition to the noted results of the experiments. The students who "knew" that they were working with unintelligent animals expressed themselves accordingly, that is, negatively, in their reports, whereas their colleagues, who had experimented with rats of supposedly above—average talents, rated their charges as friendly, intelligent, ingenious, and the like, and mentioned furthermore that they had often touched the animals, petted them, and even played with them. When we consider the surpassing role rat experiments play in experimental psychology and especially in the psychology of learning, and how often inferences are drawn from them to human behavior, these inferences now seem somewhat questionable.

Rats are known to be very intelligent animals, and the students' reports suggest that in the way they handled their animals, they literally "handed" them their assumptions and expectations. But the results of another research project, reported in 1963 by the research team Cordaro and Ison, suggest that it is not only a matter of such direct influence. In this project the laboratory subjects were earthworms (planaria), who are of great interest for the student of evolution and of behavior alike, in that they are the most primitive form of life possessing the rudiments of a brain. The supposition therefore suggested itself that these worms were capable of training of the simplest kind, as, for instance, a change in direction (to the left or to the right) upon arriving at the crossbeam of a T-shaped groove arrangement. Experiments of this kind began in several American universities in the late fifties. As in the rat experiments, Cordaro and Ison caused the experimenters to believe that they were working with especially intelligent or especially incapable worms, and even here, at this primitive stage of development (which, moreover, left little room for emotional attachment), there grew from the conviction, once it was established, objectively discernible and statistically significant differences in the experimental behavior of the planaria.[3]

For the very reason that these experiments undermine our basic concepts, it is all too easy to shrug them off and return to the comfortable certainty of our accustomed routines. That, for instance, test psychologists ignore these extremely disturbing results and continue to test people and animals with unmitigated tenacity and scientific "objectivity" is only a small example of the determination with which we defend ourselves when our world view is being threatened. The fact that we are responsible to the world in its entirety and to a much higher degree than is dreamed of in our philosophy is for the present almost unthinkable; but it can penetrate our consciousness through a better understanding of the processes of human communication—a study that will encompass many disciplines that heretofore have been either considered as being quite independent of each other or not considered at all. Rosenhan's contribution [see Reading 39] illuminates the alarming possibility that at least some so-called mental illnesses are nothing but constructions, and that the psychiatric institutions actually contribute to the constructions of those realities that are supposed to be treated therein. The chronic problem that still plagues modern psychiatry is that we have only the vaguest and most general concepts for the definition of mental health, while for the diagnosis of abnormal behavior there exist catalogs perfected to the last detail. Freud, for instance, used the concept of the ability to love and work as a basic criterion for mature emotional normalcy (a definition that does not do justice to a Hitler, on the one hand, or to the proverbial eccentricities of men of genius, on the other). The other medical specialties work with definitions of pathology that refer to certain deviations from fairly well-known normal functions of the healthy organism. Quite irrationally, in psychiatry it is just the opposite. Here pathology is considered the known factor, whereas normalcy is seen as difficult to define, if it is definable at all. This opens the floodgates to self-fulfilling diagnoses. There is a great number of very definite patterns of behavior that in the terminology of psychiatry are so tightly associated with certain diagnostic categories (again I refer to Rosenhan) that they virtually function like Pavlovian buzzers, not only in the thinking of the psychiatrist but also in the family environment of the patient. An attempt to show how certain specific forms of behavior take on the meaning of pathological manifestations on the basis of their cultural and societal significance, and how these manifestations in turn become self-fulfilling prophecies, would go beyond the scope of this essay. Of the already quite extensive literature on this topic, *The Manufacture of Madness* by Thomas Szasz (1970) is particularly notable. Suffice it to say that an essential part of the self-fulfilling effect of psychiatric diagnoses is based on our unshakable conviction that everything that has a name must *therefore* actually exist. The materializations and actualizations of psychiatric diagnoses probably originate largely from this conviction.

"Magic" diagnoses, in the actual sense of the word, have of course been known for a very long time. In his classic paper "Voodoo Death," the American physiologist Walter Cannon (1942) described a number of mysterious, sudden, and scientifically difficult to explain deaths that followed curses, evil spells, or the breaking of moral taboos. A Brazilian Indian, cursed by a medicine man, is helpless against his own emotional response to this death sentence and dies within hours. A young African hunter unknowingly kills and eats an inviolably banned wild hen. When he discovers his crime, he is overcome with despair and dies within twenty-four hours. A medicine man in the Australian bush points a bone with magic properties at a man. Believing that nothing can save him, the man sinks into lethargy and prepares to die. He is saved only at the last moment, when other members of the tribe force the witch doctor to remove the spell.

Cannon became convinced that voodoo death exists as a phenomenon,

> characteristically noted among aborigines—among human beings so primitive, so superstitious, so ignorant, that they feel themselves bewildered strangers in a hostile world. Instead of knowledge, they have fertile and unrestricted imaginations which fill their environment with all manner of evil spirits capable of affecting their lives disastrously.

At the time when Cannon wrote these lines, hundreds of thousands of human beings who were neither superstitious nor ignorant had every reason to see themselves as bewildered victims of an unimaginably hostile world. From the haunted, shadowy world of the concentration camps Viktor Frankl (1959, pp. 74–75) reports a phenomenon that corresponds to voodoo death:

> The prisoner who had lost faith in the future—his future—was doomed. With his loss of belief in the future, he also lost his spiritual hold; he let himself decline and became subject to mental and physical decay. Usually this happened quite suddenly, in the form of a crisis, the symptoms of which were familiar to the experienced camp inmate. We all feared this moment—not for ourselves, which would have been pointless, but for our friends. Usually it began

with the prisoner refusing one morning to get dressed and wash or to go out on the parade grounds. No entreaties, no blows, no threats had any effect. He just lay there.

One of Frankl's fellow prisoners lost his will to live when his own prediction, seen in a dream, did not come true and thereby became a negative self-fulfillment. "I would like to tell you something, Doctor," he said to Frankl,

> I have had a strange dream. A voice told me that I could wish for something, that I should only say what I wanted to know, and all my questions would be answered. What do you think I asked? That I would like to know when the war would be over for me. You know what I mean, Doctor—for me! I wanted to know when we, when our camp, would be liberated and our sufferings come to an end.... Furtively he whispered to me, "March thirtieth."

But when the day of the prophesied liberation was near and the Allied forces were still far from the camp, things took a fateful turn for Frankl's fellow sufferer, the prisoner F.:

> On March twenty-ninth, F. suddenly became ill and ran a high temperature. On March thirtieth, the day his prophecy had told him that the war and suffering would be over for him, he became delirious and lost consciousness. On March thirty-first, he was dead. He had died of typhus.

As a physician, Frankl understood that his friend died because

> the expected liberation did not come and he was severely disappointed. This suddenly lowered his body's resistance against the latent typhus infection.

We admire human beings who face death calmly. Dying "decently," in a composed manner, without wrangling with the inevitable, was and is considered in most cultures an expression of wisdom and unusual maturity. All the more surprising and sobering therefore are the results of modern cancer research, which suggest that the mortality rate is higher in those patients who prepare themselves for death in a mature, serene way or who, like the concentration camp prisoner F., fall victim to a negative self-fulfilling prophecy. For those patients, however, who cling to life in a seemingly senseless, irrational, and immature way or who are convinced that they simply "cannot" or "must not" die because they have important work to do or family members to take care of, the prognosis is considerably more favorable. To the American oncologist Carl Simonton (1975), whose name is associated, above all, with the appreciation of the impact of emotional factors, now more and more recognized for their importance in the treatment of cancer, three things are of the utmost significance in this connection: the belief system of the patient, that of the patient's family, and, third, that of the attending physician. That each one of these belief systems can become a self-fulfilling prophecy seems credible in the light of what we have discussed so far. Furthermore, the studies and research reports about the susceptibility of the human immune system to mood swings, suggestions, and visual imagery (O. Simonton & S. Simonton, 1978; Solomon, 1969) are increasing.

How much can and should a physician tell his patients, not only about the gravity of their illnesses, but also about the dangers inherent in the treatment *itself*? At least in certain countries this question is becoming more and more rhetorical. The risk of getting hit with a malpractice suit because a patient has not been informed about his disease and its treatment down to the last technical detail causes many doctors in the United States, for example, to protect themselves in a way that can have serious consequences. The protection consists in asking the patient for a written consent to treatment in which the most catastrophic possible consequences of the illness and of the measures deemed necessary by the doctor are listed in every detail. It is not hard to imagine that this creates a kind of self-fulfilling prophecy that has a paralyzing effect on the confidence and will to recover of even the most sanguine patient. Who has not read the description of even a seemingly harmless medication and then had the feeling of swallowing poison? How does the layman (or, presumably, even the professional) know that he is not going to be the fourth of the three fatalities reported to date that were inexplicably caused by a medication so far used safely by millions? But *fiat justitia, pereat mundus.*[4]

Since in the patient's eye a doctor is a kind of mediator between life and death, his utterances can easily become self-fulfilling prophecies. The astonishing degree to which this is possible is portrayed in a case reported (but unfortunately not sufficiently documented) by the American psychologist Gordon Allport (1964). What is unusual here is that a misunderstanding shifted the prophecy from death to life:

> In a provincial Austrian hospital, a man lay gravely ill—in fact, at death's door. The medical staff had told him frankly that they could not diagnose his disease, but that if they knew the diagnosis they could probably cure him. They told him further that a famous diagnostician was soon to visit the hospital and that perhaps he could spot the trouble.
>
> Within a few days the diagnostician arrived and proceeded to make the rounds. Coming to this man's bed, he merely glanced at the patient, murmured, "Moribundus," and went on.
>
> Some years later, the patient called on the diagnostician and said, "I've been wanting to thank you for your diagnosis. They told me that if you could diagnose me I'd get well, and so the minute you said 'moribundus' I knew I'd recover."

Knowledge of the healing effect of positive predictions is undoubtedly just as ancient as faith in the inescapable consequences of curses and evil spells. Modern use of positive suggestions and autosuggestions ranges from the "I will recover;

I feel better every day" of Emile Coué, through numerous forms of hypnotherapeutic interventions (Haley, 1973), to influencing the course of an illness—and not only cancer—by positive imagery. The extent to which such imagery that a (future) event has already taken place can reach into the physical realm is suggested by several studies according to which it is possible to increase a woman's chest measurement by an average of four to five centimeters through the use of certain self-hypnotic techniques (Staib & Logan, 1977; Willard, 1977). I mention these "successes" with all due skepticism and simply as curiosities testifying to the towering importance of the female breast in the North American erotic ethos.

Brief mention should also be made of the modern physiological and endocrinological studies that indicate more and more the possibility of stimulating the functions of the immune system of the human organism by certain experiences and that these functions are by no means completely autonomous (that is, outside conscious control), as was assumed until quite recently. Medical research is likely to make astonishing discoveries in this field in the near future. For instance, it is now known that the organism itself produces a number of morphene-like substances—the so-called endorphins (Beers, 1979)—that are analgesic and whose production is stimulated by certain emotional processes. There is thus a wide-open, unexplored territory in which the phenomenon of self-fulfilling prophecies begins to achieve scientific respectability.

Just as decisive as a doctor's suggestive comments, expectations, and convictions are the measures he takes and the remedies he administers. Of special interest here are *placebos*[5] (Benson & Epstein, 1975), those chemically inert substances that resemble certain medicines in shape, taste, or color but which have no pharmaceutical effect. We must remember that until about 100 years ago nearly all medications were practically ineffective in the modern sense. They were only slightly more elegant tinctures and powders than the ground toads, the lizard blood, the "sacred oils," or the pulverized horn of the rhinoceros of even earlier times. During my childhood, people in the rural areas of Austria still believed that a necklace of garlic would protect them from the common cold, to say nothing about the well-known success of magic in the treatment of warts. Even in our time, old "tried and true" remedies or sensational new discoveries (as, for example, Laetrile) are always being unmasked as pharmaceutically ineffective. But that is not to say that they were or are *functionally* ineffective. "One should treat as many patients as possible with the new remedies, as long as these are still working," reads the maxim of a famous physician, attributed to Trousseau, Osler, or Sydenham. Scientific interest in placebos is rapidly increasing. In his contribution to the history of the placebo effect Shapiro (1960) points out that more articles on this topic were published in scientific journals between 1954 and 1957 alone than in the first fifty years of the twentieth century. Most of these reports discuss traditional pharmaceutical effectiveness studies, in which one group of patients receives the new medication while another takes a placebo. The purpose of this well-meaning procedure is to find out whether the course of the illness of the "actually" treated patients is different from that of the placebo group. Only people whose world view is based on classical linear causal thinking (for which there is only an "objective" relationship between cause and effect) react with consternation when they realize that the patients "treated" with placebos often show a quite "inexplicable" improvement in their condition. In other words, the claim of the doctor who administers the placebo that it is an effective, newly developed medicine and the patient's willingness to believe in its effectiveness create a reality in which the assumption actually becomes a fact.

Enough examples. Self-fulfilling prophecies are phenomena that not only shake up our personal conception of reality, but which can also throw doubt on the world view of science. They all share the obviously reality-creating power of a firm belief in the "suchness" of things, a faith that can be a superstition as well as a seemingly strictly scientific theory derived from objective observation. Until recently it has been possible to categorically reject self-fulfilling prophecies as unscientific or to ascribe them to the inadequate reality adaptation of muddleheaded thinkers and romanticists, but we no longer have this convenient escape hatch open to us.

What all this means cannot yet be appraised with any certainty. The discovery that we create our own realities is comparable to the expulsion from the paradise of the presumed suchness of the world, a world in which we can certainly suffer, but for which we need only feel responsible in a very limited way (Watzlawick, 1976).

And here lies the danger. The insights of constructivism may have the highly desirable advantage of allowing for new and more effective forms of therapy (Watzlawick, 1978), but like all remedies, they can also be abused. Advertising and propaganda are two especially repugnant examples: Both try quite deliberately to bring about attitudes, assumptions, prejudices, and the like, whose realization then seems to follow naturally and logically. Thanks to this brainwashing, the world is then seen as "thus" and therefore is "thus." In the novel *1984* (Orwell, 1949) this reality-creating propaganda language is called *Newspeak,* and Orwell explains that it "makes all other modes of thinking impossible." In a recent review of a volume of essays published in London on censorship in the People's Republic of Poland (Strzyzewski, 1977–1978), Daniel Weiss (1980) writes about this magic language:

> Compare for example the great number of adjectives, characteristic for Newspeak: Every development is nothing less than "dynamic," every plenary session of the party "historic," the masses always

"proletarian workers." A sober communication scientist will find nothing but *redundance* in this inflation of mechanized epithets, drained of meaning. But after listening repeatedly, this automation is felt to have the equality of an incantation: The spoken word is no longer used to carry information, it has become the instrument of magic. (p. 66)

And finally the world simply *is thus.* How it was *made* to be this way was well known to Joseph Goebbels (1933/1976), when he lectured the managers of German radio stations on March 25, 1933:

> This is the secret of propaganda: To totally saturate the person, whom the propaganda wants to lay hold of, with the ideas of the propaganda, without him even noticing that he is being saturated. Propaganda has of course a purpose, but this purpose must be disguised with such shrewdness and virtuosity that he who is supposed to be filled with this purpose never even knows what is happening. (p. 120)

In the necessity of disguising the purpose, however, lies the possibility of overcoming it. As we have seen, the invented reality will become "actual" reality only if the invention is believed. Where the element of faith, of blind conviction, is absent, there will be no effect. With the better understanding of self-fulfilling prophecies our ability to transcend them grows. A prophecy that we know to be only a prophecy can no longer fulfill itself. The possibility of choosing differently (of being a heretic) and of disobeying always exists; whether we see it and act on it is, of course, another question. An insight from the seemingly far-removed domain of the mathematical theory of games is of interest here. Wittgenstein (1956) already pointed out in his *Remarks on the Foundations of Mathematics* that certain games can be won with a simple trick. As soon as someone calls our attention to the existence of this trick, we no longer have to continue playing naively (and continue losing). Building on these reflections, the mathematician Howard (1967) formulated his *existential axiom* which maintains that "if a person becomes 'aware' of a theory concerning his behavior, he is no longer bound by it but is free to disobey it" (p. 167). Elsewhere he also says that

> a conscious decision maker can always choose to disobey any theory predicting his behavior. We may say that he can always "transcend" such a theory. This indeed seems realistic. We suggest that among socio-economic theories, Marxian theory, for example, failed at least partly because certain ruling class members, when they became aware of the theory, saw that it was in their interest to disobey it. (1971)

And almost a hundred years before Howard, Dostoevski's underground man writes in his *Letters from the Underworld* (1913),

> As a matter of fact, if ever there shall be discovered a formula which shall exactly express our wills and whims; if ever there shall be discovered a formula which shall make it absolutely clear what those wills depend upon, and what laws they are governed by, and what means of diffusion they possess, and what tendencies they follow under given circumstances; if ever there shall be discovered a formula which shall be mathematical in its precision, well, gentlemen, whenever such a formula shall be found, man will have ceased to have a will of his own—he will have ceased even to exist. Who would care to exercise his willpower according to a table of logarithms? In such a case man would become, not a human being at all, but an organ-handle, or something of the kind. (p. 32)

But even if this kind of mathematical formulization of our lives could ever be achieved, it would in no way comprehend the complexity of our existence. The best theory is powerless in the face of an antitheory; the fulfillment of even the truest prophecy can be thwarted if we know about it beforehand. Dostoevski (1913) saw much more in the nature of man:

Moreover, even if man *were* the keyboard of a piano, and could be convinced that the laws of nature and of mathematics had made him so, he would still decline to change. On the contrary, he would once more, out of sheer ingratitude, attempt the perpetration of something which would enable him to insist upon himself. . . . But if you were to tell me that all this could be set down in tables—I mean the chaos, and the confusion, and the curses, and all the rest of it—so that the possibility of computing everything might remain, and reason continue to rule the roost—well, in that case, I believe, man would *purposely* become a lunatic, in order to become devoid of reason, and therefore able to insist upon himself. I believe this, and I am ready to vouch for this, simply for the reason that every human act arises out of the circumstance that man is forever striving to prove to his own satisfaction that he is a man and not an organ-handle. (p. 37)

However, even the evidence of the underground man is likely to be a self-fulfilling prophecy.

Notes

1. The following untrue story is a further illustration: In 1974, Secretary of State Kissinger, who is on one of his innumerable mediating missions in Jerusalem, is on his way back to the hotel after a private, late-evening stroll. A young Israeli stops him, introduces himself as an economist out of work, and asks Kissinger to help him find a job through his numerous connections. Kissinger is favorably impressed by the applicant and asks him whether he would like to be the vice-president of the Bank of Israel. The young man thinks of course that Kissinger is making fun of him, but the latter promises quite seriously that he will manage the matter for him. Next day Kissinger calls Baron Rothschild in Paris: "I have a charming young man here, a political economist, talented, going to be the next vice-president of the Bank of Israel. You have to meet him; he would be a jewel of a husband for your daughter." Rothschild growls something that does not sound like total rejection, whereupon Kissinger immediately calls the

president of the Bank of Israel: "I have a young financial expert here, brilliant fellow, exactly the stuff to make a vice-president for your bank, and most of all—imagine *that*—he is the future son-in-law of Baron Rothschild's."

2. *Editor's note:* Italian for "If it's not true, it is well written."

3. Here I will briefly mention an interesting sequel to these experiments: For reasons irrelevant to our topic, several researchers (McConnell, Jacobson, & Humphries, 1961) studied the fascinating theory that at the planaria's primitive stage of development information stored in a worm's ribonucleic acid (RNA) could possibly be directly transferred to other worms. For this purpose they fed untrained animals their already successfully trained fellow worms. Even we laymen can imagine the sensation among experts when the training of the worms provided with such food actually turned out to be much easier and faster. The euphoria lasted for a short while until the experiments, repeated under more rigorous controls, showed themselves to be inconclusive, and serious doubts arose concerning the transferability of intelligence through ground meat. The suspicion suggests itself, but was, as far as I know, never proven, that the original results were due to self-fulfilling prophecies, similar to those whose effects on the worms were already known. (The analogy, however, to the superstition of certain African tribes that eating a lion's heart will confer the lion's courage cannot be dismissed out of hand.)

4. *Editor's note:* Latin for "Let justice be done though the world perish."

5. Latin for "I shall please."

REFERENCES

Allport, G. W. (1964). Mental health: A generic attitude. *Journal of Religion and Health, 4,* 7–21.

Beers, R. F. (Ed.). (1979). *Mechanisms of pain and analgesic compounds.* New York: Raven.

Benson, H., & Epstein, M. D. (1975). The placebo effect: A neglected asset in the care of patients. *American Medical Association Journal, 232,* 1225–1227.

Cannon, W. B. (1942). Voodoo death. *American Anthropologist, 44,* 169–181.

Cordaro, L., & Ison, J. R. (1963). Observer bias in classical conditioning of the planaria. *Psychological Reports, 13,* 787–789.

Dostoevski, F. M. (1913). *Letters from the underworld.* New York: Dutton.

Feyerabend, P. K. (1978). *Science in a free society.* London: New Left.

Frankl, V. E. (1959). *From death camp to existentialism.* Boston: Beacon.

Goebbels, J. Quoted in Schneider, W. (1976). *Wörter machen leute. Magie und macht der sprache.* Munich: Piper.

Haley, J. (1973). *Uncommon therapy: The psychiatric techniques of Milton H. Erickson, M.D.* New York: Norton.

Heisenberg, W. (1958). *Physics and philosophy: The revolution in modern science.* New York: Harper & Row.

Howard, N. (1967). The theory of metagames. *General Systems, 2,* 167.

Howard, N. (1971). *Paradoxes of rationality, theory of metagames and political behavior.* Cambridge: MIT Press.

Jones, R. A. (1974). *Self-fulfilling prophecies: Social, psychological and physiological effects of expectancies.* New York: Halsted.

McConnell, J. V., Jacobson, R., & Humphries, B. M. (1961). The effects of ingestion of conditioned planaria on the response level of naive planaria: A pilot study. *Worm Runner's Digest, 3,* 41–45.

Orwell, G. (1949). *1984.* New York: Harcourt, Brace.

Popper, K. R. (1974). *Unended quest.* La Salle, IL: Open Court.

Rosenthal, R. (1966). *Experimenter effects in behavioral research.* New York: Appleton-Century-Crofts.

Rosenthal, R., & Jacobson, L. (1968). *Pygmalion in the classroom: Teacher expectation and pupils' intellectual development.* New York: Holt, Rinehart & Winston.

Shapiro, A. K. (1960). A contribution to a history of the placebo effects. *Behavioral Science, 5,* 109–135.

Simonton, O. C., & Simonton, S. (1975). Belief systems and management of the emotional aspects of malignancy. *Journal of Transpersonal Psychology, 1,* 29–47.

Simonton, O. C., & Simonton, S. (1978). *Getting well again.* Los Angeles: J. P. Tarcher.

Solomon, G. F. (1969). Emotions, stress, the nervous system, and immunity. *Annals of the New York Academy of Sciences, 164,* 335–343.

Staib, A. R., & Logan, D. R. (1977). Hypnotic stimulation of breast growth. *American Journal of Clinical Hypnosis, 19,* 201–208.

Strzyzewski, T. (1977–1978). *Czarna ksiega cenzury PRL* (Black Book of Polish Censorship, 2 vols.). London: "Aneks."

Szasz, T. S. (1970). *The manufacture of madness: A comparative study of the Inquisition and the mental health movement.* New York: Harper & Row.

Watzlawick, P. (1976). *How real is real?* New York: Random House.

Watzlawick, P. (1978). *The language of change: Elements of therapeutic communication.* New York: Basic Books.

Watzlawick, P., Bavelas, J. B., & Jackson, D. D. (1967). *Pragmatics of human communication: A study of interactional patterns, pathologies and paradoxes.* New York: Norton.

Weiss, D. (1980). Sprache und propaganda—Der sonderfall Polen. *Neue Zürcher Zeitung, 39,* 66.

Willard, R. R. (1977). Breast enlargement through visual imagery and hypnosis. *American Journal of Clinical Hypnosis, 19,* 195–200.

Wittgenstein, L. (1956). *Remarks on the foundations of mathematics.* Oxford, UK: Blackwell.

SELF-FULFILLING PROPHECIES

33

When Belief Creates Reality: The Self-Fulfilling Impact of First Impressions on Social Interaction

Mark Snyder

(1977)

For the social psychologist, there may be no processes more complex and intriguing than those by which strangers become friends. How do we form first impressions of those we encounter in our lives? How do we become acquainted with each other? When does an acquaintance become a friend? Why do some relationships develop and withstand the test of time and other equally promising relationships flounder and fall by the wayside? It is to these and similar concerns that my colleagues and I have addressed ourselves in our attempts to chart the unfolding dynamics of social interaction and interpersonal relationships. In doing so, we chose—not surprisingly—to begin at the beginning. Specifically, we have been studying the ways in which first impressions channel and influence subsequent social interaction and acquaintance processes.

AUTHOR'S NOTE: This research was supported in part by National Science Foundation Grant SOC 75–13872, "Cognition and Behavior: When Belief Creates Reality," to Mark Snyder. For a more detailed description of the background and rationale, procedures and results, implications and consequences of this investigation, see M. Snyder, E. D. Tanke, & E. Berscheid, Social perception and interpersonal behavior: On the self-fulfilling nature of social stereotypes. *Journal of Personality and Social Psychology,* 1977. For related research on behavioral confirmation in social interaction, see M. Snyder & W. B. Swann, Jr., Behavioral confirmation in social interaction: From social perception to social reality. *Journal of Experimental Social Psychology,* 1978.

When we first meet others, we cannot help but notice certain highly visible and distinctive characteristics such as their sex, age, race, and bodily appearance. Try as we may to avoid it, our first impressions are often molded and influenced by these pieces of information. Consider the case of physical attractiveness. A widely held stereotype in this culture suggests that attractive people are assumed to possess more socially desirable personalities and are expected to lead better personal, social, and occupational lives than their unattractive counterparts. For example, Dion, Berscheid, and Walster (1972) had men and women judge photographs of either men or women who varied in physical attractiveness. Attractive stimulus persons of either sex were perceived to have virtually every character trait that pretesting had indicated was socially desirable to that participant population: "Physically attractive people, for example, were perceived to be more sexually warm and responsive, sensitive, kind, interesting, strong, poised, modest, sociable, and outgoing than persons of lesser physical attractiveness" (Berscheid & Walster, 1974, p. 169). This powerful stereotype was found for male and female judges and for male and female stimulus persons. In addition, attractive people were predicted to have happier social, professional, and personal lives in store for them than were their less attractive counterparts. (For an excellent and comprehensive review, see Berscheid & Walster, 1974.)

What of the validity of the physical attractiveness stereotype? Are the physically attractive actually more likeable, friendly, sensitive, and confident than the unattractive? Are they more successful socially and professionally? Clearly, the physically attractive are more often and more eagerly sought out for social dates. And well they should be, for the stereotype implies that they should be perceived as more desirable social partners than the physically unattractive. Thus, it should come as little surprise that, among young adults, the physically attractive have more friends of the other sex, engage in more sexual activity, report themselves in love more often, and express less anxiety about dating than unattractive individuals do. But the effect is even more general than this. Even as early as nursery school age, physical attractiveness appears to channel social interaction: The physically attractive are chosen and the unattractive are rejected in sociometric choices.

A differential amount of interaction with the attractive and unattractive clearly helps the stereotype persevere because it limits the chances for learning whether the two types of individuals differ in the traits associated with the stereotype. But the point I wish to focus on here is that the stereotype may also channel interaction so as to confirm itself *behaviorally*. Individuals appear to have different patterns and styles of interaction for those whom they perceive to be physically attractive and for those whom they consider unattractive. These differences in self-presentation and interaction style may, in turn, elicit and nurture behaviors from the target person that are in accord with the stereotype. That is, the physically attractive may actually come to behave in a friendly, likeable, sociable manner, not because they necessarily possess these dispositions, but because the behavior of others elicits and maintains behaviors taken to be manifestations of such traits.

In our empirical research, we have attempted to demonstrate that stereotypes may create their own social reality by channeling social interaction in ways that cause the stereotyped individual to behave in ways that confirm another person's stereotyped impressions of him or her. In our initial investigation, Elizabeth Decker Tanke, Ellen Berscheid, and I sought to demonstrate the self-fulfilling nature of the physical attractiveness stereotype in a social interaction context designed to mirror as faithfully as possible the spontaneous generation of first impressions in everyday social interaction and the subsequent channeling influences of these impressions on social interaction. In order to do so, pairs of previously unacquainted individuals (designated for our purposes as a *perceiver* and a *target*) interacted in a getting-acquainted situation constructed to allow us to control the information that one member of the dyad (the male perceiver) received about the physical attractiveness of the other individual (the female target). In this way, it was possible to evaluate separately the effects of actual and perceived physical attractiveness on the display of self-presentational and expressive behaviors associated with the stereotype that links beauty and goodness. In order to measure the extent to which the self-presentation of the target individual matched the perceiver's stereotype, naïve observer-judges who were unaware of the actual or perceived physical attractiveness of either participant listened to and evaluated tape recordings of the interaction.

Fifty-one male and fifty-one female undergraduates at the University of Minnesota participated, for extra course credit, in what had been described as a study of the "processes by which people become acquainted with each other." These individuals interacted in male-female dyads in a getting-acquainted situation in which they could hear but not see each other (a telephone conversation). Before initiating the conversation, the male member of each dyad received a Polaroid snapshot of his female interaction partner. These photographs, which had been prepared in advance and assigned at random to dyads, identified the target as either physically attractive (attractive-target condition) or physically unattractive (unattractive-target condition). Each dyad engaged in a ten-minute unstructured telephone conversation that was tape-recorded. Each participant's voice was recorded on a separate channel of the tape.

In order to assess the extent to which the actions of the female targets provided behavioral confirmation of the male perceivers' stereotypes, twelve observer-judges listened to the tape recordings of the getting-acquainted conversations. The observer-judges were unaware of the experimental hypotheses and knew nothing of the

actual or perceived physical attractiveness of the individual whom they heard on the tapes. They heard only those tape tracks containing the female participants' voices. Nine other observer-judges listened to and rated only the male perceivers' voices. (For further details of the experimental procedures, see Snyder, Tanke, & Berscheid, 1977.)

In order to chart the process of behavioral confirmation of stereotype-based attributions in these dyadic social interactions, we examined the effects of our manipulation of the target's apparent physical attractiveness on both the male perceivers' initial impressions of their female targets and the females' behavioral self-presentation during their interactions, as measured by the observer-judges' ratings of the tape recordings of their voices.

The male perceivers clearly formed their initial impressions of their female targets on the basis of general stereotypes that associate physical attractiveness with socially desirable personality characteristics. On the basis of measures of first impressions that were collected after the perceivers had been given access to their partners' photographs but before the initiation of the getting-acquainted conversations, it was clear that (as dictated by the physical attractiveness stereotype) males who anticipated physically attractive partners expected to interact with comparatively cordial, poised, humorous, and socially adept individuals. By contrast, males faced with the prospect of getting acquainted with relatively unattractive partners fashioned images of rather withdrawn, awkward, serious, and socially inept creatures.

Not only did our perceivers fashion their images of their discussion partners on the basis of their stereotyped intuitions about the links between beauty and goodness of character, but the stereotype-based attributions initiated a chain of events that resulted in the behavioral confirmation of these initially erroneous inferences. Analysis of the observer-judges' ratings of the tape recordings of the conversations indicated that female targets who (unbeknown to them) were perceived to be physically attractive (as a consequence of random assignment to the attractive-target experimental condition) actually came to behave in a friendly, likeable, and sociable manner. This behavioral confirmation was discernible even by outside observer-judges who knew nothing of the actual or perceived physical attractiveness of the target individuals. In this demonstration of behavioral confirmation in social interaction, the "beautiful" people became "good" people, not because they necessarily possessed the socially valued dispositions that had been attributed to them, but because the actions of the perceivers, which were based on their stereotyped beliefs, had erroneously confirmed and validated these attributions.

Confident in our demonstration of the self-fulfilling nature of this particular social stereotype, we then attempted to chart the process of behavioral confirmation. Specifically, we searched for evidence of the behavioral implications of the perceivers' stereotypes. Did the male perceivers present themselves differently to the target women whom they assumed to be physically attractive or unattractive? An examination of the observer-judges' ratings of the tapes of only the males' contributions to the conversations provided clear evidence that our perceivers did have different interactional styles with targets of different physical attractiveness.

Men who interacted with women whom they believed to be physically attractive appeared to be more cordial, sexually warm, interesting, independent, sexually permissive, bold, outgoing, humorous, obvious, and socially adept than their counterparts in the unattractive-target condition. Moreover, these same men were seen by the judges to be more attractive, more confident, and more animated in their conversation than their counterparts. They were also considered by the observer-judges to be more comfortable in conversation, to

enjoy themselves more, to like their partners more, to take the initiative more often, to use their voices more effectively, to see their women partners as more attractive, and finally, to be seen as more attractive by their partners than men in the unattractive-target condition.

It appears, then, that differences in the expressive self-presentation of sociability by the male perceivers may have been a key factor in the process of bringing out those reciprocal patterns of expression in the target women that constitute behavioral confirmation of the attributions from which the perceivers' self-presentation had been generated. One reason that target women who had been labeled attractive may have reciprocated this sociable self-presentation is that they regarded their partners' images of them as more accurate and their style of interaction to be more typical of the way men generally treated them than women in the unattractive-target condition did. Perhaps, these latter individuals rejected their partners' treatment of them as unrepresentative and defensively adopted more cool and aloof postures to cope with their situations.

Our research points to the powerful but often unnoticed consequences of social stereotypes. In our demonstration, first impressions and expectations that were based on common cultural stereotypes about physical attractiveness channeled the unfolding dynamics of social interaction and acquaintance processes in ways that actually made those stereotyped first impressions come true. In our investigation, pairs of individuals got acquainted with each other in a situation that allowed us to control the information that one member of the dyad (the perceiver) received about the physical attractiveness of the other person (the target). Our perceivers . . . fashioned erroneous images of their specific partners that reflected their general stereotypes about physical attractiveness. Moreover, our perceivers had very different patterns and styles of interaction for those whom they perceived to be physically attractive and to be unattractive. These differences in self-presentation and interaction style, in turn, elicited and nurtured behaviors of the targets that were consistent with the perceived initial stereotypes. Targets who (unbeknown to them) were perceived to be physically attractive actually came to behave in a friendly, likeable, and sociable manner. The perceivers' attributions about their targets based on their stereotyped intuitions about the world had initiated a process that produced behavioral confirmation of those attributions. The initially erroneous impressions of the perceivers had become real. The stereotype had truly functioned as a self-fulfilling prophecy:

> The self-fulfilling prophecy is, in the beginning, a *false* definition of the situation evoking a new behavior which makes the originally false conception come *true*. The validity of the self-fulfilling prophecy perpetuates a reign of error. For the prophet will cite the actual course of events as proof that he was right from the very beginning. . . . Such are the perversities of social logic. (Merton 1948, p. 195)

True to Merton's script, our "prophets," in the beginning, created false definitions of their situations. That is, they erroneously labeled their targets as sociable or unsociable persons on the basis of their physical attractiveness. But these mistakes in first impressions quickly became self-erasing mistakes because the perceivers' false definitions evoked new behaviors that made their originally false conceptions come true: They treated their targets as sociable or unsociable persons, and, indeed, these targets came to behave in a sociable or unsociable fashion. Our prophets also cited the actual course of events as proof that they had been right all along. Might not other important and widespread social stereotypes—particularly those concerning

sex, race, social class, and ethnicity—also channel social interaction in ways that create their own social reality?

Any self-fulfilling influences of social stereotypes may have compelling and pervasive societal consequences. Social observers have for decades commented on and demonstrated the ways in which stigmatized social groups and outsiders may fall victim to self-fulfilling cultural stereotypes. Consider Scott's (1969) observations about the blind:

> When, for example, sighted people continually insist that a blind man is helpless because he is blind, their subsequent treatment of him may preclude his own exercising the kinds of skills that would enable him to be independent. It is in this sense that stereotypic beliefs are self-actualized. (p. 9)

All too often, it is the victims who are blamed for their own plight . . . rather than the social expectations that have constrained their behavioral options.

References

Berscheid, E., & Walster, E. (1974). Physical attractiveness. In L. Berkowitz (Ed.), *Advances in experimental social psychology* (Vol. 7). New York: Academic Press.

Dion, K. K., Berscheid, E., & Walster, E. (1972). What is good is beautiful. *Journal of Personality and Social Psychology, 24*, 285–290.

Merton, R. K. (1948). The self-fulfilling prophecy. *Antioch Review, 8*, 193–210.

Scott, R. A. (1969). *The making of blind men.* New York: Russell Sage.

Snyder, M., Tanke, E. D., & Berscheid, E. (1977). Social perception and interpersonal behavior: On the self-fulfilling nature of social stereotypes. *Journal of Personality and Social Psychology, 35*, 656–666.

THE SOCIAL PRODUCTION OF THE CULTURAL STATUS QUO

The material in the preceding sections implies that we are all participants in the construction and maintenance of everyday cultural realities. We learn systems of belief from our cultural groups, and we also learn strategies for maintaining these beliefs, even when experience seems contradictory. Through our interactions with one another, we perpetuate these belief systems and rarely subject them to careful scrutiny. Accordingly, we submit, often uncritically, to the ideas and practices that reinforce the cultural status quo. News media and the law are two cultural institutions charged with portraying and upholding social "truth." Yet, as the readings in this section illustrate, these cultural representatives may actually be providing us with information and practices that lock us even more tightly into culturally unexamined belief structures.

In "Consuming Terrorism," David Altheide chronicles the content and impact of the news media on the construction of an ideology of "terror" following the events of 9/11. According to Altheide's analysis, far from providing a critical examination of the events and the responses among various social agencies, the news media simply picked up on and perpetuated an "us versus them" ideology that reflected the status quo of the presidential administration and the media penchant for creating "consumers" out of their audience.

Sociologists Patricia Ewick and Susan Sibley explore a common social myth in "Common Knowledge and the Law: Do the 'Haves' Come Out Ahead?" Is it true, they wonder, that people with more resources do better in situations involving legal representatives? What they find is not the more common notion that people with money simply get better representation. Rather, the obscure and exclusive language of the law is intimidating to many people who might otherwise have valid claims. This intimidation has a self-fulfilling effect in limiting the experience people actually have with the law, which perpetuates the status quo belief that the law is beyond the grasp of most people, especially people without means.

READING QUESTIONS

1. How does the construction and consumption of "terror" described by Altheide reflect the "machineries of universe maintenance" discussed by Berger and Luckmann (see Reading 29)?
2. Explain why those with resources (the "haves") feel more comfortable in legal situations and are more effective when dealing with them.
3. Practice thinking about social institutions such as medicine, law, family, education, and religion from the perspective of an anthropologist from another culture. For instance, outsiders to modern Western cultures might consider Western medical practices, especially the reliance on pharmaceuticals, to be an intriguing form of magic. What kinds of public performances and interactional patterns maintain these cultural systems? What features of reality help to explain why the people of this culture tend to think that "our way is the only way"?
4. Make a list of social expectations that seem especially significant and taken for granted (for example, "everyone wants to get married," "everyone wants a good job," "everyone wants to own a home," "science provides true information"). Identify some of the social beliefs embedded in these expectations. Construct a detailed explanation for how these expectations are sustained through everyday interaction.

THE SOCIAL PRODUCTION OF THE CULTURAL STATUS QUO

34

Consuming Terrorism

David L. Altheide

(2004)

The attacks on the United States of America on September 11, 2001 (9/11), provide an opportunity to examine the role of political elites and popular culture in the social construction of a national identity grounded in consuming terrorism and the politics of fear. This article explores how the mass media contributed to changing the meaning of terrorism from a strategy or event to a condition of the world during the aftermath of 9/11. The word *terrorism* was so pervasive and so emotionally flavored that it was consumed and in turn became consuming.

The attacks created mayhem, but in the United States, the meaning of terrorism was provided by propaganda. Political elites and businesses transformed terrorism from an act into a condition and a worldview that would influence social life and become an account—particularly a justification—for adjustments to the social order (Scott and Lyman 1968). The tragic loss of lives and property fueled patriotic slogans, thousands of commercial advertisements, public contributions of more than $2 billion, major domestic and foreign policy changes, and the largest increase in the military budget in thirty-five years (Westphal 2001). Stores sold out of flags, businesses linked advertising to patriotic slogans (e.g., General Motors' "Keep America Rolling"), baseball fans sang "God Bless America" instead of "Take Me Out to the Ball Game," and children helped raise money for the Afghani kids who were "starving." Analysis of news reports and advertisements suggests that popular culture and mass media depictions of fear, patriotism, consumption, and victimization contributed to the emergence of a national identity and collective action that was fostered by elite decision makers' propaganda. Initial declarations about recovery and retaliation to promote patriotism became a "war on terrorism" that could justify altering U.S. foreign policy to embrace a "preemptive strike" on Iraq, violate treaties, and estrange allies.

Terrorism became a perspective, an orientation, and a discourse for "our time," the "way things are today," and "how the world has changed." According to Kellner (2003), the subsequent campaign to integrate fear into everyday life routines was consequential for public life, domestic policy, and foreign affairs.

The terrorism discourse was not limited to a specific situation but referred to a general worldview. Terrorism defined reality and became an incorrigible proposition that could not be questioned, challenged, or falsified and was "compatible with any and every conceivable state of affairs" (Mehan and Wood 1975:52). As a discourse, terrorism became an institutionalized disclaimer ("We all know how the world has changed . . ."), a term or phrase that documents a general (rather than a specific) situation and conveys a widely shared meaning (Hewitt and Stokes 1975).

The U.S. position extended well beyond the attacks and those who were responsible, to a redefinition of domestic and international order. As numerous citizens bought duct tape and plastic wrap to safeguard their homes from attacks, domestic life became oriented to celebrating or commemorating past terrorist acts, waiting for and anticipating the next one, and taking steps to prevent it.

Media coverage of 9/11 emphasized the commonality of the victims rather than the cause or rationale for the attacks. The popular refrain was that all Americans were victimized by the attacks, and like the "potential victims" of crime featured in a decade of news reports about the crime problem, all citizens should support efforts to attack the source of fear (Garland 2001). The cause, therefore, was simply the enemy's dislike of the United States of America, its freedom and lifestyle. Indeed, anyone who suggested that the "cause" of the attacks was more complex and that the United States had angered many political groups by previous actions (e.g., support for Israel) was denounced. Talk-show host Bill Maher, who argued that the terrorists were not really cowards, was among those pilloried and lost his job; Clear Channel, a radio consortium, published a list of one hundred fifty songs with critical themes (e.g., Simon and Garfunkel's "Bridge over Troubled Water") that should not be played (Kellner 2003:68).

The symbolic construction of terrorism transformed the 9/11 attacks into a worldview that was apparent in numerous news and public affairs messages. Virtually all explicit and implicit political statements, holiday messages, commercials and advertisements, economic projections, domestic issues, fiscal discussions, and even sporting events communicated the danger of terrorism and thereby increased its significance.

Propaganda of any event is tied to the historical and social context as well as basic structural arrangements (Jackall 1994). Propaganda thus reveals certain symbolic foundations for meaning and identity in social life. Crisis provides opportunities for heads of state to present themselves as leaders, to dramatically define the situation as tragic but hopeful, and to bring out the "resolve" of national character. The 9/11 attacks on the World Trade Center were shown repeatedly and became an icon of treachery, evil, and victimization.

The symbolic boundaries drawn by decades of war coverage on the Middle East (Adams 1981, 1982) had, essentially, been produced by the military-media complex, that is, the institutional linkage of military personnel, popular culture, and journalism regarding shared information and news sources, technology, and even careers (i.e., generals become "media consultants"; see Altheide 1999). The military-media complex is a feature of programming in an entertainment era dominated by popular culture and communication forms that share sophisticated information technologies promoting visual media and evocative content. Audiences' awareness of the potential meanings of 9/11 attacks were in part shaped by the background work of the military-media complex that produced the Gulf War (Altheide 1994; Gattone 1996; Kellner 1992). American audiences had become all too familiar with coalition formation, "surgical strikes," and bomb-site videos shown in briefings, news reports, movies, and commercials.

METHOD AND DATA

A qualitative content analysis was undertaken of news accounts; the extensive advertising campaign that followed the events of 9/11; and subsequent political, military, and social action. We began the preliminary collection and review of print and television reports immediately following the attacks, during a seminar project for a "Justice and the Mass Media" class in fall 2001. This exploratory project focused on news media reports pertaining to "charitable giving," "victims/ victimization," and "fear." Nine students examined a range of print and electronic news media, including Lexis-Nexis, as a way to become familiar with qualitative media analysis that is based on ethnographic content analysis (ECA). ECA refers to an integrated method, procedure, and technique for locating, identifying, retrieving, and analyzing documents for their relevance, significance, and meaning (Altheide 1987, 1996).

The three key themes that emerged from this analysis are examined below.

1. *Fear supports terrorism as a condition.*

Fear played an important role in the social construction of terrorism. The meaning of the attacks was framed in the context of previous domestic and international events and especially of well-established cultural narratives surrounding fear, justifying both it and the place of fear in the lives of many citizens. While most popular culture accounts of fear have been linked to crime, especially various drug wars, the 9/11 attacks offered an alternative enemy, terrorists. President Bush initially referred to the attackers as "those folks," then "evildoers." He referred to the hijackings as a "terrorist attack" and, later, an "act of war." The 9/11 attacks inspired political decision makers to generalize and promote simplistic definitions of the situation in the mass media about what happened; who was to blame; what should be done about it and who should do it; who should support such action; and, importantly, how life will change as a result of each of these definitions.

A history of numerous "crises" and fears involving crime, violence, and uncertainty was important for public definitions of the situation after 9/11. A major source of insecurity was a pervasive fear that was promoted in news reports, popular culture, and politicians' mantras about the "cure" for what ails America (Shapiro 1992). This mantra may be referred to as the discourse of fear, or the pervasive communication, symbolic

awareness, and expectation that danger and risk are a central feature of everyday life (Altheide 2002). Orientation to fear also involves an object of fear, which typically becomes some "other." Schwalbe et al. (2000) have shown that "othering" is part of a social process whereby a dominant group defines into existence an inferior group. This requires the establishment and "group sense" of symbolic boundaries of membership.

News media reports after 9/11 enabled elite decision makers to construct terrorism as the object of fear and to cast all Americans as victims. Citizens were asked to not only give blood and money, but to grant elites and formal agents of social control (FASC) all authority to deploy whatever measures they deemed necessary to protect citizens, take revenge, and prevent such a deed from reoccurring. The metaphor of "investment" covered a context of meaning that joined contributing to the "victims" of 9/11, buying products to "keep America rolling," and supporting military action and budget increases. These messages promoted a national identity (Shapiro 1992; Thiele 1993) based on the politics of fear that was later used by President Bush to pursue a "first strike" policy against those he deemed enemies of the United States. Indeed, some eleven months after the United States attacked Iraq in pursuit of "weapons of mass destruction" (WMD) that were not found, President Bush explained his actions:

> I'm a war president. I make decisions here in the Oval Office in foreign policy matters with war on my mind. . . . I believe it is essential that when we see a threat, we deal with those threats before they become imminent. It's too late if they become imminent. (NBC, *Meet the Press,* Feb. 8, 2004)

Fear and conflict can bring people together (Simmel 1964). U.S. leaders added to communalism and promoted like mindedness among U.S. citizens by insisting that terrorists could be anywhere and ratcheted up various security measures.

Americans were implored to seek not only retribution but also salvation from fear by supporting a series of draconian measures and were reminded daily of the "danger" by a color-coded fear alert created as part of the new office of "Homeland Security."

The threat level rose to "high," or orange, five times between March 2003 and March 2004. The atmosphere of alarm and fear was heightened as federal law enforcement officials warned that more attacks were likely. On October 12, 2001, the House of Representatives advanced "antiterrorist" legislation to grant broad surveillance and detention powers to the federal government. Soon thereafter, the United States Patriot Act passed by a vote of 337 to 79 with little debate, despite pleas from civil liberties advocates that the legislation could be a dangerous infringement on civil rights. Some members of Congress acknowledged that they had not read the legislation.

Criticism was limited as President Bush gained a 90 percent approval rating in opinion polls. There was little dissent about administration incursions into civil liberties and violations of due process, [even] when everyday-life routines were interrupted by color-coded "terrorism alerts." Authorities called for relaxing civil rights and [strengthening] detention regulations. Several thousand immigrants and some citizens were questioned and detained without due process. The social definition of impending attacks by terrorists among us was essentially unchallenged in public discourse, with the exception of some Internet traffic.

With a few exceptions, most criticism was directed against the detractors. Academics and others who raised concerns were targeted for their critical comments, even though these were not well publicized. One nonprofit group, the American Council of Trustees and Alumni (a founding member of which is Lynne Cheney, wife of [then-] Vice President Dick Cheney), posted a Web page accusing dozens of scholars, students, and a university president of unpatriotic behavior, of being "the weak link in America's response to the attack," and for invoking "tolerance and diversity as antidotes to evil" *(Arizona Republic,* Nov. 24, 2001, p. A11).

Mass media support of the emerging national identity was commensurate with moral character and a discourse of salvation—or "seeing the light" to guide our way through the new terrorism world. The "younger generation" was implored to meet the new challenge, as this was, after all, their war, and the mass media carried youthful testimonies of newfound loyalty and awakening that resembled those of a religious revival. For example, *Newsweek* published a statement by a young woman who "confessed" her naïveté about the "real world" and another by a former university student who criticized "antimilitary culture" with a call to arms:

> Before the attack, all I could think of was how to write a good rap—*I am not eager to say this,* but we do not live in an ideal world. . . . I've come to accept the idea of a focused war on terrorists as the best way to ensure our country's safety. (Newman 2001:9, emphasis added)

2. Consumption and giving were joined symbolically with terrorism.

Unlike reactions to previous "external attacks" such as Pearl Harbor, which stressed conservation, personal sacrifice, and commitment, a prevailing theme of consumption-as-character and financial contributions as commitment and support pervaded mass media messages surrounding the 9/11 attacks. Advertising and programming served to normalize the terrorist condition, and these messages equated giving and buying with patriotism and national unity (Espeland 2002). A nation's grief was directed to giving and spending dollars as cultural scripts of generosity and sympathy were processed through organizational entertainment formats emphasizing market participation and consumption (Kingston 2002).

Advertising and the market economy joined with giving and "selfless" assistance to others. Americans gave millions to charities to help the victims of 9/11. Businesses in the United States offered rebates and contributions to charities from individual purchases. The slumping U.S. economy was in a recession before 9/11, and it plummeted thereafter (Advertising Research Foundation [ARF] 2001). Fear of air travel topped public perceptions that more attacks might follow, and it seemed more prudent to stay close to home. Purchases of "big ticket" items such as automobiles and appliances dropped rapidly.

The U.S. advertising industry sprang into action (Jackall and Hirota 2000). For example, the Ad Council adopted a strong coalition stand against terrorism, noting in an online communication that "it was originally founded as the War Advertising Council during World War II in the aftermath of the bombings of Pearl Harbor." Following an "all advertising industry meeting," a strategy was adopted on September 18, 2001, to "inform, involve and inspire Americans to participate in activities that will help win the war on terrorism" (ARF 2001, cited in Shales 2001:G2).

Fear of crime and terrorism were joined through gun purchases. The gun industry and the National Rifle Association (NRA) urged fearful Americans to buy their slogans and products. Many Americans responded to the September attacks by arming themselves. As one reporter noted, "People may say, 'Let Tom Ridge watch out for our shores. I'll watch out for my doors'" (Baker 2001). Gun sales rose nationwide, from 9 to 22 percent, despite the concern of police officials that such a proliferation of guns would lead to higher levels of local violence (Baker 2001). Examples from advertisements illustrate the point: "Ithaca Gun Company is selling its Homeland Security model for our current time of national need—In every respect, these new Homeland Security Model shotguns are up to the demanding tasks which lay before us as a nation." The Beretta gun company promoted its "'United We Stand'—a nine-millimeter pistol bearing a laser-etched American flag. The company sold 2,000 of them to wholesalers in one day in October" (Baker 2001). Another gun manufacturer, Tromix, publicized a soon-to-be-released fifty-caliber rifle nicknamed the "Turban Chaser."

Organized campaigns by national organizations such as the Red Cross provided a symbolic way for all Americans to dramaturgically enact their collective identity as "caring." Millions of Americans participated in communal outpourings to reaffirm the nascent values of giving aid and membership. The Red Cross efforts reflect the widespread communalism spirit, although some money was donated in anger, as a type of "vengeful philanthropy"—giving not out of sympathy but out of anger—against the terrorists (Strom 2002).

The Red Cross funds supplemented the billions of dollars the federal Victim Compensation Fund established to reduce suits against airlines and other businesses. Special Master of the fund, Kenneth Feinberg, estimated that his "economic scale" of compensation that took into account occupation, age, and other assets would provide an average payment of nearly $1.8 million for each of the 2,884 persons who died in the attacks (Thomas 2001), with lesser amounts typically allotted to the 4,185 injury claims. However, there were grave problems associated with distributing these millions. Family members of those killed in the attacks were reluctant to accept money from the government's victim compensation fund, since doing so meant forfeiting their right to pursue additional claims in the future. In some cases, there were uncertainties about cultural differences in inheritance rights and disputes about compensation to foreigners (Chen 2002a, 2002b). Although only ten families completed compensation applications during the first six months of Feinberg's work (Chen 2002a:B1), most finally accepted the government's offer before the program ended (Chen 2004).

I suggest that victimization articulated the emergent symbolic construction of the "attack on America" as a feature of national identity that was linked to specific action and "membership" with entitlements (including vengeance against the "terrorists"), nurturing and control of the U.S. victims—all citizens—and entitlements to new definitions of sovereignty and human rights. Rationalizing the definitions of the true victims of 9/11 was commensurate with a sense of national unity to be forged through patriotism, giving, and vengeance. Commensuration was tied to rallying around the victims of the 9/11 attack. A catchall compensation plan for all Americans injured in various politically motivated attacks would not do. These victims would be special because they would become symbols of legitimacy for future acts.

Although some of these people were later deemed eligible, consider some of the disputes about the meaning of "terrorism victim" such as those who had been killed in the attacks on U.S. embassies in Africa in 1998. More contentious were claims by persons who were killed and injured in the Oklahoma City bombing by Timothy McVeigh and who were not included within the commensurate symbols of the fallen World Trade Center. They were merely dead Americans. As one retired foreign service officer, whose wife was killed in the August 7, 1998, bombing of the U.S. embassy in Nairobi put it, "We were the first victims of Al Qaeda." Yet he disagreed that the Oklahoma City bombing victims should be compensated: "Oklahoma City is completely different. McVeigh and Nichols were just home-grown malcontents. They were criminals. Where do you draw the line?" (quoted in Belkin 2002:92). This distinction between types of victims was quite consistent with interpretive schemes that would enable the president and others to claim that these were "special times," requiring "special acts." Such definitions, usually accompanied by visuals of the attacks, mementos from the "true victims," and icons of loss, were circulated extensively in the news media and in commercials.

3. *The absence of a clear target for reprisals contributed to the construction of broad symbolic enemies and goals referred to as "terrorism."*

The politics of fear was central to commensuration practices in forging a national identity. This was accomplished symbolically, by expanding the tragic events into an interpretive scheme that connected attacks with renewal, revenge, and deference to leaders who would attack the enemy and save us from other attacks. The communal reaction was informed by drawing on national experiences of fear, consumption, and the role of national leadership in molding a response that would also constitute and justify future actions and relationships among nations, state control, and citizens.

While media and military institutions familiarized audiences with coalitions against evil, the collective response to the terror attacks was framed as a communal patriotic experience that provided opportunities to "come together" and be "united" in a "coalition of war and humanitarianism" (Shapiro 2002). Numerous messages also appealed to a nostalgic past of U.S. moral and military dominance, authentic lifestyles, and traditional values (e.g., family, respect), as well as institutions of social control (e.g., police and fire departments, the military).

National symbols were renewed through the mournful language of victims and vengeful promises of future action by the military on our behalf. Leaders, with the aid of the mass media, repeatedly bolstered the idea that the moment of attack and tragedy was an opportunity for Americans to renew their commitments to freedom and the American way of life. As noted above, this could be demonstrated by giving; identifying with the "9/11 victims"; and becoming even more resolute in taking action to promote Americanism, avenge the deaths, and, above all, attack "evil" so that these events would never be repeated.

Patriotism was connected to an expansive fear of terrorism and enemies of the United States. The term *terrorism* was used to encompass an idea, a tactic or method, and ultimately a condition of the world. The waging of the "War on Terrorism" focused on the "idea" and "the method," depending on the context of discussion and justification. The very broad definition of terrorism served the central authorities' purposes while also justifying the action of others (e.g., Israel) in their own conflicts (Robin 2002). The mass media were key contributors to this process.

For students of propaganda, it is commonplace that the mass media are central propaganda instruments, not only in terms of content, but also in terms of the format and overall presentation and "look" (Altheide and Johnson 1980). With network and local nightly newscasts draped in the colors of the flag and anchors wearing flags on their lapels, reporting events primarily through the viewpoint of the United States ("us" and "we"), news organizations presented content and form that were interpreted by the publisher of *Harper's Magazine* as sending "signals to the viewers to some extent that the media are acting as an arm of the government, as opposed to an independent, objective purveyor of information, which is what we're supposed to be" (Rutenberg and Carter 2001).

Journalists' repetitive patriotic messages supported the national identity and the communal definition of "danger" and "victim" that were consistent with a terrorism world. Numerous news reports promoted more fear about potential terrorists and enemies of the United States. Because there were few specific targets as "nation-states," the focus narrowed on a key individual, Osama bin Laden, and his "terrorist network" of camps located in Afghanistan. However, commensurate with our avowed principle of not attacking innocent people, the U.S. government stressed that it was not at war with Afghanistan or Muslims but with terrorists and those who harbor them. Reminiscent of the Old West's "Wanted Dead or Alive" posters of criminals, Osama bin Laden provided the symbolic focus of attack that was lacking

even during the Cold War. All "terrorists" would have his face and symbolic identity. Thus, even though Afghanistan was attacked, the official target was global terrorism, whether it was connected to bin Laden or not.

THE EXPANDING DEFINITION OF TERRORISM

Many countries supported the proposition that terrorism is a condition. Numerous "internal" conflicts and revolutionary movements were quickly reclassified as instances of "terrorism," and any government that opposed them would, presumably, be joining the United States in its fight against global terrorism. Within a matter of days, states struggling against revolutionary movements within their borders, such as Colombia, Peru, and Israel, vowed to join the United States in its fight against terrorism (Bennett 2001). Placing virtually all "opposition" forces in the terrorist camp was consistent with the military-media script of pervasive fear and opposition. The serious opposition that disappeared with the end of the Cold War was reconstituted worldwide.

A military and defense budget was proposed that was commensurate with the communal fear of terrorism. While the Bush administration had long advocated more support for the military, 9/11 increased the urgency and the budget, and a military budget that dwarfed that of other nations grew even more over the next few weeks (Knickerbocker 2002). The House of Representatives passed a $383 billion defense budget on May 9, 2002, and the Senate passed (71–22) a $31.5 billion counterterrorism bill on June 6, 2002. This was $2 billion more than the measure approved in May by the House. This legislation reflected the mood of leaders who sought to be decisive and appear strong to their constituents who were receiving virtually no contextual or historical information about underlying issues that may have contributed to the attacks.

News reports reflected the mass media's use of routine "elite" news sources to get the story about the attacks and promote entertaining reports about America striking back. The widespread support for military expenditures and the public's tacit approval of civil liberty restrictions—including profiling of Arab Americans—reflected a fear-induced communalism surrounding terrorism. Communal compliance was preached and became widely practiced as fear of the future and the unknown pervaded news reports. Audiences consumed a symbolic bombardment of news that was forging a national identity commensurate with fear, a right to retaliate and attack present and future enemies, and support for restriction of civil liberties to protect us from our enemies.

CONCLUSION

This article has explored the ways shifting meanings of context are shaped by the massive social and cultural changes that have occurred in the United States since 9/11. A central tenet of symbolic interaction theory is that social power is the ability to define a situation (Blumer 1969; Couch 1984; Maines and Couch 1988; Mead and Morris 1962). Accordingly, this article suggests that powerful new definitions and meanings of context can be consequential if they are pervasive; constant; and, above all, not contradicted by systematic discussion and debate. The central argument I advance here is that mass media reports contributed to major changes in social definitions and meanings of a host of discrete events that were symbolically encapsulated as "9/11" and "terrorism."

The use of language and images positioned discrete acts in an extant discourse of fear associated with crime and victimization (especially potential victimization) that effectively transformed terrorism from an act or a strategy to a condition—a terrorism world. The use of language and the blending of symbols commensurate with a national identity contributed to consumption; giving; and compliant support for action against past, present, and future terrorists.

The article has also suggested that the dominant interpretation of 9/11 attacks was that the world was different and required new symbolic meanings—including accounts and disclaimers—social control practices; international relations; and, above all, a new rationale and perspective for a much different world, a terrorism world.

Finally, this article has argued that the context of previous symbolic meanings informs subsequent definitions that emerge about events and the discourses that seem applicable. While the terrorism world emerged from a drastic event, its meaning was constructed from crime myths, decades of distorted news reports and public information about foreign policy and the Middle East, news coverage of several popular wars such as Desert Storm, and an avalanche of commercial messages and self-promoting advertisements and "good deals," as well as an administration steeped in a commitment to transform the United States into a hegemon that would act unilaterally to maintain its position (Armstrong 2002).

Communalism and commensurability were joined reflexively through consumption as social participation as the advertisements and products articulated the terrorism world. On the one hand, media-generated symbolic constructions of victims and terrorism contributed to a "national experience" oriented to communal values and reaffirmation of cultural narratives. On the other hand, these powerful symbolic definitions supported open-ended commensurate increases in military and police authority while expanding governmental surveillance and diminishing civil liberties. American citizens came to accept reduced civil liberties because they believed the official claim that the world had changed.

A new foreign policy was born nine months after the attacks of 9/11 were skillfully implanted in a fertile womb of fear and victimization. Patriotic rituals and official pronouncements reshaped the nature of public debate and reoriented public opinion around the new threat of world terrorism. The circle was completed when advertising and public service announcements connected drug use with support of terrorism. Consistent with symbolic commensuration, attacking one was attacking the other. And we could do it together.

REFERENCES

Adams, William C. 1981. *Television Coverage of the Middle East.* Norwood, NJ: Ablex.

_____. 1982. *Television Coverage of International Affairs.* Norwood, NJ: Ablex.

Advertising Research Foundation (ARF). 2001. "The ARF Supports Ad Council Coalition Against Terrorism." http://www.arfsite.org.

Altheide, David L. 1987. "Ethnographic Content Analysis." *Qualitative Sociology* 10:65–77.

_____. 1994. "Postjournalism: Journalism Is Dead, Long Live Journalism." Pp. 134–70 in *Controlling Broadcasting: Access Policy and Practice in North America and Europe,* edited by Meryl and Nicholas Hewitt Aldridge. Manchester, UK: Manchester University Press.

_____. 1996. *Qualitative Media Analysis.* Newbury Park, CA: Sage.

_____. 1999. "The Military-Media Complex." *Newsletter of the Sociology of Culture* 13:1.

_____. 2000. "Identity and the Definition of the Situation in a Mass-Mediated Context." *Symbolic Interaction* 23:1–27.

_____. 2002. *Creating Fear: News and the Construction of Crisis.* Hawthorne, NY: Aldine de Gruyter.

Altheide, David L. and John M. Johnson. 1980. *Bureaucratic Propaganda.* Boston: Allyn & Bacon.

Altheide, David L. and Robert P. Snow. 1991. *Media Worlds in the Postjournalism Era.* Hawthorne, NY: Aldine de Gruyter.

Armstrong, David. 2002. "Dick Cheney's Song of America: Drafting a Plan for Global Dominance." *Harper's,* October 2002, pp. 76–83.

Baker, A. 2001. "A Nation Challenged: Personal Security; Steep Rise in Gun Sales Reflects Post-Attack Fears." *New York Times,* December 16, Metropolitan Desk, p. 1.

Belkin, Lisa. 2002. "Just Money." *New York Times,* December 8, p. 92.

Bennett, James. 2001. "Israel Wants Cease-Fire to Precede Truce Talks." *New York Times,* September 16, p. 1.

Chen, David W. 2002a. "Lure of Millions Fuels 9/11 Families' Feuding." *New York Times,* June 17, p. Al.

_____. 2002b. "Struggling to Sort Out 9/11 Aid to Foreigners." *New York Times,* June 27, p. A1.

_____. 2004. "Man Behind Sept. 11 Fund Describes Effort as a Success, With Reservations." *New York Times,* January 1, p. Bl.

Couch, Carl J. 1984. *Constructing Civilizations.* Greenwich, CT: JAI Press.

Espeland, Wendy Nelson. 2002. "Commensuration and Cognition." Pp. 63–88 in *Toward a Sociology of Culture and Cognition,* edited by K. A. Cerulo. New York: Routledge.

Garland, David. 2001. *The Culture of Control: Crime and Social Order in Contemporary Society.* Chicago: University of Chicago Press.

Gattone, Charles. 1996. "Media and Politics in the Information Age." *International Journal of Politics, Culture and Society* 10:193–202.

Hewitt, John P. and Randall Stokes. 1975. "Disclaimers." *American Sociological Review* 40:1–11.

Jackall, Robert, ed. 1994. *Propaganda.* New York: New York University Press.

Jackall, Robert and Janice M. Hirota. 2000. *Image Makers: Advertising, Public Relations, and the Ethos of Advocacy.* Chicago: University of Chicago Press.

Kellner, Douglas. 1992. *The Persian Gulf TV War.* Boulder, CO: Westview Press.

_____. 2003. *From 9/11 to Terror War: The Dangers of the Bush Legacy.* Lanham, MD: Rowman & Littlefield.

Kingston, Anne 2002. "You're a Goof. Buy our Beer: What the Canadian Ad Awards Reveal About Us." *Saturday Post* (Vancouver), April 20, p. 1.

Knickerbocker, Brad. 2002. "Return of the 'Military-Industrial Complex'?" *Christian Science Monitor,* February 13, p. 2.

Maines, David R. and Carl J. Couch. 1988. *Communication and Social Structure.* Springfield, IL: C. C. Thomas.

Mead, George Herbert and Charles W. Morris. 1962. *Mind, Self, and Society from the Standpoint of a Social Behaviorist.* Chicago: University of Chicago Press.

Mehan, Hugh and Houston Wood. 1975. *The Reality of Ethnomethodology.* New York: Wiley.

Newman, Rachel. 2001. "The Day the World Changed, I Did, Too." *Newsweek,* October 1, p. 9.

Robin, Corey. 2002. "Primal Fear." *Theory and Event* 5(4). http://muse.jhu.edu/journals/theory_and_event/summary/v005/5.4robin.html.

Rutenberg, Jim and Bill Carter. 2001. "Draping Newscasts With the Flag." *New York Times,* September 20, p. C8.

Schwalbe, Michael, Sandra Godwin, Daphne Holden, Douglas Schrock, Shealy Thompson, and Michele Wolkomir. 2000. "Generic Processes in the Reproduction of Inequality: An Interactionist Analysis." *Social Forces* 79:419–52.

Scott, Marvin and Stanford M. Lyman. 1968. "Accounts." *American Sociological Review* 33:46–62.

Shales, Tom. 2001. "Patriotism Advertising." *Washington Post,* December 30, p. 2.

Shapiro, Michael J. 1992. *Reading the Postmodern Polity: Political Theory as Textual Practice.* Minneapolis: University of Minnesota Press.

———. 2002. "Wanted, Dead or Alive." *Theory and Event* 5(4). http://muse.jhu.edu/login?uri=/journals/theory_and_event/v005/5.4shapiro.html.

Simmel, Georg. 1964. *Conflict.* New York: Free Press.

Strom, Stephanie. 2002. "Families Fret as Charities Hold a Billion Dollars in 9/11 Aid." *New York Times,* June 23, p. 29.

Thiele, Leslie Paul. 1993. "Making Democracy Safe for the World: Social Movements and Global Politics." *Alternatives* 18:273–305.

Thomas, Evan. 2001. "The Story of September 11." *MSNBC.com,* December 31.

Westphal, David. 2001. "Buildup Quickly Erasing Post–Cold War Peace Dividend; as the United Slates Mounts Its Campaign Against Terrorism, Defense Spending Will Increase Rapidly." *Star Tribune* (Minneapolis), October 8, p. A5.

THE SOCIAL PRODUCTION OF THE CULTURAL STATUS QUO

35

Common Knowledge and the Law: Do the "Haves" Come Out Ahead?

Patricia Ewick and Susan S. Silbey

(1999)

In 1974, Marc Galanter published a paper entitled "Why the 'Haves' Come Out Ahead: Speculations on the Limits of Legal Change" in which he analyzed the limits of a legal system, such as that of the United States, to achieve redistributive outcomes. He traced the limits to features of the U.S. legal system's "basic architecture." The specific features to which he referred were a series of structural dualisms or institutional contradictions that permitted symbolic claims to universalism, public authority, and equality to coexist with particularism, private power, and inequality.

Emerging out of these contradictions, Galanter described a complex structure of social action in which repeat players engage in the litigation game very differently from one-shot players, or those "who have only occasional recourse to the courts" (Galanter 1974:97). Repeat players initiate the play, enjoy economies of scale, develop facilitative informal relations, have access to client-specialized legal representation, play the odds in their repetitive engagements, and with regard to the rules of the game, play for rule changes as much, or perhaps more than, for immediate gains.

Although Galanter pointed out that the repeat players are not necessarily the "haves" of the world (nor are the one shotters always the "have nots"), there is considerable overlap among these statuses. Thus, by establishing that the "haves" do come out ahead and specifying wherein lies their legal advantage, Galanter drew a blueprint of the gap between law on the books and law in action, a gap that many have been exploring, mapping, and questioning ever since.

In this piece, we examine a question, provoked by Galanter's original paper: To what extent and with what consequence are the contradictions or dualisms characteristic of our legal system perceived and understood by citizens (the repeat players, the one shotters, and, we would like to include for this analysis, the no shotters). That Galanter used a vernacular phrase in the title to his paper suggests that he recognized that the perception that "'haves' come out ahead" was common knowledge. Assuming that this perception is common, here we consider the *significance of this knowing for believing*. In other words, what roles do popular understandings of why "the 'haves' come out ahead" play in sustaining or challenging the legitimacy, power, and durability of law?

LEGAL CONSCIOUSNESS OF ORDINARY AMERICANS

We have been collecting stories of people's experiences of law to track how people think and act in relation to the law. Over a period of 3 years, we interviewed approximately 430 persons randomly selected from four counties in New Jersey, counties that represented the variation in the racial and economic composition of the state. The sample included millionaire venture capitalists, lawyers, real estate brokers, hairdressers, homemakers, and welfare recipients. In the context of a lengthy, largely open-ended interview, we asked about their daily lives, problems or events that they experienced and defined as problematic, and how they reacted to these events.

Because we were interested in how people encountered and constructed legality in their daily lives, the interview was deliberately designed to capture a picture of the legality that might be unmoored from formal legal settings. Consequently, for some of the people with whom we spoke, the law in a formal sense was conspicuously absent. They reported no experience with courts, police, written laws, or regulations. In Galanter's scheme, we might refer to these people as the no shotters. For others, experience in formal legal settings and with authorities and legal agents was a frequent, ongoing feature of their lives and relationships. Most of the people with whom we spoke fell somewhere in between, having had some legal experience.

From the nearly 10,000 pages of transcribed interviews, we were able to identify three overarching stories of law, accounts of law that seemed to reoccur in the individuals' stories and accounts of legality. These metastories of law are more than simply summaries of what individuals said; they are, we argue, the common cultural materials, the interpretive frames that represent and shape how people experience legality. People draw upon these frames in constructing and interpreting their own experiences and accounts of law. Each describes a familiar way of acting and thinking with respect to the law. Each frame or schema draws upon different cultural images to construct a picture of how the law works. Each invokes a different set of normative claims, justifications, and values to express how the law ought to function.

Each attributes different capacities and identifies different constraints on legal action. Finally, each story locates legality differently in time and space.

Before the Law

In one story, "before the law" (borrowing from Kafka's parable), legality is imagined and treated as an objective realm of disinterested action, removed and distant from the lives of individuals. In this story, the law is majestic, operating by known and fixed rules in carefully delimited spaces. Here, legality is envisioned and enacted as if it were a separate sphere from ordinary social life: discontinuous and distinctive yet authoritative and predictable. The law is described as a formally ordered, rational, and hierarchical system of known rules and procedures. Respondents conceive of legality as something relatively fixed and impervious to individual action.

This version of legality is, of course, law's own story of its grandeur, something that transcends by its history and processes the persons and conflicts of the moment, offering objective rather than subjective judgment. In this account, the law is defined by its impartiality. Needless to say, in this rendering of law, the "haves" are no more likely to come out ahead than the "have nots."

One of our respondents, a woman we call Rita Michaels, provides several examples of this conception of legality and how it is articulated in thought and action. Rita is a middle-aged, white, divorced woman working as an office manager and supporting two sons in college. She lives in a meticulously neat and well-maintained home in a relatively affluent town. She had been married for 17 years, during which time her husband had been chronically unemployed, eventually refusing to work at all. Her decision to get a divorce, she said, was difficult and painful. According to Rita, none of her friends, neighbors, or family members, who were Roman Catholic, supported her decision to divorce.

The neighborhood was a very nice neighborhood, people knew me from when my kids were little, knew my husband, but no one really, no one knows what goes on inside someone's house. So, when I was divorced, or when I was in the process of doing this, a couple of my neighbors really were very upset. And my husband went and told these people that I was this terrible person and that I was throwing him out. (Rita Michaels)

Later in the interview, Mrs. Michaels said:

the neighbors, their acceptance of the fact that I was going to do this terrible thing, that I was this terrible person, um. . . . And I don't know, I think that maybe was the most painful.

In contrast, she told us:

The divorce was a rather pleasant experience, believe it or not . . . the court experience, what it felt like to go to the courtroom and face the judge or whomever. I don't mean that it was pleasant, I just think that I was pleasantly surprised because the judge had evidently read all the whatever they have, before time . . . it was evident that he had done his homework. . . . I don't think I was in that court more than, I would say maybe 45 minutes and he awarded me the divorce. He said that there was no reason for me to have to live under these conditions. . . . It left me with a good feeling. That I did do the right thing, and that he thought it was right also. Funny, I remember his exact words because it left a lasting impression.

In contrast to family and neighbors, the judge affirmed her experience and her decision to seek a divorce. She found a validation that she had not expected. Rejected and stigmatized by her family and friends and feeling outside the moral universe they guarded, Mrs. Michaels found that the law offered an alternative moral order in which she was neither wrong, nor morally deviant.

This set of legal values, rights, and expectations, was less particular and partial than the world of her family and neighbors. Her husband had not fulfilled his obligations under these larger, more general set of norms. She was comforted that she could point to these norms as grounding and legitimacy for her action. Here, Mrs. Michaels articulated a very traditional conception and function of legal ordering: protection of the individual against local group norms, a protection that derives from legality residing outside these local norms. Whereas her neighbors lacked information ("no one knows what goes on inside someone's house") and could be swayed by the misrepresentations by her husband that she was "a terrible person," Rita perceived the judge as informed and impartial.

The impartiality that is imputed to law is not just a claim for the objectivity of the law's agents; people believe that the objectivity inheres in what the law should and should not be used for. Many respondents, including Rita Michaels, often police the boundary separating the public world of law from the private worlds of self-interest and individual action by disqualifying their lives from the realm of the legal and refusing to invoke the law.

When asked whether she would call the police in response to a neighborhood conflict, Rita readily rejected the idea, claiming, "I don't use my police that way." At one level, her statement seems contradictory: expressing both identification (my police) and distance (her refusal to call the police). Yet when we unpack her meaning, putting it in the context of her other experiences, it becomes clear that the two meanings expressed are less oppositional than interdependent. In point of fact, Rita Michaels identifies with the police precisely because they do not attend to the messiness of everyday neighborhood conflicts.

Many people expressed the lack of connection between law and ordinary life. For these persons, encountering the law in the course of their lives— whether it involved being stopped by a police officer, being audited by the Internal Revenue Service, or serving on a jury—represented a disruption. Furthermore, in deciding whether to mobilize the law, people often thought about it as "breaking frame," that is, rupturing normal relationships, practices, and identities. When asked what action he had taken in response to what he described as the deterioration of this neighborhood, Don Lowe disavowed the possibility of doing anything out of the ordinary.

> I'm not a person who goes down and pickets or creates a disturbance like that. I'm a normal taxpaying person, I work, come home, pay my bills, pay my taxes, and you know, try to keep a low profile.

For people like Rita Michaels and Don Lowe who understand the law in this way, a decision to mobilize or use legal forms often is preceded by the crucial interpretive move of framing a situation in terms of some public, or at least general set of interests.

Claudia Greer, a black minister and licensed practical nurse living in Camden, New Jersey, explained the conditions under which she would "bother" the police:

> I might go to the police, but then again I might not. If they were destructive or fighting, or you know, then I might. I'd call the police . . . if there are gun shots or something like that, then, 'cause everybody's threatened then.

Notably, in this statement, it was not only the severity of the action (the gunshots) that Claudia Greer gave as a reason for bothering the police, but it was [also] the collective nature of the harm it posed that justified her decision to turn to the law.

For some people, refusing to use the law, even if it requires accepting injury or harm, is an indication of moral strength and independence. Sophia Silva criticized a friend of hers, Joanne, for suing a neighbor after that neighbor had run over [and injured] Joanne's child. Sophia Silva's criticism of Joanne's action is drawn implicitly as she describes her own parents' response to a similar situation years before:

> I hope you don't have to interview Joanne, but my friend Joanne, but my friend Joanne's daughter was on a bicycle and a neighbor was coming out of her driveway and the child was knocked down, and they sued the driver. . . . And I myself would not. . . . I remember as a child sitting on the pavement, and I was run over by the car of the people next door. Now you have to remember that my parents had no money, this was Depression time, and my father was bringing home five dollars a week. . . . And the car backed over my leg, and my parents refused any medical help. To this day I have a limp.

Later in her interview, Mrs. Silva told us that she had, in fact, sued a grocery store in her town after she had slipped on a piece of fruit. In explaining her decision to sue, she said, "I did sue, because it would be hard to think of some senior citizen slipping on that." The sincerity of Sophia Silva's altruistic motive is not, of course, the issue. What is important is the perception that such a casting is necessary. Through such a vocabulary of motive, the law is constructed and apprehended as impartial, standing above and outside the truck of everyday life and mundane motive.

With the Law

We also heard a second story of law, a story we call "with the law." Here legality is described and "played" as a game, a bounded arena in which preexisting rules can be deployed and new rules invented to serve the widest range of interests and values.

This account of law represents legality as a terrain for tactical encounters through which people marshal a variety of social resources to achieve strategic goals. Rather than existing outside of everyday life, this version of the law sees it as operating simultaneously with commonplace events and desires. In other words, the boundaries that

might be seen to separate law from the everyday (a boundary so meticulously policed by the likes of Rita Michaels, Don Lowe, and Sophia Silva) is here understood to be relatively porous and fragile, as new uses and applications of law emerge. In this second story, respondents expressed less concern about the legitimacy of legal procedures or the universal values that underwrite legality. Instead, they talked about the value of self-interest and the effectiveness of legal rules and forms for achieving their desires.

These accounts of law describe a world of legitimate competition. Less likely to reference the law's power, they often refer to the power of self and other to successfully deploy and engage the law. They explicitly likened the law to a game, a gimmick, like a chess tournament, in short as an arena for marshaling one's resources and demonstrating one's skill in pursuit of competitive self-interest. In articulating this understanding of the law, people were wise to the "haves" coming out ahead, that resources, experience, and skill matter in who wins this law game.

One man, Ray Johnson, recounted a dispute he had with his landlord about his lease. Mr. Johnson described his landlord as a skilled and experienced player in this game of rights, entitlements, and interests. Yet, despite the landlord's skill and reputation, Ray Johnson was prepared for the engagement, he told us.

> This guy was a leading man in the community, and he had ties in City Hall, he used to get people evicted out of here in a week. They didn't know any better. He'd intimidate them. He'd do whatever he did with City Hall, and they'd get the paperwork pushed through, and they'd be gone. So, he went into his little song and dance about what he was going to do and so on and so forth. And I said, "Yeah, well, no matter how you look at it, if you want me to persuade you that I have a right to this apartment, we can have that discussion. According to the lease here you cannot cancel the lease. You have to give me the option to renew. Says so right here! You do not have

the option not to let me renew." We talked about it. Well, I had no fear that it wasn't [going to work out]. He couldn't evict me!

The right to the apartment to which Raymond Johnson alluded was not a right he saw as grounded in legal principle, natural law, or abstract theories of justice. It was a right that he deduced from the rules of the game, the writing on the lease and the city statutes. Later in the interview, Mr. Johnson declared, somewhat defiantly: "There is no justice. You either win or you lose. As long as you can accomplish your objectives, you win. I'm not concerned about justice."

Mr. Johnson's cynicism was also expressed in the view that not only was the law an arena for pursuing self-interest, but that deceit and manipulation would prevail. Opponents could be expected to lie, bluff, or manufacture a story; smart and wily players should be prepared for that. One respondent stated simply,

> I learned you need proper representation because people tend to tell lies when they go to court.

What is significant about this statement and others like it is that it is not a general assessment of human nature and the propensity to lie. The pointed reference to lying "when they go to court" suggests that the tendency to lie is linked to a particular place and time where deceit is expected and permitted.

In this game of skill, resources, manipulation, and deceit, virtually all our respondents agreed that the most crucially consequential resource one can mobilize in a legal encounter is a lawyer. No matter how competent the individual, no matter how much experience or knowledge a citizen might acquire, he or she occupies an amateur status in relation to lawyers. Lawyers represent, then, the professional players in the game of law.

John Collier believed that his failure to hire a lawyer was decisive in his inability to defend himself against charges of illegal dumping. John vehemently denied the charges and appeared in criminal court without a lawyer. At the time of our interview, he admitted that "he should've had a lawyer," but at the time of the incident, he did not think that it was necessary "because I didn't feel I was guilty of a crime." John Collier's original belief that lawyers are necessary only for the guilty was undermined by his experience in court.

> They had pictures of my truck with everything in it. When this lawyer [the prosecutor] asked me, "Is that your truck?" I said "Yeah." And they said "OK," And they got me. I should never have admitted that that truck was mine. If I had had a lawyer they would really have no evidence. You know, lawyers are much smarter than the average person. So they sucked me into it.

Another respondent echoed the view that lawyers are skilled at manipulation and trickery. Andrew Eberly reported:

> Somebody came by to write a report. They asked me how far was I away from the accident. And, I said, "Well, I don't know how far I was, I wasn't too far from here to there." He said, "I have to have a number." So I said, "Well, twelve feet, if you have to have a number, about twelve feet." Went to court and the attorney asked me how far I was from the accident and I said, "Anywhere from ten to fifteen feet." He says, "Well, under sworn affidavit you said you were twelve feet." I said "To me that sounds the same. Twelve feet is the same as ten to fifteen." That's the kind of situation that you run up against in trials. The attorneys play games with the minds of people.

In this understanding of the law, it is an open arena for the legitimate pursuit of interest, but it is also one fraught with pitfalls. Lawyers lie in ambush or simply outmaneuver you. Opponents have connections to City Hall and the like. And your own naïveté—a naïveté that simply fails to understand that the law is a game—can undermine [your] chances of winning. Still, although some are discouraged from engaging in the play, others find pleasure in the encounters. Alan Fox, one of the few attorneys we interviewed, grew up in an upper-middle-class community where he still lived. Mr. Fox made numerous references throughout the interview to his friends, some of whom he has known since childhood. He mentioned to us that if any of his friends could benefit from an uncomplicated litigation, he initiates it for them for no fee. In one particular instance, Alan Fox mentioned the property reassessments about to be undertaken by the town.

> So I thought what I would do, in a magnanimous gesture, is I would file an appeal for everybody in my poker game. Just do them all at the same time.

Thus, to Alan Fox the law is a gift he can bestow upon others. Deploying the law in this way provides opportunities to achieve personal objectives, not the least of which is displaying his attachment to his friends. In fact, Alan Fox plays law as he plays poker. He said, "Because people who are really my friends, I couldn't do enough for them." Besides, Alan Fox told us, "it's fun."

Up Against the Law

Finally, we heard a third cultural narrative in people's accounts of law, one we call "up against the law." In this narrative, law is presented as a product of unequal power. Rather than objective and fair, legality is understood to be arbitrary and capricious. Unwilling to stand before the law, and without the resources to play with the law, people often act against the law, employing ruses, tricks, and subterfuges to evade or appropriate law's power.

People revealed their sense of being up against the law as being unable to either maintain the law's distance from their everyday lives and unable to play by its rules. Bess Sherman is a black, elderly woman who had had difficulty obtaining medical treatment for what turned out to be breast cancer. After months of doctors'

appointments and applications, she finally obtained Supplemental Security Income (SSI). Recounting the experience, she told us:

> I know if I had money or had been familiar, I probably would have gotten on it earlier, like the system is now. That's what they have to do. If people want to get on [SSI], and they know themselves that they are sick, they go to this lawyer, Shelly Silverberg. . . . People say "Well, why don't you go to a lawyer, Bess? Why don't you go to Shelly Silverberg?" Bess can't go, because Bess don't have no money.

Thus, being without resources, Ms. Sherman understood that she had little or no choice but to submit to the round of appointments, forms, diagnoses, and hearings. Finding themselves in such a position of powerlessness, people often described to us their attempts at "making do," using what the situation momentarily and unpredictably makes available—materially and discursively—to fashion solutions they would not be able to achieve within conventionally recognized schema and resources. Foot-dragging, omissions, ploys, small deceits, humor, and making scenes are typical forms of resistance for those up against the law.

Recognizing themselves as the "have nots" facing some more legally, economically, or socially endowed opponent, people use what they can to get what they need. The feints, tricks, and opportunistic ploys are rarely illegal. Most often, resistance of this sort does not transgress the rules as much as it evades them. It does not challenge power as much as it stuns it.

After repeated calls to the police about problems in his neighborhood were ignored, Jesus Cortez called again pretending to be a woman. He finally succeeded in mobilizing the police. Aida Marks, on the advice of her family doctor, tried unsuccessfully to get her son transferred to another hospital after he had been shot. When the nurse mistakenly handed Mrs. Marks her son's case records, she saw an opportunity. Knowing that neither the transfer nor surgery could occur without the records, she acted.

> I had that big bag from Avon with me and this silly old nurse up there, she gave me all of Ronald's records so I pushed them down into my bag. They couldn't find those records, they was having fits!

Refusing to leave retail stores, sitting in guidance counselor's offices, calling the president of a company, and stopping police officers for speeding are all examples of the disturbances and reversals of power that people enacted to escape the law's costs or lighten its burden. Recognizing the futility of demanding a right (to service, protection, attention, or respect), people found other ways of achieving their ends. Notably such efforts to resist the power of law are rarely cynical; more often, people undertake these violations of convention and, sometimes, law with a strong sense of justice and right.

The Ideological Effects of Contradiction

What we found, then, woven through the stories of 430 people, were radically different, even contradictory images of law, how it works, and how it ought to work. There was pervasive "ideological penetration" in that people routinely articulated that the law was not about justice, but that it was fixed to advantage the wealthy, big complex organizations, and even quintessential repeat players: the criminal. This penetration, however, was not complete in that it was counterpoised by articulations of law as embodying the highest ideals of justice and fairness. In short, the law appears to people as both sacred and profane, God and gimmick, interested and disinterested, here and not here. At times, legality emerged as a formal, fair, impartial, and transcendent arbiter of disputes where "haves" and "have nots" stand equally before the law. Legality was also described as a

commonplace, available arena where self-interest prevailed, and having it (money, resources, experience, and determination) made all the difference. Finally, legality was apprehended as a terrain of power, where might makes right; here it is not even a question of losing the game, but of not even being able to play.

If we focus in particular on the first two stories of law ("before" and "with" the law), it appears that we found an opposition in people's consciousness of legality that corresponds to the contradiction Galanter described in terms of the law's structure or architecture: a series of dualisms limiting the achievement of equal justice under law. What complicates this picture is the fact that these different stories of law were expressed by nearly everyone in the sample. The varied images of legality did not, in other words, neatly correspond to persons, with some being "before" the law and others "with" the law. Individuals, almost without exception, expressed more than one of these cultural narratives.

In fact, we found that one person would articulate these contradictory views, not just at different points in the interview, about different matters or experiences, but within a single account or utterance. For example, the statement that the law is "just a gimmick" (and its variants) seems to acknowledge legality as a game (perhaps even one that is "fixed" to benefit the wealthy and powerful). At the same time, through the inclusion of "just" and the tone of disgust and disappointment with which this phrase is typically uttered, the individual expresses an aspiration that law be otherwise.

This finding—commonly expressed alternative and opposing stories of law—brings us back to the question we posed at the beginning of this paper: What is the ideological significance of knowing that the "haves" come out ahead? Is legality rendered imperfect, flawed, and vulnerable because it is understood to be a game as well as transcendent, a realm of power as well as a realm of disinterested decision making? Does an awareness of the structural contradictions of law—knowing, despite formal assurances of equality before the law, that the "haves" really do come out ahead—lead to critique and disillusionment?

In answering these questions, we suggest precisely the opposite, arguing that the multiple and contradictory meanings of legality protect it from—rather than expose it to—radical critique. Rather than a flaw, or something to be explained away, we need to think about how the apparent oppositions and contradictions—the so-called gap—might actually operate ideologically to define and sustain legality as a durable and powerful social institution.

Taken together, these apparent contradictions permit individuals wide latitude in interpreting social phenomena and personal experience in ways that are consistent with prevailing ideologies of legality. Challenges to legality for being only a game, or a gimmick (the realist account "with the law"), can be rebutted by invoking legality's reified, transcendent purposes (the idealist account of "before the law"). Similarly, dismissals of law for being irrelevant to ordinary people and mundane matters, housed in leather tomes and marble halls outside the truck of everyday life, can be answered by invoking its game-like character and routinized availability.

The apparent incomparability of two of the stories we heard preserves the ideological contradictions by concealing the social organization that connects the general ideal of objective, disinterested decision making in "before the law" to the material practices represented in the story we called "with the law," including the inequality of access, the mediating role of lawyers, and the gamesmanship. The conjunction of the two stories—the contradiction itself—mediates the incomplete, flawed, practical, and mundane world with the normative legitimacy and consent that all social institutions require. Thus, legality becomes a place where processes are fair, decisions are reasoned, and the rules are known beforehand at the same time as it is a place where justice is only partially achieved, if it is at all, where public defenders do not show up, where sick old women cannot get disability benefits, where judges act irrationally and with prejudice, and where the "haves" come out ahead.

By obscuring the connections between the particular and the general, firsthand evidence and lived experience of ordinary people (experiences that might potentially contradict that general truth and the legitimacy it underwrites) are excluded as exceptional, idiosyncratic, or irrelevant. As a consequence, the power and privilege that attach to legal processes are preserved through what appears to be or is asserted to be the irreconcilability or irrelevance of the particular—local and experiential—with the general, universal, or transcendent norm of disinterested, objective judicial decision making.

Don Lowe, one of our respondents, told us, for instance, that the process of jury selection was manipulated and stacked, as he put it. Jurors were selected according to their demographic characteristics. By carefully selecting jurors on the basis of their gender, race, and social class, according to Mr. Lowe, unscrupulous lawyers could manipulate outcomes, thus subverting justice. Yet after a lengthy and impassioned indictment of this practice, Mr. Lowe concluded by stating that "justice prevails" and "the system works."

In their study of small claims courts, Conley and O'Barr (1990) found the same pattern of critique (of the particular event) and commitment (to the system). The litigants they interviewed reported surprise and frustration with the way their claims were transformed and interpreted in the process of litigation, often rendering them unrecognizable. Despite their frustrations and disappointment, however, litigants rarely blamed the system or condemned the law as unfair. Instead, they tended to blame either themselves for not being prepared or "the particular judge who heard their case" (p. 96).

How are we to interpret this abiding faith in and commitment to a system that is, in people's own experience, unfair or worse? Is it merely an instance of naïveté or illogic? The frequency with which this sort of interpretation is made suggests that it is neither of these. For Don Lowe, as for many of our respondents, the law—the reified, transcendent law—is only partially or incompletely represented in the observable material world. Only partially represented in everyday life, legality cannot be completely assessed or dismissed on the basis of that material or mundane reality. In part, then, the power and durability of law derive from it not being understood as common and observable.

We reiterate, however, that law's power is only in part derived from its status as transcendent and ideal. Were it located only in the rarefied plane of abstraction and ideal, only in leather tomes and marble halls, somewhere other than in everyday life, it would risk irrelevance. A parallel but opposite effect from transcendence must be achieved for legality to become and remain an enduring social form. At the same time that legality is represented and treated as outside of everyday life, as the before the law story suggests, it must also be located securely within the realm of the everyday and the commonplace. Thus, it is precisely because law is both god and gimmick, sacred and profane, objective, disinterested, and a terrain of legitimate partiality that it persists and endures. It is precisely because people believe that there is equality under law but also understand that sometimes the "haves" come out ahead that legality is sustained as a powerful structure of social action.

References

Conley, John M., & William M. O'Barr. (1990). *Rules Versus Relationships: The Ethnography of Legal Discourse.* Chicago: University of Chicago Press.

Galanter, Marc. (1974). "Why the 'Haves' Come Out Ahead: Speculations on the Limits of Legal Change." *Law & Society* 9(1):95–160.

THE SOCIAL PRODUCTION OF DIFFERENCE AND INEQUALITIES

When you combine everything that you have learned from this book up to this point, you will find that you now have a basis for explaining how major social patterns are created and maintained by small and seemingly insignificant everyday beliefs and actions. An important point to realize is that all of us may be contributing to the status quo, even when we sometimes believe we don't agree with it. People don't necessarily intend to perpetuate inequality; however, preconceived ideas about social differences such as gender or ethnicity or social class may lead us to engage in behavior that inadvertently contributes to these patterns. The readings in this section provide examples of the maintenance of two kinds of *patterned* social discrimination. As you read, pay close attention to the everyday actions that perpetuate these social lines of division.

Scott Harris is a sociologist interested in the way in which interactions reflect and uphold preconceived notions of social status. In "Status Inequality and Close Relationships," Harris explores how close friends handle social status differences between them. What happens, for example, when one person is promoted to a position of authority over a personal friend? How do friends manage disparities in income and related social position? Does their behavior with one another break down status barriers or reinforce these barriers?

In "The Persistence of Gender Inequality in Employment Settings," sociologist Cecilia Ridgeway asks why women have not been able to move into the highest ranks of professional management, even with legal interventions such as affirmative action. She finds the answer to this puzzle in an analysis of the preconceived *status expectations* that both men and women hold about management characteristics. All else being equal, when promotion decisions are discussed in groups, people often revert to stereotypical assessments that result in a default assumption that men are better suited for certain jobs. Through their conversations and promotion decisions, the group upholds a gender status quo.

READING QUESTIONS

1. Review Ridgeway's discussion of "gender status beliefs" and make a list of other categories of "status beliefs" (for example, race, class, and so forth). Discuss how her theory might be used to explain persistent discrimination for these other statuses.

2. Some social situations may appear isolated and private but also reflect a strongly entrenched social hierarchy. Discuss the relationship between maids and their employers. Employers often engage in behaviors in the presence of their maids that they would never engage in around "polite company." This is a form of interactional "disappearance"—the maid is expected to act as if she does not exist. Think of some other relationships in which this kind of status distancing occurs.

36

Status Inequality and Close Relationships: An Integrative Typology of Bond-Saving Strategies

Scott R. Harris

(1997)

Our close relationships are clearly a significant part of our happiness and quality of life. Who can deny the importance of our family and friends, our romantic partners, and our commiserating co-workers? Little in life would be worthwhile without companions such as these to share it with us. The fact that individuals seem to need meaningful connections with others has led some to believe that the maintenance of social bonds is "the most crucial human motive" (Scheff 1990, p. 4).

It is surprising, then, that little sociological research has investigated relationship maintenance and repair. Within the fields of communication and psychology, much (quantitative) research has been done in this area, focusing primarily on marital relationships in general states of decline (see Duck 1988 for a review). While the maintenance and repair of marital relationships is a significant topic, more attention should be given to the interactional practices that function to preserve all types of close social bonds: friendly, familial, *and* romantic. Additionally, more research could examine relationship repair within the contexts of specific types of problems, rather than assuming a general state of decay. In this paper I examine a distinctly sociological research question: *How do individuals in an intimate relationship remain close when they are confronted with a disruptive status of inequality?*

EQUALITY AND CLOSE SOCIAL BONDS

Numerous sociologists have suggested that a state of equality is an integral component of close relations. Friendship is said to involve the "felt experience" of equality (Reohr 1991, p. 48), and it is thought to be difficult or impossible when significant status differences exist (Bell 1981, p. 85). Marriage is coming to be known as a partnership between equals (Leslie 1979, p. 51; Nock 1987, p. 125), and the level of happiness within the relationship is thought to depend on the degree of gender equality within it (Collins and Coltrane 1991, p. 13). Friendly sociability is regarded as the art of rendering status differences irrelevant and acting "as if" all were equal (Simmel 1950, pp. 45–46, 49); indeed, it is argued that even the friends of friends must treat each other as equals (Suttles 1970, p. 97).

Two rationales typically pervade such discussions of equality and close relationships. The first is based on the belief that cultural norms determine behavior; from this standpoint, individuals are socialized to behave as equals in close relationships. Thus, while it may be appropriate to act "bossy" with one's employees at work, to do so with one's friends would violate a norm of conduct. Other treatments stem from exchange theory, which views individuals as rational hedonists who weigh the costs and benefits of their actions. From this perspective, mutually satisfying interactions tend to occur between status equals because only they can evenly exchange rewards and escape the cost of admitting inferiority (Homans 1974, p. 302). Those who possess similar intelligence, wealth, or attractiveness are predicted to enjoy their associations more than those who are dissimilar.

A more recent approach centers on the emotions which underlie social interaction. Work by Scheff and Retzinger (1991) suggests that feelings of inferiority, unworthiness, and embarrassment (due to improper role enactment) are rooted in the emotion "shame." Their research demonstrates how unacknowledged shame is a frequent cause of anger, alienation, and aggression between individuals and groups, particularly married couples. From this third perspective, one might assume that feelings of equality must be maintained in close relationships in order to prevent shame from arising and damaging them.

Although much of the sociological literature assumes that equality is a prerequisite to successful close relations, little research has explored how individuals may try to save a social bond when it is disrupted by status inequality. Scheff and Retzinger (1991) argue that the destructive power of shame (which may result from status inequality) can be overcome if the participants acknowledge the emotion within a frank discussion of their relationship. Acknowledgment is in fact a reparative strategy discovered by this research; however, other types of remedial *and preventative* approaches should not be ignored. The literature on facework and embarrassment—a variant of shame (Scheff and Retzinger 1991)—suggests that strategies such as avoidance, offering "accounts" (excuses and justifications), and introducing humor can be used to cope with discrediting or embarrassing predicaments (Goffman 1967; Scott and Lyman 1968; Metts and Cupach 1989, 1994). My study examines how these and other strategies can be used to mitigate an alienating status difference. *The goal of my research is to construct a typology that integrates all types of interactional practices that may be used in an attempt to save a relationship threatened by status inequality. . . .*

A SYMBOLIC INTERACTIONIST VIEW OF EQUALITY

An investigation into the interpersonal management and social creation of relative status requires a theoretical framework that is sensitive to the nature of face-to-face interaction. Symbolic interactionism provides that kind of framework. . . . Human beings *think,* and their thinking is not merely the expression of psychological motives or drives. Self-interaction—in the form of interpreting, considering, and defining the situation—is a crucial determinant of action (Blumer 1969, pp. 64–65). A symbolic interactionist perspective assumes that, if we are to gain any insight into how relative status impacts close relationships, our focus must shift from preconceived causal directives to the substance and meaning of interaction within and among individuals.

Simple introspection and casual observation indicate that many types of relationships can be quite satisfying despite being characterized by status inequality. Parent-child, teacher-student, and mentor-protégé dyads are some obvious examples where intimacy might flourish untroubled by apparent status differences. Even among two close friends, there is probably one who tends to give more advice to the other or one who makes more decisions about what they should do together. Whether this tendency drives a wedge between them depends on how it is interpreted; its impact cannot be predetermined. . . .

THREE PROCESSES

We now have two sociological questions: when and how does an inequality actually become disruptive? It may be impossible to identify certain inequalities which will always disrupt a close relationship. It is possible, however, to outline three interpretive processes which must occur for an inequality to merit bond-saving attention: At least one participant in the dyad must (a) become aware of the inequality, (b) define it as problematic, and (c) decide that the relationship is worth the effort it would take to deal with the inequality.

To disrupt a close relationship, a status difference must first be noticed. As I argued earlier, individuals are complex, multifaceted creatures; how individuals isolate, identify, and evaluate their relative status is not a simple matter. William James' (1890, p. 402) discussion of the selectivity of human attention underscores the issue: "Millions of items of the outward order are present to my senses which never properly enter into my experience. Why? Because they have no *interest* for me. *My experience is what I agree to attend to.*" Our companions may be thinner, shorter, quicker, smarter, poorer, more humorous, or less popular; they may have great success in school and at work, or they may have serious troubles with their children and their marriages. Of all the attributes human beings possess, some quality or condition must first be identified before it can be judged unequal and problematic.

After the inequality is noticed, it must be experienced as distressing in order to threaten a relationship. Several factors seem to be involved in this process. First, the level of difference must be defined as significant. (*Does my spouse dance a little better than me or does she completely out-class me?*) Second, the inequality must be felt to occur in an important or "salient" area (Stryker 1981, pp. 23–24). One's ability to blow large bubbles with bubblegum is not likely to produce an emotionally charged status difference; however, wealth or success at one's career may spark envy. (*Does my spouse dance better than me even though* I *am the one pursuing a career as a professional dancer?*) Third, how generalizable the inequality is thought to be affects its disruptive power. A status difference can be defined as a fluke or isolated occurrence, or it can be

seen as an indicator of a larger, lasting condition. (*Do I usually dance better than I'm dancing tonight? Is my poor dancing being taken as a sign that I am always uncoordinated?*) Finally, an inequality will become problematic depending on whether it is defined in competitive terms. A companion's success can be an occasion for approval and applause or a time to engage in comparative evaluation. (*Am I proud of my spouse's dancing or am I envious and determined not to be bested?*)

Once a status inequality is noticed and experienced as problematic, an individual may either walk away from the relationship or attempt to deal with the uncomfortable feelings in some way. Here, the level of intimacy and one's investment in the relationship play a crucial role. While casual associations can merely be ended when an unwanted inequality arises, valued relationships cannot be so easily disregarded. Moreover, some relationships require recurrent interaction regardless of personal choice, such as those occurring within work or school settings. These situations may cause individuals to attempt to overcome a disruptive inequality, though they might prefer to simply disengage from the relationship.

In this paper, I focus on situations where an individual feels motivated to respond to a problematic inequality in some way, rather than merely ending the association.

DATA AND METHODS

The goal of this research is to identify the types of bond-saving strategies that individuals can use when a status inequality is perceived and felt to be disruptive by at least one participant in a close relationship. I hope to arrive at a general, universally relevant typology by analyzing numerous specific examples of such practices. Ideally, then, my data would have been collected by observing a large variety of subjects as they experienced and dealt with an alienating status inequality in naturally occurring, diverse relationships.

Unfortunately, this would not be a very practical approach. First, it would be very difficult to position myself unobtrusively in many different social situations where I could expect to observe an inequality causing a problem in a relationship. Second, and more importantly, it could be impossible to remain with the participants long enough to observe them using one or more bond-saving strategies. It might take days or even months before my subjects attempted to resolve their problem—assuming they chose to do so.

Instead, I decided to obtain data by using open-ended, retrospective self-reports. During 1993, I collected 176 vignettes from students enrolled in undergraduate courses at a California State University. Respondents were asked to describe (in 500–750 words) an instance when a status inequality made a close relationship of theirs problematic in some way, the strategies one or both of the participants used to maintain the closeness of the bond, and how effective the strategies were. The self-reports were a required component of the students' course work, but contributing their papers to this study was voluntary.

Gathering data in this manner provided me with (a) numerous real-life examples of (b) individuals coping with various status inequalities (c) within different types of close social bonds (d) in diverse social settings (e) over time. My respondents did not restrict themselves to reporting classroom-oriented status differences (e.g., grades or intelligence); rather, they described a wide array of status inequalities occurring in many areas of social life, such as work, athletic, social, familial, and romantic settings. After reading and rereading their accounts, I felt that I had successfully immersed myself in my research topic. . . .

RESEARCH FINDINGS

My analysis of the respondents' vignettes yielded four basic types of bond-saving strategies that individuals can use to try to maintain or repair a close relationship threatened by a disruptive status inequality: They may (a) *accept* the status inequality; (b) *avoid* the situation which fosters feelings of inequality; (c) *alter* the status inequality by redefining or concretely mitigating it; or (d) *acknowledge* and discuss their problematic situation. Within the 176 vignettes, I found that each strategy appeared the following number of times: accept, 65; avoid, 48; alter, 107; acknowledge, 66. Moreover, each of these techniques can be undertaken by either the higher or lower status individual in the relationship. Examples from each perspective are included in my discussion.[1][2]

Accepting Status Inequality

The first type of bond-saving strategy makes no attempt to minimize the status difference or improve the relationship in any way. *Accepting status inequality* occurs when an individual experiences uncomfortable feelings of inequality in a close social bond, but does not vocalize or act upon those feelings. Rather than merely ending the relationship, the individual decides to "put up with" or "try to ignore" an unwanted element within the social bond.

Accept Higher Status

As might be expected, the vignettes offered little evidence of or support for the strategy of accepting higher status. It seems counter-intuitive that accepting one's own superiority could represent an effort to maintain an intimate bond. Nevertheless, certain vignettes did indicate that this is a possible bond-saving approach, as the following excerpts illustrate:

> [My friend] would always complain of being "stupid," and would tell me how smart I was. This status difference made me very uncomfortable. [1][2]
>
> Although I like [my friend], and it feels good to be admired, it is not what I consider a comfortable relationship. We have, consequently, drifted apart. [2]

Both of these individuals spurned attempts to place them in a superior status position in their relationships. But these examples do suggest that if individuals experience uncomfortable feelings of status superiority, and their partners insist on continuously reinforcing those feelings, then merely accepting higher status could be a plausible bond-saving strategy.

Accept Lower Status

Rather than end or try to repair a relationship disrupted by status inequality, individuals may also decide to accept a lower status position; that is, they may sacrifice their status to save the bond.

The following extract between two co-workers displays this technique. In this vignette, the respondent describes a problematic situation that arose because her friend received a promotion that both of them had wanted. After this event, the respondent was treated by her now higher-status friend with significantly less deference than before.

> I tried playing the part of the insignificant member of the duo, but I knew this couldn't go on forever if I expected to maintain my sense of self-worth. I went along with [my friend] always making the decisions as to what we would do, whose opinion was correct, and whose lifestyle was more impressive. It seemed that the difference in status had occurred overnight; I kept hoping it would disappear the same way. [3]

For this person, accepting lower status was a temporary strategy, reflecting a hope that the relationship would return to its original state of approximate equality. Eventually, her patience wore thin. "I could not continue pretending that our relationship was perfectly acceptable," she says, and so she ended the friendship.

In contrast, another respondent permanently accepted being assigned lower status in a close relationship.

> In [my friend's] mind, I will always be inferior. I can't be nearly as smart; I'm still in school and,

at that, it is only a state school, not a university. Many view this friendship as nothing short of pathetic, but to me it has made me a stronger person, for I have learned tolerance, not to take myself too seriously, and if I can't like myself how are others supposed to? [4]

Here, an individual maintains a close relationship threatened by inequality by continuously accepting a lower "place" in the relationship.

Avoiding Status Inequality

A second way respondents coped with differential status in their close relationships was to avoid the situation that fostered feelings of inequality. Often it is a specific activity or conversational topic which accentuates the problematic status characteristic. In order to save the bond, then, individuals can attempt to edit out that portion of their relationship. Although avoidance has been described as a method of saving face and avoiding embarrassment (Goffman 1967), research has not yet examined it as a strategy for maintaining a sense of equality in a close relationship.

Avoidance by the Higher Status Individual

In the following extract, the respondent describes how he used avoidance to prevent his higher status from undermining a valued relationship. When this student and his best friend from high school started attending college, they both knew only a handful of people. However, this quickly changed for one of them when the respondent joined a fraternity and made many new friends. To his dismay, this student quickly discovered that his new status characteristic, popularity, would have a negative impact on his relationship with his friend from high school.

> [My friend] would make statements such as, "I don't have to pay for my friends." He felt awkward around me since he perceived I thought I was better than he was. At first, I had had no reservations about discussing my fraternity around my friend. As I gradually

became aware of the fact that these discussions were a reinforcement of our status inequality (although they were never intended to be). I began diminishing talk about the fraternity until it eventually ceased altogether. [5]

Thus, the respondent purposefully used avoidance to prevent a sensitive topic from creating uncomfortable feelings of inequality between him and his friend.

Another respondent recalled using the same technique when she was admitted into an accelerated academic program while her friend was not.

My best friend was very upset. I knew she was jealous that I had gotten into the "smart" class and she was still in the regular A-track. There were a few things we attempted to do in order to hold on to our friendship. [One was] I refrained from discussing what we did in [class]. [6]

Both of these examples illustrate the importance of role-taking (Mead 1934) in the maintenance and repair of close relationships. If these higher status individuals were not able to imagine the perspective of their partners, they could not have sensed the nature of their relationship problem, nor could they have determined what strategy might repair it. A person who does not take the role of the other in this manner risks stomping clumsily on his or her partner's feelings and losing the relationship.

Avoidance by the Lower Status Individual

Respondents also described situations where the lower status individual used avoidance to prevent status inequality from disrupting a close social bond. In the following vignette, a financial inequality threatened to disrupt a valued friendship. The respondent made only $22,000 a year, while her friend, upon marriage, had a combined income of over $100,000. To compensate, the less affluent woman avoided those occasions which accentuated the status difference between the two of them.

I tried to plan activities that didn't involve money, such as inviting [my friend] and her husband over for dinner and cards, or to the park for a picnic. I would also decline the invitations that involved expenses beyond my means. Thus, I wouldn't get involved in an awkward situation. When she and her husband tried to pick up the tab when we went out, it made me feel inferior. [7]

This excerpt illustrates the significance of two other tenets of symbolic interactionism for the management of interpersonal relations—that individuals can (a) treat themselves as objects and (b) conceive and choose from different possible lines of action (Blumer 1969). This respondent made a conscious effort to anticipate future interactions and imagine how she might react to them. Because she could do this, she was able to plan events which would not produce unwanted feelings of inequality and yet would still help maintain the closeness of a valued social bond.

In another instance where status differentiating activities were avoided, a student's relationship with her fiancé became strained when they started taking classes together at the university. The respondent consistently received lower grades than her boyfriend even though she spent more time studying. Consequently, she began to feel "dumb," and "began inadvertently taking those feelings out on [her fiancé]." She tried to improve her grades by studying even harder, but to no avail.

There was only one solution and that was simply not take anymore classes together. There was a tremendous amount of unnecessary stress being put on us. Thus far, the solution has worked quite well. Although he still gets better grades than I do, it is different. We are not in the same class, and I do not feel as if I have to compete against him. [8]

As is evident in several of the vignettes above, the problem with avoidance is the way it detracts from the substance of the social bond (5, 6, & 8). To suddenly avoid a topic or activity reduces the repertoire of common interests within the relationship. This evidence substantiates Goffman's point that "Fear over possible loss of face often prevents the person from initiating contacts in which important information can be transmitted and important relationships re-established" (1967, p. 39). One respondent provided a partial solution to this dilemma, by avoiding *and replacing* inequality-producing situations with more congenial activities in order to preserve the closeness of the bond (7). Thus, avoidance may occur with or without an effort to replace the ties that have been edited out of the relationship.

Altering Relative Status: Redefining or Concretely Mitigating the Inequality

Rather than accept or avoid the problematic situation, individuals in a close relationship may attempt to neutralize disruptive feelings of inequality by directly manipulating their relative status. That is, they may try to redefine or take actions to mitigate the apparent inequality. There are four approaches to accomplishing this goal: Higher status individuals can attempt to (a) reduce their own status or (b) raise that of their partner; conversely, lower status individuals can attempt to (c) raise their own status or (d) reduce that of their partner. Like the strategies of acceptance and avoidance, status alterations can be undertaken without openly acknowledging that a problem exists.

Higher Status Individual Reduces Self-Status

One way to repair a relationship threatened by status inequality is for higher status individuals to reduce their own status. The following vignette describes how an educational inequality had the potential to disrupt a marriage. The respondent could tell that her husband felt less intelligent because she was attending college and he had stopped his education with a high school diploma. While the respondent did not perceive

any important status difference, her husband did. His feelings of inferiority prompted her to reduce her own status in order to preserve their bond.

> While I knew that I was not smarter than he, my husband did not. So to counter his thinking, I exaggerated my own struggles I was having in class. I gave him the impression that my good grades were attributed to "easy classes" and "lucky guesses" on exams. By downplaying my grades, I subsequently proved I was not more intelligent. [9]

It is evident that the negotiation of relative status depends heavily upon the accounts individuals give for how they achieve their high (or low) status characteristics. "Accounts," as conceived by Scott and Lyman (1968), are used to excuse or justify unanticipated, untoward, or deviant behavior. My research shows that accounts also play an important role in mitigating the capacity of a negative *or positive* occurrence to differentiate one individual's status from another's (e.g., "I was just lucky" or "You were just unlucky"). Hence, I use the term "*discounts*" to refer to statements that attempt to defuse a potentially disruptive status difference.[3] The following vignette further illustrates this strategy:

> My friend was able to go to the college we both wanted to attend. I was unable to go due to financial reasons. When my friend comes home, she tries to tell me I'm not missing anything and that the school is really hard and she is struggling to get the grades. [10]

Here, a discount is used to undermine a status differentiating trait—choice of college—in an effort to prevent feelings of inequality and jealousy from disrupting a close social bond.

Rather than merely redefining a status inequality with a verbal discount, higher status individuals may take more active steps to lower their status. For example, one respondent found herself in a position of power over her teammates (and a particularly close friend) when she became the leader of her rifle team. In order to keep from alienating them, she purposefully tried behaving like an equal rather than a superior.

> I was suddenly elevated above [my friend] as well as the other team members. Simply bearing the title "Captain" immediately gave me a "one-up" position over them. My responsibility was to basically tell them what to do. Because [she] and I were such good friends, I found it difficult to use any authority over her. I did not want to "lord it over her." First, to somehow step down from my higher position, I made an effort to emphasize to her and the others that we were all a team. I did my best to incorporate their ideas into our routines instead of just being a drill sergeant forcing them to do what I always wanted. [11]

To maintain her social bonds with her teammates, this individual purposefully distanced herself from her superior role and portrayed herself as a friend and an equal. As Goffman notes, an individual who expresses role distance in this manner "does not draw into some psychological world that he creates himself but rather acts in the name of some other socially created identity" (1961, p. 120). By driving a wedge between her position and herself, "between doing and being" (1961, p. 108), the respondent attempted to undermine her own status and prevent it from disrupting her relationships.

Higher Status Individual Raises Partner's Status

When an apparent inequality disrupts a relationship, higher status individuals can also attempt to overcome it by elevating the status of their companions. In the following vignette, this strategy was used to mitigate a status difference between three co-workers. When three friends received temporary job appointments in the same office, they enjoyed working side-by-side. The problem arose, however, when one was "let go" while the respondent and the remaining friend were offered permanent positions.

> We told her that maybe the supervisor thought that, because she was older and more experienced, she could find a better job than what we had been offered. We tried to make our job look really pathetic and reassure her that she would find a different job that was ten times better. [12]

Thus, this student and her friend used discounts which focused on the cause of the differential status and the characteristic itself. First, they raised the third person's status by "excusing" why she was not hired (she was over-qualified). Second, they reduced their own status and raised that of their friend by "justifying" why it was not a status differentiating characteristic (she would find a better job).

In addition to applying simple discounts, higher status individuals can also make more concrete efforts to raise their partner's status, as shown in the next vignette. In this situation, the respondent went to work at the same airport as a friend, who had been there two months longer. An inequality became apparent when the respondent excelled at the work and was quickly promoted.

> Things became uneasy between us when I was asked to check all of [my friend's] work before she entered it into the computer. Sometimes I would let mistakes go by and later change them in the computer. I corrected her work and did not tell my employer about it; when he asked me how she was doing, I lied. I worked slower when we were together, and I even let her take credit for some of my work. [13]

This excerpt illustrates a myriad of strategies. First, by secretly correcting her friend's mistakes and giving her undue credit, the respondent attempted to raise her companion's status. Additionally, the respondent lowered her own status (by giving away credit) while successfully avoiding confrontations about her friend's performance (through her stealth). All of these strategies represent a coordinated effort to prevent a status difference from disrupting a close relationship.

This excerpt also illustrates how the management of "awareness contexts" (Glaser and Strauss 1964) goes hand in hand with the maintenance of close relationships. This respondent needed to create several closed awareness contexts in her work relationships in order to carry out her many strategies. First, she needed to prevent her boss from finding out about her friend's lackluster performance. Second, she had to keep her friend from observing her own mistakes. Third, she needed to hide her own perceptions (and actions) from *both* her boss and her friend.

Since our personal status depends on what others think of us, *who knows what* will obviously affect perceptions of equality and inequality. In this case, managing the awareness contexts was tantamount to the successful use of avoidance and alteration.

Lower Status Individual Reduces Partner's Status

When individuals in close relationships find themselves in lower status positions, they may feel compelled to undermine the status level of their companions in order to assuage their feelings of inferiority while remaining in the dyad. This strategy often comes in the form of a verbal "put down." When we "cut someone down to size," we are letting them know that they have become too "big" for the relationship; they have claimed a status much "higher" than our own.

This strategy was illustrated in an earlier vignette [5]. The statement, "I don't have to pay for my friends," was an attempt to mitigate a disruptive, status differentiating trait—popularity. A second example comes from a person whose friend felt threatened by their different educational backgrounds.

> [My friend] has told me that an education does not guarantee a job, especially in the field of my choice, thereby downplaying the importance of my schooling. [14]

A more subtle method of reducing someone's status is provided in the following vignette. Here a disruptive inequality arose when the respondent's friend began to succeed at track. At first, the respondent was proud of her friend, but, in time, she felt that her friend was taking herself too seriously.

> Slowly I began letting her know she wasn't the only one with talent. I no longer agreed or smiled when she bragged about herself. She began noticing that I paid less attention to her and that I didn't seem all that interested in track talk. [15]

By subtly withholding deference, the respondent attempted to undermine the alienating status claim being made by her friend.

Lower Status Individual Raises Self-Status

Individuals may decide to raise their own status if they perceive that they have lower status in a particular area. This strategy tends to be used by individuals who experience distressing feelings of inferiority or unworthiness. For example, one student reported being extremely nervous about meeting his girlfriend's family for the first time because all of her adult relatives had master's or doctoral degrees. To compensate, he writes [16], "I made my major sound more prestigious than it really is." Another felt inferior to her friend because of their financial inequality. She made a conscious effort to always "dress up" in order to "be in her league" [17]. Both stories indicate how impression management (Goffman 1959) is pervasive in the construction of relative status.

A more detailed example of raising self-status is found in the following vignette. Here, a close relationship was strained when the respondent's friend became a dancer in a prestigious ballet. The friend's new accomplishment made him the center of attention at social gatherings for some time. The respondent's feelings of inferiority increased as he became known as "[The dancer's] friend." To compensate, the respondent tried highlighting some of his own attributes for their companions.

> I started by introducing my experience in theater to impress the group. When the focus of the conversation was on [my friend] I would then introduce my involvement in a current local play. [18]

This respondent attempted to mitigate the inequality in his friendship by pointing out his own accomplishments, thereby sharing some of the spotlight with his friend.

A respondent who used the strategy of avoidance [8] also provides another example of the lower status individual attempting to raise her relative status. Recall that this woman felt inferior to her fiancé because he was getting better grades in a class without trying as hard.

> I tried studying harder and longer. Also, most of my study hours were now away from home so he wouldn't see me studying. I felt that if I could get a better grade than him on the next test without letting him see me study more, then he would see that I wasn't really dumb. [19]

It is important to note that this respondent put more time and effort into her studies *in secret.* Obviously, she felt that perceived intelligence, the relevant status characteristic, hinged upon how easily one can assimilate knowledge. Thus, her efforts at raising her status involved two processes: increasing her own level of learning so she could achieve better grades, and creating a closed awareness context by controlling what her fiancé knew about her actions.

Acknowledging Status Inequality

The previous bond-saving strategies can all be used unilaterally and covertly; that is, individuals may attempt to accept, avoid, or alter status inequalities in close relationships without explicitly admitting to their partners that the relationships are strained. Therefore, acknowledging and discussing the problematic situation is the most openly interactive strategy in my typology.[4] This approach makes both participants aware that the relationship is at risk and allows them to cooperate in repairing it.

Higher Status Individual Acknowledges the Problematic Situation to Partner

The following description of a close friendship provides an example of the higher status individual acknowledging a disruptive status inequality. The relationship between these two women first began in high school; it continued despite the fact that the respondent went on to college while her friend dropped out and became a single mother. Nevertheless, a problem finally arose when various individuals outside of the relationship began treating the respondent with much more deference than her friend because of their respective life choices. One woman in particular complimented the respondent's choice of major and, in the next breath, criticized her friend's "irresponsible behavior." After this incident, the two began to see much less of each other.

> Finally, I asked her if she wanted to sit down and discuss what was going on. [My friend] was really angry that people felt that I was a better person because I was going to school. I was angry because people were always putting [her] down for the choice she made. We both realized we had unconsciously fallen into the categories in which people placed us. After talking for a while, we decided we weren't going to let people's comments bother us. I was also going to quit talking about my work and school so much. [My friend] was going to become more actively involved in conversations and not assume people don't want to hear what she has to say. [20]

In this vignette, openly acknowledging the status inequality led to many possible solutions. First, the two women realized that *they* did not perceive an inequality between them; only certain others outside their relationship were doing so. This insight may have helped to reduce the animosity between the two. Second, the respondent agreed to avoid those topics which emphasized the status inequality—namely, her accomplishments at school and work. Third, her friend was going to make an effort to raise her own status by being more vocal in social settings. Their discussion made both participants in the relationship aware of the problem and allowed them to cooperate on various reparative strategies.

A second example where acknowledgment was initiated by the higher status individual is described in the next vignette. Throughout high school and junior college, this respondent maintained a very close friendship with a fellow athlete. Their relationship became strained, however, when the respondent's friend received an athletic scholarship to a university.

> In my eyes, [my friend] was superior because he had a scholarship and I didn't. He could tell that something was wrong with me and sat me down for a talk. He told me that he wished he could be as tough a competitor as me and also a good student. When he got the scholarship, he didn't feel that our relationship had changed. He woke me up to the fact that there were tradeoffs in our friendship and that we were equals who excel in different things. Tom saved our relationship, and today we are still great friends. [21]

In this example, these two friends seem to have arrived at a rather effective solution to their status inequality. By agreeing that they are "equals who excel in different things," they have paved the way for smooth relations in the future. If this sentiment can be maintained, then, when either of them acquires a new status characteristic (such as financial or marital success), they can be proud of each other rather than envious. This solution bears much resemblance to Simmel's notion of the pure form of sociation: "Sociability is the game in which one 'does as if' all were equal and, at the same time,

as if one honored each of them in particular" (1950, p. 49). These two friends have honored each other by recognizing that they each excel in certain areas of their lives, yet they remain equal because they refrain from attempting to weigh one person's (overall) worth against the other's. They have simply "decided" to base their relationship on a vague sense of equality and mutual admiration.

Lower Status Individual Acknowledges the Problematic Situation to Partner

The student vignettes revealed that acknowledgment could be employed by either participant in a relationship threatened by inequality, but it was often difficult for the lower status individual to do so calmly. The following respondent reported using this strategy in an angry manner with her friend and co-worker. These two women enjoyed a "very close and strong" relationship until the respondent's friend received a promotion and began to treat her with less respect.

> In order to deal with this situation, I went to her and laid out exactly how I felt, I told her that she was rude, and bossy, and uncooperative, and treats me poorly. When I began to tell her how I felt, she became very angry and defensive. [22]

Another respondent reported using "confrontation" in a similar work-related situation:

> Confrontation usually occurs when I can no longer conceal my feelings of discontentment and frustration and must therefore voice them. This often brings few positive results and has the potential to create bad feelings. [23]

These extracts seem to suggest that the lower status individual resorts to an angry form of acknowledgment when a condition of status inequality becomes intolerable for her. Perhaps because we learn to be ashamed of being ashamed (Scheff and Retzinger 1991, p. 104; see also Lewis 1971), individuals may postpone acknowledging feelings of inferiority until they become unbearable. It may also be the case that admitting their feelings opens these individuals up to further humiliation; their partners may react insensitively, and their response may suggest that "You feel inferior because you are." These possibilities may account for those reported instances where the lower status individual acknowledged the problematic situation to her partner in a somewhat hostile manner.

One vignette provides an example where the lower status individual calmly acknowledged an inequality. In the following excerpt, the respondent reports a problematic situation that arose within a good relationship he shared with his supervisor. Although this student did not expect his supervisor to treat him like a complete equal, he felt he was being unfairly derogated by her behavior towards him. The respondent felt that he was an extremely proficient and experienced worker and expected to be treated as such.

> I felt that I was being treated with less respect and that she saw me at a lower status than I deserved, which I was unable to accept. I ventilated my concerns and asked if she was uncomfortable with me for any particular reason, to which she responded that she was relieved that I had brought this up. This opened up a wide range of dialogue and allowed her to ventilate that she did feel anxious at giving someone my age and with my range of experience and expertise assignments to do. She also expressed that she felt at times that I was trying to "one-up" her. The effects of the direct confrontation were very favorable. The awkwardness we had felt dissipated, and our attitudes toward each other improved greatly. [24]

The respondent was able to calmly raise the issue of the status inequality by taking the time to ask how his partner, the higher status individual, felt. By respectfully addressing her concerns at the outset, rather than merely conveying his own dissatisfaction, the respondent apparently avoided putting his supervisor on the defensive. Instead,

they were able to calmly communicate and discover that, in fact, they both felt threatened by each other's status characteristics and that they both thought they were being treated with less deference than they deserved. Once they knew this, they were able to successfully change their relationship for the better.

Summary and Conclusion

I have attempted to construct a typology of strategies individuals can use to try to maintain or repair a close relationship when an inequality is perceived and felt to be problematic by at least one participant of the dyad. My analysis of 176 retrospective reports on this topic revealed that a disruptive inequality may be accepted, avoided, altered (that is, directly mitigated), or acknowledged by one or both participants in the relationship.

These four types are broad categories which encompass a wide array of behavior. Acceptance can take the form of a temporary [3] or permanent [4] tolerance of the uncomfortable element in the relationship. Status inequality can be avoided by editing its source out of the relationship [5, 6, & 8]; however, doing so may subtract from the substance of the social bond unless an effort is made to replace the missing activities or conversational topics [7]. A disruptive inequality can be mitigated by directly altering the participants' relative status through redefinition [9, 10, 12, & 14] or more concrete actions [13, 15, 18, & 19]. Acknowledging the existence of a problematic status inequality can resolve misunderstandings [20, 21, & 24] and allows for the cooperative use of avoidance and alteration [20].

While constructing this typology, I attempted to integrate previous research on related topics. Avoidance was originally conceived by Goffman (1967) as a way to avoid embarrassment and save face. This study shows that it can also be a strategy to minimize perceptions of inequality in a close relationship [5–8]. "Discounts," a variation on "accounts" (Scott and Lyman 1968), were described as strategies for directly altering relative status. These statements mitigate feelings of inequality by redefining a negative *or positive* status differentiating trait [9, 10, 12, & 14]. Role distance (Goffman 1961) was identified as another way of altering status by disregarding or undermining a status differentiating role [11]. In their research, Scheff and Retzinger (1991) present acknowledgment as the sole method of assuaging shame in close relationships. In my study, acknowledgment (here defined more broadly) was found to be one of many approaches for overcoming disruptive feelings of status inequality; in fact, acknowledgment facilitates the cooperative use of other types of strategies [20].

Individuals' skill at perceiving the nature of their relationship problems and applying the appropriate reparative strategies [5–6] depends on their ability to take the role of the other (Mead 1934). Those who are unwilling or unable to imagine their partners' perspectives will not adequately understand the source of their relationship troubles. Because individuals can mentally pre-construct different possible lines of action (Blumer 1969), they can guide the flow of interaction in directions that will not produce distressing feelings of inequality in themselves or their partners. This ability allows for the preventative use of avoidance [7]. Finally, managing "who knows what" is an integral part of the success of some strategies [13]. Individuals frequently keep their critical opinions of their partners to themselves; by doing so, they may hope to avoid feelings of superiority or inferiority that would otherwise arise in a completely open awareness context (Glaser and Strauss 1964).

It is noteworthy that a symbolic interactionist perspective was purposefully adopted in the collection and analysis of these data. Consequently, relationship satisfaction was not presumed to be a simple function of equality, as some normative and rational choice theorists might conclude. Neither were certain inequalities considered inherently alienating; a status difference must first be identified and defined as problematic in order to disrupt a close relationship. However, my research design did assume that status inequality *can be* distressing, and that respondents could recall a time when such a predicament had occurred.

These findings validate the symbolic interactionist notion that status is a social object, the meaning of which is not intrinsic to any particular trait, but is, rather, the result of interpretation (Blumer 1969). By focusing on the process of interpretation, it is possible to see how status values are not merely handed down from the "macro" level or otherwise preordained. It is true that one's reference group may define attractiveness as being slender or wealth as a sign of prestige. However, such meanings may be renewed, renegotiated, or renounced by individuals in every relationship. As Blumer noted, "It is the social process in group life that creates and upholds the rules, not the rules that create and uphold group life" (1969, p. 19). The various forms of behavior reported in the vignettes clearly illustrate that relative status is a creature of interaction and interpretation.

Indeed, my findings reveal something important about the nature of social order. A typology of the creative strategies individuals use to maintain their close relationships begs the following questions: What would happen if people did not act this way? Would society be possible if close relationships flew apart at the slightest provocation? As Scott and Lyman (1970, p. 113) point out, "The threads of human association are constantly being rent. . . . If there were no way by which individuals might . . . repair their broken relationships, social relations would indeed be treacherous, perhaps coming to approximate Hobbes' state of nature." The stability of society rests, in part, upon the continuity of relations among its members. Since human agency, in at least the few ways discovered here, plays a role in the preservation of close relationships, it also contributes to the maintenance of social order. . . .

NOTES

1. I have tried to give the flavor of the strategies by examining instances of each type. However, the reader should not infer from my presentation that only one strategy was reported in a given vignette. Different types of strategies were often employed simultaneously or in succession. Additionally, the reader should not assume that a particular strategy was successful simply because I cite it. This is primarily a study of how individuals *attempt* to save relationships threatened by inequality.

2. I have assigned identification numbers to my excerpts for easier reference. The fact that I have numbered the excerpts sequentially does not mean that they were taken from the first vignettes in my data.

3. Status discounts should not be confused with "discounting" as explicated by Pestello (1991). Pestello's term refers to the statements and practices by which collectives make untoward or inconsistent actions nonproblematic.

4. Note that I have defined acknowledgment as a verbal admission that a problem with status inequality is harming the relationship. Scheff and Retzinger (1991) have more stringent requirements for acknowledging shame.

REFERENCES

Bell, Robert. 1981. *Worlds of Friendship.* Beverly Hills: Sage.

Blumer, Herbert. 1969. *Symbolic Interactionism: Perspective and Method.* Englewood Cliffs, NJ: Prentice Hall.

Collins, Randall, and Scott Coltrane. 1991. *Sociology of Marriage and the Family,* 3rd ed. Chicago: Nelson Hall.

Duck, Steve. 1988. *Relating to Others.* Pacific Grove, CA: Brooks/Cole.

Glaser, Barney G., and Anselm L. Strauss. 1964. "Awareness Contexts and Social Interaction," *American Sociological Review* 29:669–79.

Goffman, Erving. 1959. *The Presentation of Self in Everyday Life.* New York: Doubleday.

_____. 1961. *Encounters.* Indianapolis: Bobbs-Merrill.

_____. 1967. *Interaction Ritual.* New York: Doubleday.

Homans, George C. 1974. *Social Behavior: Its Elementary Forms.* New York: Harcourt Brace Jovanovich.

James, William. 1890. *The Principles of Psychology,* vol. I. New York: Henry Holt.

Katz, Jack. 1983. "A Theory of Qualitative Methodology: The Social System of Analytic Fieldwork." Pp. 127–148 in *Contemporary Field Research,* edited by Robert M. Emerson. Prospect Heights, IL: Waveland.

Leslie, Gerald R. 1979. *The Family in Social Context,* 4th ed. New York: Oxford University Press.

Lewis, Helen B. 1971. *Shame and Guilt in Neurosis.* New York: International Universities Press.

Lofland, John. 1976. *Doing Social Life: The Qualitative Study of Human Interaction in Natural Settings.* New York: Wiley.

Mead, George H. 1934. *Mind, Self, and Society.* Chicago: University of Chicago Press.

Metts, Sandra, and William R. Cupach. 1989. "Situational Influence on the Use of Remedial Strategies in Embarrassing Predicaments." *Communication Monographs* 56:151–162.

_____. 1994. *Facework.* Thousand Oaks, CA: Sage.

Nock, Steven L. 1987. *Sociology of the Family.* Englewood Cliffs, NJ: Prentice Hall.

Pestello, Fred P. 1991. "Discounting." *Journal of Contemporary Ethnography* 20:26–46.

Reohr, Janet. 1991. *Friendship: An Exploration of Structure and Process.* New York: Garland.

Scheff, Thomas J. 1990. *Microsociology: Discourse, Emotion, and Social Structure.* Chicago: University of Chicago Press.

Scheff, Thomas J., and Suzanne M. Retzinger. 1991. *Emotions and Violence: Shame and Rage in Destructive Conflicts.* Lexington, MA: Lexington Books.

Scott, Marvin B., and Stanford M. Lyman. 1968. "Accounts." *American Sociological Review* 33:46–62.

_____. 1970. "Accounts, Deviance, and Social Order." Pp. 89–119 in *Deviance and Respectability,* edited by Jack D. Douglas. New York: Basic Books.

Simmel, Georg. 1950. *The Sociology of Georg Simmel.* Translated and edited by Kurt H. Wolff. New York: Free Press.

Stryker, Sheldon. 1981. "Symbolic Interactionism: Themes and Variations," Pp. 3–29 in *Social Psychology: Sociological Perspectives,* edited by

Morris Rosenberg and Ralph Turner. New Brunswick: Transaction.

Suttles, Gerald D. 1970. "Friendship as a Social Institution." Pp. 95–135 in *Social Relationships,* by George J. McCall, Michal M. McCall, Norman K. Denzin, Gerald D. Suttles, and Suzanne B. Kurth. Chicago: Aldine.

Znaniecki, Florian. 1934. *The Method of Sociology.* New York: Farrar and Rinehart.

THE SOCIAL PRODUCTION OF DIFFERENCE AND INEQUALITIES

37

The Persistence of Gender Inequality in Employment Settings

Cecilia Ridgeway

(2001)

Gender hierarchy is a system of social practices that advantages men over women in material resources, power, status, and authority. Oddly, gender hierarchy has persisted in Western societies despite profound changes in the economic arrangements on which it seems, at any given time, to be based. It has continued in one form or another despite major economic transformations such as industrialization, the movement of women into the paid labor force, and, most recently, women's entry into male-dominated occupations. What accounts for gender hierarchy's uncanny ability to reassert itself in new forms when its former economic foundations erode?

Although many factors are involved, one part of the answer lies in the way gender hierarchy in economic and other social arrangements is mediated by interactional processes that are largely taken for granted. Gender processes taking place as people interact during economic and other activities can operate as an "invisible hand" that rewrites gender

inequality into new socioeconomic arrangements as they replace the earlier arrangements upon which gender hierarchy was based. To illustrate this point, I will describe some interactional processes that mediate gender inequality in paid employment and play a role in its persistence. First, however, we should consider how gender and interaction are related.

GENDER AND INTERACTION

Gender is an important part of the organization of interaction. It is striking that people are nearly incapable of interacting with each other if they cannot guess the other's sex. The television program *Saturday Night Live* illustrated this problem in its comedy sequence about "Pat," an androgynous person who wreaks confusion and havoc even in trivial, everyday encounters because the others present cannot place Pat as a man or a woman. The difficulty of dealing with a person whose gender is ambiguous suggests that gender categorization is a basic first step in the cultural rules we use for organizing interaction (West and Zimmerman 1987).

In order to interact with someone, you need some initial idea of "who" you are dealing with. You must classify the person in relation to yourself in socially meaningful ways so that you can draw on cultural knowledge about how "people like this" are likely to behave and how you should act in return. In other words, organizing interaction requires you to categorize the other as well as yourself in socially significant ways. Some of the social rules that you use for categorizing self and other must be so simplified and apparently obvious that they provide an easy means for initially defining "who" self and other are so interaction can begin at all. The cultural rules for classifying people as either male or female provide a quick initial category system—one that everyone takes for granted. Once interaction begins, definitions of self and other that are more complicated and specific to the situation can be introduced.

As research has shown, the cognitive processes by which we perceive others are hierarchically organized (Brewer 1988; Fiske and Neuberg 1990). They begin with an initial, automatic, and usually unconscious classification of the other according to a very small number of primary cultural categories and move on to more detailed typing depending on the circumstances. The evidence shows that gender is one of these primary categories in Western societies so that we automatically and unconsciously gender-categorize any specific other to whom we must relate.

In institutional settings, such as workplaces, there are often clear social scripts that define who self and other are and frame interaction (e.g., supervisor and worker). Yet gender categorization continues in these settings because the actual process of enacting a social script with a concrete other evokes habitual person perception and with

it, the cultural rules that define gender as something that must be known to make sense of others. Research shows that when institutional roles become salient in the process of perceiving someone, those roles become nested within the prior understanding of that person as a man or woman and take on slightly different meanings as a result (Brewer 1988). We may be able to imagine an ungendered institutional script whereby "the student talks to the teacher" but we cannot interact with any actual students or teachers without first classifying them as male or female. The gender categorization of self and others, even in institutionally scripted settings, is a fundamental, unnoticed process that involves gender in the activities and institutional roles that people enact together.

Gender categorization in work-related encounters sets the stage for two interactional processes that contribute to and help preserve gender inequality in paid employment. Gender categorization cues gender status beliefs that can unconsciously shape people's assumptions about how competent women in the situation are compared to similar men. Gender categorization also unconsciously biases whom people compare themselves to. Comparisons, in turn, affect the rewards to which people feel entitled and the wages for which they will settle.

GENDER STATUS PROCESSES

Gender status beliefs are widely held cultural beliefs that posit one gender as generally superior and diffusely more competent than the other. Such beliefs are well established in Western societies. Gender categorization in interaction makes gender status beliefs implicitly accessible to shape actors' perceptions of one another.

In interaction, people are never just males or females without simultaneously being many other social identities (e.g., young or old, of a given ethnic group, a worker or a student). The impact of gender status beliefs (and other cultural assumptions about men and women) on people's perceptions and behaviors in a given situation depends on the relevance of gender to the situation compared to other identities that are also salient. In work settings, work-related identities are likely to be in the foreground of people's perceptions and shape behavior most powerfully. Gender often acts as a *background identity* that flavors the performance of those work identities. Research shows, however, that even when other identities are the strongest determinant of behavior, gender status beliefs are still sufficiently salient to measurably affect people's expectations and behavior under two conditions: in mixed gender settings and when gender is relevant to the purposes or context of the setting (e.g., a women's caucus group) (Berger et al., 1977; Deaux and Major 1987). This means that gender status beliefs are effectively salient in many but not all work-related interactions.

When gender status beliefs are effectively salient like this in a work setting, they have three types of effects on goal-oriented interaction that affect employment inequality. First, they cause both men and women to unconsciously expect slightly greater competence from qualified men than from similarly qualified women. These implicit expectations tend to become self-fulfilling, shaping men's and women's assertiveness and confidence in the situation, their judgments of each other's ability, their actual performances, and their influence in the setting (see Ridgeway 1993 for details).

Second, gender status beliefs, when salient, cause people to expect and feel entitled to rewards that are commensurate with their relative status and expected competence in the setting. Thus, if gender status beliefs cause people in a work setting to assume the men are more important and competent than women, both men and women in the situation will also presume that men are entitled to higher levels of rewards such as pay or "perks." Consequently, when gender status is

salient, men may react negatively if they are placed on the same reward level as a similarly qualified woman. They may experience this situation as an implicit status threat.

Third, because gender status beliefs advantage men, men in interaction are less likely to notice, and more likely to discount if they do notice, information about self or other that might diminish or eliminate the effects of gender status beliefs on expectations for competence or rewards. This effect of gender status beliefs is due to the way people's interests in a situation unconsciously bias what they perceive. The effect makes it more difficult for women in the interaction to introduce information that would alter the lower expectations held for them. For example, there is a tendency in meetings for persons to attribute interesting or new ideas to a male speaker, even if a woman was the first to raise the point. Men who are "rewarded" for having expressed the good idea do not seem to notice that a woman may have mentioned the idea first. If the woman were to try to claim credit for the idea, and thereby lay claim to her competence, it is likely that she would be regarded as being pushy or out of line.

GENDER-BIASED COMPARISONS AND REWARDS

In addition to cueing gender status beliefs, gender categorization of self and other in workplace relations affects who people compare themselves to when they evaluate their own rewards or outcomes on the job. In general, people search out information about people whom they see as similar to them in order to evaluate whether they are receiving the rewards to which they are entitled. Automatic gender categorization causes people to unconsciously compare their own rewards more closely to those of the same gender than to those of the opposite gender. If pay, perks, or other rewards are distributed unequally among men and women on the job, then the tendency to compare with same-gender others will cause men to form higher estimates of what the "going rate" is for people with their qualifications. Women, gathering more comparisons from other women, form lower estimates of the going rate for the same qualifications. Not recognizing that their estimates of what others earn on the job have been biased by their tendency to compare with same-gender others, women form lower expectations for the pay and rewards to which they are entitled than do similar men. Such reward expectations become self-fulfilling because they affect people's willingness to settle for a given level of pay or to press for more (see Major 1989 for research on this process).

GENDER INEQUALITY IN EMPLOYMENT

Gender inequality in employment is something of a puzzle. Theoretically, competitive market forces should wipe out gender discrimination because employers who prefer men and pay higher wages to get them will be driven out of business by smarter employers who hire cheaper but equally qualified women for the same jobs. Yet gender inequality in wages and gender segregation in occupations (i.e., the tendency for men and women to work in different occupations) have stubbornly persisted and improved only slowly over decades. England (1992) argues that gender inequality persists despite the flattening effect of market forces because it is continually being created anew, even if is worn down slightly over time. A consideration of how interaction drives gender categorization in work contexts and brings in gender status and comparison processes can help explain why the work world is so relentlessly gendered. It can also help explain why such gendering persists despite ongoing economic and organizational change.

Most work-related interaction takes place in organizational contexts with established job structures and institutional rules that heavily constrain what happens. Under business-as-usual conditions, gender status and comparison-reward processes occurring in these interactions are just part of the means by which existing gender-biased job structures and practices are enacted and sustained. Interactional gender processes, however, become important in themselves, rather than merely the agents of organizational structures and rules, at the interstices of organizations and under conditions that force change on an organization. In these transition zones where organizational structures are less clearly defined, gender categorization, status, and comparison processes play a part in shaping the interaction through which actors create new organizational rules and structural forms and map gender hierarchy into them as they do so.

Occupational arrangements and wage outcomes are mediated by interaction in many ways, whether it be face-to-face, computer-mediated (e.g., email), or indirect interaction through exchanges on paper. Workers learn about jobs and evaluate them through contact with others. Employers hire workers through direct (e.g., interviews) or indirect interaction (e.g., reviewing resumes and references). On the job, performance, evaluations, task assignments, and promotions involve interactions among people in complex ways. All these mediating interactions through which the world of work is conducted are potential sites where interactional mechanisms can map gender hierarchy into the occupational patterns and wages that result.

THE SEX LABELING OF WORKERS AND JOBS

Gender inequality in employment begins with the gender labeling of workers. This point seems so obvious and natural that we don't bother to explain it. Yet why should all workers be either male workers or female workers and not just workers? Why is gender a primary descriptor of workers at all? The answer lies in the way inter-action evokes gender categorization, infusing gen-der into the hiring processes as it mediates employers' recruitment and placement of workers. Because interaction triggers gender categori-zation, employers can never interview or read the resume of a gender-neutral worker. Similarly, workers cannot interact with a gender-unclassified co-worker, boss, subordinate, or client.

The taken-for-granted, unconscious gender labeling of workers begins a process that also leads to the labeling of jobs themselves as men's or women's jobs. As the economy changes and devel-ops, jobs that have been traditionally labeled as men's or women's jobs may fade in importance and new jobs, such as computer programmer, are continually created. Theoretically, these new occupations could be gender neutral. Yet, in an example of the force of gender in the organization of work, most of these new occupations are them-selves quickly labeled as either men's or women's occupations. The persistent gender labeling of new jobs continually renews the gender-segregated nature of our occupational structure.

Gender categorization in workplace interaction plays a role in the continual gender labeling of jobs by priming workers and employers alike to infuse stereotypic assumptions about gender into the institutional scripts by which a job is enacted and represented to others. Employers often begin the process by implicitly or explicitly seeking workers of a particular gender on the basis of assumptions about labor costs that are themselves suffused by the effect of gender status beliefs. Employees of one gender come to predominate in the job. Since gender categorization in interaction primes people's cultural beliefs about gender even in segregated contexts, workers and employees may use gender-stereotypic terms to justify the activities in a gender-segregated job even when those activities originally seemed gender irrele-vant. Thus, electronic assembly comes to be repre-sented as a woman's job requiring *women's*

"attention to detail and manual dexterity." Selling securities becomes a *man's* job requiring mascu-line "aggressiveness."

As the stories and social scripts that represent a job in the media and elsewhere come to be gen-dered as masculine or feminine, the differential status attached to men and women spreads to the job as well. Research shows that a job or task, when labeled feminine, is viewed by both job evaluators and those in the job themselves as requiring less ability and effort and as worth less compensation than the identical job or task is when labeled mas-culine. Other research shows that the gender com-position of a job alone has a significant impact on what it pays, as does the association of the job with stereotypically feminine tasks such as nurturance (see Ridgeway 1997 for more details). Continual gender categorization in workplace interactions reinforces the tendency to apply gender labels to activities and perpetuates gender-based evalua-tions of jobs and activities.

MEN AND WOMEN AS INTERESTED ACTORS IN THE WORKPLACE

The interests of those in more powerful positions in employment organizations (e.g., bosses), who are more often men, are represented more force-fully than the interests of those who are in less powerful positions (e.g., secretaries). When gen-der status is salient in workplace interactions it creates a number of apparently gender-interested behaviors on the part of men, whether as employ-ers, workers, or customers. The men themselves as well as observers of both genders will tend to see men in a situation as a bit more competent and deserving of rewards than similarly qualified women. They may miss or discount information in the situation that undermines these percep-tions and perceive an implicit status threat when equivalent men and women are put on the same reward level.

All these effects usually occur as a modification or biasing of behavior during the enactment of an occupational or institutional identity that is more salient in the situation than the background identity of gender. A man acting in his role as an electrical engineer or union representative, for instance, may slightly bias his treatment of other men over women, usually in an implicit way that he himself does not recognize. Only occasionally will gender be so salient in the situation that men act self-consciously to preserve their interests as men. Yet the repeated background activation of gender status over many workplace interactions, biasing behavior in subtle or more substantial degrees, produces the effect of men acting in their gender interests, even when many men feel no special loyalty to their gender.

What about women in the workplace? Don't they pursue their interests as well? Yes, but the effect of gender status beliefs in interaction handicaps their efforts. It is in women's interests to introduce into a situation added information about their skills and accomplishments that undermines status-based assumptions about their competence compared to men and the rewards that they deserve. It is often difficult to introduce such information, however, precisely because gender is usually a background identity in workplace interactions. The participants do not explicitly think of gender as part of "what is going on here." The implicitness of gender in workplace interaction complicates the task of recognizing when bias is occurring and introducing countervailing information in the real time of actual interaction. The process is difficult as well because men's own status interests tend to make them more cognitively resistant to such information.

As a result, women on the job may periodically sense that something prejudicial is happening to them, but be frustrated in their efforts to act effectively against it. They will be vulnerable to "role encapsulation" whereby others define them in their work identities in implicitly gendered terms (e.g., "too nice" or "passive") that limit their effectiveness as actors in their own interests.

EMPLOYERS' PREFERENCES FOR MALE WORKERS

Reskin and Roos (1990) argue that employers show general preferences for hiring male workers, especially for "good," well-paying jobs. There are exceptions, of course, as when employers actually prefer female workers for jobs like nursery school teacher that involve tasks that are stereotypically associated with women. For other jobs, however, Reskin and Roos suggest that employers' preferences for male workers is a key factor that maintains gender inequality in wages and access to jobs with status and authority. While competitive market forces work against such preferences, they are nevertheless maintained by institutional rules and practices that embody them and by the implicit effects of gender status on workplace relations.

When an employer's automatic gender categorization of a potential employee cues gender status beliefs, these beliefs affect the employer's judgment of the worker's potential productivity. Expectations about competence based on gender status make the male worker appear "better" than an equally qualified woman. Also, an equally competent job or test performance by the two appears to the employer to be more indicative of ability and skill in the man than in the woman (see Ridgeway 1997 for a description of this research). On the surface merit is the basis of judgment. Yet the workers' gender is connected with merit by the way employers' evaluations of workers involve interactions that are unconsciously shaped by gender status beliefs. The result is what is called "error discrimination" where two workers who would perform equally are judged to be different and paid accordingly.

Gender status beliefs operating in the workplace can contribute to this process because they bias employers' expectations for workers' performances and these expectations tend to be self-fulfilling. This tendency often produces employer experiences with male and female workers that confirm the employers' initial judgments about them. A competent performance by a woman worker appears less competent coming from her than from her male co-worker. Also, and more insidious, the pressure of an employer's low expectations for them can actually interfere with some women workers' performances. Some male workers, on the other hand, may feel buoyed by their employer's confidence in them and perform even better than they otherwise might have. Thus, the effect of an employer's status-based expectations on some men and some women can create "real" differences in the average performance and productivity of groups of similar male and female workers. When interactional gender categorization makes gender salient in the hiring process, the employer's experience of these average differences also becomes salient. The employer may react by preferring male workers across the board (statistical discrimination). This form of discrimination is especially powerful in maintaining gender inequality in the workplace because it is more resistant to the equalizing effects of market forces than are other types of discrimination (England 1992).

WHY DO WOMEN WORKERS ACCEPT LOWER WAGES?

An employer's ability to attract and retain women workers for lower wages is also critical for maintaining gender inequality in employment. Why do women settle for less than similarly qualified men? Here, too, gender processes in interaction play a role by shaping different senses of entitlement on the part of similarly qualified men and women.

Although many women work in predominantly female jobs (e.g., nurses, secretaries, or elementary school teachers), their work performance is often evaluated through direct or indirect interaction with male supervisors, clients, or customers. Also, their work may have become typed a stereotypically female task. In any of these situations, gender categorization during interaction will activate status beliefs affecting women workers' own performance and expectations for rewards as well as their employer's and fellow workers' expectations for them. In fact, the evidence shows that women underestimate the quality of their performances in comparison with men. This makes them susceptible to arguments that they deserve less pay.

Gender categorization in work relations also unconsciously biases women's choices of whom to seek out in order to compare the pay they are receiving and evaluate whether it is fair. As we saw, women's tendency to compare their pay more closely with other women than similar men can cause them to underestimate the going rate for work by people with given qualifications. Such underestimates of possible pay rates is a second factor that causes women to peg the compensation they deserve at lower rates than do men.

If women workers inadvertently underestimate the rewards they are entitled to, employers can more easily force them to settle for lower wages (Major 1989). If corresponding gender status and biased comparison processes cause male workers to overestimate what they deserve, then employers find it harder to force lower wages on them. Out of such processes, women inadvertently accept lower wages than men. Women's unintentional acceptance of lower pay helps sustain gender hierarchy in employment over time by moderating women's resistance to pay differences.

WOMEN'S ENTRANCE INTO MALE OCCUPATIONS

In recent decades, women have entered male occupations in large numbers. Yet wage inequality and the gender segregation of jobs has not declined as much as one might expect. As Reskin and Roos point out (1990), the problem is that as women enter a male occupation in number, men often flee it so that it "turns over" to become a women's occupation. This has happened to the job of bank teller over the past couple of decades. Sometimes, when women enter a male occupation, instead of men leaving the occupation altogether, the occupation becomes reorganized so that some specialties within it are predominantly female while others are predominantly male. Thus, as women have entered medicine in recent years, pediatrics has become a women's specialty while neurosurgery has remained overwhelmingly male. Again, wage inequality and gender segregation of jobs are preserved despite women's entrance into the formerly male profession of medicine.

While many processes are behind these transformations of occupations, once again, gender processes during interaction are involved. Given employer preferences for male workers, women often gain access to men's occupations when the demand for workers in that occupation outstrips the pool of interested male workers available at an acceptable wage. As the shortage of male workers brings women into the job, gender-based status interests become increasingly salient in the workplace and may create tensions. Gender status beliefs activated by the mixed-sex context cause women's presence to subtly devalue the status and reward-worthiness of the job in the eyes of both workers and employers. Male workers may react to this perceived threat to their status and rewards by hostility towards women in the job. More men may begin to leave the job.

As women become more numerous in the job, supervisors' gender status beliefs and women workers' lower sense of entitlement exert self-fulfilling effects on women's pay and other rewards and these effects increasingly spread to the job itself. This situation makes it easier for employers to introduce organizational and technological changes to the job that further reduce the status and rewards that it offers. Although this scenario is not inevitable, when it occurs, it often results in the job becoming a woman's job with lowered status and pay. Or the job may resegregate by specialty with lower pay and status for the female specialties.

Such transitions in occupations maintain gender hierarchy over a change in the technological and organizational structure of jobs. In the many interactions through which these transitions occur, activated gender status processes and biased reward comparisons create a complex mix of discrimination, status-based competitions of interests, differences in entitlement, and differential perceptions of alternatives. The result is a system of interdependent gender effects that are everywhere and nowhere because they develop through multiple workplace interactions, often in taken-for-granted ways. Their aggregate result is the preservation of wage inequality and the gender segregation of jobs.

Conclusion

Adding an interactional perspective to labor market and organizational explanations for inequality in employment helps explain why gender is such a major force in the organization of work. Hiring, job searches, placement, performance evaluation, task assignment, promotion, and dealing with customers, clients, bosses, co-workers, and subordinates all involve direct or indirect (e.g., via resumes) interaction. Interaction with a concrete other evokes primary cultural rules for making sense of self and of other, pushing actors to gender-categorize one another in each of these interactions. Gender categorization pumps gender into the interactions through which the world of work is enacted. It cues gender status beliefs and biases the choice of comparison others. The process is insidious because gender is usually an implicit background identity that acts in combination with more salient work identities and tinges their performance with gendered expectations.

In highly structured organizational work contexts, gender processes in interaction become part of the processes through which more formal structures that embody bias, such as job ladders and evaluation systems, are enacted. Gender processes in interaction contribute to the gender labeling of jobs, to the devaluation of women's jobs, to forms of gender discrimination by employers, to the construction of men as gender-interested actors, to the control of women's interest, to differences between men's and women's pay expectations, and to the processes by which women's entrance into male occupations sometimes leads to feminization of the job or resegregation by specialty.

In less bureaucratically organized work contexts, such as those at organizational interstices, in start-up companies, in newly forming professions, or in some types of works (e.g., screen writers), interpersonal processes come to the fore and are sufficient in themselves to create gender inequality in wages and gender typing of work. As they do so, interactional processes conserve gender inequality despite significant, ongoing changes in the organization of work and the economy, writing inequality into new work structures and practices as they develop.

If this inequality is to be reduced, it is vital to understand that gender inequality is maintained by structural processes and interactional processes acting together. Change will require intervention at both the structural and interactional level through policies such as affirmative action that change the interpersonal configuration of actors and, potentially, create stereotype disconfirming experiences for all.

While much has been learned about gender inequality in employment, the study of gender-based interactional processes may help to answer some of the stubborn questions that persist. These questions include the reasons why new jobs that develop as occupations change continue to acquire connotations as men's or women's jobs, how employers' apparent preferences for male workers persist even under competitive market pressures, why women's work is devalued, whether and how people act in their gender interests in employment matters, and why women accept lower wages than men for similar work.

REFERENCES

Berger, Joseph, M. Hamit Fisek, Robert Z. Norman, and Morris Zelditch, Jr. 1977. *Status Characteristics and Social Interaction.* New York: Elsevier.

Brewer, Marilynn. 1988. "A Dual Process Model of Impression Formation." Pp. 1–36 in *Advances in Social Cognition,* Vol. 1, edited by Thomas Srull and Robert Wyer. Hillsdale, NJ: Erlbaum.

Deaux, Kay, and Brenda Major. 1987. "Putting Gender Into Context: An Interactive Model of Gender-Related Behavior." *Psychological Review* 94: 369–389.

England, Paula. 1992. *Comparable Worth: Theories and Evidence.* New York: Aldine.

Fiske, Susan, and Steven Neuberg. 1990. "A Continuum of Impression Formation, From Category-Based to Individuating Processes: Influences of Information and Motivation on Attention and Interpretation." Pp. 1–73 in *Advances in Experimental Social Psychology,* edited by Mark Zanna. New York: Academic Press.

Major, Brenda. 1989. "Gender differences in Comparisons and Entitlement: Implications for Comparable Worth." *Journal of Social Issues* 45: 99–115.

Reskin, Barbara, and Patricia Roos. 1990. *Job Queues, Gender Queues: Explaining Women's Inroads into Male Occupations.* Philadelphia: Temple University Press.

Ridgeway, Cecilia L. 1993. "Gender, Status, and the Social Psychology of Expectations." Pp. 175–198 in *Theory on Gender/Feminism on Theory,* edited by Paula England. New York: Aldine.

_____. 1997. "Interaction and the Conservation of Gender Inequality: Considering Employment." *American Sociological Review* 62: 218–235.

West, Candance and Don Zimmerman. 1987. "Doing Gender." *Gender and Society* 1: 125–151.

PART VII

SOCIAL COMPLEXITY, AMBIGUITY, AND CONTRADICTION

Advocating the mere tolerance of difference is the grossest reformism. Difference must be not merely tolerated, but seen as a fund of necessary polarities between which our creativity can spark like a dialectic. Only then does the necessity for interdependence become unthreatening.

—Audre Lorde (1984), "The Master's Tools
Will Never Dismantle This House"

These conflicts which break forth are not between the ideal and reality, but between two different ideals, that of yesterday and that of today, that which has the authority of tradition and that which has the hope of the future.

—Émile Durkheim (1965/1915),
The Cultural Logic of Collective Representations

What I claim is to live to the full contradiction of my time.

—Roland Barthes (1957/2000),
Mythologies

BOUNDARIES AND CONTRADICTIONS

Jodi O'Brien

I recall wondering as a child whether the people on television continued their activities when the set was turned off. What did they do when I was not around to operate the box they lived in? Why was it that whenever I wanted to invite one of the TV people to my birthday party, the adults in my life said the TV people couldn't come because they lived somewhere else? If they lived somewhere else, why were they always in my living room? And when some of the TV people frightened me, my parents always said not to worry because the TV people weren't real. How confusing it was to figure out what separated me and the adults I knew from the TV people!

Erving Goffman (1963), in one of his characteristically astute observations, notes that children must be taught not to call to people through walls. The reason for this, he suggests, is that children don't recognize the wall as a boundary between themselves and other people whom they know to be on the other side of the wall. Once people become aware of "walls," however, whether they are tangible or mental constructs, walls can have a profound influence on how reality is perceived.

BOUNDARIES

Two people huddled closely together in a public place, such as a coffeehouse, have an invisible wall around them. The wall is constructed from body language and gestures that we have learned to interpret as "intimacy." The action prescription that accompanies this knowledge is that it is impolite to "intrude" on someone's "walls" of intimacy. Goffman (1963) wrote an entire book, *Behavior in Public Places,* based on his observations of the manner in which persons who occupy the same physical space are able to construct unseen walls that delineate degrees of closeness and belonging. Walls also exist in the form of categorical boundaries about who we think we are or are not. Similarly, interactional routines consist of behavioral boundaries that denote what is within and without the realm of general acceptance in the situation, the group, or the culture.

Try this thought experiment: If you go to the bathroom in a public place in which there are two rooms, each with a single toilet, and the only difference is the signs that read "Men" and "Women," would you use the other bathroom if the one marked for your gender was occupied? I recently went to a public bathroom and found a couple of women waiting in line for the one marked "Women." The men's restroom was free. "Why don't we use that one?" one of the waiting women suggested. "We can keep a lookout for each other." Keep a lookout? For what? I wondered—the gender police? What would happen if the women suddenly climbed over the wall and used the men's toilet? In this case, the gender wall was invisible, but it was real to the extent that these women shared some mild anxiety about "getting caught" using the "wrong" bathroom.

The walls or boundaries that delineate experience and environment into "islands of meaning" are social accomplishments. When people define something, they trace boundaries around it; they wall it off and define what it is *not* in order to highlight and solidify what it *is*. Eviatar Zerubavel (1991), a sociologist, has written a compelling book on the topic, *The Fine Line: Making Distinctions in Everyday Life* (see also Reading 1). Zerubavel points out that the term *define* is derived from the Latin expression for boundary, *finis*. He tells this story:

> There is a joke about a man whose house stood right on the Russian–Polish border. When it was finally decided that it was actually in Poland, he cried out: "Hooray. Now I don't have to go through those terrible Russian winters anymore." (p. 28)

Zerubavel continues,

> Such reification of the purely conventional is the result of our tendency to regard the merely social as natural. Despite the fact that they are virtually mental, most gaps—as well as the quantum leaps necessary for crossing them—are among the seemingly inevitable institutionalized "social facts" that constitute our social reality. (pp. 28–29)

The signs "Men" and "Women" signify more than the location of toilets. They reflect deeply etched mental lines representing gender, one of the most basic boundaries of difference in our culture. In contemplating whether or not to use the bathroom of the "other," we are contemplating crossing over into another territory entirely.

Another illustration of a social boundary that we tend to regard as natural is the Four Corners, a popular tourist destination for travelers in the southwestern United States. In this location, four states—Utah, Colorado, New Mexico, and Arizona—all meet at a common boundary. Thousands of tourists flock to the site and engage in the contortions necessary to claim that their bodies are in four states at once. They buy souvenirs and take pictures and home videos. Is there something special about this small patch of land? If you have visited the Four Corners site, you know that it is off the beaten path, and with the exception that it's the conjunction of the four states, it's relatively unremarkable terrain. However, the conception of being in one "state" or another is a powerful reference point for the visitors. Nothing about the physical land suggests that the states should be demarcated as they are currently, but our mental maps have a firmly etched knowledge of these social boundaries.

I lived in Switzerland in my youth. This small country is home to peoples representing at least four distinct ethnic cultures—French, German, Italian, and Romanian. The first three countries border Switzerland. In crossing from one region to another, a matter of only a few kilometers in some cases, I was always struck by the ethnic distinctness of the towns. By walking across a geopolitical line separating a German from an Italian village, I could travel between two completely different worlds. The Swiss are as obsessively tidy as the stereotypes emphasize. Cars are parked neatly within carefully painted lines, and people speak in hushed tones, queue up patiently, and always deposit their litter in one of the many handy trash cans—which are always sparkling clean. Just across the border, the Italians sing and chatter merrily as they jostle one another. Traffic rules are a fiction, and motorists park in any unoccupied space that is close to their destination and often simply stop to chat with passersby.

Near my home, in Zurich, was a complicated five-way intersection. In the middle stood an enclosed podium from which a single traffic cop directed traffic—except during lunchtime. At exactly noon every working day, the traffic cop would climb down from the podium and go home for lunch, no matter that this was the time many drivers were also driving home for the noon meal. For the traffic cop, it was time to go home. It didn't seem to make much of a difference whether the traffic cop was there, however. The Swiss took turns at the intersection with the same clocklike precision that prevailed when the traffic cop was present.

The theoretical perspective developed in this book thus far suggests that the way humans make sense of and carve up our realities is a social process. We have looked at detailed information regarding the cognitive processes of "making meaning" and the interactional processes through which meaning is communicated, negotiated, and solidified. The processes have been elaborated at the personal, interpersonal, and cultural levels. By now, you know that realities are socially constructed and that organized systems of thought and rules for behavior differ from group to group. This picture is a useful representation of social reality, but it is too simple. Although it is accurate to say that boundaries are socially drawn and that different people and communities draw them differently, the impression left by much of the literature we have covered to this point is that these worlds exist as distinctly as do the worlds of the Swiss and the Italians. It may seem that negotiation proceeds, once it is routinized, as smoothly as the Swiss navigating the busy intersection at Kreuzplatz during lunchtime. However, social reality is often more complicated than this picture suggests.

CONTRADICTIONS

When different identities and cultural realities are mapped onto each other, it is evident that boundaries clash. Identities and interaction routines are not islands. They cannot be turned on and off like the people on TV. Different realms and territories overlap, and when they do, seemingly distinct selves and routines come crashing together. In the process of trying to define who we are, as individuals and as groups, we encounter contradictions. We trespass across boundaries that we hold dear. We transgress against our own systems of meaning.

Boundaries depict differences in the beliefs, interests, and relative power *among* individuals and *among* groups. Trespasses and transgressions make evident the contradictions *within* ourselves and our groups. Émile Durkheim (1915/1965), one of the founders of sociology, wrote that in the act of defining deviance, a culture (or individual) defines and reinforces its own moral boundaries. George Herbert Mead's theory of the self (see Reading 11) is grounded in the notion of an ongoing internal conversation regarding struggle between the experiences and desires of the "I" and the moral boundaries drawn by the "me." The "self" is not one or the other; rather, it is a manifestation of the conversation between the socialized "me" and conflicting desires and ideals that occur through ongoing social encounters. Karl Marx represents society as an ongoing struggle between those who control the means of production and those who do not. Society is not the victor of one or another of these struggling groups; it is an expression of the continuous conflict between them. Social institutions and practices reflect the contradictions between the haves and the have-nots.

In this final part of the book, we develop the thesis that contradictions and transgressions make people continually aware of what the boundaries are. Wrestling with these contradictions is the dynamic force of self and society. The wrestling process reveals and shapes who and what we are.

Contradictions and Conflict in Self Production

The orderly precision of Swiss society belies the fact that foreigners, or even errant locals, often transgress codes of conduct. Many a hapless visitor has thoughtlessly dropped litter to the ground, only to have an observant Swiss pick it up and return it to its "owner" with the polite inquiry, "Did you lose this?" Parking the family car was always a traumatic event for my mother because, inevitably, just as she was about to exit the car, a vigilant local would tap on the window and describe to her the way in which she had misparked. This "helper" would then redirect her into the appropriate angle.

If you imagine this process of social correction as an internal conversation, you will have a picture of Mead's "generalized other" telling the "me" what to do. Both Mead and Sigmund Freud recognized that a person often engages in activities that conflict with or contradict expected routines of behavior. To the extent that the person has been socialized by the codes and expectations of the group, he or she will experience a voice, somewhat like the Swiss tapping the litterer on the shoulder, reminding the transgressor of what is expected. Thus, to a large extent, *intrapersonal* conflict as it is discussed by Mead and Freud emphasizes the conflict between the unsocialized will—individual passions, urges, and so forth—and the internalized voices of significant groups. This picture of cultural imprinting is a bit like that of a free-spirited animal that wants to belong to the herd but resists being fenced into a pasture.

In this discussion, we focus on yet another type of intrapersonal conflict. Certainly, much self-development occurs through channeling desires and urges into expected social forms, and learning to give these feelings and drives names and to harness them accordingly. However, socialized adults are likely to encounter many circumstances in which more than one set of "generalized other" voices compete for the reins. In those cases, the person is not struggling with the conflict between "unsocialized" drives and social expectations, but rather with the clamorings and demands of distinct and contradictory voices representing varying states of being, distinct commitments, and different generalized others.

Consider this passage from *Living With Contradictions: A Married Feminist,* written by Angela Barron McBride in 1973:

> I am a married feminist. What does that mean? Am I part of a new breed of women, or someone about to burst because of the contradictions in my person? There are weeks and months when I'm not sure which description best fits me, but such tensions are the essence of being a married feminist.
>
> I am a woman who feels pulled in two directions—between traditional values and conventions on one hand, and a commitment to feminist ideology on the other. A woman who finds custom appealing and comforting, yet despises the patriarchal patterns that make women second-class citizens. I am a woman who wants a loving, long-term relationship with a man, but bitterly resents being considered only someone's other *half.* A woman who values family life, but deplores the sterile, functional view of man as the head of the family and woman as its heart. A wife who wants to belong to one man, yet not be his private property.
>
> The apparent contradictions felt by a married feminist are legion. I've listened to fashion plates sing the hedonistic pleasures of not being a mother, and felt like putting them over my knees and spanking them for their selfishness. I've heard gingham types say all they ever wanted out of life was to be a wife and a mother, and felt choked by their smugness. I bristle when people spit out the word "feminist" as if it were a communicable disease: I protest when others sneer at marriage as if it were an outdated misery. Press the button and I can feel guilty about anything. I feel guilty that I never seem to have the time to make an assortment of Christmas cookies from scratch, *and* I feel guilty about feeling guilty about that. (pp. 1–3, emphasis in original)

Note the teeter-totter between two roles, two selves—each is significant relative to specific groups, but both are defined in opposition to each other. McBride's conversation with herself is a veritable ricochet from one wall to another. In searching for her own sense of self, she wrestles with her generalized notions of what these possible selves represent. For middle-class white women in the 1960s and 1970s, the cacophony of voices about who and what they should be was loud and, in many ways, contentious.

Consider the content of these generalized voices today. Are people still inclined to represent the extremes in women's identities as "gingham types" and "radical feminists"? To some extent, these contradictions have been bridged, and the boundaries are now less sharply etched into the consciousness of young women (and men). This result stems from the attempts by the women of McBride's generation to establish some balance on the teeter-totter.

The search for new names for one's self is often prompted by the attempt to reconcile contradictions. The process can be much more complex than simply choosing one option or the other. Often the individual does not have a choice. Although contradiction and conflict may lead to change, the form of the change is always informed by the existing boundaries.

Terminology and Social Positions

In recent decades, many scholars have focused their attention on understanding the ways in which social position affects persons differently. It's obvious, for instance, that a wealthy person has a different perspective on her options when she is shopping than someone with a low-paying hourly job and a family to feed. But do these economic differences affect the self-image of each person, and if so, how? Certainly, both persons have the potential to have high self-esteem and a positive self-image, but it is also true that each is likely to have vastly different day-to-day experiences. These experiences combine to become the focus of the internal dialogue that makes up a sense of self. In this way, social position can have profound effects on self development. Regardless of what one thinks of oneself, certain features or characteristics denoting social status "mark" the interactional milieu in predictable ways. These marked interactions can affect one's sense of self.

To continue the example, someone who is wealthy is likely to be treated with respect whenever she shops. Overall, a day of shopping is likely to be a positive experience for her, and the appraisals she receives from others will likely reflect her own sense of high self-worth. Conversely, there is a tendency among store clerks to treat persons who look poor as potential thieves. Thus, regardless of her own sense of personal integrity, a person "marked" as poor frequently encounters rude stares and attitudes of suspicion when she is shopping. Whereas the wealthy person takes her high self-worth for granted and has her self-impression reaffirmed through interaction, the poor person may have to continually remind herself that she really is a decent and valuable human being, despite interactions in which she is treated as if she may not be honest.

Many concepts have been developed to describe this process of differentiation in interaction. A few of these terms are reviewed here with the aim of providing a working vocabulary. Then we turn our focus to the ways in which these processes of interactional differentiation influence self-image.

Hegemonies

Some of the terms you may have encountered to refer to a person's social position are *hegemonic position, hierarchical status, center/margin, subject/object,* and *marked/unmarked.* Here is one way to make sense of this terminology: Although there are many different, often competing, stories and perspectives that make up a culture, there are usually some stories or perspectives that are more acceptable and dominant than others. The dominant perspective is referred to as the *hegemonic* position. Whether they agree with it or not, most persons are aware of the hegemonic position, and its legitimacy is usually taken for granted. It is the position that is seen as "most normal" and "most desirable." In the contemporary United States, some of the hegemonic positions include "rational," "heterosexual," "middle-class," "Protestant," "male," and "white."

Some scholars refer to this hegemonic cluster as "the center." Recall the discussion in Part II, and you will recognize the center as the default categorical perspective. Those who do not have these centrist characteristics (for example, those who are not white) are considered "other" or "marginal." Some scholars study various hegemonies and look at the consequences for persons who are in marginal positions in the hegemony. Another way of saying this is that persons who are low in a particular social hierarchy are defined in terms relative to the hegemonic position. For instance, it can be said that economic status is a significant or hegemonic status marker in this society. There is a social hierarchy that exists according to economic status. "Middle-class" is the dominant or taken-for-granted position in this hierarchy (not necessarily the "best" position, but the one that is assumed to be "normal"). Persons who are poor are seen as low in the hierarchy and marginal.

Marked Positions and Subjectivity

For the purpose of understanding how these positions operate in interaction, the terms *marked/unmarked* and *subject/object* are useful. When a person has characteristics that are consistent with the default position in a social hierarchy, then the status of the person is said to be "unmarked." The default position is *unmarked* because, cognitively, it is what people expect to see, all else being equal. A person's status is said to be marked if it is distinct from the expected norm. Thus, as was noted in Part II, when we refer to a "basketball player," we are inclined to think of a male basketball player. If we are talking about a basketball player who is female, we tend to mark this by saying, "the woman basketball player." Similarly, when white people mention someone who is not white, race is one of the first characteristics mentioned ("I was just talking to that black guy over there"). Alternately, when referencing a white person, mention is seldom made of race ("I was just talking to that guy over there"). The latter sentence is racially unmarked and thus reflects a cultural hegemony wherein white is considered "normal."

Subject refers to the person who is in an active role; *object* refers to the person upon whom the subject is acting. This is probably the definition you were taught in English grammar. In interaction routines, however, presumably all persons are subjects. They are all interacting. In any given moment, it can be said that a particular person who is projecting a definition of the situation is the subject, and the persons to whom the subject is directing her or his actions are, in Goffman's (1963) terms, the audience (which is a more active position than "object"). In the vocabulary of symbolic interaction, persons are *subjects* to the extent that they are able to actively project their own contextual sense of self into the interactional dynamics. Someone is an *object* if he or she is seen by others only in terms of some marked social characteristic. If you came to talk with me about how much you want to go to law school, and I responded by asking you how it was for you to be the only Chicana in your class, I would be responding to you as an *ethnic object* and denying you your self-presentation as a serious student interested in law. Or imagine I responded by stating that I'm sure you would do well because Asians are so smart. In this instance, I am treating you as an ethnic object and also imposing a particular ethnic stereotype on you. In both cases, I put you in a position in which (1) I am not granting you the specific subjective position that you are presenting, and (2) you have to adjust the interaction to respond to having been put into a categorical box that may or may not have anything to do with what you are trying to talk with me about.

The paradox of subject/object is that to some extent we are always objectifying others when we interact with them. As you have learned by now, we put others into categorical boxes (label them) in order to locate their identity, and our own, in the interaction. A problem arises, however, when we interact with someone only in terms of stereotypical categories—when we do not give them the opportunity to project their own subjectivity. *Persons who can be identified by marginal, marked statuses are more likely to be treated as objects and less likely to be perceived as subjects.* A way to think about this is to ask yourself how free you are to write your own narrative in a given interaction. As we have seen, power determines who can do and say what in many interactions. To what extent does a highly marked status give you even less power in an interaction? Or, conversely, when do you find yourself treating someone else in terms of a social category (as an object) rather than as a subject?

We turn now to a discussion of some of the ways in which marked/unmarked statuses shape perception, interaction, and self-image. Keep in mind that the significant analytical point is the varying degrees to which persons in interaction have *control* over the roles and images they are able to present to others. We will look at just a few manifestations of this process: privilege and entitlement, marked positions and awareness, subjective freedom, stigmatized identities, interactional mirrors, and authenticity. Each of these processes reflects tensions and contradictions that occur as persons attempt to "realize" themselves in interaction with others.

Privilege and Entitlement

A noteworthy feature of hegemonic or unmarked positions is that those who occupy them are often unaware of their own relative subject freedom in interaction. They are more likely to pass through their everyday interactions without much friction. Their actions usually go unchallenged or don't need to be accounted for. They are generally given more space to express themselves, and their definition of the situation is likely to be accepted as the basis for the working consensus. For such people, the relationship between who they would like to be, who they think they are, and who they think they should be is likely to be isomorphic and noncontradictory. This unified and clearly delineated self-image is reflected back to them and reaffirmed in myriad small ways, especially through the ease with which they conduct their everyday interactions. This is not to say that such persons may not occupy contradictory roles—they simply have more control to make sure that these identities don't come crashing together.

Consider a small example: It is sometimes incorrectly assumed by middle-class people who live in suburbs that working-class people living in urban areas are more likely to engage in extramarital sex. In fact, the rates of extramarital sexual encounters may be the same across both classes, but middle-class people often have more resources for compartmentalizing their contradictory activities. Single-family homes ensure more privacy than do apartments with shared entries and thin walls. If you have money and credit cards, you can lead a duplicitous life farther away from prying eyes than if you do not have these resources. In short, it may be easier for a person with material wealth to move between one reality and another without experiencing too much social contradiction.

In *Carte Blanche,* a painting by René Magritte, a group of horseback riders is engaged in a fox hunt. In the foreground is a woman in fine riding clothes atop a handsome stallion. She sits astride her horse with ease and grace looking as if she hadn't a care in the world. In the background are several riders, less well clad, who are hunched low in the saddle, earnestly navigating their way around the trees of the forest through which they are riding. The woman, who represents privilege, is unaware of the trees because her horse is simply passing through them. The obstacles that exist for others don't exist for her. This is "carte blanche." The implication is that her life is like a blank check—relatively speaking, she can do as she pleases, because her social position eclipses obstacles that others must navigate.

One interactional consequence of this privilege is a sense of social entitlement. In a powerful essay about growing up as "poor white trash," author Dorothy Allison (1994) writes,

> [My people] were the *they* everyone talks about . . . the ones who are destroyed or dismissed to make the "real" people, the important people, feel safer. . . . Why are you so afraid? my lovers and friends have asked me the many times I suddenly seemed a stranger, someone who would not speak to them, would not do the things they believed I should do, simple things like applying for a job, or a grant, or some award they were sure I could acquire easily. Entitlement, I have told them, is a matter of feeling like we rather than they. You think you have a right to things, a place in the world, and it is so intrinsically a part of you that you cannot imagine people like me, people who seem to live in your world, who don't have it. I have explained what I know over and over, in every way that I can, but I have never been able to make clear the degree of my fear, the extent to which I feel myself denied . . . [that] I was born poor into a world that despises the poor. (p. 14, emphasis in original)

Entitlement in this sense can be defined as a taken-for-granted expectation that one has a *right* to pursue certain goals and to participate in various interactions. The person who feels entitled does not worry about being seen as an imposter or about being rejected or dismissed. Consider what sorts of internal conversations a person is likely to have if he or she feels entitled to participate in most realms of social life versus someone who would like to participate but is not sure if he or she has a right to do so. To what extent does this sense of entitlement provide someone with a script for pursuing such things as asking advice from professors, asking for letters of recommendation for graduate school, and so forth? A sense of entitlement is enhanced through repeated interactions in which a person is affirmed for her or his efforts. The more affirmed one feels, the more he or she will pursue new and risky opportunities that may lead to even greater social advantages. Relatedly, a person who feels entitled to certain things is more likely to get upset if things don't go as he or she planned. Relatively speaking, those with a strong sense of entitlement are more likely to hold greater expectations that situations will unfold according to their plans.

Marked Positions and Social Awareness

For those who occupy marginal, marked statuses, the simplest interaction may pose a contradiction between how they would like to see themselves and how others see them. A lack of role support combined with the necessity of pushing harder to project a definition of the situation can have profound effects on someone's sense of self. Social psychologists have studied the relationship between self-esteem and people's tendency to attribute successes and failures to external or internal factors. For instance, if you perform well on an exam and attribute this outcome to your own intelligence and the fact that you studied, you have made an *internal attribution*—the result is a consequence of something you did. If, on the other hand, you perform poorly and say that it was because the exam was too hard, you have made an *external attribution*—the outcome is due to factors beyond yourself.

A second attributional dimension is the extent to which you perceive the cause to be stable and within your control. For instance, if you perform poorly on an exam but attribute your performance to lack of study, you have made an internal attribution and concluded that the circumstances are potentially within your control: "I could pass that exam. I just need to study harder." If, however, you attribute your grade to the instructor's dislike of you, you have concluded that your evaluation is based on external factors beyond your control. Social psychologists are inclined to agree that external attributions lead to feelings of helplessness—the individual feels that nothing he or she can do will alter the outcome.

In a class exercise, I asked students to write a description of an occasion when they were uncertain about whether some outcome in their lives was due to personal (internal) factors or social (external) factors. Most of the students were middle class, but some interesting differences in their responses did appear. When students read their responses, several of the women told of instances in which they had not gotten jobs or had not been allowed to participate in certain activities. They were unsure whether the outcome was because they were female or because they didn't have the right skills. Students of color had thought of similar instances. One Chinese American male told of winning an essay contest in his first year of college. Subsequently, he was invited to a national forum to read the essay. When he arrived, he noted that all the other "winners" were also students of color. He was unable to decide whether he had won because he wrote a terrific essay or because of his ethnicity. Many of the Latin American and Asian American students related similar experiences. All of them were familiar with the day-to-day uncertainty about whether to attribute events in their lives to personal or social factors. For them, everyday self-awareness includes an ongoing internal conversation about whether their experiences result from ethnic, racial, or gendered processes or from personal skill and talent. One consequence of this ongoing deliberation is a feeling of walking along volatile boundary lines and never being certain if one is inside or outside.

The white men, meanwhile, looked increasingly ill at ease during this classroom activity. One by one, they read papers that began, "I'm not sure what the question is . . ." or "I'm not sure what you're getting at here. . . ." In subsequent reflective essays, however, many of these young men noted that they had gained a much greater recognition of how complicated self-awareness and self-evaluation are for people who cannot be certain whether or not an outcome in their lives is because of something within their control or because they are marked as particular objects. The white male students also began to take note of the many additional boundaries, such as social class and society's expectations for them (for instance, financial productivity, heterosexuality, and masculinity), that shape who and what they think they can be.

Whatever a person's status, greater self-awareness occurs as a result of recognizing the complex interplay among the positions that constitute social boundaries. Like other social routines that become ossified, and even naturalized over time, these positions are likely to be taken for granted by some and not by others. The less able a person is to take them for granted, the more likely he or she is to be aware of the boundaries—and the conflicts and contradictions—within all social systems. One outcome of dealing with contradiction is an ability to comprehend more social complexity.

Subjective Freedom

Subjective freedom can be described as how much freedom one has to successfully convey a definition of the situation. If others in the interactional setting see the person only in terms of a particular stereotypical status—as an object—then the person cannot expect to be seen on her or his own terms. For instance, in education research, it has been demonstrated that college students respond very differently to the same material depending on whether it is taught by a white man or a woman of color. The white man, who occupies the unmarked or expected position for the role of a college professor, is usually seen as "in control," "apolitical," "fair," and "informative" when he teaches material such as the ideas being discussed in this essay. A woman of color teaching exactly the same thing is often evaluated by students as being "too political," "too biased," "lacking authority," and "uninformed." Not only do perceptions differ dramatically, but in this case the man has more subjective freedom than the woman. A woman who is aware of these stereotypical reactions among students can develop strategies to counter this tendency, but in doing so, she has to shape the interaction in response to stereotypical perceptions. She is not as free to "be herself" in the same way that the man is. In presenting her subjective position (in this case as a teacher), she must navigate around the ways in which others mark her only as an object of her race and gender.

Persons who occupy significantly marked positions are usually aware of the contradictions between how they see themselves and how others see them. The dilemma is complicated further by the fact that these marked positions are also a part of someone's subjectivity. A professor who is also a woman of color does not necessarily want to be treated *as if* she were white. This "color-blind" attitude reinforces the hegemony that white is the default and desired position. The challenge in developing *multicultural consciousness* is to overcome mindless stereotypes so that persons do not have to navigate their way out of boxes that objectify them in order to present their own subjectivity.

Ironically, dismantling stereotypes requires a *more* discriminating attitude. This does not mean discrimination in the sense of stereotyping, but discrimination as a form of discernment and awareness. We have to train ourselves to *pay more attention* to details that otherwise go unnoticed because they may not fit the stereotype. An employer who is mindfully discerning, for instance, will force herself to get over the fact that the job interviewee is in a wheelchair and focus instead on features such as the person's seemingly high intelligence and expert experience. At the same time, she will be aware that the person is in fact in a wheelchair and that this is obviously of some consequence for him. The ways in which it is of consequence should be the subject's own story to tell, however. The more he perceives that he is being treated genuinely as a subject within the situation—in this case, as a potential employee—rather than as a "handicapped" object, the freer he will be to present his own complex rendering of himself.

Stigmatized Identities

Some statuses are not only highly marked, but are marked in ways that are stigmatizing for the individual and for those associated with the individual. This stigmatization can have significant consequences for interaction and self-image. Consider a person who responds with the following profile to the "Who Am I?" question (see Part III):

daughter	computer geek
granddaughter	cat lover
graduate student	religious
white feminist	music lover
from Indiana	

Are you formulating an image of this person? Can you tell something about the important things and people in her life from this list (for example, parents, grandparents, cats, school, and so forth)? This is her own subjective rendering of herself. All of these self-referential characteristics are features that she would probably be able to bring up in conversation with others and not expect conflict to occur (except maybe in terms of types of computers or favorite bands, but this would only reaffirm her commitment to these aspects of "self"). In other words, there doesn't appear to be a lot of role conflict in this initial list. Suppose, however, that she added "lesbian" to the list. Is this something that she can tell her grandmother about? Obviously, that depends on the grandmother and the relationship between the two of them. Regardless, we can assume that this particular aspect of self may exist in conflict with some of the other relationships that she may value. Even if her parents are accepting of her lesbian status in their interactions with their daughter, they may find themselves in conflict when they encounter old friends who ask if their daughter is married yet. Do they "come out" as the parents of a lesbian or deflect the question in a way that will preserve their own unmarked (that is, heterosexual) status?

For many people, once they are aware of this particular status, all other aspects of the person fade to the background. A stigmatized identity has a tendency to become a "master identity." Everything else about the person takes a back seat to, or is evaluated in terms of, the master identity. Stigmatized master identities also reflect archetypal social beliefs, such as the belief that someone can be a lesbian or religious but not both simultaneously. These sorts of ideas reflect entrenched social expectations about which social roles go together and which do not. There is a tendency to assume that a person with a stigmatized role is nothing other than that particular role.

A person who engages in activities that are considered stigmatized has to do a great deal of interactional work to manage information. This example illustrates a highly marked, problematic aspect of self (stigma) that has consequences in interaction with others. It also illustrates the fact that all of us have multiple, contradictory, shifting selves. We are many things both to ourselves and to one another. We enact various selves contextually. We may push out one aspect of self in one setting (spiritual) and another in another setting (participation in a seminar on gay/lesbian experiences). We may keep certain features hidden (lesbian) in order to preserve a valued relationship (with a grandmother). *Stigma* is an interactional feature. An aspect of self is stigmatized only to the extent that persons define it as beyond the boundaries of expected or acceptable practices. Yet stigma can have very real consequences in shaping how persons make sense of the contradictions they perceive in their own self-image and how they grapple with these contradictions in interaction with others.

Many stigmatized identities exist in the form of highly marked stereotypes (handicapped, homeless, ex-convict, hooker, drug addict, mental patient, welfare recipient, and so on). But any aspect of self about which someone feels extreme shame or embarrassment has the potential to operate as a stigmatized identity. If you are struggling with being gay, lesbian, or transgender; or being from a working-class background; or being a single parent; or because of your religious background; and so forth, then you may feel impelled to try to hide this aspect of yourself from others. Many social psychologists suggest that "shame" about an aspect of self-identity develops when a person internalizes social scripts that convey certain statuses as marked and undesirable. The person's own internal gaze or mirror is a reflection of social images whereby the identity is defined as loathsome. As a consequence of looking at this internal image, the person develops a sense of self-loathing. Persons who engage in behaviors that are stigmatized may or may not feel shame or embarrassment themselves. The extent to which they are able to deflect the shame directed at them by others depends on what sort of larger repertoire of self-understanding they have, their history of interactions with significant others, and their position in various social hierarchies.

For instance, when I am traveling in certain areas, I can expect to be called names or even spat at by persons who perceive me to be a lesbian. At times I feel unsafe in certain areas. However, for the most part I have the freedom to avoid these situations, and to the extent that I do have to deal with bigotry, I have a well-developed set of responses. My self-image as a lesbian (a nonstigmatized identity for me) is shaped by the fact that I am a tenured professor in a respectable university. I am aware that one part of who I am—my sexual identity—is socially stigmatized, but I view that part as normal and unremarkable. In interaction, I project a definition that invites others to treat me accordingly. And for the most part, they do. Students and colleagues may privately despise me for this part of who I am, but I don't provide any opportunity for them to project this definition onto my interaction. My ability to achieve this interactional de-stigmatization is based on much critical reflection about how I want to incorporate this aspect of myself into my everyday interactions; many positive experiences in which my own self-view has been affirmed by people who matter to me; and, perhaps most important, the fact that I have a great deal of power in the particular context in which I spend most of my time—a college campus.

All of us experience some degree of tension and contradiction (such as shame and guilt) in the various behaviors that we consider to be aspects of our core self. The way in which we work through these contradictions shapes our developing sense of self. Our resources for wrestling with these contradictions reflect personal interactional history and the repertoire of stories we have for ourselves, as well as our own relative power in situations.

Interactional Mirrors

One of the features of a hegemonic or central position is that persons who occupy these positions can be relatively certain of encountering others like them wherever they go. One outcome of this is that the person's reality is likely to be reflected back by others and thereby continually reaffirmed. In contrast, persons who occupy marginal positions and who interact primarily with persons who hold mainstream positions may often feel isolated and conflicted about how to interpret their own experiences. In the words of poet Adrienne Rich (1984/1994),

> When those who have the power to name and to socially construct reality choose not to see you or hear you . . . when someone with the authority of a teacher, say, describes the world and you are not in it, there is a moment of psychic disequilibrium, as if you looked in the mirror and saw nothing. It takes some strength of soul—and not just individual strength, but collective understanding— to resist this void, this non-being, into which you are thrust, and to stand up, demanding to be seen and heard. (p. 199)

Being able to interact with others whose experiences and struggles match your own is not simply a privilege; it is an occasion to (re)affirm the reality of your own impressions and feelings. Many of us transgress boundaries every day because we are "outsiders." The vertigo of these experiences can be overcome, to some extent, if we are able to interact with others who share our conflicting circumstances and contradictory experiences. Conversations with those who share our experiences provide us with new names and meanings that help us bridge the contradictions. This opportunity to associate and redefine reality is one of the reasons why special interest groups and clubs are important for people who share marginalized, marked, or stigmatized statuses. These groups provide interactional mirrors that reflect the complexities of crossing through contradictory states of being. In encounters with others who experience similar contradictions and tensions, people broaden their repertoire, learn new scripts for acting, and have an opportunity to express more subjective freedom.

In the United States, suicide is the leading cause of death among gay, lesbian, and transgendered youths aged 15 to 24 (Herdt & Roxer, 1993). These young people often experience their sexual or gender feelings as being completely outside the boundaries of the self-images that have been inculcated by significant others, such as parents, family, friends, teachers, and church and community leaders. Without positive imagery and role models for how to incorporate their differences into the rest of their self-image, these young people may suffer the contradictions deeply. Irreconcilable feelings of helplessness can lead to extreme despair. The opportunity to encounter people whose self-image reconciles the identities of "homosexual" and "productive, accepted member of society" can turn these young people away from the brink of suicide.

Similarly, female students and students of color benefit from programs designed specifically for them to interact with others who share similar points of view. For these alternative perspectives to be interactionally supported and to gain the stature of commonly understood realities, they must sometimes be enacted separately from mainstream culture. Renato Rosaldo (1993), an anthropologist who has participated actively in the development of such programs at Stanford University, calls the programs "safe houses":

> Why do institutions need safe houses? Safe houses can foster self-esteem and promote a sense of belonging in often alien institutions. Safe houses are places where diverse groups—under the banners of ethnic studies, feminist studies, or gay and lesbian studies—talk together and become more articulate about their intellectual projects. When they enter the mainstream seminars such students speak with clarity and force about their distinctive projects, concerns, and perspectives. The class is richer and more complex, if perhaps less comfortable, for its broadened range of perspectives. (p. xi)

Rosaldo is delineating the interactional steps whereby persons have an opportunity to express their subjectivity without having to navigate the imposition of stereotypes and prejudices. In the kind of interactional setting that he describes, persons develop a clearer and more articulate sense of who they are *in all their complexity*. When they bring this complexity into mainstream interactions, it can have the effect of altering the stereotypical routine.

It is important to note that status as an insider or an outsider is situational and may change with circumstance. In *Falling From Grace*, Katherine Newman (1988) describes the experiences of men in middle and upper managerial positions who have lost their jobs. For most of these men, selfhood pivots around their ability, as holders of privileged positions, to move with ease through a world in which they wield considerable control. When they lose their jobs, they lose access to a tremendous amount of interactional privilege (such as control over space and conversation) that was their basis for maintaining a positive self-image. Many of these men are unaccustomed to contradictory self-images and, as a result, are ill prepared for the quick downward spiral that they experience when they fall outside the lines of their primary reference group. Lacking alternative points of reference and feeling ashamed of having been "downsized," these men are at high risk for suicide. Support groups for these men do not simply provide a way to get through the hard times—they are interactional situations in which the men learn to project and juggle a new self-image, one that is quite different from the self they have been accustomed to being.

Authenticity

The preceding discussion reveals a picture of the social self as multiple, shifting, and contradictory. How we see ourselves and the selves we present to others shift from context to context and can be contradictory within a given situation. We are more committed to some aspects of self than others. We may be inclined to hide or deflect certain significant identities in some situations. These observations lead to the question, "Who are you really?" The question of "authenticity" is something that concerns many scholars as well as individuals. One answer to the question comes in the form of a paradox: We all live contradictory lives, but we tend to act *as if* our lives were not filled with ambiguity and contradiction. One cultural expectation that many of us share is the *norm of consistency*. Is consistency the same thing as authenticity? For many people, it is. We tend to believe someone is "authentic" when we observe her or him behaving consistently across different settings and circumstances ("She must be genuinely kind, because she is kind even when someone is mean to her."). It is possible that persons strive to make their behavior consistent because others expect them to behave consistently. Over the course of time, with repeated interactions and affirmation, we may develop self-routines that are so consistent that we believe them to be authentic expressions of self. Furthermore, to the extent that others strive to show us consistency and to hide the inconsistencies, we may come to believe that people are, indeed, consistent or authentic.

In a related way, we may strive to hide aspects of self that might strike others as contradictory according to preexisting social scripts about what sorts of behaviors go together ("He can't possibly be gay and also be a minister."). In doing so, we reaffirm these social scripts and fail to express the fact that selves are indeed multiple and contradictory.

From the perspective of symbolic interactionists who recognize the existence of multiple, shifting, contradicting self-expressions, one answer to the question, "Who are you really?" is this: We are really the *way* in which we work through the contradictions that characterize our day-to-day interactions. We are the *process of wrestling contradiction*. This process is reflected in internal conversation and external expression. Two people can have a similar profile of self-referential identities and characteristics but very different self-images and interactional responses. Consider again the woman described in the "Who am I?" question above. She might keep her more stigmatized statuses (lesbian, religious) closeted from others whom she suspects will not be able to handle the "contradictions" these statuses imply, or she might reveal all and express an attitude of "I have a right to be *all* these various selves, even if it confuses you." How she views her own selves and how she chooses to portray them to others—in all their complexity and ambiguity—reveals the process of who she really is.

In this way, it can be concluded that *selves are always in a state of becoming*. This becoming is shaped through the processes of interaction and revealed through the internal dialogues in which we observe, comment on, feel, and try to make sense of our own complexity.

Recall some of the general principles that have been formulated throughout this book. All humans use language-based systems to create conceptual meaning. This process creates definitional boundaries. All people compartmentalize. Different individuals encounter these boundaries differently. The process of self-understanding is a continual interplay between personal experience and attempts to fit experience into existing conceptual categories and representations. All of us struggle to make sense of ourselves, to find ways of self-expression, and to be heard and understood. The self undergoes constant revision as it encounters friction, contradiction, and conflict among the various boundaries that give the self meaning.

Conflict and Change in Cultural Production

Cultural production, like self production, is a dialectical process of definition. Within groups and societies, people struggle over what significant symbols mean and who has the authority to project public definitions. The struggle over frames of meaning organizes people's lives.

In this struggle to create definitions, cultural institutions are a resource—a source of privilege for some and an obstacle for others. Various institutions—family, government, religion, and the economy, for example—can wield great influence in the creation or maintenance of socially shared definitions. This influence may be unintended, or it may be consciously directed toward supporting a particular status quo. Again, however, power is an issue. Not everyone is equally able to participate in the construction of meaning. Some people's beliefs and interests are given more legitimacy than those of others.

Hegemonic practices of inequality persist because people play out the scripts expected of them—even when they may be privately opposed to these practices (see also the essay in Part VI on the status quo). People participate in practices of domination and inequality for a variety of reasons: They may not realize the extent to which they contribute to the maintenance of particular definitions of the situation (hence the popular bumper sticker "Question authority"). Or, as is often the case, they may not have the resources necessary to break the chains of the existing reality. This complicity in oppression is what Marx refers to when he says that the "tradition of the dead generations weighs like a *nightmare* on the brain of the living" (italics added; see opening quote in the Part VI essay). Prevailing realities suggest certain lines of action and forestall others. The possibility for change is in the conception of alternative lines of interaction. Alexis de Tocqueville once observed, "A grievance can be endured so long as it seems beyond redress, but it becomes intolerable once the possibility of removing it crosses people's minds." To be realized, however, even the most eloquent theories must be acted out. Change must be performed on the social stage.

In a well-known essay called "Talking Back," the writer and activist bell hooks considers what happens when an oppressed person refuses to engage in expected forms of deference (see Reading 42). Oppression is a construction that requires the cooperation of many social actors—those doing the oppressing and those who are being oppressed. According to hooks, we choose to either join in the construction of oppression or to withdraw our support. She points out that we can all actively work to breach realities that work against our interests. Even if our resistance is only small, sometimes we find ways to talk back.

Conclusions

One of the paradoxes of human social life is that cultural practices both constrain us and make our lives meaningful. Another writer and activist, Gloria Anzaldúa, who passed away in 2004, left a powerful legacy regarding cultural complexity. In one of her essays, "*La Conciencia de la Mestiza*/Toward a New Consciousness" (1987), she describes the experiences of those who walk the boundaries and live the contradictions of being outsiders to various communities by virtue of class, gender, race, religion, sexuality, and so on. According to Anzaldúa (1987), such people develop a multiple, or *mestiza,* consciousness that makes them more aware of both the advantages and limitations of entrenched cultural practices. The *mestiza* is "a product of the transfer of the cultural and spiritual values of one group to another" (p. 78). This cultural transfer or border navigation can be tremendously difficult.

Anzaldúa (1987) describes the clash this way:

> The clash of voices results in mental and emotional states of perplexity. Internal strife results in insecurity and indecisiveness. The mestiza's dual or multiple personality is plagued by psychic restlessness. . . . These numerous possibilities leave *la mestiza* floundering in uncharted seas. In perceiving conflicting information and points of view she is subjected to a swamping of her psychological borders. (p. 78)

How does *la mestiza* cope?

> The new *mestiza* copes by developing a tolerance for contradictions, a tolerance for ambiguity. She learns to be an Indian in Mexican culture, to be a Mexican from an Anglo point of view. She learns to juggle cultures. She has a plural personality, she operates in pluralistic mode. . . . Not only does she sustain contradictions, she turns the ambivalence into something else. (p. 79)

One of the implications of *la mestiza,* or multiple consciousness, is cultural awareness. Those who cannot take their social positions for granted, who cannot assume that their definition of the situation will be shared by others, are likely to have a more expansive awareness of the situation and its possibilities. This is what Anzaldúa refers to as the "consciousness of the borderlands." Borderland consciousness, and the struggle it involves, is a central aspect of change. Anzaldúa concludes,

> The struggle is inner. The struggle has always been inner, and is played out in the outer terrains. Awareness of our situation must come before inner changes, which in turn come before changes in society. Nothing happens in the "real" world unless it happens first in the images in our heads. (p. 87)

Although Anzaldúa is writing specifically about the borders that divide the consciousness of Chicana/os who are also Indians and also trying to live in Anglo worlds, her words resonate with many people who traverse multiple social borders. Contradiction is not necessarily a bad thing, especially when struggle leads to awareness. To the extent that each of us recognizes and learns to wrestle with the contradictions that are an inevitable part of social existence, we expand the definitions of who and what we imagine we can be. We increase our social muscle and enrich our repertoire of possibilities.

A similar process occurs at the societal level. As groups engage in boundary skirmishes regarding respective definitions of morality; entitlement; and the power to define cultural institutions such as politics, law, religion, and family, there is the possibility of increased awareness. This potential is shaped, in large part, by a group's power to participate in cultural definitions of what is "real" and "acceptable." If you live in the United States, consider what it means to live in a country that promotes the ideal of "freedom and justice" for all. Cultural pluralism is the bedrock of this freedom. For the ideal to become real, it is necessary to foster a national *mestiza* consciousness and all the struggle and debate that go along with it.

References and Suggestions for Further Reading

Allison, D. (1994). *Skin: Talking about sex, class and literature*. Ithaca, NY: Firebrand Books.

Anzaldúa, G. (1987). *Borderlands/La Frontera: The new mestiza*. San Francisco: Aunt Lute Books.

Barthes, R. (2000). *Mythologies* (A. Lavers, Trans.). London: Vintage. (Original work published 1957)

Durkheim, É. (1965). *The elementary forms of the religious life* (J. W. Swain, Trans.). New York: Free Press of Glencoe. (Original work published 1915)

Goffman, E. (1963). *Behavior in public places*. New York: Free Press.

Herdt, G., & Roxer, A. (1993). *Children of horizons*. Boston: Beacon.

Lorde, A. (1984). *Sister/Outsider: Essays and speeches by Audre Lorde*. Berkeley, CA: Crossing Press.

McBride, A. B. (1973). *Living with contradictions: A married feminist*. New York: HarperCollins.

McIntosh, P. (1992). White privilege and male privilege. In M. L. Anderson & P. H. Collins (Eds.), *Race, class, and gender: An anthology* (pp. 70–81). Belmont, CA: Wadsworth.

Newman, K. (1988). *Falling from grace*. New York: Free Press.

Rich, A. (1994). Invisibility in academe. In *Blood, bread, and poetry: Selected prose (1979–1985)*. New York: Norton. (Original work published 1984)

Rosaldo, R. (1993). *Culture and truth: The remaking of social analysis*. Boston: Beacon Press.

Zerubavel, E. (1991). *The fine line: Making distinctions in everyday life*. Chicago: University of Chicago Press.

CONTRADICTIONS AND CONFLICT IN SELF PRODUCTION

The previous sections (Parts III and IV) suggest an explanation for the development of a social self through interaction. This section explores the more complicated process that occurs when our self-expectations and self-images are in conflict. People often identify with conflicting reference groups, for example. Similarly, we may receive ambiguous and confusing messages from various sources about who and what we should be. The articles in this section explore how people make sense of these contradictions. They also illustrate a powerful theme in the social psychology of the self: People have an amazing capacity to construct some kind of coherency out of the most extreme contradictions. This observation suggests that we are infinitely creative in constructing our own life stories.

"Double Consciousness and the Veil" is an excerpt from the writings of a famous sociologist, W. E. B. DuBois. DuBois was a highly influential thinker during the period known as the Harlem Renaissance in the 1920s. His ideas were instrumental in the advancement and politics of the "New Negro." Although his ideas were criticized by the next generation of black artists and intellectuals as being too bourgeois and too assimilationist in reference to a white middle class, DuBois is widely regarded as one of the great intellectuals of his time. This selection is an early essay in which he considers the experience of being "other" and of cultivating a "Negro" self in a white world.

How do openly gay Christians make sense of the contradictions between Christian doctrine and being homosexual? I explore this question in "Wrestling the Angel of Contradiction: Queer Christian Identities." This study traces the ways in which openly gay and lesbian Christians define the contradictions they experience and the ways in which they reconcile these contradictions. This process of reconciling contradictions may have some surprising effects on mainstream Christian congregations.

In "Contested Selves in Divorce Proceedings," Joseph Hopper describes the excruciating conflict often experienced by persons involved in divorce proceedings. The person going through the divorce must manage the new "ex" identity, as well as the conflict between the emotional self he or she wants to project and the self that attorneys and other professionals are trying to help the person construct. According to divorce attorneys, their clients often believe that if they take on the self required for a successful divorce proceeding, they will be dishonoring the more emotional self that is in pain, angry, feeling cheated, and so forth.

READING QUESTIONS

1. Return to your list of responses to the question, "Who am I?" (Part III). Are there any items on this list that you would be embarrassed or ashamed to have someone close to you know about? If not, imagine what kinds of items might be on the lists of others that could be potentially conflicting.

2. Self concept emerges from a person's unique intersection of social positions such as class, gender, race, religion, sexuality, age, and so forth. Review the concepts in the Part VII essay for this section and consider which aspects of your social position are more or less "central" and more or less "marginal." What impact might your specific position have had on your interactions and experiences?

3. Discuss the proposition that social power is the extent to which you can author your own position. What are some interactional factors that enable people to be more or less in control of how others define them?

4. Consider some experiences of self-ambiguity or self-conflict in your own life. Trace the specific reference groups or significant others that are the source of this conflict.

5. The material in this section offers both a theory of self-stability and of self-change. Explain.

CONTRADICTIONS AND CONFLICT IN SELF PRODUCTION

38

Double Consciousness and the Veil

W. E. B. DuBois

(1903)

O water, voice of my heart, crying in the sand,

All night long crying with a mournful cry,

As I lie and listen, and cannot understand

The voice of my heart in my side or the
voice of the sea,

O water, crying for rest, is it I, is it I?

All night long the water is crying to me.

Unresting water, there shall never be rest

Till the last moon droop and the last tide fail,

And the fire of the end begin to burn
in the west;

And the heart shall be weary and wonder
and cry like the sea,

All life long crying without avail,

As the water all night long is crying to me.

—Arthur Symons

Between me and the other world there is
ever an unasked question: unasked by
some through feelings of delicacy; by others
through the difficulty of rightly framing it. All,
nevertheless, flutter round it. They approach me
in a half-hesitant sort of way, eye me curiously or
compassionately, and then, instead of saying
directly, How does it feel to be a problem? they say,
I know an excellent colored man in my town;

or, I fought at Mechanicsville; or, Do not these
Southern outrages make your blood boil? At these
I smile, or am interested, or reduce the boiling to
a simmer, as the occasion may require. To the
real question, How does it feel to be a problem?
I answer seldom a word.

And yet, being a problem is a strange experience—peculiar even for one who has never been
anything else, save perhaps in babyhood and in
Europe. It is in the early days of rollicking boyhood that the revelation first bursts upon one, all
in a day, as it were. I remember well when the
shadow swept across me. I was a little thing, away
up in the hills of New England, where the dark
Housatonic winds between Hoosac and Taghkanic
to the sea. In a wee wooden schoolhouse, something put it into the boys' and girls' heads
to buy gorgeous visiting-cards—ten cents a
package—and exchange. The exchange was merry,
till one girl, a tall newcomer, refused my card—
refused it peremptorily, with a glance. Then it
dawned upon me with a certain suddenness that I
was different from the others; or like, mayhap, in
heart and life and longing, but shut out from their
world by a vast veil. I had thereafter no desire to
tear down that veil, to creep through; I held all
beyond it in common contempt, and lived above it
in a region of blue sky and great wandering shadows.
That sky was bluest when I could beat my mates at
examination-time, or beat them at a foot-race,

or even beat their stringy heads. Alas, with the years all this fine contempt began to fade, for the words I longed for, and all their dazzling opportunities, were theirs, not mine. But they should not keep these prizes, I said; some, all, I would wrest from them. Just how I would do it I could never decide: by reading law, by healing the sick, by telling the wonderful tales that swam in my head—some way. With other black boys the strife was not so fiercely sunny: their youth shrunk into tasteless sycophancy, or into silent hatred of the pale world about them and mocking distrust of everything white; or wasted itself in a bitter cry: Why did God make me an outcast and a stranger in mine own house? The shades of the prison-house closed round about us all: walls strait and stubborn to the whitest, but relentlessly narrow, tall, and unscalable to sons of night who must plod darkly on in resignation, or beat unavailing palms against the stone, or steadily, half hopelessly, watch the streak of blue above.

After the Egyptian and Indian, the Greek and Roman, the Teuton and Mongolian, the Negro is a sort of seventh son, born with a veil, and gifted with second-sight in this American world—a world which yields him no true self-consciousness, but only lets him see himself through the revelation of the other world. It is a peculiar sensation, this double-consciousness, this sense of always looking at one's self through the eyes of others, of measuring one's soul by the tape of a world that looks on in amused contempt and pity. One ever feels his twoness—an American, a Negro; two souls, two thoughts, two unreconciled strivings; two warring ideals in one dark body, whose dogged strength alone keeps it from being torn asunder.

The history of the American Negro is the history of this strife—this longing to attain self-conscious manhood, to merge his double self into a better and truer self. In this merging he wishes neither of the older selves to be lost. He would not Africanize America, for America has too much to teach the world and Africa. He would not bleach his Negro soul in a flood of white Americanism, for he knows that Negro blood has a message for the world. He simply wishes to make it possible for a man to be both a Negro and an American, without being cursed and spit upon by his fellows, without having the doors of Opportunity closed roughly in his face.

This, then, is the end of his striving: to be a co-worker in the kingdom of culture, to escape both death and isolation, to husband and use his best powers and his latent genius. These powers of body and mind have in the past been strangely wasted, dispersed, or forgotten. The shadow of a mighty Negro past flits through the tale of Ethiopia the Shadowy and of Egypt the Sphinx. Through history, the powers of single black men flash here and there like falling stars, and die sometimes before the world has rightly gauged their brightness. Here in America, in the few days since Emancipation, the black man's turning hither and thither in hesitant and doubtful striving has often made his very strength to lose effectiveness, to seem like absence of power, like weakness. And yet it is not weakness—it is the contradiction of double aims. The double-aimed struggle of the black artisan—on the one hand to escape white contempt for a nation of mere hewers of wood and drawers of water, and on the other hand to plough and nail and dig for a poverty-stricken horde—could only result in making him a poor craftsman, for he had but half a heart in either cause. By the poverty and ignorance of his people, the Negro minister or doctor was tempted toward quackery and demagogy; and by the criticism of the other world, toward ideals that made him ashamed of his lowly tasks. The would-be black *savant* was confronted by the paradox that the knowledge his people needed was a twice-told tale to his white neighbors, while the knowledge which would teach the white world was Greek to his own flesh and blood. The innate love of harmony and beauty that set the ruder souls of his people a-dancing and a-singing raised but confusion and doubt in the soul of the black artist; for the beauty revealed to him was the soul-beauty of a race which his larger audience despised, and he could not articulate the message of another people. This waste of double aims, this seeking to satisfy two unreconciled ideals, has wrought sad havoc with the courage and faith and deeds of ten thousand people—has sent them often wooing false gods and invoking false means of salvation, and at times has even seemed about to make them ashamed of themselves.

Away back in the days of bondage they thought to see in one divine event the end of all doubt and disappointment; few men ever worshipped Freedom with half such unquestioning faith as did the American Negro for two centuries. To him, so far as he thought and dreamed, slavery was indeed the sum of all villainies, the cause of all sorrow, the root of all prejudice; Emancipation was the key to a promised land of sweeter beauty than ever stretched before the eyes of wearied Israelites. In song and exhortation swelled one refrain—Liberty; in his tears and curses the God he implored had Freedom in his right hand. At last it came—suddenly, fearfully, like a dream. With one wild carnival of blood and passion came the message in his own plaintive cadences—

Shout, O children!

Shout, you're free!

For God has bought your liberty!

Years have passed away since then—ten, twenty, forty; forty years of national life, forty years of renewal and development, and yet the swarthy spectre sits in its accustomed seat at the Nation's feast. In vain do we cry to this our vastest social problem—

Take any shape but that, and my firm nerves

Shall never tremble!

The Nation has not yet found peace from its sins; the freedman has not yet found in freedom his promised land. Whatever of good may have come in these years of change, the shadow of a deep disappointment rests upon the Negro people—a disappointment all the more bitter because the unattained ideal was unbounded save by the simple ignorance of a lowly people.

The first decade was merely a prolongation of the vain search for freedom, the boon that seemed ever barely to elude their grasp—like a tantalizing will-o'-the-wisp, maddening and misleading the headless host. The holocaust of war, the terrors of the Ku-Klux Klan, the lies of carpetbaggers, the disorganization of industry, and the contradictory advice of friends and foes, left the bewildered serf with no new watchword beyond the old cry for freedom. As the time flew, however, he began to grasp a new idea. The ideal of liberty demanded for its attainment powerful means, and these the Fifteenth Amendment gave him. The ballot, which before he had looked upon as a visible sign of freedom, he now regarded as the chief means of gaining and perfecting the liberty with which war had partially endowed him. And why not? Had not votes made war and emancipated millions? Had not votes enfranchised the freedmen? Was anything impossible to a power that had done all this? A million black men started with renewed zeal to vote themselves into the kingdom. So the decade flew away, the revolution of 1876 came, and left the half-free serf weary, wondering, but still inspired. Slowly but steadily, in the following years, a new vision began gradually to replace the dream of political power—a powerful movement, the rise of another ideal to guide the unguided, another pillar of fire by night after a clouded day. It was the ideal of "book-learning"; the curiosity, born of compulsory ignorance, to know and test the power of the cabalistic letters of the white man, the longing to know. Here at last seemed to have been discovered the mountain path to Canaan; longer than the highway of Emancipation and law, steep and rugged, but straight, leading to heights high enough to overlook life.

Up the new path the advance guard toiled, slowly, heavily, doggedly; only those who have watched and guided the faltering feet, the misty minds, the dull understandings, of the dark pupils of these schools know how faithfully, how piteously, this people strove to learn. It was weary work. The cold statistician wrote down the inches of progress here and there, noted also where here and there a foot had slipped or someone had fallen. To the tired climbers, the horizon was ever dark, the mists were often cold, the Canaan was always dim and far away. If, however, the vistas disclosed as yet no goal, no resting-place, little but flattery and criticism, the journey at least gave leisure for reflection and self-examination; it changed the child of Emancipation to the youth with dawning self-consciousness, self-realization, self-respect. In those sombre forests of his striving his own soul rose before him, and he saw himself—darkly as through a veil; and yet he saw in himself some faint revelation of his power, of his mission. He began to have a dim feeling that, to attain his place in the world, he must be himself, and not another. For the first time he sought to analyze the burden he bore upon his back, that deadweight of social degradation partially masked behind a half-named Negro problem. He felt his poverty; without a cent, without a home, without land, tools, or savings, he had entered into competition with rich, landed, skilled neighbors. To be a poor man is hard, but to be a poor race in a land of dollars is the very bottom of hardships. He felt the weight of his ignorance—not simply of letters, but of life, of business, of the humanities; the accumulated sloth and shirking and awkwardness of decades and centuries shackled his hands and feet. Nor was his burden all poverty and ignorance. The red stain of bastardy, which two centuries of systematic legal defilement of Negro women had stamped upon his race, meant not only the loss of ancient African chastity, but also the hereditary weight of a mass of corruption from white adulterers, threatening almost the obliteration of the Negro home.

A people thus handicapped ought not to be asked to race with the world, but rather allowed to give all its time and thought to its own social problems. But alas! while sociologists gleefully count his bastards and his prostitutes, the very soul of the toiling, sweating black man is darkened by the shadow of a vast despair. Men call the shadow prejudice, and learnedly explain it as the natural defence of culture against barbarism, learning against ignorance, purity against crime, the "higher" against the "lower" races. To which the Negro cries Amen! and swears that to so much of this strange prejudice as is founded on just homage to civilization, culture, righteousness, and progress, he humbly bows and meekly does obeisance. But before that nameless prejudice that leaps beyond all this he stands helpless, dismayed, and well-nigh speechless; before that personal disrespect and mockery, the ridicule and systematic humiliation, the distortion of fact and wanton license of fancy, the cynical ignoring of the better and the boisterous welcoming of the worse, the all-pervading desire to inculcate disdain for everything black, from Toussaint to the devil—before this there rises a sickening despair that would disarm and discourage any nation save that black host to whom "discouragement" is an unwritten word.

But the facing of so vast a prejudice could not but bring the inevitable self-questioning, self-disparagment, and lowering of ideals which ever accompany repression and breed in an atmosphere of contempt and hate. Whisperings and portents came borne upon the four winds: Lo! we are diseased and dying, cried the dark hosts; we cannot write, our voting is vain; what need of education, since we must always cook and serve? And the Nation echoed and enforced this self-criticism, saying: Be content to be servants, and nothing more; what need of higher culture for half-men? Away with the black man's ballot, by force or fraud—and behold the suicide of a race! Nevertheless, out of the evil came something of good—the more careful adjustment of education to real life, the clearer perception of the Negroes' social responsibilities, and the sobering realization of the meaning of progress.

So dawned the time of *Sturm und Drang:* storm and stress today rocks our little boat on the mad waters of the world-sea; there is within and without the sound of conflict, the burning of body and rending of soul; inspiration strives with doubt, and faith with vain questionings. The bright ideals of the past—physical freedom, political power, the training of brains and the training of hands—all these in turn have waxed and waned, until even the last grows dim and overcast. Are they all wrong—all false? No, not that, but each alone was oversimple and incomplete— the dreams of a credulous race-childhood, or the fond imaginings of the other world which does not know and does not want to know our power. To be really true, all these ideals must be melted and welded into one. The training of the schools we need today more than ever—the training of deft hands, quick eyes and ears, and above all the broader, deeper, higher culture of gifted minds and pure hearts. The power of the ballot we need in sheer self-defense—else what shall save us from a second slavery? Freedom, too, the long-sought, we still seek—the freedom of life and limb, the freedom to work and think, the freedom to love and aspire. Work, culture, liberty— all these we need, not singly but together, not successively but together, each growing and aiding each, and all striving toward that vaster ideal that swims before the Negro people, the ideal of human brotherhood, gained through the unifying ideal of Race; the ideal of fostering and developing the traits and talents of the Negro, not in opposition to or contempt for other races, but rather in large conformity to the greater ideals of the American Republic, in order that some day on American soil two world-races may give each to each those characteristics both so sadly lack. We the darker ones come even now not altogether empty-handed: There are today no truer exponents of the pure human spirit of the Declaration of Independence than the American Negroes; there is no true American music but the wild sweet melodies of the Negro slave; the American fairy tales and folklore are Indian and African; and, all in all, we black men seem the sole oasis of simple faith and reverence in a dusty desert of dollars and smartness. Will America be poorer if she replaces her brutal dyspeptic blundering with light-hearted but determined Negro humility? or her coarse and cruel wit with loving jovial good-humor? or her vulgar music with the soul of the Sorrow Songs?

Merely a concrete test of the underlying principles of the great republic is the Negro Problem, and the spiritual striving of the freedmen's sons is the travail of souls whose burden is almost beyond the measure of their strength, but who bear it in the name of an historic race, in the name of this the land of their fathers' fathers, and in the name of human opportunity.

39

Wrestling the Angel of Contradiction: Queer Christian Identities

Jodi O'Brien

(2004)

I wanted gays to be in the vanguard, battling against racial and economic injustice and religious and political oppression. I never thought I would see the day when gays would be begging to be let back into the Christian Church, which is clearly our enemy.

(Edmund White, author)

Seven reasons why you should absolutely, positively stay away from church . . . [reason number four]. The way some churches can get God to fit into those little boxes.

(Posted flyer, Spirit of the Sound: Gay and Lesbian Followers of Jesus)

I had to go to a non-Christian church for four years before I understood what it means to be a good Christian. A good Christian has a very big god.

(Larry, gay male and practicing Catholic)

INTRODUCTION

Several years ago I attended Gay Pride Parades in three different cities during the same month (San Francisco, Chicago, and Seattle). . . . Each parade felt distinct to me. The differences were not surprising. In many ways, they reflect the mosaic of responses to the proliferation of lesbian and gay presence and politics in recent decades. Perhaps this is why I was so surprised at one notable similarity that occurred at all three parades. Among the marchers in each parade were groups representing friends and supporters of lesbians and gays: PFLAG, AT&T Queer Allies, US Bank LGBT

Employee Support, and so forth. In each case, the crowd responded enthusiastically to this display of support and acceptance. People clapped and cheered and whistled in appreciation. The marchers glowed in acknowledgement. This is not what surprised me. Rather, it was the contrast in the crowd's response to another group of marchers: lesbian and gay Christians and, specifically, Mormons (who march under the banner of Affirmation) and Catholics (who call their association Dignity). In these three very distinct US cities I wandered up and down the streets during each parade, watching as merry crowds fell silent at the appearance of these marchers. Everywhere the response was the same: silence, broken only by an occasional boo. I was stunned. These otherwise very "normal" looking but openly queer men and women (some of whom really did look like the stereotypical Mormon missionary) were being booed at their own Pride Parades. . . .

It is likely that many parade bystanders were genuinely confused at what must have seemed an obvious contradiction: openly queer, openly religious. For some parade-goers, the presence of these lesbian and gay Christians might even have been a form of betrayal given the active anti-homosexual preaching of both the Vatican and Mormon leaders. In any case, my curiosity was aroused. What compelled someone to want to parade both statuses? My initial impression was that lesbian and gay Christians must experience a form of "double stigma." . . . What seemed to confuse and unsettle the crowd was the open expression of such an apparent contradiction. Why would any self-respecting queer want also to embrace Christianity with its seemingly inevitable denouncement and exclusion? And why, especially, would they want to announce this involvement to fellow queers, knowing the disdain and rejection that this was likely to incur?

Compelled by these questions I began to research what I called "double stigma." Specifically, I was interested in lesbians and gays who are openly queer and openly Christian. How did they make sense of and manage this "double stigma" I wondered? The concept of "double stigma" was sociologically rigorous enough to garner me research support for the project. Armed with this idea, the financial blessing of the American Sociological Association, and a solid track record of ethnographic experience, I set off in search of answers. Five open-ended interviews into the project, I knew the concept of "double-stigma" was completely off the mark. I was missing the main point. When I raised the idea of "double-stigma"—How do you deal with it? Why do you deal with it?—the first round of interviewees

all looked at me with similar confusion. Yes, they understood the question. Yes, they could understand how others would see it that way. But it did not resonate for them. Each of these five people, none of whom knew one another, said the same thing. This was not about stigma. It was about "living a contradiction that defines who I am."

Forty-two interviews and many hours of congregational participation later I was still hearing the same thing: the contradiction of being Christian and being queer is who I am. When I gave talks describing the research project I noticed the vigorous head-nodding among self-described queer Christians at the mention of the phrase, "living the contradiction." My orienting perspective at the launch of this project reflected my penchant for sociological abstraction and personal experiences that disincline me toward participation in mainstream religions (I am a former Mormon with a typical "flight from religion" experience through the process of becoming a lesbian). Through sustained contact and participatory experience with self-described "queer Christians" and the congregations that welcome them, I developed an understanding of the deeply complex process of living the contradiction of being queer and Christian. In fact, over time, I have come to have considerable appreciation for this process.

RESEARCH SETTING AND METHODOLOGY

This article is based on a more comprehensive project in which I develop the thesis that the contradictions between Christianity and homosexuality are the driving tensions in the formulation of a historically specific expression of queer religiosity. These expressions are manifested in individual identities and practices, in community practices (i.e., Christian congregations), and in ideological discourses (i.e., theological and doctrinal discourses). The transformative processes occurring at each of these levels are mutually constitutive.

In this article I focus specifically on the processes whereby lesbian and gay Christians[1] forge an integration of Christian doctrine, spirituality and sexuality.[2] My central interpretive claim in this paper is that this integrative struggle is experienced by lesbian and gay Christians as a raison d'être. Wrestling this contradiction has given rise to a particular expression of queer Christian identity. Among the many implications of these expressions of queer Christian identity is their impact on mainstream Christian congregations and Christian ideologies and practices. I describe these implications briefly in the conclusions.

As I have noted in the introduction, my original intent was to understand the motivations and experiences of lesbian and gay Catholics and Mormons who wished to be recognised explicitly for both their religiosity and sexuality. I began the project by talking with several such individuals, including my hairstylist, a self-described "flaming queen with a flair for building miniature houses" who is also active in his local Catholic parish. Larry's openly gay behavior was considered outrageous even by the standards of the gay-friendly hair salon that he worked in. Quite frankly, I could not imagine what his fellow parishioners made of his queerness. Yet Larry seemed to have found quite a home there. He spoke often and enthusiastically about his involvement with the parish. He invited me to attend services and, eventually, several meetings of the lay ministry, to experience for myself what his "contradictory" world was like. Another point of entry came through a colleague who had granted me a formal interview and then invited me to attend services at Seattle's First Baptist where he was an active participant. Later his congregation invited me to participate as a speaker in their ongoing "Adult Education" series—a version of Sunday School. They wanted to explore the theme of sexuality and asked if I would kick-off the topic. Jim, my colleague and interview subject, was instrumental in organising the series and in setting me up with subsequent interviews.

Through participation in these congregational activities I was introduced to more lesbian and gay Christians who granted me interviews and put me in contact with other friends and colleagues throughout the western United States and British Columbia. I also learned first-hand of the tensions taking place within the congregations that were supportive of lesbian and gay members.[3] The late 1990s was a time of ferment within Christian congregations regarding the presence and affirmation of lesbian and gay members. In this respect, the timing of my research was serendipitous. In recognition of these community and organisational tensions, I expanded my interviews to include heterosexual congregants and clergy members. I also expanded my participation to several regional congregations representing Episcopalian, Methodist, Unitarian, and Presbyterian denominations, in addition to my initial participation with Baptist, Catholic, and Mormon groups. My formal research process included 63 open-ended interviews and sustained contact with five congregations and two lesbian/gay Christian groups (Affirmation and Dignity) for a period of three years.

During this time I came to recognise what I term a "field of relations," which includes lesbian and gay Christians, the congregations in which they have found a "spiritual community," the general membership of these congregations, the congregational ministries, and the relationships between these congregations and their denominational organisations. There is awareness among these congregations that they are part of a historical moment that is fraught with considerable tension and debate regarding the very definition of Christianity. In this regard, I think it accurate to talk in terms of a social movement that is taking place within the pews (with a distinctly different genesis and process from LGBT political movements as they are typically presented in the social movements literature).

My research methods are consistent with ethnographic interpretive methodologies in which the intent is to articulate fields of relations and the intrapersonal and interpersonal relations that occur within these fields. My approach is especially informed by feminist methodologies, according to which my intent is to ascertain what persons within the field of inquiry have to say for themselves while remaining cognisant of my own relationship with these persons and my influence with the field of relations. At the same time, my work is strongly influenced by sociological theories that orient me toward ascertaining patterned discourses regarding how people make sense of themselves—what stories they tell themselves about who they are and what they can do—especially regarding conflict and contradiction (O'Brien 2001a; Plummer 1995). My observations and conclusions are interpretations that reflect my sociological orientation. Throughout the research process I presented myself as a sociologist with special interests in religion and sexuality. Early in the research process people became aware of my project and approached me about being interviewed and/or having me visit their congregations. This awareness and interest confirms my observation that a self-aware field of relations regarding queer Christian identities exists. My interpretations are limited to the specific context of this research project. However, my aim with this in-depth inquiry is to provide empirical insight and grounding for the conceptual frameworks through which scholars attempt to understand the integration of religion and sexuality generally.[4]

THE "GAY PREDICAMENT":
AN IRRECONCILABLE CONTRADICTION

Homosexuality is intrinsically disordered.

(Catechism of the
Catholic Church 1994, 566)

The "question of homosexuality" has been a central focus of discussion in Catholic and Protestant denominations since the 1960s. Historically, homosexuality is forbidden in most Christian doctrines. In these texts the homosexual has been variously defined as "disordered," "evil," and "sinful" (Conrad and Schneider 1980; O'Brien 2001b). In many texts homosexuality is rendered as absolutely irreconcilable with the basic tenets of Christianity. Recent revisions of a few doctrines offer a slightly more forgiving interpretation wherein homosexual behavior is separated from homosexual identity.[5] The new Catechism, for instance, defines homosexual inclinations (identity) as a "condition" that is not chosen and is experienced as a "trial" (Catechism of the Catholic Church 1994, 566). Grappling with this affliction can be a lifetime struggle and those who are "successful" in taming the beast of homosexuality can expect the same joys and blessings as other good Catholics.[6] In this rendering the act is the sin, while desire is an affliction. In an accompanying passage, the text admonishes all Catholics to treat persons who suffer the condition of homosexuality with "respect, compassion and sensitivity" (1994, 566). Progressive Catholics see this doctrine as at least an acknowledgement that homosexuality exists. The separation of act and identity is considered by some to be a statement of acceptance. Still, even in this supposedly progressive statement, the "homosexual" is rendered as someone (something) lacking, someone whose desires are a potential source of shame and exile.

Doctrines that condemn homosexuality constitute the ideological backdrop against which Christians initially experience their homosexuality. At worst, they are irredeemable sinners: at best, they suffer from problems or afflictions. Given this discourse of rejection, non-Christians might assume that the simplest path would be the renunciation of religion. For many Christians struggling with feelings of homosexuality the path is not so simple.

Psychologists of religion offer a holistic explanation for sustained Christian participation, even when the participation involves conflict. According to this thesis, Christianity is a well-established and deeply meaningful cosmology that weaves together spirit, intellect, body and community (Fortunato 1982). Christianity offers answers to big questions such as the meaning of life and death. Religious participation is also a means of transcending the oppressions and banalities of everyday living. For many Christians, the traditional ceremonies of religious expression are both evocative and comforting. Thus, motivation for participation is not so much the puzzle. In fact, to frame the question this way, as many studies of religion and homosexuality (including my own initial research proposal) do, is arguably to impose a secular perspective on a religious question.[7] Rather, the puzzle becomes: How does the homosexual make sense of the fact that, by definition, he/she is considered an exile who is beyond the promised redemption of Christian theology? Christian therapist John Fortunato refers to this as the "gay predicament." The "gay predicament," simply put, is that one cannot be a good Christian and also be queer.

The intensity of this contradiction can only be fully understood within a framework of Christian experience. Within a heteronormative culture, lesbians and gays are (often painfully) aware that they are social cast-offs. Within Christianity, active homosexuals are also aware that, in addition to their being social cast-offs, their souls have been cast off as well. This predicament poses a tremendous existential crisis. To experience homosexual desires, and certainly to pursue fulfillment of these desires, will result in being cast out from the cosmology through which one makes sense of one's life. One obvious solution is to cast off Christian theology in favor of the homosexual identity. This is easier said than done, however. Bending the rules is one thing, but shedding an entire structure of meaning may leave one cast adrift in a sea of meaninglessness—which may be even less tolerable than the knowledge that one is potentially damned. This is a defining predicament for lesbian

and gay Christians. It is also a profound set of contradictions. Abandoning Christianity may mean losing a sense of meaning and purpose, yet keeping this particular religion means facing the prospect of damnation.

Queer Secularism

In addition to the predicament of exile, lesbian and gay Christians who are open about their religiosity face rejection from other queers. Lesbian and gay political activists, scholars and writers tend to be critical and dismissive of Christianity. The following remark from gay author John Preston (known especially for his anthologies of gay male short stories) is indicative of the discourse of disdain prevalent among lesbian and gay activists and artists. Preston was invited by Brian Bouldrey to write a chapter for his anthology, *Wrestling with the Angel: Religion in the Lives of Gay Men*. This is his response:

> I'd have nothing to say in your anthology. As an atheist I have no angels with which to wrestle, and, to be honest, I think adults who worry about such a decrepit institution as organized religion should drink plenty of fluids, pop an aspirin, and take a nap, in hopes that the malady will pass. (Quoted in Bouldrey 1995, xi).

Thus, lesbian or gay Christians who seek comfort and insight among fellow queers may be setting themselves up for further disdain and rejection because of their religious affiliation. The queer Christian is doubly damned: according to Christian doctrine, homosexuality is an affliction; among fellow (non-Christian) lesbians and gays, religious affiliation may be the affliction. Not only can one not be a good Christian and be queer, apparently one cannot be a good queer and be religious. Or, as Elizabeth Stuart, author of a guide for LGBT Christians, so aptly phrases it, "queer Christians find themselves caught as it were between the devil and the rainbow, aliens in both lands" (1997, 13).[8]

Persons who have been "spun off from their galaxy of meaning" (Fortunato 1982)—in this case, heteronormative acceptance and Christian systems of meaning and purpose—seek reintegration into new systems of meaning. For instance, heterosexual persons who are inclined, for whatever reasons, to denounce their religious roots usually construct new systems of meaning within secular frameworks. Persons who find themselves spun off from heterosexual culture often find meaning in queer groups that have articulated anti-straight philosophies and practices. . . .

Responses to the Gay Predicament[9]

Anecdotal and experiential information suggests three general sorts of responses to the gay predicament: denunciation and flight, acceptance of the doctrine of shame, and articulation of an alternative (queer) religiosity. The first, denunciation and flight, is a well-known story among many lesbians and gay men. Many "coming out" stories involve a process of renouncing religious roots. These stories can be interpreted as a statement of renunciation and opposition against a system of meaning in which lesbians and gays find no place for themselves. These expressions involve a process of reshaping one's sense of self and identity in opposition to religious teachings and practices. For many individuals, this is a painful and alienating process that involves not only casting off an entire system of meaning and belonging, but forging a new (non-Christian) ideology. As one former Mormon missionary-turned-lesbian put it:

> Non-Mormons don't get that Mormonism answers your questions about everything. Now I have to wonder about every little thing. Do I still believe in monogamy? Or is that something I should throw out along with Mormonism? Do I still believe in life-after-death? Marriage? Commitment? What do I believe in? It's all a big gaping hole for me now. (Lori)[10]

For many the struggle is about how to (re)integrate with society more generally. This is often done through alignment with other queer groups and the articulation of a discourse whereby the religious community, not the individual, is seen as the problem. In this instance, throwing off the cloak of religious shame is seen as an act of liberation:

> Healthy living means finding ways to throw off the guilt. It's not just the guilt of feeling like you've betrayed your family and friends and their expectations for you. It's the guilt that comes from messages all around you that you don't belong. That you're an aberration. Until one day you start to get it and say, hey, I'm here. I'm doing okay. I must belong. When you figure that out you have the courage to walk away from the [church] and realize the problem is them. They're not big enough to let you belong. (Brian)

This group of "recovering Christians" may be the least tolerant of lesbians and gays who attempt to find a place for themselves within Christianity.

Another familiar, and similarly complex, response is to learn to accept Christian teachings that render homosexuality an affliction. In such instances, the struggle to be a good Christian (and a good person generally as defined through adherence to Christian principles) revolves around the struggle to sustain celibacy. Homosexual reintegration into Christianity involves accepting the definition of an afflicted self, donning a cloak of shame regarding one's homosexuality (or, minimally, a cloak of sickness), and embarking upon the struggle indicated by this affliction. The literature on ex-gay therapies and ministries, most of which consists of personal narratives and "undercover" participant observation, indicates that those who seek out these "therapies" are likely to come from strong Christian backgrounds. Often they are referred to the therapies by a Church leader in whom they have confided (see, for instance, Harryman 1991). In these cases, the homosexual Christian who is not "cured" is encouraged to remain "closeted" if he/she wishes to maintain a position in the religious community.

My focus is on those individuals who endeavor to maintain both a strong Christian identity and an open and "proud" lesbian or gay identity. These people recognise their distinct position with respect to those who renounce Christianity and those who accept Christian definitions of affliction. A defining feature of this group is the desire to (re)integrate within a Christian system of meaning while maintaining a queer identity and, ideally, to integrate both identities within a common community. Given this, especially viewed within the framework of the other paths of response, it is possible to assert that lesbian and gay Christians are a distinct group who have at least some awareness that they are forging a unique response to their predicament. It must be noted, however, that, at least initially the responses to this predicament are local and individual. In this regard, the convergence of responses into similar themes is sociologically noteworthy.

In this paper, I am particularly interested in the content of themes that lesbian and gay Christians have articulated. As I note in the concluding section, it is the expression of these themes and the performance of a queer Christianity within congregations that creates a critical mass, or groundswell, that can be interpreted as a particular form of queer Christian religious movement. In other words, none of the individuals in this project started out with an inclination to reform religion or to make a socio-political statement. Rather, each was primarily interested in the question of (re)integrating within a Christian community. Given this context, meaningful research questions include: how do lesbian and gay Christians make sense of and manage their predicament? What motivates their involvement in a system of meaning from which they have been spun off, socially and spiritually? What (if any) source of (re)integration do they articulate for themselves?

RAISON D'ÊTRE

Despite the threats of damnation and rejection among other queers, lesbian and gay Christians remain undaunted in their commitment to both a queer identity and Christian religiosity. Each of the 42 lesbian and gay Christians that I interviewed described having a sense of deep spirituality. Many of them offered details of what they felt to be an "early sense of vocation." As one interviewee phrased it, "religion has always been a natural and necessary part of existence for me."

At the same time, lesbian and gay Christians recognise that these proclamations of Christian spirituality put them at odds with other queers. Detailed statements about religious conviction are usually accompanied by accounts of having to defend this spirituality as a "thoughtful, meaningful enterprise and not some sort of brain-numbing self-denial" (Sean). He continues, "When I see it through the eyes of other gays, I often wonder if my religiosity is a character flaw."

Each of the interviewees articulated an awareness of a secular hegemony in this culture ("educated professional people in general are often embarrassed about their spiritual leanings"). To be religious in a secular society is a struggle. To be religious and queer is to expect ongoing struggle. The theme of struggle is constant throughout my own interviews, in my ethnographic participation in various congregations and in related writings.

The theme of struggle is also familiar and persistent throughout Christian doctrine and teachings. For example, in the Catechism, persons are instructed that appropriate sexual behavior (chastity) is an "apprenticeship in self-mastery which is a training in human freedom" (Catechism of the Catholic Church 1994, 562). This mastery (which culminates in sexual expression contained within a marriage blessed by the Church) will bring happiness and fulfillment. Failure to achieve it will lead to enslavement by the passions. "Struggle" may be a definitive trope of Christianity itself. Certainly one of the religion's most enduring themes is that persons will confront challenges and afflictions. The implied lesson is that the way they handle these struggles shapes their character. In this regard, lesbian and gay Christians can be seen as playing out a variation on an old theme: the contradiction of spirituality and sexuality is their particular struggle; the manner in which they engage the struggle defines their character. Struggle is paramount in each of the three responses to the "gay predicament"—struggle to reinterpret or renounce a dominant system of meaning; struggle to suppress and hide homosexual desire. A common distinction among the lesbian and gay Christians in this study is the extent to which struggle with a contradiction is a definitive aspect of self-understanding and identification (cf. White and White 2004). Two themes in particular emerged from my interviews and observations. First, wrestling the contradiction of spirituality and sexuality defines that self-proclaimed lesbian or gay Christian. Second is the sense among them that they are better Christians—indeed, better persons—as a consequence of this struggle. In other words, the struggle is the crucible in which their character is forged.

Articulating the Self as a Process of Contradiction

There is a version of social psychology that suggests the "articulated self" develops through the process of managing tensions and contradictions in aspects of life that the person considers most meaningful. In my own work I make the claim that the "self" can be usefully defined in terms of this process. In other words, the ways in which we make sense of and manage these contradictions are the definitive features of the social self (O'Brien 2001a). One common experience among the persons I interviewed was an early awakening of both spirituality and homosexuality.[11] Several participants indicated that their awareness

of both their spirituality and their homosexuality was simultaneous. For each of them this was a profound realisation, and one that was followed almost immediately by a sense of dread and panic:

> I was about 14 or so. I had this heightened sense that I was very special. Very spiritual. God has something special in mind for me. At the same time I had this sense of myself as sexual and that felt so good and so right. And then it occurred to me that these two feelings didn't fit and were going to get me into big trouble. That's when I started trying to figure out what God wanted with me. What was this struggle supposed to teach me? I was really a mess about it for a long time. I think I have some answers now. But I still struggle with it every day. (Jim)

Fortunato remarks that it is "no surprise that gay people ask an inordinate number of spiritual questions." For those who fit comfortably within an accepted system of meaning such as Christianity, the extent to which they think about their spirituality is probably in terms of some benign Sunday school lesson, or perhaps something that is mildly comforting in times of need.[12] Christians who have acknowledged their homosexuality do not have the luxury of semi-conscious spirituality. The discovery that one's sexuality is so deeply contradictory "requires awakening levels of consciousness far beyond those necessary for straight people" (Fortunato 1982, 39). Thus, lesbian and gay Christians may have a more articulated sense of what it means to be a Christian precisely because they have to make ongoing sense of deeply felt contradictions.

For the most part this struggle for articulation is seen as positive and definitive. Every interviewee remarked in some way or another that her/his core sense of being was shaped significantly by the struggle to reconcile homosexuality and religiosity. Comments such as "I wouldn't be me if I didn't have this struggle" were typical.

This is what has forged me, my defining battle. I'd probably be a very conservative evangelical Christian if I wasn't gay—everything is different as a result, especially my spirituality. Wrestling this marginality has become the thing that shapes me more than anything else. (Jim)

For these individuals, self-understanding comes through the process of engaging with persistent contradiction. The experience of contradiction is ongoing, both in conversations with oneself and in interactions with others. Lesbian and gay Christians constantly find themselves in situations in which they must explain (and often defend) their seemingly contradictory statuses to others. This experience is seen both as an occasion that can be tiresome and also as an occasion for growth and self-articulation. As one lesbian Baptist put it:

You can never take yourself for granted. If I go to an event with lesbians and somehow it comes up that I'm an assistant pastor, I have to listen to this barrage of criticism about the history of Christianity and what it's done to us. I get soooo tired of that. What's amazing is that it never seems to occur to them that maybe I've thought about this. Maybe I have complicated reasons for being who I am. But they don't ask. As tiresome as it can be, it's still a good experience for me. I tend to go home and ask myself, why are you doing this? And I find that I understand my own answers better and better. Does that make any sense? (Carol)

Or this comment from a gay Methodist:

It's like coming out over and over again. Every time someone new joins [the congregation] we're going to go through the same ol' dance about how the Sunday School coordinator is this gay guy. Thankfully, I'm so well-known now that the other members warn the newcomers. But there's always someone who wants to bait you, y'know, corner you at a social or something and quiz you on doctrine. Like they know doctrine!. . . I wanted to be able to scoff at their ignorance. The funny thing is, now

that I know what I do, it turns out I want to educate them instead of show them up. I guess this whole thing has made me much more conscious of being a good Christian. (Mark)

This comment is from a student of Theology and Ministry:

It seems like everyday, everywhere I go I'm a problem for somebody. It's a problem for white America that I'm black. It's a problem for gay America that I'm in the ministry. It's a problem for the ministry—a big, big problem—that I'm gay. Always a problem. Weird thing is, and you might think this is funny, but being a problem has made me really strong. I mean, as a person. I'm always having to think about who I am and not let it get to me. That makes you strong in yourself. You really know who you are. (Everett)

Another common feature in these narratives is the prevalence of contradiction.

These experiences are similar in tone and expression to some of the narrative reflections on multiple consciousness (for example, Anzaldua 1987). Persons who occupy contradictory social positions find themselves traversing the boundaries, or borders of multiple worlds. In so doing they develop a consciousness that reflects their marginal position. Persons in such positions usually have a heightened awareness of their own marginality; they are also more likely to be critically aware of expressions and practices that less marginalised persons take for granted. Most individuals perceive this heightened awareness as an advantage. At the very least, as noted in the illustrative quotes, contradictory positions are an occasion for reflection and articulation.

A significant outcome of these reflections among lesbian and gay Christians is the articulation of contradiction itself as useful and worthwhile in the shaping of a Christian identity. Not only is contradiction a catalyst for self-reflection, but ultimately it is a source of challenge for Christian congregations. Lesbians and gays who denounce Christianity and leave often make sense of their departure by recognising that their religion is "too small" to accept "the likes of me." This (re)conception of the church and/or God as being too small to accommodate difference is a common basis for renouncing religious affiliation among lesbians and gays. Among those who remain (or become) active participants in their religious communities, there is a slightly different and highly significant twist to this discourse. The strands of this twist include the articulation of the theme that "my gay presence in this too small church is an opportunity for members to stretch their own limits of love and acceptance" and the even more radical notion, "homosexuality is a gift from God." The articulation and convergence of this uniquely queer response to Christianity is the subject of the next section.

ARTICULATING A QUEER CHRISTIAN IDENTITY

Biography and faith traditions intersect to produce discursive strategies toward religion.

(Wade Clark Roof)

Homosexuality is a gift from God.

(John McNeill,
formerly of the Society of Jesus)

In the foregoing comments I have suggested that lesbian and gay Christians are aware that they occupy a unique, marginal and contradictory position with regard to fellow (heterosexual or closeted) Christians and to (former-Christian or non-Christian) lesbians and gays. This contradiction is experienced as a source of insight and as an occasion for articulating a self that these individuals perceive as stronger, more purposeful and, in many cases, indicative of the true meaning of Christianity. In other words, I suggest that rather than attempt to resolve the apparent contradiction of being queer and Christian, these

individuals see "living the contradiction" as a purpose in itself, a raison d'être.

One additional theme that emerged from my conversations with lesbian and gay Christians is this: "my contradictory presence is good for the Church." This revision of the discourse on homosexuality (from problem to useful challenge) serves to reintegrate the homosexual into Christianity (at least in terms of her/his personal articulation of the religion). Further, it renders the homosexual a sort of modern-day crucible with which Christianity must grapple. In doing so, mainline Christian denominations must revisit and redefine the message of love and redemption. In this regard, lesbian and gay Christians redefine "affliction" as an ability; the ability to embrace contradiction and ambiguity is articulated as a manifestation of Christian goodness and character.

This articulation can be interpreted in terms of Roof's thesis of religious individualism (Roof 1999). Individuals enter into a "creative dialogue with tradition" and articulate discursive strategies that enable them to retain significant (often contradictory) aspects of self while maintaining religious commitments.[13] In this instance, the homosexual biography intersects with familiar aspects of Christianity—faith in God's divine wisdom, acceptance of challenge, struggle, oppression, awakening and rebirth—to produce a particularly queer discursive response toward religion. The lesbian and gay Christians who took part in my research, as well as those interviewed by Wilcox (2000), are a unique group in that they have not rejected religion altogether, nor have they accepted the terms of a "divinely ordered closet" (i.e., donning the cloak of shame and silence in order to maintain Christian commitments and status). Instead, they have articulated a position that can be interpreted as a unique queer Christian identity. This identity merges elements of essentialist reasoning, Christian doctrines of love and acceptance, Christian histories of oppression, and collective struggle to attain godly virtues. The emergence of a common discourse among individuals who are, for the most part, engaged in solitary struggle, is noteworthy. I attribute this emergent queer Christian discourse, in its initial phases, to the common threads in Christianity generally. In articulating a queer Christianity, lesbians and gays take up similar threads regarding the formation of identity and their position within their congregations.

The most common theme I heard among both the lesbian and gay Christians I came to know and the congregants who fully accepted them was that we are "all God's children." A point of reconciliation with one's homosexuality and Christianity seems to be the acknowledgement that "God created me; He must have created me this way for a reason." This "realization" is marked by many lesbian and gay Christians as a turning point: "All of a sudden it hit me, I believe in God, I believe He is perfect and has created a perfect world. Why would I have these desires if they weren't part of a perfect plan?" Or as one lesbian pastor phrased it, "Yes I've been reborn through my faith in God's love. Turns out I was born queer."[14]

Coupled with the theme of struggle, this discourse becomes a narrative whereby homosexuality is "both a gift and my cross to bear." In this regard, homosexuality becomes a personal crucible for forging character. This discourse is buttressed by the Christian belief that God creates everything for a purpose. The good Christian's task is to nurture faith in God and to live out the purpose evident in her/his own creation—in this case, the creation of homosexuality. Queer Christians find doctrinal support for their homosexuality in the principle, "God is love." A loving God loves and accepts all Her/His creations; a Church founded on these principles must make room for all that God has created and loves. From this thread comes the idea that a Church is only as big as its god, and its god is only as big as the extent of her/his love. Thus, a truly Christian

church is a church that is big enough to love and accept homosexual members.

The third and most critical thread in this discourse combines with the others to weave the theme whereby the homosexual is a necessary and useful challenge for contemporary Christianity. In the words of former Jesuit and self-declared gay liberation theologian John McNeill, "God is calling us to play an historical role" (1996, p. 192). This role is to extend to Christian congregations and denominations the challenge of stretching to accept all who enter and wish to belong—in short, to become as big as God's love, which is infinite. This discourse reclaims the proverbial phrase, "love the sinner but hate the sin," but it reframes sin as failure to love and accept all God's creations. In this conceptualization, God and Christianity *per se* are not the problem; rather, the problem is the institution through which God's intent is interpreted. In the words of a gay Methodist minister, "I never had any doubts about my relationship with God. It's the church that's been a problem for me." Thus, the institution of Christianity becomes the problem and lesbian and gay Christians become the chosen few whose special calling it is to redeem institutional Christianity by liberating its narrowly defined god.

Articulating a queer Christian identity involves transforming a discourse of shame and silence (with the promise of exile) into a narrative of pride and expression. For lesbian and gay Christians, pride is based on a belief that homosexuality has a place in God's plan. The particular place at this particular moment in history is to foment Christian renewal and reformation. In this way, lesbian and gay Christians manage their original predicament by renaming themselves and their positions within their congregations in terms of a gay Christian activism. This discursive strategy is consistent with both lesbian and gay social movements and a Christian tradition of faith-based struggle and martyrdom. It elevates the homosexual from a position of "irredeemable problem" to one of "path to redemption." In this particular instance, it is institutional Christianity that is in need of redemption. Just as the individual must struggle in order to grow and to achieve character and, ultimately, exaltation, so too must the institution of Christianity struggle. The "latter-day homosexual" is the occasion for this institutional metamorphosis. Within this discourse, lesbian and gay Christians become both modern-day Christian soldiers and sacrificial lambs. . . .

Implications: Theology

What are the ideological consequences of a gay and lesbian presence in mainstream Christianity? I have suggested that lesbian and gay Christians are authoring a historically specific queer religiosity to make sense of their predicament of exclusion. This queer Christianity is likely to have transformative effects at the individual, community and organizational levels—all of which are mutually constitutive. Similarly, there are implications for Christian ideologies as well. I offer the following as preliminary observations. Whether one is in agreement with it or not, the articulation of a queer Christian theology, especially as it has emerged within the ranks of individuals trying to make sense of their own contradiction, has implications.

Queer Christian theologies resituate and redefine the parameters for discussions of sexuality and morality. Regardless of one's views, the conversation is different as a consequence of acknowledging homosexuality. Another significant implication is the authoring of a "gay liberation theology" whereby homosexuality is identified as a gift from God. Again, regardless of whether one agrees, this particular discourse is already leading to a re-examination in many denominations of what it means to say that theology should be a "living guide" that reflects its times.

In my own assessment, one of the most noteworthy ideological considerations is the implication of focusing on "unconditional love" as a discursive strategy for accepting and affirming a homosexual presence. Concerning the case of homosexuality, the belief that "god is love" sits in tension with the notion of a patriarchal god who, like the unchallenged parent, sets down rules that are not to be questioned. An ideology of unconditional love implies a love that is growing and stretching; a love that is manifest among members of a community who interpret for themselves the extent and expression of this love. This is a long-standing tension in Christian theology. Deliberations regarding homosexuality that are framed in terms of "god's unconditional love" tip the equation one degree further toward a rendering of a Christian god who is not an anthropomorphic figure handing down his particular rules. Rather, this god is an expression of agreement and affirmation among a collective body united in spirit and intent. In short, "god" becomes the extent of the community's expression of love. The larger the reach of the group's love, the bigger their god.

A Final Note Regarding "Oppositional Consciousness"

In an attempt to explain lesbian and gay involvement in Christian organizations, some lesbian and gay political activists have suggested that religion is one of the "last citadels" of gay oppression (see Hartman 1996 for a review). These observers see the struggle for inclusion in mainstream religions as a final step toward attaining cultural and political acceptance. In this literature, lesbian and gay Christian involvement is interpreted as a form of political expression whereby queers are taking on traditional homophobia by acting from within. This thesis presumes an "oppositional consciousness" (Mansbridge 2001) that conflates outcomes (religious reform) with motivation and presumes a motivation (desire to reform religion) that is not necessarily reflective of the actual experiences of lesbian and gay Christians. My research suggests that there are several stages in self-awareness and articulation that occur before any form of "oppositional consciousness" develops among lesbian and gay Christians. To the extent that such a consciousness is developing, I suggest that it is historically unique and should be understood within the context in which it is developing. Specifically, the motivation should be understood in terms of the homosexual Christian's desire for self-understanding in Christian terms and reintegration into a system of meaning from which he/she has been cast off.

Sociological theses such as Mansbridge's "oppositional consciousness" or Roof's "creative dialogue" are useful in providing a general framework of analysis, but they miss the mark in interpreting motivations and commitments. Roof's thesis is intended to explain what he views as a "shopping" mentality regarding contemporary religion, in which the individual shops around in search of a congregation or denomination that fits personal needs. Queer Christian identities appear to be motivated more by the desire for (re)integration within Christian traditions, at which point the individual may begin to "shop" for a welcoming congregation. Similarly, while it is certainly possible to view the growing lesbian and gay visibility within Christian organizations as a manifestation of "oppositional consciousness," I think it would be inaccurate and misleading to assume a political motivation for this involvement. An intended contribution of this study is to make clear that lesbian and gay Christian participation (and related activism) must be understood on its own terms, in its own context and in terms of the particular historical moment.

Notes

1. In this paper I use the phrase "lesbian and gay" because it is the most accurate description of the group about which I am writing. The term "lesbian/gay/ bisexual/transgender" (LGBT) is politically strategic and meaningful, but often not descriptively accurate in specific case studies.

2. Several colleagues and interviewees have indicated that the experiences of Jewish lesbians and gays are similar. In this project, I have maintained a focus on mainstream Christian denominations because of my familiarity with Christian theology. For studies in Jewish queer experience, see Schneer and Aviv (2002) and Balka and Rose (1991).

3. During the course of my formal research, Seattle First Baptist was one of a handful of recent Baptist denominations in the United States that were threatened with revocation of their charter for affirming lesbian and gay membership. Other congregations that were the spiritual homes to several of my interviewees struggled with similar tensions within their denominational organizations, especially congregations attempting to appoint lesbian and gay ministers and those that supported standing ministers who had recently "come out" to the congregation.

4. This ethnography is limited, especially in what it suggests regarding variations of gender, race, and geography on the articulation of and circumstances surrounding a queer Christian identity. I expect that there are significant variations in terms of the dimensions of gender and race, and I suspect these interact differently in different geographical regions. This study highlights one variation on the theme of individual reconciliation of homosexuality and Christianity. It should be read in terms of what it can suggest for further research regarding different variations on this theme.

5. There is a notable historical correlation between gay political movements, Christian denominations' heightened discussion of the "homosexual question"—including the revision of the Catechism—and the removal of "homosexuality" as a category of pathology in the 1974 *Diagnostic and Statistical Manual* used by the American Psychiatric Association to identify and diagnose psychological disorders.

6. Article Six, section 2359: "Homosexual persons are called to chastity. By the virtues of self-mastery that teach them inner freedom, at times by the support of disinterested friendship, by prayer and sacramental grace, they can and should gradually and resolutely

approach Christian perfection" (Catechism of the Catholic Church 1994, 566).

7. This explanation is consistent with a social psychological literature demonstrating that dominant belief systems are usually not rejected in the face of contradiction. Rather, individuals attempt to make sense of the contradictions through "secondary elaborations" (Mehan and Wood 1975, 197). The motivation for continued engagement in the belief system is the desire to maintain a coherent system of meaning regarding the meaning and purpose of one's life. Even problematic positions within the system of meaning can be less threatening than having no sense of meaning or basis for self-understanding. This literature can be used to explain seemingly incomprehensible behavior such as attendance at one's own "degradation ceremony" (e.g., the Mormon who participates in her/his own excommunication process).

8. Stuart also points out the similarities with other Christians, such as Christian feminists or Christian ecologists, who must also explain and justify their religious commitments.

9. I am not implying that these responses are mutually exclusive or fixed. Rather, it is probable that during the course of a queer Christian career individuals try on aspects of each of these responses. It is beyond the scope of this paper to develop an explanation for primary self-expression through one response or another—a settling in to a particular expression of identity. I assume that various reference groups play a part in this process and that, over time, the proliferation of an articulated queer Christianity will in itself serve as one such point of reference for a new generation of queer youth. I offer some suggestions toward such an explanation in the conclusions.

10. All quotes from subjects used in this article are intended to be illustrative (rather than analytically definitive). For this reason I do not give detailed subject descriptions. These descriptions are available on request. All of the interviewees in this study elected to use their real names. For reasons of "voice" this is my preferred ethnographical practice.

11. Although nothing conclusive can be ascertained from my few interviews, this phenomenon of simultaneous awakening of homosexuality and spiritual vocation may be more prevalent among young men. Nineteen of the 25 men I interviewed spoke of this experience. Only two of the women mentioned a similar feeling. In fact, the women tended to develop a strong sense of spirituality and desire for religious involvement sometime after coming to terms with their homosexuality. Two of the men offered an explanation of their early sense of vocation as being a means of making them feel better about their homosexuality. As one put it, "God wouldn't have made me this way if he didn't have something special in mind for my life." Another noted that he considered his experience somewhat normal "for someone who was meant to be a priest . . . after all, aren't all priests supposed to be gay? I figured that my attraction to men, including one of the teachers at my [Catholic] school, was just God's way of making it clear that I was meant to be a priest."

12. Evangelicalism is another domain of Christianity whose members experience struggle and are likely to view this struggle as a definitive aspect of themselves and their religious commitment. (Smith, C. 1998. *American Evangelicalism: Embattled and Thriving.* Chicago: University of Chicago Press.)

13. For another interesting example, see Gloria Gonzalez-Lopez's (2004) study of Catholic Mexican immigrant women and their sex lives.

14. In the past two decades, many lesbian and gay Christians embraced the hypothesis that homosexuality is genetic rather than socially determined. This essentialist position was consistent with the idea that if homosexuality exists, God must have intended it. Catholicism has accepted the essentialist proposition of biological determinism explicitly without accepting the corollary that homosexuality is a positive characteristic. The latter is the queer twist on the essentialist proposition. But belonging to a denomination that accepted the initial proposition made it easier to make the case for the possible goodness and purpose of homosexuality. Other denominations, notably Mormonism, state explicitly that homosexuality is a "lifestyle choice" that a person should resist by every possible means, no matter how strong the inclination. For a discussion of the intersection of essentialist and constructionist reasoning within Christian considerations of sexuality, see Boswell (1997).

REFERENCES

Anzaldua, G. 1987. *Borderlands/La Frontera: The new Mestiza*. San Francisco: Aunt Lute Books.

Balka, C., and Rose, A., ed. 1991. *Twice blessed: On being lesbian, gay and Jewish*. Boston, MA: Beacon.

Boswell, J. 1997. Concepts, experience, and sexuality. In *Que(e)rying religion: A critical anthology*, ed. G. D. Comstock and S. E. Henking. New York: Continuum.

Bouldrey, B., ed. 1995. *Wrestling with the angel: Faith and religion in the lives of gay men*. New York: Riverhead Books.

Catechism of the Catholic Church. 1994. United States Catholic Conference, *Libreria Editrice Vaticana*. Mahwah, NJ: Paulist Press.

Comstock, G. D. 1997. *Que(e)rying Religion: A Critical Anthology*. New York: Continuum.

Conrad, P., and Schneider, J. 1980. Homosexuality: From sin to sickness to lifestyle. In *Deviance and medicalization: From badness to sickness*, ed. P. Conrad and J. Schneider. Philadelphia: Temple University Press.

Cornell-Drury, P. 2000. Seattle First Christian Church unanimously becomes "open & affirming Letter to the congregation, 6 November, Seattle, WA.

Fortunato, J. 1982. *Embracing the exile: Healing journeys of gay Christians*. San Francisco: Harper Collins.

Gill, S., ed. 1998. *The lesbian and gay Christian movement: Campaigning for justice, truth, and love*. London: Cassell.

Gluckman, A., and Reed, B., ed. 1997. *Homo Economics*. New York: Routledge.

Gonzalez-Lopez, G. 2004. *Beyond the bed sheets, beyond the borders: Mexican immigrant women and their sex lives*. Berkeley: University of California Press.

Harryman, Don D. 1991. With all thy getting, get understanding. In *Peculiar people: Mormons and same-sex orientation*, ed. R. Schow, W. Schow and M. Raynes. Salt Lake City: Signature Books.

Hartman, K. 1996. *Congregations in conflict: The battle over homosexuality*. New Brunswick, NJ: Rutgers University Press.

Mansbridge, J. 2001. The making of oppositional consciousness. In *Oppositional consciousness: The subjective roots of social protest*, ed. J. Mansbridge and A. Morris. Chicago: University of Chicago Press.

McNeill, J. 1996. *Taking a chance on god: Liberating theology for gays, lesbians, and their lovers, families, and friends*. Boston, MA: Beacon.

Mehan, H., and Wood, H. 1975. Five features of reality. In *Reality of ethnomethodology*, ed. H. Mehan and H. Wood. New York: Wiley.

Nestle, J. 2002. How a "liberationist" fem understands being a Jew. In *Queer Jews*, ed. D. Schneer and C. Aviv. New York: Routledge.

O'Brien, J. 2001a. Boundaries and contradictions in self articulation. In *The production of reality*, ed. J. O'Brien and P. Kollock. Newbury Park, CA: Pine Forge Press.

O'Brien, J. 2001b. Homophobia and heterosexism. In *International encyclopedia of the social and behavioral sciences*. London: Elsevier Science.

Plummer, K. 1995. *Telling sexual stories: Power, change, and social worlds*. London: Routledge.

Roof, W. C. 1999. *Spiritual marketplace: Baby boomers and the remaking of American Religion*. Princeton, NJ: Rutgers University Press.

Schneer, P. and Aviv, C. 2002. *Queer Jews*. New York: Routledge.

Smith, R. L. 1994. *AIDS, gays and the American Catholic church*. Cleveland, OH: Pilgrim Press.

Stuart, E. 1997. *Religion is a queer thing: A guide to the Christian faith for lesbian, gay, bisexual and transgendered people*. Cleveland, OH: Pilgrim Press.

Tigert, L. M. 1997. *Coming out while staying in: Struggles and celebrations of lesbians and gays in the church*. Cleveland, OH: United Church Press.

White, D. and White, O. K. 2004. Queer Christian confessions: Spiritual autobiographies of gay Christians. *Culture and Religion* 5 (2).

Wilcox, Melissa. 2000. Two roads converged: Religion and identity among lesbian, gay, bisexual and transgender Christians. Doctoral Dissertation, University of California, Santa Barbara.

CONTRADICTIONS AND CONFLICT IN SELF PRODUCTION

40

Contested Selves in Divorce Proceedings

Joseph Hopper

(2001)

Since selves are socially constructed and situationally located, the social world is populated with more selves than people. Each of us moves from work to home, from the doctor's office to the grocery store, from our immediate family to our extended family, and different selves emerge that continually shape and are shaped by the interactions and practical activities of each location. This is the crux of what some describe as the postmodern condition: multiplying sites of interaction create multiple selves; we shift rapidly from one to another and in doing so we become agglomerations of many different selves (Gergen 1991; Gubrium and Holstein 1994; Holstein and Gubrium 2000).

There is, however, a phenomenological unity to our experience and to our sense of self that we carry from one situation to the next. For the most part, we do not experience the world as a disconnected collection of behavioral roles appropriately invoked in various circumstances. Rather, we experience the world as continuous, and we feel a unitary self that is the locus of such continuity and experience. There is thus a tension in our everyday lives as we work to maintain a unified, continuous sense of self in a social world that fosters multiple selves, a world that operates as if we had and could act with different, separable selves.

Divorce provides a dramatic and instructive example of this phenomenon. Divorcing people develop strong and distinct notions of themselves *as* divorcing people in ways that help to preserve their moral standing, and they carry that sense of self into the many situations and conversations in which divorce is relevant. When they seek legal help, however, they encounter a system that denies the relevance of the "moral self." Instead, they find professionals who must work with them in terms of a "legal self"—a self that is grounded not in the particulars of their own situations and in terms of who did what to whom, but in a system of generalized, bureaucratic rules focused on apportioning money and property so as to maximize the material well-being of divorcing spouses and their children.

This chapter examines the legal self that attorneys and other professionals involved in the legal process attempt to construct against the efforts of divorcing people who maintain quite different conceptions of self. I suggest that the clash between these two exacerbates the legal difficulties of divorce, whatever the conciliatory intentions of attorneys may be.

My description is based on field observations and interviews gathered via a four-year study of divorce that began in 1991. (The research was supported by a grant from the National Institute of Mental Health, 1F31MH10797-01, and by a grant from the Fahs-Beck Fund for Research and Experimentation.)

THE MORAL SELF

Divorcing persons in our culture have a pervasive and weighty set of concerns shaped by a wider institutional context of marriage and family: Marriage and family provide the central place where most members of our society anchor their identity, their social and kinship ties, their child rearing, and their bases of financial and emotional support (Mead 1971); nearly all persons in our culture seek to get married, cherish the idea of marriage, and indeed get married. Not surprisingly, then, one's self in marriage gets articulated in moral terms via a discourse of kinship and domestic life, and also not surprisingly, so does one's self as a divorcing person.

Once divorce begins, people usually identify themselves as either the partner who wants the divorce or as the partner who does not. Although the distinction conceals a great deal of complexity as to what is "really" going on in any divorce, understanding the initiator and noninitiator identities is central because they are the symbolic poles in relation to which agency gets organized. Taking on an identity in divorce as either the person who left or the person who got left imposes order and meaning upon behaviors, circumstances, and events that would otherwise seem chaotic and inexplicable (Hopper 1993a, 1993b).

One component of the order thus imposed is a moral order. Marriage is vaunted both as an institution and as a personal accomplishment, and it is a relationship that is supposed to last forever. Divorce violates the profound value we attach to marriage, and it represents a personal failure for both spouses. The initiator/noninitiator distinction helps divorcing people account for that violation, and it helps them repair damage to their identities for having failed. In short, focusing on themselves

as either initiators in divorce or as noninitiating partners helps divorcing persons formulate cogent explanations that emphasize compelling cultural values, and that help neutralize their own culpability. In the end, divorcing people thus constitute selves in expressly moral terms.

Noninitiators, for example, do this by articulating a rhetoric of family and commitment that shifts blame for the divorce onto initiators for having given up. They talk with considerable bitterness about their spouses not being willing to work at their marriages: "That's the part I don't like," said one noninitiator, "somebody walking out on that commitment." Even when they acknowledge the poor quality of their marriages or their own doubts about whether it could last, noninitiators uphold the sanctity of marriage and they present themselves as its defenders:

> My father came to the same place. He either had a choice of abandoning his family and going off and doing his own thing, or doing what I would like to say is right, and hanging in there and sticking it out and working on it. And I felt like I had to do that. That maybe it would have been better for me 11 years ago to have left. But that I had a commitment. I made a commitment to marry.

Initiators, on the other hand, articulate a rhetoric of individual and personal needs within marriage that shifts blame onto noninitiators for having failed to provide for a "real" marriage:

> There were needs that weren't being met, like there was no relationship there. Emotionally there wasn't any understanding and support. The fact that he isolated himself so much and the fact that he treated me with such contempt. The attitude was that he didn't really care about anybody but himself.

Initiators often describe their spouses as verbally and emotionally abusive, selfish, overinvolved in other activities, uncommunicative, and unaffectionate, and with this they begin reconceptualizing their marriages into "marriages that never were," in effect symbolically annulling their marriages and arguing that they were not marriages at all (Hopper 1998). They talk about their relationships being fundamentally flawed such that divorce becomes something not chosen, but something that happens inevitably to remedy the mistake of a "false" marriage. Deciding to divorce, then, is something not worthy of blame:

> I was the dumper. But it's one of those situations where it's because I was the one who had the nerve to do it. And I always wind up saying, "Well, it doesn't mean it was my fault." He tried to turn it into, "It's your fault, you wouldn't try." And I don't buy into that.

Thus the selves that divorcing people created for themselves are, among other things, bound up with matters of fault and blame. Add to that the moral significance of marriage, and it is easy to understand why who left whom and the dynamics that emerge around the distinction should figure so prominently in divorcing people's self-constructions.

Now when divorcing people approach the legal system, they do not approach it as a realm separate from these concerns; rather, they approach it hoping to air these concerns so that the truth of their marriages, their divorces, and who did what to whom will have consequences in how their dissolved relationships will be configured. Divorce professionals know this well: "People expect to go to court and have the judge know . . . about their relationship, about their children, about what happened in their breakup, you name it," one attorney explained. And the *truth* divorcing people want known is expressed for them via the moral self vis-à-vis the other, blamed spouse (Sarat and Felstiner 1988). One custody evaluator explained: "Everyone wants validation that their perception is the correct one and that the other person is an asshole." And an attorney said, "That's what I am dealing with a lot. The response that's coming from that chair has something to do with how rotten somebody was to them five years ago more than anything else."

Thus, however fragmented our institutional worlds may be, divorcing people presume a constant relevance to who they are as either initiator or noninitiating partner. They want and expect the moral failings, commitments, and courses of action that are now manifest in one person leaving the other to matter, and they approach the legal system expecting to find sympathetic professionals who will process their cases in such terms. The financial planner I interviewed gave an example of a client who had been left by her husband, and who expected a disproportionate financial settlement as a result: "She says, 'Well, yeah, but I deserve it. He's caused this divorce. He's the one that walked out.' I hear that a lot."

THE LEGAL SELF

The legal self of a divorcing person that lawyers and other professionals create differs sharply from the moral self that clients create. As with other institutional agents in other settings, they need particular selves to do their work. The legal self I describe in this section is an abstract person, subject to general rules laid down by a legislature—a person who has a definable and calculable future set of interests that can be determined by such rules. Divorce professionals see their clients in bureaucratic terms and interact with them, sometimes forcefully, expecting clients to take on similar understandings of self and to act accordingly.

They do this by simultaneously denying the moral self and proffering an alternative, and, when pressed, by insisting that institutional realities prevent them from doing otherwise. Erving Goffman's (1961) observations about how selves are constructed and transformed, though derived from his analysis of total institutions, are relevant here: The old self is denied its usual means of expression and affirmation, and at the same time a new self is constructed by subjecting persons to new sets of rules and behavioral criteria that get incorporated into their ongoing sense of how to get through divorce intact.

Denying the Moral Self

The first step for divorce professionals involves denying the moral self and the particulars of who left whom typically presented. Most simply emphasize to their clients the irrelevance of who left whom to the legal matters at hand, some saying they refuse to talk with clients about it. One attorney explained: "There are times when you have to say, 'You really don't want to talk to me about this. This is no5t important in the whole scheme of things as far as the divorce is concerned.'" The financial planner elaborated: "It's not that I don't care. I would rather not hear it all, because it doesn't affect what I'm doing." If noninitiators hope to use the legal system to contest the divorce itself, attorneys explain to them its futility:

Our society doesn't recognize that. As far as our laws are concerned, there's no way to avoid a divorce in a nonfault state where the only grounds for dissolution is irretrievable breakdown of marriage. You got to tell them, "Look, that may be your belief system, and it may be the important law for you, but this state does not agree with that."

Even the more dramatic and seemingly relevant moral aspects of divorce, such as spouses having affairs, squandering family income, or acting cruelly or emotionally abusive are considered unimportant.

In many cases, professionals see the moral contours of divorce as not only irrelevant to the legal process, but as potentially damaging as well. It can be damaging if professionals know and work with clients in moral terms, as the financial consultant described:

I have found that when I go to court, when the other side cross-examines me, if I haven't heard a lot of that stuff, I'm better off. Because they really get into it. They'll say, "Well, did you know that?" And if I can say, "No, I didn't," there's nothing else they can question me on. If I say, "Yes, I did," they really dig in. And if it has nothing to do with the financial issues, there's no reason for them to be asking me those questions. And I would rather not be entrapped. Because those are attorneys who really know how to trap you with questions. So I would rather not mess with that stuff.

It can be disadvantageous, too, if clients themselves insist on pursuing moral claims. Custody evaluators described listening for whether divorcing spouses are preoccupied with laying blame, as this would reflect poorly on their abilities to attend to a child's needs; lawyers know that this, in turn, will likely affect an evaluator's recommendation to a court regarding custody. Thus, as one attorney told me:

I perceive any client's interests as having me sit on them more than in some other kinds of cases. By that I mean, I think it is in my client's interests to have them not pursue their obsession with getting even.

Defining Clients' Best Interests

As the moral self is denied, a new legal self is preferred, one that is tailored to the requirements of legal institutions. As such, it is a self that divorce professionals conceptualize in terms of "interests" quite apart from the moral dynamics of divorce. Lawyers in particular see themselves as having an obligation to process cases and clients in ways that may contradict their clients' wishes. And they see it as their job to help clients understand themselves— and therefore what they need and want—in terms of such interests:

My obligation is to do what's in their best interest, not necessarily do what they want to do. Because they don't necessarily know what's in their best interest at the time they're in there because of their emotional state. . . . I know what they need and I know why they need it.

Another attorney said:

Part of my job is to help them get to know what's right and what they want. And when I say, "what's right"—I'm talking about their legal . . . what is potentially out there for them legally.

How do these interests, needs, and wants get built up and defined? It happens through conversations and interactions by which professionals continually broaden, shift, and refocus cases by emphasizing the contexts, rules, and standards that govern divorce as a legal proceeding. They explain, for example, that "there is no divorce without the system," as one attorney put it:

Some people would like to just do it their own way even if they shouldn't. Or even if they are going to pay a terrible price. One of the things that I do when I'm talking to people like that is that I tell them that the court is going to have to review their agreement and it might not be approved.

Another attorney said:

[I] show them the larger context in which their case, their life, their relationship is going to proceed. Especially if you start talking about a new divorce client. Many people will come in and say I need X, Y, Z, whatever. And they just are never going to get it. You better tell them. Or if they want it, you may have to tell them that it has to come in this way, in this context, you have to ask for it this way or you'll never get it. To reframe their experience from being one of a simply personal and relational problem, to now one that is going to include me, it's going to include someone else's lawyer, usually, it's going to include a system. It's going to include much more than they ever anticipated.

The working assumption among professionals is that every divorce will go to a full-blown trial:

"I assume every case will go to court . . . even though 90 percent of them don't," one custody evaluator said. Thus they remain attentive to how cases and clients must be configured for future institutional scrutiny. As one attorney described:

I'm always building the faces [creating the appearances] that I have to prove to a judge sometime later. . . . You have to be thinking from the moment you first sit down, that this person, even if he's here, how you're going to present it to a judge someday.

Professionals explain that within the broader context thus laid out is a set of dispassionate, clearly articulated rules that are fault-blind and that will determine outcomes, be they "right, wrong, or indifferent." "You're stuck with the state system, so here is the range that this state is going to deal with," one attorney explained. Many used language as if they were working with algebraic formulas: "The marriage has been X amount of time, she has made X amount of sacrifices." Another put it this way:

The court is going to say, "Okay, here's the deal: The marriage is X amount of years time, it was this kind of marriage, here's what you did, here's what the other person did during the course of the marriage. Here's what you need, here's what they need. Here's what you can afford, here's what they can afford." So that's what we've got to talk about. We've got to talk about what your expenses are. We've got to talk about what your needs are and we've got to talk about what your income is. We've got to talk about what the future is going to be for you under whatever the scenario might be.

Several emphasized that the rules are general rules, the procedures are bureaucratic, and so the particulars of each case are emphatically pushed to the background:

I give a lecture . . . that goes through every element of domestic relations, whether it's applicable to this particular situation or not. So they understand the general foundations and rules, and also they understand the grounds for dissolution, they understand the longevity of the proceeding, on a minimal basis what has to be done, what procedures we go through, the collection of data, collection of evidence if we're in that type of case, and what they can expect.

Hence for professionals, the self of a client is a generalized self. It is a self that expresses something more abstract, an outcome achieved by applying universal rules within a legal context to the situation at hand. One lawyer, in fact, complained about divorce mediation because it is premised on the opposing idea that spouses know best their own situations and can therefore craft better and more particular solutions:

Mediation [is] a narcissistic hangover of values from the '80s: "What I want and how I want to do it is very important; it doesn't matter about the social context in which it arose or in which it's going to die—the legal ramifications of it. No, it's personal to me. Me me me me me. And therefore, I I I I I want to do it my my my my way. And so we are going to make this a very personated kind of a thing."

The result is that lawyers and other divorce professionals work with clients and construct notions of who clients are in calculable terms that focus on matters of money, property, and time with children. They collect information about income and expenditures, property, bank accounts, retirement plans, and debts. They work out the specifics of who will get what and when and how two households can be maintained, apportioning cars and houses and in some cases trifling items like Zippo lighters and blue Corning pots. They haggle over maintenance (alimony) and child support payments, which are themselves calculated with formulas laid out by the law. Even the issue of custody is handled not in terms of who left whom (i.e., who "betrayed" the family) or in terms of who is the

better parent (as divorcing people typically argue) but in terms of "the best interests of the child." Interests of children are, in turn, determinable according to financial formulas and according to the scientific canons of developmental psychology.

There is a way in which this legal self is still related to questions of morality, but the grounds shift decisively. First, what is "right" is what conforms to the rules, precisely because the rules are designed to ensure equitable outcomes despite the whims of divorcing spouses, attorneys, and judges. Second, what is "right" has to do with the future and how that future must be mapped out, rather than having to do with the past and how grievances might be redressed. Third, what is right has essentially to do with matters of "fairness" in terms of clients' legally defined interests. An attorney described his job thusly:

You're extricating people from a legal binding relationship, and you want them to be happy as you can. You want them to be under the least strain that they can be in. You want to make sure the children are cared for, so maybe there's a joint caring of the kids. You want to make sure there's a fair disposition of the money accumulated during the course of the marriage, i.e., marital assets. You want to make sure the payments are fair and commensurate with ability to pay and need. And you want to make sure that, hopefully, that everybody goes on with their lives and is happy. That's really the job.

Asserting Ownership of the Legal Self

The legal self constructed by divorce professionals, though constructed in response to institutional demands about how cases and clients must be processed, is more than a heuristic that allows professionals to accomplish their work. It is something they believe in, and they see this legal self as a self that clients can and should adopt for their own good. Most attorneys thus insist that clients take "ownership" of the process and of the decisions finally made:

> I want it to be from his heart, too. For him, it's better that it's real. . . . The last thing I want him to say is, "Yeah, I went to a parenting class because my lawyer told me I had to." And the truth is, I want . . . if my client wants custody, my client has to show *me* that he's committed in that kind of scenario. You show me how committed you are to making some changes, because what I'm trying to sort out is: is this just a power struggle? or this guy doesn't want custody, he just wants to zing the wife?

Most attorneys want their clients to move on with their lives, and most want to spare them the trauma and expense of a court trial. "Winning" cases thus involves settling them, I was told. And settling cases is a matter of having clients internalize an understanding of the legal rules and procedures according to which their cases will be processed, than having clients arrive at the kinds of decisions a court would arrive at were their divorces actually to go to trial. This is not always easy. It is facilitated in part by the fact that most clients pay for the legal services rendered, giving them an incentive to work out fair solutions quickly and agreeably.

The Unifying Intrusions of the Moral Self

As professionals work with their clients in divorce cases, they construct working models of who their clients are in terms of tangible interests with determinate rights and obligations as specified by the legal institution within which they must work. Meanwhile, divorcing people construct moral selves that provide, among other things, some means of defense against the ignominy of divorce. Thus, people getting divorced have at least two "divorcing selves" that get constructed in at least two different contexts according to the institutional demands of each.

I suggested earlier, however, that within the lived experiences of most divorcing persons there are not multiple selves but a unified self—a self that cannot easily shed its various assemblages depending upon institutional contexts. Hence, professionals come to discover that their clients usually expect the legal system to serve the moral self, and that clients often transform dispassionate discussions of interests, legal rights, and contractual obligations squarely back into moral terms. This is part of what makes the process so complicated and potentially difficult. Clients must be able to "separate their own stuff from the business end of the divorce," one attorney explained, and when they cannot, "when the relationship issues are just so overwhelming, oftentimes you can't reach agreement."

A number of factors make it particularly difficult for divorcing people to separate out different selves for the sake of getting the legal work done. First, divorcing people are not separated from the everyday world and institutional sources that shape the moral self. Goffman (1961) suggests that total institutions are able to reconstruct inmates' selves in part because total institutions separate inmates almost entirely from their "home worlds." Divorce lawyers cannot do this; in fact divorcing people are often pulled more tightly into the social worlds that define the moral self as they turn to parents and family members for financial, practical, and emotional help, even as they seek out attorneys for legal help.

Lawyers recognize this and the difficulties it creates. "There's very often parental influence," one attorney explained, and every lawyer I interviewed said that having a client's parents somehow involved in the process made the job more difficult. "It's just a bad situation," one said. "You're trying to get them to see things impartially and Mom or Dad or both are coming in and saying, 'You ought to do this, you ought to do that.'" Another attorney described: "Those pulls are incredible on them. And quite often very destructive in the legal case as well as to that person who can't deal with that right then." This same attorney noted that professionals, too, can get swept into the familiar context that shapes moral selves and lose sight of their clients' legal selves as a result. The more an attorney knows the detailed story of a client's life, she told me, the more "you want to react emotionally, just like the client does":

> You begin to get strong feelings about the other attorney, and about the other client. It happens frequently in divorce cases, but it's even more of an issue when you're handling postdecree cases, cases that you've been on for years and years and years. That person is like an aunt or an uncle. You know everything about the family. You know what's going on. And you really get entrenched there.

A second factor that makes it difficult for clients to separate the legal self from the moral self is that attorneys may work in ways that actually reinforce the strength and clarity of clients' moral identities in divorce. When attorneys have clients who are wavering about whether or not to get divorced, they often push their clients toward taking a more resolute stand—not necessarily because divorce attorneys have an interest in clients pursuing divorce, but because they cannot work effectively within ambiguously defined situations. Ambiguity and ambivalence "just drive you crazy," said one attorney as he related to me a story about a client he was working with:

> I had a discussion with her, "Look, damn it, you've got to make a decision. I can't do this and this at the same time. Tell me which one you want to do." [Interviewer: What can't you do at the same time?] I can't pursue this case in litigation and not pursue. I can't do discovery and not do discovery. Tell me which one. [Interviewer: And what does she say?] Well, it depends on what moment you catch her. We executed a very unusual order that allowed us to go into his business and inventory everything without his knowledge. So we went in last

Sunday and did all of that. And she calls me up Monday and says, "Do you think I'm walking away from this relationship too soon?"

But it is precisely when resolute decisions are made and ambivalence resolved that the moral identities in divorce take form and become important phenomena in divorce (Hopper 1993a, 1993b). The either-or nature of the legal system effectively pushes people toward resolving the ambivalence they might have had, and, as most attorneys know, few clients turn back once legal action is begun. Attorneys also sometimes strengthen the salience of clients' moral selves by maneuvering them into doing the "right" thing—what is required of the legal self—by drawing upon clients' moralistic interpretations of how a divorce is playing out. "You sometimes have to play into their craziness," one attorney explained:

> For example, "You don't want him to see the kids because you think this bad thing is going to happen?" And the bad thing is not too bad. I mean I wouldn't do it with any safety issues. Sometimes you have to say, "Well, you know I really believe you, but we don't have the evidence. So what we need to do is we have to try it, and then if he does it then your case is going to be made." And you kind of feed into the sort of craziness and suspiciousness and paranoia in a way to get them to do the right thing. And it's not totally dishonest—I don't feel that good about having to do it—but a lot of times you have to do it. Especially at critical stages. And then later you can talk to them about it. But especially if they are doing something really destructive for their case. Sometimes you have to give them okay reasons to do the right thing.

In short, though the legal system technically nullifies questions of fault—questions that are at the heart of clients' moral selves—the practical realities of how lawyers and other professionals get their clients processed through that system often intensify the moral selves of clients. One might think that the dual constructions of self would cause confusion among divorcing people as they work to manage competing versions of the self in various contexts, and this on top of the crisis in meaning that divorce itself would seem to present. But as one custody evaluator observed, there does not seem to be much in terms of confusion:

> Usually, they're arguing their case to me and arguing their case to their attorney and as they do that they become more and more convinced that what they're saying is right and the way it should be.

For many divorcing people, then, the unifying intrusions of the moral self beckon strongly. "They need fault. They want fault. They want somebody to pay when they're bad," one attorney explained, and they want that somebody to pay in tangible ways via a penalty imposed by the court. A number of attorneys suggested to me that one result is that many more clients than ever before are playing out matters of fault in battles over custody. One said:

> That's the only place where the whole system seems to let fault be played out. I think that if parents could—and I'm talking about marriages with children—if parents could get in the court and say why they think they were wronged, and there might be legal consequences to it to the other parent, they probably would not use their children as the go-betweens as much.

There may be no-fault divorce in a technical sense, but for divorcing people the issue of fault does not go away. And the issue of fault in divorce can easily translate into the domain of parenting and custody, for the central issues about who left whom and why still get expressed, as one divorcing woman explained to me:

> Morally are you being a bad parent because you're having an affair with this man? What are you going to teach the child if you're doing this during our marriage? Or, the child's going to get hurt if he stays with you because you beat me; what's going to make it to where you don't beat them?

Clients thus reassert their moral selves, bringing matters of fault back into the legal process by linking their identity in divorce with their identity as a parent. The legal system may thus exacerbate divorce conflict in a rather surprising way, because it refuses to allow matters of fault within the purview of divorce proceedings. In the end, since the legal system has no place for fault to play out within the domain of the dissolving marital relationship itself, the moral battle may get displaced into arenas like custody where divorcing partners can fight over who is at fault [for] the marriage's failure by fighting over who is the better parent. As courts have tried to remove matters of fault and blame even from custody considerations, hoping instead to rely on the scientific formulations of child psychology and expert opinion, one attorney hypothesized that the custody battles would get even worse:

> There are more allegations of spousal and child abuse made to get custody. It's upped the ante so that if someone really wants to show someone else is at fault, and they'll do anything to do it, they've just upped the ante. So now you say, "This person has abused me." Whereas before all you had to say was they were mean.

SELVES IN CONFLICT

There are at least two selves in divorce, which I have called the moral self and the legal self; they are constructed in different institutional spheres by social actors who attend to the ongoing concerns of those institutions. From one perspective, the two selves in divorce give evidence that theorists of self in postmodernity are right that we are each constituted by multiple selves—that the self in our postmodern society, with its burgeoning possibilities for interactions contextualized within multiple institutions, has become a "saturated" self, as Kenneth Gergen (1991) has put it.

But the descriptions in this chapter suggest a more distressing possibility as well: Perhaps it is not so much that we have become saturated with multiple selves, but that we have become fragmented into partial selves. As we become increasingly subject to diverse and disparate encounters in various spheres, our attempts to pull our experiences into some semblance of unity through a singular point of reference become more precarious. This chapter has emphasized, in particular, the unifying attempts of the moral self, as divorcing persons seek to bring the legal system into line with their everyday moralistic expectations. The legal self has unifying tendencies as well: Witness legal professionals insisting that the legal self is the good self, the fair self, the self that ought to come from one's heart so that one can move on. Either way, it seems that as institutional spheres proliferate in number and scope, according to a logic that does not necessarily serve the living persons who comprise them, the self is frustrated in its unifying efforts. In the case of divorce, each competing self attempts to incorporate the other under its own terms, and neither seems to accomplish it. The legal self requires objectivity and compromise, which the moral self refuses and stymies; the moral self requires justice, not scientific administration, and thus seeks ever new ways to use the legal system to fight its battles.

No doubt the conflict in divorce between two competing selves can take its toll on two levels. First, since the two constructions of self presumably inhere in one and the same person, the conflict may be internalized as an existential struggle in personal terms. Second, it can be externalized and manifest in social terms, as battles over custody attest. In this, perhaps the social theorists of

modernity were more prescient than postmodern theorists appreciate. Translated into language about the self, we might say that Marx wrote about the alienated self, Durkheim the anomic self, Weber the self trapped in an iron cage of rationality, and Simmel the subjective self outpaced by objective culture. Each suggested in his own way that we face the danger of becoming fragmented, impoverished, and frustrated at the partial demands multiple institutions put upon us and the limited possibilities they give for unitary self-expression.

REFERENCES

Gergen, Kenneth J. 1991. *The Saturated Self: Dilemmas of Identity in Contemporary Life.* New York: Basic Books.

Goffman, Erving. 1961. *Asylums.* New York: Anchor Books.

Gubrium, Jaber F., and James A. Holstein. 1994. "Grounding the Postmodern Self." *The Sociological Quarterly* 34:685–703.

Holstein, James A., and Jaber F. Gubrium. 2000. *The Self We Live By: Narrative Identity in a Postmodern World.* New York: Oxford University Press.

Hopper, Joseph. 1993a. "Oppositional Identities and Rhetoric in Divorce." *Qualitative Sociology* 16:233–56.

_____. 1993b. "The Rhetoric of Motives in Divorce." *Journal of Marriage and Family* 55:801–13.

_____. 1998. "The Symbolic Origins of Conflict in Divorce." Paper presented at the annual meeting of the American Sociological Association, San Francisco.

Mead, Margaret. 1971. "Anomalies in American Postdivorce Relationships." In *Divorce and After,* ed. Paul Bohannan, 107–25. Garden City, NY: Anchor Books.

Sarat, Austin, and Felstiner, William L. F. 1988. "Law and Social Relations: Vocabularies of Motive in Lawyer/Client Interaction." *Law & Society Review* 22:737–69.

COMPLEXITIES AND CHANGE IN CULTURAL PRODUCTION

The reading examples in the next-to-last section of Part VI, "The Social Production of the Cultural Status Quo," explored some of the ways in which everyday social interaction results in the persistence of the status quo. This section looks at examples of complexity and change in cultural production.

"Take Your Good Friday to the Streets" is a selection from Pierrette Hondagneu-Sotelo's book *God's Heart Has No Borders*. Hondagneu-Sotelo spent several years talking with and observing social activists working to better the lives of Latin American immigrants in the Los Angeles area. This selection describes the complex relationship between a group of religious leaders and union organizers working together to support labor reform. The religious leaders explain their activism in terms of their beliefs about God and service to fellow human beings. Accordingly, they are able to reconcile seemingly contradictory social positions as they work toward social change.

"Talking Back" is a short essay from renowned contemporary author and scholar bell hooks. In this brief autobiographical sketch, hooks recalls an event in which it became impossible to maintain the expected social routine. She found that she simply had to "talk back."

READING QUESTIONS

1. According to Hondagneu-Sotelo, religious activists use their moral authority to influence labor reform, and this enables them to be more effective than secular union organizers. Explain how moral authority works in this case.

2. Make a list of some of the central cultural shifts that have taken place in recent history. Who or what groups were largely responsible for these shifts, and how did they manage to be effective in changing the status quo?

3. Discuss one taken-for-granted belief or practice that you have reconsidered as a result of studying the material in this book.

41

Take Your Good Friday to the Streets

Pierrette Hondagneu-Sotelo

(2008)

After decades of declining rates of unionization, a revitalized labor movement emerged in the United States at the turn of the millennial century. Unions had dedicated more than a century to organizing white male citizen workers, and, in fact, had been historically key to pushing for nativist, restrictionist policies, but they have now deliberately diversified their strategies and also the kinds of workers they include. Spearheaded by progressive leaders working at the grassroots level and in the AFL-CIO, the movement gained momentum with the rise of service-sector unions; the concerted cultivation of community allies; and a new commitment to organizing women, minorities, and immigrant workers. Less well publicized are the new mobilizations of clergy marching in the street to support these unionization efforts. Religion is a critical part of this newly revitalized style of unionism, which relies on building allies and cultivating community support. Often in clerical robes and regalia, rabbis, priests, and ministers from various denominations are marching in the streets, holding prayer vigils, engaging in civil disobedience, and visiting workers at their homes and workplaces. Through their actions, they collectively offer their moral authority and spiritual support to the struggles faced by low-wage workers, many of whom are immigrants.

How did this happen? The development of these religious support groups for workers follows on the heels of the new openness in the labor movement, but it also reflects the clergy's pent-up desire for meaningful social engagement. Religious people who had grown weary of the limitations of religious charity—and who longed to once again, or perhaps for the first time, experience participating in something like the civil rights movement—coalesced to form labor support organizations such as Clergy and Laity United for Economic Justice (CLUE) in the 1990s. Many of these clergy groups around the country are coordinated through the Chicago offices of Interfaith Worker Justice (IWJ), an organization founded by Kim Bobo in 1995. As Bobo told me, "There were a lot of folks in the religious community who had done twenty or twenty-five years of soup kitchens and shelters and were beginning to realize that this was just a complete dead end." These were religious people looking for a way to put their faith into action for social change. "We had to find," Bobo explained, "some new ways to challenge what was going on in society."

CLUE is located in Los Angeles, and it is among the strongest of the sixty religious-based labor support organizations in the country. These groups support workers by relying on religious moral authority, scripture, and a mixture of modern political persuasion techniques (such as street protests, phone calls, and delegations to authority figures) and ancient religious symbols (such as stone tablets, bitter herbs, and milk and honey). In Los Angeles and Santa Monica, CLUE has acted quite militantly in demanding economic justice for workers and the working poor. Sometimes their opponents, the managers and employees of corporations, allege that the CLUE clergy are not authentic religious leaders or that they are merely puppets of the union. For example, when CLUE members organized civil disobedience and clergy delegations at a major luxury hotel in support of service workers and their union, the hotel management circulated a flyer warning workers not to be duped by "phony priests." Leaders in CLUE were outraged and exacted an apology from the management. CLUE members also bristle at the insinuation that they were simply manufactured by the union or that they follow union orders. "We're not on their payroll," they say. Rather, they see themselves as an autonomous organization, constituted by people of deep religious faith who have embraced the cause of worker justice as their own, precisely because it is a direct expression of their religious beliefs and doctrines. For many of them, supporting the struggles of low-wage immigrant workers has become an integral part of their religious identity and practice. A CLUE board member and minister of a small congregation told me, "Faith is what you do." Many of the clergy said that the experience of participating in CLUE has brought them spiritual renewal and positive transformation.

In cities like Los Angeles, where Latino immigrant workers constitute the majority of those in the low-wage, super-exploited jobs, labor organizers of the 1980s and 1990s concentrated on a particular set of industries that seemed organizable. Consequently, much of the sparkle and success in the new labor movement comes from immigrant workers in the hotel and restaurant industry, in home health care, and in the janitorial sector. Organizations such as CLUE support the cause of economic justice broadly, but some of their biggest and most successful efforts have concentrated on

union campaigns where Mexican and Central American immigrant workers predominate.

Scriptures and Protest

As one of their first direct actions in support of the hotel workers, CLUE inaugurated Java for Justice. Seemingly inspired by the lunch counter sit-ins of the civil rights movement, small groups of clergy dressed in clerical collars and ministerial garb ordered coffee at the hotel restaurants. They used these opportunities to preach about the injustices of hotel managers who refused to sign union contracts or allow for workers' demands. Reverend Dick Gillet recalls one of his first experiences with the Java for Justice campaign this way: He and about a half-dozen other clergy, several of them in clerical collars, visited the restaurant of one of the luxury hotels and ordered coffee. "We finished our drinks and coffee and stuff and then I got up," he related, "and said, 'May I have your attention?'" Speaking in as loud a voice as he could muster, he recalled saying, "I know this is a bit unusual, and certainly not my real congregation, but I would like you to know that we are here in support of the people who are waiting on you, who make your beds, who are tending to you while you are in this hotel. They need your help, and you can help them if you go downstairs to the front desk after you are through here and tell them that you personally want the hotel to sign a fair contract."

CLUE would continue to develop and refine this tactic. In 2002, after Elba Hernandez, an employee who had worked for Santa Monica's Doubletree Hotel for eleven years, was fired, allegedly for union organizing, CLUE participated in a "lunch-in" action at the hotel restaurant. Twenty-two CLUE members filtered into the hotel restaurant, and after ordering drinks and lunch, they stood up in unison, holding placards that read, "Support Your Workers' Rights." Reverend Jarvis Johnson led them in prayer and declared, "These walls of Jericho," the ones that separate rich and poor, "need to come tumbling down." The clergy activists were quickly ushered out of the building, but outside they gathered to pray while Reverend Sandy Richards read a letter of support from the Muslim Public Affairs Council's senior advisor, Maher Hathout. Letters in support of reinstating the fired worker were also sent to the hotel from bishops of the Methodist, Episcopal, and evangelical Lutheran churches. Following this event, Father Michael Gutierrez, also a CLUE member and a priest at a Santa Monica church, had a private meeting with the general manager of the hotel, a fellow Catholic. At the meeting, he expressed his dissatisfaction with the hotel management decisions, and he suggested the manager face the moral contradiction of being a Catholic and treating employees so unfairly. A few months after these actions, Elba Hernandez was reinstated with back pay.

CLUE members have used a variety of tactics to express their support for union mobilization. To show their support for workers to the public and to corporate management, they have marched in picket lines, spoken out publicly in support of the union mobilizations, and participated in several instances of civil disobedience and a well-publicized fast at USC (University of Southern California). Many clergy were also arrested at USC in their attempts to win union contracts for the food service workers. Some clergy also visited the offices of hotel and USC managers.

The battle with the Westside hotels reached a high point in April 1998 when CLUE, together with the Westside Interfaith Council and the Jewish Labor Committee, organized what would become the first annual Holy Week-Passover Procession. At that first event, sixty priests, rabbis, and ministers outfitted in robes, shawls, collars, and yarmulkes walked alongside another one hundred lay supporters and workers on that iconic boulevard of consumer dreams, glitzy Rodeo Drive in Beverly Hills. By the time the procession occurred, two of the three Beverly Hills hotels had already signed

the contract with Local 11, so these hotels were publicly rewarded with symbolic offerings of milk and honey, referring to the land where Moses set the Jews free. The managers at the Summit Rodeo Hotel received bitter herbs after a brief street-side seder, symbolizing the plight of the ancient Jews. Soon after, the Summit Rodeo signed the union contract.

In all of CLUE's actions, biblical references and faith-based morality are used as justifications. One of CLUE's earliest declarations in support of the living wage cited Deuteronomy 24:14–15: "Don't withhold the wages of poor and needy laborers—including those of 'aliens.'" In the struggle at USC, CLUE relied on the biblical story of David and Goliath to call attention to how "the University of Southern California, like Goliath of old, has unleashed its enormous economic and corporate power on its own little David, the 340 Food Service and Housing working men and women members of H.E.R.E. Local 11" (Dalton 2003:44–45). And Moses and stories of exodus (e.g., "You must welcome the alien, the stranger as yourself") as well as references to Incarnation have been frequently invoked in various CLUE campaigns.

GOD'S HEART HAS NO BORDERS

"A new movement, an old commandment, or both?" This was the question printed in big bold type on the envelope of a mass mailing from the Interfaith Worker Justice during spring 2006, when millions of people marched nationwide in massive rallies in support of immigrant rights. The accompanying letter, sent to supporters nationwide, cited the Leviticus quote that is reproduced above and informed readers that many immigrant workers lost their jobs for participating in the marches. It also listed the different ways in which the IWJ participated in the "emerging social justice movement" for immigrant rights. "We must stand for all workers—both immigrant and native-born—when they fight for justice in their workplaces," declared the letter, "we are called to do it through all of our sacred traditions."

CLUE leaders also marched through the streets of Los Angeles during spring 2006. Later that year, CLUE and IWJ joined forces to help coordinate the new sanctuary movement to protect immigrant families facing orders of deportation. While CLUE continued to mobilize in favor of all low-wage workers, CLUE members also saw their mission as including immigrant workers because, as one member told me in an interview, Los Angeles "is a pretty immigrant-looking city."

Most fundamentally, the clergy leaders saw their support of low-wage workers, immigrant or U.S. born, as a direct extension of their religious faith. "We don't see religions as isolated over here and handling one thing," explained Reverend William Campbell, a minister in an African American congregation. "We see it performing in all facets of life. Jesus clearly identified with the poor," he said, and clearly that is how [Reverend Campbell] saw his mission as well. Regardless of whether they were Christian or Jewish, clergy saw their work in CLUE as rooted in scripture and ancient religious traditions.

RELIGION AT WORK

CLUE participants used religion and their position as religious leaders to better the lives of low-wage immigrant workers. In this next section, I discuss three relevant CLUE activities: providing spiritual support to workers, deploying religious symbols in public spaces to underscore a labor struggle, and exercising moral voice and persuasion in favor of the unions.

During the late 1980s and 1990s, the Latino immigrant unions in Los Angeles, such as SEIU Justice for Janitors and HERE Local 11, innovated protests that featured the dramatization of labor struggles in the streets. These involved using props like big papier-mâché figures, placing beds in the middle of a street protest to show how many beds hotel housekeepers must make in a shift, or having a person dressed as Scrooge represent a greedy employer. CLUE followed suit by boldly brandishing religious symbols far beyond the confines of their churches and temples. Material objects with roots in ancient scripture, such as stone tablets, bitter herbs, and milk and honey, played central roles in CLUE protests and processions.

Clerical dress was a key part of these public activities. For these public events, concerted organizational steps were taken to ensure that clergy arrived attired in ways that left little ambiguity about whether they were union people or ordained religious leaders. The flyer announcing the 2001 interfaith procession that occurred during Holy Week-Passover, for example, reminded the participants to bring appropriate symbols of their identities. The flyer said, "Religious Leaders: Wear Vestments; All Workers: Bring a Symbol of Your Work; and Congregations, Organizations: Bring a Banner." Procession participants complied with this request, and the outcome was visually stunning.

The participants were all costumed and carrying props, but these were not theatrical performances but rather enactments of verifiable identities and social locations. Reverend Bob Miller, a retired minister who became quite active in various union-led direct actions, recalled attending his first demonstration in support of the hotel and restaurant employees' union in 1997. There he saw a peaceful demonstration, where, he said, the workers were blocking traffic while "costumed according to whether they were a concierge, housekeeper, whatever." The idea of telegraphing one's identity, whether a worker or clergy member, appealed to him. "The workers received me so warmly," he recalled. "And I thought, Well, I'll have to buy some new shirts and collars and wear them because I want the hotel management to know that I wasn't just a union employee."

Religious garb was donned in the streets and in front of the luxury hotels, but it was not just theatrical costuming. It was used together with traditional religious practices, such as prayer, song, and scripture, and concrete, symbolic reminders of ancient texts. Together, this array of identifiably familiar practices and objects communicated the religious significance of these struggles. When the clergy offered blessings and prayers, they were momentarily transforming a secular site into a sacred place. Moments of Durkheimian collective effervescence ensued. When I asked Don Smith, a Presbyterian minister, to describe his experiences in the CLUE processions and protests, he recalled his experience at the first Holy Week-Passover events. "As you can imagine, it's a tremendous feeling of solidarity. You're there with all the workers, you're there with a whole bunch of clergy . . . you're marching down Rodeo Drive, and . . . you're having an effect. People are stopping on the street, asking, 'What is this?'" Part of the excitement comes from breaking the norms of mundane social interaction, and part of the meaning comes from the religious rituals. As Reverend Smith put it, "There is the sense that this is not usually done. What are these religious people doing out here, dressed up? And that's what one has to do, to interrupt the status quo, to make a point." The marches, he said, were empowering and uplifting because they gave the "sense that you're making an impact."

In all of these venues, the CLUE clergy were exercising moral voice. But part of their challenge was to use their religious authority to persuade others of the urgency of economic justice. CLUE's mission, as Reverend Perez summed up, involved "bringing moral pressure to bear, pressuring political leaders and working with unions, and pushing corporations and businesses to do the right thing." To be effective, they sought venues where they might direct their moral persuasion toward particular audiences. These included targeting the

leaders at their own congregations, the owners and managers of the hotels, and their own congregation members. Clergy were well-suited to this task, as they are socially recognized as moral leaders, as experts in distinguishing right from wrong. Some of them felt that it was "not fair that clergy are respected more than the workers," but none of them failed to recognize the moral credibility which their positions afforded them.

Most of the clergy did not preach about economic justice on a weekly basis, but each Labor Day there was a concerted effort to do so. This is part of a national effort begun in 1996 and coordinated by IWJ and the AFL-CIO. On Labor Day weekend across the country, participating clergy are urged to speak to their congregations about the religious commitment to economic justice, tying the importance of unions today to biblical and scriptural readings. Union members are invited as guest speakers to discuss how they mesh their religious faith and union commitments.

During Labor Day weekend 2001, about one hundred Los Angeles–area congregations participated in this program, with guest speakers appearing at about fifty. I attended two services organized by CLUE clergy. Both featured special emphasis on immigrant worker rights and, in particular, Latino immigrant labor struggles. The two services were radically different, reflecting the different sizes of the congregations, the style of worship, and the congregations' demographic composition. Both, however, were unambiguously directed at the same cause: bringing religious communities and unions together to work for immigrant worker justice. Elsewhere, other religious services at predominantly black churches were focused on honoring the struggles of bus transit and airport security workers, many of whom are African American.

The first Labor in the Pulpit service that I attended occurred at a relatively small Unitarian church in affluent Santa Monica. In this small church filled with natural light, about two hundred or two hundred fifty people, many of them elderly or middle-aged white folks, filled the pews. After welcoming remarks, the lighting of a candle within a chalice (with some difficulty because of a faulty lighter), and the singing of songs such as "This Little Light of Mine," a middle-aged congregation member hobbled to the altar. She revealed that she suffered from multiple sclerosis, and she read a beautifully rendered narrative of thanks to all of the workers who made her life possible—the taxi drivers, the concrete workers, the designers and builders of her motorized wheelchair, and the builders of ramps and rails. More songs ensued, and then small children entered with offerings of food for a food bank before gathering around the group Los Jornaleros del Norte. This is a band formed by Latino immigrant men who met in the day laborer organizing project of the Coalition for Humane Immigrant Rights in Los Angeles. Pablo Alvarado, an immigrant rights and day laborer organizer and member of the band, introduced them by saying, "All of us are immigrant workers and all of us are parents, too." And then he introduced Jose, one of the band members. With that, Jose took the microphone and explained, in Spanish and through a translator, that he was a single parent of six children in Mexico. "I would like to tell the children here," he said, directing himself to the kids who sat on the steps around the altar, "to thank God because they live with their parents. I would love to be with my children, but I cannot." While the band played one of their compositions about the plight of children "back home" with parents working in the United States, the audience bobbed their heads to the beat.

Like the testimonials offered by union workers at the CLUE breakfast meetings, these were two different social worlds coming together. Speaking in Spanish through a translator, the first speaker said, "We day laborers use this Labor Day to protest the exploitation of immigrant workers." Another cited Leviticus and denounced abusive employers who violate the laws of government and the laws of God. They played more songs, ending with a lively rendition of "Sí, Se Puede" on accordion, electric piano, bass, and guitar, and the expressions on the band members' and the congregation's faces suggested genuine warmth, appreciation, and feelings of solidarity.

DENOMINATIONAL DIFFERENCES?

CLUE and IWJ brought together clergy and laity from a variety of religious faiths and traditions, but when I asked if these denominational differences played out into conflicts, nearly everyone told me no. Reverend Don Smith, who had worked in numerous interfaith groups, including explicitly immigrant rights organizations, said, "In these social ministries, you'll never find the need to kind of say that, well, 'You're Catholic, I'm Jewish, and you're Episcopal.' There's this kind of innate understanding that all religions have in common, [which] is this need to address human pain, human suffering."

Just about everyone concurred. Political progressives were less likely to be mired in denominational differences. "The majority of those who will come into CLUE are your more progressive clergypersons anyway," said one clergyman, "and because they are more progressive, they are less likely to bring in denominational garbage." In fact, some clergy found this denominational diversity and shared understanding of social justice, theology, and social action to be particularly gratifying, giving them opportunities for clerical solidarity. Reverend Altagracia Perez, a youthful thirtyish female black and Latina pastor, said, for example, that she had tired of repeatedly explaining to other neighboring Episcopal pastors that she was not the youth minister or the pastor's wife. She said she had more in common with a particular Lutheran minister (and co-CLUE participant) who pastored in the same Central Los Angeles neighborhood and was similarly bound up with problems of poverty and worker injustice than she did with pastors in suburban Episcopal churches. "We have the same kind of population, we're serving the same neighborhood, and we have a lot of the same issues," she said of the Lutheran minister. "We share a common theology." In fact, she went even further, stating, "I think that the priests, ministers, and religious leaders that see themselves as part of the call to social justice feel more connected to each other than they do to people within their own denomination." A ministry focused on social and economic justice brought diverse clergy together in ways that being ordained in the same denomination did not.

Denominational differences did come up when CLUE planned liturgical programming. During the plans for the Journey Toward Justice march in Santa Monica, there was some dispute over the incorporation of Wiccans from Santa Monica. A couple of CLUE clergy felt that an interfaith organization needed to be open and inclusive. In fact, during the discussions, these two people said that even having "clergy and laity" in the name of the organization was regressive and exclusive, as some religions, such as Buddhism, do not have ordained clergy. Other clergy disagreed, including one clergy member who anticipated that if pagan rituals were included in the interfaith blessings, Latina women in the union would fear becoming involved with anything that smacked of *brujeria,* or witchcraft. Another person told me that union organizers had asked, "How's it going to look if we invite a witch?" Big theological discussions ensued within CLUE, with some clergy arguing that pagan traditions were part of indigenous religion and at the root of Christianity and other faith traditions while other clergy were still opposed. The resulting program reflected something of a compromise, with blessings to the four directions included in the liturgy. In general, in efforts to be inclusive, the CLUE liturgies walked a fine line, avoiding overtly Christ-centered ceremonies and yet remaining true to ancient faith traditions of the major religions, principally those of Christianity and Judaism.

Spiritual Renewal

"CLUE doesn't realize it, but I needed them just as much as they need me." These are the words of Reverend Jarvis Johnson, and they speak to the deep gratification that many of the clergy derived from their participation with CLUE. In the struggle for economic justice and for the rights of Latino immigrant workers in Los Angeles, we have seen how important the integration of religion and religious moral voice has proven to be. Religion is critical to this burgeoning social movement, but so, too, many of the clergy said that CLUE activism was a way for them to reaffirm their faith.

No one was more effusive in this regard than Reverend Altagracia Perez, who found her CLUE involvement to be deeply transformative. She had been experiencing something of an emotional and spiritual crisis, but she was newly revitalized and inspired when she met the workers through CLUE. These mostly Latino immigrant workers "were taking risks and making sacrifices—and not just doing it, but doing it willingly and joyfully," she recalled. "And I, who had all this privilege, was doing everything begrudgingly. . . . It really shamed me. . . . It was a conversion experience for me to see that, and it invited my involvement." Although she had been active in community organizing around youth and HIV in the Bronx, she had never really experienced a seamless fit of faith and action. Becoming a faith-based activist in CLUE, she said, was "what I always dreamed of when I was in seminary. I had studied liberation theology, and . . . I was finally doing it!"

Similarly, Reverend Dick Gillet, a veteran of religiously inspired economic justice activism, also found a sort of redemption in his CLUE work. He had worked with factory workers in Puerto Rico in the 1970s, then in Los Angeles in the 1980s as part of "a very small but quite effective coalition to address massive plant closures in Los Angeles" and high unemployment [Los Angeles Coalition Against Plant Shut Downs]. But it "was not right for massive protest at that time, and the religious community, well there was just a handful of us that were involved in that." As a retired clergy, he felt renewed through CLUE, which had provided him with new experiences. "I find that in my late sixties I am learning, and I'm kind of in awe that I can learn, and I feel myself developing skills. I feel myself really rooted in this higher plan, and so it's an exciting time."

CONCLUSIONS

[W]e have seen how a group of clergy, most of them from Christian and Jewish traditions, use religious tools to promote the labor rights of Latino immigrant workers in the service industries. These clergy, many of them influenced by strategies and experiences of clergy in the civil rights movement and of César Chávez and the UFW (United Farm Workers), enjoy access to a well-stocked religious tool box.

First, they not only come to their social activism motivated by their religious beliefs, but they are frequently verbally reasserting this to one another in meetings and forums. When I asked why they do what they do for the immigrant workers, [clergy members] frequently invoked scripture, and they spoke of the importance of faith-based sacrifice for the good of others. They said their activism around economic justice was a way to express and practice their faith. For these clerical leaders, this activism goes to the core of what it means to be a religious person.

Second, they rely on the concrete religious resources at their disposal to organize protests,

meetings, and lobbying visits to the homes of workers or the offices of hotel managers and employers. Important religious-based resources include the well-honed oratory skills and charismatic talents of many of the clergy and the mundane but vital resources of church meeting halls, folding chairs, and office equipment.

[The CLUE] clergy and laity are not at all shy about using their religious authority and moral legitimacy for the cause. At this, they excel. They engage in civil disobedience, direct actions, and street protests when necessary. They are committed to nonviolence, but they will shut down the streets and avenues of Los Angeles, if necessary, and they freely use religious symbols and morality in these activities. They also use religion to directly pressure and persuade employers and managers to negotiate in good faith with the unions. In both lobbying activities and direct actions, they act as moral specialists.

CLUE members and the unions they support are media savvy and telegenic. As modern clergy, they do not wear collars and robes on all days of the week, but when doing their political work, they deliberately wear the clerical garb with the intent to persuade others of their moral authority. These religious activists are also cognizant of the need to respect religious pluralism and multiculturalism against the backdrop of re-Christianization. Therefore, they include religious rituals drawn from various religious traditions in protests, being careful not to get too denominational or exclusive. In the process, they make secular spaces momentarily sacred and imbue their movement for social change with collective corporeal activities that invoke ancient religious connections with the past.

REFERENCE

Dalton, Frederick John. 2003. *The Moral Vision of Cesar Chavez.* Maryknoll, NY: Orbis Books.

42

Talking Back

bell hooks

(1989)

In the world of the southern black community I grew up in, "back talk" and "talking back" meant speaking as an equal to an authority figure. It meant daring to disagree and sometimes it just meant having an opinion. In the "old school," children were meant to be seen and not heard. My great-grandparents, grandparents, and parents were all from the old school. To make yourself heard if you were a child was to invite punishment, the back-hand lick, the slap across the face that would catch you unaware, or the feel of switches stinging your arms and legs.

To speak then when one was not spoken to was a courageous act—an act of risking and daring. And yet it was hard not to speak in warm rooms where heated discussions began at the crack of dawn, women's voices filling the air, giving orders, making threats, fussing. Black men may have excelled in the art of poetic preaching in the male-dominated church, but in the church of the home where the everyday rules of how to live and how to act were established it was black women who preached. There, black women spoke in a language so rich, so poetic, that it felt to me like being shut off from life, smothered to death if one was not allowed to participate.

It was in that world of woman talk (the men were often silent, often absent) that was born in me the craving to speak, to have a voice, and not just any voice but one that could be identified as belonging to me. To make my voice, I had to speak, to hear myself talk—and talk I did—darting in and out of grown folk's conversations and dialogues, answering questions that were not directed at me, endlessly asking questions, making speeches. Needless to say, the punishments for these acts of speech seemed endless. They were intended to silence me—the child—and more particularly the girl child. Had I been a boy they might have encouraged me to speak believing that I might someday be called to preach. There was no "calling" for talking girls, no legitimized rewarded speech. The punishments I received for "talking back" were intended to suppress all possibility that I would create my own speech. That speech was to be suppressed so the "right speech of womanhood" would emerge.

Within feminist circles, silence is often seen as the sexist "right speech of womanhood"—the sign of woman's submission to patriarchal authority. This emphasis on woman's silence may be an accurate remembering of what has taken place in the households of women from WASP backgrounds in the United States, but in black communities (and diverse ethnic communities) women have not been silent. Their voices can be heard. Certainly for black women, our struggle has not been to emerge from silence into speech but to change the nature and direction of our speech, to make a speech that compels listeners, one that is heard.

Our speech, "the right speech of womanhood," was often the soliloquy, the talking into thin air, the talking to ears that do not hear you—the talk that is simply not listened to. Unlike the black male preacher whose speech was to be heard, who was to be listened to, whose words were to be remembered, the voices of black women—giving orders, making threats, fussing—could be tuned out, could become a kind of background music, audible but not acknowledged as significant speech. Dialogue—the sharing of speech and recognition—took place not between mother and child or mother and male authority figure but among black women. I can remember watching fascinated as our mother talked with her mother, sisters, and women friends. The intimacy and intensity of their speech—the satisfaction they received from talking to one another, the pleasure, the joy. It was in this world of woman speech, loud talk, angry words, women with tongues quick and sharp, tender sweet tongues, touching our world with their words, that I made speech my birthright—and the right to voice, to authorship, a privilege I would not be denied. It was in that world and because of it that I came to dream of writing, to write.

Writing was a way to capture speech, to hold onto it, keep it close. And so I wrote down bits and pieces of conversations, confessing in cheap diaries that soon fell apart from too much handling, expressing the intensity of my sorrow, the anguish of speech—for I was always saying the wrong thing, asking the wrong questions. I could not confine my speech to the necessary corners and concerns of life. I hid these writings under my bed, in pillow stuffings, among faded underwear. When my sisters found and read them, they ridiculed and mocked me—poking fun. I felt violated, ashamed, as if the secret parts of my self had been exposed, brought into the open, and hung like newly clean laundry, out in the air for everyone to see. The fear of exposure, the fear that one's deepest emotions

and innermost thoughts would be dismissed as mere nonsense, felt by so many young girls keeping diaries, holding and hiding speech, seems to me now one of the barriers that women have needed and still need to destroy so that we are no longer pushed into secrecy or silence.

Despite my feelings of violation, of exposure, I continued to speak and write, choosing my hiding places well, learning to destroy work when no safe place could be found. I was never taught absolute silence, I was taught that it was important to speak but to talk a talk that was in itself a silence. Taught to speak and yet beware of the betrayal of too much heard speech, I experienced intense confusion and deep anxiety in my efforts to speak and write. Reciting poems at Sunday afternoon church service might be rewarded. Writing a poem (when one's time could be "better" spent sweeping, ironing, learning to cook) was luxurious activity, indulged in at the expense of others. Questioning authority, raising issues that were not deemed appropriate subjects brought pain, punishments—like telling mama I wanted to die before her because I could not live without her—that was crazy talk, crazy speech, the kind that would lead you to end up in a mental institution. "Little girl," I would be told, "if you don't stop all this crazy talk and crazy acting you are going to end up right out there at Western State."

Madness, not just physical abuse, was the punishment for too much talk if you were female. Yet even as this fear of madness haunted me, hanging over my writing like a monstrous shadow, I could not stop the words, making thought, writing speech. For this terrible madness which I feared, which I was sure was the destiny of daring women born to intense speech (after all, the authorities emphasized this point daily), was not as threatening as imposed silence, as suppressed speech.

Safety and sanity were to be sacrificed if I was to experience defiant speech. Though I risked them both, deep-seated fears and anxieties characterized my childhood days. I would speak but I would not ride a bike, play hardball, or hold the gray kitten. Writing about the ways we are hurt by negative traumas in our growing-up years, psychoanalyst Alice Miller makes the point in *For Your Own Good* that it is not clear why childhood wounds become for some folk an opportunity to grow, to move forward rather than backward in the process of self-realization. Certainly, when I reflect on the trials of my growing-up years, the many punishments, I can see now that in resistance I learned to be vigilant in the nourishment of my spirit, to be tough, to courageously protect that spirit from forces that would break it.

While punishing me, my parents often spoke about the necessity of breaking my spirit. Now when I ponder the silences, the voices that are not heard, the voices of those wounded and/or oppressed individuals who do not speak or write, I contemplate the acts of persecution, torture— the terrorism that breaks spirits, that makes creativity impossible. I write these words to bear witness to the primacy of resistance struggle in any situation of domination (even within family life); to the strength and power that emerges from sustained resistance and the profound conviction that these forces can be healing, can protect us from dehumanization and despair.

These early trials, wherein I learned to stand my ground, to keep my spirit intact, came vividly to mind after I published *Ain't I a Woman* and the book was sharply and harshly criticized. While I had expected a climate of critical dialogue, I was not expecting a critical avalanche that had the power in its intensity to crush spirit, to push one into silence. Since that time I have heard stories about black women, about women of color, who write and publish (even when the work is quite successful), having nervous breakdowns, being made mad because they cannot bear the harsh responses of family, friends, and unknown critics, or becoming silent, unproductive. Surely, the absence of a humane critical response has tremendous impact on the writer from any oppressed, colonized group who endeavors to speak. For us,

true speaking is not solely an expression of creative power; it is an act of resistance, a political gesture that challenges the politics of domination that would render us nameless and voiceless. As such, it is a courageous act—as such, it represents a threat. To those who wield oppressive power, that which is threatening must necessarily be wiped out, annihilated, silenced.

Recently, efforts by black women writers to call attention to our work serve to highlight both our presence and absence. Whenever I peruse women's bookstores I am struck not by the rapidly growing body of feminist writing by black women but by the paucity of available published material. Those of us who write and are published remain few in number. The context of silence is varied and multidimensional. Most obvious are the ways racism, sexism, and class exploitation act as agents to suppress and silence. Less obvious are the inner struggles, the efforts made to gain the necessary confidence to write, to rewrite, to fully develop craft and skill—and the extent to which such efforts fail.

Although I have wanted writing to be my life-work since childhood, it has been difficult for me to claim "writer" as part of that which identifies and shapes my everyday reality. Even after publishing books, I would often speak of wanting to be a writer as though these works did not exist. And though I would be told, "you are a writer," I was not yet ready to fully affirm this truth. Part of myself was still held captive by domineering forces of history, of familial life that had charted a map of silence, of right speech. I had not completely let go of the fear of saying the wrong thing, of being punished. Somewhere in the deep recesses of my mind, I believed I could avoid both responsibility and punishment if I did not declare myself a writer.

One of the many reasons I chose to write using the pseudonym bell hooks, a family name (mother to Sarah Oldham, grandmother to Rosa Bell Oldham, great-grandmother to me), was to construct a writer-identity that would challenge and subdue all impulses leading me away from speech into silence. I was a young girl buying bubble gum at the corner store when I first really heard the full name bell hooks: I had just "talked back" to a grown person. Even now I can recall the surprised look, the mocking tones that informed me I must be kin to bell hooks—a sharp-tongued woman, a woman who spoke her mind, a woman who was not afraid to talk back. I claimed this legacy of defiance, of will, of courage, affirming my link to female ancestors who were bold and daring in their speech. Unlike my bold and daring mother and grandmother, who were not supportive of talking back, even though they were assertive and powerful in their speech, bell hooks as I discovered, claimed, and invented her, was my ally, my support.

The initial act of talking back outside the home was empowering. It was the first of many acts of defiant speech that would make it possible for me to emerge as an independent thinker and writer. In retrospect, "talking back" became for me a rite of initiation, testing my courage, strengthening my commitment, preparing me for the days ahead—the days when writing, rejection notices, periods of silence, publication, ongoing development seem impossible but necessary.

Moving from silence into speech is for the oppressed, the colonized, the exploited, and those who stand and struggle side by side a gesture of defiance that heals, that makes new life and new growth possible. It is that act of speech, of "talking back," that is no mere gesture of empty words, that is the expression of moving from object to subject—the liberated voice.

EPILOGUE

The mind that has conceived a plan of living must never lose sight of the chaos against which that pattern was conceived.

—Ralph Ellison (1952),
Invisible Man

As any action or posture long continued will distort and disfigure the limbs; so the mind likewise is crippled and contracted by perpetual application to the same set of ideas.

—Samuel Johnson (1751),
The Rambler, No. 173

God can be shaped. God is Change.

—Octavia Butler (1993),
Parable of the Sower

On January 10, 2009, my close friend and long-time colleague, Peter Kollock, was killed instantly when he struck a tree while driving a motorcycle near his home in the Malibu hills of California. Peter and I conceived the original edition of this book together in the early 1990s when we were both eager young professors fresh out of graduate school. The impetus for the book was a request from a publisher who hoped to break free from some of the more limiting aspects of textbook production and create a line of books that would be highly socially relevant and engaging for students. The publisher promised us that in producing this text, we would have creative freedom. Peter and I were enthusiastic about the prospect of creating a text that deviated from some of the mind-numbing, "dumbed down" material that was available to students at the time. In thinking about how to approach that first edition of the book, we identified one primary aim: We wanted to introduce readers to the usefulness of symbolic interactionism as a set of tools for self- and social awareness. We called this awareness "mindfulness."

In addition to being a professor of sociology, Peter was a dedicated student of Buddhism (in the tradition of the Vietnamese teacher, Thich Nhat Hanh). Buddhist practices emphasize meditation and "mindfulness" as a means to liberation from pain and suffering. Many contemporary practices, both religious and secular, also focus on what are sometimes called "contemplative" exercises, or forms of insight and meditation intended to induce greater awareness of our personal and social patterns. Common to all of these contemplative practices is the promise that by slowing down and bringing our awareness to taken-for-granted feelings, experiences, and routines, we will gain insight into the patterns that shape our daily lives. This insight enables us to make mindful choices about how we are living. In other words, we wake up to our selves and our social surroundings.

Peter and I were always fascinated with the ways in which the study of sociology in general, and symbolic interactionism in particular, are similar to these contemplative practices. In both, the focus is on gaining awareness of the internal conversations and social routines and patterns that shape our lives and our relationships with others. For us, sociology has been a practice of becoming more mindful. In the recent years before his death, Peter had extended his sociology class offerings at UCLA (where he was a professor) to include a course on "Mindfulness." In addition to readings and guest lectures from some of the leading contemporary scholars studying the positive effects of meditation on brain activity and creativity, Peter's syllabus included a significant amount of material derived from studies in symbolic interactionism. The class was wildly popular and always had a long waiting list. Students applying to take the class often commented that their college education was giving them a lot of information, but this information didn't necessarily include recipes or tools for how to incorporate it into a useful and meaningful life. They also hoped the class would yield insights into how to live satisfying, balanced lives in a time that, for many people, has felt increasingly chaotic and out of control.

Peter and I pondered similar questions as we considered how best to organize this text in a way that demonstrates the usefulness of symbolic interactionism as a set of tools for mindfulness. At the time of his death, Peter was working on a book he called *The Sociology of Mindfulness*. By way of conclusion to this fifth edition, and in tribute to Peter's efforts, I offer some thoughts on symbolic interactionism as a set of tools for mindful, meaningful living.

Fractured Selves

The conditions of contemporary life leave many of us feeling harried, overwhelmed, and incapable of "catching up" to ourselves. Rapid advances in electronic communication enable us to connect with others all across the globe at lightning speed. We welcome this potential for expanded social networking, but we also feel overwhelmed with the quickened pace and rising confusion of being in multiple worlds simultaneously. Most of us find ourselves occupying a variety of social positions and taking on a wide range of social identities daily. What are the consequences of this multiplicity of self? People increasingly report that they feel "fractured."

Social psychologist Kenneth Gergen (1991) talks about this contemporary experience as the "saturated self." In Gergen's assessment, the hectic pace of everyday life leaves us "saturated" with social demands. As a result of the increasing complexity of social life, we experience ourselves as filled to overflowing with a "multiplicity of incoherent and unrelated languages of the self" (p. 6). In this flood of social stimuli, our awareness of an inner core, or beacon, is diluted. We need re-centering, but even when we do manage to find solitude, we can no longer hear ourselves. This inner deafness is exacerbated by the encroaching presence of television, computers, and other forms of media output in nearly every public space. This external hubbub is reproduced as an internal chatter that we find difficult to silence even when we are alone.

As an exercise, I ask my students to sit someplace public but not necessarily too busy and "do nothing" for 10 minutes. Joking about having an assignment to "do nothing," they happily embark to various sites to do their "homework." The subsequent essays are very revealing and suggest the difficulty in turning off the inner chatter that tells us we should always be busily engaged, or at least appear to be. Many students write that they were surprised to find that they couldn't settle down, even for 10 minutes. Several note that they felt frustrated, even angry, because they were "wasting time." Many of them are also intrigued when they realize just how strong their inner critic is and how in sync it is with the pace of contemporary life.

Arlie Hochschild (1983; see Reading 27) suggests that the "emotional labor" that we are required to engage in as we perform a variety of social roles, especially in employment, also diminishes our ability to hear ourselves. Emotions can be an important source of information for making sense of our experiences. However, prolonged and uninterrupted emotion management makes it difficult for us to recognize emotional cues that may be signalling something important, such as stress, grief, anxiety, and so on. The more we ignore these cues and the less practiced we are in listening to ourselves, the more likely we are to be at the mercy of social forces, including our own unexamined, internalized social reflexes such as guilt, shame, and competition. For Hochschild, the result is "burnout" or disassociation.

Sociologists Jay Gubrium and James Holstein (2001) sum up the state of the contemporary self as "trying times and troubled selves." In their analysis, the self has become increasingly "institutionalized." The idea of the "institutionalized self" offers an interesting play on words: We are not necessarily locked up in institutions (such as prisons and asylums); in fact, we are technically more "free" than our ancestors were due to the technological advances that allow us to "virtually" roam all over the world at the touch of a finger. These same technological advances also enable many people to work from their homes, in coffee shops, and so forth, and thereby avoid the presumably stifling environment of the office. In theory, these conditions should make us less "institutionalized." However, the resulting din and the speed at which we are living our lives has created a chaos that, in the absence of being able to tune in internally, means we are living more from the outside in. That is, we are much more likely to behave in response to socially instituted practices that have been (mindlessly) incorporated and now act as institutional reflexes.

An analysis of all the conditions that have given rise to this state of being is beyond the scope of this brief essay (though I do hope the issues tempt you to pursue more sociology). However, an antidote to this chaos can be found in our ability for awareness or mindfulness of the social practices in which we participate. As a basis for this, I offer a brief review of some of the lessons of symbolic interactionism, especially as they relate to the construction of taken-for-granted social beliefs and practices. To the extent that we become aware of these practices, and of our own ability to "reframe" them, we become more awake, more engaged, and better able to listen to ourselves and others.

SYMBOLIC INTERACTIONISM, MEANING, AND TRUTH

What's real? How do you determine what is true and right and good? These are the questions that opened this book (see Part I). Symbolic interactionism as a form of intellectual inquiry implies that realities are multiple, shifting, contradictory, and situationally specific. Whereas some contemporary scholars focus on deconstructing cultural beliefs and practices, symbolic interactionists focus on studying *how* people learn and sustain culturally specific practices and beliefs through everyday patterns of interaction. If you really follow the logic of the symbolic interactionist perspective, you will note that it implies that (1) interactions are always fraught with misunderstandings, miscues, misinformation, and possibly even attempts to mislead and manipulate; and (2) meaning is *always negotiated:* It is always in flux and always reflects the interactional context and the relationship between persons in the interaction.

Because symbolic interactionism implies that there is no universal meaning or "truth," the perspective has been criticized as perpetuating cynicism and social dissolution. Students of symbolic interactionism sometimes conclude that it is not worthwhile to participate in social life because, ultimately, there is no *real* meaning. The conclusion they draw is that nothing really matters. The dilemma, as they represent it to themselves, is whether to participate in social relations that are, theoretically, always in flux.

This is especially a dilemma for people who are newly aware of the complex, contradictory, and shifting aspects of social relations. However, it is not so much a crisis of meaning that has been brought about by symbolic interactionist studies and critical inquiries, but a crisis that arises because people who learn these perspectives remain stuck in unquestioned or taken-for-granted beliefs that meaning is not real or authentic unless it transcends human construction. *The real dilemma is not that there is no universal meaning, but that persons fail to comprehend the significance of their own expressive and creative potential.* As a way of reframing this dilemma, consider the following story:

In the book *The Sword and the Stone,* by T. H. White (1938/1978), a wise old badger tells his young apprentice, Wart, how all the creatures of the earth came to be as they are. According to the badger, God assembled a multitude of embryos before him on the sixth day of Creation and explained that He was going to hand out gifts. The embryos could each choose two or three gifts. These gifts would serve as a set of tools that would mark the creature's unique existence on earth. The embryos chattered excitedly among themselves about the possible combinations of tools each might ask for. When the time came, each embryo stepped forward and requested its gifts from God. Some asked for arms that were diggers or garden forks, some chose to use their arms as flying machines, and others asked for bodies like boats and arms that were oars. One of the lizards decided to swap its entire body for blotting paper. Still others asked to be able to use their mouths as drills or offensive weapons. Finally, it was the turn of the embryo called "human." This small, naked creature approached God and stammered shyly, "I have considered your generous offer, and I thank you for it, but I choose to stay as I am."

"Well chosen," thundered God. "In deciding to retain your embryonic form you will have use of all the gifts that mark the being of each of the other creatures. You will exist always as potential: the potential to take up and put down the tools of the other creatures, the potential to create uniforms and tools of your own design and to wear and discard them as you see fit. You have chosen wisely, human. We wish you well in your earthly journey."

An important lesson of symbolic interactionism is that humans exist as embryonic potential. We are capable of creating, taking on, and casting off various identities and cultural institutions. Our potential is limited only by our imagination and our ability to assemble the materials necessary to realize our visions. As social beings, the ability to create shared meaning is the distinctive mark of our species. However, the history of Western consciousness suggests a somewhat paradoxical acceptance of this ability. We are eager to embrace our creative potential but at the same time reluctant to recognize our own authority as social creators and the responsibility that this implies.

Imagine using this logic if you intended to build a sand castle on the beach. It will only be washed away by the tides or eroded by the wind. It's fragile and temporary, so why bother? *Why* do people build sand castles? Certainly not so that they will endure, but rather for the sheer pleasure of doing so. The experience lingers long after the sand form has crumbled away. Why do people form friendships, get married, or invest time and energy in pursuing a vocation (such as law or ministry), even though they may have doubts about its "permanence"? Presumably, these activities are more stable than the sand castle, but are they more stable because they are "naturally" so, or because we care enough to remain continually engaged in their ongoing creation?

This is a significant distinction and one that is at the core of symbolic interactionism, with its emphasis on social interaction as a basis for creating and maintaining social routines. Symbolic interactionism provides us with the tools for exploring *why* and *how* specific social activities become stable and take on the form of social institutions that have firmly grounded social stability and corresponding social authority. In other words, according to the symbolic interactionist perspective, *there are stable, predictable patterns of behavior and systems of belief.* The central focus of this perspective is not only to demonstrate the existence of these patterns, but *to show the ways in which ordinary people create and re-create them.* Just because these patterns are the result of human activity does not make them any less meaningful. The pertinent question is whether people are *mindfully engaged* in these practices or *mindlessly* rattling around in old routines and beliefs that may have lost their meaning.

The fact that we create and re-create our own systems of meaning and ideals doesn't make these beliefs and practices any less real. In fact, our ability to analyze, critique, and *change* our practices for the common good is a mark of our creative potential. Again, the pertinent point is the extent to which we are mindfully engaged in the process of social relations. When you are engaged and critically aware of the role you play in various systems of meaning, then you are also able to take responsibility for your actions and to participate in ongoing discussions about what is "right" and "good." Authority, morality, and authenticity are *embedded* in these social relations. The actual process of involvement can be seen as an enactment of morality and authenticity.

We like to think that most people who were given a choice between (1) living a life in mindless ignorance of the social processes that shape who and what we are and (2) becoming mindfully and critically aware of these processes, would choose mindful awareness. This process of becoming aware can itself be an act of meaningful engagement. Through critical reflection and analysis, we learn to discern taken-for-granted beliefs and practices; through engaged, mindful participation, we contribute to the ongoing creation of a mindful existence. In the remainder of this essay, I discuss two consequences of mindlessness that must be addressed in pursuit of a mindful, meaningful existence: ossification and entropy.

Ossification

We have discussed the tendency for human routines and ideas to harden, or "ossify," into habits and entrenched systems of belief (see the essays for Parts V and VI). We have also discussed some of the reasons why this occurs in human relations (desire for predictability, cognitive efficiency, mindlessness). Ossified social practices (a.k.a. "social institutions") are not necessarily bad. The problems arise when we forget the purpose of the initial routine or practice, or fail to remain mindful about the fact that these are socially created routines. What may have served as a useful basis for achieving some particular end becomes an ideology and an end in itself. In other words, useful recipes for living become calcified as ideologies. We may persist in maintaining these ossified constructions simply because they have become permanent, hardened features of our social landscape. But at the same time, we may be contributing to the maintenance of our own prisons.

People usually know when to tear down a building that has ceased to serve any useful function and may even be a source of danger. However, we sometimes continue to put up with social institutions that are cracked and crumbling, simply because we fail to realize that it is within our power to step beyond the confines of these structures and build others. The point is not that all old social institutions should be torn down; it is that we should be mindful of the purposes of the social institutions that our actions (or inactions) help to perpetuate. Unfortunately, such purposes become increasingly difficult to recognize—and change becomes more difficult—the more hardened, or ossified, the institution becomes.

Consider the social routine prevalent in U.S. universities of giving exams. In a seminar for graduate students on how to teach, I ask prospective college teachers to provide a rationale for giving exams. At first, this seems like a simple task, but the seminar participants usually end up struggling once they begin to think about it. The practice of giving exams has become such an ossified element of the educational landscape that many instructors engage in the practice mindlessly. They really don't know why they do it. If exams are written and administered with a particular purpose, such as providing feedback for the student and the instructor or as an incentive to organize chunks of information, then teachers are participating in the mindful maintenance of this social institution. But to give exams simply because "that's what's always been done" is to perpetuate a potentially meaningless social routine.

Once the purpose for a particular social routine is isolated, it is possible to devise potentially more useful routes to achieve it. For example, one unfortunate outcome of the exam procedure may be the unnecessary rank ordering of students. If the purpose of exams is to motivate students to organize and articulate their knowledge, then it may be possible to create an alternative exercise that more directly serves the intended purpose and avoids the pitfalls. It is possible, however, that the purpose of exams is indeed to rank order persons—perhaps to facilitate their entrance into a stratified institution, such as the labor market. In that case, instructors should be mindfully aware that their examination procedures serve to perpetuate social stratification, and that they are performing a gatekeeping role for other social institutions.

The point is to understand how one's participation in particular cultural routines perpetuates the existence of social institutions. Here, in the exploration of ossified structures, is where the tools of deconstruction serve a useful end. Such explorations need not lead to the conclusion that the entire structure should be dismantled, however. Mindful construction leads us to ask what purpose the social routine serves and whether we want to participate in that purpose.

Entropy

If any pattern in nature seems to play itself out in human relations, it is entropy. In nature, entropy is the natural process of decay. Applied to social relationships, entropy is a tendency toward erosion. According to the laws of thermodynamics, coherent molecular systems require constant input of energy to maintain their structure. If this energy is diverted, the system (whether molecule, leaf, or earlobe) will erode or fall apart into increasingly random elements. This tendency toward randomness is entropy. Similarly, the meaning and purpose of our social relationships are constantly threatened with erosion unless participants infuse these routines with mindful energy. Failure to do so is the reason we so often find ourselves thinking, "The thrill is gone."

What are some of the activities or relationships in your life that you take for granted? Do you have a spouse or family member whom you love but "don't have enough time for"? Imagine an attorney who decides to commit his services to assisting those who cannot afford legal counsel. After mindful consideration, he has decided to devote his time and talent to fighting what he perceives to be an injustice. In effect, he has chosen to actively chip away at one social system that he perceives to be culturally unfair: economic inequality in the legal system. Now imagine this same man explaining to his spouse and children that he does not have time to celebrate birthdays and anniversaries because he is busy fighting for an important social cause. He is often absent from family meals and other everyday rituals as well. One day he awakens to the discovery that he is no longer meaningfully engaged with his family— they seem to be living their lives without him.

This example illustrates the simple but profound point that if we do not mindfully participate in the production of those realities that we wish to maintain as the foundation of our lives, they will be eroded by the forces of entropy. Love and family involvement require ongoing, active participation in the ritual interactions that maintain these institutions. We can't take for granted even seemingly well-established social institutions such as "the family." These social institutions do not endure without active maintenance.

Mindful Engagement

Khalil Gibran once wrote that pain is the experience of breaking the shell that encapsulates understanding. The implication is that, in the process of stretching one's experiences, intelligence, and understanding, there will always be the pain of breaking old habits and relinquishing old ways of knowing. Mindfulness requires both critical self-examination and the courage to break step with known, predictable routines. This can be difficult. At the same time, the words of Anaïs Nin remind us that "the time came when the risk to remain tight in the bud was more painful than the risk it took to bloom."

In conclusion, I offer two take-away messages for mindful engagement: (1) Be mindfully choosy about the realities that you intend to produce or reproduce, and (2) recognize that the production of any reality requires your participation. To the extent that you participate mindfully, your life will take on increased meaning and purpose.

Trudy the bag lady, introduced in Reading 2 by Jane Wagner, is a true hero from the perspective of the mindful construction of reality. She has scrutinized the social institutions in which she dwells and found them to be unacceptable. Rather than turn away in despair, she has created a rich, lively alternative reality for herself. Now, as she describes it, her days are "jam-packed and fun-filled." Trudy is both a product of the general social realities that form this society and a commentator on them. Her commentary is compelling because it is both informed and hopeful. She is neither a social robot nor a cynic. She has taken responsible control of the construction of her own reality, and she invests in this production with enthusiasm and vigor. She is an intriguing character in that, although she is a street person, we do not feel pity for her. In fact, we may even feel a bit envious of her insightful, energetic reality, mad though it may appear by conventional standards. Trudy is bursting with potential.

Our own realities can be similarly produced, whether by doing something as simple as participating wholeheartedly in small daily rituals with those you love or as revolutionary as "talking back to outrage" in the form of large-scale, collective protest. The message is that it takes insight, courage, and responsibility to engage in the mindful production of reality. This is the basis of a meaningful existence.

REFERENCES

Butler, O. (1993). *Parable of the sower.* New York: Warner Aspect.

Ellison, R. (1952). *Invisible man.* New York: Random House.

Gergen, K. (1991). *The saturated self.* New York: Basic Books.

Gubrium, J., & Holstein, J. (2001). *Institutional selves: Troubled identities in a postmodern world.* New York: Oxford University Press.

Hochschild, A. (1983). *The managed heart.* Berkeley: University of California Press.

Johnson, S. (1751, November 12). *The rambler,* No. 173. London: John Payne and J. Bouquet.

White, T. H. (1938/1978). *The sword and the stone.* New York: Laurel Leaf (Random House).

CREDITS

Reading 1: Reprinted with the permission of The Free Press, a Division of Simon & Schuster, Inc., from *The Fine Line: Making Distinctions in Everyday Life* by Eviatar Zerubavel. Copyright © 1991 by Eviatar Zerubavel. All rights reserved.

Reading 2: Reuse of excerpts from pp. 13, 16–21, 23, 26, 29, 212–213 from *The Search for Signs of Intelligent Life in the Universe* by Jane Wagner. Copyright © 1986 by Jane Wagner Inc. Reprinted by permission of HarperCollins Publishers.

Reading 3: Reprinted by permissions of Waveland Press, Inc. from Earl Babbie's *Observing Ourselves*. (Long Grove, IL; Waveland Press, Inc., 1986 [reissued 1998].) All rights reserved.

Reading 4: From Charon, Joel, *Symbolic Interactionism*, pp. 13, 14, and 16–25, © 2010. Reproduced by permission of Pearson Education, Inc.

Reading 5: Reprinted by permission of Yale University Press from *An Essay on Man* (pp. 42–44) by Ernst Cassirer. Copyright © 1944 by Yale University Press.

Reading 6: Reprinted by permission of Simon & Schuster Adult Publishing Group from *From the Man Who Mistook His Wife for a Hat and Other Clinical Tales* by Oliver Sacks. Copyright © 1970, 1981, 1983, 1984, 1985 by Oliver Sacks.

Reading 7: From "Final Note on a Case of Extreme Isolation" by Kingsley Davis from American *Journal of Sociology, 52*, pp. 432–437. Copyright © 1947 American Sociological Association.

Reading 8: From *Mindfulness* by Ellen Langer. Copyright © 1990 Ellen J. Langer. Reprinted by permission of Da Capo Press, a member of the Perseus Books Group.

Reading 9: Reprinted by permission of The University of Chicago Press. Excerpts from *Metaphors We Live By* (pp. 3–5, 22, 46–51, 139–146, 156, 160, 193–195) by George Lakoff and Mark Johnson. Copyright © 1980 by The University of Chicago Press. All rights reserved.

Reading 10: Excerpts from *Racism in the English Language* (pp. 413–420) by Robert B. Moore. Reprinted by permission of The Council on Interracial Books for Children, c/o Lawrence Jordan Literary Agency, 345 West 121st, New York, NY 10027.

Reading 11: Reprinted by permission of The University of Chicago Press. Excerpts from George Herbert Mead's *Mind, Self, and Society: From the Standpoint of a Social Behavorist* (pp. 136–144, 195–196) edited by Charles W. Morris. Copyright © 1962 by The University of Chicago Press.

Reading 26: "Being Middle Eastern American" by Amir Marvasti in *Symbolic Interaction, 28,* pp. 525, 526, 530, 533–543. Copyright © 2006. Reprinted by permission.

Reading 27: Excerpts from *The Managed Heart: Commercialization of Human Feeling, 20th Anniversary Edition,* (pp. ix–x, 24–25, 95–96, 98–101, 104–105, 110–111, 126–128, 131) by Arlie Russell Hochschild. Copyright © 1983 by The Regents of the University of California. Used by permission of the Regents of the University of California and the University of California Press.

Reading 28: From "Shaping the Selves of Young People Through Emotion Management." by David Schweingruber and Nancy Berns, *Journal of Contemporary Ethnography, 34,* pp. 679–693, 696–701. Copyright © 2005.

Reading 29: From *The Social Construction of Reality* by Peter L. Berger and Thomas Luckmann, Copyright © 1966 by Peter L. Berger and Thomas Luckmann. Used by permission of Doubleday, a division of Random House, Inc.

Reading 30: "Five Features of Reality" from *Reality of Ethnomethodology* (pp. 8–33) by Hugh Mehan and Houston Wood. Copyright © 1975 by John Wiley & Sons. Reprinted with permission of John Wiley & Sons, Inc.

Reading 31: "A Conception of and Experiments With 'Trust' as a Condition of Concerted Stable Actions" by Harold Garfinkel from *Motivation and Social Interaction* (pp. 220–235), edited by O. J. Harvey, 1963. Reprinted by permission of the author.

Reading 32: "Self-Fulfilling Prophecies" by Paul Watzlawick, translated by Ursula Berg Lunk, from *The Invented Reality: How Do We Know What We Believe We Know?* (pp. 95–116), edited by Paul Watzlawick. Copyright © 1984 by W.W. Norton & Company, Inc. Copyright © 1981 by R. Piper & Co., Verlag, Munich. Used by permission of W.W. Norton & Company, Inc.

Reading 33: "When Belief Creates Reality" by Mark Snyder from *Experiencing Social Psychology* (pp. 189–192) edited by A. Pines and C. Maslach. New York: Alfred A. Knopf. Copyright © 1977. Reprinted by permission of the author.

Reading 34: "Consuming Terrorism," by David L. Altheide in *Symbolic Interaction, 27,* pp. 290–291, 293, 295, 298, 300–305. Used by permission. All rights reserved.

Reading 35: "Common Knowledge and Ideological Critique: The Significance of Knowing That the 'Haves' Come Out Ahead." by Patricia Ewick and Susan Silbey. Copyright © 1999. *Law & Society Review, 33,* pp. 1025, 1027–1036, 1039–1040. Reprinted by permission.

Reading 36: "Status Inequality and Close Relationships: An Integrative Typology of Bond-Saving Strategies," by Scott R. Harris in *Symbolic Interaction,* Vol. 20, No. 1: 1–20. © 1997 Society for the Study of Symbolic Interaction. Used by permission. All rights reserved.

Reading 37: This reading, "The Persistence of Gender Inequality in Employment Settings" was originally published in 1990 as "Interaction and the Conservation of Gender Equality: Considering Employment" *American Sociological Review, 62:* 218–235. Cecilia Ridgeway has adapted the article specifically for this text.

Reading 38: "Double-Consciousness and the Veil" from *The Souls of Black Folk* by W. E. B. DuBois, 1903. New York: Bantam Books.

NAME INDEX

Adams, W. C., 411
Agnew, S., 99
Alba, R., 211
Allen, W., xi
Allison, D., 462
Allport, G., 399
Altheide, D. L., 155, 409, 410, 411, 412, 416
Alvarado, P., 510
Anderson, L., 288
Anzaldúa, G., 470–471, 487
Armstrong, D., 417
Aronson, E., 45
Aronson, J., 212
Artaud, A., 338
Asch, S., 45

Babbie, E., 35
Baron, R., 212
Barthes, R., 54, 82, 453
Becker, H., 181–183, 219, 221
Beers, R. F., 400
Belkin, L., 415
Bennett, J., 416
Benson, H., 400
Berger, P., 40, 42, 173, 176, 187, 189, 272, 273,
    341, 359, 361, 446
Berns, N., 258, 318, 325
Berscheid, E., 405, 406
Bin laden, O., 416
Blank, A., 85
Blauner, B., 211
Blumer, H., 49, 52, 206, 215, 417, 431, 435, 442
Blumstein, P., 115
Bobo, K., 505
Boltzmann, L., 131, 136
Borges, J. L., 84
Bouldrey, B., 483
Bourdieu, P., 200, 203
Brewer, M., 445
Brissett, D., 290
Burgest, D. R., 101

Bush, G. W., 412, 413, 416
Butler, O., 517

Cahill, S., 291, 325, 334
Calhoun, C., 159
Campbell, W., 508
Campenni, C. E., 144
Cancian, F. M., 229
Cannon, W., 397–398
Cantor, G., 136
Carter, B., 416
Carter, J., 96–97
Carter, P. L., 215
Cassirer, E., 51, 69, 71
Castañeda, C., 370, 376
Chanowitz, B., 85
Charon, J., 39
Chauncey, G., 162
Chen, D. W., 414
Cheney, D., 413
Cheney, L., 413
Chomsky, N., 58–59, 131, 370
Cicourel, A. V., 366
Clark, K. B., 100
Classen, C., 292, 293
Collier, J., 423–424
Collins, R., 430
Coltrane, S., 430
Conchas, G. Q., 215
Conley, J. M., 427
Connell, R. W., 147
Conrad, P., 352–353, 482
Cooley, C. H., 112–113, 120, 126, 129, 151, 153,
    187, 267
Cooper, H. M., 212
Copernicus, 38
Copp, M., 327
Cordaro, L., 396
Corsaro, W. A., 230
Cortez, J., 425
Couch, C. J., 417

SUBJECT INDEX

ABOUT THE AUTHOR

Jodi O'Brien is Professor of Sociology at Seattle University. She teaches courses in social psychology, social inequalities, gender and sexualities, religion, and social theory. She writes and lectures on the cultural politics of transgressive identities and communities. Her other books include *Everyday Inequalities* (Basil Blackwell) and *Social Prisms: Reflections on Everyday Myths and Paradoxes* (Pine Forge Press), and she is the editor of *The Encyclopedia of Gender and Society* (Sage).

SAGE Research Methods Online
The essential tool for researchers

**Sign up now at
www.sagepub.com/srmo
for more information.**

An expert research tool

- An **expertly designed taxonomy** with more than 1,400 unique terms for social and behavioral science research methods

- **Visual and hierarchical search tools** to help you discover material and link to related methods

- Easy-to-use navigation tools
- Content organized by complexity
- Tools for citing, printing, and downloading content with ease
- Regularly updated content and features

A wealth of essential content

- The most comprehensive picture of quantitative, qualitative, and mixed methods available today

- More than **100,000 pages of SAGE book and reference material** on research methods as well as editorially selected material from SAGE journals

- More than **600 books** available in their entirety online

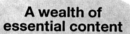

Launching 2011!

 SAGE research methods online

CPSIA information can be obtained
at www.ICGtesting.com
Printed in the USA
FFOW03n1548200116
20605FF